Lecture Notes of the Institute for Computer Sciences, Social Informatics and Telecommunications Engineering 141

T0213050

More information about this series at http://www.springer.com/series/8197

Ramón Agüero · Thomas Zinner
Rossitza Goleva · Andreas Timm-Giel
Phuoc Tran-Gia (Eds.)

Mobile Networks and Management

6th International Conference, MONAMI 2014
Würzburg, Germany, September 22–24, 2014
Revised Selected Papers

 Springer

Editors
Ramón Agüero
University of Cantabria
Santander
Spain

Andreas Timm-Giel
Hamburg University of Technology
Hamburg
Germany

Thomas Zinner
University of Würzburg
Würzburg
Germany

Phuoc Tran-Gia
University of Würzburg
Würzburg
Germany

Rossitza Goleva
Technical University of Sofia Faculty
    of Telecommunications
Sofia
Bulgaria

ISSN 1867-8211   ISSN 1867-822X (electronic)
Lecture Notes of the Institute for Computer Sciences, Social Informatics
and Telecommunications Engineering
ISBN 978-3-319-16291-1   ISBN 978-3-319-16292-8 (eBook)
DOI 10.1007/978-3-319-16292-8

Library of Congress Control Number: 2015932980

Springer Cham Heidelberg New York Dordrecht London

Printed on acid-free paper

Springer International Publishing AG Switzerland is part of Springer Science+Business Media
(www.springer.com)

Preface

This volume is the result of the Sixth International ICST Conference on Mobile Networks and Management (MONAMI), which was held in Würzburg, Germany during September 22–24, 2014, hosted by the University of Würzburg.

The MONAMI conference series aims at closing the gap between hitherto considered separated and isolated research areas, namely multi-access and resource management, mobility and network management, and network virtualization. Although these have emerged as core aspects in the design, deployment, and operation of current and future networks, there is still little to no interaction between the experts in these fields. MONAMI enables cross-pollination between these areas by bringing together top researchers, academics, and practitioners specializing in the area of mobile network and service management.

In 2014, after a thorough peer-review process, 20 papers were selected for inclusion in the main track of the technical program. In addition, MONAMI 2014 hosted a well-received workshop on Enhanced Living Environments, which featured 10 papers. All in all, 30 papers were orally presented at the conference. The Technical Program Committee members made sure that each submitted paper was reviewed by at least three competent researchers, including at least one TPC member.

The conference opened with one half-day tutorial: "SDN Experimentation Facilities and Tools," addressing one of the main leitmotifs of the MONAMI conference, organized and presented by Dr. Kostas Pentikousis and Dr. Umar Toseef (EICT GmbH, Germany) and Philip Wette and Martin Dräxler (University of Paderborn, Germany). Prof. Klaus Moessner, from the Centre for Communication Systems Research at the University of Surrey, UK, officially opened the conference day with his vision on "Networks in Times of Virtualisation." In addition, the conference featured a panel session on "Cloudification of Mobile Networks - Expectations, Challenges and Opportunities," organized by Dr. Andreas Maeder and with the participation of the following reputable researchers: Dr. Klaus Moessner, Dr. Dirk Kutscher, Dr. Wolfgang Kellerer, Dr. Wolfgang Kiess, and Prof. Alberto Leon-Garcia. The second day of the conference started with a keynote by Dr. Dirk Kutscher from NEC Europe Ltd., Germany, who gave a speech entitled "From Virtualization to Network and Service Programmability – A Research Agenda for 5G Networks." This was followed by a special session on Software Defined Networking and Network Function Virtualization, organized by Prof. Wolfgang Kellerer (Technische Universität München, Germany) and Dr. Marco Hoffmann (Nokia, Germany) featuring the talk "Commodity Hardware as Common Denominator of SDN and NFV," given by Dr. Hagen Woesner (BISDN GmbH, Germany).

The First Workshop on Enhanced Living Environments, organized by the IC1303 AAPELE COST Action, featured a keynote by Prof. Phuoc Tran-Gia (University of Würzburg, Germany) and a talk from the AAPELE Science Officer, Dr. Guiseppe Lugano.

It is worth highlighting that the attendance increased in MONAMI 2014 and all newcomers acknowledged the collegial atmosphere which characterizes the conference, making it an excellent venue, not only to present novel research work, but also to foster stimulating discussions between the attendees.

The papers included in this volume are organized thematically into five parts, starting with LTE Networks in Part I. Virtualization and Software Defined Networking aspects are discussed in Part II. Part III presents new approaches related to Self-Organizing Networks, while Part IV addresses Energy Awareness in Wireless Networks. Part V includes papers presenting avant-garde Algorithms and Techniques for Wireless Networks, and Part VI entails papers related to Applications and Context Awareness. The next three parts of the volume deal with Ambient Assisted Living systems: Part VII focuses on architectural issues, Part VIII discusses Human Interaction Technologies and, finally, Part IX closes the volume with three papers on Devices and Mobile Cloud for AAL.

We close this short preface to the volume by acknowledging the vital role that the Technical Program Committee members and additional referees played during the review process. Their efforts ensured that all submitted papers received a proper evaluation. We thank EAI and ICST for assisting with organization matters, CREATE-NET and University of Würzburg for hosting MONAMI 2014. The team that put together this year's event was large and required the sincere commitment of many folks. Although too many to recognize by name, their effort should be highlighted. We particularly thank Petra Jansen for her administrative support on behalf of EAI, and Prof. Imrich Chlamtac of CREATE-NET for his continuous support of the conference. Finally, we thank all delegates for attending MONAMI 2014 and making it such a vibrant conference!

We hope to see you all in Santander, 2015.

December 2014

Phuoc Tran-Gia
Andreas Timm-Giel
Rossitza Goleva
Thomas Zinner
Ramón Agüero

Organization

General Chairs

Phuoc Tran-Gia   University of Würzburg, Germany
Andreas Timm-Giel   Hamburg University of Technology, Germany

TPC Chairs

Thomas Zinner   University of Würzburg, Germany
Ramón Agüero   University of Cantabria, Spain

ELEMENT Workshop Chairs

Nuno Garcia   University of Beira Inteiror, Portugal
Rossitza Goleva   Technical University of Sofia, Bulgaria
Periklis Chatzimisios   Alexander TEI of Thessaloniki, Greece
Thomas Plagemann   University of Oslo, Norway

Special Session Chairs

Wolfgang Kellerer   Technische Universität München, Germany
Marco Hoffmann   Nokia Siemens Networks, Germany

Tutorials Chair

Oliver Blume   Alcatel-Lucent Bell Labs, Germany

Financial Chair

Maciej Muehleisen   Hamburg University of Technology, Germany

Webchair

Jarno Pinola   VTT Technical Research Centre of Finland,
                               Finland

Panel Chair

Andreas Mäder   NEC Laboratories Europe, Germany

Contents

AAL: Devices and Mobile Cloud

LTE Networks

Scalable and Self-sustained Algorithms for Femto-Cell Interference Mitigation

Sameera Palipana[1], Yasir Zaki[2]([✉]), Umar Toseef[1], Jay Chen[2], and Carmelita Goerg[1]

[1] Communication Networks (ComNets), University of Bremen, Otto-Hahn-Allee NW1, 28359 Bremen, Germany
{dmsp,umr,cg}@comnets.uni-bremen.de
[2] Computer Science Department, New York University, Abu Dhabi (NYUAD), UAE
yasir.zaki@nyu.edu, jchen@cs.nyu.edu

Abstract. Cellular networks are reaching their physical limits providing capacity that is almost near the Shannon theory. However, cellular usage is still increasing exponentially with hungry applications demanding higher data rates. As a result, designers are facing significant challenge in meeting the required demands. One promising solutions, being fostered by the 3GPP, is to increase the spectral efficiency through higher frequency reuse using smaller and denser network cells such as femto, pico and nano cells. One of the main challenges behind using smaller cells is managing interference. In this paper, we propose two novel solutions that alleviate the interference of femto-cells on macro-cell user equipment (MUEs). The solutions do not rely on any additional information exchange or signaling, nor do they rely on the backhaul and it's delay. The first proposal is Femto-cell Power Control Scheme (FPCS) that utilizes an analytical approach to adapt the femto base station's transmit power based on Channel Quality Indicator (CQI) reports from affected MUEs. The second method is Random Physical Resource Block Selection Scheme (RPSS) that allocates the femto-cell's resources from a random subset of Physical Resource Blocks (PRBs) so that the MUEs benefit from a reduced interference level. Our evaluations have shown that the two proposals do alleviate the femto-cell interference significantly, increasing the SINR and enhancing the end performance. To the best of our knowledge, no similar work exist in literature that addresses the femto-cell's interference without information exchange.

Keywords: HetNet · Femto-cells · Interference mitigation

1 Introduction

Femto-cells are small, low power/cost and plug and play cellular base stations that can be placed inside homes and small business. It can be connected to the operator's network through Internet Protocol (IP) by means of a third party backhaul connection such as Asymmetric Digital Subscriber Line (ADSL) or through fiber optics. Femto-cells aim at providing better indoor coverage,

© Institute for Computer Sciences, Social Informatics and Telecommunications Engineering 2015
R. Agüero et al. (Eds.): MONAMI 2014, LNICST 141, pp. 3–17, 2015.
DOI: 10.1007/978-3-319-16292-8_1

increasing network capacity and also providing new services to users. Accordingly, they provide higher data rates while reducing the macro-cells load. However, there are several technical challenges that must be addressed before femto-cells can coexist among other macro- and pico-cells. These challenges can be categorized into: inter-cell interference, handover in areas with multiple femto-cells, self configuration, healing and optimization, spectrum accuracy, and providing quality of service using the shared backhaul connection [1,2].

In a heterogeneous network with femto-cells and macro-cells coexistence, the downlink inter-cell interference can occur across femto-macro tiers (cross-tier interference), as well as in femto-femto tiers (co-tier interference). The main reasons for this downlink inter-cell interference are the deployment of femto-cells without proper planning, spectrum reuse or co-channel deployment by femto-cells, Closed Subscriber Group (CSG) access and uncoordinated operation among femto-cells and macro-cells [3].

Methods available for the downlink data channel protection can be divided into two areas: power control and radio resource management. Radio resource management involves methods such as component carrier aggregation, almost blank subframes and PRB level resource partitioning. To overcome the downlink cross-tier interference, several power controlling schemes are proposed in the literature. Claussen et al. [4] provides a transmit power calculation method considering the distance between the femto-cell and the most interfering macro-cell which offers a minimum coverage for its serving Home User Equipment (HUE). Yavuz et al. [5] use a power setting based on the received signal strength from the macro-cell which is measured by the Home NodeB and adjusts the transmit power to achieve a minimum quality level for the macro-cell control channel. However, in these methods there is a high probability that the femto-cell decreases its power without a MUE in the vicinity, resulting in an unnecessary performance degradation. Lalam et al. [6] proposes a dynamic power control algorithm that uses the CQI reports from HUEs in Frequency Division Duplex (FDD) High Speed Downlink Packet Access (HSDPA) and the excellent transmission quality associated to a femto-cell to adjust the downlink power transmission according to a given targeted CQI. However, the femto-cell is restricted here to achieve a target Quality of Service (QoS) even without MUE influence. Morita et al. [7] introduced an adaptive power level setting scheme that depends on the availability of MUEs. Here, the HeNB measures the variation of uplink received power from the MUEs and thereby, the transmit power of the femto-cell can be adjusted intelligently. This scheme requires the femto-cell to enable the Network Listen Mode (NLM) to sniff the environment as a UE.

Several resource partitioning schemes are proposed in literature trying to alleviate the downlink cross-tier interference. A dynamic resource partitioning method that denies Home enhanced NodeBs (HeNBs) to access the downlink resources that are assigned to macro UEs in their vicinity was introduced by Bharucha et al. [8]. Here, the interference on most vulnerable MUEs can be effectively controlled at the expense of HeNB's capacity. Nonetheless, this method requires an X2 link for backhaul communication which is delay prone. In [9] the eNodeB schedules the UEs affected by HeNBs to a special part of the spectrum such that the HeNBs map the downlink resource blocks from uplink sensing. However, the problem lies at the uplink to downlink Resource Block mapping that's performed by the HeNB which implies that the mapping scheme must be exchanged among the cells. Mahapatra and Strinati [10] describes a method which measures the interference of each RB at the HeNB, classifies the RBs and allocates them to the appropriate users with suitable transmit powers. This method is computationally intensive and the interference measurement is done at the HeNB and not the UE. Wang et al. [11] describes a scheme that uses time domain muting where the MUEs in a coverage hole are protected by scheduling them only on the muted sub-frames, but it may waste resources by scheduling macro users only on muted sub-frames.

This paper puts forward two novel interference mitigation schemes: FPCS and RPSS. FPCS is an adaptive power control scheme that detects affected MUEs based on their CQI feedback utilizing the Network Listen Mode (NLM) of the femto-cell. RPSS is an efficient yet simple resource partitioning scheme which does not rely on extra signaling, measurements and estimations.

2   Interference Mitigation Architecture

2.1   Femto-Cell Power Control Scheme (FPCS)

The main idea of this scheme is to achieve a controlled femto-cell interference at a MUE depending on the CQI reported by this user. However, the reported CQI already includes interference from the femto-cell which can be referred as 'SINR with femto-cell interference'. Thus, depending on this value, the femto-cell can estimate 'SINR without femto-cell interference' at this particular MUE. Then, the femto-cell can adjust its transmit power so that the SINR seen by the affected macro-cell user remains at a certain percentage of the estimated 'SINR without femto-cell interference'. This percentage is referred here as the SINR reduction factor, c.

When a femto-cell is started, during the initialization process it gathers information on its position, potential interferer positions with their transmission powers, and the wall penetration loss associated with the building it's serving. This takes place every time the femto-cell is booted or when it is plugged in. A femto-cell belongs to a specific cellular operator, and will be sold and licensed by this operator. Thus, femto-cells will be configured by the operator to exchange a set of information during the beginning of the femto-cell operations and maybe during regular intervals at the scale of hours or days.

After the initialization, when the femto-cell receives a CQI report from a nearby MUE, it estimates the MUE's SINR without femto-cell's interference, γ'_{woi}. Then, it adjusts its transmit power depending on γ'_{woi}. As a consequence, during the next transmission time interval (TTI) the femto-cell would still generate interference to the MUE, however it will be consistent with the pre-set operational limits of allowed interference. The MUE would report back the new CQI to its serving macro-cell and the femto-cell would again hear this and adjust it's transmit power accordingly. Figure 1a further illustrates this functionality.

Precise location information at the initialization process of the femto-cell can be obtained from the operator using the IP address of the femto-cell through the backhaul link. Here, the operator would know the location of the femto-cell due to the ADSL or fiber optic subscription of the user. The positions and transmit powers of potential interferes are sent by the operator to the femto-cell during this process. Hence the wall penetration loss, L'_{ow} can be estimated using the reception power of the strongest interfering macro-cell, $P_{rx,M}$ as follows:

$$L'_{ow}[dB] = P_{tx,M}[dB] - P_{rx,M}[dB] - PL_{M,F}[dB] \tag{1}$$

where, $P_{tx,M}$ is the transmit power of the strongest interfering macro-cell, $P_{rx,M}$ is the received power by the femto-cell from this strongest interferer, $PL_{M,F}$ is the path loss between this interferer and the femto-cell.

We define the relationship of estimated SINR without femto-cell's interference (γ'_{woi}), SINR with femto-cell interference (γ_{wi}) and SINR reduction factor (c) in Eq. 2. This relationship can be utilized to determine γ'_{woi} and as a result an expression for the femto-cell's transmit power can be derived based on known and estimated parameters.

$$\gamma'_{woi}[dB] = \begin{cases} \frac{1}{c} \times \gamma_{wi}[dB], & \text{if } \gamma_{wi}[dB] > 0 \\ c \times \gamma_{wi}[dB], & \text{if } \gamma_{wi}[dB] < 0 \end{cases} \tag{2}$$

Here, γ_{wi} can be approximated as:

$$\gamma_{wi} \approx \frac{P'_{rx,M}}{I_{M,noise} + P'_{rx,F}} \tag{3}$$

where, $(P'_{rx,M})$ is the estimated received power from the macro BS at the MUE, $(I_{M,noise})$ is the interference from all other BSs + noise and $P'_{rx,F}$ is the estimated received power from the femto-cell at the MUE. SINR w/o femto-cell's interference at the MUE, estimated by the femto-cell, is defined according to:

$$\gamma'_{woi} = \frac{P'_{rx,M}}{I_{M,noise}} \tag{4}$$

The femto-cell estimates the received power from the macro-cell using the macro BS's transmit power ($P_{tx,M}$) and the estimated path loss between the MUE and the macro-cell ($PL'_{MUE,M}$).

$$P'_{rx,M}[dB] = P_{tx,M}[dB] - PL'_{MUE,M}[dB] \tag{5}$$

The received power from the femto-cell at the MUE is estimated using the femto BS's transmit power ($P_{tx,F}$), estimated path loss between the MUE and the femto-cell ($PL'_{MUE,F}$), and estimated wall penetration loss (L'_{ow}) as:

$$P'_{rx,F}[dB] = P_{tx,F}[dB] - PL'_{MUE,F}[dB] - L'_{ow}[dB] \tag{6}$$

Thus the femto-cell's transmit power can be expressed as follows:

$$P_{tx,F}[dB] = PL'_{MUE,F}[dB] + L_{ow}[dB] + P_{tx,M}[dB]$$
$$- PL'_{MUE,M}[dB] + f(\gamma_{wi}, c) - \gamma_{wi}[dB], \quad (7)$$

where

$$f(\gamma_{wi}, c) = \begin{cases} [1 - \gamma_{wi}^{(1-\frac{1}{c})}][dB] \text{ if } \gamma_{wi}[dB] > 0 \\ [1 - \gamma_{wi}^{(1-c)}][dB] \text{ if } \gamma_{wi}[dB] < 0 \end{cases}$$

Next, we are going to describe each of the assumptions taken by the FPCS and how these assumptions can be justified.

Affected MUE Detection: A femto-cell can listen to CQI signals of macro UEs in its vicinity through the NLM mode, since users are sending these CQI reports in the uplink to their connected macro-cell. The femto-cell also belongs to the same operator, thus it can be configured to listen to the CQIs from these users. A femto-cell is capable of listening to the uplink transmissions of only nearby macro users because the signal power tends to decrease as the user goes further away. Therefore the femto-cell can identify which users are in its vicinity. Moreover, a femto-cell determines if a MUE is affected by the HeNB interference when the CQI values reported by this user tend to drop for a certain duration.

MUE Position Estimation: It is necessary to estimate the affected MUE's position by the femto-cell for FPCS to function properly. To determine the transmit power that achieves the estimated SINR at the MUE, it is required to estimate the path loss of the MUE-macrocell ($PL'_{MUE,M}$) and MUE-femtocell ($PL'_{MUE,F}$) links according to Eq. 7. The femto-cell estimates the affected UE's path loss by behaving as a MUE and performing uplink power control. Accordingly, uplink reception power from the femto-cell and the MUE will be the same at the macro-cell at this instance. Hence the path loss between the femto-cell and the MUE can be estimated using the femto-cell uplink transmit power, $P_{tx,F,UL}$ and the femto-cell uplink reception power $P_{rx,F,UL}$ as follows:

$$PL'_{MUE,F} = \frac{1}{2}(P_{tx,F,UL} - P_{rx,F,UL}) - L'_{ow} \quad (8)$$

Figure 2b further illustrates the MUE's path loss estimation by the femto-cell. Now, the path loss between macro-cell and the MUE ($PL'_{MUE,M}$) can be estimated as the distance to the macro-cell is known.

However, the influence of fading is not considered for the path loss estimation because the femto-cell is not aware of the amount of fading present at the MUE. Fading is a property that is inherent to the MUE depending on its signal propagation, thus the femto-cell is unable to acquire any information on this.

2.2   Random PRB Selection Scheme (RPSS)

Unlike FPCS, this scheme performs interference mitigation exploiting resource partitioning. In OFDMA, downlink resource allocation is characterized by scheduling UEs with Physical Resource Blocks (PRBs) and each resource block

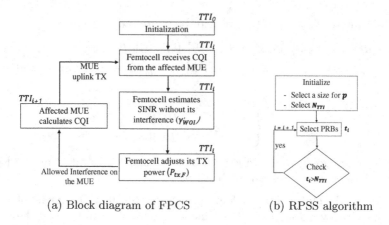

(a) Block diagram of FPCS   (b) RPSS algorithm

Fig. 1. Proposed algorithms

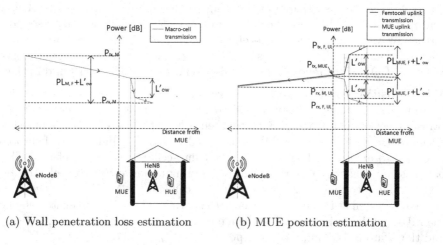

(a) Wall penetration loss estimation   (b) MUE position estimation

Fig. 2. These figures explain the estimation of wall penetration loss and the position of the macro UE. Femto-cell performs uplink power control and behaves similar to an MUE during the period when the MUE's position is estimated

is assigned only to one UE at a time. In assigning PRBs to users, usually the best PRBs having the highest SINR are allocated to achieve a higher Modulation and Coding Scheme (MCS), a higher data rate and spectral efficiency. In this scheme, downlink resource partitioning is performed as follows: The femto-cell chooses PRBs for a subset, p_i in the ith interval such that $p_i \subseteq S$, where S is the set of all PRBs. PRBs for this subset are chosen randomly. The chosen PRBs are used for a predetermined time, i.e. a pre-defined number of TTIs (N_{TTI}) to schedule the HUEs. They are released when the usage duration of the ith interval (t_i), $t_i \geq N_{TTI}$, to choose the next set of PRBs (p_{i+1}) for the next interval, $i + 1$. The optimum size of the subset, p and the optimum usage duration of these chosen PRBs, N_{TTI} are determined using a sensitivity analysis.

Essentially, this optimum combination is required to reduce the interference efficiently at the MUEs while satisfying the HUEs' data rate and Quality of Service (QoS) demands. Figure 1b further elaborates the RPSS algorithm.

Moreover, this scheme does not guarantee that the chosen subset will not interfere with other macro users in the vicinity. Since the subsets are chosen randomly, there is still a probability that it might be the same PRBs that the MUE in the vicinity is using. Nonetheless, the idea is to have a simple solution that does not require any prior knowledge, assumptions or any complexity.

Comparison of FPCS and RPSS: As both FPCS and RPSS do not rely on backhaul communication, they can perform without substantial delays. In FPCS, the femto-cell has control over interference that it generates at the macro UE. The assumptions that are made for this scheme are reasonable, following the 3GPP specifications. Another advantage of this scheme is that interference mitigation is performed based on the channel condition at the macro user, not the femto-cell. In contrast, RPSS has the advantage of simplicity, it does not rely on signaling, measurements, or assumptions. In spite of that, the parameters for PRB subset and duration must be chosen carefully so that both MUEs and HUEs benefit from a balanced performance.

3 Channel Model

There are three path loss models used in this work according to [12] which are used conditional to the type of link that exists between a transmitter and a receiver. Expression 9 is used as the path loss model for an outdoor link (useful or interfering) between a macro-cell and a MUE.

$$PL_1[dB] = 15.3 + 37.6 log_{10} R \tag{9}$$

where, R is the distance between the UE and the macro-cell. Equation 10 is used for a HUE that's served by a HeNB in the same house.

$$PL_2[dB] = 38.46 + 20 log_{10} R \tag{10}$$

Finally, Eq. 11 is used for a MUE which is situated outside a house but receiving signals from a HeNB

$$PL_3[dB] = max(15.3 + 37.6 log_{10} R,\ 38.46 + 20 log_{10} R) + L_{ow} \tag{11}$$

where, L_{ow} is the wall penetration loss.

All links are modeled with shadow fading using Log-Normal distribution with spatial correlation according to [13]. The fast fading model used in this work is a Jakes'-like model [14,15]. Hence the fast fading attenuation depends on both time and frequency as it considers delay spread for frequency selectivity and Doppler spread for time selectivity. Mobility of the users prompts Doppler spread. The power delay profile caused by multi-path propagation which is the reason behind frequency selectivity is modeled using the ITU Pedestrian B channel specification [16]. This is a commonly used medium delay empirical channel model for office environments. Unlike path loss and slow fading, fast fading is different for each PRB of each user since the channel is frequency selective.

4   Simulation and Results

This section explains the simulation environment of this work e.g. simulator, user mobility, simulation parameters and evaluates the performance of the two interference mitigation schemes introduced in the previous sections.

4.1   ComNets LTE-A System Level Simulator

Simulations for this work are carried out using ComNets LTE-A system level simulator [17–19] in OPNET modeler software. The simulator is designed to investigate and analyze the overall network and end user performance. Radio, transport and end-to-end protocols of LTE-A have been designed and implemented according to the 3GPP specifications. Figure 3a illustrates a reference scenario of the simulator. The figure shows that modelling of the core networks is represented by Access Gateway (aGW), and the E-UTRAN part is represented by transport routers, eNodeBs and UEs. The Remote Server represents an internet server or any other internet device to which the LTE users are communicating with. The aGW and eNodeBs are connected through the transport network which consists of IP routers. These routers are configured with standard OPNET models and routing protocols. Furthermore, entities such as aGW and eNodeBs are developed along with the respective user-plane protocols defined by the 3GPP standards. Global UE List acts as a central database that collects and updates global information of all UEs and other nodes upon their changes. It updates the users' mobility information within each cell along with the channel condition of each user.

The cells schedule their UEs using Optimized Service Aware Scheduler (OSA) [20,21] in this simulator. The OSA scheduler differentiates between different QoS classes mainly by defining several MAC QoS bearer types such as Guaranteed (GBR) and non-Guaranteed (nonGBR) Bit Rate. At the same time, it gains from the multi-users-diversity by exploiting the different users' channel conditions in order to maximize the cell throughput in a proportional fair manner.

As mentioned in Sect. 3, the shadow fading maps and the fast fading model for femto- and macro-cell UEs were produced using open source Vienna Simulator [22] and they were deployed in ComNets LTE-A System Level Simulator. Separate shadow fading maps with sizes of 2400 m × 2080 m and 100 m × 100 m were generated for both femto- and macro-cells respectively. The shadow fading parameters used to generate these maps are specified in [12].

4.2   Mobility Model

HUEs and MUEs have two different mobility models. MUEs travel inside the coverage area of the macro-cell that it is connected to. HUEs on the other hand travel inside a 15 m × 15 m building. Once the HUE reaches a wall, they choose a random direction to traverse inside that same building. A femto-cell can accompany several HUEs inside the building. MUEs do not enter the house and they also do not change their direction once they come across a wall of a house on

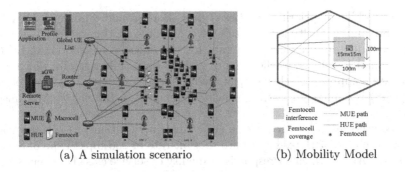

(a) A simulation scenario   (b) Mobility Model

Fig. 3. Simulation Environment

their way. This is done to avoid the extreme interference they have to confront inside houses with femto-cells. This implies that when a MUE from outside enters a house, it joins the Closed Subscriber Group of that house and hence the HeNB doesn't behave as an interference source. Macro-cells do not serve any of the HUEs placed in their respective coverage areas, and HUEs are only served through the femto-cells. Figure 3b illustrates the mobility of a femto and a macro user having the above mentioned behavior. In Fig. 3b the red line marks the macro-cell coverage boundary, the 100 m × 100 m yellow rectangle represents the femto-cell interference area and the light blue rectangle represents the femto-cell coverage area. The difference of the femto-cell coverage area and the interference area is that femto-cells do not serve any users beyond their coverage although the MUEs can receive their power as interference.

4.3   Simulation parameters

Table 1a summarizes the simulation assumptions and general parameters used within the evaluation. There are three users classified according to the type of application used by them: FTP, VoIP and Video. Table 1b summarizes the configuration parameters of those applications. Femto-cells in the simulations are placed inside small indoor apartments and the apartments are modeled with an area of 15 m × 15 m. The walls of the apartments are modeled to have a 20 dB wall penetration loss. Femto-cells and their apartments are placed only in the center cell, where four apartments are considered for the evaluation and are placed within the micro-cell. Inside each apartment there is a femto-cell and a HUE. Each apartment is 150 m away from the center cell.

Parameter 'Command Mix' in Table 1b denotes the percentage of FTP downloads to FTP uploads. Hence a Command Mix of 100 % means that the application performs only FTP downloads. The Inter-request time denotes the time taken for the next file request to start once a file download is completed. Request for the next file download is sent only after the current download is finished. The simulator consists of eight types of quality of service classes and each class has a different QoS characteristic and this means that each has different priority over the air interface. The types of quality of service classes arranged in the order of lowest to highest priority are: Best Effort, Background, Standard, Excellent Effort, Streaming Multimedia, Interactive Multimedia, Interactive Voice and Reserved. VoIP application's data rate for the encoder scheme GSM EFR is 12.2 kbps and it belongs to the Adaptive Multi-Rate codecs family which is an audio data compression scheme optimized for speech coding. The Type of Service (TOS) is configured as 'EF' which corresponds to Interactive Multimedia traffic.

Video users are configured with a Frame inter-arrival time of 15 frames/s and a Frame size of 2133 Bytes contribute to a bit rate of 256 kbps. Type of Service of Video is 'AF31' which corresponds to quality of service class Excellent Effort. All the femto-cell users are configured as Video users with a bit rate of 18 Mbps to enable maximum interference to the MUEs.

4.4 Results and Analysis

In this section, we present the simulation results for our evaluations. The purpose of these evaluations is to study and compare the effects of the two interference mitigation schemes proposed in this paper: FPCS and RPSS. The performance of FPCS is examined using three scenarios having three different SINR reduction factors: $c = 95\%$; 90% and 85%. These percentages reflect the amount of SINR reduction that is expected at a macro UE due to the presence of a femto-cell. Results of the three FPCS scenarios are compared with the results of RPSS. Additionally, two reference scenarios are used to benchmark the best and worst performances. 'No HeNB' is the ideal scenario, and femto-cells do not interfere with the macro UEs here. 'Fixed' is the worst scenario with maximum interference from femto-cells having fixed transmit powers. Hence, altogether six scenarios are compared, and they are listed in Table 2 along with the terms used to represent them in the results. Ten simulations are performed with ten different seeds for each scenario. The confidence interval calculations in all the result graphs are carried out using Student's t distribution.

Table 1. Simulation parameters

Parameter	Value
Downlink operating frequency	2.0 GHz
Number of cells	7
Inter eNodeB distance	500m
MUEs in the center cell	10
MUEs in each surrounding cell	5
Apartment size	15×15 m^2
Femto-cells in the center cell	4
HUEs per femto-cell	1
Femto-cell distance to macro-cell	150m
Total number of PRBs	25
eNodeB transmit power per PRB	-4 dBm
Femto-cell's total transmit power (without power control)	0 dBm
Noise per PRB	-120.447 dBm
Noise floor	9 dB
Wall penetration loss	20 dB
UE speed	3 kmph

(a) Simulation parameters

User	Parameter	Value
FTP	Command Mix (Get/Total)	100%
	Inter-request Time (seconds)	1
	Type of Service	Best Effort
	File Size	1 MB
VoIP	Encoder Scheme	GSM EFR
	Voice Frames per Packet	1
	Type of Service	AF33
	Traffic mix (%)	All discrete
	Conversation environment	Land phone (Quiet room)
Video	Frame inter-arrival time	15 frames/s
	Frame size	2133 Bytes
	Type of Service	EF
	Traffic mix	All discrete

(b) Traffic model parameters

Table 2. Types of scenarios used in the simulations and used terms

Scenario	Term
FPCS: 95 % SINR reduction	'95 %'
FPCS: 90 % SINR reduction	'90 %'
FPCS: 85 % SINR reduction	'85 %'
RPSS	'Random'
No interference from femto-cells	'No HeNB'
Femto-cells with fixed transmit power	'Fixed'

The types of collected results from the above mentioned six scenarios are as follows: for FTP users the SINRs and the download response times are compared during the interference periods from HeNBs. For VoIP users, the Mean Opinion Scores (MOS), end-to-end delays and SINRs are compared. Finally for Video users the end-to-end delays and SINRs are compared. MOS measures the subjective quality of a voice call and returns a scalar one digit score to express the quality of the call [19]. The MOS values range from 1 to 5, with 5 being the best quality and 1 the worst quality. MOS values in the simulations were calculated based on the end-to-end delays and jitter of the delay of VoIP users, and the experience of humans were not considered.

Figure 4a illustrates the SINR of VoIP users, Figs. 4b and c depict the performances of their applications in terms of end-to-end delay and MOS. In the SINR comparisons of '95 %', '90 %' and '85 %' against the 'Fixed' scenario, the three power control scenarios of FPCS have outperformed 'Fixed' with the gain margin ranging from 30.52 % to 42.75 %. This shows a clear improvement over the worst case scenario. This demonstrates the ability of FPCS to mitigate the femto-cell interference. However, RPSS shows the best performance with the exception being that they achieve much lower data rates for the HUEs.

VoIP is an example for a GBR real time application that is sensitive to delays. Usually an end-to-end delay of more than 150 ms for a VoIP application results in bad call quality [19] and deteriorates user satisfaction. The significant fact is that the two interference mitigation schemes show values less than 150 ms, while the

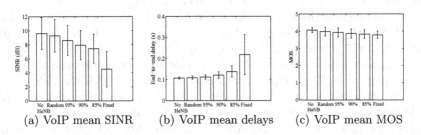

(a) VoIP mean SINR (b) VoIP mean delays (c) VoIP mean MOS

Fig. 4. Results comparison of VoIP users for 'No HeNB', 'Random', '95 %', '90 %','85 %' and 'Fixed' scenarios

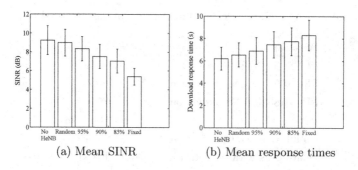

(a) Mean SINR   (b) Mean response times

Fig. 5. Results comparison of FTP users for 'No HeNB', 'Random', '95 %', '90 %','85 %' and 'Fixed' scenarios

'Fixed' scenario shows that MUE is having very bad call quality which is much higher than 150 ms. This indicates the performance enhancement in the VoIP application of the macro users due to the interference alleviation. MOS values depend on the end-to-end delays and the delay jitter of VoIP users. Hence MOS is also an important metric on the performance of the VoIP application. Any improvement of SINR at the macro UEs due to mitigation of interference should finally reflect on the performance of the user's application. MOS values give an indication on the performance enhancement of the VoIP application under the two interference mitigation schemes over 'Fixed' scenario.

Figure 5a depicts the mean SINRs of FTP users for the six scenarios. Here RPSS achieves a gain margin of 38.92 %, whereas FPCS with sensitivities of '95 %', '90 %' and '85 %' achieve 32 %, 23.19 % and 17.94 % respectively compared to 'Fixed'. This clearly shows that the two interference mitigation schemes perform better compared to the 'Fixed' scenario in terms of SINR for FTP users. Non-GBR bearers usually carry non real time or best effort type of services; FTP is an example for such a service. Hence FTP does not have high delay requirements in contrast to real time or GBR services. Figure 5b depicts the mean download response times of FTP users across the six scenarios. As expected, the download response time of the 'Fixed' scenario has the highest delay with 8.31s FPCS and RPSS scenarios all have better download response times showing a clear edge over the worst case user application performance.

Figure 6a depicts the Video users' mean SINRs for the compared six scenarios. FPCS with sensitivities of '95 %', '90 %' and '85 %' achieve gain margins of 28.34 %, 19.37 % and 13.59 % respectively and RPSS achieves a gain margin of 43.24 % compared to 'Fixed'. This shows that the two interference mitigation schemes perform better compared to 'Fixed' in terms of SINR for Video users. Figure 6b shows the mean end-to-end delays of video users. 'Fixed' scheme has the highest delay of about one second and the confidence interval is also high suggesting a higher variation of delays. The mean end-to-end delays for all other scenarios are less than 0.2 s with a much lower delay variation suggesting a clear improvement over 'Fixed'. This shows how the worst case scenario's video performance is affected, emphasizing the importance of the interference mitigation.

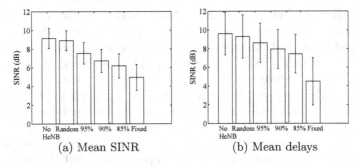

(a) Mean SINR   (b) Mean delays

Fig. 6. Results comparison of Video users for 'No HeNB', 'Random', '95 %', '90 %', '85 %' and 'Fixed' scenarios

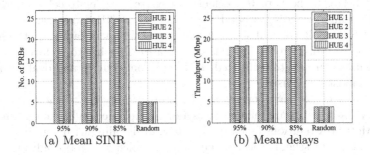

(a) Mean SINR   (b) Mean delays

Fig. 7. Comparison of HUEs for '95 %', '90 %','85 %' and 'Random' scenarios

However, in all of the above comparisons, FPCS does not perform interference mitigation optimally. RPSS out performs FPCS in all the scenarios. This can be attributed to the amount of fading prevalent at the macro UEs which is not estimated by the femto-cell in the FPCS interference mitigation process.

Figures 7a and b represent respectively the number of used PRBs and the throughputs of the four HUEs. It can be observed that the number of PRBs and throughputs of RPSS are much less than the other three in all scenarios. The other significant fact is the throughputs and the number of used PRBs of FPCS have similar values in all three. Hence it is evident that the performance of HUEs are limited in RPSS due to the limited number of PRBs. On the other hand the FPCS provides a much balanced scheme that mitigates macro UE interference successfully while being able to provide a better service to femto-cell users.

5   Conclusion

In this paper, two novel interference mitigation schemes are proposed and evaluated, mainly: FPCS and RPSS. Results of these two schemes were compared against an ideal case, 'No HeNB', where there is no interference from femto-cells, and a worst case where there is maximum interference from femto-cells, 'Fixed'. The macro users were configured with three types of applications, VoIP, video and FTP and their performance was evaluated under the two interference mitigation schemes. The results have shown that as the SINR of the macro users improve, performance of the user applications have also improved compared to the worst case situation. Our results show that the two interference mitigation schemes perform efficiently compared to the worst case situation.

Although RPSS performs better than FPCS with regards to MUE SINR and the users' applications performance, the femto-cell users suffer because only a subset of PRBs is allocated to their users. In addition, in real life situations the cells can become increasingly loaded with MUEs and as a result when choosing a subset of PRBs, there might still be a high probability that this subset would interfere with certain MUEs. On the other hand, FPCS gives a balanced performance between the performance of the MUEs and the HUEs, creating a fair trade off between the two. It efficiently alleviates the femto-cell's interference on MUEs while providing a good service to the HeNB users. The main issue with FPCS is, as it's not able to estimate the amount of fading at the MUEs, the efficiency of interference mitigation decreases. This has to be further studied and a solution on how to estimated these additional effects and deal with these situations must be devised.

The two schemes have several novel features compared to the current SoA: simplicity, lower hardware intensiveness and non-reliance on backhaul communication. Most SoA solutions focus on in/out-band signaling with high information exchange, but our schemes do not rely on any, which is a major advantage.

References

1. Lopez-Perez, D., Valcarce, A., de la Roche, G., Zhang, J.: OFDMA femtocells: a roadmap on interference avoidance. IEEE Commun. Mag. **47**, 41–48 (2009)
2. Lopez-Perez, D., Guvenc, I., de la Roche, G., Kountouris, M., Quek, T., Zhang, J.: Enhanced intercell interference coordination challenges in heterogeneous networks. IEEE Wirel. Commun. **18**, 22–30 (2011)
3. Burchardt, H., Bharucha, Z., Haas, H.: Distributed and autonomous resource allocation for femto-cellular networks. In: Signals, Systems and Computers (2012)
4. Claussen, H., Ho, L.T.W., Samuel, L.: Self-optimization of coverage for femtocell deployments. In: Wireless Telecommunications Symposium (2008)
5. Yavuz, M., Meshkati, F., Nanda, S., Pokhariyal, A., Johnson, N., Raghothaman, B., Richardson, A.: Interference management and performance analysis of UMTS/HSPA+ femtocells. IEEE Commun. Mag. **47**, 102–109 (2009)
6. Lalam, M., Papathanasiou, I., Maqbool, M., Lestable, T.: Adaptive downlink power control for HSDPA femtocells. In: Future Network Mobile Summit (2011)
7. Morita, M., Matsunaga, Y., Hamabe, K.: Adaptive power level setting of femtocell base stations for mitigating interference with macrocells. In: VTC Fall (2010)
8. Bharucha, Z., Saul, A., Auer, G., Haas, H.: Dynamic resource partitioning for downlink femto-to-macro-cell interference avoidance. EURASIP J. (2010)
9. Guvenc, I., Jeong, M-R., Sahin, M., Xu, H., Watanabe, F.: Interference avoidance in 3GPP femtocell networks using resource partitioning and sensing. In: PIMRC (2010)
10. Mahapatra, R., Strinati, E.: Radio resource management in femtocell downlink exploiting location information. In: ANTS (2011)

11. Wang, Y., Pedersen, K., Frederiksen, F.: Detection and protection of macro-users in dominant area of co-channel CSG cells. In: VTC (2012)
12. 3GPP R4-092042. Simulation assumptions and parameters for FDD HeNB RF requirement. 3GPP Technical report (2009)
13. Claussen, H.: Efficient modelling of channel maps with correlated shadow fading in mobile radio systems. In: PIMRC (2005)
14. Lichte, H.S., Valentin, S.: Implementing MAC protocols for cooperative relaying: a compiler-assisted approach. In: SIMUTools (2008)
15. Köpke, A., Swigulski, M., Wessel, K., Willkomm, D., Haneveld, P.T.K., Parker, T.E.V., Visser, O.W., Lichte, H.S., Valentin, S.: Simulating wireless and mobile networks in OMNeT++ the MiXiM Vision. In: SIMUTools (2008)
16. ITU-R Recommendation M.1225. Guidelines for evaluation of radio transmission technologies for IMT-2000. ITU, Technical Report (1997)
17. Zahariev, N., Zaki, Y., Li, X., Goerg, C., Weerawardane, T., Timm-Giel, A.: Optimized service aware LTE MAC scheduler with comparison against other well known schedulers. In: Koucheryavy, Y., Mamatas, L., Matta, I., Tsaoussidis, V. (eds.) WWIC 2012. LNCS, vol. 7277, pp. 323–331. Springer, Heidelberg (2012)
18. Zaki, Y., Weerawardane, T., Görg, C., Timm-Giel, A.: Long term evolution (LTE) model development within OPNET simulation environment. In: OPNETWORK (2011)
19. Zaki, Y.: Future mobile communications: LTE optimization and mobile network virtualization. Ph.D. dissertation, University of Bremen (2012)
20. Zaki, Y., Zahariev, N., Weerawardane, T., Görg, C., Timm-Giel, A.: Optimized service aware LTE MAC scheduler: design, implementation and performance evaluation. In: OPNETWORK (2011)
21. Zaki, Y., Weerawardane, T., Gorg, C., Timm-Giel, A.: Multi-QoS-Aware fair scheduling for LTE. In: VTC (2011)
22. Ikuno, J., Wrulich, M., Rupp, M.: System level simulation of LTE networks. In: VTC (2010)

Enhancing Video Delivery in the LTE Wireless Access Using Cross-Layer Mechanisms

Michelle Wetterwald[1]($\boxtimes$), Leonardo Badia[2], Daniele Munaretto[2], and Christian Bonnet[3]

[1] HeNetBot, Sophia Antipolis, France
Michelle.Wetterwald@henetbot.fr
[2] University of Padova, Padua, Italy
{badia,munaretto}@dei.unipd.it
[3] Eurecom, Sophia Antipolis, France
Christian.Bonnet@eurecom.fr

Abstract. The current evolution of the global Internet data traffic shows an increasing demand of video transmissions, which potentially leads to the saturation of mobile networks. To cope with this issue, this paper describes techniques to handle the video traffic load in the last hop, of the communication network, i.e., the wireless access. The general idea is to benefit from a cross-layer architecture for efficient video transport, where multiple wireless access technologies, represented by Wi-Fi and next generation cellular technologies (4G and beyond), interact with the upper layers through an abstract interface. This architecture enables the introduction of enhancements in the LTE-A wireless access: evolved Multimedia Broadcast and Multicast Services (eM-BMS) extended with dynamic groupcast communications, video relay at the Packet Data Convergence Protocol (PDCP) level and a smart video frame dropping mechanism to provide mobile users with a satisfactory level of Quality of Experience (QoE). These video-aware mechanisms leverage the abstract interface and allow mobile operators to fine-tune their networks while coping with the upcoming mobile video traffic increase.

Keywords: Wireless access · LTE-advanced · Video transport · Mobile network operators · Cross-layer optimisation · eMBMS

1 Introduction

Recent market studies [1] and future technology forecast reports [2] show that the share of video in global Internet traffic is growing at a rapid pace. It already represents the majority of the Internet traffic and is going to become dominant in the near future. In parallel, due to the diffusion of smart mobile phones and tablets, users consume videos via wireless networks, either local or cellular. Mobile network operators face the growing challenge of providing wireless accesses tailored to the expected level of QoE at the user side when consuming Mobile TV, Video on Demand or user-generated content (upstreaming).

Taking this challenge into consideration, the objective of the MEDIEVAL project [3] was to enhance the existing network architecture to efficiently deliver video

© Institute for Computer Sciences, Social Informatics and Telecommunications Engineering 2015
R. Agüero et al. (Eds.): MONAMI 2014, LNICST 141, pp. 18–31, 2015.
DOI: 10.1007/978-3-319-16292-8_2

applications to the mobile users. The designed architecture is composed of four sub-systems, Video Services Control on top to provision the network services, then Transport Optimization (TO) to enhance video quality using transport and caching mechanisms and Mobility Management (MM) to allow video flow continuation when roaming [4] and finally, Wireless Access to optimise access network functions for video delivery in the last hop through heterogeneous wireless access technologies. Hence, novel mechanisms in the Wireless Access sub-system are designed and focus on enhanced access techniques which exploit cross-layer optimisations through the interaction with upper layers, e.g., application and transport layers. Contention-based techniques, such as the IEEE 802.11 standard for Wireless Local Area Networks (WLANs) [5], and coordination-based, e.g., the Long Term Evolution Advanced (LTE-A) of Third Generation Partnership Project (3GPP) cellular systems are covered.

As a main pillar of its global architecture, a wireless abstract interface guarantees a transparent interaction between the underlying wireless technologies and the video traffic-aware upper layers. This interaction is built upon the IEEE 802.21 standard, pictured in Fig. 1, which proposes three different Media Independent Handover (MIH) Services [6] and offers to the upper layer management protocols generic triggers, information acquisition and the tools needed to perform mobility. The Event Service (MIES) provides the framework needed to manage the classification, filtering and triggering of network events, and to dynamically report the status of the links. The Command Service (MICS) allows the upper layer management entities to control the behaviour of the links. The Information Service (MIIS) is distributes the topology-related information and policies from a repository located in the network. They result in a cross-layer architecture where the Media Independent Handover Function (MIHF) operates as a relay between the media-specific Link layer entities and the media-agnostic upper layer entities, e.g., MIH-Users. In the mobile terminal, the MIH-User is usually represented by a Connection Manager (CMGR) whose main role is to decide which path is best suited to reach the application server or the Correspondent Node (CN) located across the Internet [7].

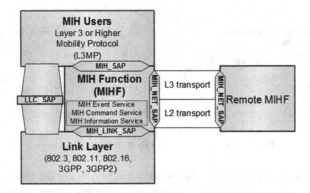

Fig. 1. IEEE 802.21 cross-layer model

Indeed, in the proposed architecture, a cross-layer relationship is established with upper components, i.e., the MM and TO subsystems, to exchange information about the capabilities of the components at the lower layers, as well as to configure them [8]. This interface, pictured in Fig. 2, is optimised by a central abstraction layer. This layer operates at both the Mobile Terminal (MT) and the Point of Attachment (PoA) to the network, which corresponds to the access point in WLAN and the base station, or eNodeB, in LTE-A networks. The associated functions are split into two main streams, as shown in Fig. 2. A Monitoring function dynamically retrieves the information related to the access networks availability and quality in order to provide it to the upper layers through the abstract interface. Moreover, it senses the environment searching for new available access networks; whenever they are found, it analyses their capacity, bandwidth usage, and available resources. The MM is mostly interested in the wireless signal events, while the TO considers the traffic measurements allowing a more precise estimation of the wireless cell load. Secondly, a Dynamic Configuration function takes into account the requests from the upper layers and the characteristics of the video flows to setup the network interface or establish radio channels to accommodate an upcoming data flow. It works by defining a utility function which makes it possible to allocate resources by providing the optimal set of parameters describing each technology. Generic Quality of Service (QoS) parameters for link throughput, classes of service, or error rates, are defined and translated through the interface into technology-specific parameters. The MM is thus able to activate and deactivate the network interfaces and resources due to the roaming of the user or some optimization decision made in the core network entities. The TO is able to command that some video frames, marked at the Internet Protocol (IP) packet level, become prioritised before leaving the PoA, avoiding deep packet inspection and thus preserving the user QoE.

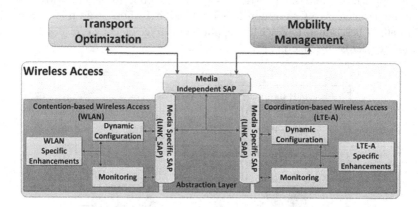

Fig. 2. Wireless Access sub-system architecture

As a consequence, the Wireless Access (WA) subsystem of the architecture is split into three main functional blocks. The abstraction layer component provides the generic interfaces between video specific functions (i.e., transport and mobility), while the wireless components include the features and mechanisms designed to further enhance the video flow transmission over the air. In fact, besides being tightly coupled with the monitoring and dynamic configuration functions, the wireless components have been enriched with technology-specific functionalities benefiting from the cross-layer architecture. Video applications are characterised by high throughput, i.e. large bandwidth to ensure good visual quality, and a strong sensitivity to jitter. Novel features and techniques should address these constraints. The focus of this paper is on the work performed from a system view on the upper layers of the LTE-A radio interface, contained in the "LTE-A Specific Enhancement" block shown on the right of Fig. 2. The enhancement applied to the cellular system covers group communications based on the 3GPP evolved Multimedia Broadcast and Multicast Services (eMBMS) standard. It further extends the cell capabilities and coverage thanks to the introduction of a relay at Layer 3 level between the eNodeB and the User Equipment (UE) and finally, when these methods are not sufficient, smartly drops part of the video traffic to ensure a target quality to the users. All three techniques can be used independently or complement one another.

The objective of this paper is to describe the enhancements achieved by the project for the upper layers of the LTE radio interface and provide directions to help the network operators better deliver video traffic in their cellular networks. The discussion is organised as follows. Section 2 discusses the optimization of group communications in the cellular LTE technology, i.e., the improvements proposed for the eMBMS multicast support. In Sect. 3, relays operating at the Packet Data Convergence Protocol (PDCP) level, just below networking layer, are introduced. Their impact on the quality of the video transmitted in the cell is analysed and evaluated. In Sect. 4, we propose a mechanism to smooth the load in the cell and avoid visual degradation of the video. Finally, we conclude the paper by assessing these different techniques, highlighting their benefits and suitability for future mobile networks.

2 Introducing Dynamic Groupcast Communications in the LTE Cell

The first enhancement applied to the LTE-A system addresses group communications. Since video content uses a large amount of the available transport capacity, distributing the same data to several users located in the same area wastes radio resources. Conversely, multicasting or broadcasting the service allows saving the resources that would be used if unicast Data Radio Bearers (DRB) were established for other users and/or purposes. Multicast communications allow sharing the resources on the wireless hop when a geographically-close and potentially large group of mobile listeners watches the same program. In LTE-A, the services broadcast by eMBMS are enhanced to support dynamic multicast sessions together with user mobility.

In the cellular part of the WA architecture, multicast is optimised by supporting and extending the eMBMS bearer service specified in the 3GPP standards [9, 10]. Its objective is to enable point-to-multipoint communications (p-t-m) over the radio interface (or Access Stratum), allowing resources to be shared in the network. The MBMS support has been subject to serious revisions within the 3GPP standardization, with the inclusion of new tools and procedures to improve its performance. Actually, the handling of multicast flow has disappeared in the transition between the initial and evolved versions of this standard, mostly due to business causes, costs and complexity of deployment. In the LTE and LTE-A systems, only broadcast sessions are proposed.

The Multicast-Broadcast Single Frequency Network (MBSFN) areas, pictured in Fig. 3, hosting the eMBMS, are configured semi-statically. When the network is built, some eNodeBs are set-up in order to support point-to-multipoint transmissions, while others, pertaining to reserved cells in the same area, do not offer that service. The MBMS configuration is beaconed over the related cells in two different messages (or System Information Blocks, SIB), independently of the number of listening mobile users in the cell. To avoid the allocation of broadcast resources (MBMS Radio Bearer or MRB) when the number of users is low, the eNodeB implements a counting procedure, where the connected MTs in the cell are invited to signal themselves back to the base station in uplink. This procedure is used to perform admission control and allocation of the MRB resources. In more recent advances, mobile nodes are able to inform the network of their interest and have the capability to receive MBMS sessions from a certain set of frequencies of the MBSFN, allowing the network entities to further enhance resource allocation in the cell. This information is transferred to the target eNodeB during the handover preparation phase within a specific MBMS context associated to the MT.

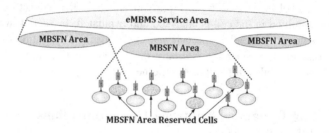

Fig. 3. eMBMS Areas

We extend these features to improve the semi-static broadcast support provided by the MBSFN. By using a cross-layer operation between the LTE-A component and the MM sub-system through the dynamic configuration function, the eMBMS can include the dynamic multicast resource allocation in a manner similar to what earlier planned by the standard. In our study, we simplify the Multicast session start and stop procedures at the eNodeB and their notification to the mobile. Another important feature is the counting of listening mobiles in each cell by the eNodeB. This information is used to trigger the multicast session if needed or move the flow back to a point-to-point bearer if only one user in the cell is listening. To avoid interference over other types of traffic (e.g., voice calls) that could take place simultaneously, it is important to establish a coordinated control of unicast and multicast communications in a cell providing the MBMS service.

When the connected MT joins a multicast session, an MBMS context is created in the network entities. Whether it happens while being attached to the LTE cell or during a handover, the procedures that enable it to receive the session are executed in the wireless access modules, as shown in Fig. 4. A request to activate the multicast resources is received by the LTE-A Access module in the PoA. If relevant, and based on internal algorithms taking into account the resources already allocated, it triggers the MBMS Session Start procedure, establishing a new MRB and informing the MT. The "MBMS session start" is executed dynamically in the eNodeB, upon the request from the MM sub-system, which removes the constraint to allocate resources when the network is built. If it happens during a handover, the MT still connected to its old PoA receives this information during the preparation phase and is thus able to configure and receive the MBMS service as soon as it attaches to the target cell.

The MT joins the service only once, as long as the context can be transferred between PoAs. This is another feature of the MM [11], which avoids the constraint of the MT self-signalling during the whole data reception period, whether in mobility or not. This enhancement allows a smooth support of the counting procedure, but with the eNodeB capable of identifying by itself the attached MTs that own a multicast context in the cell. It can then adapt the resource allocation to the real bandwidth consumption and the actual number of mobile listeners in its cell. When it detects that a flow, identified by a specific flow label and source address, marked as "multicast-enabled" is received simultaneously by several MTs, it transfers the video data into an MRB, even if the core network is not multicast-enabled. This improves sharing resource in the wireless access. Table 1 provides a summary of the mechanism traces recorded at the eNodeB.

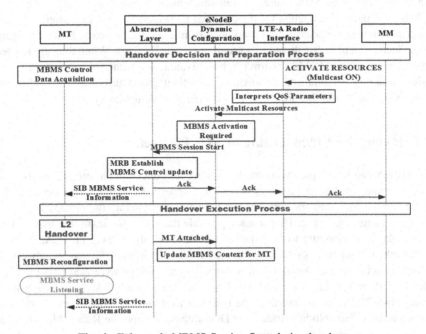

Fig. 4. Enhanced eMBMS Session Start during handover

Table 1. Traces obtained in eNodeB when applying the dynamic Session Start (time in ms.)

Steps	Start	End
- Final step of MT arrival in the cell (MT connected)		0.000
- MBMS context for service 97 established for the MT	0.011	0.070
- Successful MBMS context setup in the lower layers	2.673	2.666
- First multicast packet from IP to be sent to the MT	14858.290	14858.297
- eMBMS session start triggered	14858.301	14858.343
- Procedure on-going, packet sent as unicast, which prevents it from being delayed	14858.344	14858.360
- Notification: successful completion of the procedure	14922.571	14922.586
- IP multicast packet forwarded on the MBMS bearer	15859.957	15859.983
- IP multicast packet forwarded on the MBMS bearer	16857.716	16857.743

Another impact is expected also on the configuration of the radio access when taking into account the spectrum usage and the resource allocation. Multicast flows require bandwidth reservation based on the dedicated eMBMS Bearer parameters received from upper layers and the worst Channel Quality Indicator (CQI) of Multicast clients measured in the lower layers. This results in a bad spectrum usage because users with a robust link underutilise the bandwidth resources. Our solution combines H.264/ SVC (Scalable Video Coding) together with cross-layer optimization to dynamically increase/decrease the video quality perceived by each user according to the different channel feedback messages, using mechanisms similar to those described in Sect. 4.

This is of particular interest for the Personal Broadcast Service [12] studied by the project and that is expected to gain momentum in the coming years. Here, user generated video content is distributed to a group of mobile listeners. When they are located in the same area, an eMBMS session can be activated. A typical use case is a group of tourists receiving personalised information from their guide during a visit [13] or the dissemination of a road hazard event in a cooperative vehicular system.

3   Relaying the Video Traffic at PDCP-Level

The eMBMS can be coupled with another feature introduced in the project. An LTE-A relay, operating on top of Layer 2, is able to improve the coordination between the unicast and the multicast transmissions in the cell by offloading the eMBMS sessions from the regular user traffic. This is made possible thanks to the flexibility provided by the cross-layer architecture to start the session dynamically in the LTE PoA.

The relaying scheme is introduced at the PDCP level in the LTE access network. It is worth noticing that in parallel to this work, Layer-3 relays were also being studied within 3GPP, and included in the LTE-A architecture at stage 2 level (i.e. high level design) [14]. The work achieved in the standard focuses on a new interface, the Un, between a dedicated eNodeB (called the Donor eNodeB) and the Relay. Moreover, as we mainly focus on video transmissions, we decide to assess the impact of the delay introduced on video streams by the relaying architecture.

Relaying techniques offer an interesting method for extending and improving wireless networks capabilities [15]. These techniques have been selected as part of the enhancements introduced to the LTE-A architecture. Their effectiveness has been investigated in the literature, showing good results in terms of both network coverage beyond the eNodeB and overall capacity. Outdoor measurements have shown in [16] that a time-shared LTE relaying system with 20 MHz bandwidth can both achieve 60 Mbps of data rates and cover the coverage holes in urban macro environments with a diameter of 300 m. A performance evaluation has been also accomplished in [17] via simulations showing interesting trade-offs between transmission power of both eNodeB and Relay Node (RN) and their positions. Two different LTE relay deployments are proposed in [18] considering the following criteria: early deployment (i.e., compatibility with current LTE Evolved Packet Core, or EPC, architecture), system complexity and traffic performance. The architecture complexity has been reduced considering packet aggregation of multiple UE flows with the same QoS requirement. Finally, header compression and stripping under the *Un* interface are added. Generally, the approach used in the literature focus on a very tight set of aspects of the LTE architecture, due to the complexity of the overall system. Here, on the contrary, we study the problem of LTE relay from an architectural point of view, considering all the aspects involved in a real deployment, from the IP level to the wireless access.

Relaying mechanisms usually operate on the LTE radio interface and can be performed at several levels: physical layer, link layer or just below the IP protocol stack. At physical layer level, the relay only repeats the received Radio Frequency (RF) signal. Such technology has been in operation for some time because it is very cheap and relatively simple. However, it increases the level of interference in the system, both propagating the inter-cell interference already present in the RF signal and introducing an additional contribution from the backbone signal to the relayed signal. Layer 2 relays introduce additionally demodulation, decoding, encoding and modulation, thus eliminating the noise. The Layer 3 relay operates on top of the PDCP level. It benefits from all the error correction mechanisms and transmission quality brought by the link layers, since the IP packet is extracted from the RN radio bearer and forwarded onto another UE radio bearer. However, this operation may have a cost in terms of QoS, which we evaluate for video applications. This relaying scheme has also an impact on the signalling flows and procedures for the attachment, detachment and coordination of resources management functions, both at the relay and mobile nodes.

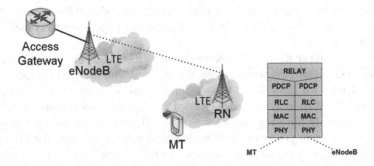

Fig. 5. LTE Relay Node in the wireless access

Figure 5 depicts how the RN plays a role in the wireless access architecture. A radio configuration similar to 3GPP is adopted. The eNodeB and RN signals at the physical layer level are assumed to be differentiated either by operating each link on a different frequency or by time-division multiplexing. The control plane analysis we perform mostly focuses on the impact on the latency and on the radio interface procedures for network attachment, session setup and tear down, and detachment of the mobile node or the LTE relay from the network. We consider here that the LTE relay serves as an extension of the network to increase its capacity and thus is not moving. The analysis also involves the wireless abstract interface, which allows the upper control layers to be agnostic from the specifics of the LTE technology.

At the initialization phase, the LTE module triggers the attachment of the RN to the LTE eNodeB, signalling that it is actually a RN. When the procedure is over, the RN starts broadcasting the system information in its cell. When a MT connects to the network, the RN informs the eNodeB that a new MT has appeared and retrieves its new cell configuration parameters, differentiating those related to the link with the eNodeB from those related to the link with the MT. A similar but reversed procedure is triggered when the connection has to be reconfigured because a new video session has started at the MT. In the data plane, the RN receives the packets from the PDCP layer on one side and forwards them to the opposite path. It can accommodate eMBMS sessions in an identical manner, potentially providing a different PoA for those MTs that are interested in receiving the multicast communications and alleviating the impact of eMBMS on other types of sessions.

The impact on the control plane turns into additional latency for establishing signalling and data radio bearers during session setup or when executing a handover. Execution traces, recorded by one of our partners in an operational network during the attachment of a MT, show that a radio reconfiguration takes only a very few milliseconds (less than 4 ms) compared to a total attachment time of 1.33 s. It can thus be accounted that in the control plane the impact of adding a relay at PDCP level will be minimal.

The theoretical analysis of the impact of the LTE relay on data traffic can be split into two parts. Firstly, the impact of the forwarding in the LTE Relay itself and secondly, the impact of adding a second radio link before the delivery of packets to the MT. The second radio link doubles the burden of radio transmissions on the traffic flow. It increases the effect of the Relay-to-eNodeB radio link on the QoS metrics for the delay or the jitter, but can be compensated by an adaptation of the coding and modulation techniques and parameters used on each link. Packet loss is compensated by the fact that the relay operates at PDCP level and that Layer 2 recovery mechanisms are fully operational.

In order to evaluate the resulting performance of such a scheme, we implemented a simple scenario within a network simulation performed with the open-source simulator ns-3 [19]. There, we show the improvement in terms of throughput achieved in a cellular network when relay nodes are enabled to help the eNodeB deliver the packets to multiple users. In this scenario, we first place 20 users in the coverage area of an eNodeB (transmission power of 30 dBm, bandwidth 5 MHz), using the Friis propagation loss model. In a second phase, we place 2 relays at few km from the base station. The base station sends 500 packets of 1024 bytes every 20 ms to each node. The simulation runs do not take into account signalling, which was studied independently as aforementioned and we assume that the channel between eNodeB and relays is ideal. This simplification can be justified by the fact that the RN is considered static with an optimised radio link towards the eNodeB.

Figure 6 shows the comparison of data reception for the different nodes according to their distance to the eNodeB. The blue points show the reception in the case without relays, whereas the magenta squares show the simulations with two relays. The figure confirms that in all cases the situation of the worst nodes, i.e., that suffered from losses in the standard case, has been improved to a large extent.

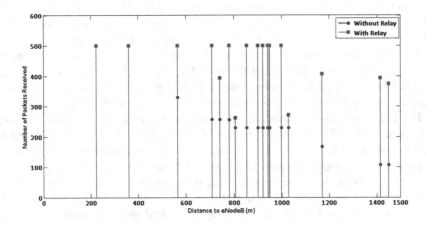

Fig. 6. Comparison of coverage with and without relay

This functionality permits to extend the network coverage while still benefiting from the transmission quality and error recovery present in the link layer protocols. MTs closer to the RN than to the eNodeB can access the cell while still obtaining a good communication quality. A larger number of users can be accommodated through the same eNodeB by distributing their load between several relay nodes, hence improving the scalability performance of the wireless access. The traffic passing through the eNodeB can be increased, compared to a standard MT-eNodeB attachment, since the transmission between the Relay and the eNodeB is expected to be of good quality and can use modulation and coding schemes with low redundancy. The results obtained prove that this type of relay has a moderate impact on the general control plane procedures, while improving drastically the transmission and coverage of the LTE cell, which benefits network operator and users.

Even though such relays had been under specification in 3GPP since the beginning of the project, our study has shown how they could positively impact the video traffic delivery. Beside enlarging the coverage and improving the reception quality in the related cells, we propose that such relays are used to separate the eMBMS groupcast listeners from the regular users with unicast traffic, which would put aside current limitations faced by operators to deploy the eMBMS. One of the major reasons for not deploying MBMS in previous releases of 3GPP was its radio impact on other types of communications when sharing the same cell. Coupling an LTE RN to the eNodeB to handle specifically the MBMS traffic allows a dedicated node with differentiated physical and medium access parameters to serve as MBMS PoA for video delivery. Users listening to MBMS broadcast or multicast sessions can be attached to the LTE RN while the others remain attached to the eNodeB (or another LTE Relay attached to it) and are unaffected.

4 Smart Video Frame Dropping

In the previous sections, mechanisms were introduced to extend the capability of the LTE-A cell. However, there are cases when this is not sufficient and sudden heavy traffic load conditions have to be handled. The simple, yet very unpopular, solution consists in denying access to new users or even breaking some existing communications. Accepting all data traffic means that part of the data packets will not be able to go through, being dropped in a random fashion at the link layer, which may generate a temporary degradation or even stalling of the image on the screen [20].

The last mechanism outlined in this paper to improve the transport of video applications in the LTE-A cells selects instead specific video frames in the eNodeB to address overload in the last hop. We propose a cross-layer mechanism where we try to resolve the issue of high occupancy of Radio Link Control (RLC) buffers, by reporting it through the abstract interface to the TO. The upper layers can mark the priority of the IP packets according to their video content (e.g., SVC video layer). The lower priority packets can be dropped based on parameters transferred through another cross-layer interaction in the eNodeB.

A cross-layer Video Frames Selection function performs this temporary rate adaptation on the last hop, yet avoiding deep packet inspection. It classifies and filters the received video frames according to a dedicated mark previously introduced in the IP packet header. When a congestion is detected in the network, the data packets are marked for prioritisation by the TO. The lower priority packets can then be dropped before the video frames are actually handled by the Link layer protocols, according to the receiver capabilities. This reduces the bandwidth occupation and loosens the level of traffic load in the last hop. The process initially designed performs the full process inside the PoA itself: detect the congestion, decide on the filtering and drop the packets. However, considering that a global SVC layer optimization algorithm exists in the TO, an alternative solution has been adopted that keeps the decision and marking update of the IP packets in the TO, based on the results of its algorithms, while the decision is executed in the LTE-A specific wireless component. This last operation, restricted to the overloaded cell, is accomplished in the eNodeB, after the packets coming from the Core Network have been decapsulated from the General Packet Radio Service (GPRS) Tunnelling Protocol-User (GTP-U) tunnel and before they get encapsulated in the PDCP protocol.

Figure 7 indicates with a (*) the components of the implementation involved in this mechanism. New functions have been introduced in the RRC (Radio Resource Control) and LTE-A specific wireless components at the eNodeB that retrieve the measurement of buffer occupancy from the RLC layer and signal an event to the upper layers through the abstract interface when this occupancy reaches a certain threshold corresponding to heavy load conditions. In the case of the initial solution, where the whole process is performed in the eNodeB, a classifier located at the Non-Access Stratum (NAS) driver above the PDCP layer is able to drop silently the least significant video frames, based on the marking of the packets arriving from the IP protocol stack. The classifier operates by comparing the Differentiated Services Code Point (DSCP) field of the IP packet header with an active mask, thus avoiding deep packet inspection of other header or even data fields in the classifier, and of the network layer fields in the wireless access layers. In the alternative solution, on request from the TO, some measurements of the planned Physical Resource Blocks (PRB) and total data volume from the MAC layer are reported through the abstract interface, enabling the TO to drop the least important packets directly in the core network. The implemented process affects the eNodeB only, and is split between the LTE radio interface protocols (RRC and MAC layers), and the LTE-A specific component which retrieves and analyses the measurements, then executes the required actions.

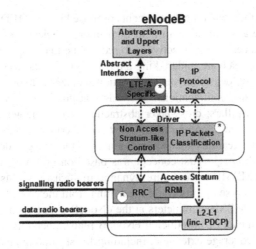

Fig. 7. Implementation of the video frames selection in the eNodeB

Functional results could be obtained with a local testing system. This successful test has been performed on a small testbed focusing mostly on network measurements and congestion detection. Another part of the testbed complemented this evaluation, taking care of the packet dropping as reported in [21]. The test performed here allowed validating the correct operation of the LTE-A specific module in cooperation with the radio interface protocol layers and the abstract interface. The traces obtained are summarised in Table 2. From a functional point of view, the correct execution of the following features has been verified: detecting the congestion situation in the eNodeB according to the specified threshold, triggering notification about the high load event to the TO, returning link traffic parameters on request from the upper layers and finally stopping the specific measurements when the situation has returned to normal condition, in order to reduce the mechanism overhead on the control plane.

Table 2. Traces recorded at the eNodeB during a congestion event (time in s.)

Event	Time
- LTE-A module receives an event subscription for congestion notification.	0.000
- It polls periodically the lower layers to check the cell correct operation.	35.991
- Congestion detected (RLC buffers for MT0 above threshold); a notification is sent to the upper layers.	41.296
- Upper layer (TO) requests periodic measurement retrieval	41.297
- Link traffic parameters forwarded through the L2.5 Abstraction Layer.	44.421
- After the problem resolution by the TO, the measures fall back to normal conditions.	72.975
- Request received from the TO to stop forwarding the measurements	72.976
- Request executed by the LTE-A module	75.579

5   Conclusion

This paper has described several enhancements proposed by the MEDIEVAL project to mobile network operators in order to help them more efficiently distribute the video traffic in the wireless cells. Our objective is to reduce the load imposed by this specific type of applications, which are undertaking a huge growth in the coming future. Under this objective, we have focused on next generation wireless networks where we aim at providing video-friendly optimizations. Towards that goal, we have based our architecture on three main pillars: cross-layer abstraction, access network monitoring and network interface dynamic configuration. They have served as a basis to the development of innovative features that should improve the current design of operator networks in the last hop. The first concept was based on group communications. We have enhanced the eMBMS to configure dynamic multicast sessions, with better performance for the session setup procedure, benefiting from the cross-layer design which allows receiving the eMBMS parameters at the eNodeB ahead of the session start. We have evaluated the impact of introducing eNodeB relays operating at the PDCP level on the QoS and cell coverage extension, including for separating eMBMS traffic from legacy service. Finally, we have implemented a cross-layer mechanism to selectively drop IP packets containing lower priority video frames in order to handle heavy load conditions in a specific cell and potentially avoid congestion or access rejection. This filtering applies in the eNodeB, at the junction between the GTP-U tunnel and the PDCP protocol. From these enhancements, we have demonstrated that the abstract interface introduced between the upper layer control entities and the wireless access modules provides additional capabilities to efficiently manage the network traffic and to introduce novel network mechanisms in a video-optimised way. Moreover, the combination of enhanced link-specific mechanisms allows the wireless link access to go beyond a simple wireless transmission of data.

Acknowledgments. The research leading to these results has received funding from the European Community's Seventh Framework Programme (FP7-ICT-2009-5) under grant agreement n. 258053 (MEDIEVAL project).

References

1. Cisco Visual Networking Index: Global Mobile Data Traffic Forecast Update, 2013–2018. http://www.cisco.com/en/US/solutions/collateral/ns341/ns525/ns537/ns705/ns827/white_paper_c11-520862.html/. Accessed May 2014
2. Celtic Plus Purple book, March 2012. http://www.celtic-initiative.org/PurpleBook+/Purplebook.asp. Accessed May 2014
3. http://www.ict-medieval.eu
4. Costa, R., Melia, T., Munaretto, D., Zorzi, M.: When mobile networks meet content delivery networks: challenges and possibilities. In: ACM MobiArch, August 2012
5. IEEE Standard for Information Technology-Telecommunications and information exchange between systems-Local and metropolitan area networks-Specific requirements - Part 11: Wireless LAN Medium Access Control (MAC) and Physical Layer (PHY) specifications, IEEE Std. 802.11, 2007
6. Piri, E., Pentikousis, K.: IEEE 802.21. Internet Protoc. J. 12(2), 7–27 (2009)
7. Kassar, M., Kervella, B., Pujolle, G.: An overview of vertical handover decision strategies in heterogeneous wireless networks. Comput. Commun. 31(10), 2607–2620 (2008)
8. Corujo, D., Bernardos, C.J., Melia, T., Wetterwald, M., Badia, L., Aguiar, R.L.: Key function interfacing for the MEDIEVAL project video-enhancing architecture. In: Pentikousis, K., Aguiar, R., Sargento, S., Agüero, R. (eds.) MONAMI 2011. LNICST, vol. 97, pp. 230–243. Springer, Heidelberg (2012)
9. Lecompte, D., Gabin, F.: Evolved multimedia broadcast/multicast service (eMBMS) in LTE-advanced: overview and Rel-11 enhancements. IEEE Comm. Mag. 50, 68–74 (2012)
10. 3GPP TS 23.246: Multimedia Broadcast/Multicast Service (MBMS); Architecture and functional description, Release 12
11. Figueiredo, S., Wetterwald, M., Nguyen, T., Eznarriaga, L., Amram, N., Aguiar, R.L.: SVC multicast video mobility support in MEDIEVAL project. In: Proceedings of Future Network and Mobile Summit 2012, Berlin, Germany, 4–6 July 2012
12. 3GPP TR 22.947: Study on Personal Broadcast Service (PBS), Release 10
13. Badia, L., Bui, N., Miozzo, M., Rossi, M., Zorzi, M.: Improved resource management through user aggregation in heterogeneous multiple access wireless networks. IEEE Trans. Wireless Commun. 7(9), 3329–3334 (2008)
14. 3GPP TS 36.300: Evolved Universal Terrestrial Radio Access (E-UTRA) and Evolved Universal Terrestrial Radio Access Network (E-UTRAN); Overall description; Stage 2, Release 10
15. Quer, G., Librino, F., Canzian, L., Badia, L., Zorzi, M.: Inter-network cooperation exploiting game theory and Bayesian networks. IEEE Trans. Commun. 61(10), 4310–4321 (2013)
16. Wirth, T., Venkatkumar, V., Haustein, T., Schulz, E., Halfmann, R.: LTE-advanced relaying for outdoor range extension. In: Proceedings of VTC Fall, September 2009
17. Beniero, T., Redana, S., Hämäläinen, J., Raaf, B.: Effect of relaying on coverage in 3GPP LTE-advanced. In: Proceedings of VTC Spring, April 2009
18. Huang, X., Ulupinar, F., Agashe, P., Ho, D., Bao, G.: LTE relay architecture and its upper layer solutions. In: Proceedings of IEEE GLOBECOM, December 2010
19. NS-3 simulator. http://www.nsnam.org/. Accessed May 2014
20. Quality of Experience for Mobile Data Networks: White Paper, Citrix, 2013
21. Fu, B., Kunzmann, G., Wetterwald, M., Corujo, D., Costa, R.: QoE-aware traffic management for mobile video delivery. In: Workshop on Immersive and Interactive Multimedia Communications over the Future Internet, IEEE ICC 2013, Budapest, Hungary, 9–13 June 2013

Novel Schemes for Component Carrier Selection and Radio Resource Allocation in LTE-Advanced Uplink

Safdar Nawaz Khan Marwat[1(✉)], Yangyang Dong[1], Xi Li[1],
Yasir Zaki[2], and Carmelita Goerg[1]

[1] Communication Networks, TZI, University of Bremen,
Otto-Hahn-Allee NW1, 28359 Bremen, Germany
{safdar,ydong,xili,cg}@comnets.uni-bremen.de
[2] Computer Science Department, New York University Abu Dhabi,
PO Box 129188, Abu Dhabi, United Arab Emirates
yasir.zaki@nyu.edu

Abstract. The LTE (Long Term Evolution) provides mobile users high throughput and low latency. In order to meet the requirements of future mobile data traffic, the 3rd Generation Partnership Project (3GPP) has introduced advanced features to the LTE system, including Carrier Aggregation (CA), enhanced MIMO (Multiple Input Multiple Output), and coordinated multipoint (CoMP). The enhanced system is called LTE-Advanced (LTE-A) system. This paper investigates Component Carrier Selection (CCS) and radio resource scheduling for uplink in LTE-A. In this work, a CCS algorithm depending on the pathloss and the slow fading of the radio signals is developed. Based on the channel conditions and the Quality of Service (QoS) requirements of the users, a Channel and QoS Aware (CQA) uplink scheduler is also designed, which is time and frequency domain decoupled. The simulation results demonstrate that the proposed schemes provide a good QoS and throughput performance as compared to other reference schemes.

Keywords: LTE-A · Carrier aggregation · Uplink · Scheduling · QoS

1 Introduction

The 3rd Generation Partnership Project (3GPP) has designed the Long Term Evolution (LTE) standard to support high data rates of up to 100 Mbps in downlink and 50 Mbps in uplink [1]. The 3GPP Release 8 series specify the LTE standards, with enhancements in Release 9. However, these specifications do not meet the 4G requirements set by ITU-R (International Telecommunication Union Radiocommunication Sector), e.g. data rate of up to 1 Gbps. To achieve such requirements, the LTE system has been extended by introducing several new features. The 3GPP Release 10 documents feature new technologies designed for improving the performance of LTE. The improved system is termed as LTE-Advanced (LTE-A). The main features of LTE-A include Carrier Aggregation (CA), enhanced Multiple Input Multiple Output (MIMO), as well

© Institute for Computer Sciences, Social Informatics and Telecommunications Engineering 2015
R. Agüero et al. (Eds.): MONAMI 2014, LNICST 141, pp. 32–46, 2015.
DOI: 10.1007/978-3-319-16292-8_3

as coordinated multipoint (CoMP). With these new features the LTE-A can support transmission over a bandwidth of up to 100 MHz as compared to only 20 MHz of LTE.

The primary focus of this paper is to design a Component Carrier Selection (CCS) algorithm to perform CA and a radio resource allocation scheme for LTE-A uplink. The function of CA is to aggregate several bands to achieve a wider bandwidth for data transmission. However, a wider bandwidth does not necessarily ensure a better performance in uplink. Terminals lacking sufficient power, for example, may not benefit from it. Therefore, it is essential to determine whether the frequency bands should be aggregated or not, which is why an efficient CCS scheme is required. The scheme presented in this work is based on a time variant radio channel model with real-time channel conditions of the users. The scheme takes into account the pathloss and slow fading of the users under mobility consideration. The radio resource allocation scheme presented in this work performs scheduling decisions with awareness of the CCS and Quality of Service (QoS) requirements of the mobile terminals.

2 Literature Review

Despite the relative novelty of the topic, a considerable amount of literature is available for downlink CA. The main difference between uplink and downlink transmission is the power constraint of a user terminal. The contiguity constraint of frequency resource allocation to single user is relinquished in LTE-A. The performance gain of CA in terms of throughput and fairness is investigated in [2] over independently deployed carriers for downlink with system level simulations. The LTE-A uplink CA is investigated in [3] with the help of a simple CCS algorithm. The results depict a performance improvement as compared to LTE users. In [4], an advanced CCS algorithm is proposed to optimize the system performance with CA in uplink. The results show an improvement in performance over the algorithm in [3]. However, the authors do not address the user mobility. Chunyan et al. [5] investigates a CCS scheme for diverse coverage of CA deployment, such that Component Carriers (CCs) of an eNodeB have antennas with beams in different directions.

Recent work on radio resource scheduling mainly focuses on LTE. For LTE downlink, [6] proposes a QoS aware scheduler. In [7], the performance of the scheduler in [6] is compared with other traditional schedulers. For LTE uplink, [8] suggests a QoS and channel aware scheduler, which takes Power Control (PC) and contiguity constraint into consideration. For LTE-A downlink, the authors of [9] employ user grouping based downlink resource allocation algorithm with CA, results show that the proposed algorithm is fairer to users than the proportional fair algorithm. Various load balancing methods over multiple CCs are analyzed in [10]. For LTE-A uplink, [11] proposes a cross-carrier scheduling method along with a per-carrier scheduling method, enabling scheduling on several carriers. Liu and Liu [12] proposes a subcarrier allocation method which assumes equal power allocation among all subcarriers. The proposed method achieves better sector throughput and cell-edge user throughput. In [13], the work in [12] is further elaborated with new results indicating performance improvement in terms of sector throughput and cell-edge user throughput.

Our motivation is to design schemes for both CA and radio resource scheduling functionalities incorporated into LTE-A environment according to CCS scheme under mobility consideration. The scheduler is designed in such a way that the CA functionality is taken into account while making radio resource allocation decisions.

3   LTE and LTE-A Features

3.1   Air Interface

Orthogonal Frequency Division Multiple Access (OFDMA) is used in LTE downlink, providing wideband transmission while staying robust to frequency selectivity of radio channels. The uplink uses Single Carrier Frequency Division Multiple Access (SC-FDMA) as the transmission scheme due to the low Peak-to-Average-Power-Ratio (PAPR) as compared to the OFDMA signal. However, the SC-FDMA used in LTE has a constraint which only allows adjacent radio resource allocation in frequency domain. OFDMA is also used in LTE-A downlink. For LTE-A uplink, due to the several types of CA, the uplink air interface turns out to be the aggregation of multiple SC-FDMA bands, which is denoted as Aggregated Discrete Fourier Transform-Spread OFDMA (N*DFTS-OFDMA). This aggregation results in the air interface being able to support both contiguous and non-contiguous resource allocation in uplink to user terminals. Thus, DFTS-OFDMA overcomes the disadvantages of the OFDMA (high PARP) and the SC-FDMA (contiguity) in LTE.

3.2   Carrier Aggregation

To achieve higher data rate, a wider bandwidth is required. According to the 3GPP specifications, the LTE-A system is able to aggregate two or more CCs to obtain a wider transmission bandwidth. The current 3GPP standards allow up to 5 carriers. LTE terminals can only receive/transmit on a single CC. But LTE-A terminals are able to receive/transmit data on one or multiple CCs simultaneously (Fig. 1). The CA in LTE-A can be classified into three types: the intra-band contiguous, the intra-band non-contiguous and the inter-band non-contiguous (Fig. 2).

In LTE, the User Equipment (UE) has only one Radio Resource Control (RRC) connection with the eNodeB. However for LTE-A, there are several serving cells due to CA, with each one corresponding to a CC. Initially, an RRC connection is established with a single CC, using the same RRC establishment procedure as specified for LTE. This CC is called Primary Component Carrier (PCC). Additional CCs can then be configured from the eNodeB, which are called Secondary Component Carriers (SCCs). The SCCs are added and removed as required, while the PCC is only changed at handover. For UEs using the same set of CCs, different PCCs are possible. The PCC serves the Primary Serving Cell (PSC) and the SCC serves the Secondary Serving Cell (SSC) (Fig. 3).

3.3   Component Carrier Selection

A CCS scheme is used to allocate one or multiple CCs to the incoming users according to certain criteria. In downlink, the allocation of multiple CCs results in a higher

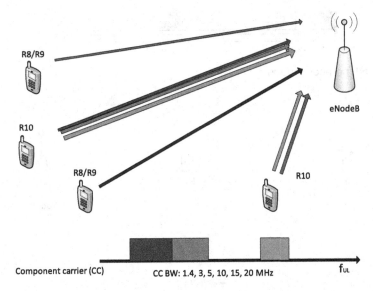

Fig. 1. Carrier aggregation

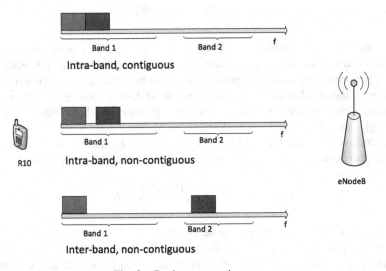

Fig. 2. Carrier aggregation types

throughput due to larger transmission bandwidth without power constraint. However, this might not always work for the uplink, especially for the users who are power limited at the cell edge. Therefore, an efficient way to select the CCs for the users is needed.

In this work, only the intra-band contiguous carrier aggregation is considered. A simple algorithm is that the users having distance to eNodeB larger than a threshold

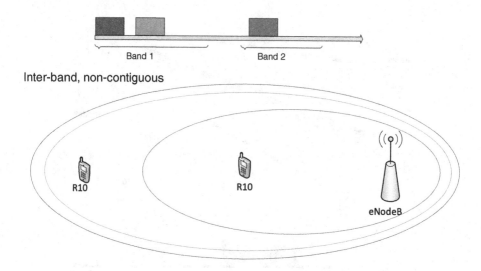

Fig. 3. Primary and secondary cells

distance are assigned to primary CC, otherwise both CCs. This algorithm is easy to implement and requires simple calculations; however, different threshold distances give different performances. If the best performance is to be achieved, the determination of the distance threshold requires a great amount of testing. Moreover, the network environment changes over the time, while the distance threshold would not adapt accordingly, once it is set.

An effective pathloss threshold based CC selection algorithm was proposed in [4] to distinguish between power limited and non-power limited LTE-A users.

$$L_{threshold} = L_{95\%} - \frac{10 \log K + P_{backoff}}{\alpha} \tag{1}$$

where $L_{95\%}$ is the estimated 95 percentile user pathloss, K is the total number of CCs and α is the pathloss compensation factor used in the PC scheme. $P_{backoff}$ is the estimated power backoff to model the effects of increased PAPR and CM (Cubic Metric) when a user transmits over multiple CCs simultaneously. If a user is scheduled for transmission only on one CC, there is no power backoff; otherwise, it is set with a fixed value, for example, 4 dB or 6 dB. With a higher power backoff, less LTE-A users will be assigned on multiple CCs due to the limitation of user transmission power. The users are stationary in the cell. When the pathloss of the LTE-A users is higher than $L_{threshold}$, they are considered to be power limited and assigned on a single CC; otherwise they are considered to be non-power limited and can use multiple CCs for data transmission. Hence, the cell-edge users would not experience performance loss from being scheduled over multiple CCs, while the non-power limited users can benefit from the advantages of a wider bandwidth.

This scheme is further extended in this work, and provides improvement to achieve better system performance. Instead of assuming that the users are stationary, a time variant radio channel model is used to get the real-time channel conditions of the users. Furthermore, not only the pathloss is considered when determining the threshold and the number of CCs, the slow fading is also taken into consideration. Therefore, instead of labeling the users as power limited and non-power limited, the CCS would be based on the real-time channel conditions of the users. The proposed algorithm can be illustrated as:

$$L_{threshold,mob} = (L + SF)_{95\%} - \frac{10 \log K + P_{backoff}}{\alpha} \tag{2}$$

where SF is the slow fading of the user. At the time, when the sum of the user's pathloss and slow fading is higher than the threshold, one CC is assigned; otherwise, the user can use multiple CCs for data transmission.

4 Channel and QoS Aware Scheduling

Resource allocation and scheduling is conducted by the Medium Access Control (MAC) packet scheduler at the eNodeB. It dynamically distributes the radio resources among the active users. It aims to maximally utilize the scarce radio resources, while meeting the QoS requirements of the bearers. The scheduling is performed in every Transmission Time Interval (TTI). In this work, we propose an LTE-A uplink Channel and QoS Aware (CQA) scheduler that guarantees the QoS of different traffic types and considers their channel conditions. The scheduler is decoupled into two domains, i.e. Time Domain Packet Scheduling (TDPS) and Frequency Domain Packet Scheduling (FDPS). Figure 4 illustrates the scheduler implemented in this work. The radio resources are distributed according the PC scheme.

4.1 Power Control

The downlink transmission power control is usually not a major issue since it comes from the eNodeB, and the PSD for each UE is kept constant at the eNodeB to reduce inter-cell interference. For the uplink, the users are usually limited by the transmission power, therefore, the power control scheme is necessary to adjust the transmission power. It aims at maximizing the power of the desired signals while limiting the inter-cell interference. The interference based power control scheme in [14] is utilized in our work.

4.2 Time Domain Packet Scheduling

In TDPS, bearers are classified according to TDPS metric based on QoS requirements and channel conditions. The QoS parameter used for the bearer classification is the

Quality Class Identifier (QCI), which is an index associated with predefined values for the priority, delay budget and packet loss rate. Nine QCI classes are defined by the 3GPP - four for the GBR (Guaranteed Bit Rate) bearers and five for the non-GBR bearers. Network operators are allowed to define additional new classes based on their specific needs. Since each traffic type has different QoS requirements, each bearer (associated with a traffic type) is assigned with a single QCI class. In the MAC scheduler, the bearers are distributed into five MAC QoS classes according to [6]: two classes - MAC QoS Class 1 and Class 2 (not considered in this work) for the GBR bearers and three classes - MAC QoS Class 3, 4 and 5 for the non-GBR bearers. Table 1 shows how MAC QoS classes are mapped onto QCI classes.

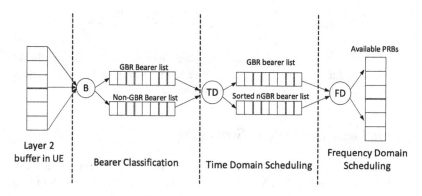

Fig. 4. Primary and secondary cells

The TDPS priority metric value for the bearer k, similar to [8], is expressed as:

$$\lambda_k(t) = \frac{R_{inst,i}(t)}{R_{avg,k}(t)} W_k(t) \tag{3}$$

where $R_{inst,i}(t)$ is the instantaneously achievable throughput at time t of user i to which bearer k belongs, $R_{avg,k}(t)$ is the average throughput of bearer k at time t obtained by using the Exponential Moving Average (EMA) time window of 1 s, $W_k(t)$ is the dynamic QoS weight of bearer k at time t and explained below. The bearers are placed in GBR and non-GBR bearer lists and sorted according to TDPS metric.

Table 1. QCI and MAC QoS mapping

Bearer type	QCI class	MAC QoS class	Traffic type
GBR	QCI-1	MAC-QoS-1	Voice
Non-GBR	QCI-7	MAC-QoS-3	Streaming video
Non-GBR	QCI-8	MAC-QoS-4	Browsing
Non-GBR	QCI-9	MAC-QoS-5	File transfer

$W_k(t)$ is the TDPS weight of bearer k and is calculated according to the following formula, which takes the QoS requirements of bearer k into consideration.

$$W_k(t) = \frac{R_{min,k}}{R_{avg,k}(t)} \frac{\tau_k(t)}{\tau_{max,k}} \rho_k(t) \qquad (4)$$

where $R_{min,k}$ is the bit rate budget, $\tau_{max,k}$ is the end-to-end delay budget, $R_{avg,k}(t)$ is the average throughput, and $\tau_k(t)$ is the packet delay of bearer k, $\rho_k(t)$ is a variable with value set to 10 if $\tau_k(t)$ is above the threshold value of bearer k at time t, otherwise equal to 1. The value 10 of $\rho_k(t)$ raises the metric value of bearer k by 10 times and ensures immediate scheduling. This value works well for the traffic load scenarios investigated in this paper. This variable is to avoid large packet delays of delay-sensitive traffic (e.g. video). The bit rate budget, packet delay budget and delay threshold values [8] used in this work for the QoS classes are given in Table 2. Bit rate budget for a QoS class is defined according to its traffic model in this work. However, the network operators can modify the behavior of the scheduler by tuning these values.

Table 2. Bit rate budget, delay budget and delay threshold

Traffic type	Bit rate budget	Packet end-to-end delay budget	Packet delay threshold (s)
Voice	55	0.1	0.02
Streaming video	132	0.3	0.1
Browsing	120	0.3	–
File transfer	10	0.3	–

4.3 Frequency Domain Packet Scheduling

In this work, a frequency domain scheduler based on [6] has been implemented. But in this work, the CCS is also considered in the scheduling decisions. Due to the strict QoS requirements of GBR bearers, the GBR list is scheduled first by starting with the top of the list bearer having highest priority. Power limited users are scheduled only on PCC. This is followed by the scheduling of non-GBR bearers. The frequency domain scheduling procedure for non-GBR bearers is summarized as follows:

1. At the beginning of each TTI, once the GBR list is scheduled, N number of bearers are chosen from the top of the non-GBR candidate list and put into a subset candidate list. The bearer selection is based on TDPS metric value.
2. The scheduler searches for the best PRB, in terms of Signal-to-Interference-and-Noise-Ratio (SINR), of the first bearer. This PRB is reserved for the best bearer; therefore, the bearer's average SINR of the reserved PRBs is set as the effective SINR. Power limited users are able to obtain PRBs only from PCC. The Modulation and Coding Scheme (MCS) corresponding to average SINR is determined to find out the resulting Transport Block Size (TBS).
3. The achievable TBS is compared against the buffer size of the bearer.

    a. If TBS is greater than the buffer size, the bearer can be completely served in this TTI, the PC constraint of the UE is checked.

      (i)   If the number of PRBs reserved for the user of this bearer exceeds the PC limit, do not allocate the reserved PRB, serve the UE with remaining reserved PRBs if any and discard it from the candidate list for this TTI.

      (ii) Otherwise the reserved PRB is allocated to the bearer and scheduled.

    b. If the TBS is smaller compared to the buffer size, the bearer waits until the remaining bearers from the subset candidate list go through the above procedure.

4. Once all the bearers in the candidate list get a PRB reserved or get discarded after being scheduled, the above process is repeated again for the remaining bearers and the effective SINR of more than one PRB is calculated using link-to-system mapping. This procedure continues until all the PRBs are allocated or all the bearers in the subset candidate list are served.

5. Once the subset list is completely served, and there are still some bearers to be served in the non-GBR candidate list, then in case of availability of PRBs, the $N + 1^{th}$ bearer in the candidate list is moved to the subset candidate list and provided PRBs according to the above procedure. This continues until there are no more PRBs available or no more bearers to serve in candidate list.

5 Simulation Results

The OPNET Modeler is used as the simulation and analysis tool in this work. The LTE-A model implementation is based on the LTE simulation model designed in [15]. The simulations are performed under the parameter settings and traffic models given in Table 3 and are in accordance with [16].

5.1 Component Carrier Selection Results

The proposed pathloss and slow fading based CCS algorithm is analyzed along with the algorithm proposed in [4]. For comparison, the simple CCS algorithm based on distance between UEs and eNodeB is also evaluated as a reference scheme. 40 voice, 40 video and 10 file transfer UEs are deployed in the cell in investigated scenarios.

    Figure 5 shows the throughput comparison among the three algorithms: pathloss and slow fading based (PL_SF) proposed in this work, pathloss based (PL) [4] and the third one based on the distance to the eNodeB, using 100 m and 200 m as the thresholds. The figure shows that the cell throughput is higher in the system with the proposed scheme (PL_SF), or the distance to the eNodeB of 200 m as the threshold. Compared with the system using the pathloss as the threshold, the one considering additional slow fading gives a better performance, because in practice, both pathloss and slow fading influence the transmitted signal. Thus the latter one provides more accurate channel conditions. Therefore, the CCS decision is more accurate than the one with only the pathloss as the threshold. For the system with the distance to the eNodeB as the threshold, different distance thresholds give different performances. For example, 200 m gives good performance compared to 100 m in this case. However this method is not adaptive and requires large effort on deciding the optimum distance threshold.

Figure 6 shows the average voice delay. Since the voice users are defined as the GBR users and served with highest priority. Therefore, the voice packet end-to-end delay does not vary much for different CCS algorithms. The video and the file transfer users are non-GBR, so their performance varies with different CCS schemes. Figures 7 and 8 present the average video end-to-end delay and average file upload time. The case with pathloss and slow fading as the threshold gives lower video delay and file upload time, compared to the one with the pathloss as the threshold. Also, different distance thresholds result in good results for 200 m and poor for 100 m.

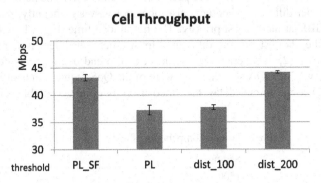

Fig. 5. Comparison of cell throughput for CCS schemes

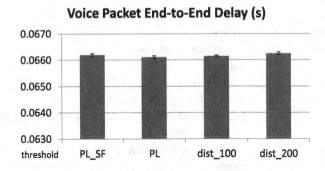

Fig. 6. Comparison of voice packet end-to-end delay for CCS schemes

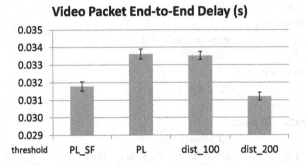

Fig. 7. Comparison of video packet end-to-end delay for CCS schemes

5.2 Scheduler Comparison and Results

In order to compare the QoS performance of various schedulers, the video traffic in the cell is reduced in such a way that the video users are reduced to 10. Figure 9 gives the cell throughput comparison among the proposed CQA scheduler and the reference schedulers: Blind Equal Throughput (BET), Maximum Throughput (MaxT) and Proportional Fair (PF) schedulers. The comparison reveals that due to the low load in the cell, the throughput performance of all the schedulers is quite comparable.

Figure 10 shows the average voice packet end-to-end delay. The performance of the voice users under different schedulers also does not vary significantly, since they are served with GBR at the highest priority. The file upload time (Fig. 11) with the CQA scheduler is the shortest but the difference from other schedulers is not substantial. However, in Fig. 12, the average video packet end-to-end delay results depict a very contrasting view. The CQA scheduler is aware of the QoS requirements of video users; hence the packet-end-to-end delay for video users is quite acceptable. On the other

Table 3. Simulation parameters and traffic models

Parameter	Setting
Simulation length	1500 s
Cell layout	7 eNodeBs all with single cell
Cell radius	375 m
User velocity	120 kmph
Max UE power	23 dBm
Carrier frequency	2 GHz
Component carriers	2 * 20 MHz contiguous
Noise figure	9 dB
Noise per PRB	-120.447 dBm
Pathloss	$128.1 + 37.6\log10(R)$, R in km
Slow fading	Log-normal shadowing, 8 dB std. deviation, correlation 1
Fast fading	Jakes-like method [17]
Mobility Model	Random Way Point (RWP)
UE buffer size	Infinite
Power Control	Interference based [14], $\alpha = 0.6, \beta = 0.4, P_0 = -104\,\text{dBm}$
Traffic environment	Loaded
Subset candidate list size	20
Voice traffic (40 users)	
Silence/talk spurt length	Exponential(3) sec
Encoder scheme	GSM EFR
Video traffic (40 user)	
Frame size	1200 bytes
Frame inter-arrival time	75 ms
File transfer traffic (10 users)	
File size	20 Mbytes
File inter-request time	Uniform, min 80 s, max 100 s

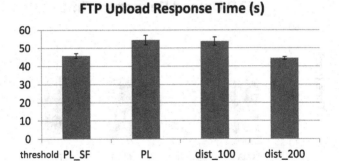

Fig. 8. Comparison of file upload response time for CCS schemes

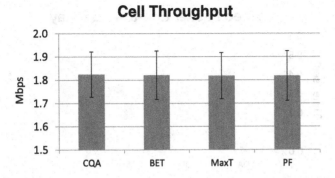

Fig. 9. Comparison of cell throughput for various schedulers

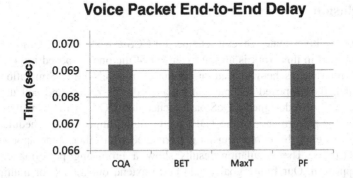

Fig. 10. Comparison of voice end-to-end delay for various schedulers

hand, the BET scheduler is designed to provide equal throughput to all the users, therefore the delay requirements of video users are not taken into account. MaxT scheduler also neglects the requirements of the video bearer, and PF scheduler in also not considering the video QoS. In summary, the CQA scheduler is QoS-aware and able to treat traffic types according to their respective requirements.

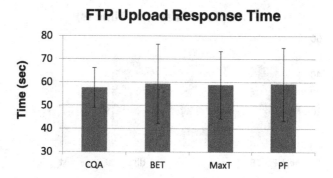

Fig. 11. Comparison of file upload time for various schedulers

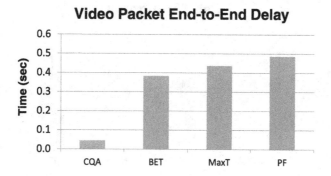

Fig. 12. Comparison of video end-to-end delay for various schedulers

6   Conclusion

In this paper, we investigated several schemes for CCS and MAC scheduling. The CCS scheme proposed in this work is an improvement of the one proposed in [4]. We also analysed a reference scheme based on distance from eNodeB. Simulation results illustrated that the proposed scheme can enhance the user QoS and cell throughput performance. We also designed a QoS based scheduler (CQA) with channel awareness We analysed the performance of the TDPS metric algorithm of CQA scheduler having dynamic QoS weight by comparing its performance with other contemporary TDPS metric algorithms. The simulation results show a promising performance of the designed approach. Our future goal would be to extend our model for multiple contiguous and non-contiguous CCs.

Acknowledgments. This work is supported by University of Engineering and Technology, Peshawar, Pakistan and the International Graduate School for Dynamics in Logistics, University of Bremen, Germany.

References

1. 3GPP, 3GPP TSG RAN Future Evolution Work Shop, Toronto, Canada, Technical Paper, November 2004
2. Chen, L., Chen, W., Zhang, X., Yang, D.: Analysis and simulation for spectrum aggregation in LTE-Advanced system. In: IEEE 70th Vehicular Technology Conference, Anchorage, AK, USA, 20–23 September 2009
3. Wang, H., Rosa, C., Pedersen, K.I.: Performance of uplink carrier aggregation in LTE-Advanced systems. In: IEEE 72nd Vehicular Technology Conference, Ottawa, ON, Canada, 6–9 September 2010
4. Wang, H., Rosa, C., Pedersen, K.I.: Uplink component carrier selection for LTE-Advanced systems with carrier aggregation. In: IEEE International Conference on Communications, Kyoto, Japan, 5–9 June 2011
5. Chunyan, L., Wang, B., Wang, W., Zhang, Y., Xinyue, C.: Component carrier selection for LTE-A systems in diverse coverage carrier aggregation scenario. In: IEEE 23rd International Symposium on Personal Indoor and Mobile Radio Communications, pp. 1004–1008. Sydney, NSW, Australia, 9–12 September 2012
6. Zaki, Y., Weerawardane, T., Goerg, C., Timm-Giel, A.: Multi-QoS-aware fair scheduling for LTE. In: IEEE 73rd Vehicular Technology Conference, Yokohama, Japan, 15–18 May 2011
7. Zahariev, N., Zaki, Y., Li, X., Goerg, C., Weerawardane, T., Timm-Giel, A.: Optimized Service Aware LTE MAC Scheduler with Comparison against Other Well Known Schedulers. In: Koucheryavy, Y., Mamatas, L., Matta, I., Tsaoussidis, V. (eds.) Wired/Wireless Internet Communication. Lecture Notes in Computer Science, vol. 7277, pp. 323–331. Springer, Heidelberg (2012)
8. Marwat, S.N.K., Weerawardane, T., Zaki, Y., Goerg, C., Timm-Giel, A.: Performance evaluation of bandwidth and QoS aware LTE uplink scheduler. In: Koucheryavy, Y., Mamatas, L., Matta, I., Tsaoussidis, V. (eds.) Wired/Wireless Internet Communication. Lecture Notes in Computer Science, vol. 7277, pp. 298–306. Springer, Heidelberg (2012)
9. Songsong, S., Chunyan, F., Caili, G.: A resource scheduling algorithm based on user grouping for LTE-Advanced system with carrier aggregation. In: International Symposium on Computer Network and Multimedia Technology, Wuhan, China, 18–20 January 2009
10. Wang, Y., Pedersen, K.I., Mogensen, P.E., Sorensen, T.B.: Carrier load balancing methods with bursty traffic for LTE-Advanced systems. In: IEEE 20th International Symposium on Personal, Indoor and Mobile Radio Communications, pp. 22–26. Tokyo, Japan, 13–16 September 2009
11. Wang, Y., Pedersen, K.I., Sorensen, T.B., Mogensen, P.E.: Carrier load balancing and packet scheduling for multi-carrier systems. IEEE Trans. Wirel. Commun. 9(5), 1780–1789 (2010)
12. Liu, F., Liu, Y.: Uplink scheduling for LTE-Advanced system. In: IEEE International Conference on Communication Systems, pp. 316–320. Singapore, 17–19 November 2010
13. Liu, F., Liu, Y.: Uplink channel-aware scheduling algorithm for LTE-Advanced system. In: 7th International Conference on Wireless Communications, Networking and Mobile Computing, Wuhan, China, 23–25 September 2011
14. Boussif, M., Quintero, N., Calabrese, F.D., Rosa, C., Wigard, J.: Interference based power control performance in LTE uplink. In: IEEE International Symposium on Wireless Communication Systems, pp. 698–702, 21–24 October 2008
15. Zaki, Y., Weerawardane, T., Goerg, C., Timm-Giel, A.: Long Term Evolution (LTE) model development within OPNET simulation environment. In: OPNET Workshop 2011, Washington, DC, USA, 29 August–1 September 2011

16. Marwat, S.N.K., Weerawardane, T., Zaki, Y., Goerg, C., Timm-Giel, A.: Design and performance analysis of bandwidth and QoS aware LTE uplink scheduler in heterogeneous traffic environment. In: 8th International Wireless Communications and Mobile Computing Conference, Limassol, Cyprus, 27–31 August 2012
17. Cavers, J.K.: Mobile Channel Characteristics. Kluwer Academic Publishers, Boston (2002)

Optimising LTE Uplink Scheduling by Solving the Multidimensional Assignment Problem

Raphael Elsner$^{(\boxtimes)}$, Maciej Mühleisen, and Andreas Timm-Giel

Institute of Communication Networks,
Hamburg University of Technology, Hamburg, Germany
{raphael.elsner,maciej.muehleisen,timm-giel}@tuhh.de

Abstract. Inter-cell interference mitigation in LTE networks is important to improve the system throughput. Upcoming Cloud Radio Access Networks (C-RANs) allow controlling multiple cells at a single location enabling novel inter-cell coordination algorithms. Coordinated recourse allocation can be used to achieve optimal spectral efficiency through reduced inter-cell interference.

In this paper the uplink resource allocation is optimised by deciding which user terminals served by different base stations should transmit on the same resources. A central meta-scheduler situated in the cloud is responsible for the optimisation. The optimisation is performed using heuristic algorithms to solve the underlying multidimensional assignment problem. The complexity is further reduced to a feasible size by only coordinating a subset of base stations. This way the problem can be solved for real world cellular deployments.

The performance for different groupings of cooperatively managed base stations is investigated. Results show that coordinating resource assignment of multiple base stations improves the cell spectral efficiency in general and coordinating three sectors at the same site outperforms coordinating three base stations of different sites.

Keywords: LTE · Radio resource management · Inter-cell interference coordination · Base station grouping · Interference mitigation · Linear assignment problem · Multidimensional assignment problem · IMT-Advanced · C-RAN

1   Introduction

In recent years the demand for higher data rates in mobile networks has significantly increased. Therefore higher data rates in mobile communication are a major goal within the optimisation of mobile networks. The efficiency of such communication systems can be described by the Cell Spectral Efficiency (CSE) which is defined as achieved data rate per unit of radio spectrum and cell.

LTE [1] is a mobile communication system applying OFDM with a frequency reuse factor of one. Therefore, the complete frequency spectrum used by the system is available in every cell. This allows high flexibility in resource assignment, but is causing severe inter-cell interference, especially in neighbouring cells.

© Institute for Computer Sciences, Social Informatics and Telecommunications Engineering 2015
R. Agüero et al. (Eds.): MONAMI 2014, LNICST 141, pp. 47–59, 2015.
DOI: 10.1007/978-3-319-16292-8_4

Coordinated resource allocation of multiple base stations, e.g. in a cloud based radio access network [2], can avoid interference, and therefore has the potential to improve the overall system throughput and thus the CSE. The coordination of all base stations within a large scenario is too complex to solve it in reasonable time [3]. Therefore we investigate the performance if only certain base stations, forming a group, are coordinated. The CSE for different amounts and locations of grouped base stations is evaluated.

1.1 Related Work

Resource assignment in OFDMA systems has been a research topic for several years. In [4] a comprehensive overview of the state of the art of optimised single cell resource allocation in OFDMA-based systems is provided. With the proposed frequency reuse factor of one for LTE, inter-cell interference mitigation has become an important subject.

The authors of [5] and [6] give extensive overviews on current inter-cell interference coordination techniques. They categorise different approaches and provide many references. The centralised coordination schemes mentioned in [6] where developed for Time Division and Code Division Multiple Access Schemes (TDMA / CDMA). In [7] the authors provide an overview on inter-cell interference mitigatation and scheduling in LTE. Their focus lies on different soft and fractional frequency reuse schemes. The optimal power allocation to user terminals with respect to maximising the downlink throughput using inter-cell coordination was analysed in [8]. Therein the authors define a "cell of interest" as well as its "neighbour set" of close by interferers. The described optimisation problem takes into account the resulting interference power but is only optimal for the cell of interest, not the overall system.

Optimisation using linear optimisation methods is described in [9–12]. In [9] the authors describe a dynamic fair scheduling scheme for a two cell scenario. The Hungarian algorithm is used to optimise the schedule with Max-Min fairness as objective, which is to maximise the spectral efficiency (CSE) of the UE having the lowest CSE. In [10] interference avoidance in femtocell networks is described. Therein the problem is formulated in terms of integer linear programming.

The resource allocation in device-to-device communication underlaying LTE was investigated in [11]. The problem is formulated as an integer linear program and it is stated that it is infeasible to solve. Instead heuristic distributed algorithms are presented and evaluated. The authors of [12] investigate the uplink resource assignment problem of multiple cells using geometric programming. They present centralised and distributed algorithms for sub-optimal resource allocation schemes. Power and subcarrier allocation is considered in their work.

In our previous work different optimisation algorithms were analysed ([3,13]). In [3] a cooperatively managed resource allocation formulated as an assignment problem is introduced. Therein the resource allocation is optimised in a central scheduler with information about interference situations of all user terminals. From there a better resource allocation is derived by deciding which user terminals of different cells should transmit on the same resources. The optimisation objective is to increase the overall system throughput. The investigations have shown, that optimisating the resource allocation using heuristic algorithms leads to good optimisation results with acceptable computation time. In our previous work optimisation has only been done with small scenarios resembling an indoor femto-cell environment. Here we present results for a macro-cell deployment [14]. The scenarios are described in detail in Sect. 2.

Most analysed interference coordination techniques in literature rely on distributed schemes without a central coordination entity. In LTE-Advanced the coordination can rely on information exchanged via the X2 interface and then a distributed optimisation can be performed. Although a central scheduling would require a high signaling, it can possibly lead to better results as information of more other cells is known and interference situations can be determined.

We have analysed a scenario where a central scheduling unit can be easily used, the Cloud Radio Access Network (C-RAN) [2]. In this scenario, remote radio heads are connected to the cloud. All management and coordinating functions are placed in the cloud making all information for coordinated scheduling available. This results in normal signaling for Channel Quality Indication (CQI) feedback to the cloud but no inter-base station signaling.

1.2   The Resource Assignment Problem

As explained above, LTE is intended for use with a frequency reuse factor of one. Thus, users of adjacent cells can cause high uplink interference to neighbouring base stations. Cooperatively managing resource allocation of multiple cells can therefore reduce the impact of interference, leading to increased CSE. In LTE resources for transmissions are assigned on the basis of physical resource blocks (PRBs) defined in [15]. A restriction in uplink transmission resulting from the Single Carrier Frequency Division Multiple Access (SC-FDMA) scheme is that PRBs assigned to one user terminal (UT) have to be consecutive in frequency domain. The optimal allocation of PRBs to UTs with respect to an optimal throughput influenced by the block error rate (BLER) and the effective signal to interference and noise ratio (SINR) mapping are nonlinear optimisation problems [12]. To reduce this complexity only the mapping of UTs served by different base stations to each other is taken into consideration. For the formulation as an multidimensional assignment problem it is necessary to have only one interferer per neighbouring cell for a user. This means that for a scenario of five cells a user has four interfering user terminals from the other cells. To achieve this, each user gets the same amount of resources. For example for a set up with five users and 50 PRBs each user gets 10 consecutive PRBs.

Therefore, our aim is to find an optimal assignment which UTs should transmit on the same resource blocks. A basic example of a possible assignment is given in Fig. 1. In this Figure the users $UT_{1,1}$ and $UT_{2,1}$ are transmitting on the same resources. The SINR calculated for $UT_{1,1}$ from signal $S_{1,1}$ and interference $I_{2,1}$ leads to an achievable data rate. Summed up with the data rate of the user terminal $UT_{2,1}$ the sum data rate $r_{1,1}$ is calculated. The user terminals $UT_{1,2}$ and $UT_{2,2}$ lead to the sum data rate $r_{2,2}$. The other possible resource assignment in this simple example with user terminals $UT_{1,1}$ and $UT_{2,2}$ on the same resources and $UT_{1,2}$ and $UT_{2,1}$ on the same resources will lead to other sum data rates. Due to a different interference situation the sum data rates $r_{1,2}$ and $r_{2,1}$ are calculated. Thus, the different possible resource assignments are causing different interference situations between the UTs and therefore lead to a different overall system throughput. The aim is to optimise this overall system throughput. By doing this, the cell spectral efficiency is optimised.

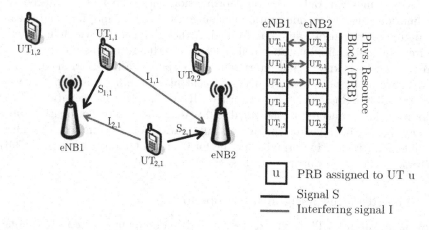

Fig. 1. Example of a possible resource assignment for two cells and two user terminals per cell.

The decision on which user terminals of different cells should transmit on the same resource block is leading to an assignment problem. To optimize the overall system throughput the sum of all user data rates has to be maximised. For a two-cell scenario this means that the sum of the user terminal data rates r_i of the first cell and r_j of the second cell has to be maximised. Therefore we first define sum data rates r_{ij}. Where r_{ij} represents the sum of the data rates achieved by user terminal i of the first cell and j of the second cell transmitting on the same PRBs. Next, the sum data rates r_{ij} can be written as elements of a matrix R. From this matrix the best data rates have to be chosen under the following restriction: As only one user terminal of a cell can transmit on the same resources as one user terminal of another cell, only one element per row and column of matrix R can be chosen. This is represented by restrictions (2)–(4) which define a permutation matrix C with elements $c_{ij} \in \{0,1\}$. This means, choosing a sum data rate r_{ij} from R sets the element c_{ij} of C to one. Thus for two base stations the linear assignment problem is given by

$$\max \sum_{i=1}^{N} \sum_{j=1}^{N} c_{ij} r_{ij} \tag{1}$$

$$\text{s.t.} \ \sum_{j=1}^{N} c_{ij} = 1, \text{for } i = 1, 2, ..., N, \tag{2}$$

$$\sum_{i=1}^{N} c_{ij} = 1, \text{for } j = 1, 2, ..., N, \tag{3}$$

$$c_{ij} \in \{0, 1\} \tag{4}$$

For scenarios with more than two cells the sum data rates are written in a tensor. It has as many indices as cells. This is leading to a multidimensional assignment problem [16] which is defined for three dimensions by [17]:

$$\max \sum_{i=1}^{N} \sum_{j=1}^{N} \sum_{k=1}^{N} c_{ijk} r_{ijk} \tag{5}$$

$$\text{s.t. } \sum_{j=1}^{N} \sum_{k=1}^{N} c_{ijk} = 1, \text{for } i = 1, 2, ..., N, \tag{6}$$

$$\sum_{i=1}^{N} \sum_{k=1}^{N} c_{ijk} = 1, \text{for } j = 1, 2, ..., N, \tag{7}$$

$$\sum_{i=1}^{N} \sum_{j=1}^{N} c_{ijk} = 1, \text{for } k = 1, 2, ..., N, \tag{8}$$

$$c_{ijk} \in \{0, 1\} \tag{9}$$

To formulate the problem as a multidimensional assignment problem it is necessary to have an equal amount of user terminals selected for scheduling in each cell at the time of optimisation.

2   Simulation Scenarios

Different scenarios were taken into account for evaluating the impact of cooperative resource management in groups. First, small scenarios representing simple indoor femto-cell deployments scenarios with a closed subscriber group were analysed. The scenario is adapted from the ITU IMT-Advanced indoor scenario described in [14]. All links are set to have Non-line-of-sight (NLoS) channel conditions. The user terminals are randomly distributed within cell areas of 100 m radius. As described in the previous section all coordinated cells must serve the same number of user terminals to formulate the problem as an multidimensional assignment problem. A simple approach assuring an equal amount of terminals scheduled in each TTI is chosen: The number of users served by each base station is equal. This way no time domain scheduling is necessary.

The layout of the scenario set up is shown in Fig. 2. Results have been obtained for different numbers and locations of cooperatively managed base stations. The different analysed groupings are depicted in Fig. 3. The assignment problem in these scenarios has been solved using a brute force algorithm such that the optimal user assignment for the cooperatively managed base stations is found.

The more cells are cooperatively managed by the central scheduling entity in the cloud, the more potential for optimisation exists. Thus the interference can be reduced and the system throughput increased. So, it is expected that the cooperative resource management of all base stations will lead to a higher system throughput than the cooperative management of two cells. Furthermore, the coordination should at least not give a worse throughput than the uncoordinated scenario.

In a next step the coordination of different groups has been applied to a larger scenario. The urban macro-cell scenario has been described by the ITU in [14]. For this evaluation 21 sectors at 7 base station sites are simulated. The coordination in groups enables us to analyse different coordination setups of this

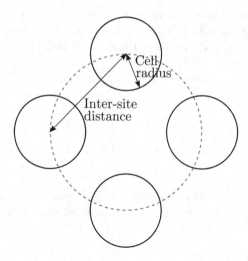

Fig. 2. Schematic layout of the small scenario

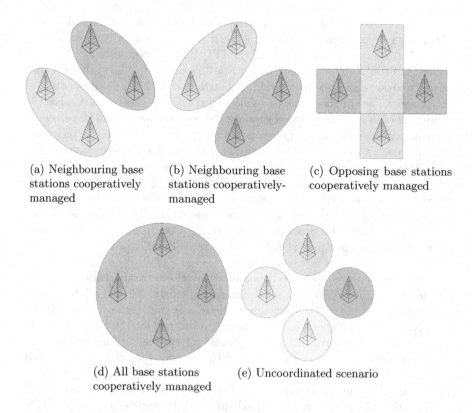

(a) Neighbouring base stations cooperatively managed

(b) Neighbouring base stations cooperatively-managed

(c) Opposing base stations cooperatively managed

(d) All base stations cooperatively managed

(e) Uncoordinated scenario

Fig. 3. Different groupings of base stations for the small scenarios

scenario. A cooperative coordinated resource allocation of all base stations, even with heuristic algorithms, was not possible, since even with only ten user terminals per cell a tensor with 10^{21} elements must be constructed which results in the number of $10!^{20}$ possible assignments. The maximum amount of cooperatively managed base stations was therefore limited to six. In this scenario the inner six base stations were coordinated and the outer ones were independent of each other. Further simulation parameters are depicted in Table 1.

Table 1. Simulation parameters of small scenarios

Environment	Similar to indoor hotspot (after ITU M.2135 [14])
Channel model	Path loss only: $PL = 22.1 + 43.3 \cdot log_{10}d$
User distribution	Random uniform
User mobility	None
Base station antenna	Omnidirectional
Duplex scheme	FDD
System bandwidth	20 MHz
Numbers of users per basestation	5
Inter-site distance	100 m, 200 m
Cell size	100 m
Grouping of base stations	see Fig. 3
Assignment problem solver	None (random assignment), brute force (optimal)

As described in Sect. 1.2 the same amount of user terminals have to be scheduled in all cells in each subframe in order to formulate the problem as a multidimensional assignment problem. Rather than achieving this by time-domain scheduling the simple approach of deploying the same amount of user terminals per cell was chosen. In all simulations in every cell ten users are served. For optimising the resource allocation in the urban macro-cell scenarios, the greedy algorithm [3] has been used. Therefore, the schedule is not necessarily optimal. Further simulation parameters are depicted in Table 2.

In the urban macro-cell scenarios four different locations and numbers of cooperatively managed cells have been investigated. Two different locations of three cell groupings have been investigated. On the one hand the three cells managed by the same base station site were jointly managed. Secondly the cells of different sites were grouped. Furthermore, a grouping of only two base stations hasbeen analysed. The coordination group set ups are shown in Fig. 4.

In all scenarios only the inner three base stations were taken into account for evaluating the user performance. Thus, there is an influence on all evaluated base stations by surrounding base stations and their assigned user terminals. The simulations have been repeated 150 times for sufficient confidence levels. Each simulation run is executed with a different random number seed and therefore different user terminal positions.

Table 2. Simulation parameters for urban macro-cell scenarios

Environment	Urban macro (after ITU M.2135 [14])
Large scale channel model	Urban macro
Small scale channel model	None
User distribution	Random uniform
User mobility	None
Base station antenna	Sectorised (after ITU M.2135 [14])
Duplex scheme	FDD
System bandwidth	10 MHz

Scenarios with same random number seed but different groupings are compared. This way it is assured that different performance is caused by different groupings and not by more or less favourable user terminal deployments.

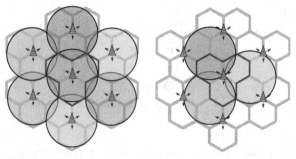

(a) Three base stations of one site cooperatively managed

(b) Three base stations of different sites cooperatively managed

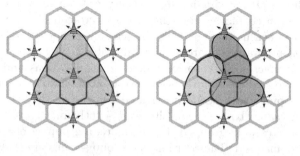

(c) Six base stations cooperatively managed

(d) Two base stations cooperatively managed

Fig. 4. Urban macro-cell scenario groupings. Base stations are indicated at their sites. Arrows indicate the main radiation directions of sector antennas. Ungrouped cells are left blank. The centre cells are marked by a blue border.

3   Results

The results in Fig. 5 show the average cell throughput for the different groupings of Fig. 3 and for two different cell centre distances. The provided black lines in the figure (as in all following as well) indicate the 95 % confidence interval. The results proof the assumption that it is better to coordinate all base stations than only few. This holds independently of the distance. It can be seen that no significant (or even none at all) improvement is achieved for a coordination of only two base stations, no matter which are coordinated. For a more specific analysis the ratio for a certain grouping to achieve the best throughput is analysed.

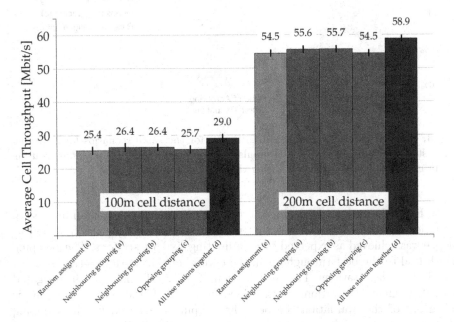

Fig. 5. Average cell throughput for different groupings as in Fig. 3 for the small scenarios

The ratio how often a particular grouping lead to the highest overall CSE was evaluated. This grouping is referred to as the "winner" for the particular user terminal deployment. In Fig. 6 the results for the winning coordination set up in achieving the best throughput for the small scenarios are shown. As expected, coordinating all base stations leads to the highest throughput. Furthermore it shows that it is important which base stations are coordinated. As coordinating all base station leads to the highest throughput in most of the cases this grouping is taken out off the evaluation in this Figure. Here, in almost 90 % of the simulation runs the coordination of one of both possible neighbouring groupings has lead to the best system throughput. On the other hand it can be seen that in a few simulation runs the neighbouring groupings are leading to the worst throughput. So by not coordinating all base stations it is even possible to get a worse solution than without any coordination. But nevertheless it gives a better performance for a large majority of simulation runs.

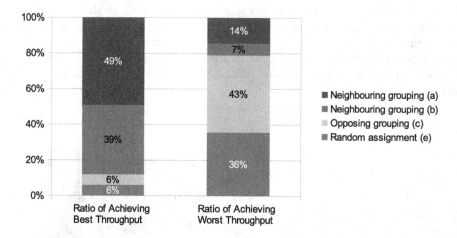

Fig. 6. Ratio of different groupings (see Fig. 3) for the small scenarios for achieving the best/worst throughput over 100 simulation runs with a cell distance of 200 m using the brute force algorithm for optimising the user assignment

In Fig. 7 the ratio of achieving the best throughput for the urban macro-cell scenarios is shown. It is obvious that in most simulation runs the best performance was achieved as expected by coordinating six base stations. The grouping which lead to the best throughput in the fewest simulation runs is the grouping of only two base stations. The coordination of three cells has been investigated with different configurations as explained in Sect. 2. If the six cell grouping is taken out of the evaluation the best throughput is achieved by the grouping of three cells of one site in most of the runs (see Fig. 8). Here, only in 28 % of the simulations the three base station grouping of different sites is leading to the best throughput.

The average CSE gain over an uncoordinated scenario is shown in Fig. 9. The coordination of six base stations is leading to a gain in CSE of more than 10 %. This confirms the expectation that the more base stations are coordinated the higher the gain in CSE is. Furthermore, it shows again that the two different groupings with three base stations show different performances. The coordination of cells belonging to one base station site is leading to a better performance than the coordination of cells served by base stations of different sites. The first location of base stations is leading to an average improvement in CSE of 6 % compared to only 2.6 % in the later location. This is beneficial with regard to the information that must be exchanged in order to enable coordination. The

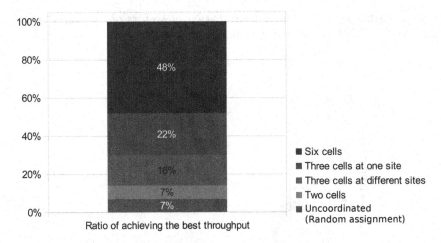

Fig. 7. Ratio of different groupings (see Fig. 4) for the urban macro-cell scenario for achieving the best throughput over 150 simulation.

reason is that the coordinated user terminals for the first grouping often lie in an area where antenna attenuation of user terminals of the neighbouring sector is not very high and therefore a high interference power is received. Interference at other sites experiences a higher attenuation due to the higher path loss. The maximum antenna attenuation among sectors from the same site is 17 dB [14] while the attenuation difference resulting from path loss among different sites

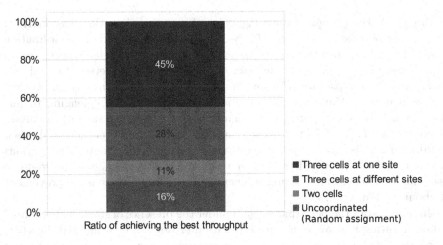

Fig. 8. Ratio of different groupings (see Fig. 4) for the urban macro-cell scenario for achieving the best throughput over 150 simulation without the grouping of six cells.

can be much higher. Therefore a coordination of sectors of the same site can avoid very low SINR values due to reduced interference power.

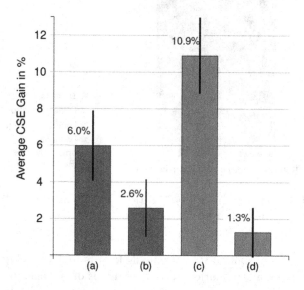

Fig. 9. Average gain in CSE for the different groupings (see Fig. 4) for the urban macro-cell scenario

4   Conclusion and Outlook

In this paper the cooperative management of resource allocation was analysed as it would be possible in Cloud RANs. With the introduction of coordination groups for a cooperative resource management of several cells a performance improvement in a small and urban macro-cell scenario was achieved. It was shown that it plays an important role how many and which base stations are cooperatively managed. Managing the resource allocation of cells belonging to one base station site shows better performance than for different sites in the urban macro-cell scenario. An improvement in CSE of 6 % has been achieved when coordinating cells served by base stations of one site. The more base stations are cooperatively managed the higher the gain. Jointly managing the resource assignment of six cells in the urban macro-cell scenario leads to an improvement of about 10 % in CSE.

In future work the performance gain under the presence of small-scale channel fading resulting in channel quality estimation errors will be evaluated. Furthermore, the possibility of larger coordination groups has to be investigated and compared against other interference mitigation methods like interference cancelation with multiple antennas. As well, the combination of our method with other existing methods can be analysed to achieve higher gains in CSE.

References

1. 3GPP, Evolved Universal Terrestrial Radio Access (E-UTRA); LTE physical layer; LTE Physical layer; General description, Technical report 3GPP 36.201 (2009)
2. Rost, P., Bernardos, C.J., De Domenico, A., Di Girolamo, M., Lalam, M., Maeder, A., Sabella, D., Wübben, D.: Cloud technologies for flexible 5G radio access networks. IEEE Commun. Mag. **52**(5), 68–76 (2014)
3. Mühleisen, M., Henzel, K., Timm-Giel, A.: Design and evaluation of scheduling algorithms for LTE femtocells. In: ITG Fachbericht Mobilkommunikation 2013, Osnabrück (2013)
4. Girici, T., Zhu, C., Agre, J.R., Ephremides, A.: Proportional fair scheduling algorithm in OFDMA-based wireless systems with QoS constraints. J. Commun. Netw. **12**(1), 30–42 (2010)
5. Hamza, A.S., Khalifa, S.S., Hamza, H.S., Elsayed, K.: A survey on inter-cell interference coordination techniques in OFDMA-based cellular networks. IEEE Commun. Surv. Tutorials **15**(4), 1642–1670 (2013)
6. Boudreau, G., Panicker, J., Guo, N., Chang, R., Wang, N., Vrzic, S.: Interference coordination and cancellation for 4G networks. IEEE Commun. Mag. **47**(4), 74–81 (2009)
7. Kwan, R., Leung, C.: A survey of scheduling and interference mitigation in LTE. J. Electr. Comput. Eng. **2010**, 10 (2010). Hindawi Publishing Corporation, New York
8. Shi, Z., Luo, Y., Huang, L., Gu, D.: User fairness-empowered power coordination in OFDMA downlink. In: 2011 IEEE Vehicular Technology Conference (VTC Fall), San Francisco, pp. 1–5 (2011)
9. Guo, W., Wang, X., Li, J., Wang, L.: Dynamic fair scheduling for inter-cell interference coordination in 4G cellular networks. In: 2nd IEEE/CIC International Conference on Communications in China (ICCC), Xi'an, pp. 84–88 (2013)
10. Liang, Y.-S., Chung, W.-H., Yu, C.-M., Zhang, H., Chung, C.-H., Ho, C.-H., Kuo, S.-Y.: Resource block assignment for interference avoidance in femtocell networks. In: 2012 IEEE Vehicular Technology Conference (VTC Fall), Quebec City, pp. 1–5 (2012)
11. Zulhasnine, M., Changcheng H., Srinivasan, A.: Efficient resource allocation for device-to-device communication underlaying LTE network. In: IEEE 6th International Conference on Wireless and Mobile Computing, Networking and Communications (WiMob), Niagara Falls, pp. 368–375 (2010)
12. Tabassum, H., Dawy, Z., Alouini, M.-S.: Sum rate maximization in the uplink of multi-cell OFDMA networks. In: 7th International Wireless Communications and Mobile Computing Conference (IWCMC), Istanbul, pp. 1152–1157 (2011)
13. Garcia Luna, J. A., Mühleisen, M., Henzel, K.: Performance of a heuristic uplink radio resource assignment algorithm for LTE-advanced. In: ITG Fachbericht Mobilkommunikation 2011, Osnabrück (2011)
14. ITU, ITU-R M.2135 Guidelines for evaluating of radio interface technologies for IMT-Advanced, Technical report (2009)
15. 3GPP, Evolved Universal Terrestrial Radio Access (E-UTRA); LTE physical layer; Physical channels and modulation, Technical Report 3GPP 36.211 (2009)
16. Pierskalla, W.P.: Letter to the editor - the multidimensional assignment problem. Oper. Res. **16**(2), 422–431 (1968)
17. Balas, E., Saltzman, M.J.: An algorithm for the three-index assignment problem. Oper. Res. **39**(1), 150–161 (1991)

Virtualization and Software
Defined Networking

SDN and NFV Dynamic Operation of LTE EPC Gateways for Time-Varying Traffic Patterns

Arsany Basta[1(✉)], Andreas Blenk[1], Marco Hoffmann[2], Hans Jochen Morper[2], Klaus Hoffmann[2], and Wolfgang Kellerer[1]

[1] Technische Universität München, Munich, Germany
{arsany.basta,andreas.blenk,wolfgang.kellerer}@tum.de
[2] Nokia Solutions and Networks, Munich, Germany
{marco.hoffmann,hans-jochen.morper,klaus.hoffmann}@nsn.com

Abstract. The introduction of Network Functions Virtualization (NFV) and Software Defined Networking (SDN) to mobile networks enables operators to control and dimension their network resources with higher granularity and on a more fine-grained time scale. This dynamic operation allows operators to cope with the rapid growth of traffic and user demands, in addition to reducing costs. In this paper, we model and analyze a realization of the mobile core network as virtualized software instances running in datacenters (DC) and SDN transport network elements (NE), with respect to time-varying traffic demands. It is our objective to determine the datacenters placement that achieves the minimum transport network load considering time-varying traffic and under a data-plane delay budget. A second objective is to achieve power savings, considering the variation of traffic over time, by using the available datacenter resources or by acquiring additional resources.

Keywords: Network Functions Virtualization · Software Defined Networking · Datacenters · Mobile core gateways · Time-varying traffic

1 Introduction

Today's network operators are faced with the steadily increasing network traffic given the limited flexibility provided by currently deployed architectures. This lack of flexibility leads to an inefficient use of the available resources, which in turn leads to decreasing revenues for operators [1], when the changing dynamics of the user demands cannot be fully considered. This means that network operators let their network regularly undergo periods of over- and under-utilization. New concepts, namely Network Function Virtualization (NFV) and Software Defined Networking (SDN), emerged over the last few years that may allow network operators to operate their network resources in a more fine granular way [2] and to apply dynamic network changes over time.

The flexibility in resource allocation for network components is obtained by NFV, where network components are hosted as virtual components on virtualized commodity hardware and can be migrated between different virtualized environments, hence datacenters. Flexibility in control is provided by SDN,

© Institute for Computer Sciences, Social Informatics and Telecommunications Engineering 2015
R. Agüero et al. (Eds.): MONAMI 2014, LNICST 141, pp. 63–76, 2015.
DOI: 10.1007/978-3-319-16292-8_5

where the network traffic can be shaped dynamically on run time with a centralized control. Both concepts allow the operators to exploit more gains from dimensioning and operating the mobile network considering time-varying traffic patterns to achieve more efficient load balancing or energy savings.

The adoption of both concepts to increase the flexibility of existing networks has been discussed in some related work. Google [3] set up an architecture based on SDN for their WAN interconnecting their datacenters, where SDN allows them to plan their network operation and resource allocation according to their applications in advance driving their network utilization to nearly 100 %. A similar approach is introduced in [4], where the network is dynamically adapted to the demands of big data application. The consideration of traffic-patterns in the embedding of virtual networks was shown in [5]. Regarding the application of SDN and NFV in mobile networks, some studies have discussed the architecture of virtualized mobile network as in [6] and their different advantages and use-cases. First steps migration have been presented in [7] which utilize the virtualized resources hosted in datacenters only to offload the network traffic within the mobile core. Additionally, conceptual architectures and use-cases of an SDN-based mobile core have been discussed in [8]. In our previous work, a qualitative analysis of the benefits of SDN and NFV to the mobile core have been discussed in [9]. Additionally, we have studied the influence of SDN and NFV on the gateways and datacenter placement within the mobile core in [10], however considering only uniform traffic demands. Hence, existing work still lacks quantitative evaluation of the impact of virtualization and SDN on mobile networks and their flexibility gain considering the time-varying property of the traffic.

In this paper, we consider a mobile network architecture with virtual components and SDN control, which offers a fine-granular control of the available resources. Our main attention is drawn to the application of NFV and SDN concepts on the high volume data-plane within the mobile core network. Hence, as a first investigation, we focus on LTE core network elements which handle both control-plane and data-plane, namely the Serving Gateway (SGW) and PDN Gateway (PGW).

Our objective is to find the optimal datacenter(s) location, hosting the virtual gateway components, which achieves a minimum transport network load while considering time-varying traffic pattern and under a data-plane delay budget. We provide further approaches to maximize power savings by adapting the datacenter(s) operation according to the traffic patterns and datacenter resources.

The remainder of the paper is structured as follows. In Sect. 2, we introduce the architecture that enables a traffic-pattern aware orchestration of datacenters and network traffic. In Sect. 3, we give a short overview of measurement papers that backup our assumption of predictable traffic. In Sect. 4, we introduce our new models that optimize the datacenter placement and resource allocation for our proposed architecture. In Sect. 5, we show the results of our analysis, and we finally conclude our work in Sect. 6.

2   Architecture

This section describes the architecture that applies virtualization and SDN to mobile core network gateways in order to achieve dynamic resource allocation with respect to traffic demands. In particular, we discuss the required components and the interaction between them.

2.1   Gateways Virtualization

The considered architecture applies the concept of NFV, where the current mobile core network gateways are transformed to virtual instances hosted by a datacenter platform and SDN Network Element (NE) at the transport network as shown in Fig. 1. Hence, the operator gets the advantage of deploying and operating the core gateways in a datacenter environment, where datacenters provide a flexible and dynamic allocation for the intra-datacenter network as well as computational resources for each virtualized gateway.

Within the transport network, each gateway would be replaced by an SDN NE, which is responsible for transporting and steering the traffic that comes from the access network or external data networks and is intended to the virtual gateway instances at the datacenters. These replacement SDN NEs offer the capability of changing the traffic routes and forward the traffic to different datacenters when needed, which requires that all datacenters should be reachable from any SDN NE at the transport network.

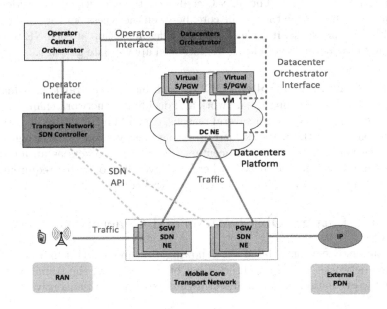

Fig. 1. Architecture of virtual mobile core gateways and SDN transport NEs

2.2 Orchestration

It is noted that in the introduced architecture, multiple orchestration and control elements are needed as illustrated in Fig. 1. In the following, we explain the Datacenters Orchestrator (DC-O), the SDN Controller (SDN-C), and the Operator Central Controller (OCC).

Datacenters Orchestrator (DC-O) is required to assign sufficient resources to the virtual mobile core gateways from the pool of resources at the datacenter platform, which include both networking and computational resources. It allocates the computational power such as processing cores, memory or storage to the gateways software instances, which must be sufficient to handle the high data volume traffic and achieve a comparable performance to the current hardware gateway component. Additionally, it is responsible to setup the connectivity within the datacenter between different physical hosts and setup the connection to external networks as well. Finally, it handles the synchronization and migration of the virtual gateway instances in case a network change is triggered by the operator.

Transport SDN Controller (SDN-C) is essential to control the transport network, i.e., control the SDN NEs to handle the traffic forwarding to the virtual core gateways. Having an SDN transport network control provides dynamic traffic handling as the SDN-C has the capability to flexibly adapt and program the network setup on run-time. The SDN-C configures the network which carries the high-volume traffic within the mobile core, between the access network and external packet data networks. It makes sure that rules are set up at each NE to steer the traffic to the datacenter hosting the intended appropriate gateway.

Operator Central Controller (OCC) contains the central logic which is responsible for dimensioning the network and deciding on network changes. Network changes are motivated for several reasons, e.g., adding new sites or network elements, balancing the network load or saving energy costs by shutting down parts of the network including datacenters. The OCC also acts as an interface towards the DC-O and the SDN-C where it delivers the operator requirements which are translated and enforced by both control components.

3   Traffic Pattern Observations and Generation

We first summarize recent related work showing measurements taken from mobile and wired networks. Based on observations of these papers, the traffic patterns used for the evaluation of our architecture are explained subsequently.

3.1   Traffic Measurements from Today's Networks

Many measurement papers [11–15] show traffic behavior that is correlated in time and space as well. The measurements are taken from 2G/3G/4G networks, for different vantage points, for up to four major U.S. carriers including UMTS networks, and for mega events.

In [11], an event based analysis of cellular traffic for the Super Bowl is provided, which shows that there are traffic peaks related to events, e.g., the Half-time Show or a Power Outage. In [12], the authors investigate the traffic proportion of companies, e.g. Google, Facebook, Akamai, and Limelight. The traffic shows a time-dependent behavior, where Google has the highest proportion. Reference [13] analyzed user activity at different locations in order to investigate users' mobility. Reference [14] shows that traffic patterns for wired and wireless network are affecting each other where more users utilize the mobile network during commuting time. Further, different points in space are showing a different but timely correlated traffic intensity. In [15], a correlation even for different applications can be concluded.

3.2 Traffic Pattern Generation

To quantify effectiveness of our approach, traffic patterns for the mobile core demands have to be created. A demand is defined as the traffic flow between each sgw and its respective pgw, which is considered to be time-varying, bidirectional and non-splittable. Hence, traffic demand patterns could integrate a correlation in time and location of the corresponding gateway $sgw \in SGW$.

First, we explain how the traffic pattern for each city, whose demand is forwarded to one sgw, is determined. For this, the population and location of cities C, and the time-dependent behavior of the traffic intensity is taken into account. The intensity function

$$i(t) = intensity_t \tag{1}$$

takes the traffic intensity $intensity_t$ from a look-up table (as introduced in Sect. 5, Table 1) according to the current time t. The current time t of a city corresponds to its current local time. For calculating the traffic based on the population for the current time t, the following function is used

$$f(c,t) = i(t) \cdot p(c) \tag{2}$$

where $p(c)$ provides the population of city c. Using these functions, the traffic patterns integrate a correlation in time and location for each city.

The traffic at each sgw is the sum of all cities C connected to it. Thus, for each $sgw \in SGW$ the function

$$TR_{sgw}(t) = \sum_C f(c, time_{c,sgw}(t)) \cdot b_{c,sgw} \tag{3}$$

calculates the aggregated traffic at time t, where $time_{c,sgw}(t)$ is the local time of city c calculated depending on the local time of sgw, and $b_{c,sgw}$ is an indicator whether city c is connected to sgw or not. Note again that cities and gateways may belong to different time-zones, thus, the traffic intensity of a city c always depends on c's local time that has be calculated depending on the current time, i.e., the time zone of the sgw.

4 Datacenter Placement and DC Power Saving Models

As previously discussed in Sect. 3, time-varying traffic patterns could be observed in today's mobile networks. Such variation in network traffic could be considered for dynamic network dimensioning to achieve higher gains for operators in terms of network utilization or power saving. We split the whole time frame into multiple time slots, each with varying traffic demands.

We introduce three models, where the first model aims at finding the optimal datacenter(s) placement that minimizes the total transport network load under a data-plane delay budget. By exploiting the traffic variation, the second and third models aim at achieving power savings by allowing fewer datacenters in operation within the resulted available datacenter resources or using additional resources.

The network load is considered as a significant objective cost metric for mobile networks dimensioning as it reflects on traffic delay and cost imposed on operators. We define the total network load as:

$$\sum_{t \in T} \sum_{d \in D} Tr_{d,t} * lengthPath_{d,t} \tag{4}$$

where d is a demand between each SGW and PGW, which are considered to be time-varying, bi-directional and non-splittable. $Tr_{d,t}$ is the traffic volume of demand d at a time slot t, while $lengthPath_{d,t}$ is the length of the path taken for a demand d at time slot t. A demand path within the core network is defined between an SGW NE, a datacenter and a PGW NE. Hence, chosen paths in fact determine the location of datacenters and assigned demand to each DC. While data-plane delay is defined as propagation delay on the path for each demand.

Note that datacenters are assumed to be placed in a location where an operator has already an existing site to reduce the floor space cost, i.e., the datacenter is placed in a location where an operator has gateways. We also keep the gateways geographical locations unchanged, i.e., replace conventional gateway with an SDN NE. All models are formulated as path-flow models.

4.1 DC Placement for All Time Slots (DCP-ATS)

The objective of this first model is to find the optimal DC placement with minimum transport network load under a given data-plane delay budget, considering the traffic demands over all time slots as follows:

$$\min \sum_{c \in C} \sum_{d \in D} \sum_{t \in T} \delta_{c,d,t} N_{c,d,t} \tag{5}$$

where the set C includes all possible locations of the K datacenters. The binary variable $\delta_{c,d,t}$ denotes that a datacenter c is chosen for demand d at time slot t. The parameter $N_{c,d,t}$ is pre-calculated load resulted from a combination of datacenter location, demand and time slot. The constraints are given by:

$$\sum_{c \in C} \delta_c = K \tag{6}$$

$$\delta_{c,d,t} \leq \delta_c \quad \forall d \in D, c \in C, t \in T \tag{7}$$

$$\sum_{c \in C} \delta_{c,d,t} = 1 \quad \forall d \in D, t \in T \tag{8}$$

$$\delta_{c,d,t} L_{c,d,t} \leq L_{budget} \quad \forall d \in D, c \in C, t \in T \tag{9}$$

where (6) ensures that K datacenters are chosen as δ_c is a binary variable to indicate a chosen datacenter. Constraint (7) reflects that if a datacenter c is chosen, demand d at time slot t could be assigned to this datacenter c. In case of K selected datacenters, only one datacenter can be assigned for each demand, guaranteed by (8). Finally, (9) ensures that the chosen path satisfies the data-plane delay budget where parameter $L_{c,d,t}$ is pre-calculated latency resulted from a combination of datacenter location, demand and time slot.

4.2 Power Saving at Each Time Slot Within DC Resources (PS-ETS)

This model acts as a next step after solving DCP-ATS in Sect. 4.1 as it takes the resulted chosen DCs and their available resources as an input from the solution of the model 4.1. The objective of such model is again to minimize the total transport network load, while having the degree of freedom of operating a number of DCs less than K at each time slot, from the set of previously chosen DCs and within the available DC resources. This implies that among the deployed DCs and considering the traffic characteristics, operators would be able to minimize the power consumption of unutilized DCs, resulting in power and cost savings.

In this model, the objective is updated to find the optimal solution for each time slot as follows:

$$\min \sum_{c \in C_s} \sum_{d \in D} \delta_{c,d,t} N_{c,d,t} \quad \forall t \in T \tag{10}$$

Additionally, constraint (6) is replaced with constraints 11, which allows for operating fewer DCs and (12) that ensures that one DC is at least in operation.

$$\sum_{c \in C_s} \delta_c \leq K \tag{11}$$

$$\sum_{c \in C_s} \delta_c \geq 1 \tag{12}$$

Note that for all expression the set of datacenters C is replaced by C_s which contains the chosen DCs by model DCP-ATS in Sect. 4.1. Additional constraint (13) is needed to ensure that the assigned resources at each DC do not exceed the available resources $R_{d,t}$.

$$\sum_{d \in D} \sum_{t \in T} \delta_{c,d,t} R_{d,t} \leq R_c \quad \forall c \in C_s \tag{13}$$

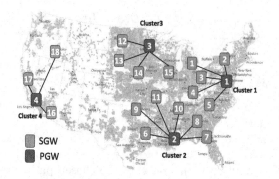

Fig. 2. Presumed core gateways topology based on LTE coverage map in [16]

4.3 Power Saving at Each Time Slot with Additional DC Resources (PS-ETS-AR)

This models is an extension for the previous PS-ETS model, where it provides a room of having additional resources at each DC which should not exceed the available resources multiplied by a factor P. It also considers the set of DCs as an input from the solution of model DCP-ATS in addition to applying constraints (11) and (12) as in the previous model. However, constraint (13) is substitured by (14) to allow additional resources under the boundary provided by $R_c * P$.

$$\sum_{d \in D} \sum_{t \in T} \delta_{c,d,t} R_{d,t} \leq R_c * P \quad \forall c \in C_s \tag{14}$$

5 Simulation and Evaluation

For simulation, a java framework has been implemented with GUROBI [17] used as the optimization solver. We created a US mobile core gateways network shown in Fig. 2, based on LTE coverage map in [16] which correlates with the US population distribution as well [18]. The core gateways network consists of 4 PGWs and 18 SGWs, where a traffic demand exists between each SGW and the corresponding PGW in its cluster, resulting in a total of 18 demands. The core network is assumed to be fully meshed which implies that any gateway location could be chosen to deploy a DC with an available link to all other locations. The network load $N_{c,d,t}$ and path latency $L_{c,d,t}$ parameters are pre-calculated for all combinations of DC locations, demands and time slots. This decreases the optimization solving complexity and run time as well.

5.1 Traffic Patterns

Based on Eq. (3), a traffic pattern for each gateway is determined. Here, the indicator $b_{c,sgw}$ is set to one if a gateway sgw is the closest to a city c.

Table 1. Look-up table contains daytime and corresponding traffic intensity.

Daytime	0:00	1:00	2:00	3:00	4:00	5:00	6:00	7:00	8:00	9:00	10:00	11:00
Intensity	0.65	0.55	0.35	0.25	0.2	0.16	0.16	0.2	0.4	0.55	0.65	0.75
Daytime	12:00	13:00	14:00	15:00	16:00	17:00	18:00	19:00	20:00	21:00	22:00	23:00
Intensity	0.79	0.79	0.85	0.86	0.85	0.83	0.8	0.79	0.76	0.76	0.69	0.6

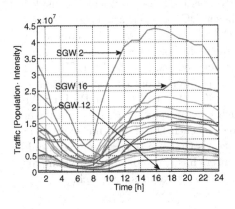 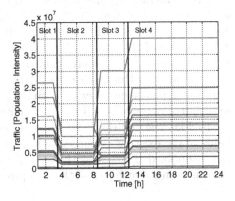

Fig. 3. Daily traffic pattern   **Fig. 4.** Split in 4 time slots

The population and the geo-location information of all U.S. cities is taken
from [19,20]. Table 1 contains the daytime and the corresponding traffic intensity
according to [14].

Figure 3 shows the traffic patterns of 18 gateways, which consider the population and intensity based on the time during a day. The time zone is set to
EDT (New York's local time). As SGW 2 is located at the east coast, and, thus
is connected to cities such as New York, it has the highest traffic demand. SGW
16 is located at the west coast and serves cities such as Los Angeles, therefore,
having the second highest demand. Between both gateways, we can also see the
time shift according to the different time zones of the cities both gateways are
serving. As SGW 12 is the most northern gateway that connects only cities with
a small population, it has the lowest demand over time.

The daily time frame was split into 4 time slots according to the traffic
distribution, where hours with minor variation traffic patterns were grouped
into a time slot. The evaluation is done based on the averaged traffic patterns
that are shown in Fig. 4.

5.2   Simulation Parameters and Cases

The transport network data-plane delay budget L_{budget} has been set to 15 ms.
An underlying optical transport network has been considered which is used to
calculate the data-plane propagation delay for each path. The DC resources are
depicted in traffic demand units. For evaluation, we have conducted a comparison between four cases shown in Table 2, in terms of the resulting DC required
resources, DC utilization, transport network load and DC power consumption.

Table 2. Simulation and Evaluation Cases

Model	DCP-ATS	PS-ETS	PS-ETS-AR	DCP-ATS
K DCs	3	3	3	2

First, the problem has been solved for the DCP-ATS model which considers all 4 time slots in a day, with 3 DCs. The chosen DC locations and their resources have been taken as an input to solve the DC power saving models, namely PS-ETS and PS-ETS-AR, which exploit the operation of fewer datacenter than 3 for each time slot, to achieve operational power savings. For the PS-ETS model, it is solved with the resulting available DC resources from the optimization of datacenter placement over all 4 time slots (DCP-ATS). While for PS-ETS-AR model, it allows additional resources for each DC up to factor P, which has been set to 2 i.e. the additional acquired resources at each DC should not exceed the value of the existing resources or in other words that the total resources should not be doubled. The case with $K-1$ datacenters has been considered to compare the gains and drawbacks of the two proposed power savings approach.

5.3   Datacenter Location

The DC locations which achieve the minimum transport network load under the data-plane delay budget of 15 ms and with 3 DCs can be seen in Fig. 5. It could be noted that cluster 4 required its own DC to be able to handle its traffic under the 15 ms data-plane delay budget due to its remoteness from the other three clusters. However, cluster 1, 2 and 3 which are more adjacent could be handled by only 2 DCs. Another property to note is that in case a DC is handling only a single cluster, the DC is placed at the location of the PGW of such cluster as for example DC1 and DC3, as this achieves the minimum transport network load. On the other hand, the centrality of the DC is observed in case it handles more than one cluster as in the case of DC 2.

5.4   Datacenter Resources

Figure 6 shows the required resources at each DC for the 4 evaluation cases. Models DCP-ATS with 3 DCs and PS-ETS have equal required DC resources since PS-ETS is achieving power savings within the available DC resources from DCP-ATS. On the other hand, model PS-ETS-AR which allows for additional resources results in increasing the acquired resources of DC2 by 40 % compared to models DCP-ATS with 3 DCs and PS-ETS. Additionally, it can be seen that in case DCP-ATS with 2 deployed DCs only, DC2 and DC3 are chosen due to cluster 4 remoteness and centrality of DC2 towards clusters 1,2 and 3. The resources required by DC2 in this case compared to DCP-ATS with 3 DCs are 100 % more. In this case, it is the operator's decision whether to get an extra datacenter or increase the resources of a datacenter, which depends on the costs induced for deploying the DC compared to adding resources to it.

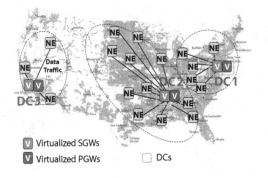

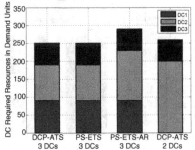

Fig. 5. DC placement at K = 3 DCs   **Fig. 6.** Required DC resources

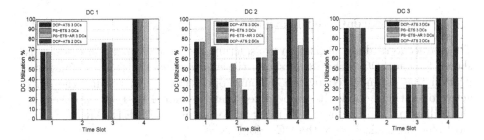

Fig. 7. DC utilization percentage at each time slot

5.5 Datacenter Utilization at Each Time Slot

The utilization percentage at each time slot is shown in Fig. 7, respectively. The figure also shows the active operation periods at each time slot for each DC. It is shown that model PS-ETS is able to divert the allocated demands from DC1 to DC2 at time slot 2, which means that the operator would operate two DCs only at time slot 2 instead of three and hence power saving for one time slot daily. This can be noted due to the constraint on the already existing resources at DC2. The dynamic allocation is supported by the cloud orchestration, which synchronizes the state of DC1 and DC2, while SDN provides the dynamic network steering of the traffic to DC2 for time slot 2 and back to DC1 for the other time slots. Again it is not possible to re-allocate the demands of DC3 at any time slot due to its remoteness and the data-plane delay budget of 15 ms.

Moreover, model PS-ETS-AR is able to divert the traffic demands of DC1 to DC2 for time slots 1, 2 and 3, due to the acquired additional resources at DC2 which leads to more daily power savings. However, note that the utilization % at DC2 can be observed to be lower compared to the other models for time slots 2 and 4, due to the increased amount of available resources and the traffic demands at these time slots.

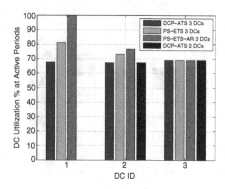 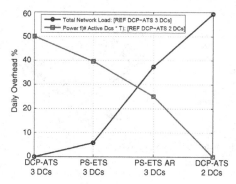

Fig. 8. DC utilization percentage at daily active periods

Fig. 9. Daily total transport network load compared to DC power consumption

5.6 Daily Datacenter Utilization

The datacenters daily utilization considering the active operation periods is shown for each DC in Fig. 8. It shows the efficiency of the DC resources utilization that is impacted by the dynamic operation by considering the daily active operation periods. It can be noted that the model PS-ETS improves the DC utilization and operation efficiency while the model PS-ETS-AR shows the most efficient utilization of the DC resources.

5.7 Transport Network Load Vs. DC Power Consumption

Figure 9 shows the resulted total transport network load compared to the DC power consumption for all 4 cases. The power consumption is defined as number of active DCs multiplied by active time daily. The comparison is shown as daily overhead %, where the transport load has the reference of DCP-ATS with 3 DCs as it achieves the minimum transport load while for power consumption has the reference of DCP-ATS with 2 DCs as it intuitively results in the minimum power consumption according to the aforementioned definition.

The trade-off between the resulting network load overhead compared to the power consumption overhead can be noted, as model PS-ETS with 3 DCs results in 6 % load overhead while it offers power savings of 10 %, compared to DCP-ATS with 3 DCs, respectively. Regarding model PS-ETS-AR with 3 DCs, it shows an increase in the transport load of 37 % while it offers in return power savings of 25 %, compared to DCP-ATS with 3 DCs, respectively. Hence, an operator would adopt either of the 4 cases depending on the cost resulted from increasing the transport network load compared to costs endured due to power consumption.

6 Conclusion

In this paper, we introduce an architecture that supports the virtualization of the mobile core network gateways, where the gateways are realized by software instances hosted in datacenters and SDN based network elements at the transport network. We have formulated a model for the time-varying traffic patterns that can be observed within the mobile network core according to the user population and traffic intensity changing with time.

For the introduced virtualized architecture, a model has been presented to find the optimal datacenter placement which minimizes the transport network load given a number of DCs under a data-plane delay budget, namely datacenter placement over all time slots (DCP-ATS). To exploit the dynamic flexibility offered by virtualization and SDN and the variation of the traffic over time, the time frame is split into time slots. Two further models have been formulated which minimize the transport load however with the possibility of operating fewer number of DCs at each time slot for power saving purposes, namely power saving at each time slot (PS-ETS) and power saving at each time slot with additional DC resources (PS-ETS-AR).

The three models have been solved for an exemplary US core gateways network under a delay budget of 15 ms. The DCP-ATS with 3 DCs results in the minimum transport network load and the highest power consumption. While the DCP-ATS with 2 DCs shows the least powers consumption but with the maximum transport network load. The power saving models with 3 DCs show the trade-off between transport network load and power consumption which shows the advantage of considering the time-varying property of the traffic for network dimensioning. Additionally, it shows quantitative gains obtained from the flexibility of virtualization and SDN in mobile core networks.

For future work, further mobile core network components such as the MME could be considered in the placement model, with control-plane delay budget taken into consideration as well.

References

1. Nokia Solutions and Networks, Enabling Mobile Broadband Growth, white paper, December 2013. https://nsn.com/system/files/document/epc_white_paper.pdf
2. Feamster, N., Rexford, J., Zegura, E.: The road to SDN. Queue - Large-Scale Implementations **11**, 20–40 (2013)
3. Jain, S., Zhu, M., Zolla, J., Hölzle, U., Stuart, S., Vahdat, A., Kumar, A., Mandal, S., Ong, J., Poutievski, L., Singh, A., Venkata, S., Wanderer, J., Zhou, J.: B4: experience with a globally-deployed software defined WAN. In: Proceedings of the ACM SIGCOMM 2013 Conference, New York, USA, pp. 3–14 (2013)
4. Wang, G., Ng, T.E., Shaikh, A.: Programming your network at run-time for big data applications. In: Proceedings of the First Workshop on Hot Topics in Software Defined Networks - HotSDN 2012, New York, USA, pp. 103–108 (2012)
5. Blenk, A., Kellerer, W.: Traffic pattern based virtual network embedding. In: Proceedings of CoNEXT Student Workhop (2013)
6. Nokia Solutions and Networks, Technology Vision for the Gigabit Experience, white paper, June 2013. https://nsn.com/file/26156/nsn-technology-vision-2020-white-paper?download
7. Banerjee, A., Chen, X., Erman, J., Gopalakrishnan, V., Lee, S., Van Der Merwe, J.: MOCA: a lightweight mobile cloud offloading architecture. In: Proceedings of the Eighth ACM International Workshop on Mobility in the Evolving Internet Architecture - MobiArch 2013, New York, New York, USA, p. 11 (2013)

8. Hampel, G., Steiner, M., Bu, T.: Applying software-defined networking to the telecom domain. In: INFOCOM, WKSHPS (2013)
9. Basta, A., Kellerer, W., Hoffmann, M., Hoffmann, K., Schmidt, E.-D.: A virtual SDN-enabled LTE EPC Architecture: a case study for S-/P-Gateways functions. In: IEEE SDN for Future Networks and Services (SDN4FNS) (2013)
10. Basta, A., Kellerer, W., Hoffmann, M., Morper, H.-J., Hoffmann, K.: Applying NFV and SDN to LTE mobile core gateways; the functions placement problem. In: 4th Workshop on All Things Cellular, SIGCOMM (2014)
11. Erman, J., Ramakrishnan, K.: Understanding the super-sized traffic of the super bowl. In: Proceedings of the 2013 Conference on Internet Measurement Conference - IMC 2013, pp. 353–360 (2013)
12. Gehlen, V., Finamore, A., Mellia, M., Munafò, M.M.: Uncovering the big players of the web. In: Pescapè, A., Salgarelli, L., Dimitropoulos, X. (eds.) TMA 2012. LNCS, vol. 7189, pp. 15–28. Springer, Heidelberg (2012)
13. Qian, L., Wu, B., Zhang, R., Zhang, W., Luo, M.: Characterization of 3G data-plane traffic and application towards centralized control and management for software defined networking. In: 2013 IEEE International Congress on Big Data, pp. 278–285, June 2013
14. Rossi, C., Vallina-Rodriguez, N., Erramilli, V., Grunenberger, Y., Gyarmati, L., Laoutaris, N., Stanojevic, R., Papagiannaki, K., Rodriguez, P.: 3GOL: power-boosting ADSL using 3G onloading. In: Proceedings of the ninth ACM Conference on Emerging Networking Experiments and Technologies - CoNEXT 2013, New York, NY, USA, pp. 187–198 (2013)
15. Zhang, Y., Arvidsson, A.: Understanding the characteristics of cellular data traffic. ACM SIGCOMM Comput. Commun. Rev. **42**, 461 (2012)
16. LTE Coverage Map. http://www.mosaik.com/marketing/cellmaps/, http://platform.cellmaps.com/
17. Gurobi Optimizer. http://www.gurobi.com/products/gurobi-optimizer/
18. UMTS Forum Report 44 Mobile traffic forecasts 2010–2020, pp. 63, January 2011. http://www.umts-forum.org/component/option,com_docman/task,doc_download/gid,2537/Itemid,213/
19. Annual estimates of the resident population: April 1, 2010 to july 1, 2013 - united states - metropolitan and micropolitan statistical area; and for puerto rico (2014). http://factfinder2.census.gov/faces/tableservices/jsf/pages/productview.xhtml?src=bkmk. Accessed 05/09/2014
20. MaxMind, MaxMind GeoLocations, 2014. http://dev.maxmind.com/geoip/legacy/geolite/. Accessed 05/09/2014

Towards a High Performance DNSaaS Deployment

Bruno Sousa[1]([⊠]), Claudio Marques[1], David Palma[1], João Gonçalves[1], Paulo Simões[2], Thomas Bohnert[3], and Luis Cordeiro[1]

[1] OneSource Consultoria Informática, Lda, Coimbra, Portugal
{bmsousa,claudio,palma,joagonca,cordeiro}@onesource.pt
[2] CISUC, Department of Informatics Engineering, University of Coimbra, 3030-290 Coimbra, Portugal
psimoes@dei.uc.pt
[3] Zurich University of Applied Sciences, Zurich, Switzerland
thomas.bohnert@zhaw.ch

Abstract. The existence of the Domain Name Service (DNS) is a vital service for the Internet, being much more than a simple translation mechanism, allowing more high-profiled functionalities such as load-balancing or enhanced content distribution. With the current trend towards Cloud Computing, employing DNS as a Service (DNSaaS) in this paradigm contributes to the decentralisation of this service, improving its robustness and overall flexibility. In order to consider it multiple tenants must be supported among other advanced features, authentication of operations and support multiple DNS backends, providing an adequate interface as well (e.g., a RESTfull interface). While such characteristics seem promising, to the best of our knowledge this is the first paper to assess the performance of DNSaaS. The performed evaluation comprise a thorough set of experiments, demonstrating how the configuration of several simultaneous tenants can be supported, performing several operations, within acceptable response time. Moreover, by assessing the performance of the used DNS backend, results highlighted that the evaluated DNSaaS solution was able to support to ≈36500 DNS queries per second.

Keywords: DNSaaS · DNS · OpenStack · Designate · Cloud · PowerDNS

1 Introduction

With the current trend towards Cloud Computing, more and more applications are moving towards the cloud environment as Services or as Virtualized Network Functions (VNF). The possibility of having fully elastic services, capable of scaling on-demand, both horizontally and vertically, is very attractive for today's Internet services and Domain Name System (DNS) is no exception.

Being an extensible and hierarchically distributed naming system, used for resources connected to the Internet or to private networks, the employment of

© Institute for Computer Sciences, Social Informatics and Telecommunications Engineering 2015
R. Agüero et al. (Eds.): MONAMI 2014, LNICST 141, pp. 77–90, 2015.
DOI: 10.1007/978-3-319-16292-8_6

DNS on the cloud would allow a cost and time efficient solution for translation of well-formed domain names into IP addresses. Indeed such translation is fundamental in many Internet services.

Nowadays solutions such as OpenStack [1] allow the deployment of different services in the cloud. Services such as IP Multimedia Subsystem (IMS) or Content Distribution Networks (CDNs) are currently being deployed as services in the cloud [2], leading to the coining of the term anything or everything as a Service (XaaS).

DNS is typically used in parallel with other services and has also evolved into this paradigm. As previously mentioned, employing DNS as a Service (DNSaaS) in the cloud environment allows a more efficient management of the resources required to support DNS across different services and data centres, being flexible enough to scale appropriately, on-demand and according to the current needs of the service, being more resilient and fault tolerant. However, multi-tenancy support, as well as a seamless integration with the cloud infrastructure, for instance with an adequate monitoring system suitable for the cloud, is still a challenge. Common DNS solutions, widely used in traditional systems, such as BIND [3] or PowerDNS [4] do not foresee these possibilities and lack support for a cloud paradigm.

DNSaaS solutions are already in place, such as Designate [5]. Indeed, Designate is a DNSaaS frontend for integration with OpenStack which, by maintaining a dedicated database, allows the creation of on-demand DNS servers capable of being configured appropriately through a well-defined Application Programming Interface (API). Moreover, Designate resorts to reliable DNS systems, such as BIND and PowerDNS, as backends for the whole operation.

The contribution of this paper includes an objective evaluation of DNSaaS, which besides characterising the performance of frontend and backend DNSaaS components highlights the impact that virtual machines hosting DNSaaS have in the overall DNS performance.

Despite the ongoing efforts on allowing a cloud-based DNS, its performance is still unknown and there is a lack of proper knowledge about the actual advantages of operating DNS as a Service in the cloud. Section 2 presents an analysis of existing assessments of DNS and of the cloud paradigm specifically. Section 3 focuses on the details of the architecture of DNSaaS. A proper methodology and thorough evaluation of DNSaaS, using a real testbed with different emulated scenarios is presented in Sect. 4, followed by the discussion of results in Sect. 5 and paper concludes with Sect. 6.

2 Related Work

While the movement towards the cloud is extremely significant, there is not still a full understanding of all the possible advantages and disadvantages it brings. Bearing this in mind, several works aim at assessing the benefits of cloud computing and provide comprehensive analysis of existing frameworks and services.

For instance, OpenStack is evaluated in different works. Lasze et al. [6] introduce a framework to compare different cloud frameworks, which performs comparison of different features, such as authentication and software deployment. Nonetheless, no details are provided to assess specific services of such frameworks. Xiaoen et al. [7] take a different direction and assess specific characteristics such as fault resilience support of OpenStack. Server crashes and network partitions are the two common fault types considered. Nonetheless, once again, no insights are provided regarding the evaluation of services, such as Database as a Service or others.

Despite this effort in better understanding what the cloud paradigm has to offer, the escalating adoption of distinct services into the cloud does not allow a proper analysis of these services. In particular for DNSaaS and to the extent of our knowledge, in the literature there is still no thorough evaluation that considers DNS as Service in the cloud environment.

Other works have already studied the performance of DNS in different scenarios, analysing the relevant metrics and defining appropriate methodologies. The evaluation of DNS backends, such as BIND and PowerDNS have been performed in distinct works [8,9]. These evaluations assess mainly the performance of these backends in terms of determining the maximum number of supported queries per second, within authoritative or caching servers. While these works make progresses in the evaluation of DNS services in non-virtualised platforms, they fail to evaluate the behaviour of this services in a cloud context. Other kind of evaluation goes beyond the basic evaluation of DNS. For instance, Daniel Migault et al. [10] assess the cost of incorporating security mechanisms in DNS. Other important evaluations of DNS [9,11] include their feasibility in supporting translation services between Internet addresses and telephone numbers (ENUM service). Nonetheless, none of such evaluation is performed in a cloud context.

The high level of expected dynamism in the cloud environment represents several challenges for a distributed Cloud-based Naming System [12]. Moreover, the amount and distinct ways DNS can be employed, for content distribution networks or for user mapping [13], also complicates the process of properly assessing its performance. Previous works take into account the latency between clients and servers, which typically depend considerably on the users' proximity to the DNS servers [14]. However, in a cloud environment this issue may be addressed by efficiently managing the distributed instances of the DNS service. Metrics such as the average Query Response Time and Loss Rate have been proved to allow the correct assessment of the performance of DNS server instances [15]. In addition to networking-related metrics, health and security concerns may also be considered to correctly evaluate the performance of such a system [16].

To the best of our knowledge related works do not provide a complete and concise evaluation of frontend and backend components of DNSaaS. This paper aims to fill this gap.

3   Domain Name Service as a Service

When considering DNS as a Service in a cloud environment, the main characteristics that must be present concern not only the basic DNS functionalities but also interfacing mechanisms with all the relevant components of the cloud, and with other services.

For this purpose the presented DNSaaS is inspired in Designate, a DNSaaS implementation for the OpenStack framework [5]. Its architecture consists of three main components, the Frontend, the Central Agent and the DNS Backend. Each of these components is fundamental for the configuration, adaptation and execution of the service. Figure 1 depicts the main modules comprised in DNSaaS.

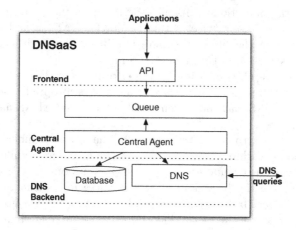

Fig. 1. Architecture and components of DNSaaS

3.1 Frontend

The frontend component includes all the interfacing elements for applications to perform Create, Read, Update or Delete (CRUD) operations related with DNSaaS (e.g., new DNS records). Through the Application Programming Interface (API) in the frontend, applications are able to configure the operations of DNSaaS and maintain DNS information (e.g., creation of records). The use of the different functionalities provided by the API may require validation, to assure that the information to create or update a certain record is correctly filled. For instance, when creating an A record, besides providing the name, the respective IPv4 address must also be provided.

All the valid requests received by the API are sent to the central agent for further processing. Message queues are used to establish the communication between the API and central agent. This approach enables the support of several APIs or different versions, allowing an extensible approach and added flexibility. Moreover the API relies on Representational state transfer (REST) technology, due to its associated performance and scalability, which supports JavaScript Object Notation (JSON) to allow data interchange between clients and DNSaaS API.

3.2 Central Agent

The central agent is responsible for handling the communication between the frontend and the backend. For such, all the requests coming from the frontend API are parsed from the message queue for further validations. In this sense, the central agent has an interface with Keystone [17], which is the identity management software in OpenStack, to assure that requests are authenticated, guaranteeing that a certain user/tenant does not perform operations on data that it does not hold, or to which it has no access authorization.

The central agent also coordinates the persistent storage (e.g., id of tenants) and DNS backend information. Besides, the central agent also integrates with other cloud services, such as monitoring to feed such service with monitored data (e.g., number of records created by a tenant).

3.3 DNS Backend

The DNS backend includes the traditional DNS servers, such as BIND [3], PowerDNS [4] and Name Server Daemon (NSD) [18]. These DNS servers have their own specific data storage mechanisms, for instance they can rely on flat files or on database storage mechanisms. The central agent in its persistent storage function, assures that DNS data storage are filled according to the chosen DNS backend server.

PowerDNS server is employed by default as the DNS backend solution, due to its efficient support in using database storage mechanisms, and performance. Moreover, PowerDNS supports authoritative server functionality (i.e. controls name resolution inside a domain) and recursor operation, when there is no knowledge of domains other authoritative servers are used to provide a resolution for the request performance. For instance, NSD only supports the authoritative server functionality. BIND natively supports both functionalities, but only the more recent versions added support for storing and retrieving zone data information on database.

4 Evaluation Methodology

This section discusses the methodology employed to evaluate the performance of frontend and backend components of DNSaaS.

4.1 Scenario

The evaluation scenario is depicted in Fig. 2 and includes multiple clients connected via Gigabit links to the Havana OpenStack cloud platform [1].

The clients are configured in order to have two distinct roles and will be mentioned as $n\_cli\_designate$ and as $n\_dns\_clients$. The first role aims at determining the impact of having a number of n clients using the Designate API to Create (C), Get (G), Update (U), and Delete (D) DNS records. The second role

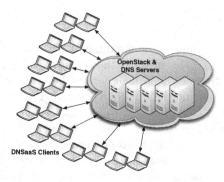

Fig. 2. Evaluation scenario of DNSaaS

considers typical clients performing DNS queries directly to DNS backends (e.g., PowerDNS). This second approach aims at assessing how DNSaaS performs with standard DNS-related operations, for instance translating the host name into IP information. The number of clients is configured according to the findings in [8], as summarised in Table 1.

CPU and RAM usage metrics are obtained with the *collectl* tool [19] that allows to monitor the performance of DNSaaS servers, regarding resources consumption in terms of memory, CPU usage and others such as disk usage, network interface receive and transmission packet ratios.

A client application has been developed using the Designate client API [20], to perform requests on the frontend components of DNSaaS. The Designate client API allows to abstract from all the details of the DNSaaS API. These serve multiple purposes, where the Update is used to modify the Time To Live (TTL) field of domains and records, while Get operations retrieve all the information of domains/records, such as creation and modification dates, TTL values for domains and records, as well as record data, record type, record names and record priorities (e.g., only for MX and SRV records).

The implemented client application supports the operations of the CRUD model. The Create(C) operation introduces information for $n\_domains$ (creation of domain and respective A, AAAA, TXT, MX, NS, SRV and PTR records) according to the number of records $n\_records$. The Update (U) operation modifies information for the $n\_domains$ with the respective $n\_records$. The Get (G) and Delete (D) operations are also performed with the same logic, to print out information and to delete all the records associated with a domain previously introduced, respectively. The number of clients performing the same operation simultaneously is controlled through the parameter $n\_cli\_designate$. No mixture of operations between several clients is considered, for instance ones performing Create(C) and others performing Update(U), to have more control on the DNSaaS performance assessment. Moreover, each client has associated specific record names to avoid overlapping information in the DNS backend.

In addition to the assessment of service-related functionalities of DNSaaS, *DNSPerf* [21] was employed to evaluate the performance of PowerDNS, and therefore determines its feasibility as a backend for DNSaaS. As such, the evaluation with DNSPerf tool determines the query throughput, query loss ratios and query processing time given a certain number of DNS records $n\_records$. Moreover, the number of concurrent clients performing query operations is evaluated according to $n\_dns\_clients$.

Different experiments were performed according to the values depicted in Table 1 for the configuration parameters. The values in some parameters were related to each other. For instance, the 500 k $n\_records$ require 1000 $n\_domains$.

Table 1. Configuration parameters

Parameter	Values
n_cli_designate	{1,25,10,50,100,200}
n_dns_clients	{1,50,100,200,500}
n_records	{500,5 k,50 k}
conf_server	{normal,enhanced}
n_domains	{1,5,100,500,1000}

Table 2. Server configurations as per $conf\_server$

Parameter	Normal	Enhanced
CPU	1	2
Memory	1 GB	6 GB
Disk	50 GB	50 GB
Interfaces	1 GB	1 GB

The characteristics of the servers hosting DNSaaS were also considered, as summarised in Table 2. In particular, the *normal* and *enhanced* server instantiations were employed to determine the impact that different computing power attributes (i.e., CPU, memory) have on the performance of DNSaaS.

4.2   Performance Metrics

For the performance evaluation of the presented DNSaaS approach, different performance metrics were taken into consideration as presented next:

- **Processing time** - Time taken by the frontend of DNSaaS to process a certain request (in ms).
- **Queries Throughput** - Number of DNS queries supported by the backend of DNSaaS (in qps).
- **Queries Lost** - Number of DNS queries not replied by the backend of DNSaaS or lost.
- **Queries Latency** - Time taken by the backend of DNSaaS to process a DNS query (in ms).
- **CPU and RAM usage** - How efficiently CPU and RAM resources are used.

These metrics were employed to assess the performance of DNSaaS in the diverse test cases presented for the evaluation scenario and also rely on the findings of [8,9].

5   Results

The presented results are discussed considering a 95 % of confidence interval achieved from the 10 runs executed for each test case. The Processing Time, Queries Latency and Queries Throughput metrics are presented in box plot graphics to depict the variation in performance. Other metrics, such as Queries Lost, CPU and RAM usage, are presented in ratios with bar-plots and error-plots. The variation in performance is depicted in error-plots, by considering the minimum and maximum ratio values achieved in each test, within the confidence interval.

5.1   Designate Performance

The performance of the DNSaaS operations is depicted in Fig. 3, where the response time is pictured for the different number of records, and Create (C), Get (G), Update (U), Delete (D) operations, in the different server configurations where the normal server is represented by n_X and the enhanced server configuration as e_X.

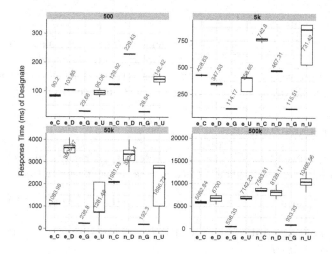

Fig. 3. Processing time per operation type and server configuration

The response time with the enhanced server is lower in all the test cases in comparison to the normal server. For instance, with 500 records the processing time of Create is ≈90 ms and ≈129 ms in enhanced and normal server configurations, respectively. This is an expected behaviour as the memory and CPU configuration differs between servers. In fact, such difference is more evident when the number of clients and the overall number of records increases. With 500 k records the processing time has the worst performance due to the high number of records and high number of simultaneous clients (i.e., 50). For instance, the

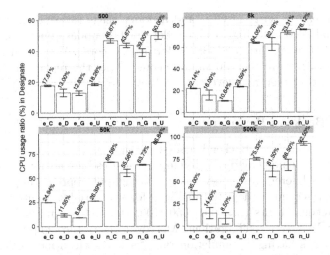

Fig. 4. CPU usage ratio per operation and server configuration

Update operation achieves times of ≈7142 ms and ≈10465 ms for enhanced and normal servers, respectively. The Create operation in this case has ≈5083 ms and ≈7564 ms for enhanced and normal servers, respectively, which is ≈60 times worst then with 500 records. This fact is justified by the overhead that is introduced due to the high number of clients and record size.

The type of requested operation also impacts the performance of DNSaaS as depicted in Fig. 3 with the processing time, in Fig. 4 with CPU usage ratio and Fig. 5 with memory usage. The Update operation is the one that introduces more overhead in terms of memory, CPU and consequently, has the highest response time. This operation involves getting the record (locate it in the database) and a modification of data (in this case refreshing the TTL of the several records).

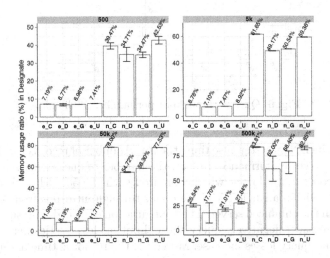

Fig. 5. Memory usage ratio per operation and server configuration

The overhead in terms of CPU and memory usage ratios is quite notorious in the normal server, as Figs. 4 and 5 depict. The update operation can lead to ≈93 % CPU usage ratio and ≈83 % for 500 k records. With such number of records and with more then 50 simultaneous clients the replies in the normal server exceed the acceptable levels [8], as they were in the order of minutes.

5.2 DNS Backend Performance

The results of the DNS Backend assessment are based on the evaluation of PowerDNS and include Queries Throughput, Queries Latency and Queries Lost metrics for the different test cases. Query Throughput, representing the number of queries per second, is depicted in Fig. 6 for the variable number of records and simultaneous clients (i.e., 001, 050, 100, 200, 500) in normal (n_X) and enhanced (e_X) server configurations. Moreover, query throughput is only considered in clients having a completion rate $\geq 97.5\,\%$, which means that almost all the requested DNS queries receive a reply. In other words, high query losses are disregarded as they imply that the server is not able to cope with the corresponding load.

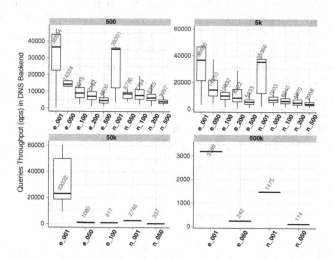

Fig. 6. Queries throughput per number of clients

As with the DNSaaS response time, the total number of records has an impact on the DNS server performance. In fact, the number of queries per second (qps) for 500 k records is the lowest when compared with the 500, 5 k and 50 k cases. For instance, within a single client the query throughput drops from ≈36500 to ≈3200 qps, in the enhanced server. The configuration of records and simultaneous clients also impacts negatively query throughput, as less queries per second are supported and query losses increase. Moreover, the response time of queries also

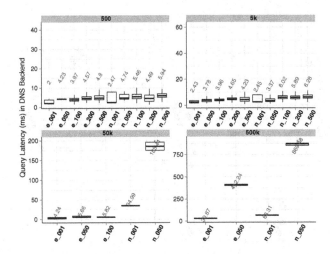

Fig. 7. Query latency (in ms) per number of clients

increases according to Fig. 7, as expected. The computation characteristics of servers justify such behaviour.

There are no significant variations in performance in performance regarding the response time of the DNS Backend with low number of records (500 and 5 k). Nonetheless, the associated overhead is distinct, as depicted in Figs. 8 and 9 for CPU and RAM usage ratios, respectively. For instance, within 500 clients the normal server consumes more CPU and memory, which outputs the same tendency as in designate results (recall Subsect. 5.1), low computation power characteristics of normal server are not satisfactory to support 500 simultaneous

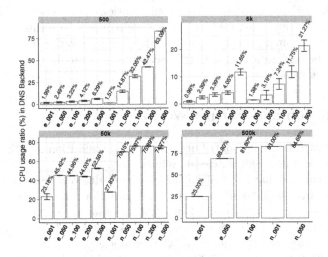

Fig. 8. CPU usage ratio

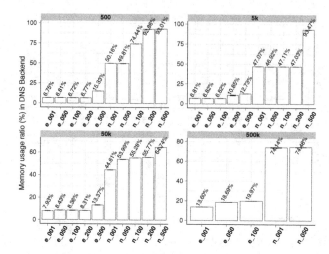

Fig. 9. Memory usage ratio

clients. Nonetheless, in the 50 k and 500 k record cases, the query throughput drops to unacceptable levels of performance, as response time is quite high [8] and the overhead in both servers is also more evident is terms of used CPU and memory.

The CPU usage ratios is higher in the normal server due to the existence of a single processor. Thus, the CPU usage increases linearly in the enhanced server with the increase in records, in the normal server, the CPU is always "busy" processing requests, even with low number of records, as depicted in Fig. 8.

Memory usage follows the same trend as CPU usage. The higher number of clients leads to an higher usage of memory in the backend server, as depicted in Fig. 9. The difference in the server configurations is also noticeable, as the normal server requires more memory to process requests, in terms of ratios. For instance, even for single clients, memory usage achieves ratios of ≈50 %, which reveals that the configurations of normal server are not satisfactory and can lead to performance gaps.

6   Conclusion and Future Work

DNS as a Service (DNSaaS) contributes to the decentralisation of DNS, improves its robustness and flexibility in cloud architectures.

The performance characterisation of DNSaaS, in different scenarios, provides insights that are useful to dynamically configure cloud resources, avoiding a wasteful usage of resources, while being able to guarantee that the expected baseline performance of a DNS service is always achieved. It has been demonstrated that a misplaced configuration, with insufficient computation-power, can lead to a ineffective support of DNS regarding the desirable number of queries per second or the total number of supported simultaneous clients. As such, we claim that this paper establishes the first steps towards a high performance DNSaaS deployment by a concrete and objective performance evaluation, that fully characterises the baseline performance of DNSaaS in the cloud.

Our next steps include the analysis of the impact of distributing the DNSaaS through several virtual machines and better understanding how automatically triggered scaling operations can improve the overall performance of DNSaaS, regarding the number of queries per second and of simultaneous clients that can be accommodated.

Acknowledgments. This work was carried out with the support of the MobileCloud Networking project (FP7-ICT-318109) funded by the European Commission through the 7th ICT Framework Program.

References

1. OpenStack: Openstack cloud software. https://www.openstack.org. Last Visit 08 August 2014
2. Lu, F., Pan, H., Lei, X., Liao, X., Jin, H.: A virtualization-based cloud infrastructure for ims core network. In: Cloud Computing Technology and Science (CloudCom), 2013 IEEE, vol. 1, pp. 25–32, December 2013
3. I.S.Consortium: BIND - The most widely used Name Server Software. https://www.isc.org/downloads/bind/. Last Visit 08 August 2014
4. P. Bv, PowerDNS. https://www.powerdns.com. Last Visit 08 August 2014
5. OpenStack, Designate, a DNSaaS component for OpenStack. http://designate.readthedocs.org/en/latest/. Last Visit 08 August 2014
6. von Laszewski, G., Diaz, J., Wang, F., Fox, G.C.: Comparison of multiple cloud frameworks. In: 2012 IEEE 5th International Conference on Cloud Computing (CLOUD), pp. 734–741. IEEE (2012)
7. Ju, X., Soares, L., Shin, K.G., Ryu, K.D., Da Silva, D.: On fault resilience of openstack. In: Proceedings of the 4th Annual Symposium on Cloud Computing, p. 2. ACM (2013)
8. da Mata, S.H., Magalhaes, J.M., Cardoso, A., Guardieiro, P.R., Carvalho, H.A.: Performance comparison of enum name servers. In: Computer Communications and Networks (ICCCN), IEEE 2013, pp. 1–5 (2013)
9. Yu, Y., Wessels, D., Larson, M., Zhang, L.: Authority server selection in DNS caching resolvers. ACM SIGCOMM Comput. Commun. Rev. **42**(2), 80–86 (2012)
10. Migault, D., Girard, C., Laurent, M.: A performance view on dnssec migration. In: Network and Service Management (CNSM), IEEE 2010, pp. 469–474 (2010)
11. Rudinsky, J.: Private enum based number portability administrative system evaluation. In: International Conference on Ultra Modern Telecommunications & Workshops, ICUMT 2009, IEEE 2009, pp. 1–7 (2009)
12. Celesti, A., Villari, M., Puliafito, A.: A naming system applied to a reservoir cloud. In: 2010 Sixth International Conference on Information Assurance and Security (IAS), pp. 247–252, August 2010
13. Berger, A., Gansterer, W.: Modeling DNS agility with DNSMap. In: 2013 IEEE Conference on Computer Communications Workshops (INFOCOM WKSHPS), pp. 387–392, April 2013

14. Huang, C., Maltz, D., Li, J., Greenberg, A.: Public DNS system and global traffic management. In: INFOCOM, 2011 Proceedings IEEE, pp. 2615–2623, April 2011
15. Lee, B.-S., Tan, Y.S., Sekiya, Y., Narishige, A., Date, S.: Availability and effectiveness of root dns servers: a long term study. In: Network Operations and Management Symposium (NOMS), 2010 IEEE, pp. 862–865, April 2010
16. Casalicchio, E., Caselli, M., Coletta, A.: Measuring the global domain name system. IEEE Netw. 27(1), 25–31 (2013)
17. OpenStack, Keystone, The OpenStack Identity Service! http://keystone. openstack.org. Last Visit 08 August 2014
18. Labs, N.: NSD: Name Server Daemon. http://www.nlnetlabs.nl/projects/nsd/. Last Visit 08 August 2014
19. Seger, M.: Collectl. http://collectl.sourceforge.net/. Last Visit 08 August 2014
20. OpenStack, python-designateclient. http://python-designateclient.readthedocs. org/en/latest/index.html. Last Visit 08 August 2014
21. Nomium, Network measurement tools. http://nominum.com/support/ measurement-tools. Last Visit 08 August 2014

Network Configuration in OpenFlow Networks

Adel Zaalouk and Kostas Pentikousis[(✉)]

EICT GmbH, Berlin, Germany
{adel.zaalouk,k.pentikousis}@eict.de

Abstract. Software-defined networking (SDN) and in particular networks based on an OpenFlow control plane are expected to take significant share in upcoming deployments. Network programmability has emerged as a particularly desirable property for such new deployments, in which logically centralized software will be able to both control and manage operation. This paper focuses on one aspect of network management, namely configuration, in light of the ongoing work in the FP7 ALIEN project to augment a variety of devices with an OpenFlow control plane. In particular, we review management for programmable networks and present how software-defined control can be complemented with software-defined configuration.

Keywords: SDN · OpenFlow · Hardware Abstraction Layer · NET-CONF

1 Introduction

Packet-switched computer networks are based on network elements which run distributed control software that is complex to configure. While network operators ought to maintain a complete view of the actual network state, in practice, they have only coarse-grained tools at their disposal. For instance, network device configuration can often require human intervention based on command line interface (CLI) interaction. CLIs are cumbersome to use, error-prone, and may vary widely across different vendors, so management complexity increases even more. Network administration might lead to configuration errors, which are difficult to detect. But more in the interest of this work is that the current network configuration paradigm is not really programmable.

The emergence of software-defined networking (SDN) [1] introduced new opportunities in network research [2]. SDN advocates a logically centralized control plane with advanced programming capabilities based on a control-data plane separation. By breaking the tight coupling between the control and data plane both can evolve independently. Programmability fosters the development of software that can dynamically alter network-wide behavior, thus enabling testing of research ideas in a speedier manner without having to always resort to simulation tools. In particular, a programmable control plane based on OpenFlow [3] is expected to accelerate network innovation and the rollout of new services. Open-Flow per se, however, is not well-suited for the management plane. To address this

© Institute for Computer Sciences, Social Informatics and Telecommunications Engineering 2015
R. Agüero et al. (Eds.): MONAMI 2014, LNICST 141, pp. 91–104, 2015.
DOI: 10.1007/978-3-319-16292-8_7

gap, the Open Networking Foundation (ONF; www.opennetworking.org) introduced the OpenFlow Management and Configuration Protocol (OF-CONFIG) [4], which uses the Network Configuration Protocol (NETCONF) [5] as the transport protocol.

Originally OpenFlow was designed for Ethernet and ASIC network devices, leaving behind a large set of other platforms such as wireless and point-to-multipoint (DOCSIS, optical). To address this problem, the FP7 ALIEN project (www.fp7-alien.eu) is working on the design and implementation of a Hardware Abstraction Layer (HAL) which enables network devices that do not support the OpenFlow protocol and switch model natively, to be included in the OpenFlow control plane of a network deployment. In particular, ALIEN aims to enable such devices (called "ALIEN devices" in the remainder of this paper) to be controlled through OpenFlow thereby extending an OpenFlow control plane to new classes of devices [6]. Within this framework, we are interested in the design and implementation of a HAL for ALIEN devices that can be both controlled and managed in a software-defined manner. As ALIEN devices will be introduced in the OFELIA OpenFlow experimental facility [7], their management should be programmatically enabled. In more general terms, this paper contributes to the ongoing discussion about what does SDN entail [8], and in particular how operators can employ software to both control and manage not only soon-to-be-deployed OpenFlow compatible devices but legacy equipment as well.

We start our exploration with an overview of related work (Sect. 2) and continue with a discussion of the motivation behind, and the salient characteristics of, the programmable networks paradigm in light of the emergence of SDN (Sect. 3). We consider recent work at the IRTF SDNRG and map accordingly the HAL design in Sect. 4. Finally, we introduce network configuration based on NETCONF for the ALIEN HAL (Sect. 5) and present workflows for software-defined configuration for OpenFlow networks (Sect. 6). We conclude this paper in Sect. 7 and outline future work.

2   Related Work

OpenFlow deployments require management just like traditional networks. But, given their edge in programmability, and the fact they would be controlled by software, management should also follow along, thus enabling programmability both in the control plane and the management plane. The ONF-standardized OF-CONFIG protocol takes advantage of NETCONF as a configuration protocol and YANG [9] for OpenFlow switch data modeling.

Prior to its adoption by ONF, NETCONF was studied and compared against other popular configuration management protocols. Hedstrom et al. [10] compare the performance of NETCONF with SNMP in a testbed, considering protocol bandwidth use, number of packets, number of transactions, operations time, and so on. They conclude that NETCONF is much more efficient for configuration management than SNMP (e.g., requires much less transactions over managed objects). Another empirical study [11] compares NETCONF and

SNMP indicating that NETCONF is more efficient in handling a large number of configuration transactions. With respect to implementation, there are several open-source frameworks for developing NETCONF clients and servers [12,13]. Tran et al. [14] introduce a plan for testing and verifying existing NETCONF implementations. Based on performance as well as other considerations, NET-CONF was chosen as a reasonable candidate for configuring OpenFlow networks.

Several projects have sought to incorporate NETCONF as a tool for network configuration management in their networks. Munz et al. [15] present an XML-based data model for NETCONF to cover all common configurable parameters for network monitoring. Xu et al. [16] introduce a NETCONF implementation using a RESTful web service in the context of Internet of Things (IoT), while applications of NETCONF in a military context were introduced in [17].

This earlier work does not address the opportunities arising with SDN with respect to network configuration programmability. According to [8], the SDN architecture should decouple control and management functionalities. Although several research projects focus on extending and enhancing network control using OpenFlow, the research effort towards improving the SDN management plane remains minimal to the best of our knowledge. For example, HybNET [18] is an automated network management framework for "hybrid" networks (i.e., SDN and legacy infrastructures). HybNET uses NETCONF for the management of legacy network switches. Sonkoly et al. [19], on the other hand, introduce an OpenFlow virtualization framework which employs NETCONF for managing native OpenFlow devices. Unlike HybNET which uses NETCONF to manage legacy switches, or the OpenFlow virtualization framework that uses NET-CONF to manage native OpenFlow devices, this paper proposes to integrate the management capability provided by NETCONF into non-native HAL-enabled OpenFlow devices (Sect. 4). Although OF-CONFIG uses NETCONF for managing native OpenFlow devices, we employ NETCONF to manage HAL-enhanced network devices. As such, the contributions of this paper compared to earlier work include a thorough study of NETCONF in the context of OpenFlow networks, the architectural mapping of the ALIEN HAL design and the SDN Layers work currently under adoption in the SDN RG (www.irtf.org/sdnrg), and the introduction of a proposal for employing NETCONF for software-defined configuration.

3   The Programmable Networks Paradigm

Arguably, the Internet has become extremely difficult to evolve both in terms of its physical infrastructure and network protocols. As the Internet was designed for tasks such as sending and receiving data with best effort guarantees only, there has been continuous interest to evolve the current IP packet-switched networks to address the new challenges including Quality of Service (QoS), multicasting, and network security. One of the first steps towards making networks more programmable was the introduction of Active Networking (AN) [20]. The main idea behind AN was to enable network devices to perform custom computations on packets. To do so, two different models were introduced [1]. First, in the "packet capsules model", network programs were attached to (possibly each) packet and sent across the network to target devices such as ANTS [21]. Second, in the "programmable network devices model" [22], network devices were pre-configured with several service-logic modules. When a packet arrives, its headers are matched and sent to the appropriate module. Largely, the AN vision did not come to pass, for various reasons [1]. For instance, a clear migration path was not evident. Further, at that point of time, no operator pressing need was practically addressed by AN. That said, at the core, AN networks aimed for having programmability in the data plane. This concept evolved over the years and took hold in network devices that are known as middleboxes now. The concept of middlebox programmability has received quite some attention recently. For example, xOMP [23], an eXtensible Open MiddleBox software architecture allows for building flexible, programmable, and incrementally scalable middleboxes based on commodity servers and operating systems. Similarly, SIMPLE [24], a programmable policy enforcement layer for middlebox-specific traffic steering, allows network operators to specify middlebox routing policies which take into account the physical topology, switch capacities and middlebox resource constraints.

Another important step that has been taken towards network programmability is the separation of the control and data planes. This decoupling enables the two planes to evolve separately, and allows new paradigms where logically centralized control can have a network-wide view making it easier to infer and direct network behavior. Examples of such separation have been proposed earlier in Routing Control Point (RCP) [25] and, of course, ForCES [26]. So far, the OpenFlow approach towards control and data plane separation focused on control plane rather than data plane programmability as compared to AN. Despite the intellectual contributions that resulted from such separation, the AN deployment strategy was not pragmatic, e.g. required network-wide deployment of new hardware. OpenFlow defines a standard interface between the control and the data plane that goes hand-in-hand with the concept of Network Operating Systems (NOS) [27] with the goal of providing an abstraction layer between network state awareness and control logic.

Haleplidis et al. [8] provide a detailed description of the SDN layers architecture, drawing a clearer picture of the emerging paradigm, which is often cluttered with marketing terms. By dividing the SDN architecture into distinct planes, abstraction layers and interfaces, [8] clarifies SDN terminology and establishes some commonly accepted ground across the SDN community.

As shown in Fig. 1, the *Forwarding Plane* represents parts of the network device which are responsible for forwarding traffic. The *Operational Plane* is the part of the network device responsible for managing device operation. The *Control Plane* instructs the network device(s) forwarding plane on how to forward traffic. The *Management Plane* is responsible for configuring and maintaining one or more network devices. The draft also defines three layers, as follows.

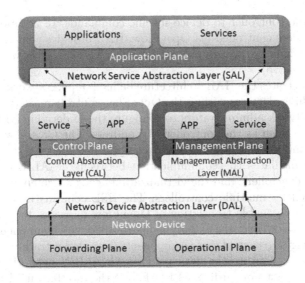

Fig. 1. High-level view of the SDN architecture

The *Device and resource Abstraction Layer (DAL)* provides a point of reference for the device's forwarding and operational resources. The *Control Abstraction Layer (CAL)* provides access to the control plane southbound interface. Finally, the *Management Abstraction Layer (MAL)* provides access to the management plane southbound interface. Figure 1 illustrates all functional components of the SDN architecture and provides a high-level overview of the SDN architecture abstractions including control and management plane abstractions. The architecture visibly decouples management, control and forwarding functions including their interfaces. Of course, this is an abstract model. In practice, the entities providing these functions/planes could be collocated. In this paper, we focus on the management and control southbound interfaces, as we explain next.

4   Abstraction Layer for ALIEN Devices

As mentioned earlier, the OpenFlow protocol was mainly designed to support ASIC and campus Ethernet switches with little or no regard for other platforms such as circuit-switched, wireless and optical. Unfortunately, these platforms are often closed and changes cannot be made to the device per se in order to make it natively compatible with an OpenFlow control plane. To overcome this challenge, the FP7 ALIEN project defines a Hardware Abstraction Layer (HAL) [6] which aims to enable communication with devices that do not natively support OpenFlow through a set of hardware abstractions. These HAL-enhanced devices will be controlled in the same manner as their native OpenFlow counterparts. Each hardware device that does not natively support OpenFlow will have a Hardware Specific Layer (HSL) that translates OpenFlow protocol messages coming from the controller to device-specific commands. In addition to having the ALIEN devices controlled via OpenFlow, HAL provides configuration management functionalities through protocols such as NETCONF as we discuss later in this paper (Sect. 5).

Figure 2 illustrates the HAL architecture defined in [6]. Network Control represents controlling elements such as the OpenFlow controllers. Network Management allows network administrators to configure the underlying ALIEN devices with parameters such as the controller's IP address. The Cross-Hardware Platform Layer contains hardware-agnostic components such as the OpenFlow-endpoint that mediates the communication between the ALIEN devices and the OpenFlow controllers, and the virtualization agent which enables the device to be controlled by multiple controllers. The HSL contains hardware specific sub-components to enable translation of OpenFlow messages to device specific messages [7], or to discover the underlying hardware device components and relay incoming messages to each of these components (i.e., Orchestration). Finally, the network devices constitute the data plane in an ALIEN network deployment. Finally, the Abstract Forwarding API (AFA) is the interface used for relaying, management and control messages from the Cross-Hardware Platform Layer to the HSL. Due to space restrictions we cannot delve into details here; interested readers are referred to [6, 7].

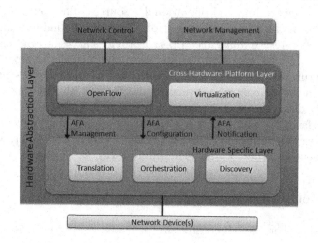

Fig. 2. HAL architecture

We map the ALIEN HAL to the SDN layers in Fig. 3. Essentially, DAL in the SDN architecture is realized by the HAL in ALIEN, which handles the translation of OpenFlow messages to device-specific messages. Generic network devices are mapped to ALIEN devices, which do not support OpenFlow natively. The control plane is realized using OpenFlow controllers and the OpenFlow protocol. The management plane is implemented using NETCONF. The application plane is mostly outside the scope of the ALIEN architecture.

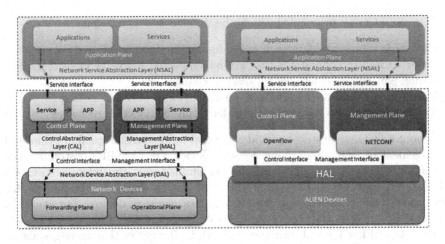

Fig. 3. Mapping of HAL to the SDN Layers Architecture

5   HAL Network Configuration

Using OpenFlow, the control plane can communicate with the data plane to perform several functionalities such as adding or removing flow-rules and collecting per-flow, per-table statistics. However, this assumes that the OpenFlow switches are already configured with various parameters such as the IP address(es) of the controller(s). Here it is important to distinguish time-sensitive control functionalities for which OpenFlow was designed (e.g., modifying forwarding tables, matching flows) from non-time-sensitive management and configuration management functionalities which are essential for the operation of the OpenFlow-enabled device (e.g., controller IP assignment, changing switch ports administrative status, configuring datapath-ids, etc.).

In principle, SNMP could be used for such configuration tasks. However, as per [9], SNMP has several drawbacks, including unreliable transport of management data (e.g., UDP); no clear separation between operational and configuration data; no support for roll-backs in case of errors/disaster; lack of support for concurrency in configuration (i.e., N:1 device configuration); and no distinction between transaction models (e.g., running, startup, and candidate). To address such shortcomings, the NETCONF protocol was developed and defined in RFC 6241 [5]. NETCONF provides several key features such as the ability to retrieve configuration as well as operational data, rich configuration management semantics including validation, rollbacks and transactions, and configuration extensibility based on the capabilities exchange that occurs during initiating the session initiation. Furthermore, NETCONF's transactional models constitutes candidate, running and startup data-stores.

The NETCONF protocol stack can be divided into four layers:

- **Content:** represents data such as configuration and operational data
- **Operations:** the operations that are be supported by NETCONF (e.g., get-config, edit-config, delete-config, discard-changes, etc.)
- **Messages:** wraps the content and operations into an RPC messages
- **Transport:** defines the protocol for delivering NETCONF messages

The NETCONF protocol provides general guidelines for configuration and management of "any" underlying network device. OF-CONFIG customizes the use of NETCONF to OpenFlow switches. In simple terms, the difference between NETCONF and OF-CONFIG, is that the latter defines XML-models for OpenFlow-specific instances rather than general network devices. For example, OF-CONFIG defines the OpenFlow Capable Switch (OCS) which can have one or more OpenFlow Logical Switches (OFLS), i.e. an entity that manages a subset of resources in the OCS. Listing 7.1 presents an XML model which defines the configuration of a OFLS with the size of the Virtual Local Area Network (VLAN) table. In the remainder of this paper we explain high-level NETCONF commands only, without delving into the OpenFlow-specific message details (i.e., OF-CONFIG).

```
1   <capable-switch xmlns="urn:onf:of111:config:yang"
2   xmlns:ndm="urn:opennetworking.org:yang:ndm"
3   xmlns:1213="urn:opennetworking.org:yang:ndm:1213">
4     <logical-switches>
5       <switch>
6         <id>LogicalSwitch5</id>
7         <resources>
8           <ndm:ndm-implementation>
9             <1213:1213>
10              <vlan-table-size>128<vlan-table-size>
11            </1213:1213>
12          </ndm:ndm-implementation>
13        </resources>
14      </switch>
15    </logical-switches>
16  <id>capable-switch-0</id>
```

Listing 7.1. XML-Model for configuring logical switches

As described in Sect. 4, the HAL architecture comprises two layers, one of which is hardware-specific (i.e., HSL) while the other is hardware-agnostic (i.e., CHPL). All management and control specific modules (e.g., OpenFlow-endpoint and NETCONF server) should reside in the CHPL. The network management block incorporates the NETCONF client. Furthermore, NETCONF can be abstracted for networks administrators by providing a customized user interface for managing the underlying devices. The integration of the NETCONF server / client is shown in Fig. 4. The Figure illustrates that the ALIEN management plane includes also a virtualization gateway (VGW) as discussed in [6].

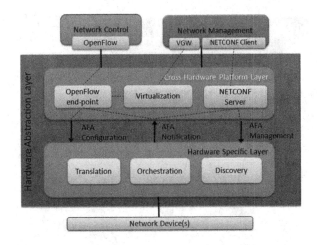

Fig. 4. NETCONF implementation and HAL integration

An example of the commands that can be provided to the administrators as an extra layer of abstraction is shown in Listing 7.2.

```
1  user@network−management−pc:~$ list −capabilities <ofcs_id >
2  user@network−management−pc:~$ list −ports <ofcs_id>
3  user@network−management−pc:~$ disable−port <ofcs_id , port_no>
4  user@network−management−pc:~$ list −logical_datapaths <ofcs_id >
```

Listing 7.2. XML-Model for configuring logical switches

6 Software-Defined Configuration

We now proceed to illustrate three software-defined configuration workflows for OpenFlow networks based on a simple but representative topology. The workflows showcase the combined use of OpenFlow in the control plane with NETCONF in the management plane. We consider interactions with devices such as middleboxes, ALIEN switches, and native OpenFlow switches. All three workflows share the same network topology as illustrated in Fig. 5. The topolgy maps elements in the network into four planes: management plane, control plane, forwarding plane, and applications plane as described in Sect. 3.

The topology in Fig. 5 is composed of the following entities: *OF Switches* which stand for OpenFlow-enabled switches, some of which are equipped with sFlow [28] agents for collecting monitoring information; *ALIEN Devices* which can be controlled via OpenFlow through HAL; *Software-configured Middleboxes* with configurable functions i.e., can act as firewalls, Intrusion Detection Systems (IDS) and so on, based on their real-time configuration; *OF Controllers* to control entities in our OpenFlow-based networks; *sFlow Collectors* for collecting the monitoring information sent by the sFlow agents running in the OF switches for further analysis; *NETCONF Clients* which are devices that run the NETCONF

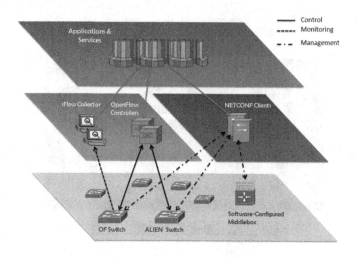

Fig. 5. Software Defined Configuration Topology

client; and, finally, *Application & Services* represented as the logical entities that
make use of the underlying management and control planes as per [8].

First consider the case where a network application employs NETCONF to
configure the sFlow agents monitoring parameters such as sampling rate, sFlow
collector IP, etc. This workflow is shown in Fig. 6. First, the application specifies
the configuration parameters and sends it to the NETCONF client. In turn, the
NETCONF client will form an *edit-config* message with the specified parameters
and will send it to the NETCONF server running on the target OF switch(es).
Once the NETCONF server receives the message, it will update the switch configuration and will send a reply back to the NETCONF client regarding the
success or failure of the operation. Subsequently, upon the instruction of the
application, the OF controller will interact with the underlying switches using
OpenFlow to control the flow of traffic.

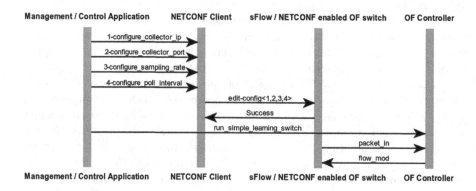

Fig. 6. Monitoring configuration workflow

Another scenario for software-defined configuration using NETCONF is applying security through real-time middlebox configuration. Usually the functions embedded in middleboxes are fixed or static. In this example we examine how NETCONF can be used to configure the middleboxes to run security modules based on the traffic monitored in the network. For example, if a Denial of Service (DoS) attack is suspected, then NETCONF client informs the middlebox to run the DoS detection module. For simplicity, the steps related to monitoring the network for suspicious behavior are omitted in this workflow (more details about these steps can be found in [29]). In the workflow shown in Fig. 7, the application is already aware of a DoS attack likelihood (with the help of network monitoring). Accordingly, the NETCONF client is instructed to configure the middleboxes to run the DoS detection modules. Consequently, the NETCONF client will form an *edit-config* message with the specified parameters and send it to the NET-CONF server running on the middlebox. Once the NETCONF server receives the message, it will update the device configuration, switch on the corresponding security modules, and send a reply back to the client to inform it about the success or failure of the operation. In addition to configuring the middlebox using NETCONF, the network switches are instructed by the OpenFlow controller to redirect suspicious traffic to the middleboxes for further inspection, thus utilizing the combined functionalities of network configuration, management, and control. The middlebox functions can be provided through a physical device or using a Network Function Virtualization (NFV) approach where functions are provided as a service. Furthermore, NETCONF could be used to configure and attach virtual function(s) and service(s) together to provide a fully fledged network function through the assembly of smaller sub-functions.

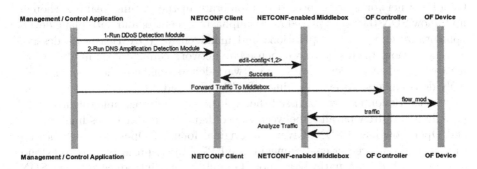

Fig. 7. Software-configured middlebox workflow

Finally, the NETCONF implementation in HAL (Fig. 4) is used to configure the underlying ALIEN device. For example, it might be desirable to switch off a faulty interface on an ALIEN switch. Alternatively, the network admin might want to list all available interfaces on the ALIEN switch. The workflow for this scenario is shown in Fig. 8. First, the NETCONF client is instructed by the application to list all the available switch ports. Consequently, an *edit-config* message

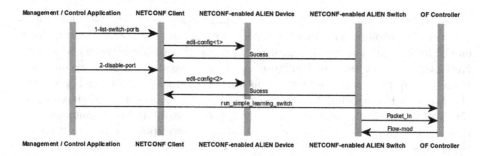

Fig. 8. Configuration of HAL-enhanced Devices Workflow

is formed and sent to the NETCONF server embedded in the HAL implementation of the ALIEN device. In turn, the NETCONF server will apply the command and send the reply back to the client. Furthermore, the NETCONF client will follow the same steps when instructed to disable a switch port. In addition to configuring the underlying ALIEN devices using NETCONF, OpenFlow will be used to control the forwarding behavior for the ALIEN devices by installing the appropriate flow rules according to the logic running on-top of the controller. In addition to using OpenFlow for network control, NETCONF automates configuration management functions thus making network management tasks much simpler.

7   Conclusion and Future Work

OpenFlow networks are expected to proliferate in the coming years. Although up to now SDN R&D has placed more emphasis on control and data plane development, we expect that operations and management (OAM) aspects deserve more attention. In this paper we focused on network configuration in OpenFlow networks, and in particular on how software-defined configuration can enhance SDN deployments. After reviewing OF-CONFIG and NETCONF in an Open-Flow network context we discussed the evolution of the programmable networks paradigm and drew parallels between the configurable middleboxes line of work and OpenFlow-based SDN. Given the original focus of OpenFlow switches on campus and data center environments, the FP7 ALIEN projects aims to extend devices which do not natively support OpenFlow and introduce them to SDN experimental facilities such as OFELIA in Europe. For this type of devices, configuration is necessary and as we have seen NETCONF can serve as the basis for further development in this domain. In this respect, we overviewed the ALIEN Hardware Abstraction Layer (HAL) and mapped it to recent work in the IRTF SDNRG. This paper also introduced a range of workflows which illustrate how software-defined configuration can work in practice, enabling network applications and services to dynamically configure and control a virtual infrastructure which includes native OpenFlow switches, ALIEN devices and configurable middleboxes. Namely, we discussed software-defined configuration of sFlow monitoring agents in OF switches, ALIEN device configuration and security-related middlebox configuration. We are currently working on the NET-CONF implementation in the ALIEN HAL. This implementation will be part of the ALIEN demos and will be introduced in the OFELIA experimental facility once it is mature for production. Until then, we plan to have several experiments performed, illustrating the feasibility and potential of our approach while measuring its performance on an OpenFlow testbed. Furthermore, we consider mapping the architecture defined in this paper to a virtual environment, where network functions are defined as a server and where NETCONF could be used to configure the necessary parameters for these virtual network functions.

Acknowledgment. This work was conducted within the framework of the FP7 ALIEN project, which is partially funded by the Commission of the European Union.

References

1. Feamster, N., Rexford, J., Zegura, E.: The road to SDN. Queue **11**(12), 20:20–20:40 (2013)
2. John, W., Pentikousis, K., et al.: Research directions in network service chaining. In: 2013 IEEE SDN for Future Networks and Services, pp. 1–7, November 2013
3. McKeown, N., Anderson, T., et al.: Openflow: enabling innovation in campus networks. ACM SIGCOMM Comput. Commun. Rev. **38**(2), 69–74 (2008)
4. ONF: OF-CONFIG 1.2. OpenFlow Management and Configuration Protocol version 1.2 (2014)
5. Enns, R., Bjorklund, M., Schoenwaelder, J.: NETCONF configuration protocol. IEEE Network (2011)
6. Parniewicz, D., Doriguzzi Corin, R., et al.: Design and implementation of an openflow hardware abstraction layer. SIGCOMM DCC **2014**, 1–6 (2014)
7. Ogrodowczyk, L., Belter, B., et al.: Hardware abstraction layer for non-OpenFlow capable devices. In: TERENA Networking Conference, pp. 1–15 (2014)
8. Haleplidis, E., Pentikousis, K., et al.: SDN layers and architecture terminology. Internet Draft: draft-haleplidis-sdnrg-layer-terminology (work in progress) (2014)
9. Schönwälder, J., Björklund, M., Shafer, P.: Network configuration management using NETCONF and YANG. IEEE Commun. Mag. **48**(9), 166–173 (2010)
10. Hedstrom, B., Watwe, A., Sakthidharan, S.: Protocol Efficiencies of NETCONF versus SNMP for Configuration Management Functions. p. 13 (2011)
11. Yu, J., Al Ajarmeh, I.: An empirical study of the NETCONF protocol. In: 2010 Sixth International Conference on Networking and Services (ICNS), pp. 253–258. IEEE (2010)
12. Bhushan, S., Tran, H.M., Schönwälder, J.: NCClient: a python library for NET-CONF client applications. In: Nunzi, G., Scoglio, C., Li, X. (eds.) IPOM 2009. LNCS, vol. 5843, pp. 143–154. Springer, Heidelberg (2009)
13. Krejci, R.: Building NETCONF-enabled network management systems with libnet-conf. In: 2013 IFIP/IEEE International Symposium on Integrated Network Management (IM 2013), pp. 756–759. IEEE (2013)
14. Tran, H.M., Tumar, I., Schönwälder, J.: NETCONF interoperability testing. In: Sadre, R., Pras, A. (eds.) AIMS 2009 Enschede. LNCS, vol. 5637, pp. 83–94. Springer, Heidelberg (2009)

15. Munz, G., Antony, A., et al.: Using NETCONF for configuring monitoring probes. In: 10th IEEE/IFIP Network Operations and Management Symposium, NOMS 2006, pp. 1–4. IEEE (2006)

16. Xu, H., Wang, C., et al.: NETCONF-based integrated management for internet of things using RESTful web services. Int. J. Future Gener. Commun. Netw. 5(3), 73–82 (2012)

17. Zhu, W., Liu, N., et al.:Design of the next generation military network management system based on NETCONF. In: Fifth International Conference on Information Technology: New Generations, ITNG 2008, pp. 1216–1219, April 2008

18. Lu, H., Arora, N., et al.: Hybnet: network manager for a hybrid network infrastructure. In: Proceedings of the Industrial Track of the 13th ACM/IFIP/USENIX International Middleware Conference, p. 6. ACM (2013)

19. Sonkoly, B., Gulyás, A., et al.: Openflow virtualization framework with advanced capabilities. In: 2012 European Workshop on Software Defined Networking (EWSDN), pp. 18–23. IEEE (2012)

20. Smith, J.M., Nettles, S.M.: Active networking: one view of the past, present, and future. IEEE Trans. Syst. Man Cybern. Part C Appl. Rev. 34(1), 4–18 (2004)

21. Wetherall, D.J., Guttag, J.V., Tennenhouse, D.L.: ANTS: a toolkit for building and dynamically deploying network protocols. In: 1998 IEEE Open Architectures and Network Programming, pp. 117–129. IEEE (1998)

22. Samrat, B., Calvert, K.L., Zegura, E.W.: An architecture for active networking. In IEEE Communications Magazine, pp. 72–78 (1997)

23. Anderson, J.W., Braud, R., et al.: xOMB: extensible open middleboxes with commodity servers. In: Proceedings of the Eighth ACM/IEEE Symposium on Architectures for Networking and Communications Systems, ANCS '12, pp. 49–60. ACM, New York (2012)

24. Ayyub Qazi, Z., Tu, C., et al.: Simple-fying middlebox policy enforcement using sdn. In: Proceedings of the ACM SIGCOMM 2013 Conference on SIGCOMM, SIGCOMM '13, pp. 27–38. ACM, New York (2013)

25. Feamster, N., Balakrishnan, H., et al.: The case for separating routing from routers. In: Proceedings of the ACM SIGCOMM Workshop on Future Directions in Network Architecture, FDNA '04, pp. 5–12. ACM, New York (2004)

26. Yang, L., Dantu, R., et al.: Forwarding and control element separation (ForCES) framework, RFC 3746, April 2004

27. Gude, N., Koponen, T., et al.: NOX: towards an operating system for networks. SIGCOMM Comput. Commun. Rev. 38(3), 105–110 (2008)

28. Wang, M., Li, B., Li, Z.: sFlow: towards resource-efficient and agile service federation in service overlay networks. In: Proceedings of the 24th International Conference on Distributed Computing Systems, pp. 628–635 (2004)

29. Zaalouk, A., Khondoker, R., et al.: OrchSec: an orchestrator-based architecture for enhancing network-security using network monitoring and SDN control functions. In: IEEE SDNMO, Krakow, Poland, pp. 1–8 (2014)

A Novel Model for WiMAX Frequency Spectrum Virtualization and Network Federation

Babatunde S. Ogunleye$^{(\boxtimes)}$ and Alexandru Murgu

Department Electrical Engineering, University of Cape Town, Private Bag X3,
Rondenbosch 7701, South Africa
OGNBAB001@myuct.ac.za, alexandru.murgu@uct.ac.za

Abstract. Network virtualization is an emerging and trending subject and it is currently defining research ideas in areas such as the future internet and wireless communication systems. The notion of combining the concept of network virtualization together with network federation which basically involves the interconnection of independent network domains, possess the potential to provide a far more enriching environment where network resources like spectrum will be better harnessed and utilized. This paper focuses on spectrum virtualization implemented on the Worldwide Interoperability for Microwave Access (WiMAX) network where virtualized WiMAX networks exist in a federated arrangement for the purpose of sharing spectrum resources. A novel entity known as the VS-Hypervisor, which is responsible for virtualizing the WiMAX spectrum is fully described theoretically and metrics such as time delay, request rejection probability was used in expressing its basic behaviour.

Keywords: Virtualization · Virtual spectrum · Virtual network federation · VS-Hypervisor · WiMAX

1 Introduction

The emergence of new generations of wireless and mobile technologies has increased the demand for advanced telecommunication infrastructure coupled with the need for radio frequency spectrum that has the capacity to support high-speed transmissions with extremely huge data content. Radio spectrum is a finite resource and its demand is constantly increasing, most especially, by mobile network operators and this constitutes a global challenge [1]. To illustrate the increasing demand for radio spectrum, at the ITU World Radiocommunication conference 2007 [2], members considered the expansion of radio spectrum for 4G networks also known as IMT-Advanced. The expansion was made to cater for the spectra needs of the new emerging 4G technologies. Further expansions was also made at the 2012 edition of the aforementioned conference for IMT-Advanced and other telecommunication technologies.

The limited nature of radio spectrum accounts for it being very expensive especially the licensed portions. Some of the factors that affect the high costs of radio spectrum includes: (a) Propagation range (b) In-building penetration; and (c) Capacity i.e. the bandwidth available in the band. In the implementation of mobile technologies, low

© Institute for Computer Sciences, Social Informatics and Telecommunications Engineering 2015
R. Agüero et al. (Eds.): MONAMI 2014, LNICST 141, pp. 105–117, 2015.
DOI: 10.1007/978-3-319-16292-8_8

frequencies (below 1 GHz) have a longer propagation range and are more suited to deployments having few base stations which obviously means lesser cost and this is more viable for low density areas. As for the higher frequencies (between 2 and 3 GHz and above) they have shorter propagation ranges, higher capacities (bandwidth) and very effective for high density regions with closely packed cells and high density of traffic [3]. Because of the varied uses of these portions of the radio spectrum there is very high competition amongst mobile network operators to secure them which accounts for its very expensive nature. The number of base stations in a cellular or mobile network is a major factor that affects its cost which ultimately affects the capital expenditure (CAPEX) and operating cost (OPEX) of the network provider. These underlying issues of radio spectrum have stimulated the need to develop methods and systems for optimizing radio spectrum and a considerable amount of research in this area is being conducted.

One of the new and exciting approaches to future network design is network virtualization. Network virtualization is a networking concept that enables the deployment of customized services and resource management solutions in isolated slices (groups or portions) on a shared physical network [4]. The idea of virtualization is not so new. It was first introduced by International Business Machines (IBM) in the 1970s and the technology provided a way of separating computer physical hardware and software (operating systems & applications) by emulating hardware using a software program. Essentially, it involves installing a software program (known as a hypervisor) on a physical computer. This software or hypervisor, in-turn then installs files that define a new virtual computer otherwise known as a Virtual Machine (VM) [5].

There are several approaches to virtualization currently used on computer systems and they include: Bare Metal Virtualization, Hosted Virtualization etc. [4, 6]. These approaches are being closely studied by researchers and attempts are being made to mirror their application into network virtualization. One major stride in developing an architecture for network virtualization was done by a European initiative known as the 4WARD Project. The 4WARD Project's main objective was to develop an architectural framework for network virtualization in a commercial setting. This project has since ended in 2010 but ongoing feasibility test is being done on its architecture [7]. To fully harness the benefits of network virtualization, the inclusion of the concept known as Network Federation into its overall design and implementation is beginning to capture the interest of many researchers.

WiMAX which is a leading 4G mobile telecommunication technology has been chosen as case study in this paper, whereby a novel model for generating virtual WiMAX radio spectrum is developed for WiMAX network virtualization and federation.

2 Related Work

Currently, quite a number of research works have gone into developing architectures for wireless network virtualization with emphasis on WiMAX. Others have also looked at the possibility of developing more flexible ways of spectrum access through spectrum virtualization, while a few have considered spectrum virtualization and management from a generalized perspective. Federation of virtualized networks has received minimal attention so far.

2.1   Wireless Network Virtualization

Ravi Kokku et al. [8] designed and implemented a network virtualization substrate (NVS) for the effective virtualization of wireless resources in WiMAX networks. The NVS system they designed aimed to strengthen the role of cellular networks in providing enriched experience for users. The NVS system was also designed to facilitate the provision of greater differentiation of services among content providers and mobile virtual network operators (MVNO). MVNOs are wireless network providers that lease the physical network from the mobile network operators (MNO) to provide wireless services meeting specific and unique needs of customers.

Their virtualization design centered more on isolating service flows which they called slices. A service flow in the context of WiMAX is a unidirectional flow of either uplink or downlink where packets are sent with a particular set of quality of service (QoS) parameters. In their research, no particular attention was made at looking specifically at the virtualization of the air-interface (spectrum) of WiMAX; where within a physical based station multiple virtual networks will exist with each having an allocation of a specific slice of the available spectrum.

Guatam Bhanage et al. [9] proposed a virtual basestation design that will house multiple MVNOs to on a single physical basestation to share its spectrum resources. Their work was basically a discussion of how to design the infrastructure for supporting a virtualized WiMAX framework. They also elaborately discussed the various options available for building such a substrate and the tradeoffs of each option. They did not go into details about how this can be done especially with regards to virtualizing the spectrum as a singular resource.

The Global Environment for Network Innovations (GENI) [10] is a suite of research infrastructure sponsored by the National Science Foundation in the United States. GENI is made of federated virtual laboratory of multiple testbeds used mainly for research purposes. GENI started a WiMAX project and part of the scope was to develop an open/virtualized WiMAX basestation with external control and data APIs. The project has made significant milestones so far, but nothing concrete with regards to WiMAX spectrum virtualization and network federation [11].

2.2   Spectrum Virtualization

Kun Tan et al. [12] argued that spectrum programmability – which means the ability to change spectrum properties of a signal to match an arbitrary frequency allocation, is an independent property that can be separated from the general PHY modulation. They proposed to add a new spectrum virtualization layer (SVL) which they called *layer 0.5*. The propose that layer will support flexible spectrum programmability and enable flexible spectrum access for general wireless networks. Their research is amongst the few that practically described how radio spectrum could be virtualized and dynamically accessed.

Yasir Zaki et al. [13] implemented their ideas of network virtualization using the Long Term Evolution (LTE) as their case study. They narrowed their perspective of network virtualization into two sections: (1) virtualization of the physical nodes of the network and (2) virtualization of the air-interface (spectrum) with the latter section being the main focus of their research. The approach they used in the LTE air-interface virtualization, involved using a hypervisor which they termed and called the LTE Hypervisor. This LTE Hypervisor is responsible for virtualizing the enhanced Node B (eNodeB) i.e. the LTE basestation into a number of virtual eNodeBs. The LTE hypervisor is also responsible for scheduling the air-interface resources between the virtual eNodeBs. They stated that there are already solutions for building virtualized base stations identifying the VANI MultiRAN solution which supports multiple virtual base stations all running a single physical infrastructure.

Similar to [13], this research paper centers more on the air-interface virtualization of WiMAX, especially for WiMAX networks existing in a federated arrangement.

3 Motivation for WiMAX Spectrum Virtualization

Wireless broadband technologies are growing currently at a very high rate, having a major influence on how people communicate. This has resulted in an inexhaustible need for radio spectrum and ultimately bandwidth by network operators and WiMAX is not left out in this struggle. According to recent WiMAX market report analysis, the global WiMAX equipment market is expected to grow from $1.92 billion in 2011 to $9.21 billion in 2016, while the service market is expected to grow form $4.65 billion in 2011 to $33.65 billion in 2016 [14]. Reports like this further stress the need and importance to efficiently optimize and utilize scare wireless resources such as spectrum which can be adequately achieved through spectrum virtualization.

Spectrum virtualization for WiMAX will greatly reduce the number of base stations needed for deployment and overall energy usage. With WiMAX virtual networks operating in a federated arrangement, it will further enhance the sharing of network resources and exponentially improve the efficient use of spectrum. This will in the long-run attract smaller network providers to come into the market to provide better services, hence creating a richer experience for end-users.

4 Network Federation Concept

The concept of network federation is a new and exciting idea that it is being currently proposed by many researchers as part of the building blocks for the future internet. Federation in the network domain is a model for establishing very large scale and diverse infrastructure for the purpose of interconnecting independent network domains in order to create a rich environment with increased benefits to users of the independent domains [15]. This concept can easily be expressed as shown in Fig. 1 where independent Network providers (NP) existing in an interconnected framework with each of them having their own Network Operators (NO). The NOs are dependent on the NPs for the use of their network infrastructure and the federated network setting allows for resource sharing amongst all the various NPs.

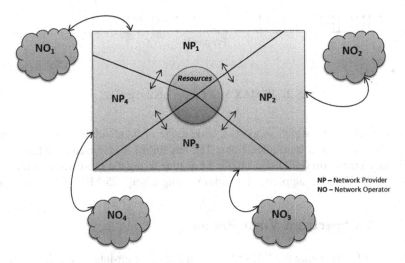

Fig. 1. Illustration of Network Federation

5 Overview of WiMAX PHY Layer

WiMAX is defined under the IEEE 802 family as IEEE 802.16. For the IEEE 802.16, the physical layer was defined for a wide range of frequencies from 2 to 66 GHz. Sub frequency range of 10–66 GHz is essentially for line-of-sight (LoS) propagation, whereas for 2–11 GHz bands, communication can be achieved for licensed and unlicensed bands and they are also used for non-line-of-sight (NLoS) communication.

WiMAX uses a number of legacy technologies amongst which are: Orthogonal Frequency Division Multiplexing (OFDM), Time Division Duplexing (TDD) and Frequency Division Duplexing (FDD). OFDM is a multiplexing technique that subdivides the bandwidth of a signal into multiple frequency sub-carriers. These multiple frequency subcarriers are modulated with data sub-streams and then transmitted. OFDM modulation is realized with efficient Inverse Fast Fourier Transform (IFFT) that generates large number of subcarriers (up to 2048) with minimal complexity.

In an OFDM system, resources (e.g. spectrum) are available in the time domain by means of OFDM symbols and in the frequency domain by means of subcarriers. These resources in the time and frequency domain can be rearranged into sub-channels for allocation to individual users. An offshoot of OFDM is the Orthogonal Frequency Division Multiple Access (OFDMA) which is a multiple access/multiplexing scheme that provides multiplexing operation of data streams from multiple users both on the downlink and uplink sub-channels. The OFDMA subcarriers are shown in Fig. 2. WiMAX IEEE 802.16e-2005 otherwise known as mobile WiMAX is based on scalable

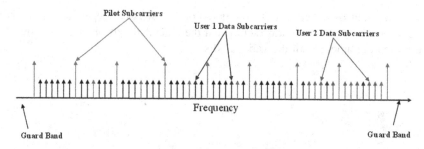

Fig. 2. WiMAX S-OFDMA Subcarriers [17]

OFDMA (S-OFDMA) which supports a wide range of bandwidths enabling the need for flexible various spectrum allocations. The scalability is achieved by adjusting the Fast Fourier Transform (FFT) size and the same time fixing the sub-carrier frequency at 10.94 kHz. S-OFDMA supports bandwidth ranging from 1.25 MHz to 20 MHz [18].

6 WiMAX Spectrum Virtualization

The process of virtualizing the WiMAX radio spectrum or air-interface will require that the basestation hardware components must also be virtualized. As similarly proposed by [13] for LTE eNodeB virtualization which follows the principle of node virtualization already done in the field of computer systems we propose a near similar architecture for the virtualization of WiMAX basestation with emphasis on spectrum virtualization. As previously discussed, the general approach for computer system virtualization involves the use of a hypervisor. In similar fashion, our proposed model for WiMAX basestation visualization is shown in Fig. 3. Considering that our emphasis is solely on spectrum, the generic hypervisor has been renamed Virtual Spectrum Hypervisor (VS-Hypervisor).

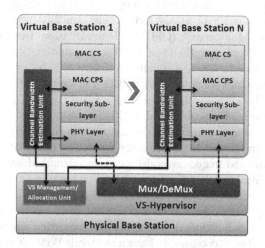

Fig. 3. Approach for WiMAX Basestation Virtualization

6.1 VS-Hypervisor

The VS-Hypervisor is the entity responsible for virtualizing the air interface and ensuring proper management of spectrum allocation. Its primary job is the scheduling of spectrum resources amongst the virtual networks to meet their individual bandwidth requirements. WiMAX resources in the frequency domain are represented as S-OF-DMA subcarriers and the numbers of subcarriers are directly proportional to the bandwidth size. The VS-Hypervisor works by receiving bandwidth estimates from the individual virtual WiMAX networks done by a bandwidth estimation unit. The estimated bandwidth values are then mapped unto the appropriate number of S-OFDMA subcarriers or sub-channels (grouped sub-carriers) and a scheduling algorithm schedules these subcarriers/spectrum resources to the appropriate virtual networks. The amount of spectrum allocated will be based on contracts or strictly on need and request. Figure 4 depicts the VS-Hypervisor having access to the entire spectrum channel bandwidth of a physical WiMAX basestation while it schedules the spectrum to the virtual networks.

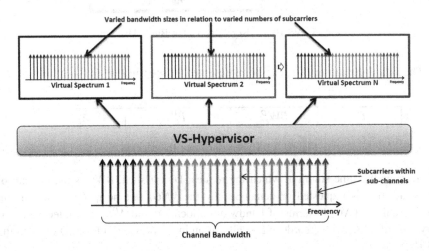

Fig. 4. WiMAX Spectrum Virtualization Using VS-hypervisor

In this paper we focus more on the basic description of the VS-Hypervisor and its functionality. We also look at this functionality in terms of handling requests from VNOs using metrics such as time delay and request rejection rate.

6.2 VS-Hypervisor Operational Characterization

Considering that the VS-Hypervisor will be constantly receiving spectrum allocation requests from VNOs, it is very necessary to analyze its operational characteristics one of which is; how it long it takes (time delay) for a request to be processed. Theoretically, lets denote the time delay as T_i, assuming that $D_i(t)$ is the demand or request for bandwidth (BW) allocation or spectrum allocation issued by VNO_i at time t arriving instantaneously at the VS-Hypervisor. Let us apportion R_i for rates (bits/sec) at which request are issued by VNO_i.

The response of the VS-Hypervisor after a demand can be denoted as $Y_i(t)$ which can also be assumed to be instantaneously received by the VNO_i; meaning that no delays occurs between the input and output of the VS-Hypervisor. These are reasonable assumptions for an ideal situation but in real terms, the travel times of the request/ response signals could be represented in the definition of $Y_i(t - T_i)$. Due to the various system modeling assumptions, the appropriate block diagram describing the VS-Hypervisor functionality in terms of time delay is shown in Fig. 5 below.

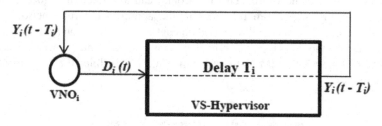

Fig. 5. VS-Hypervisor Time Delay Block Diagram

The signal definition $D_i(t)$ can be represented as seen in Fig. 6

t_i^D	BW_i^D	P_i^D	A_i^D

Fig. 6. VS-Hypervisor Input Information

Where t_i^D is the time stamp at which the request D_i is issued, BW_i^D is the amount of bandwidth that is requested or demanded by the VNO_i at time t_i, P_i^D is the current priority/rank of VNO_i in terms of bandwidth allocation and A_i^D is the antecedent priority/rank of VNO_i with regards to BW allocation in the previous allocation cycle of the VS-Hypervisor.

Signal $Y_i(t)$ has the following structure is expressed in Fig. 7 below:

t_i^A	BW_i^A	P_i^A	F_i^A	T_i^A	S_i^A	E_i^A

Fig. 7. VS-Hypervisor Output Information

Where t_i^A is the time stamp at which the allocation Y_i is issued, BW_i^A is amount of bandwidth that is allocated by the VS-Hypervisor to VNO_i, P_i^A is the priority/rank of VNO_i in the next cycle of spectrum allocation by the VS-Hypervisor, F_i^A is the frequency plan (that is, indexes of frequency channels to be used in the next allocation cycle to implement BW_i^A), T_i^A is the time plan (that is, indexes of time slots to be used in the next allocation cycle to implement BW_i^A), S_i^A is the start time of the next allocation cycle of BW (spectrum) addressing the VNO$_i$ demand currently processed and E_i^A is the end time of the next allocation cycle of BW addressing the current VNO$_i$ demand. Formally the VS-Hypervisor time flow can be expressed as shown in Fig. 8.

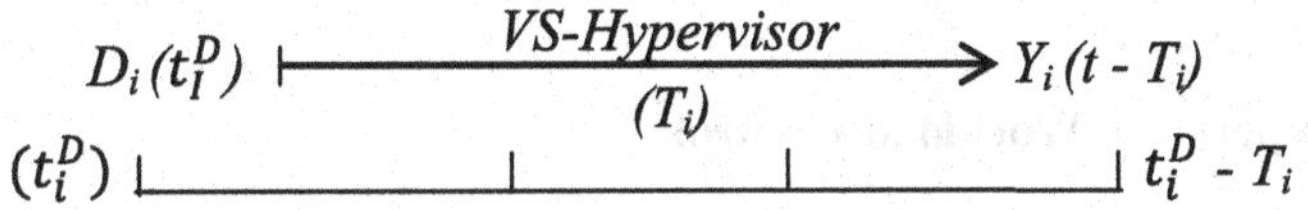

$$D_i(t_I^D) \vdash \xrightarrow[\ (T_i)\ ]{VS\text{-}Hypervisor} Y_i(t - T_i)$$

$$(t_i^D) \vdash \rule{4cm}{0.4pt}\rule[0.8ex]{0pt}{0pt} t_i^D - T_i$$

Fig. 8. VS-Hypervisor Time Flow Structure

Alternatively it can be expressed as described in Eq. (1) below:

$$Y_i(t_i^D - T_i) = \begin{cases} NILL, & \text{if } t_i^D - T_i \le 0 \\ H_i[D_i(t_i^D)], & \text{if } t_i^D - T_i > 0 \end{cases} \tag{1}$$

Where $H_i[.]$ is the VS-Hypervisor mapping function corresponding to VNO$_i$ which can be represented as shown in Fig. 9 below:

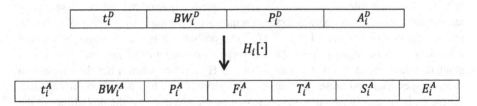

Fig. 9. VS-Hypervisor Input/Output Map

The specific definition for t_i^A, BW_i^A, P_i^A, ..., E_i^A are part of the VS-Hypervisor design process to be implemented on the spectrum virtualization. Their definitions will form part of the future work of this paper.

The available bandwidth BW_i^A for the VS-Hypervisor to allocate can be expressed as:

$$BW_i^A = BW_i^D \pm BW_{predict}(t_i^D + S_i^A) \tag{2}$$

$BW_{predict}$ can be defined as the anticipated BW needed at the moment of request i.e. $t_i^D + S_i^A$. Fundamentally, the map function $H_i[.]$ will be controlled by a state machine containing external events D(t), having an internal state evolution subject to system capability functionality constraints which can be expressed as:

$$BW_1^D + BW_2^D + \cdots + BW_n^D \le C \tag{3}$$

(That is the sum of BW demanded by the VNOs cannot exceed system capacity C)

$$T_1^A + T_2^A + \cdots + T_n^A \leq T \tag{4}$$

Where T is the overall duty cycle of the WiMAX system.

6.3 VS-Hypervisor Workload Control

The ability the VS-Hypervisor to control its workload is a very important issue that has to be considered knowing that not all requests made to the VS-hypervisor will be processed. There is the possibility that some may be rejected because there is not enough bandwidth (spectrum) to be allocated. Using classic telephony congestion probability formula like the Engset loss formula, we can be able to measure the probability at which a request made to the VS-Hypervisor will be rejected [16]. Consider the Engset Eq. (7) below:

$$P_l(\rho, M, N) = \frac{(M - N)\lambda P_N}{\sum_{i=0}^{N}(M - i)\lambda P_i} \tag{5}$$

Where M, N are the input requests and granted requests by the VS-Hypervisor respectively, ρ is the ratio between rate of requests (λ) are made by a VNO to the rate at which a request granted (μ), i.e. $\rho = \lambda/\mu$. The probability is expressed as the ratio of the lost stream of requests into the VS-Hypervisor and to the requests that where granted. Where the state i is the state of the VS-Hypervisor when it has the capacity to allocate spectrum and state N is the VS-Hypervisor reaches it maximum capacity. Where P_N is the probability that a request will be granted and P_i is the probability of the state at which the VS-Hypervisor can grant requests.

7 Federation of Virtualized WiMAX Network

The establishment of a virtualized and federated mobile network will essentially consist of the following key participants:

Virtual Network Provider (VNP). The VNP is the owner of the network physical infrastructure that has the ability to provide the existence of virtualized mobile networks.

Virtual Network Operator (VNO). The VNO is a mobile operator that operates a leased virtual network infrastructure and in turn hosts their network services on these virtual mobile infrastructure provided by a VNP.

Diagrammatically, the federation of a virtualized WiMAX network can be modelled using the Fig. 10. The figure shows three virtual network operators (VNO$_1$, VNO$_2$ & VN0$_3$) that are separately hosted by four virtual network providers (VNP$_1$, VNP$_2$, VNP$_3$ & VNP$_4$). The allocation and management of resources (spectrum) in this federated setup is coordinated by the VS-Hypervisor.

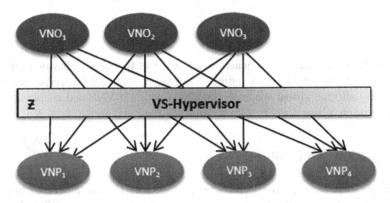

Fig. 10. Virtualized Federated Mobile Network Implemented Using the VS-Hypervisor

The aggregation of all demands of the individual VNOs can be expressed as:

$$D = [D_1, D_2, D_3]^T \tag{6}$$

Where the demand D is the transpose of the vectors D_1, D_2 and D_3. The capacity C is the aggregate capacity in terms of spectrum for all the network providers. It can also be expressed as:

$$C = [C_1, C_2, C_3, C_4]^T \tag{7}$$

The total capacity C of the entire federated network is represented as the transpose of the vectors C_1, C_2, C_3 and C_4. The VS-Hypervisor's cumulative magnitude in terms of the amount of spectrum requests/demand it can handle can be represented with the vector Z which is defined as:

$$Z = \alpha_1 Z_1 + \alpha_2 Z_2 + \alpha_3 Z_3 + \alpha_4 Z_4 \tag{8}$$

Where Z_1, Z_2, Z_3 and Z_4 are the basis vectors which are linearly independent vectors representing the VS-Hypervisor for the individual VNOs as shown in Fig. 10. The real numbers α_1, α_2, α_3, and α_4 are the coefficients of Z.

$$0 \leq \alpha_1 + \alpha_2 + \alpha_3 + \alpha_4 \leq 1 \tag{9}$$

Irrespective of how the federated networks are designed, the total number of demand made by the VNOs must never be more that the available bandwidth B. This is represented as a dot product between Z and demand D as show in Eq. 10 below:

$$Z.D \leq B, \quad Z \in \mathbb{R}^{NO \times NP} \tag{10}$$

To assess the efficiency of the VS-Hypervisor within the federated network, a mathematical expression showing the ratio between the total bandwidth and capacity of the federated network can be described as show in the Eq. 11 below.

$$\eta_{VSH} = \frac{B}{C}, \in [0, 1] \tag{11}$$

In summary, these equations in general try to express the basic behavior of the VS-Hypervisor in a federated network setting describing how the VS-Hypervisor should be able reliably allocate virtual spectrum for VNOs within a VNP and enable spectrum sharing between VNPs.

8 Discussions and Future Work

In our research so far, we have been able to provide a basic view about the concept of network virtualization existing within a federated arrangement using WiMAX as our case study. Our emphasis on WiMAX spectrum virtualization was to develop a system and framework where WiMAX spectrum can be fully utilized and better harnessed for current network operators and to encourage the entry of new players into the WiMAX market. We described the workings of the VS-Hypervisor which is an innovative system tailored for the virtualization of the WiMAX air-interface.

This work is still at its infancy stage and a lot of issues are yet to be addressed. The issues waiting to be resolved includes: The bandwidth estimation algorithm needed for proper fair allocation of the virtual spectrum, developing a scheduling algorithm for the VS-hypervisor on how spectrum resources will be allocated to the virtual networks either based on contracts or service level agreements (SLAs) and running tests simulations to evaluate the overall performance of the entire federated virtualized WiMAX network.

References

1. MacKenzie, R., Briggs, K., Gronsund, P., Lehne, P.: Spectrum micro-trading for mobile operators. IEEE Wirel. Commun. **20**(6), 6–13 (2013)
2. International Telecommunication Union: Final Acts WRC-07: World Radiocommunication Conference, Geneva (2007)
3. Martyn, R.: Spectrum for Mobile Broadband in the Americas: Policy Issues for Growth and Competition. GSMA, Atlanta (2011)
4. Jorge, C., Javier, J.: Network Virtualization – A View from the Bottom. MobiCom, Chicago (2010)
5. David, B.: Virtualization - Is it Right for You?: LAD Enterprizes, Inc. (2008)
6. Susanta, N., Tzi-cker, C.: A Survey on Virtualization Technologies: SUNY. Stony Brook, New York (2005)
7. The FP7 4WARD Project, The FP7 4WARD Project: The Project. http://www.4ward-project.eu/index.php?s=overview&c=project
8. Ravi, K., Rajesh, M., Honghai, Z., Sampath, R.: NVS: A Virtualization Substrate for WiMAX Networks. MobiCom, Chicago (2010)
9. Gautam, B., Ivan, S., Dipankar, R.: A Virtualization Architecture For Mobile WiMAX Networks. ACM SIGMOBILE Mob. Comput. Commun. Rev. **15**(4), 26–37 (2011)

10. GENI. http://www.geni.net
11. GENI, WiMAX-GENI:geni. http://groups.geni.net/geni/wiki/WiMAX
12. Kun, T., Haichen, S., Jiansong, Z., Yongguang, Z.: Enable flexible spectrum access with spectrum virtualization. In: IEEE DySpan, Washington (2012)
13. Yasir, Z., Liang, Z., Carmelita, G., Andreas, T.-G.: LTE wireless virtualization and spectrum management. Mob. Netw. Appl. **16**(4), 424–432 (2011)
14. Markets and Markets: WiMAX Market - TDD/FDD Spectrum Analysis and Global Forecast (2011–2016). http://www.marketsandmarkets.com/Market-Reports/wimax-market-335.html
15. Technopedia: What is Federation? http://www.techopedia.com/definition/2500/federation
16. Ran Pang: Engset Distribution: Department of Electrical and Computer Engineering North Carolina State University (2012)
17. Orthogonal Frequency Division Multiple Access. http://en.wikipedia.org/wiki/Orthogonal_frequency-division_multiple_access
18. WiMAX Forum: Mobile WiMAX – Part 1: A Technical Overview and Performance Evaluation (2006)

Mobile Network Architecture Evolution Options: GW Decomposition and Software Defined Networks

Wolfgang Hahn[✉]

Nokia, St. Martin-Straße 76, 81541 Munich, Germany
wolfgang.hahn@nsn.com

Abstract. This paper discusses long term architectural evolution options of the 3GPP Evolved Packet Core (EPC). It is focused to the question which functions of the existing EPC are addressed or impacted when introducing Software Defined Networking (SDN). Several aspects are discussed showing the benefits of a strict separation of mobile specific gateway functions from SDN functions. In that aspect the suggestions made in this paper differs from existing SDN based concepts. This paper analyses how the SGW/PGWs of the EPC can be decomposed in different ways. A reduction of mobile specific network elements and a separation into network independent administrative domains may help to reduce the cost for network operation in future.

Keywords: 3GPP · Evolved packet core · Gateway · SDN

1 Introduction

Operators are faced with a continuously increasing demand for mobile data traffic at moderate cost. Managing the total cost (TCO) is one challenge - the other is to become more flexible in reacting to future network needs. In this context new technologies have received attention in the Telecommunication sector: Cloud computing and Software Defined Networking (SDN), see NSN view on Technology Vision for 2020 [1]. SDN originated in the data centre networking business. The technology virtualizes the switching and forwarding resources in the data plane and makes them accessible for higher layer software through the introduction of a central controller [2]. For telecommunications networks it promises better utilization of transport resources and delivery of a higher degree of automation in the management.

The principles introduced by SDN are considered to be useful also in areas beyond the pure routing and switching in transport networks. It is the "centralization of network control" that allows for a number of benefits: centralized Software can run in cloud environment on standard computer hardware, it makes the network more flexible and easily "programmable" and in consequence allows for simplified service introduction, management and increased level of service automation.

An important question is how those SDN principles and technologies will impact the mobile network architecture, especially the evolved packet core (EPC) defined by 3GPP. Operators are already asking 3GPP to study requirements for virtualization and

© Institute for Computer Sciences, Social Informatics and Telecommunications Engineering 2015
R. Agüero et al. (Eds.): MONAMI 2014, LNICST 141, pp. 118–131, 2015.
DOI: 10.1007/978-3-319-16292-8_9

programmability and rethinking the current architecture [3]. This will become even more relevant for the next generation of mobile networks – 5G. The EU commission has initiated the 5G Infrastructure Public Private Partnership [4] to drive the development of 5G standards.

In this context the paper sketches potential evolution options of the 3GPP architecture on a high level.

Two approaches are outlined in Sects. 2 and 3 that differ in the kind how SDN technology is applied. The first approach aims to enhance the current EPC architecture with SDN and is already subject to particular research and standardization activities. The second approach presented here introduces bigger changes and might be subject to further research especially in the 5G context. After an evaluation the second new approach is investigated in more detail in the following sections.

Starting point is the 3GPP EPC architecture for LTE according to [5], see a simplified depiction in Fig. 1. Mobile devices connect via the air interface with base stations (eNB). The MME as central Mobility Management Entity authenticates the users, establishes the connectivity in the network and tracks the mobile devices locations. SGW and PGW as gateways in the user data plane path that provide more centralised processing for the user traffic like the provisioning of a mobility anchor point, QoS authorization and charging functions, this will be further detailed in Sect. 4.1.

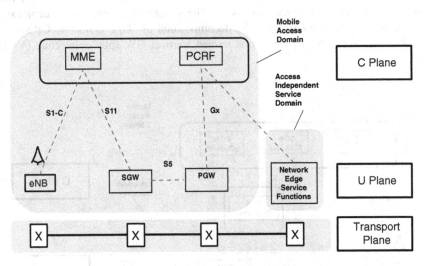

Fig. 1. Evolved Packet System Architecture (simplified)

Figure 1 also includes the Policy control and Charging Rule Function (PCRF) what is omitted in the other figures for simplicity. Furthermore a number of domains (Mobile Access, Access Independent Service Functions and Transport Network) are introduced for elaborating operation and management aspects later. And the network functions are allocated to a layered plane structure for control (CP), mobile network user data (UP) and transport.

2 SDN Based Architecture: Vertical GW Decomposition

Basic principles of SDN concepts are the separation of control and data plan of a network, an open interface between both layers (often referred to OpenFlow protocol), the centralization of the network control functions programmable by networking applications through APIs and a simplification of nodes in the user plane are expected including its universal applicability in fixed, enterprise and mobile networks.

What has been proposed for the transport network was then also discussed for the mobile network user plane (UP), mainly for the gateway (GW) functions, which are the Serving GW SGW and Packet Data Network GW PGW in the EPC. In the Open Networking Foundation (ONF) white paper [6] OF enabled GWs are suggested. Recently ONF has chartered a Wireless and Mobile Working Group [8]. It aims for the development of SDN Enhanced Distributed S/P-GW as discussed in this section. A prototype implementation is described in [7]. In a wider context relationships between SDN, network virtualization and cloud computing are shown in [10].

The basic assumption is that considerable control functions of the GWs can be separated from the UP and centralized. Aspects of this centralization strategy were studied e.g. in [9].

The remaining 3GPP network specific user plane (UP) functions are then merged with SDN based network packet forwarding nodes as a "fast path" that potentially allows hardware optimized wire speed processing. The suggested architecture is depicted in Fig. 2 below. As the main aspect is the decomposition of 3GPP GWs into CP and UP vertical to the layers the architecture is termed Vertical GW split architecture (V-GW split).

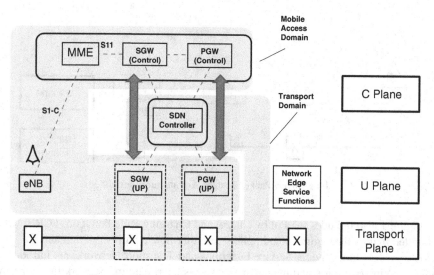

Fig. 2. GW vertical decomposition and SDN design

The SDN switches in the transport plane representing the forwarding nodes providing basic switching and routing capability. The suggested merging of GW-UP functions and SDN switches as preferred deployment is indicated within the above figure by dotted boxes. It neglects to some extend that the mobile network GW provides complex UP functions especially related to policy control and charging. As a consequence the transport nodes are required to provide those functions and the SDN control must control them.

A comprehensive study of different implementation options for network elements (called enhanced network elements NE+) and the different function split options between CP and UP are elaborated in [10]. This includes also an investigation of the implementation of UP functions related to QoS and charging.

Claimed benefits for the architecture are that both CP and UP functions can scale independent of each other (CP computing resources adapt based on signaling load, UP based on traffic throughput). Further Control Plane functions may converge, for example MME with GW-Control and with SDN control.

Some benefits materialize in case dedicated physical nodes based GWs are distributed within a certain network topology. (The platform flexibility allows CP and UP entities to be deployed independently.) The distribution of GWs (UP) is simplified: only one control interface is needed to be managed and secured at different GW locations. For current not decomposed GW a number of interfaces (S11, Gx, Rx, Ro) would need to be maintained for many distributed GWs.

But the vertical GW decomposition also gives some drawbacks: For example it requires a new interface between the decomposed GW functions which requires additional resources and increased processing. On top of that - communication via external interfaces are usually less efficient than communications within integrated nodes. Also more messages (and delays) are required when looking to call flows involving a central control unit compared with e.g. direct SGW-PGW communication. It introduces additional nodes or Virtual Network Function (VNF) types that need to be managed and orchestrated.

Looking from higher abstraction level further issues of the architecture are identified that result from the application of the SDN principle (separation of GW CP and UP) in connection with an SDN based implementation (introducing an SDN controller with two interfaces, merging GW UP and SDN switching functions):

The vertical GW decomposition introduces several dependencies between the mobile access and transport network domain. For the control plane this can be seen in Fig. 2. Here the SDN controller needs enhancements on both interfaces (Northbound and Southbound) to process mobile GW specific actions.

It mixes also the layered plane concept of UP and Transport plane. E.g. 3GPP specific bearers need to be handled in the same node as packet forwarding and is controlled by the same protocol. 3GPP specific bearer handling does not relate to GTP encapsulation only, it includes policy enforcement and charging functions as well.

From operator point of view it is advantageous to limit the interactions and dependencies between domains as much as possible (to well defined/standardized interfaces) to allow an independent vendor selection, deployment and management of the domains.

Compared with the cost of introducing this new architecture the new functions itself require also new investments for products and inter-operability testing effort. This will not lead to new EPC functionality because it provides a redesign of existing functions only. This means the costs need to be paid back by better resource utilization only.

3   Introduction of a Horizontal GW Decomposition

The analysis of the vertical GW split given in Sect. 2 highlights some drawbacks of that architecture. Within this section an architecture is suggested which targets to avoid some negative impacts, especially the domain dependencies.

The starting point to develop a novel architecture is a local IP access introduced in 3GPP Releases 10 for Femto BS (LIPA, [5]), i.e. the concept of co-locating a local GW (LGW) with a Femto BS. To extend and generalize this concept the restriction of LIPA as the lack of support for mobility needs to be overcome. It should be noted that future developments may simplify the deployment of core network functions even more by introducing those functions into base stations: the so-called cloud RAN concept provides base band processing in local data centers (DC) as well, or the other way around a base station is enhanced by cloud servers which allows localized functions like for content storage for very low latency applications and for saving backhaul transport for content delivery networks (CDN).

Figure 3 shows the architecture introduced in this section that enhances the LIPA solution.

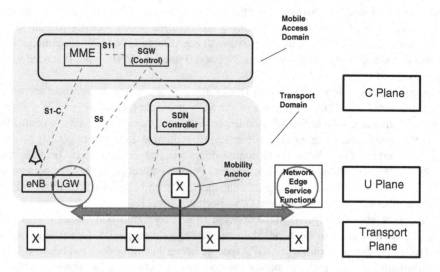

Fig. 3. Horizontal GW function decomposition, SDN design

From the LIPA architecture it is inherited that the SGW works as a controller only and can be placed within the control plane. The LGW can be controlled like the PGW with a S5 interface, which avoids the need to add mobile network specific functions into the SDN controller and OF protocol as outlined for the Vertical-GW-split in Sect. 2. For a horizontal GW functions distribution - also termed H-GW split - it is further investigated how functions of the PGW and the UP part of the SGW can be distributed within the network.

Potential candidates are three allocations or network nodes, marked with the circles in Fig. 3. (Particular locations in the architecture might be preferred for certain functions.):

– In a network edge

Parts of the GW functions can be implemented as centralized UP processing and performed in a mobile access network independent fashion. This may allow to include functions as legal interception, charging, and services that are currently under investigation for the so-called "Service Function Chaining" (e.g. NAT, Firewall, Deep Packet Inspection, Content optimization etc.).

Functions allocated this way benefit from convergence with fixed networks and the economy of scale. From the operator management point of view this allows own domains for network and IT services.

– In an SDN controlled transport network

Especially for mobility related functions SDN based switches or forwarding elements can be used. As described in Sect. 4 they may serve as mobility anchors and trigger functions for the activation of traffic paths for IDLE users. This can be achieved by functions available in all transport switches (it should be noted that mobile network specific enhancements are avoided). Please also take a look to OF related activities later in this text to allow tunneling which can be applied for a mobile anchor function.

– In the BS of the mobile access network

The local GW (LGW) function performs the missing mobile network specific UP related functions. This allows QoS functions and allocation of traffic classes to radio bearers.

Before going into the details of the architecture in the following a short evaluation of the Horizontal-GW split advantages is provided (especially in relation to the Vertical-GW split) for different aspects:

– Number of mobile network specific nodes

Integrating the mobile network specific UP functions in the BS removes a mobile network specific node/function from the architecture. This may contribute to TCO reduction. (The other candidate locations are not used in a mobile network specific way.)

– High level comparison of number of managed network nodes/functions

Just counting network functions is a quite simple approach to evaluate the management effort of certain network architecture. Those functions might be implemented by various products coming from different vendors and each may have its own management environment, requiring inter-operation tests etc. For the network function virtualization scenario this might be the number of virtual network functions and type of virtual machines an operator needs to provide for life cycle management and other functions. So reducing the numbers of entities might result in a direct contribution to TCO reduction.

Network Functions	4G EPS	V-GW split	H-GW split
MME	x	x	x
PGW	x		
PGW-C		x	
PGW-U		x	
SGW	x		
SGW-C		x	x
SGW-U		x	
eNB/LGW	x	x	x
Router/SDN Router	x	x	x
SDN controller		x	x
Sum	5	8	5

It can be seen that the V-GW split increases the number of functions compared to EPC. (Please note that this might not only result in increased management effort but also introduces longer messaging flows when communicating via central controllers compared to direct SGW-PGW communication.)

– Separation of administrative domains

The differences of the V-GW split and H-GW split implementation became already visible by comparison of Figs. 2 and 3. The H-GW split performs better to keep different administrative domains as much as possible independent (mobile access, transport and service/IT functions) and makes use of SDN w/o modifications for mobile specific handling (e.g. avoid carrying mobile specific information in OF, for policy enforcement, charging etc.)

– Network Flatness

The V-GW split keeps the number of EPS/EPC nodes in the user plane path high whereas the H-GW split reduces it resulting in a more flat architecture. This is mainly achieved by 3GPP Specific GW function running in the BS. SDN switches used for e.g. mobility anchor functions are assumed to add only little delay as running with wire speed.

– Network Migration and Roaming support

The GW split into GW control and GW user plane (switch) requires a redesign of the current 3GPP SGW and PGW. This introduces a barrier for introducing the concept in real products. The H-GW split starts with existing components that can be evolved step by step depending on network requirements. E.g. with limited PCC functions only no enhancements for the S5 i/f are needed. Also the SGW (Control) is nearly unchanged. For traffic allocation to radio bearers in the LGW it can use the functions introduced for the PMIP alternative of the EPC (like the interface to the PCRF). On the other hand a prerequisite is the assumption of deployed SDN technology that can talk over some GW functions.

The centralized SGW can also serve home routed traffic for roaming subscribers operating in the "old mode". Nevertheless in can be assumed that in future high bandwidth networks reasons for home routing will disappear and the home operator can allow local breakout what would allow to use the new proposed architecture. Hence in future only a small portion of traffic might use the SGW for traffic routing and interfacing with other networks whats allows to centralize the SGW functions.

The comparison above provides a promising number of advantages for the H-GW split. For this reason details of the architecture are elaborated in the next section.

4   Horizontal GW Decomposition Based Architecture Details

4.1   Gateway Function Distribution

When analyzing the function split within the components of the suggested architecture it is necessary to reconsider all functions provided by SGW and PGW in the EPC today. It becomes quite obvious that there are different options for distributing these functions.

This applies in particular for the functions within the policy control and charging (PCC) framework. Above in Figs. 1, 2 and 3 an element called Network Edge Service Functions is shown which can be deployed as a separate network domain for access independent functions. Those functions might be part of the PCC framework which is not further investigated as it does not contribute much novel aspects to the architecture.

The solution for PCC corresponding for EPC as shown in Fig. 1 is that the LGW would provide the PCC functions of the PGW. The benefit is that there are only minor changes required to today's existing functions, but on the other hand there would be a need to support many control interfaces for charging and policy control at every LGW and handover procedures are required for interfaces when the end device (UE) moves to another base station. Hence an additional option is to terminate the protocols (e.g. Gx) at the SGW controller (marked with option 1 in the table). The SGW would be evolved to a combined SGW/PGW controller. This way the horizontal function split is enhanced and complemented by a vertical function split similar as shown in Fig. 2. The difference to the V-GW split model is that more functions can be hosted by the LGW compared with an SDN switch. On the other hand it is still possible to avoid the need to enhance the S5 control interface, e.g. the policy enforcement is using predefined rules in the LGW that are supported without the need to implement the Gx interface. Another difference and advantage is that the LGW control is decoupled from SDN control. LGW control (e.g. by enhanced S5 interface) can evolve independently from switch control in the transport network.

Enhancements with protocol termination in the SGW-C allow the change of eNB and LGW during handover without the need to change interfaces towards the charging system or the PCRF. The vertical centralization of the LGW control may imply the need for future standardization enhancements towards the S5 interface within mobile networks.

The following tables show the proposed function distribution between the GW control (SGW-C), the local GW (LGW) and the SDN switch (acting as Mobility anchor).

SGW functionality	SGW-C	LGW	Mobility anchor
Policy enforcement signaling Option 1: trigger and receive QoS enforcement rules which were sent by PCRF and provide related responses back to PCRF	X		
Policy enforcement signaling Option 2: trigger and receive QoS enforcement rules which were sent by PCRF and provide related responses back to PCRF		x	
Enforce QoS policy rules according 3GPP TS 23.203 and 3GPP TS 29.212		x	
Local Mobility Anchor point for inter-eNodeB handover			x
Support of Idle mode: Treatment of packets w/o eNB context, (in LGW: forward the packet to the CP to inform the controller for initiating data downlink notification procedures; in IP edge or mobility anchor: there is no routing entry for the packet available, i.e. forward unknown packet to CP)		x	x
Support of Idle mode: Initiation of network triggered service request procedure	x		
User packet routing and forwarding		x	x
Transport level packet marking in UL and DL, e.g. setting the DiffServ Code Points based on the QCI of the associated EPS bearer		x	

PGW functionality	SGW-C	LGW	Mobility anchor
Policy enforcement signaling option 1: during session establishment set up a Gx control session towards a PCRF to request PCC/enforcement rules	x		
Policy enforcement signaling option 2: during session establishment set up a Gx control session towards a PCRF to request PCC/enforcement rules		x	
Counting for CDR generation		x	
UL and DL service level charging (e.g. based on SDFs defined by the PCRF, or based on local policy);		x	
Charging signalling Option 1: Interfacing Offline Charging (OFCS)	x		
Charging signalling Option 2: Interfacing Offline Charging _(OFCS)		x	
UL and DL service level gating control e.g. as defined in TS 23.203 [11];		x	
UL and DL service level rate enforcement e.g. as defined in TS 23.203 (e.g. by rate policing/shaping per SDF);		x	
UL and DL rate enforcement based on APN-AMBR		x	

(Continued)

(*Continued*)

PGW functionality	SGW-C	LGW	Mobility anchor
DL rate enforcement based on the accumulated maximum bit rate (MBRs) of the aggregate of SDFs with the same GBR QCI		x	
Packet screening, usage threshold enforcement policy rules		x	
UL and DL bearer binding and verification e.g. as in [11]		x	
IPv4 address assignment signalling via mobility manager function (e.g. MME) to the UE	x	x	
IPv4 address allocation, IPv6 prefix allocation for the UE, and DHCPv4 (server and client) and DHCPv6 (client and server) functions. Option 1: LGW acts as first hop router to assign an IP Address,		x	
IPv4 address allocation, IPv6 prefix allocation UE, and DHCPv4 (server and client) and DHCPv6 (client and server) functions: Option 2: Mobility anchor or network edge acts as first hop router, especially for tunnel based mobility solution			x

4.2 SDN Based Functionality

As could be seen from the previous description the main difference to the EPC as shown in Fig. 1 is that SGW and PGW related functions of **traffic routing and mobility** (that are basically implemented by GTP tunneling) are now provided by the "SDN" or transport domain.

The two basic alternatives of using SDN for mobility support, i.e. tunnel based switching located in a "Mobility anchor" or routing based by using a programmable SDN switch routing table – are outlined in [12]. In [13] it is argued for using tightly integrating tunnel handling via OpenFlow termed as "Vertical Forwarding" as alternative to hop by hop "Horizontal Forwarding".

This allows now for a greater flexibility to use layer 2 or layer 3 (IP) technology, e.g. to use dynamic established or predefined tunnels (like with MPLS), or without tunneling by establishing the switching path dynamically. Depending on the abstraction level of the (northbound) interface of the SDN controller all this can be realized transparent for the GW control within the mobile access domain. Figure 4 below provides an example when a handover or a "path update" is requested by the GW control. In that case it is then up to the SDN domain to configure the path or change the mobility anchor for the purpose of route optimization (similarly as in the SGW relocation procedure), see Fig. 5 below.

On the mobile access side a handover needs to be enhanced by the context information transported between Source and Target eNB and will also include LGW context data. This can be seen as the minimum impact to 3GPP standards when following this concept.

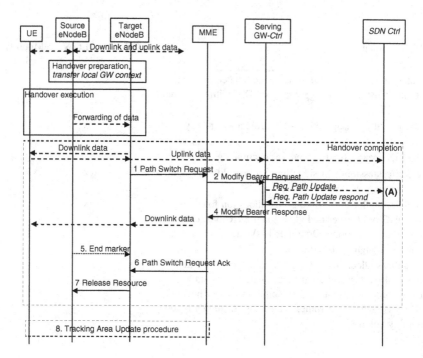

Fig. 4. Trigger of path change due to handover

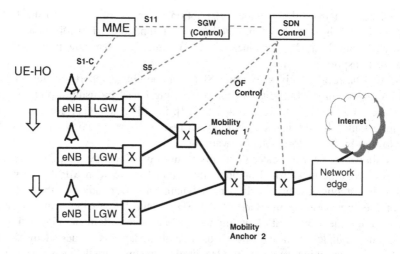

Fig. 5. Mobility anchor relocation

Also related to traffic routing is the concept of **Access Point Names** (APN). Conventionally, the APN describes the external network which the user wants to reach and is used to determine the PGW at the edge of the network. The APN might be a criteria for the Network Edge located Service Function selection.

One solution is to terminate tunnels and locate mobility anchors at the network edge. But this may result in the need to establish a lot of (virtual) connections between that point and all Base Stations. If the mobility anchors are located somewhere distributed in the network topology as shown in Fig. 5 there would be a need to provide traffic UL routing to the right network edge. This could be achieved by a per path establishment for each end user connection.

A solution to reduce such dynamic signaling effort could be the use of predefined routes: i.e. for uplink routing the LGW may set the header information according to the APN indicating the external network. The header information fields used may be DSCP, an IPv6 flow label, or an Ethernet VLAN option. Figure 6 down below shows a solution which describes the above. There are two external networks, the Internet via IP router 1 and the IMS via IP router 2. The mobility anchor or a node between mobility anchor and the edge routes the traffic according to the header information towards IP router 1 or IP router 2. QoS requirements and markings may be used in addition, e.g. the IMS traffic might get a dedicated DiffServ Core Point.

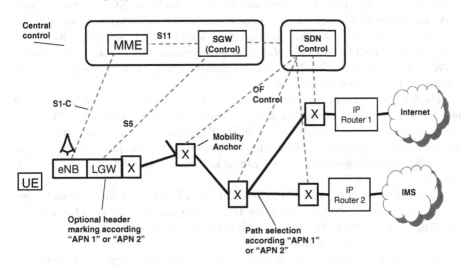

Fig. 6. APN based routing

The last concept that is described here is the support of UE **Idle Mode**. If UE Idle Mode is supported by the network the user plane path to the eNB will be interrupted (in EPC at the SGW). In case downlink data arrives at the SGW the MME pages the UE and a new UP path is established (probably towards a new eNB). An implementation option within a SDN controlled domain could be as following: when a terminal moves into idle mode the SGW Control and/or SDN control may decide to select a node within the network to terminate the DL packet routing. For this the SDN control is informed about the IP address of the terminal. The SDN control calculates based on its knowledge of the network topology and taking into account the last known position of the terminal (i.e. eNB address) and target network (APN) for this specific terminal traffic the node which shall perform the downlink routing of UP packets. This could be the IP edge or a Mobility anchor. The SDN control updates the routing table in that node so that packets have no routing entry. The first arriving packets will then be sent to the SDN control that initiates the downlink data notification procedure towards the SGW control and MME in order to start paging the UE.

5 Final Assessment and Conclusions

An evolved mobile network architecture has been outlined. Its characteristic is that functions of the mobile specific SGW and PGW are allocated to the Base Stations, the SDN controlled transport network and to Network Edge Service Functions. This reduces complexity by separating the network into independent domains for access, transport and services, reducing mobile network specific functions and build on fixed mobile convergence. All this contributes directly to TCO reduction.

The proposals can be mapped in parts to the vertical GW split architecture and materialize benefits claimed for that architecture as well: the SGW enhanced with PGW/LGW control function map to a combined SGW-C and PGW-C controller and can contribute to a control plane consolidation. SDN switches used in the horizontal function distribution to provide mobility related functions map to some extend to the SGW-U of the vertical GW split and can implement efficient traffic routing topologies needed for latency requirements etc.

The horizontal distribution of GW functions has been chosen as base line with the intent to keep the different network layers as much as possible independent. This does not exclude a further vertical shift of LGW/PGW control functions to the control plane like the described termination of charging and policy control interfaces, but still allows that mobile network specific functions can be kept fully in the mobile access network domain.

Related to this is a positional optimization of the LGW control and an obvious area for further research activities. Since the LGW is co-located with the eNB a single signaling interface might be sufficient. An enhancement of the S1-C interface could serve all need for LGW control.

The vertical GW decomposition schema outlined in Sect. 2 targets to redesign the existing 3GPP functions by using SDN principles. The new proposed horizontal function distribution introduces a bigger architectural change as it replaces 3GPP bearer concepts in the core network by SDN based flow handling.

This way a considerable amount of current 3GPP UP functions has been shifted to the SDN controlled transport plane. Hence the future deployment of the presented concepts may depend on the adoption of SDN principles in telecommunication networks and their capability to scale according to mobile network requirements.

Not all issues of the architecture developed can be discussed and evaluated in the scope of this paper nor they are already investigated. Under the Horizon 2020 program the EU commission has called for 5G research projects [4]. Under the topic "Advanced 5G Network Infrastructure for the Future Internet" [14] areas like Radio network architecture, convergence beyond last mile, network management and network virtualization and software networks are scoped. It can be anticipated that projects when established will look deeper into details of the architecture partly outlined here and proposed for a potential NW evolution.

References

1. Technology Vision for the Gigabit Experience, NSN White paper June 2013. http://nsn.com/futureworks-publications
2. Software-Defined Networking: The New Norm for Networks, white paper, ONF, April 2012
3. China Telecom. 3GPP SA1 document S1-135118. http://www.3gpp.org/ftp/tsg_sa/WG1_Serv/TSGS1_64_SanFrancisco/docs/. New study on Requirement for Virtualization and Programmable of Mobile Networks
4. 5G Infrastructure Public Private Partnership, Vision and Mission. http://5g-ppp.eu/our-vision/
5. 3GPP TS 23.401: GPRS Enhancements for E-UTRAN Access
6. OpenFlow™-Enabled Mobile and Wireless Networks, ONF Solution Brief, 30 September 2013. https://www.opennetworking.org/images/stories/downloads/sdn-resources/solution-briefs/sb-wireless-mobile.pdf
7. Mueller, J., Chen, Y., Reiche, B., Vlad, V., Magendanz, T.: Design and implementation of a carrier grade software defined telecommunication switch and controller. In: 1ST IEEE / IFIP International Workshop on SDN Management and Orchestration, Krakow, Poland, 9th May 2014. http://clayfour.ee.ucl.ac.uk/sdnmo2014/
8. ONF Wireless&Mobile Working Group Charter. https://www.opennetworking.org/working-groups/wireless-mobile
9. Hahn, W., Sanneck, H.: Centralized GW control and IP address management for 3GPP networks. In: Timm-Giel, A., Strassner, J., Agüero, R., Sargento, S., Pentikousis, K. (eds.) MONAMI 2012. LNICST, vol. 58, pp. 13–27. Springer, Heidelberg (2013)
10. Basta, A., Kellerer, W., Hoffmann, M., Hoffmann, K., Schmidt, E.-D.: A virtual SDN-enabled LTE EPC architecture: a case study for S-/P-Gateways functions. In: IEEE SDN4FNS Workshop (2013)
11. 3GPP TS 23.203: Policy and charging control architecture
12. Liu, D., Deng, H.: China Mobile, Internet-Draft SDN Mobility, 08 July 2013. http://tools.ietf.org/html/draft-liu-sdn-mobility-00
13. Hampel, G., Steiner, M., Bu, T.: Applying software-defined networking to the telecom domain. In: Proceedings of the 16th IEEE Global Internet Symposium in Conjunction with IEEE Infocom (2013)
14. EU commission: Advanced 5G Network Infrastructure for the Future Internet in ICT 2014 (2013). http://ec.europa.eu/research/participants/portal/desktop/en/opportunities/h2020/topics/77-ict-14-2014.html

Self-Organizing Networks

A Post-Action Verification Approach for Automatic Configuration Parameter Changes in Self-Organizing Networks

Tsvetko Tsvetkov[1]([envelope]), Szabolcs Nováczki[2], Henning Sanneck[3], and Georg Carle[1]

[1] Department of Computer Science, Technische Universität München, Munich, Germany
{tsvetko.tsvetkov,carle}@in.tum.de
[2] Nokia, Budapest, Hungary
szabolcs.novaczki@nsn.com
[3] Nokia, Munich, Germany
henning.sanneck@nsn.com

Abstract. In a mobile Self-Organizing Network (SON) a SON coordinator is required to prevent the execution of conflicting SON function instances. Usually, such a coordinator is responsible for conflict prevention and resolution and does not consider the fact that the activity of SON function instances may induce an undesired network behavior, like a performance degradation. In this paper, we propose an approach for the verification of Configuration Management (CM) changes induced by the activity of function instances. We have developed the SON verification function which is triggered when CM change requests get acknowledged by a SON coordinator. It analyses the resulting Performance Management (PM) data and in the case it detects an undesired network behavior it sends a request to the coordinator to revert the changes responsible for that to happen. Furthermore, our function takes the impact area of a SON function instance into account to determine the scope of verification. It also takes the impact time of function instances that have been active into consideration as it tries to identify the CM changes that have possibly caused an undesired network behavior. Simulations have shown that the tight integration of our function with a SON coordinator provides a solution for overcoming such problems and improving the overall network performance.

Keywords: Self-Organizing Networks · Long Term Evolution · SON verification · SON coordination

1 Introduction

SONs are seen today as a key enabler for automated network management in next generation mobile communication networks such as Long Term Evolution (LTE) and LTE-Advanced. SON areas include self-configuration, self-optimization and self-healing [1]. The first area typically focuses on the initial

© Institute for Computer Sciences, Social Informatics and Telecommunications Engineering 2015
R. Agüero et al. (Eds.): MONAMI 2014, LNICST 141, pp. 135–148, 2015.
DOI: 10.1007/978-3-319-16292-8_10

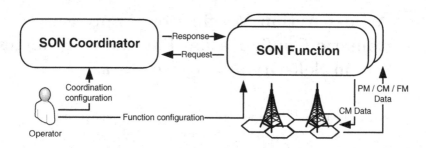

Fig. 1. Overview of a SON

configuration and auto-connectivity of newly deployed Network Element (NEs). The second one targets the optimal operation of the network. A network enabled for self-optimization automatically adapts network parameters which should lead to improved robustness, reliability and throughput. The third area, self-healing, is responsible for fault detection and resolution caused, for example, by malfunctioning hardware or faulty software.

A SON-enabled network is managed by a set of autonomous functions performing specific Network Management (NM) tasks, as shown in Fig. 1. These SON functions are often designed as control loops which monitor PM and Fault Management (FM) data, and based on their objectives perform changes of CM parameters. Usually, a SON function's objective is given by the operator through a function's configuration [2]. For instance, the objective of the Mobility Robustness Optimization (MRO) function is to keep the rate of Handover (HO) failures below a given threshold.

Since SON function instances may perform changes to network configuration parameters during their operation, a SON coordinator is required to reject the requests which would cause or engage in conflicts and allow those which would guarantee a flawless network operation. Usually, such type of coordination is referred to as *pre-action SON coordination* and is based on rules used to anticipate and avoid known conflicts between SON function instances. Extensive research has led to several coordination approaches which can be performed either at design-time or at run-time [3–6].

Nevertheless, approved network configuration changes may not necessarily lead to the performance targeted by the corresponding SON functions or by the human operator himself. A SON coordinator does not consider the fact that the actions of a large number of deployed SON functions may cause an undesired behavior [4]. Usually, a SON coordinator is designed for conflict prevention and resolution between SON function instances, e.g., taking care that two instances are not modifying the same CM parameter on the same cell. However, it does not observe whether approved changes have had a negative impact on the network performance.

A possible solution is to employ an anomaly detection and diagnosis framework, as defined in [7,8]. The purpose of such a mechanism is to detect an undesired network behavior, perform root cause analysis and provide the corresponding corrective action. Such a system includes an anomaly detector that learns the faultless behavior of the network. The gained knowledge is used at a later point in time as a basis of comparison to identify significant deviations from the usual behavior. There are several ways of how the required performance data can be collected. For instance, each NE can monitor its own operation by measuring several types of performance indicators and upload the result to the Operations Support System (OSS) database. This stored data can be then fed into the anomaly detector. In order to provide the corrective action the diagnosis part may learn the impact of different faults on the performance indicators. For example, it may employ a scoring system that rewards a given action if it has had a positive effect on the network.

Inspired by the ideas of anomaly detection and diagnosis we have developed the SON verification function. The purpose of our function is to assess the impact of SON-induced CM changes and provide the corrective action in case they have caused an undesired or unusual network behavior. When action requests get acknowledged, the SON coordinatordelegates the task of observing the performance impact of those changes to our verification function. The coordinator sends for this purpose a verification request message identifying the cells that have been reconfigured by a SON function instance. Furthermore, the coordinator informs our function about the area influenced by that reconfiguration as well as the time the change has an effect on other running function instances. Based on this information, our verification function determines where to look for an anomaly and find the changes responsible for an undesired behavior to occur. In this document, we classify the workflow of our function as *post-action verification*.

The rest of the paper is organized as follows. In Sect. 2 we give a general overview of coordination and verification in SON. In Sect. 3 we present our SON verification function, including all main building blocks. In Sect. 4 we outline the results from our experimental case study as well as include a description of the used simulation system. Our paper concludes with the related work and a summary.

2 Coordination and Verification in SON

In a SON-enabled network, functions are designed to work independently from each other. Moreover, a very common approach is to split a SON function into three major parts [3]: (1) a monitoring phase, (2) an algorithm execution phase, and (3) an action execution phase. During the monitoring phase a SON function instance observes certain Key Performance Indicator (KPIs) and collects information about the network, such as configuration changes and fault occurrences. After gathering the required amount of information, the algorithm part of a SON function instance may get triggered. Its purpose is to compute new CM parameters which are then applied during the action execution phase. In addition, there are two important properties of a SON function instance required for coordination: the impact time and impact area. As defined in [3], a SON function instance has to be considered by a SON coordinator for the whole time period it has an influence on the network. This includes not only the delay required to perform measurements, run the algorithm and compute new configuration parameters, but also the time required to deploy the new configurations and the time until they become relevant for subsequently active functions. The impact area on the other side is the spatial scope within which a SON function instance modifies configuration parameters or takes measurements. More precisely, it contains the function area (area that is directly configured), the input area (area where the measurements are taken from), and the effect area (the area that contains the NEs that are affected by a CM change). Furthermore, it may include a safety margin which is an extension to the impact area. Its purpose is to provide a higher degree of protection against undesired effects.

The workflow of a post-action verification approach resembles the one of a SON function. It begins with the analysis of PM data required for the detection of significant performance changes. This phase can be represented as the monitoring phase of a SON function. It continues by identifying the affected NEs and suggesting the corrective configuration action. This part can be classified as the algorithm phase. The last phase, namely the action execution, takes place when the selected CM changes are enforced on the corresponding NEs. It should be noted, though, that unlike the CM configuration assembled by typical SON function, the configuration here is constructed by taking past CM settings. In this paper, we call such an action a *CM undo operation*.

However, having such a workflow immediately raises the question about the coordination, more precisely, the selection of the impact area and time. In general, a SON function instance that is not properly coordinated (e.g., due to an inappropriate selection of an impact area) may lead to configuration and measurement conflicts. As stated in [6], this can further cause undesired network behavior like performance drops. For instance, if two functions are trying to modify the same CM parameters at a given cell at the same time, configurations can get overwritten. The first function instance can simply modify the setting of the parameter that is considered to be unchanged by the second one. In fact, even if two function instances are not adjusting the same parameters, they might still be in a logical, but not direct conflict. If, for example, the Coverage and Capacity Optimization (CCO) function modifies the antenna tilt, the cell border changes physically which means that the received signal quality changes as well. Obviously, this affects the HO performance of neighboring cells which is monitored by a function like MRO.

An alternative post-action verification approach is to employ SON functions that track their own CM changes and trigger an undo in case they have caused an undesired network behavior. However, a SON function following such an approach suffers from one major weakness. In a SON-enabled network where several SON functions are actively running, a single function has a rather limited view on the network to determine whether exactly its change is causing an abnormal behavior. The impact of each function's action on the environment simply depends upon the actions of other functions. For instance, an inappropriate change of the physical cell borders induced by CCO may negatively impact the HO performance and, therefore, the upcoming decisions taken by MRO as well.

Since SON functions do not exchange context information, there will be always an uncertainty when a function performs a CM undo on its own. Typically, functions are considered as black-boxes which means that no one except the vendor is able to perform changes to the function itself (e.g., adding an interface for such context information exchange).

3   Concept Overview

Our post-action verification approach involves a tight integration with SON coordination. The SON verification function we propose analyzes the network performance for acknowledged action requests of SON function instances. In case the activity of a given instance causes an undesired network behavior, our function requests a CM undo from the SON coordinator for the affected area. To achieve its task, though, the SON verification function makes use of four helper functions: (1) an anomaly level, (2) a cell level, (3) an area resolver, and (4) an area analyzer function. The anomaly level function allows us to differentiate between normal and abnormal cell KPI values. The cell level function creates an overall performance metric of individual cells. The area resolver function defines the spatial scope we are going to observe for anomalies. The area analyzer function determines whether the cells within that scope are showing abnormal behavior, identifies the responsible CM changes for that to happen and sends a request to the SON coordinator to undo these changes. In the following, we are going to describe each function in detail and provide information of how they interact with each other.

3.1   Anomaly Level Function

Just monitoring a given cell KPI and observing whether it is above or below a threshold is not sufficient to determine whether it is showing anomalous values. Usually, a supervised anomaly detection technique requires the training and computation of a classifier that allows us to differentiate between a normal and abnormal state. If we take the KPI terminology used in this paper, such a method would allow us to compute a reference state from which a given cell KPI may deviate. In this way, we can analyze whether a given KPI data set is conform to an expected pattern or not.

The anomaly level function presented in this section is responsible to calculate this difference. Its output is a *KPI anomaly level* which depicts the deviation of a KPI from its expectation. To do so, we standardize a KPI dataset by taking the z-score of each point. A z-score is a measure of how many standard deviations a data point is away from the mean of a given KPI data set. Any data point that has a z-score lower, for example, than -2 or higher than 2 is an outlier, and likely to be an anomaly. The actual process of computing an anomaly level consists of two steps.

First, we collect samples $X_1, \ldots, X_t$ during the *verification training* phase for each KPI. Here, we use t to mark a training period. Depending on the granularity at which we are able to get PM data from the network, a training period may correspond to an hour, a day, a week and so on. Second, we compute the z-score for each KPI sample $X_1, \ldots, X_t, X_{t+1}$. Note that X_{t+1} corresponds to the KPI sample from the current (non-training) sampling period. Let us give an example of how this may look like when we observe the Handover Success Rate (HOSR) for a given cell. Suppose that a cell has reported a success rate of 98.1 %, 97.6 %, and 98.5 % during the training phase. Furthermore, let us assume 95.2 % is the result from the current sampling period. The normalized result of all four samples would be 0.46, 0.21, 0.78, and −1.46. The HOSR anomaly level equals to −1.46, which is the z-score of the current sampling period.

Furthermore, it should be noted that during the verification training phase our verification function collects KPI data and does not verify any CM changes. It is of high importance for the verification function to be supplied with faultless data during this phase, i.e., the network must show an expected behavior.

Research has shown that there are several other ways of designing an anomaly level function. For instance, we may use a two-sample Kolmogorov-Smirnov test to compare the distributions of two sets of KPI samples [8]. Another example is the approach followed in [9] where an ensemble method is suggested to calculate KPI degradation levels.

3.2   Cell Level Function

The definition of KPI anomaly levels is not sufficient for depicting the state of any part of the network. The question that arises here is how we can use the result provided by the anomaly function so we can compute an overall performance metric of individual cells. In addition, we may desire to test a given cell for different anomaly types. For instance, we may wish to take only HO related KPI anomaly levels into account so we can assess the impact of a CM change induced by the MRO function.

To be able to provide such a flexibility, our verification approach makes use of a *cell level function*, denoted as φ. This function is responsible for the aggregation of the KPI anomaly levels of a single cell. In this paper, we call such an aggregation a *cell level*. For a given set K of KPIs and an anomaly level function ρ, we multiply the resulting KPI anomaly levels with a weighting factor α. The sum of the weighted anomaly levels corresponds to the cell level.

$$\varphi(K, \rho) = \sum_{k \in K} \alpha_k \rho(k) \qquad (1)$$

3.3   Area Resolver Function

A cell level function is an indicator for abnormal network behavior of a cell. However, such a function becomes useful only when we know when and where to apply it. In other words, we need a mechanism that allows us to assess the impacts of SON-induced CM changes. For this reason, we have defined the *area resolver function* that identifies the cell or a set of cells affected by a (set of)

CM change(s). The output of this function is a *target tuple* (Σ, Ω). It consists of a set Σ that includes the cells that have been reconfigured by a SON function instance and a set of cells Ω that have been possibly influenced by that reconfiguration process. In this paper, we call Σ the *CM change base* and Ω the *CM change extension area*. Altogether (i.e., $\Sigma \cup \Omega$) they compose the *verification area V* which is the spatial scope we observe for anomalies.

Our area resolver function performs the computation based on the impact area of the SON function instance whose activity has triggered the verification process. As mentioned in [3], the impact area of a SON function instance provides us information about which cells are affected after its execution. In a similar manner as described in [10], we compute the CM change base by taking the function area. We see the cells that have been reconfigured by a SON function instance as most prone for experiencing anomalies. Furthermore, we compute the CM change extension area by taking the effect area and the safety margin. The main reason why we consider the effect area is because it includes all cells that are supposed to experience side-effects after the execution of a SON function instance. For instance, the load of a cell may change if the transmission power of a neighboring cell has been adjusted. However, the effect area can differ from its original definition. For example, due to an increased network density the effect area can be much larger than assumed. This is why we take the safety margin as well.

3.4   Area Analyzer Function

So far, we have described how our verification function assesses anomalous changes in performance and how it determines the area affected by a particular CM change. However, we did not mention how an undesired network behavior is actually detected and how the corrective action is provided. These two tasks are accomplished by the *area analyzer function* δ as follows.

First, it evaluates whether a given target tuple is showing an anomalous behavior. For each cell within the verification area it applies the cell level function φ and observes whether the result falls within the acceptable range defined by c_{min} and c_{max}. A tuple is considered as such when the following condition is met: $\exists v \in V: \delta(v, \varphi) \rightarrow (-\infty, c_{min}] \cup [c_{max}, \infty)$. Should this be the case, it goes to the second step: triggering a CM undo for the CM change base. Such an operation can be triggered when we have only one verification area to observe. However, being able to instantly verify the action of each SON function instance is rather ambitious. For example, the SON coordinator and our verification function may not placed at the same level, e.g., the latter one is located at the NM level whereas the coordinator is settled at the Domain Management (DM) level, several verification requests can get aggregated and sent at once. As a result, we can face the situation where we have overlapping verification areas, i.e., we have at least one cell that is part of two target tuples. In case this cell is the one that is experiencing anomalous behavior, i.e., it has triggered the creation of both target tuples, we cannot simply undo the changes at both CM change bases. The induced reconfiguration at one of the CM changes bases might

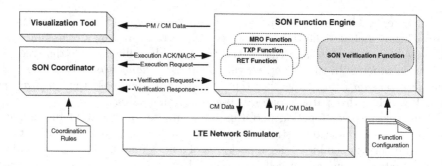

Fig. 2. S3 overview

have had a positive impact, i.e., it is not responsible for the degradation of that cell. In our concept we call such a situation a *verification collision*. Our proposal is to stepwise revert the changes made by the SON function instances. We first start to undo the CM changes triggered by the instance whose impact time has been most recently completed. Then, we observe the impact of the undo operation. Should the result lead to an improvement but still indicate that the target tuple is showing anomalous behavior, we continue by undoing the changes made by the next function instance that has been most recently executed. The undo process terminates as soon as we fall again in the acceptable range, as defined by c_{min} and c_{max}.

4   Evaluation

In this section we present the results of our experimental case study with the presented SON verification approach. We also give an overview of the simulation system we use for evaluation.

4.1   SON Simulation System

To evaluate the behavior of the introduced concept, we have developed the SON Simulation System (S3). The corresponding structure is outlined in Fig. 2. Our system consists of a state of the art LTE radio network simulator which allows us to configure 12 Evolved NodeB (eNBs) at run-time. The configuration itself is done by a set of SON functions as well as our SON verification function. All functions are running in a SON Function Engine (SFE) and are coordinated by using a priority-based SON coordinator. In addition, our system includes a visualization tool that depicts the state of the network.

LTE Network Simulator. The simulator periodically computes and exports PM data for an LTE macro cell network, consisting of 12 eNBs spread over an area of $50\,km^2$. The simulation is performed in rounds each corresponding to approximately $100\,min$ in real time. At the beginning of a round, the simulator configures the network according to the CM parameters defined by the selected scenario. During a round, 1500 uniformly distributed mobile users follow a random walk mobility model and use the network. The constant bit rate requirement of each user is set to 256 kpbs. In addition, the speed of the users is set to 6 km/h. At the end of a round, the simulator computes the performance statistics for each cell which are forwarded to the SFE. Furthermore, the simulator makes use of the path loss radio propagation model. A HO happens immediately when a User Equipment (UE) crosses the hysteresis threshold of 2.0 dB. A Radio Link Failure (RLF) happens based on a signal-to-interference-plus-noise ratio comparison to a threshold of -6.0 dB.

SON Function Engine. The SFE is a runtime environment for SON functions which handles their communication and configuration. Every time the LTE network simulator completes a round, i.e., it exports new PM data, the SFE triggers the monitoring phase of all SON functions. Should a CM change request be generated, it is immediately forwarded to the SON coordinator. Based on the coordinator's decision, the SFE deploys the requested CM parameter changes to the simulator. For all simulation test runs, we employ our verification function as well as three optimization functions: the MRO, Remote Electrical Tilt (RET), and Transmission Power (TXP) function. Note that the latter two are a special CCO type, as defined in [1]. The RET function adapts only the antenna tilt whereas TXP adjusts solely the transmission power within a cell.

Furthermore, an instance of MRO, RET and TXP is running on each cell in the network. The function and input area of every function instance is set to a single cell. The impact time of every instance is set to one simulation round.

SON Coordinator. The used SON coordinator performs pre-action coordination [4] by employing the batch coordination concept with dynamic priorities, as defined in [6]. The concept is designed for batch processing of SON function requests. More precisely, every SON function instance has an assigned bucket and dynamic priority. The bucket initially contains a number of tokens that are reduced every time a request by the SON function instance is accepted and increased otherwise. In case the bucket gets empty, the priority is changed to minimum. The priority can be increased again if requests start being rejected. The coordinator collects all requests for a round, determines the conflicts and sends an Acknowledgment (Ack) for the requests with the highest priority and a Negative-Acknowledgment (Nack) for the others.

SON Verification Function. In our system a sampling period corresponds to a simulation round. The total number of training periods equals to 70 rounds. The KPIs we take into account for computing a cell level are the Channel Quality Indicator (CQI) and the HOSR. The CQI is computed as the weighted harmonic mean of the CQI channel efficiency. The efficiency values are defined in [11]. Furthermore, the cell level function weights these two KPIs with a factor of 0.5. A cell is considered to be experiencing anomalous behavior if the cell level function returns a value that falls in the range of $(-\infty, -2.0)$.

4.2   Simulation Results

Each scenario consist of 5 test runs each of which is lasting 18 simulation rounds. The 70 training rounds have been recorded beforehand. Each test run starts with a standard setup, as defined by the network planning phase. Furthermore, we define the effect area of each function instance to include only the cell on which the instance is running, i.e., the effect area equals the function area. In addition, we allow only one CM parameter per cell to be changed at the same time, i.e., only one function instance is allowed to adjust the configuration of a cell during a simulation round. The initial function coordination priority P is set as follows: $P_{RET} > P_{TXP} > P_{MRO}$.

Scenario "Function Dependency". As stated in Sect. 2, a SON function instance is only able to partially perform verification on its own, i.e., monitoring whether its CM changes are causing an undesired network behavior. The RET and TXP functions employed by S3 are fitting perfectly well for recreating and evaluating such a scenario. Both functions are monitoring the same set of KPIs, having the same objective, but modifying different CM parameters. In other words, if TXP changes the transmission power in such a way that it induces a negative impact on the KPIs monitored by the RET function, the latter one may try to provide a corrective action which may not necessarily lead to an improvement. Moreover, since we employ a pre-action coordination mechanism that dynamically adapts the priority of the running function instances, a high-prioritized RET function may even prevent a low-prioritized TXP from undoing its change. The scenario presented in this section investigates the advantages of employing our SON verification function in such a situation. The used safety margin does not increase the impact area.

At round 5 of every test run, the TXP instances running on two neighboring cells decrease the transmission power in such a way that it negatively impacts the KPIs monitored by the RET function instances running on these cells as well. Figures 3 and 4 outline the aggregated result of the HOSR and CQI of the two cells as well as three of their direct neighbors. Up to round 5, the observed set of five cells is showing a normal and usual behavior which is also confirmed by the resulting cell level, as shown in Fig. 5. At the time where the two TXP instances make a wrong decision by decreasing the transmission power of the two cells, all five cells begin to experience an anomalous behavior. At this point, the advantage of employing our function can be seen. Instead of letting the functions slowly provide a solution, i.e., let RET and TXP adapt the coverage and the let MRO adjust the HO parameters, our function triggers a CM undo which returns the set of cells to the normal state experienced between round 1 and 4. The same observation can be made for another KPI, namely the RLFs, as shown in Fig. 6. The experienced level of RLFs before round 5 and after round 6 matches. Furthermore, another important observation can be made here. The SON system is not able to completely return the performance state experienced before round 5 if we disable our SON verification function. This is caused by the dynamic coordination

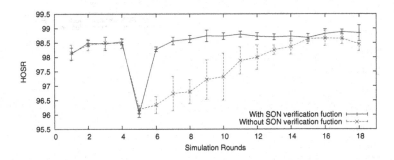

Fig. 3. HOSR result for scenario "Function Dependency"

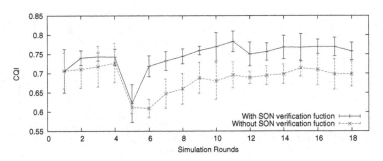

Fig. 4. CQI result for scenario "Function Dependency"

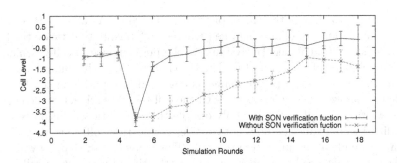

Fig. 5. Cell level result for scenario "Function Dependency"

mechanism. At some point in time, the coordinator starts to reject the requests of a function instance if it has frequently been executed.

Scenario "Verification Collision". The purpose of this scenario is to show the importance of resolving verification collisions. To do so, we configured the SON coordinator to send a verification request not immediately after it acknowledges an action request, but collect and send them in batches every odd-numbered round. To get a verification collision, though, we configure the safety margin of RET and TXP to include the direct neighbors as well. Furthermore,

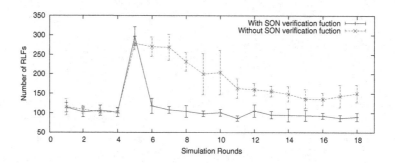

Fig. 6. RLF result for scenario "Function Dependency"

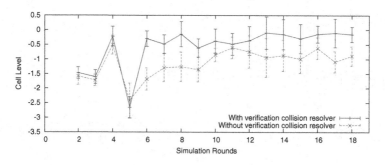

Fig. 7. Cell level for scenario "Verification Collision"

we force RET to change the tilt of one cell (denoted as A) and TXP to adjust the transmission power of another one (denoted as B). Note that we do the latter change in a way that it negatively impacts the performance of cell C which is a common neighbor of cells A and B. The tilt change is done in round 4 on cell A whereas the transmission power change is triggered in round 5 on cell B.

Figure 7 shows the cell level at cell C, the cell that has triggered the creation of the two target tuples. If we simply disable the verification collision resolving capability, i.e., our function does not consider verification collisions, we will undo all changes made after simulation round 3. This would mean that we will revert a CM change that has had a positive impact (the tilt adjustment on cell A) and one that has had a negative influence (the power change on cell B) on cell C. As a result, cell C returns to the state before the tilt change was triggered which leads to a much lower cell level compared to the results from the test runs where we have enabled the verification collision resolver. In the latter case, our function reverts only the changes made by the TXP function instance running on cell B.

5   Related Work

Within the SOCRATES project [4] ideas have been developed about how undesired behavior can be detected and resolved in a SON-enabled network. The authors introduce a so-called Guard function whose purpose is to detect unexpected and undesirable network performance. They define two types of undesirable behavior: oscillations and unexpected absolute performance. Into the first category usually fall CM parameter oscillations. The second category includes unexpected KPI combinations such as high Random Access Channel (RACH) rate and low carried traffic. The Guard function itself follows only the directive of the operator defined through policies, i.e., it requires knowledge about expected anomalies. In case such a behavior has been detected, the Guard function calls another function, the Alignment function, to take countermeasures. The latter one is divided into two sub-functions: an Arbitration and an Activation function. The first one is responsible for the detection and resolution of conflicting action execution requests. The second one is responsible for enforcing parameter changes, undoing them in case the Guard function detects an undesired behavior, and even suggesting SON function parameter changes.

Despite the given ideas, no detailed concepts are provided. Furthermore, the questions of how we should select the spatial scope that we are going to observe for anomalies, how we should determine the impact area when we are triggering a CM undo and how we should handle verification collisions remain unanswered.

In [12] a concept for operational troubleshooting-enabled SON coordination is given. If a SON function encounters a problem and has at the same time a high assigned priority by the SON coordinator, it may block other functions from being executed. Thus, it can monopolize the network which can result in an unusable SON that is trapped in a deadlock. In such a case a SON function might need assistance by another SON function. The approach proposed by the authors includes new SON troubleshooting function that analyses whether SON functions are able to achieve their objectives. If a function encounters a problem that hinders it from achieving its task, the troubleshooting function may trigger another one that might provide a solution.

6 Conclusion

In this paper we proposed an approach for verifying CM changes induced by the activity of SON function instances. We realized it by defining a new SON function: the SON verification function. It is requested by a SON coordinator to observe the impact of acknowledged CM change requests. The SON verification function determines whether a cell or set of cells is experiencing an undesired behavior and triggers a so-called CM undo request to the SON coordinator in case such a state can be confirmed. The purpose of this message is to revert the changes made by the SON function instance responsible for that to happen.

The results from our experimental case study show that the tight integration with a SON coordinator is quite advantageous when performing post-action verification. During the anomaly detection process the usage of the impact area of SON function instances proves to be a reliable starting point where to search for an unusual network behavior. Furthermore, the experiments show that if we stepwise undo CM changes based on another function property, namely the impact time, we are able to prevent positive (i.e., such having a positive effect on the network) CM changes from being undone.

Our future work will be devoted to further evaluation including more KPIs and more complex fault cases. We also plan to study alternative anomaly detection and diagnosis techniques. The link between several CM undo operations and performing the corrective action if they start repeating will be also one of our future research topics.

References

1. Hämäläinen, S., Sanneck, H., Sartori, C. (eds.): LTE Self-Organising Networks (SON): Network Management Automation for Operational Efficiency. Wiley, Chichester (2011)
2. 3GPP: Telecommunication management; Self-Organizing Networks (SON) Policy Network Resource Model (NRM) Integration Reference Point (IRP); Information Service (IS). Technical specification 32.522 v11.7.0, 3rd Generation Partnership Project (3GPP), September 2013
3. Bandh, T.: Coordination of autonomic function execution in Self-Organizing Networks. Ph.D. thesis, Technische Universität München, April 2013
4. Kürner, T., Amirijoo, M., Balan, I., van den Berg, H., Eisenblätter, A., et al.: Final Report on Self-Organisation and its Implications in Wireless Access Networks. Deliverable d5.9, Self-Optimisation and self-ConfiguRATion in wirelEss networkS (SOCRATES), January 2010
5. Tsagkaris, K., Galani, A., Koutsouris, N., Demestichas, P., Bantouna, A., et al.: Unified Management Framework (UMF) Specifications Release 3. Deliverable d2.4, UniverSelf, November 2013
6. Romeikat, R., Sanneck, H., Bandh, T.: Efficient, dynamic coordination of request batches in C-SON systems. In: IEEE Vehicular Technology Conference (VTC Spring 2013), Dresden, Germany, June 2013
7. Szilágyi, P., Nováczki, S.: An automatic detection and diagnosis framework for mobile communication systems. IEEE Trans. Netw. Serv. Manag. 9(2), 184–197 (2012)
8. Nováczki, S.: An improved anomaly detection and diagnosis framework for mobile network operators. In: 9th International Conference on Design of Reliable Communication Networks (DRCN 2013), March 2013
9. Ciocarlie, G., Lindqvist, U., Nitz, K., Nováczki, S., Sanneck, H.: On the feasibility of deploying cell anomaly detection in operational cellular networks. In: IEEE/IFIP Network Operations and Management Symposium (NOMS 2014), May 2014
10. Tsvetkov, T., Nováczki, S., Sanneck, H., Carle, G.: A configuration management assessment method for SON verification. In: International Workshop on Self-Organizing Networks (IWSON 2014), Barcelona, Spain, August 2014
11. 3GPP: Evolved Universal Terrestrial Radio Access (E-UTRA); Physical layer procedures. Technical specification 36.213 v12.1.0, 3rd Generation Partnership Project (3GPP), March 2014
12. Frenzel, C., Tsvetkov, T., Sanneck, H., Bauer, B., Carle, G.: Detection and resolution of ineffective function behavior in self-organizing networks. In: IEEE International Symposium on a World of Wireless Mobile and Multimedia Networks (WoWMoM 2014), Sydney, Australia, June 2014

Operational Troubleshooting-Enabled Coordination in Self-Organizing Networks

Christoph Frenzel[1,3]([⊠]), Tsvetko Tsvetkov[2], Henning Sanneck[3],
Bernhard Bauer[1], and Georg Carle[2]

[1] Department of Computer Science, University of Augsburg, Augsburg, Germany
{frenzel,bauer}@informatik.uni-augsburg.de
[2] Department of Computer Science, Technische Universität München,
Munich, Germany
{tsvetko.tsvetkov,carle}@in.tum.de
[3] Nokia, Munich, Germany
henning.sanneck@nsn.com

Abstract. A Self-Organizing Network (SON) performs automated network management through the coordinated execution of autonomous functions, each aiming to achieve a specific objective like the optimization of a network Key Performance Indicator (KPI) value. However, there are situations in which a SON function cannot achieve its objective which can lead to disturbed SON operation and inferior performance. We present a SON Operational Troubleshooting (SONOT) SON function that is able to detect such problematic situations and trigger respective countermeasures. Thereby, it can exploit regular SON functions as probes in order to improve problem detection. Simulations show that the tight integration of the SONOT function with SON coordination provides means to automatically overcome the problems and improve overall network performance.

Keywords: Self-Organizing Network · SON operation · SON coordination · Troubleshooting

1 Introduction

The Self-Organizing Network (SON) paradigm is an automated network operations approach which provides self-configuration, self-optimization, and self-healing capabilities for next generation mobile communication networks including Long Term Evolution (LTE) [6]. This is achieved by a collection of autonomous SON functions, each observing Performance Management (PM), Fault Management (FM), and Configuration Management (CM) data and changing network parameters in order to achieve a specific operator given objective or target [2], e.g., the reduction of the number of Handover (HO) failures between two network cells. However, the SON function objectives are connected and, so, the SON functions can interfere with each other at run-time, e.g., by contrary adjustments of the same network parameters. Such conflicts hamper seamless SON operations

© Institute for Computer Sciences, Social Informatics and Telecommunications Engineering 2015
R. Agüero et al. (Eds.): MONAMI 2014, LNICST 141, pp. 149–162, 2015.
DOI: 10.1007/978-3-319-16292-8_11

and can lead to inferior performance, hence, they are prevented before or resolved after they happen by SON coordination [3]. Among the numerous approaches for SON coordination, run-time action coordination [11] is very common. It requires all SON functions to request for permission to change some network parameter at a SON coordination function. This function then determines conflicting requests, e.g., contrary changes of the same network configuration parameter, computes a set of non-conflicting SON functions that can be executed at the same time in the same area, and triggers their execution. Thereby, the conflict resolution may be based on operator priorities [3].

There can be network conditions and situations in which a SON function might not be able to achieve its targets [5]. Although, the reasons for this are often outside of the objective scope of the particular SON function, the problems that cause the function failure can often be resolved by another SON function. For instance, on the one hand, an Mobility Robustness Optimization (MRO) function running in an area with a coverage hole might not be able to reduce HO failures, however, on the other hand, the coverage problem can be handled by a Coverage and Capacity Optimization (CCO) function. The main problem of an ineffective SON function is that it may affect other SON functions due to the coordinated execution. An example for such an negative effect on other SON functions is network monopolization: a high priority function is constantly running because it encountered an unresolvable problem and, thereby, blocks the execution of other functions leading to a deadlock. In such problem situations, a SON function might need assistance by another SON function or the operator. Currently, the operation of SON functions is usually not monitored, thus, leaving such problems unnoticed and making the affected SON functions valueless.

In order to overcome these problems, we have sketched a preliminary concept in [5] that is able to detect conditions in which a SON function cannot achieve its objectives and mitigates this problem. Thereby, a SON function, namely the SON Operational Troubleshooting (SONOT) function, is proposed that can analyze the problem using a network-wide view and determine possible remedy actions, e.g., blocking functions that cannot achieve their objectives as well as triggering other functions that might resolve the problem.

In this paper, we present an approach for troubleshooting a SON that is based on the concept presented in [5]. In contrast to the previous work, we discuss the approach and its design aspects, especially the detection of ineffective functions, in much more depth including a detailed evaluation of the approach using an LTE network simulator. Additionally, we have extended the initial concept with the ability to exploit SON functions as probes, thereby, increasing accuracy and decreasing delay of problem detection. We present results of simulations which show the positive impact of the approach on network performance.

2   SON Operational Troubleshooting Approach

The SONOT approach presented in this paper consists of two steps, as depicted in Fig. 1. First, there is an *alarm generation* step which detects that a SON

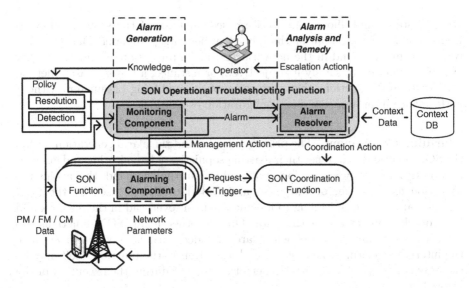

Fig. 1. The SONOT function and its interaction with other SON functions

function ran into some problematic state which it cannot handle by itself and raises an alarm. Second, this alarm is evaluated and a corrective action is taken in the *alarm analysis and remedy* step.

Alarms may be generated by two different sources: the normal SON functions and the SONOT function. In the first case, each function is extended with an *alarming component* which raises an alarm if it encounters a problem during execution. In the second case, the SONOT function, more specifically its *monitoring component*, continuously analyses the network and generates an alarm if it encounters undesired behavior, controlled by the operator through a policy. The alarms trigger the analysis and remedy of the problem which produces a corrective action, e.g., a coordination action, a management action, or an escalation action. This process is based on a policy which captures the operational experience of the operator and the SON vendor. During execution, the SONOT function can access comprehensive contextual information about the operational status of the network, e.g., the current date and time, CM data like the network topology, PM data like Key Performance Indicators (KPIs), and FM data like technical alarms from the Network Elements (NEs).

2.1 Alarm Generation

In this paper, an alarm is an indication that a SON function is not able to achieve its objective, i.e., an alarm is not supposed to directly indicate hardware or software failures of NEs. Before generating an alarm, the system has to detect the problem that hinders a SON function from fulfilling its objective. There are two general approaches for this: the *state-based* approach considers the current network state, whereas the *history-based* approach additionally considers previous network states and allows time series-based analyses of the system behavior. Hence, the latter can monitor the impact of network parameters changes, analyze performance trend in the network, and make predictions about the ability of a SON function to satisfy its objective. For instance, a history-based method can detect SON functions that are continuously modifying parameters without performance improvements, i.e., configuration oscillations.

Alarming Component. The primary idea behind the alarm generation within the SON functions is to reuse their existing sophisticated monitoring and analysis capabilities, i.e., they are exploited as probes. On the one hand, this avoids the collection and transfer of PM, FM, and CM data that is used by the SON function anyway, thus, leading to less management overhead in the network and less complex processing of the data. On the other hand, SON functions are usually self-contained entities which are provided without any specification of the internal algorithms, i.e., like black boxes. Hence, the function itself may be the only entity which can directly detect a problem during the execution of the algorithm.

Usually, a SON function is designed for the detection of a specific problem based on KPIs from the network and the determination and execution of corrective actions in form of changes of network parameters. Nevertheless, it is often able to also detect problematic situations that it cannot correct by itself. Thereby, state-based detection approaches should be preferred because they are less complex. In that way, a SON function might detect a problem from anomalous PM data from a NE that is not foreseen by the algorithm so that it runs into an exception. An example for such an error state is when the MRO function monitors a lot of too late and too early HOs or when it attempts to set the value of an HO parameter outside a limit defined by the operator.

However, in some cases history-based detection methods may also be possible to use. A SON function can learn the effects of network parameter changes on network performance and, if the reaction differs significantly from the learned behavior, it raises an alarm. The reason for a significant deviation from the normal network behavior can be numerous, e.g., a severe hardware fault.

The alarming component extends a SON function by allowing it to inform the SONOT function about an issue through an alarm. However, if an alarm is raised, the SON function should try to continue its operation. This is because a SON function typically has a limited view on the network and, therefore, is not able to make informed decisions about the remedy of the problem.

SON Operational Troubleshooting. It is not reasonable to assume that all SON functions in a mobile network will have an alarming component. It is more likely that there will always be a mixture of alarming-enabled and traditional SON functions in a real network. Hence, the SONOT function needs to monitor and analyze the behavior of all SON functions as well.

The monitoring component in the SONOT function has an advantage over the alarming components in the SON functions: a broad view on the network regarding PM, FM, and CM data. SON functions often focus on single NEs and solely monitor data that is necessary for their task due to time and memory constraints. In contrast, the SONOT function can collect and accumulate a broad range of data that is not accessible to regular SON functions, e.g., the performance of a group of NEs in a specific area, system-level KPIs or Minimization of Drive Test (MDT) [6] data.

The disadvantage of external monitoring is that the SONOT usually has no information about the algorithm or the internal status of the SON function. Hence, its analysis must always be based on assumptions about the logic of the functions. If these are not correct then this can lead to false inferences and, consequently, false alarms or unnoticed problems. For instance, a continuously running CCO function might indicate a coverage hole produced by a broken NE. Conversely, if an Mobility Load Balancing (MLB) function is often executed, this does not necessarily indicate a problem because MLB is heavily dependent on user behavior which might change often. Therefore, the monitoring component needs to be configured for a concrete SON. As depicted in Fig. 1, this configuration is given in form of a policy.

The SONOT function should employ complex, history-based approaches since the indirect identification of problems requires sophisticated, knowledge-based inference mechanisms. In this way, the monitoring component can detect oscillations produced by an ineffective SON function through a statistical, time-series analysis. However, notice that even complex detection approaches need to be configured for a specific SON. For example, oscillations can also be caused by a SON function that attempts to find an optimal value for a network parameter using some hill climbing algorithm.

2.2 Alarm Analysis and Remedy

The alarm resolver component performs an analysis of the alarms and determines suitable countermeasures. For example, the analysis of an CCO function alarm that indicates an unrecoverable coverage hole by the alarm resolver can produce an equipment failure as the root cause. As a result, the SONOT function blocks the execution of the CCO and triggers a self-healing Cell Outage Compensation (COC) function. For a comprehensive analysis and well-informed decision making, the SONOT function can draw on contextual information about the current status of the network. Thereby, it is possible to employ simple reasoning approaches like production or fuzzy rule systems, or sophisticated Artificial Intelligence (AI) systems like influence diagrams or planners [10].

Remedy Actions. The actions that the alarm resolver might execute can be classified into three categories:

- *SON coordination actions* are directly interfering with the execution of SON functions. Examples are the blocking or preempting of the execution of a SON function, or the active requesting of the execution of a SON function. Thereby, it is also imaginable to not just request the execution of a single function but to carry out a complex workflow with several functions.

- *SON management actions* are changing the configuration of the SON system itself, e.g., by changing the configuration of the SON functions such that their objectives change.
- *Escalation actions* are triggered if the SON troubleshooting function cannot or should not perform an action. For instance, an alarm can be escalated to a human operator as a trouble ticket for further inspection. Then, the operator can decide for a remedy. By utilizing machine learning techniques, it is possible to extend the expert knowledge of the SON troubleshooting function based on the operator response.

Interaction with Coordination. If the SONOT function requests the execution of a SON function, this request needs to be coordinated against other SON function requests [3]. Consequently, these requests need to by prioritized. A simple option is to give the SONOT requests maximum priority. However, this can result in unintended behavior. For instance, consider that the MRO function detects some coverage hole and sends an alarm to the alarm resolver which requests the execution of the CCO function. In parallel, a Cell Outage Detection (COD) function detects a severe outage of an NE and request the execution of a self-healing function. It is obvious that, in this case, the operator prefers the execution of the self-healing function.

In the following, an advantageous prioritization scheme proposal is derived. Therefore, consider an CCO(RET) function instance I_{RET} which performs CCO by adapting the Remote Electrical Tilt (RET). This instance has a priority P_{RET} and raises an alarm $A_{RET \to TXP}$. The alarm leads to the execution of a CCO(TXP) function instance I_{TXP} which performs CCO by adjusting the Transmission Power (TXP). It has the priority P_{TXP} and requests an adaptation of the TXP R_{TXP}. Since I_{RET} continues to run after raising the alarm (cf. Sect. 2.1), I_{RET} also requests a new RET value R_{RET} at the SON coordination function. Furthermore, imagine that an MRO function instance I_{MRO} with priority P_{MRO} requests an adjustment of the HO parameters R_{MRO}. The priorities are $P_{RET} > P_{MRO} > P_{TXP}$, i.e., I_{RET} has the highest and I_{TXP} the lowest priority. In summary, there are three action request, R_{RET}, R_{TXP}, and R_{MRO}, and one alarm, $A_{RET \to TXP}$.

A first simple approach is to prioritize the alarm-triggered requests like regular ones, i.e., R_{TXP} has priority P_{TXP}. This does not require an adaptation of the SON coordination function. In this case, the coordination function triggers R_{RET} and blocks R_{TXP} since $P_{RET} > P_{TXP}$, though, it is obvious that it should be the other way around because I_{RET} is actually in a problematic state. Therefore, the coordination function additionally needs to block the requests by alarming functions, i.e., R_{RET} would not be considered for coordination. Consequently, the request R_{MRO} would be triggered since $P_{MRO} > P_{TXP}$. However, since the highly important I_{RET} encountered a problem which blocked it from satisfying its objective, it seems reasonable that the solution to this problem,

R_{TXP}, should actually be executed. So, it is furthermore required to adapt the priority of the request by alarm-triggered functions such that their priority is the maximum of the priority of the alarming and the alarm-triggered function, i.e., R_{TXP} gets the priority $\max(P_{TXP}, P_{RET})$. As a result, R_{TXP} would be triggered since $P_{\text{TXP}} > P_{\text{MRO}}$. This finally leads to the desired behavior.

3 Evaluation

In order to evaluate the behavior of the SONOT concept, an extended simulation environment based on [14] has been developed. It consists of a state-of-the-art LTE network simulator which simulates an LTE macro cell network with an area of $50\,\text{km}^2$ and 1500 uniformly distributed mobile users moving randomly around at $6\,\text{km/h}$. The simulation is performed in periodic time-slices, called rounds, of approximately 100 min in real time.

The following three SON functions are considered:

- *MRO function*: Its objective is to minimize HO problems, e.g., too late and too early HOs [6], by altering the HO offset parameter between a pair of cells.
- *CCO(RET) function*: As a CCO function, it aims to maximize a cell's coverage and capacity. It adapts the antenna tilt in order to minimize interference.
- *CCO(TXP) function*: It is also a CCO function which adapts the transmission power.

3.1 SON Coordination

The SON coordination function implements an adaptation of the pre-action batch coordination concept with dynamic priorities [9]. In this concept, the priorities represent the importance of a SON function for the overall system performance, i.e., the higher the priority of a function, the more important it is. Every SON function instance, i.e., a running SON function in a concrete area, has an assigned bucket and dynamic priority. The bucket initially contains a number of tokens which are reduced every time a request by the function instance is triggered and increased if a request is rejected. If the bucket gets empty, the priority is set to minimum. However, the priority can be increased again if a request is rejected. In sum, the SON coordination function collects all requests by SON functions with non-empty buckets in a round, and computes and resolves the conflicts between them by accepting the requests with the highest priority. For simplicity, the SON coordination function has been configured to consider all requested actions concerning the same cell as conflicting. In other words, only one network parameter per cell can be changed in each simulation round.

3.2 SON Operational Troubleshooting Implementation

Alarm Generation. The alarming component of each SON function employs a network parameter limit check which generates an alarm if the SON function

```
1 rule" RETAlarm+TXPAlarm->Reset"
  when
3   $alarm : RETAlarm ()
    $txp : SonFuncInst () from new SonFuncInst(TXP(), $alarm.targetCell)
5   eval (context.isAlarmInCurrentRound($txp))
    $neighbor : Cell () from context.getNeighborsOfCell($alarm.targetCell)
7   $reset : SonFuncInst () from new SonFuncInst(SonFunction.RESET(), $neighbor)
  then
9   sfe.requestSonFunction($reset);
    sonco.addAlarm($alarm, $reset);
11 end
```

Listing 1. Exemplary rule of the policy for the alarm resolver

algorithm wants to cross it. This state-based problem detection is motivated by the fact that the function attempts to achieve it objective but is prevented by its configuration. However, notice that the reason for this might not be a wrong configuration but an environmental problem. For instance, the CCO(RET) function is configured with some upper and lower limit on the tilt of the antenna within which it tries to find an optimal value.

The SONOT function's monitoring component performs oscillation detection of a SON function's behavior. This history-based approach observes whether a function monopolizes the network by continuously adjusting network parameters. Furthermore, it applies exponential smoothing on the KPI data. With this history-based problem detection, they can make a prediction about the effectiveness of their proposed network parameter change: if a SON function does not manage to improve a KPI within a specific number of rounds, it generates an alarm.

Alarm Analysis and Remedy. The alarm resolver is controlled by a policy which is a set of rules mapping an alarm in a specific operational context to a request for a SON function. Listing 1 shows a complex rule taken from the Scenario "Sleeping Cells" in Sect. 3.3 encoded in the Drools rule language [7]: if there are two alarms, one by the CCO(RET) function (Line 3) and one by the CCO(TXP) function (Line 5), then all neighbors of the cell are determined (Line 6) and the reset function is triggered for each of them (Line 9). Additionally, the SON coordination function is informed about the alarm (Line 10) in order to block the CCO(RET) function and set the priorities of the reset requests.

The definition of such rules needs to be well thought through. On the one hand, the system may face a deadlock if the mapping in the policy is circular. On the other hand, in case a function in a cell is triggered because of an alarm, its impact area [3] needs to be taken into account. More precisely, all other functions on neighboring cells which have an impact area overlapping with the impact area of the triggered function have to be blocked.

3.3   Simulation Results

The presented results in this section include the evaluation of three simulation scenarios. For each of them, the SONOT concept is compared with the batch SON coordination with dynamic priorities (cf. Sect. 3.1). In the former case, the priority adaptation of the coordination mechanism is disabled, i.e., the request having the highest initial priority will be always triggered and the SONOT function has to block the execution of SON functions. In the latter setup, the SONOT function is disabled and, so, the SON coordination performs coordination with dynamic priorities.

Scenario "Inability of CCO(RET)". In the first scenario, it can be observed that the CCO(RET) function detects a coverage hole, tries to close it and, due to its inability to achieve its objective, an alarm is generated which triggers the execution of the CCO(TXP) function. Such unexpected changes in coverage may occur due to several reasons [6], e.g., the demolition or construction of buildings, the insertion or deletion of base stations, or the misconfiguration of a cell during network planning.

In order to reproduce such a scenario, a coverage hole is manually created before the start of the simulation. Furthermore, the order of the SON functions regarding their priority P is $P_{RET} > P_{TXP} > P_{MRO}$, i.e., CCO(RET) is the most important function and MRO the least important one. Regarding the resolution policy, an CCO(RET) alarm is mapped to a request for CCO(TXP) function execution and a CCO(TXP) alarm is mapped to a request for MRO function execution.

Figure 2(a) and (b) depict the changes in the network parameters and the interesting KPIs of a cell that has been affected by the coverage problem for both the SONOT approach and the coordination with dynamic priorities. In the former case, the CCO(RET) function first performs several adjustments to the antenna tilt (up to round 4) which do not lead to a significant improvement of the Radio Link Failures (RLFs) throughput, though. As soon as the SONOT functions detects this it sends an alarm that leads to the trigger of the CCO(TXP) function. As a result, the transmission power is increased twice which improves the RLFs by a factor of 1.5 and the throughput by a factor of 1.1.

However, in round 7 the CCO(RET) function reaches the antenna tilt limit. This results in the generation of an alarm by the function itself which results in triggering CCO(TXP) This final parameter change improves the cell performance such that the objectives of both functions are achieved and they stay inactive until the end of the experiment. Hence, the MRO function gets its turn to adapt the HO parameters which is not shown.

In contrast to that, the coordination mechanism with dynamic priorities is not able to improve the performance of the cell in such a manner. This is mainly caused by the coordination mechanism itself. Each SON function is allowed to try to improve the performance on its own for 6 rounds until the bucket is empty: first the CCO(RET), then the CCO(TXP), and finally the MRO function caused by the priorities. As can be seen, this coordination does not allow blocking a function

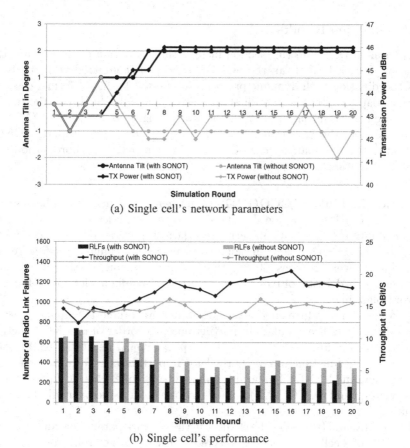

(a) Single cell's network parameters

(b) Single cell's performance

Fig. 2. Comparison between SONOT function and SON coordination with dynamic priorities for scenario "Inability of CCO(RET)"

if it is not doing any good leading to the case that the function actually decreases performance. This trend can be also be seen in the performance measurements from all cells affected by the coverage hole as shown in Fig. 3(a).

Scenario "Inability of MRO". In the second scenario, the MRO function spots a coverage problem and sends an alarm so that one of the other two functions can resolve it. In this scenario, the same coverage problem as before is induced, but the priority P of the SON functions is set to $P_{MRO} > P_{TXP} > P_{RET}$. The resolution policy describes that an MRO alarm is mapped to a request for CCO(TXP) function execution and a CCO(TXP) alarm is mapped to a request for CCO(RET) function execution.

Figure 3(b) depicts the performance of the cell around the coverage hole for of the SONOT-enabled coordination and the SON coordination with dynamic priorities. In the first three simulation rounds, the RLFs and the throughput stay

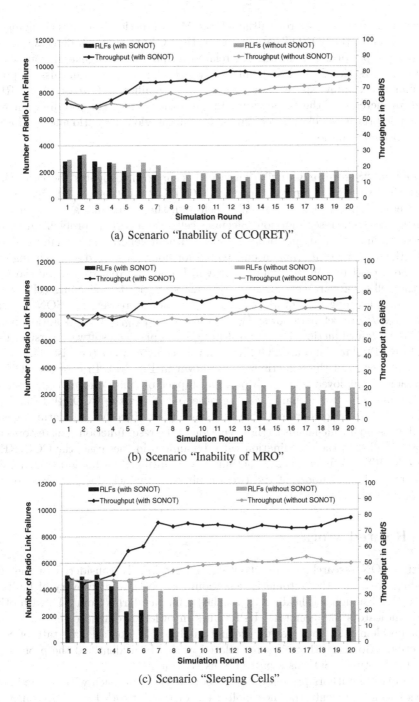

(a) Scenario "Inability of CCO(RET)"

(b) Scenario "Inability of MRO"

(c) Scenario "Sleeping Cells"

Fig. 3. Overall performance with the SONOT function and SON coordination with dynamic priorities

constant and do not improve although the MRO function is always changing the HO offsets. In the SONOT case, however, the SONOT function detects in round 4 that the performance drop is not related to mobility and generates an alarm. This triggers the CCO(TXP) function which changes the transmission power similar to the previous scenario, leading to a significant decrease of the RLFs and an increase of the throughput. In contrast to that, the coordination with dynamic priorities behaves very similar to the previous scenario and produces a non-optimal situation.

Scenario "Sleeping Cells". The third scenario investigates the case where both the CCO(RET) function and the CCO(TXP) function are not able to close a coverage hole caused by a sleeping cell and, therefore, an alarm is generated which triggers a reset function. Sleeping cells are a serious problem in mobile networks since they are performing poorly without generating any failure alarms [11]. Hence, they often remain undetected for hours or even days. Sleeping cells can be caused by software failures, in which case the remedy can be the reset of the cell's software configuration. In this scenario, two sleeping cells, cause by a software upgrade, produce a coverage hole. Moreover, the SON function priorities P are set as follows: $P_{RET} > P_{TXP} > P_{MRO}$. The resolution policy triggers a reset function, i.e., the restoration of a previous software version, if an CCO(RET) alarm and a CCO(TXP) alarm occur together (cf. List. 1).

The results of this experiment are shown in Fig. 3(c). In case the SONOT function is employed, the same positive impact on the performance as shown in the previous two scenarios can be observed. Since the CCO(RET) and the CCO(TXP) functions are not able to achieve their objective, an alarm is generated in round 3 which leads to the execution of the reset function that restores the sleeping cells. In the coordination with dynamic priorities case, the CCO(RET) and CCO(TXP) functions are continuously adapting the tilts and transmission powers of the neighbors of the two sleeping cells which does not lead to the desired effect.

4 Related Work

Within SON research, troubleshooting is traditionally considered in the self-healing area, i.e., the automatic detection, diagnosis, and recovery of faults of NEs [1]. Although self-healing approaches combine alarms from NEs with other fault indicators like abnormal KPI values in order to diagnose the root cause of a problem [12], they usually do not analyze the operational state of SON functions. However, there is some related work which identified the problem of troubleshooting a SON as a part of SON coordination.

In [9], the authors present a batch coordination approach with dynamic priorities which prevents the monopolization of the network by a SON function, i.e., that a SON function with a high priority permanently issues requests which block other functions. However, the reason for this abnormal behavior of the function is not particularly analyzed. Furthermore, it does not allow to distinguish between different problems one SON function might encounter and it does not allow triggering another SON function to solve a problem.

The Self-NET project provides a framework for the self-management of cognitive NEs by introducing a hierarchical architecture of cognitive managers [8]. Thereby, a low-level cognitive manager can delegate a problem to a higher-level manager if it does not match its local resolution rules. The UniverSelf project aims in a similar direction [13]. Thereby, the SON functions are able to alert a coordination block about a "situation where they are not able to fulfil the specified goals" [13]. If the problem cannot be solved by coordination, it is escalated to the human operator. The SOCRATES project developed, among others, an extensive SON coordination concept introducing several functions which together perform coordination [11]. Thereby, the concept describes a Guard function which detects undesired performance and behavior in the SON and, hence, compares to the monitoring component of the SONOT function. The authors particularly mention the detection of oscillations and poor absolute performance of the network, i.e., not achieved objectives. The Guard function notifies the Alignment function about detected problems, which determines suitable countermeasures, e.g., undo previous changes of network parameters, blocking of SON functions, or adapting the configuration of SON functions, by analyzing the cause of the problem. The three projects consider operational troubleshooting as a side note and, thus, do not provide further details, e.g., an implementation or case study.

The SEMAFOUR project aims at a unified self-management system and extensively works on a SON coordination concept [4]. Its SON coordination function is able to detect oscillations and frequent requests by functions which the authors infer to be due to a misconfiguration of the functions. Hence, the coordination can trigger a management component to adapt the configuration. However, due to its recent start, there are currently no further details.

5 Conclusion

This paper presented the details of a new operational troubleshooting approach for a Self-Organizing Network (SON). It allows the detection of situations in which a SON function is not able to achieve its objectives. This monitoring is performed by the SON functions themselves as well as the monitoring component of the SON Operational Troubleshooting (SONOT). This approach allows, on the one hand, the exploitation of the sophisticated detection methods employed by the SON functions and, on the other hand, the utilization of complex algorithms and network-wide data in the SONOT function. Based on the detected problems, the alarm resolver can determines possible countermeasures like the preemption and triggering of SON functions. In simulations it has been shown that the presented approach remarkably improves the network performance in terms of Key Performance Indicators (KPIs) like Radio Link Failure (RLFs) and cell throughput, and outperforms traditional coordination approaches like a batch-based coordination scheme with dynamic priorities.

In the future, further research is necessary for the development of improved methods for the detection of problematic situations, the diagnosis of problems, and the determination of countermeasures. Particularly, it seems promising to make use of machine learning in order to enable a high degree of automation.

References

1. 3GPP: Telecommunication management; Fault Management; Part 1: 3G fault management requirements. Technical specification 32.111-1 v12.0.0, 3rd Generation Partnership Project (3GPP), June 2013
2. 3GPP: Telecommunication management; Self-Organizing Networks (SON) Policy Network Resource Model (NRM) Integration Reference Point (IRP); Information Service (IS). Technical specification 32.522 v11.7.0, 3rd Generation Partnership Project (3GPP), September 2013
3. Bandh, T.: Coordination of autonomic function execution in Self-Organizing Networks. Ph.D. Thesis, Technische Universität München, April 2013
4. Ben Jemaa, S., Frenzel, C., Dario, G., et al.: Integrated SON Management - Requirements and Basic Concepts. Deliverable d5.1, SEMAFOUR Project, December 2013
5. Frenzel, C., Tsvetkov, T., Sanneck, H., Bauer, B., Carle, G.: Detection and resolution of ineffective function behavior in self-organizing networks. In: Proceedings of 15th IEEE International Symposium on a World of Wireless, Mobile and Multimedia Networks (WoWMoM 2014), Sydney, Australia, June 2014
6. Hämäläinen, S., Sanneck, H., Sartori, C. (eds.): LTE Self-Organising Networks (SON): Network Management Automation for Operational Efficiency. Wiley, Chichester (2011)
7. JBoss Community: Drools Expert. http://www.jboss.org/drools/drools-expert
8. Kousaridas, A., Nguengang, G.: Final Report on Self-Management Artefacts. Deliverable d2.3, Self-NET Project, April 2010
9. Romeikat, R., Sanneck, H., Bandh, T.: Efficient, dynamic coordination of request batches in C-SON systems. In: Proceedings of IEEE 77th Vehicular Technology Conference (VTC Spring 2013), Dresden, Germany, pp. 1–6, June 2013
10. Russell, S.J., Norvig, P.: Artificial Intelligence: A Modern Approach, 2nd edn. Prentice Hall, Upper Saddle River (2003)
11. Schmelz, L.C., Amirijoo, M., Eisenblaetter, A., Litjens, R., Neuland, M., Turk, J.: A coordination framework for self-organisation in LTE networks. In: Proceedings of 12th IFIP/IEEE International Symposium on Integrated Network Management (IM 2011) and Workshops, Dublin, Ireland, pp. 193–200, May 2011
12. Szilágyi, P., Nováczki, S.: An automatic detection and diagnosis framework for mobile communication systems. IEEE Trans. Netw. Serv. Manage. 9(2), 184–197 (2012)
13. Tsagkaris, K., Galani, A., Koutsouris, N., et al.: Unified Management Framework (UMF) Specifications Release 3. Deliverable d2.4, UniverSelf Project, November 2013
14. Tsvetkov, T., Nováczki, S., Sanneck, H., Carle, G.: A post-action verification approach for automatic configuration parameter changes in self-organizing networks. In: 6th International Conference on Mobile Networks and Management (MONAMI 2014), Würzburg, Germany, September 2014

Anomaly Detection and Diagnosis for Automatic Radio Network Verification

Gabriela F. Ciocarlie[1], Christopher Connolly[1], Chih-Chieh Cheng[1],
Ulf Lindqvist[1], Szabolcs Nováczki[2], Henning Sanneck[2(✉)],
and Muhammad Naseer-ul-Islam[2]

[1] SRI International, Menlo Park, USA
{gabriela.ciocarlie,christopher.connolly,
chih-chieh.cheng,ulf.lindqvist}@sri.com
[2] Nokia, Budapest, Hungary
{szabolcs.novaczki,henning.sanneck,
muhammad.naseer-ul-islam}@nsn.com

Abstract. The concept known as Self-Organizing Networks (SON) has been developed for modern radio networks that deliver mobile broadband capabilities. In such highly complex and dynamic networks, changes to the configuration management (CM) parameters for network elements could have unintended effects on network performance and stability. To minimize unintended effects, the coordination of configuration changes before they are carried out and the verification of their effects in a timely manner are crucial. This paper focuses on the verification problem, proposing a novel framework that uses anomaly detection and diagnosis techniques that operate within a specified spatial scope. The aim is to detect any anomaly, which may indicate actual degradations due to any external or system-internal condition and also to characterize the state of the network and thereby determine whether the CM changes negatively impacted the network state. The results, generated using real cellular network data, suggest that the proposed verification framework automatically classifies the state of the network in the presence of CM changes, indicating the root cause for anomalous conditions.

Keywords: Network automation · Self-organized networks (SON) · SON verification · Anomaly detection · Diagnosis

1 Introduction

Modern radio networks for mobile broadband (voice and data) are complex and dynamic, not only in terms of behavior and mobility of users and their devices, but also in terms of the many elements that make up the network infrastructure. Network degradations that cause users to experience reduced or lost service could have serious short- and long-term impact on the operator's business, and must therefore quickly be resolved as part of network management. Effective management of complex and dynamic networks requires some form of automated

© Institute for Computer Sciences, Social Informatics and Telecommunications Engineering 2015
R. Agüero et al. (Eds.): MONAMI 2014, LNICST 141, pp. 163–176, 2015.
DOI: 10.1007/978-3-319-16292-8_12

detection of problems such as performance degradation or network instability, and also automation support for timely and effective diagnosis and remediation of the detected problems. There are many factors that could cause degradations in radio network performance: hardware faults, software faults, environmental conditions (like weather and changes in the infrastructure), but degradations can also stem from unintended effects of network configuration changes.

The need for adaptive, self-organizing, heterogeneous networks becomes pressing given the explosion of mobile data traffic with increased use of smartphones, tablets, and netbooks for day-to-day tasks. Expectations for mobile networks have grown along with their popularity, and include ease of use, high speed, and responsiveness. Heterogeneous Networks (HetNet) can offer these capabilities, providing virtually "unlimited" capacity and "ubiquitous" coverage. However, a high level of distribution in the network infrastructure introduces higher complexity, which requires additional mechanisms such as Self-Organizing Networks (SON) concepts.

In order to prevent network-level degradation, actions that change network-element configurations must either be coordinated *a priori* or their effects must be verified (or both approaches could be used complementarily). Verification is a hard problem for several reasons: actions can be the result of automated or human decisions; networks for mobile broadband are very complex; some parameters such as user behavior cannot be controlled; and no established simple indicator of "system health" exists.

1.1   SON Verification

Before a system reaches the verification process, it may undergo a pre-action SON coordination process. Based on rules provided by human experts or automatically determined, SON coordination aims to reduce the risk of processing actions that lead to conflicts and degraded states [14]. Performance Management (PM) data is continuously collected from network cells in the form of Key Performance Indicators (KPIs), which are a set of selected indicators used for measuring network performance and trends: call-drop statistics, channel-quality-indicator statistics, handover statistics, throughput, etc. Based on the KPIs collected from all cells in the network or domain, the operation of a SON-enabled system in a certain network domain should be verified to ensure that the new actions improved the network performance rather than negatively impacting it.

The SON verification process must occur as quickly as possible in order to correlate detection results based on PM history with the history of Configuration Management (CM) changes. If verification indicates that the network entered a normal state, then the SON coordination process leverages knowledge of acceptable actions and combinations of actions given the configuration history and the system's current state. In addition, it is desirable to determine and learn which actions and combinations of actions are unacceptable, given the same history and state, along with enabling action reversal where applicable.

1.2   Contributions

This paper proposes a novel SON verification framework using anomaly detection and diagnosis techniques that operate within a spatial scope larger than an individual cell (e.g., a small group of cells, a geographical region like a town section, an existing administrative network domain, etc.). The aim is to detect any anomaly which may point to degradations and eventually faults caused by an external or system-internal condition or event. CM changes (which reflect actions, e.g., by human operators or SON functions or optimization tools), and KPIs (which reflect the impact of the SON actions on the considered part of the network) are analyzed together to characterize the state of the network and determine whether it was negatively impacted by CM changes. Main contributions include:

- automatically identifying different network states using the KPI measurements from all the cells/network in scope,
- using intrinsic knowledge of the system to automatically classify the states as either normal or abnormal,
- determining the most likely explanation for the performance degradation.

2   Anomaly Detection and Diagnosis for SON Verification

Our approach is comprised of two main steps: (1) detecting anomalies for a group of entities (i.e., cells) using topic modeling combined with (2) diagnosing any anomaly using Markov Logic Networks (MLNs), which rely on probabilistic rules to discern between different causes.

Topic modeling [16] is a type of statistical model that allows efficient topic training and inference of mixing proportion of topics. It was initially used for discovering topics in documents, where a topic is defined as a probability distribution over words. The benefit of topic modeling is that each topic is individually interpretable and characterizes a coherent set of correlated terms.

Markov Logic Networks (MLN) [13] are an approach for probabilistic reasoning using first-order predicate logic. As with traditional first-order logic, hypotheses can be described in terms of supporting evidence and conclusions about network properties. In contrast to first-order logic, MLNs permit rule weighting and an explicit representation of the probabilities associated with logical statements. As a result, one can think of MLNs as providing the infrastructure of a probabilistic knowledge base, which can operate using noisy or incomplete data and can incorporate diverse data sources into a common framework for analysis.

2.1   Overall Framework

Topic modeling is applied to the training KPI data from all the cells in scope, leading to the construction of topic modeling clusters[1] (indicators of the state of the network), which are further classified by semantic interpretation as either

---

[1] Given that we apply topic modeling to KPI data, for clarity, we will refer to topics as clusters.

normal or abnormal. Using the labeled clusters, the KPI data under test (i.e., subject to detection) leads to the mixture of weights for the different clusters indicating the overall state of the network. For real deployment, testing data can span any time or geographic scope (as a subset of the training geographic scope), and may or may not overlap with the training data. This component is well suited for this application domain, as we do not have any *a priori* notion of what the different network states could be or how many types of states there could be. Here, we generalize the concept of topic modeling to identify the states (topics) of a system (i.e., the radio network). Furthermore, using semantic information, states can be interpreted as either normal or abnormal, enabling the detection of degradation in system's state (see Sect. 2.3). Moreover, incremental topic modeling can be used to capture new states over time [8].

In case of abnormal behavior, the diagnosis component is triggered. The MLN inference is achieved by using CM change history information or any other external information in form of an event sequence, along with the MLN rules and their associated weights. The MLN rules are specific to this application domain and are typically generated based on human expert knowledge. Rule weights can be estimated or learned during operation, as new cases arise.

Figure 1 presents the detailed verification approach:

- Initially, for a given period of time, the KPI measurements of the group of cells/network in scope are selected as the training dataset (D1) for generating the topic modeling.
- The topic modeling clustering (M1) is applied to the training dataset (D1).
- The result of (M1) is a set of clusters representing the different states in which the network can exist (D2). Each cluster has an associated weight corresponding to the percentage of the network in the state represented by that cluster.
- Given the set of clusters (D2), the semantics of the KPIs are used to further interpret the semantics of each cluster (M2).
- The result of (M2) is a set of labeled clusters that indicate if the network state is either normal or abnormal (D3).
- The labeled clusters (D3) and the KPI measurements for test for the group of cells in scope are used in a testing phase against the clusters (M3) to generate the weight mixture indicating how normal or abnormal the network is.
- The result of (M3) is the weight mixture (D4) indicating the current state of the network.
- The diagnosis component is triggered only if the cells in scope are abnormal. Principal Components Analysis (PCA) (M4) is applied to the training dataset (D1) to generate similar groups of cells. The result of (M4) contains groups of cells (D5) that behave similarly; MLN inference is applied primarily on these groups. Cell grouping is used to reduce MLN complexity.
- The groups of cells along with the CM change information (D5), external events (e.g., weather event feeds) and MLN rules (generated either manually based on human expert knowledge or automatically from other sources) are used to generate the diagnosis information based on the MLN inference (M5).
- The result of (M5) is the diagnosis information for the abnormal cells within the scope (D6).

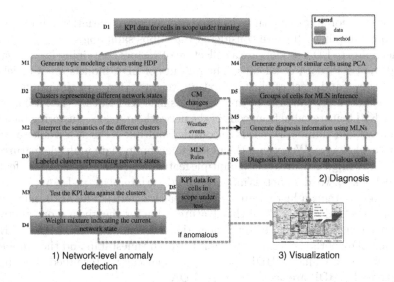

Fig. 1. Overall approach of the SON verification method applied to the group of cells in scope. Data is depicted in blue and methods in pink. The dashed lines indicated that an event is triggered in the presence of new evidence/data.

2.2 Anomaly Detection for SON Verification

The family of algorithms known as topic modeling [16] is well suited to the SON verification domain because topic modeling can discover and infer themes (topics) that constitute a hidden structure in a data set. In the set of KPI data from multiple cells in a network, we do not have any *a priori* notion of what the different network states could be or how many types of states there could be. From the KPI data, topic models learn clusters of network states, and output the codebook of the clusters and the mixing proportion of the clusters at each time stamp. A codebook records a profile for each cluster (the average of the cluster, called a *centroid*), and the clustering of an unknown query usually depends on its similarity to the cluster's profile.

Each cluster represents a state, characterized by its centroid. The mixing proportion of clusters at each timestamp can be seen as a type of trigger for the overall state of cells in scope. For our implementation, we used the Hierarchical Dirichlet Process (HDP) algorithm [18]. As the name suggests, HDP is a hierarchical graphical model which extends the Latent Dirichlet Allocation (LDA) [4], the most common topic modeling approach. For our context, the LDA model represents a collection of M timestamps of KPI data from N cells. At each time stamp, the KPI data is a mixture of K clusters, and the weight of each cluster is represented by θ. For each cell n at time m, the KPI feature w can be classified into one of the K clusters, determined by the hidden variable z.

Therefore, the goal of LDA models is to infer $p(z|w) = \frac{p(w,z)}{\sum_z p(w,z)}$, which is usually intractable due to a complicated marginalization of hidden variables. Several solutions exist for approximating the inference, including variational inference [4] and Gibbs sampling [10]. We considered the Gibbs sampling.

The inputs to LDA models are a collection of vectors containing feature values derived from KPI data of all cells. The outputs of LDA models are a codebook for K clusters, and a set of cluster mixture weights θ for each timestamp m.

By default, LDA can only be applied to a single KPI feature (i.e., it considers only one KPI feature value from cells in the network, and does clustering based on it). However, our framework needs to consider multiple KPIs as a whole to determine network status. We extend the model to accommodate multiple features by replacing the single feature w with multiple features w_i, and associate each feature to a codebook β_i. We denote this model as multi-variate LDA (m-LDA). Note that each cluster contains a histogram for every feature (KPI). The histogram represents the expected histogram of that feature value for the given scope (network or group of cells) under one cluster. The major difference between LDA and HDP is that for LDA both the number of topics at each timestamp and the number of profiles are fixed, while for HDP they are automatically determined. The inputs and outputs for HDP are the same as for LDA.

2.3   Cluster Interpretation

Using visual inspection, the topic modeling centroids can be characterized as either normal or abnormal, but an automated interpretation module is necessary. Consequently, we introduce a simple classifier for the centroids that considers the characteristics of the KPIs. This classification can be achieved only for KPIs that are not supposed to increase (e.g., drop call rate) or decrease (e.g., call success rate) within certain bounds. To characterize each KPI for a given centroid (represented as a normalized histogram with B bins, where p_i is the proportion allocated to bin i), we calculate its expected value as $E[X] = \sum_{i=1}^{B} p_i * i$.

A final score is computed as:

$$
score = \begin{cases} \frac{|1-E[X]|}{B-1}, \text{if it should not increase} \\[2mm] \frac{|B-E[X]|}{B-1}, \text{if it should not decrease} \end{cases} \tag{1}
$$

The following qualifiers are generated for the different score values:

$$
label = \begin{cases} \text{VERY GOOD, if } score < \tau_1 \\ \text{VERY BAD, if } score > 1 - \tau_1 \\ \text{GOOD, if } \tau_1 <= score < \tau_2 \\ \text{BAD, if } 1 - \tau_2 <= score < 1 - \tau_1 \\ \text{RELATIVELY BAD, otherwise} \end{cases} \tag{2}
$$

where τ_1, $\tau_2 \in [0,1]$ are the thresholds that determine the classification and are empirically determined such that the quality of the (VERY) GOOD clusters is high (i.e., $\tau_1 = 0.05$ and $\tau_2 = 0.15$). A cluster that has at least one BAD (any type) histogram is considered an abnormal centroid; otherwise it is normal.

2.4   Diagnosis for SON Verification

MLNs are well suited for diagnosis in this application domain because they can be used to compute the most likely explanation for an event given data that is noisy, incomplete or even contradictory. Probabilistic parameter values (weights) can be learned through experience and user feedback. We approach the problem of diagnosis in terms of expressing multiple hypotheses within the MLN rule set, running the inference engine, then querying for the most likely explanations given the observed conditions. We use the Probabilistic Consistency Engine (PCE) [1], a very efficient MLN solver under continuous improvement.

We apply MLNs by reasoning over groups of cells (where groups can be geographically or behaviorally defined) at different times. PCA is applied to identify groups of cells that behave similarly over all KPIs. By reasoning over groups, we can improve the efficiency of the inference process, reducing the number of entities (from cells to group of cells) on which the inference is performed. The PCE input language consists of the following elements:

- Definition of types (also called sorts)
- Enumeration of the sets corresponding to each type
- Declarations of the predicates to be used, and the types of each argument
- A set of weighted clauses comprising the probabilistic knowledge base
- Assertions (predicate forms that express information that is known to be true)

Each clause is an expression in first-order logic. MLNs search for the most likely explanation for the knowledge base in terms of the assignments of variables to predicate arguments. MLNs accumulate the probabilities that each clause is true given a particular variable assignment. One can also query the knowledge base and ask for the probability that a specific predicate is true under a specific variable assignment or ask how often a predicate is true in general.

Figure 2 presents an example of a PCE input specification, which includes three types (sorts), called $Time\_t$, $Group\_t$ and Mag_t. In particular, the $Group\_t$ sort refers to PCA-derived groups of cells. The const declaration defines 486 cell groups that we can reason over. We also have anomaly conditions derived from the network-level anomaly detection component described above. In the MLN excerpt here, we see two out of several hundred anomaly conditions. These two declare that anomalies were observed in groups $G39$ and $G46$ at time interval $T2$. Finally, we see three add statements. These are rules that link weather, anomaly, and configuration information with hypotheses about the reasons for network degradation. The final statements in the PCE input are ask statements that query the state of the network for the probabilities of different hypotheses.

When applying MLNs to temporal data, decomposition of the timeline into intervals or atomic units (individual timestamps or samples) is generally useful. In some cases, rules might be needed to define temporal order, especially for attempts to represent causality and delayed response to disruptive events. Time (or sample number) can be applied as an extra argument in certain predicates. In general, MLN solution times depend polynomially on the number of observations in the data, but will grow exponentially with the number of arguments to

```
sort Time_t;
sort Group_t;
sort Mag_t;
. . .
const G1, G2, G3 … G486: Group_t;
. . .
assert anomaly(G39,T2);
assert anomaly(G46,T2);
. . .
add [C, T] (snowdepth(C,T,HEAVY) and anomaly(C, T))
               implies weather_event(C,T) 5.0;
add [C, T] cm_correlation(C,T) and anomaly(C,T)
               implies cm_event(C, T) 5.0;
add [C, T] anomaly(C,T) and (not weather_event(C,T))
               and (not cm_event(C,T))
               implies hw_event(C,T) 5.0;
….
ask [x,y] cm_event(x,y) 0.7;
ask [x,y] hw_event(x,y) 0.7;
ask [x,y] weather_event(x,y)  0.7;
ask [x,y] normal(x,y)  0.7;
```

Fig. 2. Example of a PCE input specification

predicates. Therefore, the argument count should be kept low for all predicates and, if necessary, the problem should be decomposed to maintain a low argument count for all predicates used by the knowledge base.

When specifying an MLN, we normally start with rules and weight estimates that represent a subject matter expert's (SME's) understanding of causes and effects that determine network behavior. Moreover, the weights associated with the MLN rules can be learned over time to provide a more accurate probabilistic model for the observed situations. Several weight learning schemes exist, most of which take the form of maximum-likelihood estimation with respect to a training set. As more relevant training data is available, the MLN weights can be modified to tune the probabilistic knowledge base to generate the best answers for a given situation. Realistically, a SME might not be able to account for all possibilities in advance. As unexpected cases arise, there will be a need to add rules during the training phase to accommodate these cases. The new rules' weights will also need to be trained. Weight adjustment can be an ongoing process, but weight stability will be the primary indicator that the MLN is working as expected.

3   Performance Evaluation

This section analyzes the performance of our framework applied to a real network dataset. The experimental corpus consisted of KPI and CM data for approximately 4,000 cells, collected from 01/2013 to 03/2013. The KPIs have different characteristics; some of them are measurements of user traffic utilization (e.g. downlink or uplink data volume or throughput), while others are measurements of call control parameters (e.g. drop-call rate and successful call-setup rate).

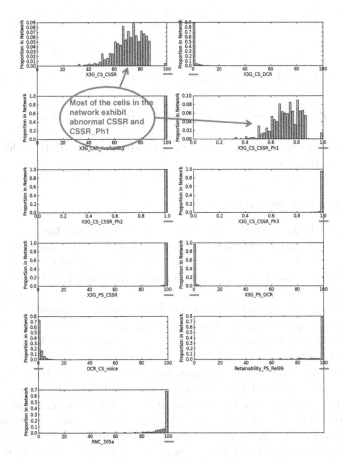

Fig. 3. Codebook of cluster #8 generated by the HDP experiment. The cluster is characterized by profiles of features, and each profile shows how the KPI value is distributed across the network within this cluster. The red underlines denote the normal value of each KPI. Under normal condition, most of the cells are supposed to be concentrated around normal values.

3.1 Cluster Analysis

We experimented with the HDP approach on all cells in the network with valid KPI data from 01/2013 to 03/2013. We trained the model on all timestamps from this time range to produce the cluster profiles, and tested on the same temporal and geographic scope to investigate the cluster semantics over the whole network. However, for real-time testing, data could span any time and geographic scope. We did not set the number of clusters, nor any constraints on how they were constructed, in advance. The final number of clusters automatically learned by our algorithm was 32. Figure 3 shows the codebook of cluster #8, with 11 KPIs. We use this particular cluster as an example because it shows one type of anomaly condition, corresponding to an abnormal network condition in mid-February. The predominant level of cluster #8 along the entire period of

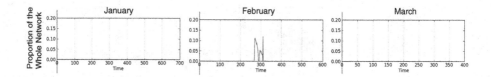

Fig. 4. The predominant level of cluster #8 as a time series.

time is shown in Fig. 4, which is generated by running the HDP model of Fig. 3 on all cells from the whole time span.

3.2 Cluster Interpretation

Since HDP modeling is an unsupervised learning technique, the generated clusters have no associated semantics (normal or abnormal). We thus implemented a simple classifier for the centroids, taking into consideration the characteristics of the KPIs. This classification can be achieved only for KPIs that are not supposed to increase (e.g., drop call rate) or decrease (e.g., call success rate). A cluster that has at least one BAD (any type) histogram is considered an abnormal centroid; otherwise it is normal. After analyzing all the clusters (where $\tau_1 = 0.05$ and $\tau_2 = 0.15$), our tool deemed 15 centroids as normal and 17 as abnormal. Visual inspection confirmed the labels.

Given the outcome of the interpretation module, we further classified the overall state of the network for February 2013, the month with more interesting dynamics. Figure 5 presents the portion of the network in an abnormal state for February 2013. We observe that overall 5–10% of the network exhibits some abnormalities, and then for some periods of time a larger portion of the network exhibits abnormalities. The diagnosis component will further identify the causes for the observed anomalies.

3.3 Diagnosis Results

When we applied PCE to the February 2013 rule set, we asked for instances of three different hypothetical conditions: (1) normal behavior, (2) weather-related degradation, and (3) configuration changes. Our query results are limited to predicates with a greater than 70% probability of being true. The results are presented in Fig. 7. The MLN used input regarding changes in the *wcel_angle* (antenna tilt angle) parameter for approximately 4,000 cells for each day in February, along with weather reports that

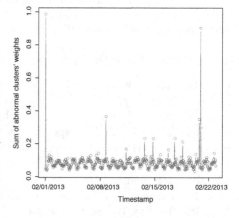

Fig. 5. Portion of the network in abnormal state for February 2013.

covered the whole area of interest for February 2013. The network found some anomalies for 10 February 2013. In Fig. 7, we can observe that not all changes in *wcel_angle* served as anomaly triggers, since only a smaller portion of the cells were affected. In our investigation, we also noticed a very interesting trend in the change, which can indicate an automated action (Fig. 6).

MLNs are generated in a semi-automated fashion for each timestamp. Figure 8 presents the input and output of PCE tool for February 10th 2013. We can observe that MLN receives input from topic modeling regarding the groups of cells that were deemed anomalous as well as input from the CM data as *wcel_angle* changes. Moreover, the MLN can also accommodate a visibility delay of up to n hours for which CM changes can propagate and affect cells ($n = 48$ in our experiments); hence, the time window in which cells are labeled as anomalous in Fig. 7. The output of the PCE tool consists of groups of cells

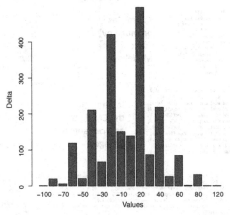

Fig. 6. Deltas between the after and before wcel_angle values for all the cells affected

affected by CM changes and normal groups of cells (no cell group was affected by weather events for that day).

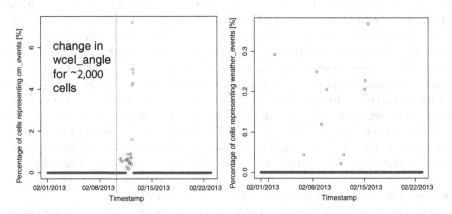

Fig. 7. Percentage of cells diagnosed as anomalous due to *wcel_angle* changes (left) and weather events (right). The dotted vertical line indicates when changes in *wcel_angle* started to occur.

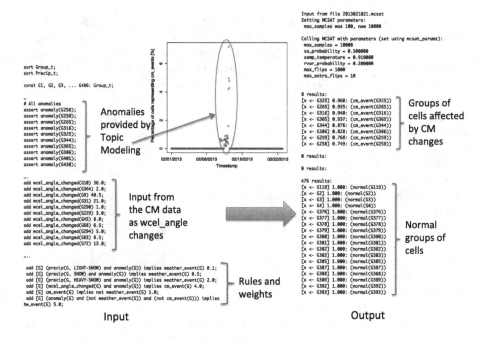

Fig. 8. Input and output of PCE tool for February 10th 2013

3.4   Computational Performance

We implemented the HDP models using the Gibbs sampling, which is a variant of Markov Chain Monte Carlo (MCMC) method that is based on previous sampling of hidden variables. Gibbs sampling is an iterative algorithm, which loops through all timestamps within the valid time range in each iteration. The number of iterations depends on the convergence of the algorithm, and is related to the number of available data. With the full dataset from January to March, the algorithm converged in 10 iterations. Let us denote the total number of timestamps as N, the average number of valid cells at each timestamp as M, the average number of topics at each timestamp as T, the number of global profiles as K, the number of KPIs as F, and the number of digitized bins for features as W. The complexity of topic sampling for each cell data is $O(KF)$, and the complexity of profile sampling for each topic is $O(KFW)$. Therefore, the total complexity for each Gibbs sampling iteration is $O(N(MKF + TKFW))$.

For the detection phase, the Gibbs sampling for computing the probabilities has the same complexity as training. However, the deployed system usually collects KPI data for one time point at a time ($N = 1$) and calls the evaluation process. For a small set of test data like this, the number of iterations to reach convergence is less than the training one, and the HDP evaluation process can respond in real time. On a Linux system with 2.27 GHz CPU, an iteration for the evaluation takes 2 s with a subset ($\sim$ 1000) of all cells. The evaluation process converged in 2 iterations.

An MLN description consists of "direct" predicates that correspond to observations and "indirect" predicates that are evaluated during the inference process. In contrast to conventional logic systems for which predicates can only be true or false, MLN predicates can be true with some probability. PCE uses an MCMC approach to inference, relying on sampling to estimate the probabilities of different indirect predicates in the system. Despite the theoretical worst-case complexity of MLN inference, the MCMC approach has distinct advantages for practical application. Our experiments exhibit running times on the order of 1 min for 486 PCA-derived cell groups and three segmented time intervals. In these experiments, the sampling parameter ranged from 1000 to 10000 runs, a range which appears appropriate for convergence.

4   Related Work

To the best of our knowledge, there are significant methods available for CM and PM analysis; however, none of them fully addresses the SON verification use case. Some of the existent work is only partially automated [2] with tool support for regular network reporting and troubleshooting, while others use disjoint analysis for PM and CM, requiring an additional linking mechanisms which is normally done manually. In terms of PM analysis, most work relates to detection of degradations in cell-service performance. If previous research addressed the cell-outage detection [11], cell-outage compensation [3] concepts and network stability and performance degradation [5,9] without relying on PM data, more recently, detection of general anomalies has been addressed based on PM data [6,7,12,17]. For CM analysis, Song et al. [15] propose formal verification techniques that can verify the correctness of self-configuration, without addressing the need for runtime verification.

5   Conclusions

This paper proposed a framework for SON verification that combines anomaly detection and diagnosis techniques in a novel way. The design was implemented and applied to a dataset consisting of KPI data collected from a real operational cell network. The experimental results indicate that our system can automatically determine the state of the network in the presence of CM changes and whether the CM changes negatively impacted the performance of the network. We are currently planning to expend our framework to more SON use cases such as troubleshooting and we are exploring other types of data that can be used in the diagnosis process. We envision that additional work is needed to integrate our framework with human operator input.

Acknowledgment. We thank Lauri Oksanen, Kari Aaltonen, Kenneth Nitz and Michael Freed for their contributions.

References

1. Probabilistic Consistency Engine. https://pal.sri.com/Plone/framework/Components/learning-applications/probabilistic-consistency-engine-jw
2. Transparent network performance verification for LTE rollouts, Ericsson whitepaper (2012). http://www.ericsson.com/res/docs/whitepapers/wp-lte-acceptance.pdf
3. Amirijoo, M., Jorguseski, L., Litjens, R., Schmelz, L.C.: Cell outage compensation in LTE networks: algorithms and performance assessment. In: 2011 IEEE 73rd Vehicular Technology Conference (VTC Spring), 15–18 May 2011
4. Blei, D., Ng, A., Jordan, M.: Latent dirichlet allocation. J. Mach. Learn. Res. **3**, 993–1022 (2003)
5. Bouillard, A., Junier, A., Ronot, B.: Hidden anomaly detection in telecommunication networks. In: International Conference on Network and Service Management (CNSM), Las Vegas, NV, October 2012
6. Ciocarlie, G.F., Lindqvist, U., Novaczki, S., Sanneck, H.: Detecting anomalies in cellular networks using an ensemble method. In: 9th International Conference on Network and Service Management (CNSM) (2013)
7. Ciocarlie, G.F., Lindqvist, U., Nitz, K., Nováczki, S., Sanneck, H.: On the feasibility of deploying cell anomaly detection in operational cellular networks. In: IEEE/IFIP Network Operations and Management Symposium (NOMS), Experience Session (2014)
8. Ciocarlie, G.F., Cheng, C.-C., Connolly, C., Lindqvist, U., Nováczki, S., Sanneck, H., Naseer-ul-Islam, M.: Managing scope changes for cellular network-level anomaly detection. In: International Workshop on Self-Organized Networks (IWSON) (2014)
9. D'Alconzo, A., Coluccia, A., Ricciato, F., Romirer-Maierhofer, P.: A distribution-based approach to anomaly detection and application to 3G mobile traffic. In: Global Telecommunications Conference (GLOBECOM) (2009)
10. Griffiths, T., Steyvers, M.: Finding scientific topics. Proc. Natl. Acad. Sci. **101**(suppl. 1), 5228–5235 (2004)
11. Mueller, C.M., Kaschub, M., Blankenhorn, C., Wanke, S.: A cell outage detection algorithm using neighbor cell list reports. In: Hummel, K.A., Sterbenz, J.P.G. (eds.) IWSOS 2008. LNCS, vol. 5343, pp. 218–229. Springer, Heidelberg (2008)
12. Nováczki, S.: An improved anomaly detection and diagnosis framework for mobile network operators. In: 9th International Conference on Design of Reliable Communication Networks (DRCN 2013), Budapest, March 2013
13. Richardson, M., Domingos, P.: Markov logic networks. Mach. Learn. **62**(1–2), 107–136 (2006)
14. Hämäläinen, S., Sanneck, H., Sartori, C. (eds.): LTE Self-Organising Networks (SON) - Network Management Automation for Operational Efficiency. Wiley, Chichester (2011)
15. Song, J., Ma, T., Pietzuch, P.: Towards automated verification of autonomous networks: A case study in self-configuration. In: IEEE International Conference on Pervasive Computing and Communications Workshops (2010)
16. Steyvers, M., Griffiths, T.: Probabilistic topic models. In: Landauer, T., McNamara, D.S., Dennis, S., Kintsch, W. (eds.) Handbook of Latent Semantic Analysis, pp. 427–448. Erlbaum, Hillsdale (2007)
17. Szilágyi, P., Nováczki, S.: An automatic detection and diagnosis framework for mobile communication systems. IEEE Trans. Netw. Serv. Manage. **9**, 184–197 (2012)
18. Teh, Y.W., Jordan, M.I., Beal, M.J., Blei, D.M.: Hierarchical dirichlet processes. J. Am. Stat. Assoc. **101**(476), 1566–1581 (2006)

Energy Awareness in Wireless Networks

On the Performance Evaluation of a Novel Offloading-Based Energy Conservation Mechanism for Wireless Devices

Constandinos X. Mavromoustakis[1(✉)], Andreas Andreou[2],
George Mastorakis[3], Athina Bourdena[3],
Jordi Mongay Batalla[4], and Ciprian Dobre[5]

[1] Department of Computer Science, University of Nicosia,
46 Makedonitissas Avenue, P.O. Box 24005
1700 Nicosia, Cyprus
mavromoustakis.c@unic.ac.cy
[2] Faculty of Computer Science and Technology, University of Cambridge,
William Gates Building, 15 JJ Thomson Ave,
Cambridge CB3 0FD, UK
aa773@cam.ac.uk
[3] Department of Informatics Engineering, Technological Educational Institute
of Crete, Estavromenos, 71500 Heraklion, Crete, Greece
gmastorakis@staff.teicrete.gr, bourdena@pasiphae.eu
[4] National Institute of Telecommunications,
Szachowa Str. 1, 04-894 Warsaw, Poland
jordim@interfree.it
[5] Faculty of Automatic Control and Computers, University Politehnica
of Bucharest, 313, Splaiul Independentei, 060042 Bucharest, Romania
ciprian.dobre@cs.pub.ro

Abstract. Mobile Cloud computing paradigm includes plenty of critical challenges that have to be addressed for allowing application execution on remote terminals/servers. An integral part of mobile cloud computing reliable service provision is the establishment of a methodology that will guarantee the efficient execution of applications in an energy-efficient way. This work elaborates on the evaluation of a framework, which utilizes a cooperative partial process execution offloading scheme, aiming at offering energy conservation. The scheme uses a dynamic scheduling methodology in order to guarantee that no intermittent execution will occur on mobile devices. In addition, this work proposes a partial scheduling offloading algorithm for failure-aware resource allocation in an energy-efficient manner, associating temporal execution-oriented metrics. The proposed framework is thoroughly evaluated through event driven simulation experiments, towards defining the efficiency of the proposed offloading policy in contrast to the energy consumption of wireless devices, as well as for the reliability degree offered.

Keywords: Mobile cloud · Offloading methodology · Reliability · Dynamic resource migration · Dependable mobile computing · Temporal execution-oriented metrics

© Institute for Computer Sciences, Social Informatics and Telecommunications Engineering 2015
R. Agüero et al. (Eds.): MONAMI 2014, LNICST 141, pp. 179–191, 2015.
DOI: 10.1007/978-3-319-16292-8_13

1 Introduction

The recent popularity of smartphones and tablets created a fertile ground of new application paradigms for mobile wireless communications. This growth has also been fueled by the numerous applications that run per wireless device, creating the need for a reliable and high performance mobile computing application environment. All wireless devices are prone to energy constraints that very often impair the reliability of the correct execution for the running application on the device. In this context, this paper proposes a mechanism, which takes into consideration the energy consumption of the wireless devices, while running an application. This mechanism exploits an offloading technique, in case where the resources need to be partially or in totally outsourced. This mechanism is utilized by end-terminals (server rack) and/or run on mobile devices, where resources are redundant. The offloading methodology is applied as a part of the application initiation (run start-up), in order to minimize the GPU/CPU efforts and the energy consumption of the mobile device that is running out of resources.

On the contrary with the utility computing, mobile cloud services should only be offered in a synchronous mode [1]. To this end, different parameterized metrics of both wireless devices and availability of offloading by other terminals and/or servers [1] should be taken into consideration. Traditional cloud computing models are considered as 'low offered' throughput models [2] and [3], more expensive, significantly offering low Quality of Service (QoS) or Quality of Experience (QoE) to the end-recipients (i.e. wireless end users). The limited processing power and bounded capacity availability of wireless devices, aggravate the execution and negatively affect the reliability offered to the user's mobile device, by causing capacity-oriented failures and intermittent execution. When there is lack of available resources (processing and/or memory-oriented), the wireless device may refer to a mobile cloud infrastructure as in [1] to enable precise execution through the resource/task migration mechanism. Within this context, a mechanism for ensuring that there is adequate processing power for executing the application of a wireless device and at the same time allowing the evaluation of the power consumption through the consideration of an energy-efficient application offloading, has not yet been extensively examined [4].

In this direction, a dynamic scheduling scheme for offloading resources from a wireless device to another mobile device is investigated in this work, to enable the improvement of the response quality and system's throughput, according to the partial or in-total execution, as well as the request deadline. The ultimate target of this work is to prevent long application execution requests, which will result in greater energy consumption for each wireless device and enable efficient manipulation of local (device), as well as cloud resources. Within this context, the proposed scheme minimizes the utilization of local (device's) resources to complete (GPU, CPU, RAM, battery consumption) and offers at the same time extensibility in the wireless devices lifetimes. To this end, this work presents an attempt to reduce the computational load of each wireless device so as to extend the lifetime of the battery. In addition, this study considers a partitionable parallel processing wireless system, where resources are partitioned and handled by a subsystem [1] that estimates and handles the resource offloading process. A certain algorithm is being proposed for the offloading process, in order to dynamically define the optimal resource manipulation in an energy-efficient manner.

The structure flow of this paper is as follows: related work is described in Sect. 2, by focusing in particular on the existing research approaches and the resource off-loading/migration scheduling policies. The proposed offloading scheme and the associated mechanisms for minimizing the energy consumption and maximizing the lifetime of each wireless device is presented in Sect. 3. The proposed scheme is based on the available resources of each mobile device, as well as on temporal device characteristics and server-based parameters along with communication-oriented diversities for establishing and maintaining the efficient resource manipulation onto each mobile device in an energy-efficient manner. In turn, Sect. 4 presents the results obtained, by conducting simulation experiments for the performance evaluation, focusing on the behavioral characteristics of the scheme along with the system's response and the energy consumption achieved. Finally, Sect. 5 elaborates on the research findings and discusses the potential future directions.

2 Related Work and Research Motivation

It is undoubtedly true that over the past few decades, several research efforts have been devoted to device-to-device or Machine-to-Machine communication networks, ranging from physical layer communications to communication-level networking challenges. Wireless devices can exchange resources on the move and can become data "Prosumers", by producing a great amount of content [2], while at the same time as content providers devices can consume the content. The research efforts for achieving energy efficiency on-the-move for wireless devices, trades-off the QoS [3] offered, by significantly reducing the performance with energy-hungry applications such as video, interactive gaming, etc. While energy-hungry applications are widely utilized by wireless devices, the explicit lifetime of devices should be extended, towards hosting and running the application in device's entire lifetime. In order to achieve resource management in wireless devices within the context of the cloud paradigm, efficient allocation of processor power, memory capacity resources and network bandwidth should be considered. To this end, resource management should allocate resources of the users and their respected applications, on a cloud-based infrastructure, in order to migrate some of their resources on the cloud [5]. Wireless devices are expected to operate under the predefined QoS requirements as set by the users and/or the applications' requirements. Resource management at cloud scale requires a rich set of resource and task management schemes that are capable to efficiently manage the provision of QoS requirements, whilst maintaining total system efficiency. However, the energy-efficiency is the greatest challenge for this optimization problem [3], along with the offered scalability in the context of performance evaluation and measurement. Different dynamic resource allocation policies targeting the improvement of the application execution performance and the efficient utilization of resources have been explored in [6]. Other research approaches related to the performance of dynamic resource allocation policies, had led to the development of a computing framework [7], which considers the countable and measureable parameters that will affect task allocation. Authors in [8] address this problem, by using the CloneCloud approach [9] of a smart and efficient architecture for the seamless use of ambient computation to augment mobile device applications, off-loading the right portion of their execution onto device clones, operating in a computational cloud. Authors in [9] statically partition service tasks and resources between client and server portions, whereas in a later stage the service is reassembled on the mobile device. The spine of the proposal in [9] is based on a cloud-augmented execution, using a cloned VM image as a powerful virtual device. This approach has many vulnerabilities as it has to take into consideration the resources of each cloud rack, depending on the expected workload and execution conditions (CPU speed, network performance). In addition, a computation offloading scheme is proposed in [10] to be used in cloud computing environments, towards minimizing the energy consumption of a mobile device, in order to be able to run certain/specified and under constrains application. Energy consumption has also been studied in [11], in order to enable computation offloading, by using a combination of 3G and Wi-Fi infrastructures. However, these evaluations do not maximize the benefits of offloading, as they are considered as high latency offloading processes and require low amount of information to be offloaded. Cloud computing is currently impaired by the latency experienced during the data offloading through a Wide Area Network (WAN). Authors in [1] and [11], elaborate on issues, where the devices carried by human beings are always considered as delay sensitive. The variability of this delay in turn impairs the QoS/QoE of the end-users.

Authors in [12] address the resource processing poverty for 'hungry' applications that require processing resources in order to run on a handheld device, while authors in [13] provide a resource manipulation scheme as a solution based on the failure rates of cloud servers in a large-scales datacenters. However, these criteria do not include servers' communications diversities in the communication process with mobile users' claims, as well as the available processing resources, the utilization of the device's memory, the remaining energy and the available capacity with the communication of each of the device with the closest –in terms of latency- cloud terminal. Research approaches in [14] and [15] have proposed different analytical models to address offloading computation and elaborate on offloading to offer energy conservation.

Within this context, this paper is making progress beyond the current state-of-the-art, by proposing an offloading resource mechanism, which is used in collaboration with an energy-efficient model proposed. The scheme uses an offloading methodology in order to guarantee that no intermittent execution will occur on mobile devices, whereas the application explicit runtime will meet the required deadlines to fulfil the QoS requirements. This paper also elaborates on the development of an offloading scenario, in which the scheduling policy for guaranteeing the efficiency in the execution of mobile users' tasks/applications can be achieved in an energy-efficient manner. The proposed framework is thoroughly evaluated through event driven simulation experiments in order to define the efficiency of the proposed offloading policy, in contrast to the energy consumption of the wireless devices, as well as for the reliability degree offered.

3   Offloading-Based Energy Conservation Mechanism for Wireless Devices

3.1   Device 'Live' Offloading Mechanism

As explored in [14], the offloading may be beneficial if large amounts of computation resources are required with the minimization of the communication delays in the end-to-end relay path. However, there are numerous applications and interactive actions of the mobile users that are draining the energy resources due to the continuous and full utilization of all computational resources of mobile devices. This work considers the scenario of the mobile user case, who uses high processing and computational power on the mobile application. The proposed scheme allows the computational processes that cannot be performed (executed/run) on the mobile device, to be offloaded onto cloud, or onto other neighboring mobile devices with redundancy in availability of resources (as opportunistically formed cloud). Applications that do not consume significant amounts of energy due to high processing power requirements (i.e. voice recognition, on-device gaming etc.) can be hosted and run on the mobile device of the end-user.

Authors in [16] performed a detailed analysis in real-time of the energy consumption of a smartphone, based on measurements of a physical device for different applications. It was shown that there are specific energy consuming components within the smartphone device that are contributing to the overall "short-run" of the device's power, with primary factor the high utilization of the processing power simultaneously with high transmission powers, exposed by the wireless interfaces of each device. Having considered the issues above, the proposed scheme allows low-consumption applications that run on the mobile device to be offloaded, if this may positively affect the energy consumption, according to the proposed methodology of the scheme and the algorithm designed that is shown in the next section. Due to the heterogeneity in the hardware of both mobile devices and the servers on the cloud that the resources will be potentially (based on the proposed scheme) offloaded, the proposed framework encompasses the execution environment volatility and considers the cloud servers' response time, in order to a-priori compare them and select the appropriate server, according to the best fit-case.

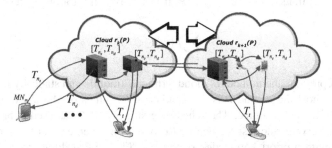

Fig. 1. Cloud configuration when a mobile device has no remaining resources to run an application, offloading resources on the cloud to achieve the best effort processing on-device power.

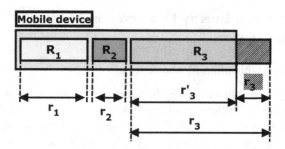

Fig. 2. Resource partitioning onto mobile device.

More specifically, this work considers the network-oriented parameters for bandwidth provisioning to achieve an acceptable resource offloading downtime (e.g., $\delta \leq 1.6\,s$ as the experimental process validates in [1]). To this end, from the network perspective, the modelled parameters can be expressed, for an offloading process *O for an* executable resource task O_{a_j}, as a 5-tuple given by:

$O_{a_j}(MN) = <n_s, T_{n_s}, T_{n_d}, BW, T_t>$ where n_s is the devices or cloud terminals that the a_j from *MN* device will be offloaded, T_{n_s} is the source location best effort access time, T_{n_d} is the destination's device or cloud's location best effort access time (time to access the resource) from the source, BW is the required connection bandwidth, T_t is the connection holding duration for the a_j executable resource task. In essence the work done in [1] considers the resource transfer time, by taking into account the volume of traffic that should be transferred to the destination node. The total data volume that will be transferred, if the request meets the BW criteria can be provided by BW × T_t. In this work, the typical values ranges that were utilized in our experimental processes were $1\,MB \leq BW \leq 15\,MB$ and $T_t = 2\,s + t_x, s = T_{n_s} + T_{n_d}$, where t_x is the time to process x-partitionable parts that are processed during the offloading process. Every executable resource task may have *x-partitions*, which in this work are considered as t_x partitioning parts/tasks where $1 \leq t_x \leq z*P$, where z is the number of different devices that the resource can be offloaded. Therefore, the number of tasks per executable resource task is limited to the number of terminals in the system. An executable resource can be shared and partitioned to $x_1, x_2, \ldots x_n$ and can be simultaneously processed with r sequential partitions, where $0 \leq r < z*P$, if and only if the following relation holds:

$$r + \sum_{i=1}^{n} p(x_i) \leq z * P \qquad (1)$$

where $p(x)$ represents the number of cloud terminals (mobile and statically located) that are needed to host the a_j, and P is the number of terminals on the cloud that will be hosting the offloaded resource. The scheduling strategy that was used is based on the Largest First Served/ Shortest Sequential Resource First Served and the service notations of [1] with a-priori knowledge of the $[T_n, T_{n_d}]$ service durations, as shown in Fig. 1.

3.2 Energy-Consumption Model Using Temporal Capacity Measurements

As the consumed power varies with traffic and depends on the variations of the signal characteristics, as well as on the traffic-aware measurements [17], it is desirable to minimize the amount of power consumption according to the resources that cannot 'run' on the mobile device or devices. To this end, the proposed scheme in this paper makes a progress beyond the current state-of-the-art, by elaborating on the association of the measurements of the partitionable tasks for two distinct cases: when resources can run on the device, but in order to achieve energy conservation they may be offloaded to a cloud or any other peer-neighboring device (so that the device that needs to run may potentially conserve energy); and the case that the device or devices cannot run the resources (as in Fig. 2) as the processing and memory requirements cannot support this execution. Thus, the measurable energy consumption can be evaluated according to the:

$$E_{r(a_j)} = E_c(a_j) \cdot \frac{C}{S_{a_j}} \forall C \in O_{a_j}, T_{n_s} < T_t, T_{n_d} < T_t \qquad (2)$$

In Eq. 2, parameter C is the number of instructions that can be processed within T_t, S_{a_j} is the processing time of the terminal that can host the offloaded executable task, provided that $T_{n_s} < T_t, T_{n_d} < T_t$ is satisfied, and $E_c(a_j)$ is the relative energy consumption in mW and it is expressed by:

$$E_c(r_i) = \frac{Cost_{c(r_i)}}{S_{c(r_i)}} \cdot W_c, \forall C \in O_{a_j} \qquad (3)$$

where S_c is the server's processing instruction speed for the computation resources, $Cost_c$ the resources' processing instruction cost for the computation resources, and W_c energy consumption of the device or server in mW.

Each mobile device examines if all neighboring 2-hops devices (via lookup table) can provide information about their offloading capabilities without affecting their energy status (thus without draining their energy to run other devices' resources). In addition, the closest cloud rack is considered if the relations exposed in (4) and (5) are not satisfied. Hence, for the neighboring devices within 2-hops vicinity coverage (based on the maximum signal strength and data rate model [1]) should stand:

$$\frac{Cost_{c(r_i)}}{S_{c(r_i)}} \cdot W_c \Big|^{r_i} > \frac{Cost_{c(r_i)}}{S_{c(r_i)}} \cdot W_c \Big|^{1,2..N} \qquad (4)$$

$$W_{r_i} > W_c \forall 1, 2, 3, \ldots N \qquad (5)$$

The energy consumption of each device should satisfy the Eqs. (4)–(5) for each of the resources (executable processes) running onto the device MN_{m-1} hosting the r_i, where $m-1$ represents the remaining devices from total m devices. Otherwise, the r_i with the maximum energy consumption is running in a partitionable manner to minimize the energy consumed by other peer-devices. These actions are shown in the steps of the proposed algorithm in table I.

The resource allocation will take place, towards responding to the performance requirements as in [1]. A significant measure in the system is the availability of memory and the processing power of the mobile-cloud devices, as well as the server-based terminals. The processing power metric is designed and used to measure the processing losses for the terminals that the r_i will be offloaded, as in Eq. 4, where is an application and T_k^j is the number of terminals in forming the cloud (mobile and static) rack that are hosting application, and $T_{a_j}(r)$ is the number of mobile terminals hosting process of the application across all different cloud-terminals (racks).

$$C_{a_j} = \frac{T_k^j}{\sum_k T_{a_j}(r)} \forall \min(E_c(r_i)) \in 1, 2, ..N \tag{6}$$

Equation 4 shows that if there is minimal loss in the capacity utilization i.e. $C_{a_j} \cong 1$ then the sequence of racks $T_{a_j}(r)$ are optimally utilized. The latter is shown through the conducted simulation experiments in the next section. The dynamic resource migration algorithm is shown in Table 1 with the basic steps for obtaining an efficient execution for a partitionable resource that cannot be handled by the existing cloud rack and therefore the migration policy is used to ensure that it will be continuing the execution. The continuation is based on the migrated policy of the partitionable processes that are split, in order to be handled by other cloud rack terminals and thus omit any potential failures. The entire scheme is shown in Table 1, with all the primary steps for off-loading the resources onto either MN_{m-1} neighbouring nodes or to server racks (as in [1] and [15]) based on the delay and resources temporal criteria.

Table 1 Dynamic Resource-based offloading scheme.

1: **Inputs:** MN_m, Location($[T_{n_x}, T_{n_d}]$), resources $r_1, r_2, r_3, ..r_i \forall MN_m$

2: for all Cloud devices that stands $r_1, r_2, r_3, ..r_i$ find the r_i that can be offloaded to run onto another device

3: for all MN_{m-1} do{

4:   while (T_t = TRUE) {

5:     while ($1 \le t_x \le z*P$)

6:       search for MN_{m-1} device that satisfies

$$\frac{Cost_{c(r_i)}}{S_{c(r_i)}} . W_c|^\eta > \frac{Cost_{c(r_i)}}{S_{c(r_i)}} . W_c|^{1,2..N}, W_\eta > W_c \forall 1, 2, 3, ...N$$

7:   offload ($r_i, MN_{k(i)}$) //to $MN_{k(i)}$ to execute resource (i)

8:     end **while**

9:     end **while** ($C_{a_j} \forall \min(E_c(r_i)) \in 1, 2, ..N) \&\&(E_c(r_i) = satisfied, \forall C \in O_{a_j})$)

10:   end **for**

11: end **for**

12:

4 Performance Evaluation Analysis, Experimental Results and Discussion

Performance evaluation results encompass comparisons with other existing schemes for offered throughput and reliability degree, in contrast to the energy conservation efficiency. The mobility model used in this work is based on the probabilistic Fraction Brownian Motion (FBM) adopted in [17], where nodes are moving, according to certain probabilities, location and time. Towards implementing such scenario, a common look-up application service for resource execution offloading is set onto each one of the mobile nodes MN_m. Topology of a 'grid' based network [1] was modeled, where each node can directly communicate with other nodes, if the area situated is in the same (3 × 3 center) rectangular area of the node. For the simulation of the proposed scenario, the varying parameters described in previous section were used, by using a two-dimensional network, consisting of nodes that vary between 10–180 (i.e. terminal mobile nodes) located in measured area, as well as five cloud terminals statically located on a rack. All measurements were performed using WLAN varying with different 802.11X specifications. During simulation the transfer durations are pre-estimated or estimated, according to the relay path between the source (node to offload resources) and the destination (node to host the executable resources).

The dynamic offloading scheme and the instant that takes place, is an important measure to estimate as well as the effectiveness of the proposed framework and the impact on the system. To this end, the total failed requests among nodes with the number of requests and with the number of mobile devices participating in the evaluated area, are shown in Fig. 3. Towards examining the impact of the different capacities, several sets of experiments were conducted using the presented resource

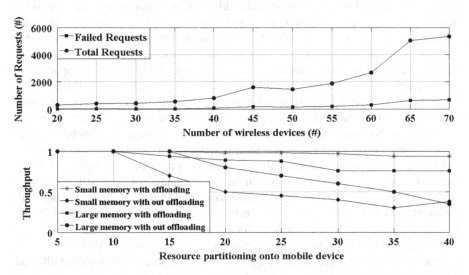

Fig. 3. Number of requests with the number of mobile devices participating in the evaluated area and throughput response with the mean number of executable resources that are partitioned per mobile device.

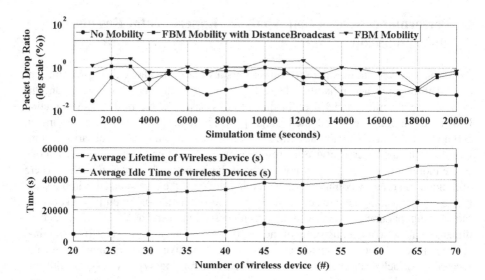

Fig. 4. Packet drop ratio of the proposed scheme for different mobility variations and no-mobility model over time and average lifetime for both active and idle time with the number of mobile devices.

offloading scheme. Large memory resources are executable resources/processes that are between 500 MB–1 GB, whereas small memory resources are executable processes that are hosting capacities between the range of 10–400 MB. The throughput response in contrast to the mean number of executable resources that are partitioned per mobile device is also shown in Fig. 3. The throughput response offered by the proposed scenario is greater for large files that are offloaded in partitionable parts onto other terminals on the cloud. Moreover, when utilizing the proposed framework, the small memory capacity requirements offer almost greater than 90 % for throughput response measurements. The packet drop ratio of the proposed scheme for different mobility variations and without mobility over time is shown in Fig. 4. It is important to emphasize that the proposed scheme scales well in the presence of FBM and even better when the FBM with distance broadcasting is applied. In addition, Fig. 4 presents the average lifetime for both active and idle time with the number of mobile devices.

Assuming that game-playing users are participating through their mobile devices utilizing game playing actions. These game playing actions require resources in GPU/CPU-level. These resource-constraints can be used as a measure to evaluate the efficiency offered by the proposed scheme under 'heavy limitations' and 'strict latencies'. Hence, the lifetime of each of the mobile device is an important metric for the evaluation of the overall performance of the scheme and the impact on nodes lifetime. Measurements in Fig. 5 were extracted for the total number of 180 mobile terminals that are configured to host interactive gaming applications, using Wi-Fi/WLAN access technology. The overall energy consumption for each mobile device for three different schemes in the evaluated area (for the interactive game playing draining resources) is shown in Fig. 5. The proposed scheme shows that it outperforms the scheme proposed in [1], as well as the scheme in [8] for the Wi-Fi/WLAN connectivity configuration.

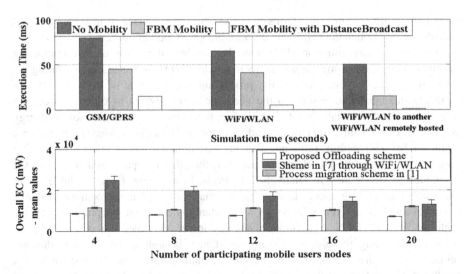

Fig. 5. Overall energy consumption for each mobile device for three different schemes in the evaluated area and execution time during simulation for nodes with different mobility patterns for three different schemes.

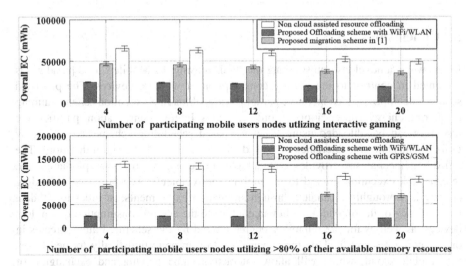

Fig. 6. Energy Consumption (EC) with the number of mobile users participating during an interactive game and Energy Consumption (EC) with the number of mobile users utilizing greater than 80 % of their resources.

When resources are offloaded, a critical parameter is the execution time, while nodes are moving from one location to another. In Fig. 5 the execution time during simulation for mobile nodes with different mobility patterns is also evaluated, for GSM/GPRS, Wi-Fi/WLAN and for communication within a certain Wi-Fi/WLAN to another Wi-Fi/WLAN remotely hosted. The latter scenario - from a Wi-Fi/WLAN to another Wi-Fi/WLAN- shows to exhibit significant reduction in terms of the execution time, whereas it hosts the minimum execution time through the FBM with distance broadcast mobility pattern.

The Energy Consumption (EC) with the number of mobile users participating during an interactive game (requirements in GPU/CPU) is shown in Fig. 6. During the interactive game-playing process, the processing requirements of each device dramatically increase. This results to the need for some devices to offload processing power into cloud terminals. In this regards, Fig. 6 presents the evaluation for the energy consumed (EC) for three schemes including a non-assisted cloud. Measurements were extracted for 150 mobile terminals that are configured to host interactive gaming applications. The proposed scheme outperforms the other compared schemes, with the associated EC to be kept in relatively low levels. In turn, Fig. 6 shows the EC with the number of mobile users utilizing greater than 80 % of their memory available resources for three different schemes. It is important to denote that the proposed scheme with the Wi-Fi/WLAN configuration enables lower EC than the other evaluated schemes, including the absence of any assistance through cloud. Devices that are utilizing greater than the 80 % of their computational resources are the best candidates to offload. Figure 6 shows that the EC is significantly minimized, by using the proposed scheme that utilizes the Wi-Fi/WLAN configuration, whereas it behaves almost the same with small number of mobile nodes, as well as with greater number of mobile nodes with lack of resources in the described scenario.

5   Conclusions

In this work, a novel task outsourcing mechanism using the Mobile Cloud paradigm is presented in contrast to the Energy consumption of wireless devices. The proposed scheme encompasses a cooperative partial process offloading execution scheme, aiming at offering energy conservation. In order to allow Energy conservation, partitionable resources can be offloaded using a latency-based scheduling scheme as well as by utilizing the state characteristics of each device (i.e. allowed execution duration). The offloading mechanism provides efficient cloud-oriented resources' exploitation and reliable task execution offered to the mobile end-recipients. The proposed offloading scheme is thoroughly evaluated through simulation experiments, in order to validate the efficiency of the offloading policy in contrast to the energy consumption of wireless devices, as well as for the reliability degree offered by the scheme. Future streams in our on-going research include the enhancement of an opportunistically formed federated mobile cloud, which will allow interactive game playing and exchanging of resources with strict resource constraints and streaming characteristics (delay-sensitive resource sharing) in a MP2P manner, on-the-move.

Acknowledgment. The work presented in this paper is co-funded by the European Union, Eurostars Programme, under the project 8111, DELTA "Network-Aware Delivery Clouds for User Centric Media Events".

References

1. Mousicou, P., Mavromoustakis, C.X., Bourdena, A., Mastorakis, G., Pallis, E.: Performance evaluation of Dynamic Cloud Resource Migration based on Temporal and Capacity-aware policy for Efficient Resource sharing. In: 16th ACM International Conference on Modeling, Analysis and Simulation of Wireless and Mobile Systems (MSWiM 2013), Barcelona, Spain (2013)
2. Abolfazli, S., Sanaei, Z., Ahmed, E., Gani, A., Buyya, R.: Cloud-based augmentation for mobile devices: motivation, taxonomies, and open challenges. IEEE Commun. Surv. Tutorials **16**(1), 337–368 (2013)
3. Dimitriou, C., Mavromoustakis, C.X., Mastorakis, G., Pallis, E.: On the performance response of delay-bounded energy-aware bandwidth allocation scheme in wireless networks. In: IEEE 2013 International Workshop on Immersive & Interactive Multimedia Communications over the Future Internet, organized in conjunction with IEEE International Communications Conference (ICC 2013), pp. 641–646, Budapest, Hungary (2013)
4. Miettinen, A.P., Nurminen, J.K.: Energy efficiency of mobile clients in cloud computing. In: 2nd USENIX Conference on Hot Topics in Cloud Computing. USENIX Association (2010)
5. Salehi, M.A., Javadi, B., Buyya, R.: Resource provisioning based on preempting virtual machines in distributed systems. Concurrency Comput. Pract. Exp. **26**(2), 412–433 (2013)
6. Slegers, J., Mitriani, I., Thomas, N.: Evaluating the optimal server allocation policy for clusters with on/off sources. J. Perform. Eval. **66**(8), 453–467 (2009)
7. Warneke, D., Kao, O.: Nephele: Efficient parallel data processing in the cloud. In: 2nd Workshop Many-Task Computing on Grids and Supercomputers, ACM, Portland, OR, USA (2009)
8. Chun, B., Ihm, S., Maniatis, P., Naik, M., Patti, A.: Clonecloud: Elastic execution between mobile device and cloud. In: 6th Conference on Computer systems of EuroSys (2011)
9. Chun, B.G., Maniatis, P.: Augmented smartphone applications through clone cloud execution. In: HotOS (2009)
10. Barbera, M.V., Kosta, S., Mei, A., Stefa, J.: To offload or not to offload? The bandwidth and energy costs of mobile cloud computing. Im: INFOCOM 2013, Turin, Italy (2013)
11. Cuervo, E., Balasubramanian, A., Cho, D., Wolman, A., Saroiu, S., Chandra, R., Bahl, P.: MAUI: making smartphones last longer with code offload. In: ACM International Conference on Mobile Systems, Applications, and Services, pp. 49–62, San Francisco, CA, USA (2010)
12. Satyanarayanan, M., Bahl, P., Caceres, R., Davies, N.: The case for vm-based cloudlets in mobile computing. Pervasive Computing **8**(4), 14–23 (2009)
13. Vishwanath, V.K., Nagappan, N.: Characterizing cloud computing hardware reliability. In: 1st ACM Symposium on Cloud Computing, pp. 193–204 (2010)
14. Kumar, K., Lu, Y.H.: Cloud computing for mobile users: can offloading computation save energy? Computer **43**(4), 51–56 (2010)
15. Papanikolaou, K., Mavromoustakis, C.X.: Resource and scheduling management in Cloud Computing Application Paradigm. In: Mahmood, Z. (eds.) Cloud Computing: Methods and Practical Approaches, pp. 107–132. Springer International Publishing, Heidelberg (2013)
16. Carroll, A., Heiser, G.: An analysis of power consumption in a smartphone. In: 2010 USENIX, Boston, MA, USA (2010)
17. Mavromoustakis, C.X., Dimitriou, C.D., Mastorakis, G.: On the real-time evaluation of two-level BTD scheme for energy conservation in the presence of delay sensitive transmissions and intermittent connectivity in wireless devices. Int. J. Adv. Netw. Serv. **6**(3&4), 148–162 (2013)

A Traffic Aware Energy Saving Scheme for Multicarrier HSPA+

Maliha U. Jada[1,2]([✉]), Mario García-Lozano[2], and Jyri Hämäläinen[1]

[1] Department of Communications and Networking, Aalto University, Espoo, Finland
{maliha.jada,jyri.hamalainen}@aalto.fi
[2] Department of Signal Theory and Communications, BarcelonaTech (UPC),
Barcelona, Spain
mariogarcia@tsc.upc.edu

Abstract. In the near future, an increase in cellular network density is expected to be one of the main enablers for the newly introduced challenging capacity goals. This development will lead to an increase in the network energy consumption. In this context, we propose an energy efficient dynamic scheme for HSDPA+ (High Speed Downlink Packet Access-Advanced) systems aggregating several carriers. In the proposed scheme the network adapts dynamically to the network traffic. The scheme evaluates whether node-B deactivation is feasible without compromising the user flow throughput. Furthermore, instead of progressive de-activation of carriers and/or node-B switch-off, we evaluate the approach where feasible combination of inter-site distance and number of carriers is searched to obtain best savings. The solution exploits the fact that re-activation of carriers might permit turning off the BSs earlier at relatively higher load than existing policies, which provides the highest energy saving. Remote electrical downtilt is also considered as a means to reduce the utilization of lower modulation and coding schemes (MCS) in the new extended cells. This approach promises significant energy savings when compared with existing policies - not only for low traffic hours but also for medium load scenarios.

Keywords: Multicarrier HSPA+ · Energy saving · Cell switch off · Carrier management

1 Introduction

Due to the increase in demand for mobile broadband services, mobile network vendors are preparing to 1000× mobile data traffic increase between 2010 and 2020 [1]. This is basically nothing new: According to [2] wireless capacity has already increased more than $10^6\times$ since 1957. Whereas 5× comes from improvements in modulation and coding schemes (MCS), 1600× increase is due to the reduction in cell sizes. It is widely accepted that the new 1000× objective comes hand in hand with a further reduction in distances between transmission points. Network densification allows higher spatial reuse and so it allows higher area

© Institute for Computer Sciences, Social Informatics and Telecommunications Engineering 2015
R. Agüero et al. (Eds.): MONAMI 2014, LNICST 141, pp. 192–206, 2015.
DOI: 10.1007/978-3-319-16292-8_14

spectral efficiency [bits/s/Hz/km^2]. On the other hand, considering that base stations (BSs) contribute the most to the energy consumption [3–5], future hyperdense network deployments may negatively impact on the operational costs and carbon emissions.

It has become an important goal for industry and academia to reduce the energy consumption of mobile networks over coming years. Energy efficiency is one of the key challenges in the evolution towards beyond fourth generation (4G) mobile communication systems. Yet, focusing in future systems is not enough since High Speed Packet Access (HSPA) and Long Term Evolution (LTE) will serve and coexist in the next decade, with probably a more tight integration in future releases of the standards [6]. In particular, HSPA is currently deployed in over 500 networks and it is expected to cover 90 % of the world's population by 2019 [7]. So it will serve the majority of subscribers during this decade while LTE continues its expansion in parallel and gain constantly large share of users.

Among the advantages in the latest releases of HSPA (HSPA+), multicarrier utilization is considered as an important performance booster [8] but it has not been extensively studied from the energy efficiency perspective so far. Given this, the focus of our study is in the reduction of energy consumption through dynamic usage of multiple carriers combined with the BS (node-B) switch-off.

Various BSs turn off strategies have been extensively studied as means for energy saving. Since cellular networks are dimensioned to correctly serve the traffic at the busy hour, the idea behind these strategies is to manage the activity of BSs in an energy-efficient manner while simultaneously being able to respond the traffic needs dynamically. Thus, the focus is on strategies where underutilized BSs are switched off during low traffic periods [3,9,10]. In order to guarantee coverage, switch-off is usually combined with a certain power increase in the remaining cells, but still providing a net gain in the global energy saving. However, this is not a straight-forward solution from practical perspective: common control channels also require a power increase and electromagnetic exposure limits must be fulfilled [11]. Remote electrical downtilt lacks these problems, it positively impacts the noise rise and received powers, and thus the coverage for common control channels could be expanded without increasing their power [12]. More recently, BS cooperation has also been proposed to cover the newly introduced coverage holes when switch-off is applied [13].

Algorithms that minimize the energy consumption do also have an impact on the system capacity. The work in [14] studies these conflicting objectives and investigates cell switching off as a multiobjective optimization problem. This tradeoff should be carefully addressed, otherwise the applicability of a particular mechanism would be questionable. Yet, not many works consider the capacity issue in detail and many of the contributions just introduce a minimum signal-to-noise plus interference ratio (SINR) threshold, which allows to compute a minimum throughput or outage probability to be guaranteed. Consequently, capacity does not remain constant before and after the switch off. Indeed [15] strongly questions the applicability of cell switch off combined with power increases as a feasible solution for many scenarios.

Very few works evaluate energy saving gains obtained by advantageous use of the multi-carrier option. The works [16] and [17] respectively deal with HSPA and LTE when two carriers are aggregated and evaluate whether the additional carrier can be de-activated when load decreases and BSs are not powered off.

The current work deals with the reduction of energy consumption in HSPA+ by means of a strategy that combines partial and complete node-B switch off with antenna downtilt. Utilization of multiple carriers is evaluated as an additional degree of freedom that allows more energy effective network layouts. The number of available carriers is dynamically managed in combination with full BS turn off. This last action provides the highest energy saving. For this reason, instead of progressive de-activation of carriers until the eventual node-B turn off, we evaluate the combination (inter-site distance, number of carriers) that gives best energy saving. The solution exploits the fact that *activation* of previously shut-off carriers might permit turning off the BSs earlier at relatively higher load than existing policies. The new scheme promises significant energy savings when compared with existing policies - not only for low traffic hours but also for medium load scenarios.

The paper is organized in five sections. Section 2 discusses about the advantages and possibilities of multicarrier HSPA+. Section 3 describes the system model. In Sect. 4 we discuss about the BS shut-off scheme and Sect. 5 is devoted to results and discussion. Conclusions are drawn in Sect. 6.

2   Multicarrier HSPA+

Latest releases of HSPA offer numerous upgrade options with features such as higher order modulation, multi-carrier operation and multiple input multiple output (MIMO). Evolution from initial releases is smooth since MCS update and multicarrier are unexpensive features [18]. These advantages have motivated 65 % of HSPA operators to deploy HSPA+, as recorded December 2013 [7].

HSPA has evolved from a single carrier system to up to 8-carrier aggregation (8C-HSDPA). So, multicarrier operation can be supported in a variety of scenarios depending on the release, indicated in Table 1 for the downlink (HSDPA). Note that the uplink just allows dual cell since release 9. Multicarrier capability being important advantage that affect the system performance [8, 19]:

- It scales the user throughput with the number of carriers reaching a top theoretical speed of 672 Mbps on the downlink when combining 8C-HSDPA with 4×4 MIMO.
- It also improves spectrum utilization and the system capacity because of the load balancing between carriers.
- Multicarrier operation improves the user throughput for a given load at any location in the cell, even at the cell edge, where channel conditions are not good. Note that other techniques such as high order modulation combined with high rate coding or the transmission of parallel streams with MIMO require high SINRs. Furthermore, it is well known that every order of MIMO

Table 1. Evolution of multicarrier HSDPA

Release	Name	Aggregation type
R8	Dual Cell HSDPA	2 adjacent downlink carriers
R10	Dual band HSDPA	2 carriers from 2 different bands
	4C-HSDPA	Up to 4 carriers from one or 2 bands
R11	8C-HSDPA	Up to 8 carriers from one or 2 bands

just doubles the rate only for users with good channel strength and no line of sight, while on cell edge MIMO just provides diversity or beamforming gain.

Regarding the availability of bandwidth, dual-carrier is currently mainstream solution. 8C-HSDPA is a likely option for scenarios in which bands from second generation (2G) systems are intensively refarmed or the use of unpaired bands as supplemental downlink is introduced [20]. On the other hand, scalable bandwidth for HSPA would also allow a more gradual refarming process and availability of new bandwidth pieces for aggregation [21]. However, the most interesting option would be a holistic management of the operator's spectrum blocks, with concurrent operation of GSM, HSPA and LTE that would allow an efficient resource sharing among technologies [22]. This multiaccess management can consider both quality of service (QoS) and energy efficiency as described herein.

3   System Model

The BS shut-off scheme presents a well-defined solution for a problem of underutilized network elements. However, as previously stated, this action should be performed without compromising the system performance. This section presents the model to assess coverage and capacity dimensioning.

3.1   Coverage Model

Let us assume the downlink of an HSPA+ system. At the link level, 30 modulation and coding schemes (MCS) are adaptively assigned by the scheduler based on the channel quality indicator (CQI) reported by user equipments (UEs). Given the channel condition and the available power for the high speed physical downlink shared channel (HS-PDSCH) $P_{\text{HS-PDSCH}}$, the scheduler selects the MCS that would guarantee a 10 % block error rate (BLER) for each user per transmission time interval (TTI).

The CQI reported on the uplink can be approximated using the SINR (γ) at the UE for the required BLER as [23]:

$$CQI = \begin{cases} 0 & \text{if } \gamma \leq -16 \text{ dB} \\ \lfloor \frac{\gamma}{1.02} + 16.62 \rfloor & \text{if } -16 \text{ dB} < \gamma < 14 \text{ dB} \\ 30 & \text{if } 14 \text{ dB} \leq \gamma \end{cases} \qquad (1)$$

Throughput of UE i depends on the number of allocated carriers and the SINR at each carrier f:

$$\gamma_i = \frac{\frac{N_{\text{code}}P_{\text{code}}}{L_{s,i}}}{(1-\alpha)\frac{P_{\text{tot}}-P_{\text{code}}}{L_{s,i}} + \sum_{j \neq s}(\bar{\rho}_j \frac{P_{\text{tot}}}{L_{j,i}}) + P_{\text{N}}}16, \qquad (2)$$

where:

- For the sake of clarity, index referring to carrier f has been omitted.
- $L_{j,i}$ is the net loss in the link budget between cell j and UE i for carrier f. Note that index s refers to the serving cell.
- P_{tot} is the carrier transmission power. Without loss of generality, it is assumed equal in all cells of the scenario.
- Intercell interference is scaled by neighbouring cell load $\bar{\rho}$ at f (carrier activity factor).
- P_{N} is the noise power.
- P_{code} is the power allocated per HS-PDSCH code. Note that all codes intended for a certain UE shall be transmitted with equal power [24]. So, considering an allocation of N_{code} codes and a power P_{CCH} for the control channels that are present in f, then $P_{\text{code}} = \frac{P_{\text{tot}}-P_{\text{CCH}}}{N_{\text{code}}}$.
- The orthogonality factor α models the percentage of interference from other codes in the same orthogonal variable spreading factor (OVSF) tree. Our model assumes classic Rake receivers, in case of advanced devices (Type 2 and Type 3/3i) [25], their ability to partially suppress self-interference and interference from other users would be modelled by properly scaling the interfering power [26].

At the radio planning phase, a cell edge throughput is chosen and the link budget is adjusted so that the corresponding SINR (CQI) is guaranteed with a certain target probability p_t. Given that both useful and interfering powers are log-normally distributed, the total interference is computed following the method in [27] for the summation of log-normal distributions. Coverage can be computed for any CQI and so, the boundary in which MCS k would be used with probability p_t can be estimated. This allows finding the area A_k in which k is allocated with probability $\geq p_t$. Figure 1 shows an example for a tri-sectorial layout with node-Bs regularly distributed using an inter-site distance (ISD) of 250 m. The shape of the final CQI rings largely depends on the downtilt and antenna pattern at each carrier. The example considers a multiband commercial antenna and optimized downtilt to maximize capacity.

Rings distribution will expand or reduce following the load in other cells. Figure 2 shows the pdf for CQIs 15 to 30 for 2, 4 or 8 carriers and the same cell load, and so different load per carrier $\bar{\rho}(f)$. Interference is spread among the different carriers and so the probability of allocating higher CQIs increases with the number of carriers. This has an impact on cell capacity and so, the next subsection is devoted to describe its model.

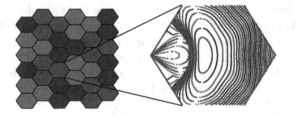

Fig. 1. Probabilistic CQI ring distribution in tri-sectorial regular layout.

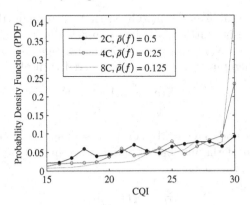

Fig. 2. CQI pdf for 2, 4 and 8 carriers and same cell load.

3.2   Capacity Model

The capacity model largely follows [28]. We define cell capacity as the maximum traffic intensity that can be served by the cell without becoming saturated. Note that the cell load is evenly distributed among all carriers, so for the sake of clarity and without loss of generality we will proceed the explanation assuming one single carrier and the index f will be omitted. A round robin scheduler is assumed, more refined options would just shift absolute throughput values.

Cell Capacity. Let's assume the traffic to be uniformly distributed in the cell. Data flows arrive according to a Poisson process with rate λ per area unit. Flow sizes are independent and identically distributed with average size $\mathrm{E}(\sigma)$. So, the cell load or fraction of time in which the scheduler must be active is:

$$\bar{\rho} = \lambda A_{\text{cell}} \times \sum_{k=1}^{30} \frac{\mathrm{E}(\sigma)}{c_k} p_k \leq 1, \tag{3}$$

where A_{cell} is the cell area, c_k is the code rate associated to MCS k, and p_k is the probability of using MCS k, $p_k = A_k/A_{\text{cell}}$. Since the cell load is bounded to one, the maximum throughput that can be served ($\bar{\rho} = 1$), or cell capacity is:

$$\bar{C} = \left(\sum_{k=1}^{30} \frac{p_k}{c_k} \right)^{-1}. \tag{4}$$

At any given load, the observed throughput (served) would be given by $\bar{\rho} \times \bar{C}$.

Flow Throughput. Actions to provide energy savings should not compromise the QoS and so the user flow throughput should not been altered. Hence, this has been used as performance metric. Since the scheduler is shared among the users in the cell, serving time depends on the cell load and allocated MCS. So the contribution to the cell load from users at A_k (fraction of time that should be allocated by the scheduler) is given by

$$\bar{\rho}_k = \frac{\lambda A_k \times \mathrm{E}(\sigma)}{c_k}. \tag{5}$$

It is immediate that $\bar{\rho} = \sum_k \bar{\rho}_k$. Given that all users in the cell share the same scheduler, by using Little law's the mean flow duration t_k for a user in A_k can be computed $t_k = N_k / \lambda A_k$ where N_k is the average number of users in A_k. Then the flow throughput τ_k for users being served with MCS k is:

$$\tau_k = \frac{\mathrm{E}(\sigma)}{t_k} = \frac{\lambda A_k \times \mathrm{E}(\sigma)}{N_k}, \tag{6}$$

Considering the underlaying Markov process [28], it can be found the stationary distribution of the number of active users in each A_k and its average value, $N_k = \frac{\bar{\rho}_k}{1-\bar{\rho}}$, which yields:

$$\tau_k = c_k(1 - \bar{\rho}), \tag{7}$$

and the average flow throughput at cell level:

$$\bar{\tau} = \sum_{k=1}^{30} p_k c_k (1 - \bar{\rho}). \tag{8}$$

where $\bar{\rho}$ captures the own cell load and p_k is affected by the load in neighbouring cells, which modifies SINR values, CQI rings and so A_k values $\forall k$.

4   Node-B Shut Off Scheme and Energy Model

At medium load levels, it is not possible to just shut off BSs without user throughput degradation. On the other hand, at this stage some carriers might have already been de-activated due to underutilization or could even be obtained from other low loaded systems if radio resources are jointly managed. The transition of a network configuration (in terms of ISD and active number of carriers) takes place at a certain load threshold. This load threshold depends upon the possibility of deactivating or reactivating specific number of carriers, and the number of BSs that could remain active or could be shutoff respectively, maintaining the requested average flow throughput. Any shut off is followed by an update of downtilt angles in remaining cells to maximize capacity under the new conditions, and so the use of highest possible MCS.

After performing node-B shut off, the higher load of the new expanded cells is again evenly distributed over the total frequency resources. This high load

Table 2. Evaluated scenarios.

	Scenario 1	Scenario 2	Scenario 3
Targeted $\bar{\tau}$	5.76 Mbps	21.80 Mbps	60.53 Mbps

includes the user traffic of the switched off node-Bs, which has to be accommodated by the remaining active ones. Considering v as the ratio $\text{ISD}^{\text{new}}/\text{ISD}^{\text{initial}}$ and that cell area A_{cell} is proportional to the cell square radius, from (3), the relation between the cell load with new ISD $\bar{\rho}^{\text{new}}$ and with initial ISD $\bar{\rho}^{\text{initial}}$ is given by,

$$\bar{\rho}^{\text{new}} = v^2 \times \bar{\rho}^{\text{initial}}. \tag{9}$$

Although the use of more carriers will account for a certain increase in energy consumption, the saving for switching off some BSs is much higher.

The metric used for the analysis of energy consumption is energy consumed per unit area (E/A). Assuming an entire parallel system at the node-B to handle each carrier, the energy consumed per unit area (kWh/km^2) is given as [4,16,29]:

$$E/A = \frac{N_{\text{site}} \cdot N_{\text{sector}} \cdot N_{\text{car}} \cdot [P_{\text{oper}} + (\bar{\rho}(f) \cdot P_{\text{in}})] \cdot T}{A_{\text{tot}}}, \tag{10}$$

where, N_{site}, N_{sector}, N_{car} are the number of sites, sectors per site and carriers respectively. P_{oper} is the operational power which is the load independent power needed to operate the node-B. On the other hand, P_{in} is the power consumed to eventually obtain the required power at the antenna connector. Finally, T is the time duration the particular load remains in the piece of network under study and A_{tot} is the total evaluated area containing N_{site} sites. Any change in N_{site} and/or N_{car} implies the corresponding update in $\bar{\rho}(f)$.

5 Results

In order to quantify the gains that can be achieved by an intelligent joint management of carriers and node-Bs, the system performance is evaluated in terms of average flow throughput ($\bar{\tau}$). Three cases have been evaluated: 2, 4 and 8 carriers are initially used to serve an aggregated cell load of 1. This load is evenly distributed among the carriers, $\bar{\rho}(f) = 0.5$, 0.25, and 0.125. Given this, three scenarios are defined considering the $\bar{\tau}$ value to be respected (Table 2).

The reference network has node-Bs regularly deployed and considering an $\text{ISD} = 250$ m. Therefore after a first shut off, the new ISD would be 500 m, and a second implies $\text{ISD} = 750$ m. Other network parameters are provided in Table 3.

Figure 3 represents the power consumption per unit area for decreasing cell load values and showing the transition points that should be used to guarantee the target user flow throughput after the network update. In each subplot four cases are represented:

Table 3. Network parameters

Parameter	Value
Operating bands	2100 MHz, 900 MHz
Inter-Site distances	250 m, 500 m, 750 m
Number of sites, for each ISD	108, 27, 12
Optimum downtilt angles, for each ISD	19.5°, 12.5°, 11.5°
Macro BS transmission power	20 W
Transmission power per user	17 W
Control overhead	15 %
BS antenna gain	18 dB
Body loss	2 dB
Cable and connection loss	4 dB
Noise power	-100.13 dBm
Propagation model	Okumura-Hata
Shadow fading std. deviation	8 dB
Cell edge coverage probability	0.99

- **Initial:** Power consumption under the initial network configuration, without changes. It can be seen that it just depends on the system load and so the power consumption is just slightly reduced.
- **BSO:** Base station shut off. Classic model in which node-Bs are successively shut off whenever the load allows to still keep the target flow throughput.
- **CSO:** Carrier shut off. Generalization of the DC-HSDPA case in [16], carriers are progressively shut off with load reduction.
- **JM:** Joint management. The proposal of the current work. Power off of BSs and carriers are jointly managed and re-activation of carriers is a valid option if that justifies earlier full BSs shut off and so a net energy saving.

Each tag in the plot shows the transition points in terms of (ISD, number of active carriers). Since the load is progressively reduced, the pictures should be read from right to left. For example, for the BSO case in Scenario 1, the transition points evolve as $(250, 2) \rightarrow (500, 2) \rightarrow (750, 2)$, note how the last case can only be implemented for cell loads of 10 %, meaning a 5 % of load per carrier.

The joint management allows earlier BS shut off and transition points fall below the other options, thus having clearly less power consumption without performance degradation. It can be seen how JM allows using ISD = 750 m as soon as the cell load falls below 0.8. For Scenario 2, ISD can be increased from 250 to 500 for high loads, and 750 m can be used once the load falls below 0.5. Scenario 3 is the most restrictive since it starts with the maximum possible carriers at the current HSPA+ standard. So there is less flexibility with respect to the other cases and the savings are just slightly better. For illustrative purposes, it has been included the off-standard case in which up to 10 carriers are used,

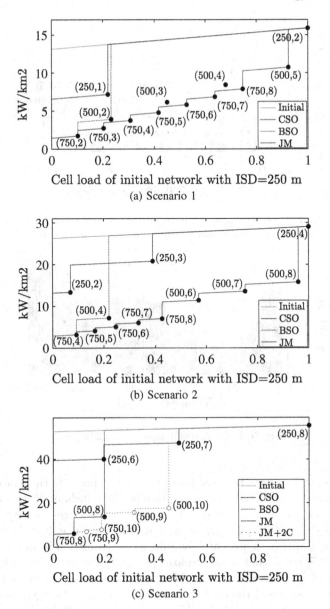

Fig. 3. Power consumption per unit area for decreasing cell load values. Transition points indicate the pair (ISD, number of carriers) to be used.

it can be seen how energy savings are again important. This way, multiaccess energy saving mechanisms that manage the pool of resources among several systems would make the most of each system load variations.

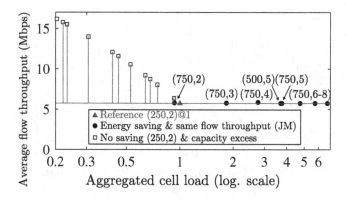

Fig. 4. Transition of cell configuration from initial network setup (scenario 1) to new setups at specific load values and maintaining the QoS requirements (5.75 Mbps).

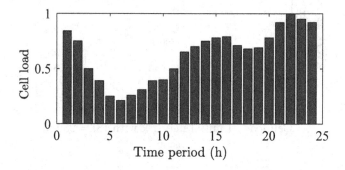

Fig. 5. HSDPA traffic profile over 24h [16].

It is important to note that the horizontal axis represents the equivalent cell load that would be obtained if the network remained unchanged. But obviously, after carrier and/or node-B switch off, the cell load changes. For example, initially the load is 1 (0.5 per carrier) and it is not until it is reduced to 0.92 that important energy savings are possible, so we transition from $(250, 2)@0.92$ to $(500, 5)@3.7$, recall that since the load per carrier is bounded to 1, the final aggregated cell value can be > 1. Besides, it is clear that the cell load increases due to its expansion and the new users to be served, but the QoS is respected, since both $(250, 2)@1$ and $(500, 5)@3.7$ provide the same flow throughput.

In order to illustrate how load evolves with every change, Fig. 4 represents the average flow throughput as a function of the aggregated cell load for each configuration proposed by JM (solid symbols). Note the logarithmic scale in the horizontal axis to improve readability. Following Fig. 3a, their evolution is as follows: $(250, 2)@1 \rightarrow (500, 5)@3.7 \rightarrow (750, 8)@6.72 \rightarrow (750, 7)@5.74$ and so on. If no energy savings mechanisms are implemented, in other words if we remain with the dense node-B deployment, an excess in capacity would be obtained due to load decrement. These situations are represented by empty symbols.

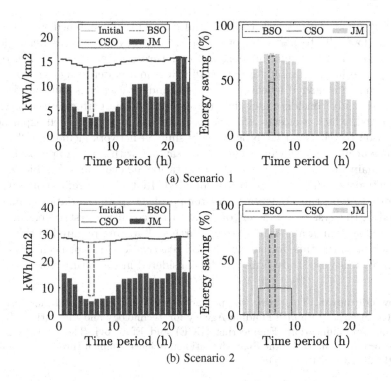

Fig. 6. Comparison between energy savings (%) of BSO, CSO and JM.

Given the previous results, in the following we consider a realistic profile of daily HSDPA traffic (load) [16] (Fig. 5) and evaluate energy consumption and corresponding savings along time.

Figure 6 represents results for scenarios 1 and 2. In case of Scenario 1, the total energy saving percentage is 45.4 % with JM, whereas it is just 2.8 % with BSO and 1.8 % with CSO. For Scenario 2, gains increase up to 55.8 % for JM, and 2.9 %, 5.9 % for BSO and CSO respectively. Scenario 3 had an equal saving of just 3.5 % in CSO and JM, with no possible gain with BSO. As previously mentioned this is because scenario 3 is very restrictive and requires a flow throughput of 60.53 Mbps. In the hypothetical off-standard case with up to 10 available carriers, energy savings with JM would reach 19.9 %. From Fig. 6 it is also noticeable how small reductions in the load can lead to important savings as it happens with cell load values around 60 %. So we can conclude that even at mid-high values, interesting savings are possible when applying the JM approach.

6 Conclusions

In this paper we investigated the potential energy savings by shutting off the BSs through the dynamic use of multiple carriers in HSDPA. We have proposed an energy saving scheme in which fewer or additional carriers have been used depending upon the network traffic variations. This is combined with remote electrical downtilts to partially cope with the use of a higher number of lower MCSs. Instead of just guaranteeing a power threshold at the cell edge, or an outage probability threshold for data traffic, it is more interesting to ensure that QoS remains unchanged whenever a node-B and/or carrier is shut-off, for this reason the study considers user flow throughput as the performance metric to be respected, which is closely affected by load variations due to cell expansions. Comparison to schemes that progressively shut off network elements (BSO and CSO) has been done, showing clear energy savings with the JM approach.

The main challenge to make the adaptation efficient and flexible is that load fluctuations should be correctly followed. Reiterative traffic patterns can be assessed along time but abnormal temporal or spatial variations could be included in the system by means of a pattern recognition system, e.g. a fuzzy logic based system or a neural network. Further efforts are required in this direction. Moreover, the time for carrier and BS reactivation has not been taken into account for this case study. This will be considered in the future work.

Acknowledgments. This work was prepared in EWINE-S project framework and supported in part by Finnish Funding Agency for Technology and Innovation (Tekes), European Communications Engineering (ECE) and Efore oyj. The work by Mario García-Lozano is funded by the Spanish National Science Council through the project TEC2011-27723-C02-01 (ERDF).

References

1. Andrew, R.: 2020: The Ubiquitous Heterogeneous Network - Beyond 4G. ITU Kaleidoscope, NSN, Cape Town (2011). http://www.itu.int/dms_pub/itu-t/oth/29/05/T29050000130001PDFE.pdf
2. Chandrasekhar, V., Andrews, J., Gatherer, A.: Femtocell networks: a Survey. IEEE Commun. Mag. **46**(9), 59–67 (2008)
3. Marsan, M., Chiaraviglio, L., Ciullo, D., Meo, M.: Optimal energy savings in cellular access networks. In: IEEE International Conference on Communication Workshops (ICC Workshops), Dresden, pp. 1–5 (2009)
4. Jada, M., Hossain, M.M.A., Hämäläinen, J., Jäntti, R.: Impact of femtocells to the WCDMA network energy efficiency. In: 3rd IEEE Broadband Network and Multimedia Technology (IC-BNMT), Beijing, pp. 305–310 (2010)
5. Jada, M., Hossain, M.M.A., Hämäläinen, J., Jäntti, R.: Power efficiency model for mobile access network. In: 21st IEEE Personal, Indoor and Mobile Radio Communications Workshops (PIMRC Workshops), Istanbul, pp. 317–322 (2010)
6. Yang, R., Chang, Y., et al.: Hybrid multi-radio transmission diversity scheme to improve wireless TCP performance in an integrated LTE and HSDPA networks. In: 77th IEEE Vehicular Technology Conference (VTC Spring), Dresden, pp. 1–5 (2013)
7. 4G Americas: White Paper on 4G Mobile Broadband Evolution: 3GPP Release 11 & Release 12 and Beyond. Technical report (2014)
8. Johansson, K., Bergman, J., et al.: Multi-carrier HSPA evolution. In: 69th IEEE Vehicular Technology Conference (VTC Spring), Barcelona (2009)

9. Gong, J., Zhou, S., Niu, Z., Yang, P.: Traffic-aware base station sleeping in dense cellular networks. In: 18th International Workshop on Quality of Service (IWQoS), Beijing, pp. 1–2 (2010)
10. Niu, Z.: TANGO: traffic-aware network planning and green operation. IEEE Wirel. Commun. **18**(5), 25–29 (2011)
11. Chiaraviglio, L., Ciullo, D., et al.: Energy-efficient management of UMTS access networks. In: 21st International Teletraffic Congress (ITC), Paris, pp. 1–8 (2009)
12. Garcia-Lozano, M., Ruiz, S.: Effects of downtilting on RRM parameters. In: 15th IEEE International Symposium on Personal, Indoor and Mobile Radio Communications (PIMRC), Barcelona, vol. 3. pp. 2166–2170 (2004)
13. Han, F., et al.: Energy-efficient cellular network operation via base station cooperation. In: IEEE International Conference on Communications (ICC), Ottawa, pp. 4374–4378 (2012)
14. González G.D., Yanikomeroglu, H., Garcia-Lozano, M., Ruiz, S.: A novel multiobjective framework for cell switch-off in dense cellular networks. In: IEEE International Conference on Communications (ICC), Sydney, pp. 2647–2653 (2014)
15. Wang, X., Krishnamurthy, P., Tipper, D.: Cell sleeping for energy efficiency in cellular networks: is it viable?. In: IEEE Wireless Communications and Networking Conference (WCNC), Paris, pp. 2509–2514 (2012)
16. Micallef, G., Mogensen, P., et al.: Dual-cell HSDPA for network energy saving. In: 71st IEEE Vehicular Technology Conference (VTC Spring), Taipei, pp: 1–5 (2010)
17. Chung, Y.-L.: Novel energy-efficient transmissions in 4G downlink networks. In: 3rd International Conference on Innovative Computing Technology (INTECH), London, pp. 296–300 (2013)
18. Borkowski, J., Husikyan, L., Husikyan, H.: HSPA evolution with CAPEX considerations. In: 8th International Symposium on Communication Systems, Networks & Digital Signal Processing (CSNDSP), Poznan (2012)
19. Bonald, T., Elayoubi, S.E., et al.: Radio capacity improvement with HSPA+ dual-cell. In: IEEE International Conference on Communications (ICC), Kyoto (2011)
20. 3GPP: RP-140092 - Revised Work Item: L-band for Supplemental Downlink in E-UTRA and UTRA. Technical report (2014). http://www.3gpp.org/
21. 3GPP: TR 25.701 v12.1.0 (Release 12) - Study on scalable UMTS Frequency Division Duplex (FDD) Bandwidth. Technical report (2014). http://www.3gpp.org/
22. NSN: Answering the Network Energy Challenge (whitepaper). Technical report (2014)
23. Brouwer, F., de Bruin, I., et al.: Usage of link-level performance indicators for HSDPA network-level simulations in E-UMTS. In: International Symposium on Spread Spectrum Techniques and Applications (ISSTA), Sydney, pp. 844–848 (2004)
24. 3GPP: TR 25.214 v11.8.0 (Release 11) - Physical layer procedures (FDD). Technical Specification (2014). http://www.3gpp.org/
25. 3GPP: TR 25.101 v12.3.0 (Release 12) - User Equipment (UE) Radio Transmission and Reception (FDD). Technical Report (2014). http://www.3gpp.org/
26. Rupp, M., Caban, S., et al.: Evaluation of HSDPA and LTE: From Testbed Measurements to System Level Performance. Wiley, New York (2011)
27. Beeke, K.: Spectrum Planning - Analysis of Methods for the Summation of Log-Normal Distributions. EBU Technical Review, no. 9 (2007)

28. Bonald, T., Proutière, A.: Wireless downlink data channels: user performance and cell dimensioning. In: Annual International Conference on Mobile Computing and Networking (MOBICOM), San Diego, CA (2003)
29. Arnold, O., Richter, F., Fettweis, G., Blume, O.: Power consumption modeling of different base station types in heterogeneous cellular networks. In: Future Network and Mobile Summit, Florence, pp. 1–8 (2010)

Enabling Low Electromagnetic Exposure Multimedia Sessions on an LTE Network with an IP Multimedia Subsystem Control Plane

Joël Penhoat[1]([✉]), Ramón Agüero[2], Fabien Heliot[3], and Milos Tesanovic[4]

[1] Orange Labs, Lannion, France
joel.penhoat@orange.com
[2] Universidad de Cantabria, Santander, Spain
ramon@tlmat.unican.es
[3] University of Surrey, Surrey, UK
fheliot@surrey.ac.uk
[4] Fujitsu Laboratories of Europe Ltd, Hayes, UK
milos.tesanovic@uk.fujitsu.com

Abstract. Most existing work on electromagnetic exposure reduction has focused on developing physical layer techniques and solutions to lower the power received and emitted by the user terminals. In this paper, we propose a novel cross-layer approach for reducing the electromagnetic exposure in LTE network by combining techniques belonging to the link and transport layers, while ensuring an acceptable Quality of Experience of a video application. We propose to categorize the RLC frames into critical and non-critical ones and to decrease the number of retransmissions for non-critical ones. In turn, this will reduce the radiated power, i.e. exposure. We also propose an enhanced 3GPP compliant architecture for accommodating our reduced exposure approach.

Keywords: Electromagnetic exposure · Quality of Experience · IP Multimedia Subsystem · LTE · H.264/AVC

1 Introduction

Public concerns about the potential health risk of being exposed to radio communication devices are on the rise given that radio waves produced by radio telecommunication networks are increasingly ubiquitous in peoples daily environment. Even though international standards [1] have established thresholds and guidelines on exposure limits, the debate over the harmfulness of electromagnetic exposure is far from being over; for instance, a recent study in [2] highlighted that several health risk assessments, which were carried out by various scientific groups, came up with divergent conclusion regarding the harmfulness level of radio telecommunications waves. To respond to the public concerns

© Institute for Computer Sciences, Social Informatics and Telecommunications Engineering 2015
R. Agüero et al. (Eds.): MONAMI 2014, LNICST 141, pp. 207–216, 2015.
DOI: 10.1007/978-3-319-16292-8_15

about the potential health risk due to electromagnetic exposure, the European Commission launched the LEXNET project [3] whose two main objectives are: (1) to define a metric for accurately measuring the exposure, as well as; (2) to study strategies for reducing such exposure without jeopardizing the quality of experience (QoE) perceived by the end-users.

The electromagnetic exposure can be decomposed into two contributions: the downlink and uplink exposures. The downlink exposure (far-field) is the exposure to radio access elements (base stations, access points) and it is linked to the power density (in W/m^2) received by the terminals. The uplink exposure (near-field) comes from the exposure to the terminal itself, which increases with the emitted power. Consequently, there exist two main types of metrics to evaluate the exposure of a whole population. The first type is related to near-field exposure (uplink), which focuses on measuring the exposure induced by telecommunications devices, like laptops, tablets or smartphones, and is expressed in terms of the specific absorption rate (SAR). The SAR is defined as the absorbed energy by the human body (in W/kg) and is calculated either on the whole human body or on ten grams of tissue. They are usually context-dependent, since they depend on the power emitted by the terminals, the application that is being used, the power received from the radio access points, the morphology of the users, and the position of the terminals relative to the users body. The second group of metrics considers the exposure induced by far-field sources (downlink), mostly caused by base stations, and are used to measure the intensity of the electric field (in V/m).

The exposure index that is being proposed within the LEXNET project considers the correlation between the two aforementioned types of metrics, which reflect the duality between downlink and uplink. Indeed, there is a clear relationship between the power emitted from personal devices and the power received by them: the closer a terminal is to its base station, the lower the emitted power and the higher the received power.

In this paper, our objective is to tackle the second main objective of the LEXNET project, i.e. reducing the exposure induced by wireless networks while keeping an acceptable QoE, by proposing a novel IP architecture for multimedia services over long term evolution (LTE) systems. In Sect. 2, existing works on the reduction of the electromagnetic exposure in wireless systems are first outlined. Section 3 introduces our scenario of interest, i.e. multimedia service (video transmission) over LTE, whereas, Sect. 4, discusses the issues and opportunities of modifying the existing IP architecture for reducing uplink electromagnetic exposure. Then, in Sect. 5 we propose a novel cross-layer solution to reduce the exposure in LTE networks, by categorizing the RLC frames (critical vs. non-critical) and decreasing the number of retransmissions for non-critical ones. We also propose an enhanced 3GPP compliant architecture that can be used to implement our reduced exposure solution. Section 6 draws the main conclusions of this work and outlines future works, in particular how the proposed scheme will be evaluated.

2 Existing Works on the Reduction of the Electromagnetic Exposure

As was mentioned earlier, LEXNET proposes a metric to assess the total exposure induced by telecommunication networks [4]. The metric, named Exposure Index (in $\frac{J \cdot kg^{-1}}{h}$), gathers both the average power emitted by the personal devices and the average power density received by these devices. It can be therefore seen as the combination of the exposures induced by the access points and the personal devices of the telecommunication networks located within the same geographical area. As previously mentioned, the assessment, done at different periods of the day, takes into account the characteristics of the applications used by the users, the particularities of the telecommunication networks, the morphology of the users and the position of the terminals relative to the users.

As far as exposure reduction is concerned, it has been shown in [5] that using lower frequency bands in universal mobile telecommunication systems (UMTS) can reduce the EM radiation density of a BS by about 13 dB. In 2010, Kelif et al. [6] showed that it is possible to decrease the downlink exposure (power density) by a factor of two without jeopardizing the Quality of Service of a LTE network, by increasing the number of base stations in an area. Consequently, exposure to electromagnetic fields can be reduced by deploying small-cells. More recently, in 2014, Habib et al. [7] have demonstrated that it is possible to reduce the Exposure Index in a heterogeneous LTE network, comprising both macro- and small-cells, by extending the coverage of a number of small-cells located at the edges of a macro-cell. The rationale of their solution is to off-load the users located at the edge of the macro-cell towards the small-cells, in order to decrease their uplink transmissions. Other techniques based on SAR shielding have also been proposed in the literature [8] for reducing the uplink exposure by using special material inside communication devices. Up to date, most of the works on exposure reduction has focused on physical layer techniques and solutions to lower the power received and emitted by the user terminals. In contrast, we propose here a scheme for reducing the electromagnetic exposure by combining techniques belonging to the link and transport layers.

3 Scenario of Interest

We consider (see Fig. 1) the typical architecture of a LTE network. The control plane relies on the IP Multimedia Subsystem [9], which uses session initiation protocol (SIP) to control the different multimedia sessions [10]. In the control plane, the service centralization and continuity application server [11] ensures the continuity of multimedia sessions at the wireless devices.

In the scope of this work, we will focus on a multimedia service; in this sense, a wireless device sends a video stream to a remote device. The video is encoded with H.264/AVC, the recommended codec by the 3GPP. The corresponding video slices are transported over UDP/IP datagrams.

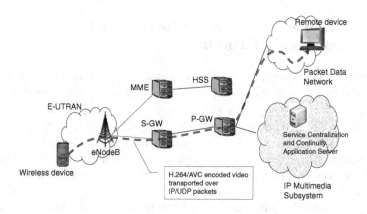

Fig. 1. Architecture of the scenario

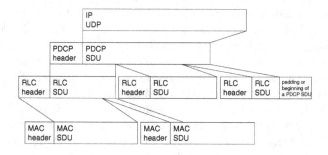

Fig. 2. IP/UDP packet transported over RLC frames

The Evolved Universal Terrestrial Radio Access Network (E-UTRAN) transmits each UDP/IP datagram over one or several Radio Link Control (RLC) frames, as it can be seen on Fig. 2.

4   Issues and Opportunities for Reducing the Exposure in LTE

In the scenario depicted in Sect. 3, when one RLC frame belonging to a particular UDP/IP datagram is lost or erroneous, the eNodeB requests the wireless device to retransmit it, when it is configured in acknowledged mode [12]. If such frame is not received after $MaxDAT - 1$ attempts, where $MaxDAT$ is the maximum number of (re)-transmission, the eNodeB discards all the RLC frames of the corresponding UDP/IP datagram, which clearly wastes a considerable amount of radio resources. If the eNodeB were able to not discard an entire UDP/IP datagram when just a small part of it was not correctly received, the remote device could receive the remaining information of the whole datagram. In turn, this information could be used by the H.264/AVC decoder to interpolate the missing video slices. As more packets are effectively received by the decoder as

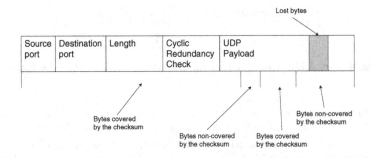

Fig. 3. CRC computation over an uncompleted IP/UDP packet

the Quality of Experience (QoE) of the video application, which is defined by the International Telecommunication Union in [13], could be improved. Here, instead of increasing the QoE, our objective is to maintain the QoE at a satisfying level, while decreasing the number of RLC retransmissions. This would in turn bring about an exposure reduction. In order to achieve it, the following issues must be tackled:

- At the RLC layer of the eNodeB, the loss of particular RLC frames belonging to a UDP/IP datagram could cause the loss of critical information, such as the IP addresses and UDP ports of the connection. To avoid this situation, those RLC frames carrying critical pieces of information, for instance those identifying the connection, shall be protected;
- In its regular operation, the UDP receiving entity would discard a datagram when its Cyclic Redundancy Check (CRC) is wrong and therefore it would not send it to the decoder. This, for instance, would be the case for incomplete UDP datagrams. This behavior would have been overcome if the erroneous chunks of the incomplete datagram had not been included in the CRC computation, as shown in Fig. 3. In this sense, those bytes not covered by the checksum (within the UDP datagram) must not be critical for the decoder, and they might be useful just to enhance the perceived QoE. To establish whether a frame is critical or not, the properties of the application must be used (for instance, the *I-frames* for some streaming services);
- At the architectural level, we need to assess the QoE and ensure that it is kept at an appropriate level, despite the increase in block error ratio (BLER) due to fewer RLC frame retransmissions.

5   Design of an Architecture for Reducing the Exposure

As already mentioned, we aim at decreasing the maximum number of RLC frame retransmissions, while keeping the QoE at an appropriate level; this goal requires modifications in the architecture design.

Source port	Destination port	Length	Cyclic Redundancy Check	Bytes covered by the CRC

Fig. 4. New UDP header indicating the bytes covered by the checksum

First of all, we propose the following modification to the 3GPP legacy specifications of the RLC layer acknowledged mode. When the eNodeB (acting as a receiver) does not receive a RLC frame, it requests the transmitter, i.e. the user terminal, to retransmit the frame. When the information carried by the RLC frame payload is critical for the decoder (for example the IP addresses and UDP ports of the connection), the maximum number of retransmissions is set to $MaxDAT - 1$. On the other hand, if the information is not so relevant for the decoder (we can state that it provides a higher QoE), the maximum number of retransmissions is reduced to $\lfloor \frac{MaxDAT-1}{N} \rfloor$, where N can vary between $[1, MaxDAT]$. In this sense, the higher the value of N, the lower the electromagnetic exposure. In order to allow for this new functionality, we require some cross-layer interaction; the RLC layer of the transmitter shall be aware on how critical/relevant is the information contains within each of the RLC frame payloads, so as to establish the maximum number of retransmissions. We propose to modify the transport protocol, by adding a new field within the UDP header (see Fig. 4) to indicate the bytes that are covered by the checksum. When the RLC layer receives a UDP/IP datagram from the packet data convergence protocol (PDCP) layer [14], it checks this new field to assess whether or not the payload contains critical bytes.

Then, at the PDCP layer, the 3GPP specifications can possibly be modified according to the following rule. When the wireless device receives a PDCP status report coming from the eNodeB, it reads the payload of this message to know what are the PDCP frames to be retransmitted. If a PDCP frame does not carry a critical IP/UDP packet, its number of retransmissions can be decreased, as long as the QoE requirements are met. For instance, when assuming that each retransmission utilizes the same amount of power P and that $MaxDAT = 4$, if most of the frames can be transmitted by using one less retransmission in comparison with the traditional approach, while keeping an acceptable QoE, then a reduction of around 25 % of power/energy can be achieved, i.e. by using $3P$ transmit power instead of $4P$.

Last, but not least, we need to include a new monitoring method to periodically evaluate the QoE of the video application in order to ensure that it remains at a satisfactory level. We consider here the use of a method, which was originally proposed by the ADAMANTIUM project [15]. The mean opinion score (MOS), a numerical evaluation of the QoE, is estimated by using (1) [16], which is based on the following parameters: the frame rate (FR) of the H.264/AVC codec, the sender bit rate (SBR) of the codec, the complexity of the video content (CT), the $BLER$, and the mean burst length (MBL).

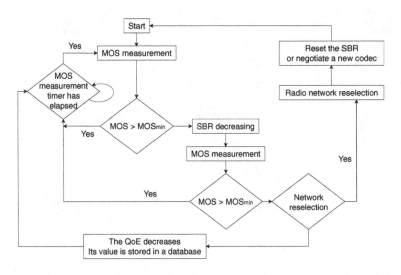

Fig. 5. Decision-making algorithm

$$MOS = a + \frac{(be)^{FR} + c\log(SBR) + CT[d + e\log(SBR)]}{1 + [f(BLER) + g(BLER)^2]h \cdot MBL} \tag{1}$$

where the values of a, b, c, d, e, f, g, h are obtained for a non-linear regression model.

In order to keep the QoE of an ongoing multimedia connection, we introduce a dynamic algorithm that is able to modify the parameters of such a session. Its main steps (Fig. 5) are as follows. The MOS is periodically evaluated by means of (1); if it is higher than a threshold, no further action is needed. On the other hand, when the MOS value is lower than such threshold, some actions are taken. A first option would be to decrease the SBR for increasing the MOS, since decreasing the SBR decreases the number of lost packets. Afterwards, a new MOS measurement is carried out; if the corresponding value is higher than the threshold, no further action needs to be taken. On the other hand, a new action shall be triggered; if selecting another radio network is possible, then the algorithm initializes the radio network reselection process. If this fails, then the final QoE value is lowered and stored in a database, which can be used by network planning tools to carry out off-line strategic analysis (this particular aspect is beyond the scope of this work).

The implementation of the different algorithm steps requires some enhancements of the 3GPP architecture. They basically consist on defining the messages that need to be exchanged between the involved entities and the interfaces between them. The exchanged messages, which are depicted in Fig. 6, are as follows. Message #1 is sent by the service centralization and continuity application server (SCC AS) to the eNodeB to request the BLER and the MBL; these metrics are needed to evaluate the MOS according to (1). It is worth noting that the SCC AS manages the SIP sessions, and it is therefore aware of the SBR and

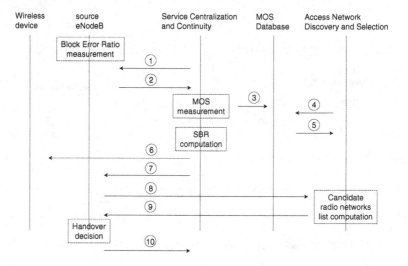

Fig. 6. Messages between the entities involved in the implementation of the algorithm

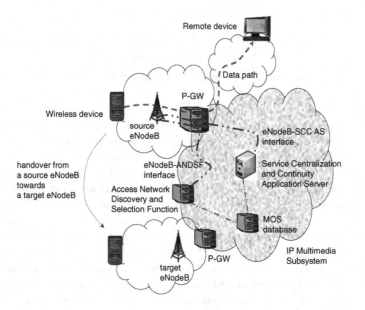

Fig. 7. Definition of the eNodeB-SCC AS and eNodeB-ANDSF interfaces

the Frame Rate (FR) of the codec. Message #2 contains the response sent by the eNodeB. After having evaluated the MOS, the SCC AS stores the value in a database (#3). The message flow also shows the information exchange with the database; in this regard, #4 is sent by the access network discovery and selection function (ANDSF) [17] to request the MOS values for a particular end user terminal, while #5 is the response sent by the database. #6 is a SIP message containing the value of the SBR of the codec, computed by the SCC AS. #7 triggers the reselection process, when maintaining the QoE level is not possible and is sent by the SCC AS to the eNodeB, requesting a handover (the eNodeB is the entity that initiates the reselection processes [18]). #8 is sent by the eNodeB to the ANDSF, which can provide a list of candidate radio networks based on criteria such as the MOS experienced by a wireless device when it is connected to a particular radio network; this list is included in message #9. Finally, #10 is sent by the eNodeB to the SCC AS to indicate a handover event. Upon reception of this message, the SCC AS prepares the new SIP session towards the target radio network.

The messages are exchanged through the two new interfaces that are highlighted in Fig. 7. The first interface is included between the eNodeB and the SCC AS and is used by the SCC AS for retrieving the information that characterizes the link layer and requesting a handover. The second interface connects the eNodeB and the ANDSF, and it is in charge of the network reselection process, which enables the eNodeB to retrieve information about candidate radio networks.

6   Conclusion

The paper proposes a novel solution to reduce the exposure in LTE networks, by decreasing the number of retransmissions of lost RLC frames. Our proposed cross-layer scheme has been designed for multimedia (video) services. In this sense, it is only desirable to reduce the number of retransmissions of the frames carrying non critical information for the delivery of the service. In order to implement the solution, the degree of relevance of the information is included in a new field of the transport layer header. The latter must be checked by the RLC layer (cross-layer interaction) to adapt the number of retransmissions according to the significance of the information contains in RLC frame payloads. Given that the BLER could increase as a result of the reduced number of retransmissions, a QoE measurement is periodically carried out and actions are established if it falls below a predefined threshold.

The implementation of the proposed solution involves enhancements in the E-UTRAN as well as some additional signaling, which could be integrated within the IMS core network, if it was used. In our future work, we will carry out the performance analysis of the proposed solution. As this heavily depends on the chosen QoE model, several models will be required to be implemented. Another aspect to solve is related to the compression of the UDP header at the PDCP layer. Even if the header is compressed, the information characterizing the importance shall be made available for the RLC layer.

Acknowledgements. This paper reports a work undertaken in the context of the LEXNET project, which is a project supported by the European Commission in the 7th Framework Program (GA n°318273). Ramón Agüero would also like to thank the Spanish Government for its support through the project "Connectivity as a Service: Access for the Internet of the Future", COSAIF (TEC2012-38574-C02-01).

References

1. International Commission on Non-Ionizing Radiation: Guidelines for limiting exposure to time-varying electric, magnetic, and electromagnetic fields (up to 300 GHz. Healt Phys. **74**(4), 494–522 (1998)
2. Wiedemann, P.M., Boerner, F., Dnrrenberger, G., Estenberg, J., Kandel, S., van Rongen, E., Vogel, E.: Supporting non-experts in judging the credibility of risk assessments (cora). Sci. Total Environ. **463464**, 624–630 (2013)
3. Low Electromagnetic Field Exposure Networks (LEXNET) project. http://www.lexnet-project.eu
4. Conil, E., et al.: LEXNET deliverable D2.4: global wireless exposure metric definition. Technical report (2013)
5. Derakhshan, F., Jugl, E., Mitschele-Thiel, A.: Reduction of radio emission in low frequency wcdma. In: Proceedings of Fifth IEE International Conference on 3G Mobile Communication Technologies (3G 2004), October 2004
6. Kelif, J.M., Coupechoux, M., Marache, F.: Limiting power transmission of green cellular networks: impact on coverage and capacity. In: 2010 IEEE International Conference on Communications (ICC), pp. 1–6, May 2010
7. Sidi, H.B.A., Altman, Z., Tall, A.: Self-optimizing mechanisms for emf reduction in heterogeneous networks. CoRR abs/1401.3541 (2014)
8. Ragha, L.K., Bhatia, M.S.: Evaluation of SAR reduction for mobile phone using RF shield. Int. J. Comput. Appl. **1**(13), 80–85 (2010)
9. Camarillo, G., Garcia-Martin, M.A.: The 3G IP Multimedia Subsystem (IMS): Merging the Internet and the Cellular Worlds, 3rd edn. Wiley, Hoboken (2008)
10. Rosenberg, J., Schulzrinne, H., Camarillo, G., Johnston, A., Peterson, J., Sparks, R., Handley, M., Schooler, E.: SIP: Session Initiation Protocol. RFC 3261 (Proposed Standard), June 2002
11. 3rd Generation Partnership Project: Technical specification group services and system aspects: 3GPP TS 23.237: IP multimedia subsystem (IMS) service continuity (Release 12). Technical report (2013)
12. 3rd Generation Partnership Project: Technical specification group radio access network: 3GPP TS 25.322: radio link control (RLC) protocol specification (Release 11). Technical report (2013)
13. ITU-T: Recommendation P.10/G.100: vocabulary for performance and quality of service. Technical report (2013)
14. 3rd Generation Partnership Project: Technical specification group radio access network; evolved universal terrestrial radio access (E-UTRA): 3GPP TS 36.323: packet data convergence protocol (PDCP) specification (Release 11). Technical report (2013)
15. ADAptative Management of mediA distributioN based on saTisfaction orIented User Modelling (ADAMANTIUM) project. http://www.ict-adamantium.eu
16. Khan, A., Sun, L., Ifeachor, E., Fajardo, J-O., Liberal, F., Koumaras, H.: Video quality prediction models based on video content dynamics for H.264 video over UMTS networks. Int. J. Digit. Multimedia Broadcast. **2010**, Article ID 608138, 17 pp. (2010). doi:10.1155/2010/608138
17. 3rd Generation Partnership Project: Technical specification group core network and terminals: 3GPP TS 24.312: access network discovery and selection function (ANDSF) management object (MO) (Release 12). Technical report (2014)
18. 3rd Generation Partnership Project: Technical specification group radio access network; evolved universal terrestrial radio access (E-UTRA) and evolved universal terrestrial radio access network (E-UTRAN): 3GPP TS 36.300: overall description (Release 12). Technical report (2013)

Wireless Networks Algorithms and Techniques

A New Learning Automata-Based Algorithm to the Priority-Based Target Coverage Problem in Directional Sensor Networks

Shaharuddin Salleh$^{(\boxtimes)}$, Sara Marouf, and Hosein Mohamadi

Center of Industrial and Applied Mathematics, Universiti Teknologi Malaysia,
Johor Bahru, Malaysia
ss@utm.my

Abstract. One of the main operations in directional sensor networks (DSNs) is the surveillance of a set of events (targets) that occur in a given area and, at the same time, maximization of the network lifetime; this is due to limitation in sensing angle and battery power of the directional sensors. This problem gets more complicated by the possibility that targets may have different coverage requirements. In the present study, this problem is referred to as priority-based target coverage (PTC). As sensors are often densely deployed, organizing the sensors into several cover sets and then activating these cover sets successively is a promising solution to this problem. In this paper, we propose a learning automata-based algorithm to organize the directional sensors into several cover sets in such a way that each cover set could satisfy coverage requirements of all the targets. Several experiments are conducted to evaluate the performance of the proposed algorithm. The results demonstrated that the algorithms were able to contribute to solving the problem.

Keywords: Directional sensor networks · Target coverage problem · Cover set formation · Learning automata

1 Introduction

Wireless sensor nodes are electronic devices that are able to collect, store, and process environmental information, and they can communicate with other sensor nodes through wireless communications. A wireless sensor network (WSN) consists of a large number of wireless sensor nodes distributed within a region of interest. Wireless sensor nodes are conventionally assumed to have a disk-like sensing range [16]. Nevertheless, in real world, sensor nodes may be limited in their sensing angle and they can sense only a sector of a disk-like region. These sensors are known as directional sensors (e.g., ultrasound, infrared, and video sensors) [1] and the networks composed of them are know as directional sensor networks (DSNs). Sensor nodes are powered by batteries with limited lifetime, which cannot be recharged or replaced in remote and harsh environments. For this reason, extending the network lifetime is of a great importance in sensor networks.

© Institute for Computer Sciences, Social Informatics and Telecommunications Engineering 2015
R. Agüero et al. (Eds.): MONAMI 2014, LNICST 141, pp. 219–229, 2015.
DOI: 10.1007/978-3-319-16292-8_16

One of the basic problems associated with any sensor network is coverage through which different types of data are collected from the environment. Coverage problem can be classified into two main subcategories: area coverage and target coverage [8]. In the area coverage, the whole area of interest should be monitored continuously. Whereas, in the target coverage, only some crucial points (targets) in the area are needed to be monitored [8]. The target coverage problem can be classified into three sub-problems: simple target coverage, k-coverage, and priority-based target coverage (PTC). In simple coverage, each target is monitored by at least one sensor node. Simple coverage has a low accuracy in its monitoring operation. This drawback shifts the attentions towards k-coverage wherein each target is monitored by at least k sensor nodes, leading to an enhancement in the reliability and accuracy of the monitoring operation. However, in real applications, targets may have different coverage requirements, which causes k-coverage to be unfit to such situations. This feature of k-coverage pushes us to take PTC into consideration, in which a target is monitored by different number of sensor nodes based on its coverage requirement (priority). The coverage requirement refers to the minimum quality of monitoring that each target requires. The coverage requirement is denoted by a value that can be set based on the nature of the problem. Therefore, one of the most important challenges is to solve the PTC problem and, at the same time, maximize the network lifetime, which is addressed in the present study.

Due to dense deployment of sensor nodes in most applications, organizing the sensors into several cover sets and then activating these cover sets successively is a promising solution to this problem, which is known as scheduling technique. Many studies have used this technique as solution to the target coverage problem in DSNs. Ai and Abouzeid [7] have conducted one of the first studies on the coverage problem in DSNs. They have modeled a Maximum Coverage with the Minimum Sensors problem to maximize the number of covered targets while minimizing the number of activated sensors. In [4], the authors have defined the multiple directional cover sets problem and proved its NP-completeness. They have proposed several heuristic algorithms to solve the problem of target coverage. For solving this problem, Gil and Han [5] have proposed two algorithms: one based on greedy method and the other one based on genetic algorithm. In [3,13], Mohamadi et al. have taken the advantage of learning automata in order to find a near-optimal solution for solving the target coverage problem.

A common assumption in the above-mentioned studies is that the targets require the same coverage quality. Consequently, the algorithms proposed in these studies cannot perform well under real scenarios in which the targets are different in their coverage quality requirements. Wang et al. [2] have introduced the problem of PTC in the DSNs, which aimed at choosing a minimum subset of directional sensors that is able to satisfy the prescribed priorities of all the targets. They have proposed a genetic algorithm for solving this problem and used a directional sensing model in which more than one direction of a sensor can work at the same time. Moreover, their algorithm generates only one cover set. Yang et al. [6] also assumed that the targets require different coverage quality requirements according to their roles in the application. In addition, they have assumed the distance between the target and the sensor affects the coverage quality. A directional sensing model in which only one direction of a sensor can work at a time have been used in their study. They have proposed a greedy-based scheduling algorithm that is able to find a sequence of feasible cover sets in order to prolong the network lifetime. Although the greedy-based algorithms are able to solve the problem, the performance of these algorithms is extremely dependent on the closeness of the initial candidates to the optimal solution. Therefore, the scheme can result in a local minimum due to its heuristic search [5].

In this paper, we propose a learning automata-based scheduling algorithm in order to find a near-optimal solution to the problem. The proposed algorithm consists of a number of stages at each of which a cover set is constructed through the selection of a subset of sensor directions; the selection is performed by learning automata (LA). The constructed cover set is rewarded if its cardinality (the number of active sensor direction in the cover set) is less than that of the best cover set found so far. As the algorithm goes on, the automata learn how to choose the best actions (sensor directions) to find an optimal cover set of the network among all possible cover sets. To evaluate the contribution of the proposed algorithm to extend the network lifetime, several experiments have been conducted.

The remainder of this paper is organized as follows: Sect. 2 introduces PTC problem in DSNs. Section 3 introduces the proposed LA-based scheduling algorithm. Section 4 discusses the results obtained from the simulation experiments. Finally, Sect. 5 concludes the paper.

2 Problem Definition

In this study, we investigate the following scenario. Several targets are distributed within a two-dimensional Euclidean field. A certain coverage quality requirement is defined for each target, indicating its importance. In this field, a number of directional sensors are randomly deployed close to the targets to satisfy their coverage quality requirements. All deployed sensors are homogeneous in their initial energy, sensing range, and the number of directions. Each directional sensor has several directions; however, at each given time, only one of its directions can be activated (known as working direction). Each directional sensor can monitor only one sector of the disk. Consequently, a target is monitored by a directional sensor only if it is located within both the sensing range and working direction of the sensor. An important factor that affects considerably the coverage quality is the distance between the directional sensor and the target. That is, with an increase in the distance, the coverage quality decreases, and vice versa. Note that a target may require to be monitored by more than one directional sensor simultaneously in order that its coverage quality requirement could be fully satisfied. A general assumption is that the coverage quality requirement of a target that could be satisfied is equal to the sum of coverage provided by the sensor directions that cover the target. In this paper, we use the following notation [6]:

- M : the number of targets
- N : the number of sensors
- W : the number of directions per sensor
- L_i : the lifetime of sensor s_i
- t_m : the m-th target, $1 \le m \le M$
- s_i : the i-th sensor, $1 \le i \le N$
- d_{ij} : the j-th direction of the i-th sensor, $1 \le i \le N$, $1 \le j \le W$
- D : the set of the directions of all the sensors, $D = \{d_{ij} | i = 1 \dots N, j = 1 \dots W\}$
- $T =$ the set of targets, $t_1, t_2, \dots, t_M$
- $S =$ the set of sensors, $s_1, s_2, \dots, s_N$
- $u(x)$: the coverage quality function; where x signifies the ratio of the distance between the sensor and target to the sensing range
- $g(m)$: the required coverage quality of target t_m

The functions $u(x)$ and $g(m)$ depend on the context of networks and the application requirements. These functions are defined as follow [6]: $u(x) = 1 - x^2$ and the value of $g(m)$ is selected between 0 and 1 randomly and uniformly.

Problem: How to organize the sensor directions into several cover sets in a way that each cover set could satisfy the different coverage quality requirements of all the targets and, at the same time, the network lifetime could be maximized. In this study, organizing the sensors refers to determining the mode of the sensor directions as either active or passive.

Definition 1: A cover set consists of a subset of sensor directions by which the coverage quality requirements of all the targets can be satisfied.

Definition 2: The network lifetime can be defined as the amount of time during which the coverage quality requirements of all the targets can be satisfied.

3   Proposed Algorithm

In this section, we propose a centralized LA-based scheduling algorithm as a solution to the problem of PTC(See [9, 10] for more details about learning automata). The operation of network in this algorithm is composed of several rounds. At each round, one cover set is generated, which is able to satisfy the coverage quality requirement of all the targets. The algorithm consists of two phases: initialization and sensor direction selection, which are elaborated in the following subsections.

3.1   Initialization

The initialization phase is composed of three steps: generating a network of LA, defining the action-set of LA, and configuring the action probability vector of LA. In the first step, in order to generate a network of LA, each target is provided with a learning automaton. The learning automaton is aimed to select one or more sensor directions needed for satisfying the coverage quality requirement of its corresponding target. The generated network of LA can be modeled by a duple $\langle A, \alpha \rangle$, where $A = \{A_i | \forall t_i \in T\}$ denotes the set of LA corresponding to the targets in the network, and $\alpha = \{\alpha_i | \forall A_i \in A\}$ signifies the set of action-sets of LA in which $\alpha_i = \{\alpha_i^1, \alpha_i^2, ..., \alpha_i^{r_i}\}$ defines the set of actions that learning automaton A_i is able to select (for each $\alpha_i \in \alpha$), and r_i is the cardinality of action-set α_i. In this algorithm, we employ LA with a variable number of actions in order to propose a pruning rule to avoid the selection of redundant sensor directions and/or more than one sensor direction of each sensor. In this algorithm, LA can be set to either active or passive state (note that they are initially set to the passive state).

In the second step, the action-set of LA is formed. For this purpose, each learning automaton assigns an action to each sensor direction that covers the target corresponding to that learning automaton. Let $\alpha_i = \{\alpha_i^j | d_{i,j} \text{ cover target } t_i\}$. Action α_i^j is corresponding to selection of sensor direction $d_{i,j}$ as an active sensor direction.

In the third step, the action probability vector of each learning automaton is configured. Let $p = \{p_i | \forall \alpha_i \in \alpha\}$ signify the set of action probability vectors and $p_i = \{p_i^j | \forall \alpha_i^j \in \alpha_i\}$ represent the action probability vector of learning automaton A_i, where p_i^j is corresponding to the choice probability of action α_i^j.

In order to speed up the convergence of the proposed algorithm, the action probability vector of automaton A_i should be adjusted in such a way that the sensor directions with high covering power have more chance to be selected. To this end, the action probability vector of learning automaton A_i is initially configured as follows:

$$p_i^j(k) = \frac{CF(d_{i,j})}{\sum CF(d_{i,j})} \quad \forall \alpha_i^j \in \alpha_i \text{ and } k = 0 \tag{1}$$

where $CF(d_{i,j})$ signifies the sum of the targets' coverage quality requirements satisfied by direction $d_{i,j}$, and $\sum CF(d_{i,j})$ denotes the sum of the targets' coverage quality requirements of all the sensor directions that monitor target t_i. From Eq. (1), it is implied that the sensor directions that satisfy more coverage quality requirements are more likely to be chosen as active sensor direction. Note that the action probability vector of the LA is updated based on the rewarding process.

It is noticeable that the action-set and action probability vector of LA change over the time in two conditions: (i) when a sensor runs out its energy and/or (ii) when the action-set of a learning automaton is to be pruned. For instance, if sensor direction $(d_{i,j})$ becomes disabled at stage $k + 1$, the action-set of learning automaton A_i is updated by eliminating the action corresponding to sensor direction $(d_{i,j})$. Then, the choice probability of the removed action (α_i^j) is set to zero, and that of other actions $(\alpha_i^{j'})$ is updated as follows.

$$p_i^{j'}(k+1) = p_i^{j'}(k).[1 + \frac{p_i^j(k)}{1 - p_i^j(k)}] \quad j \neq j' \tag{2}$$

Up to this part of the paper, three steps regarding the initialization phase, namely, generating a network of LA, forming the action-set of LA, and configuring the action probability vector of LA have been elaborated. The following subsection explains the sensor direction selection phase of the algorithm.

3.2   Sensor Direction Selection

This phase deals with selecting a subset of appropriate sensor directions in such a way that a cover set with the minimum number of active sensor directions (i.e., the minimum cardinality) could be constructed. The pseudo code of the proposed algorithm is shown in Algorithm 1. The algorithm consists of a number of stages at each of which a subset of sensor directions is selected by LA as a cover set. Afterward, the cardinality of the constructed cover set is computed, based on which the actions selected by the LA are either rewarded or penalized. This process continues until a cover set with the minimum cardinality is formed. The k-th stage of the algorithm can be explained as follows.

Set T_{cur} keeps the list of targets whose coverage quality requirements have not been satisfied. Set C_{cur} keeps the list of the sensor directions that have been already selected to satisfy the coverage quality requirements of the targets. In order to form a cover set, a critical passive automaton is selected (known as A_i) and switched to the active state. Then, automaton A_i prunes its action-set using pruning rule and selects one of its actions. Next, the sensor direction corresponding to the selected action (i.e., $d_{(}i,j)$) is added to set C_{cur}. Then, the coverage quality requirements of both the critical target (i.e., the target corresponding to automaton A_i) and the other targets covered by direction $d_{(}i,j)$ are updated. If the coverage quality requirement of the critical target is fully satisfied, the above process continues by the selection of the next critical automaton. Otherwise, the already activated automaton continues its operation by selecting another action. The process of activating a passive automaton and selecting an action continues until the coverage quality requirements of all the targets are satisfied.

Pruning rule: In this algorithm, each activated learning automaton prunes its action-set by disabling the actions corresponding to (i) the already-selected directions, (ii) directions that cover the already-satisfied targets, and (iii) the other directions of those sensors that have a direction in the current cover set. Using this rule reduces the number of actions and, consequently, speeds up the convergence of the algorithm.

To improve the performance of the proposed algorithm, the action probability vector of the activated LA should be updated using a rewarding process. For this purpose, the cardinality of the constructed cover set is computed and then compared to dynamic threshold T_k. If the cardinality of the cover set is smaller than or equal to the dynamic threshold, the selected actions of the automata activated for constructing the cover set are rewarded; otherwise, they remains unchanged. In other words, the constructed cover set is rewarded only if it satisfies the coverage quality requirement of all the targets with a number of active directions smaller than or equal to those of the cover sets previously generated. With such a rewarding process, the convergence of the action probability vector of the learning automaton to the optimal configuration can be guaranteed. It should be noted that the action probability vector of the activated LA is updated after all disabled actions are re-enabled. Dynamic threshold is initially set to a large value and, at each stage, it is set to the cardinality of the last rewarded cover set. Then, the k-th stage of the proposed algorithm will be ended. As the proposed algorithm continues, the LA learn how to choose active sensor directions in such a way that a cover set with the minimum cardinality could be generated. The algorithm is terminated once the number of constructed cover sets reaches a value higher than a predefined threshold. Finally, the cover set with the minimum number of active sensor directions is returned as the output of the algorithm.

Algorithm 1. Sensor direction selection

01.**input**: Directional sensor network
02.**output**: An appropriate cover set
03.**assumption**:
04.Assign an automaton to each target
05.Let α_i denote the action-set of automaton A_i
06.**begin**
07.Let T_k denote the dynamic threshold at stage k
08.Let k denote the stage number initially set to zero
09.**repeat**
10.$T_{cur} \leftarrow T$
11.$C_{cur} \leftarrow \emptyset$
12. **while**$T_{cur} \not\equiv \emptyset$ **do**
13. Find a critical passive automaton and activate it (call it A_i)
14. **while**(the coverage requirement of the critical target is not satisfied) **do**
15.   Automaton A_i prunes its action-set and chooses one of its actions (say $d_{i,j}$)
16.   Add $d_{i,j}$ corresponding to the selected action to C_{cur}
17.   Update the coverage requirements of the targets covered by $d_{i,j}$
18. **end while**
19. Update the list of unsatisfied targets (i.e., T_{cur})
20. **end while**
21. Configuration of activated automata is updated by re-enabling all disabled actions
22. Compute the cardinality of the constructed cover set (C_k)
23. **if** $C_k \leq T_k$ **then**
24. Reward the chosen actions of the activated automata by Eq. 1
25. $T_k \leftarrow C_k$
26. **end if**
27. $k \leftarrow k + 1$
28. **until** (the stage number k exceeds K)
29.**end algorithm**

Afterward, an activation time is assigned to the cover set and added to the total network lifetime. Based on the activation time, the algorithm updates the residual energy of the sensors that have a direction in the generated cover set and eliminates the sensors that have no residual energy from the set of available sensors. It means a round of the algorithm is terminated and another round is started. The process of constructing a new cover set continues until the coverage quality requirements of all the targets become satisfied.

4   Simulation Results

In this section, we present several experiments carried out in order to examine the performance of the proposed algorithm. The parameters considered in these experiments include (a) the number of sensors, (b) the number of targets, and (c) the sensing range. In these experiments, a DSN consisting of N sensor nodes and M targets are modeled in which the sensor nodes and targets are randomly deployed within a two-dimensional simulation area of size $100\,m * 100\,m$. In these experiments, each directional sensor has three directions. Initially, all the sensor nodes have the same level of energy, which is 1 unit, and all targets have different coverage quality requirements. The amount of energy that an active sensor consumes in each cover set is also 1 unit, and this amount for a sleep sensor is zero. Therefore, each cover set adds 1 unit of time to the total network lifetime. Each simulation experiment is executed 10 times, and the average network lifetime is then calculated for each scenario. In this study, we have adjusted the proposed algorithm to take value of 0.1 for the learning rate, and the action probability vector of the learning automaton has been updated using the reinforcement scheme $L_{(R-I)}$.

Experiment 1. This experiment is aimed at studying the impact of the number of sensors on the network lifetime. To this end, the number of sensors was ranged between 50 and 90 with incremental step 10. The number of targets and sensing range were fixed to 15 and 40 m, respectively. The results shown in Fig. 1 demonstrate a direct relationship between the number of sensors and the network lifetime. That is, increasing the number of sensors causes the network lifetime to be increased. This is because in this condition, more sensors are available to be scheduled for satisfying the coverage quality requirement of all the targets.

Experiment 2. This experiment is conducted to examine the effect of the number of targets on the network lifetime. Here, we ranged the number of targets from 4 to 20 with incremental step 4. The number of sensors and sensing range were fixed to 100 and 40 m, respectively. The obtained results shown in Fig. 2 reveal that by increasing the number of targets, the network lifetime decreases. The reason is that when the number of targets increases, more active sensors are needed to satisfy the coverage quality requirement of all the targets. As a result, the total energy of network will be sooner exhausted.

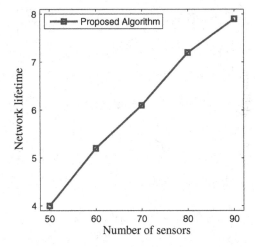

Fig. 1. Effect of the number of sensors on the network lifetime

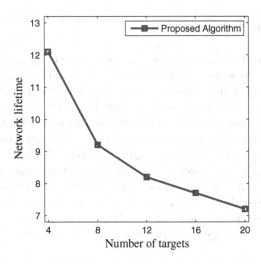

Fig. 2. Effect of the number of targets on the network lifetime

Experiment 3. The aim of this experiment is to investigate the impact of the sensing range on the network lifetime. We set the sensing range from 30 m to 50 m with incremental step 5 m. The number of sensors and targets were fixed to 100 and 10, respectively. From the results shown in Fig. 3, it can be observed that the network lifetime increases as the sensing range grows. It is reasonable because when a sensor has a large sensing range; it can satisfy the coverage quality requirement of more targets. As a result, fewer sensors are required for satisfying coverage quality requirement of all the targets.

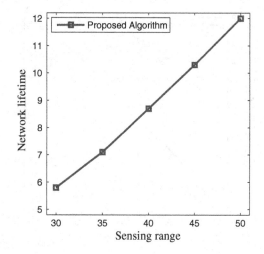

Fig. 3. Effect of sensing ranges on the network lifetime

5 Conclusion

This paper investigated the problem of target coverage in a directional sensor network in which the sensors were limited in their battery power and sensing angle, and the targets had different coverage requirements (the problem was known as priority-based target coverage problem). To solve this problem, we proposed a learning automata-based scheduling algorithm capable of organizing the directional sensors into several cover sets in such a way that each cover set could satisfy coverage requirements of all the targets. Several experiments were conducted to examine the effect of different parameters such as the number of sensors and targets and the sensing range on the network lifetime. The obtained results demonstrated the contribution of the proposed algorithm to solving the problem. In future studies, we intend to develop an appropriate algorithm for solving the target coverage problem in cases in which sensors have multiple sensing ranges.

Acknowledgment. The authors would like to thank Universiti Teknologi Malaysia and the Malaysian Ministry of Education for providing funds and support with research grants no. 01G14 and 04H43 for this research.

References

1. Guvensan, M.A., Yavuz, A.G.: On coverage issues in directional sensor networks: a survey. Ad Hoc Networks. **9**, 1238–1255 (2011)
2. Wang, J., Niu, C., Shen, R.: Priority-based target coverage in directional sensor networks using a genetic algorithm. Comput. Math. Appl. **57**, 1915–1922 (2009)

3. Mohamadi, H., Ismail, A.S., Salleh, S.: A learning automata-based algorithm for solving coverage problem in directional sensor networks. Computing **95**, 1–24 (2013)
4. Cai, Y., Lou, W., Li, M., Li, M.: Energy efficient target-oriented scheduling in directional sensor networks. IEEE Trans. Comput. **58**, 1259–1274 (2009)
5. Gil, J.M., Han, Y.H.: A target coverage scheduling scheme based on genetic algorithms in directional sensor networks. Sensors **11**, 1888–1906 (2011)
6. Yang, H., Li, D., Chen, H.: Coverage quality based target-oriented scheduling in directional sensor networks. In: Proceedings of international Conference on Communications, pp. 1–5 (2010)
7. Ai, J., Abouzeid, A.A.: Coverage by directional sensors in randomly deployed wireless sensor networks. J. Comb. Optim. **11**, 21–41 (2006)
8. Wang, B.: Coverage problems in sensor networks: a survey. ACM Comput. Surv. **43**, 32 (2011)
9. Najim, K., Poznyak, A.S.: Learning Automata: Theory and Applications. Printice-Hall, New York (1994)
10. Thathachar, M.A.L., Harita, B.R.: Learning automata with changing number of actions. IEEE Trans. Syst. Man Cybern. **17**, 1095–1100 (1987)
11. Mohamadi, H., Ismail, A.S., Salleh, S., Nodhei, A.: Learning automata-based algorithms for finding cover sets in wireless sensor networks. J. Supercomput. **66**, 1533–1552 (2013)
12. Mohamadi, H., Ismail, A.S., Salleh, S.: Utilizing distributed learning automata to solve the connected target coverage problem in directional sensor networks. Sens. Actuators A Phys. **198**, 21–30 (2013)
13. Mohamadi, H., Ismail, A.S., Salleh, S., Nodhei, A.: Learning automata-based algorithms for solving the target coverage problem in directional sensor networks. Wirel. Pers. Commun. **73**, 1309–1330 (2013)
14. Mohamadi, H., Ismail, A.S., Salleh, S.: Solving target coverage problem using cover sets in wireless sensor networks based on learning automata. Wirel. Pers. Commun. **75**, 447–463 (2014)
15. Salleh, S., Marouf, S.: A learning automata-based solution to the target coverage problem in wireless sensor networks. In: Proceedings of International Conference on Advances in Mobile Computing and Multimedia, pp. 185–191 (2013)
16. Yick, J., Mukherjee, B., Ghosal, D.: Wireless sensor network survey. Comput. Netw. **52**, 2292–2330 (2008)

Anti-jamming Strategies: A Stochastic Game Approach

Andrey Garnaev[✉] and Wade Trappe

WINLAB, Rutgers University, North Brunswick, USA
garnaev@yahoo.com,
trappe@winlab.rutgers.edu

Abstract. Due to their shared and open-access design, wireless networks are very vulnerable to many malicious attacks, ranging from passive eavesdropping to active interfering. In this paper, using stochastic game modeling we study anti-jamming strategies and their effectiveness against two types of interference attacks: (i) a random jammer, where the malicious user combines jamming modes with sleep modes; and (ii) a sophisticated jammer, where the malicious user uses the network for a two-fold purpose: law-obedient communication with other users and non-obedient jamming against a specific (primary) user. We focus our research on constructing the optimal maxmin anti-jamming transmission strategy and an optimal strategy against a selfish malicious user. Further, employing the suggested models we demonstrate that incorporating silent modes into the anti-jamming transmission protocol, where the primary user does not transmit signals for the purpose of helping an intrusion detection system identify the source of a jamming attack, can improve communication reliability. Further, since the equilibrium strategies are obtained explicitly, we identify several interesting properties that can guide designing such anti-jamming transmission protocols.

Keywords: Anti-jamming · Jamming strategies · Stochastic games

1 Introduction

Due to the fact that wireless networks are built upon a shared and open medium, wireless networks are susceptible to malicious attacks, especially those involving jamming or interference. For this reason wireless security has continued to receive growing attention by the research community. A reader can find comprehensive surveys of such threats in [1,2]. In this paper, we focus specifically on jamming attacks and anti-jamming strategies to cope with such malicious interference. In such attacks, an adversary (jammer) tries to degrade the signal quality at the intended receiver (see, for example, a recent book on jamming principles and techniques [3], on detecting jamming attacks [4], about employing artificial noise to improve secret communication [5], about defense against jamming attacks [6], jamming in multi-channel cognitive radio networks [7], jamming of dynamic traffic [8]). These types of attacks can be accomplished by an

© Institute for Computer Sciences, Social Informatics and Telecommunications Engineering 2015
R. Agüero et al. (Eds.): MONAMI 2014, LNICST 141, pp. 230–243, 2015.
DOI: 10.1007/978-3-319-16292-8_17

adversary by either bypassing the MAC (Media Access Control) layer protocol or by emitting radio frequency signals. Here we mention, as examples, only three type of jamming (malicious) attacks: (a) *Constant jammer* continuously emits radio frequency signals and it transmits random bits of data to channel. (b) *Random jammer* alternates between period of continuous jamming and inactivity. After jamming, it stops emitting radio signals and enter into sleep mode. (c) The adversary can even be more sophisticated, such as when a *primary user emulation* attack is carried out by a malicious user emulating a licensed primary user to obtain the resources of a given channel to jam or ward-off the other users from using the channels. To deal with such problems where users have coniciting interests, game theory is a proper tool [9]. In [10], one can find a structured and comprehensive survey of research contributions that analyze and solve security and privacy problems in computer and wireless networks via game-theoretic approaches. Here, as examples of game-theoretic approaches, we mention just a few such works: for modeling malicious users in collaborative networks [11], for adaptive packetized wireless communication [12], for attack-type uncertainty on a network [13], for packet transmission under jamming [14], for fight jamming with jamming [15], for ad hoc networks [16], and for fair-allocation of resources by a base station under uncertainty [17], for jamming in fast-fading channels [18]. The applications of stochastic games for modeling network security can be found in [19–22] and for secret and reliable communication with active and passive adversarial modes in [23].

In this paper we study anti-jamming strategies versus two type of jamming attacks: (i) a *random jammer*, where the malicious user combines jamming modes with sleep modes, and (ii) a *sophisticated jammer*, where the malicious user uses the network for a two-fold purpose: law-obedient communication with other users and to conduct a jamming attack against a specific (primary) user. Through simple stochastic game models, we demonstrate that incorporating silent time periods in the transmission protocol so as to increase the probability of detecting the jamming source, can increase the reliability of communication and support jamming-robust operation.

The organization of this paper is as follows: in Sect. 2 and in two its subsections, we first introduce and solve non-zero sum and zero-sum stochastic games with a random jammer. In Sect. 3, we formulate and solve a stochastic game for a sophisticated adversary combining malicious and law-obedient behavior. In Sect. 4, conclusions are presented. Finally, in Sect. 5, due to restriction on the paper's length, to illustrate applied mathematical methods for solving explicitly the suggested stochastic games, the proof of the theorem about non-zero-sum stochastic game with random jammer is offered as a supplement.

2 The Interferer Is a Random Jammer

In this section we deal with the situation where the interferer is a random jammer that can choose between jamming and sleep modes. Thus, there are two users: the PU (or user 1) and the jammer (or user 2). The game is played in time slots

0,1,.... At each time slot user 2 chooses between two modes: (a) a jamming mode (J), where user 2 tries jam user 1's communication applying the optimal strategy for such mode, and (b) a sleep mode (S), where user 2 does not apply any power at all – perhaps because user 2 is employing some form of intelligent strategy, choosing how long and when to jam and to sleep.

Beyond the difference in the payoffs in the jamming and transmission modes, there is another important aspect to consider in the game, namely, in jamming mode the jamming source can be detected, and perhaps user 2 can be identified as malicious and his malicious activity can be stopped. We assume that there is a probability $1 - \gamma$ of detecting user 2 in jamming mode by an IDS (Intrusion Detection System). Note that there is quite an extended literature on detecting an intruder's signal or its source (see, for example, books [24–26], and papers on the energy detection of unknown signals [27,28] and on game-theoretic model of the optimal scanning bandwidth algorithm [29,30]). Thus, γ is the probability of not detecting the source of the malicious activity. Of course, in sleep mode user 2 cannot be detected since he is not active in that case.

At each time slot user 1 also chooses between two modes: (a) a transmission mode (T_J), where he transmits a signal optimal under the jamming threat, and (b) a silent (or quiet) mode (S), where he does not apply any power at all. When user 1 chooses silent mode, he is not transmitting signals but is trying to increase the probability to detect the source of jamming by the IDS. So, in silent mode detection probability $1 - \gamma_S > 1 - \gamma$ is greater than in transmission mode. By using silent mode, user 1 may lose some payoff due to the delay in transmitting signals. However, user 1 can gain due to the earlier detection of the jamming event, and, hence, earlier resumption of the more efficient regime of transmission.

There is a discount factor δ on the signals transmitted and the rewards obtained for jamming. This δ can be interpreted as the urgency in communication, $\delta = 0$ corresponds to the highest urgency and means that transmission has to be performed during the current time slot, not later, while increasing δ means that losing a transmission time slot can be easily compensated in the following time slots.

In the next two sections we'll model this situation using non-zero sum and zero sum scenarios. The zero-sum scenario allows us to find a maxmin transmission protocol giving the optimal transmission under the worst conditions. The non-zero sum scenario allows us to find the transmission protocol versus a slightly more sophisticated malicious user, who wants to jam transmission without being detected. Such a jammer is inclined to be less risky.

2.1   Random Jammer: Non-zero-sum Game

In this paper, as a basic example to describe payoffs we consider a wireless medium with n separate channels (e.g. different subcarriers in an OFDM system), which we model as additive white Gaussian noise (AWGN) channels. A strategy for user k is a power vector $\boldsymbol{P}^k = (P_1^k, \ldots, P_n^k)$, where P_i^k is a power transmitted by user k through channel i, $\sum_{i=1}^{n} P_i^k = \bar{P}^k$, and $\bar{P}^k$ is the total power to transmit.

The payoff to user 1 in transmission mode is his throughput, i.e. the payoff to user 1, if the users apply powers $\boldsymbol{P}^1$ and $\boldsymbol{P}^2$ respectively, is given as follows: $v_T^1(\boldsymbol{P}^1, \boldsymbol{P}^2) = \sum_{i=1}^n \ln\left(1 + h_i^1 P_i^1 / (\sigma^2 + h_i^2 P_i^2)\right)$, where h_i^1, h_i^2 are fading channel gains, σ^2 is a background noise.

In jamming mode the payoff to user 2 is a weighted reduced throughput for the rival, i.e. the payoff to user 2, if the users apply powers $\boldsymbol{P}^1$ and $\boldsymbol{P}^2$, and is given as follows: $v_J^2(\boldsymbol{P}^1, \boldsymbol{P}^2) = C^2\left(v_T^1(\boldsymbol{P}^1, \boldsymbol{0}) - v_T^1(\boldsymbol{P}^1, \boldsymbol{P}^2)\right)$, where C^2 is a weight per a unit for reduced user 1's throughput.

Let $(\boldsymbol{P}_{T_J*}^1, \boldsymbol{P}_{J*}^2)$ be the equilibrium strategies [9], i.e. a pair of strategies $(\boldsymbol{P}_{T_J*}^1, \boldsymbol{P}_{J*}^2)$ that for any $(\boldsymbol{P}^1, \boldsymbol{P}^2)$ the following inequalities hold: $v_T^1(\boldsymbol{P}^1, \boldsymbol{P}_{J*}^2) \leq v_T^1(\boldsymbol{P}_{T_J*}^1, \boldsymbol{P}_{J*}^2)$ and $v_J^2(\boldsymbol{P}^1, \boldsymbol{P}_{J*}^2) \leq v_J^2(\boldsymbol{P}_{T_J*}^1, \boldsymbol{P}_{J*}^2)$.

For example, the equilibrium strategies in jamming mode can be calculated by using the results in [31] for the general SINR regime or for the low SINR regime with one jammer [32] and several jammers [33].

User 1 can choose between two modes: transmission T_J (regular mode) and silent mode S. In transmission mode user 1 applies power $\boldsymbol{P}_{T_J*}^1$. User 2 can choose between two modes: a sleep S and a jamming J mode. In jamming mode, user 2 applies a jamming power of $\boldsymbol{P}_{J*}^2$. If the malicious activity of user 2 is detected, then user 1 switches to employing the optimal signal for transmission when there are no malicious threats, i.e., $\boldsymbol{P}_0^1 = \arg\max_{\boldsymbol{P}} v_T^1(\boldsymbol{P}, \boldsymbol{0})$. Let $\bar{v}^1 = v_T^1(\boldsymbol{P}_0^1, \boldsymbol{0})$.

If either user 2 is not detected when he jams, or user 2 chooses sleep mode, the game goes to the next time slot with discount factor δ. This scenario can be described by a non-zero sum stochastic game denoted by (Γ^1, Γ^2) as follows:

$$(\Gamma^1, \Gamma^2) = \begin{array}{c} T_J \\ S \end{array} \begin{pmatrix} (a_{T_JS}^1 + \delta\Gamma^1, \Gamma^2) & (a_{T_JJ}^1 + \delta\gamma\Gamma^1, a_{T_JJ}^2 + \delta\gamma\Gamma^2) \\ (\delta\Gamma^1, \Gamma^2) & (a_{SJ}^1 + \delta\gamma_S\Gamma^1, \delta\gamma_S\Gamma^2) \end{pmatrix},$$

where

$$a_{T_JS}^1 = v_T^1(\boldsymbol{P}_{T_J*}^1, \boldsymbol{0}), \quad a_{T_JJ}^2 = v_J^2(\boldsymbol{P}_{T_J*}^1, \boldsymbol{P}_{J*}^2)$$

$$a_{T_JJ}^1 = v_T^1(\boldsymbol{P}_{T_J*}^1, \boldsymbol{P}_{J*}^2) + (1-\gamma)\sum_{i=1}^{\infty}\delta^i\bar{v}^1 = v_T^1(\boldsymbol{P}_{T_J*}^1, \boldsymbol{P}_{J*}^2) + (1-\gamma)\delta\bar{v}^1/(1-\delta),$$

$$a_{SJ}^1 = (1-\gamma_S)\sum_{i=1}^{\infty}\delta^i\bar{v}^1 = (1-\gamma_S)\delta\bar{v}^1/(1-\delta).$$

We will look for stationary equilibrium $(\boldsymbol{x}^1, \boldsymbol{x}^2)$, where $\boldsymbol{x}^1 = (x_{T_J}^1, x_S^1)$ is the stationary mixed strategy of user 1 assigning the probabilities $x_{T_J}^1$ and x_S^1 to using actions T_J and S, so, $x_{T_J}^1 + x_S^1 = 1$, $\boldsymbol{x}^2 = (x_S^2, x_J^2)$ is the stationary mixed strategy of user 2 assigning the probabilities x_S^2 and x_J^2 to using actions S and J, so, $x_S^2 + x_J^2 = 1$. Recall that a pair of (mixed) strategies $(\boldsymbol{x}^1, \boldsymbol{x}^2)$ is a stationary equilibrium if and only if they are the best response strategies to each other, i.e. they are solutions of the following equations:

$$\boldsymbol{x}^k = \arg\max_{\mathbf{1}^T\boldsymbol{x}^k=1, \boldsymbol{x}^k\geq 0} (\boldsymbol{x}^1)^T A^1(u^1)\boldsymbol{x}^2, \quad k = 1, 2$$

such that

$$u^k = (\boldsymbol{x}^1)^T A^k(u^k)\boldsymbol{x}^2, \quad k = 1, 2,$$

where

$$A^1(u^1) = \begin{pmatrix} a^1_{T_J S} + \delta u^1 & a^1_{T_J J} + \delta \gamma u^1 \\ \delta u^1 & a^1_{SJ} + \delta \gamma_S u^1 \end{pmatrix} \text{ and } A^2(u^2) = \begin{pmatrix} \delta u^2 & a^2_{T_J J} + \delta \gamma u^2 \\ \delta u^2 & \delta \gamma_S u^2 \end{pmatrix}.$$

Instead of solving these LP problems directly, it is easier to solve them using an approach that involves examining their dual LP problems:

$$U^1(u^1) = \arg \min_{A^1(u^1)\boldsymbol{x}^2 \leq \mathbf{1}^T U^1(u^1), \mathbf{1}^T \boldsymbol{x}^2 = 1, \boldsymbol{x}^2 \geq 0} U^1(u^1), \tag{1}$$

$$U^2(u^2) = \arg \min_{(A^2)^T(u^2)\boldsymbol{x}^1 \leq \mathbf{1}^T U^2(u^2), \mathbf{1}^T \boldsymbol{x}^1 = 1, \boldsymbol{x}^1 \geq 0} U^2(u^2) \tag{2}$$

with the following complementary slackness conditions correspondingly:

$$(\boldsymbol{x}^1)^T (\mathbf{1} U^1(u^1) - A^1(u^1)\boldsymbol{x}^2) = 0, \tag{3}$$

$$(\boldsymbol{x}^2)^T (\mathbf{1} U^2(u^2) - (A^2)^T(u^2)\boldsymbol{x}^1) = 0, \tag{4}$$

and, then, to find such u^1 and u^2 that $U^1(u^1) = u^1$ and $U^2(u^2) = u^2$.

Since the considered stochastic game has a discount factor, it has an equilibrium [9]. The following theorem gives the equilibrium strategies explicitly and proves uniqueness.

Theorem 1. *The considered non-zero sum stochastic game has an unique stationary equilibrium.*

(a) If

$$(1 - \gamma_S \delta)a^1_{T_J J}/(1 - \delta \gamma) > a^1_{SJ} \tag{5}$$

then the unique (pure) equilibrium is (T_J, J) with payoffs

$$u^k = a^k_{T_J J}/(1 - \delta \gamma), \quad k = 1, 2. \tag{6}$$

(b) If

$$(1 - \gamma_S \delta)a^1_{T_J J}/(1 - \delta \gamma) < a^1_{SJ} \tag{7}$$

then the unique (mixed) equilibrium $(\boldsymbol{x}^1, \boldsymbol{x}^2)$ with payoffs (u^1, u^2) are given as follows:

$$x^1_{T_J} = 0, \quad x^2_J = \frac{a^1_{T_J S}}{a^1_{SJ} + a^1_{T_J S} - a^1_{T_J J} - \delta(\gamma - \gamma_S)u^1},$$

$$x^1_S = 1, \quad x^2_S = \frac{a^1_{SJ} - a^1_{T_J J} - \delta(\gamma - \gamma_S)u^1}{a^1_{SJ} + a^1_{T_J S} - a^1_{T_J J} - \delta(\gamma - \gamma_S)u^1}, \tag{8}$$

$$u^1 = (-c^1_1 - \sqrt{(c^1_1)^2 - 4c^1_2 c^1_0})/(2c^1_2) \text{ and } u^2 = 0, \tag{9}$$

with

$$c^1_0 = a^1_{SJ}a^1_{T_J S}, \quad c^1_1 = (a^1_{T_J J} - a^1_{SJ})(1 - \delta) - a^1_{T_J S}(1 - \delta \gamma_S),$$

$$c^1_2 = (1 - \delta)\delta(\gamma - \gamma_S). \tag{10}$$

Figures 1 and 2 illustrate the impact of the silent mode on the user's payoffs and their equilibrium strategies for $v_T^1(\boldsymbol{P}_{T_J*}^1, \boldsymbol{P}_{J*}^2) = 0.5$, $v_J^2(\boldsymbol{P}_{T_J*}^1, \boldsymbol{P}_{J*}^2) = 3$, $v_T^1(\boldsymbol{P}_{T_J*}^1, \boldsymbol{0}) = 2.5$, $\bar{v}^1 = 6$ and $\gamma = 0.8$. Of course, with increasing discount factor δ (so, with decreasing urgency in transmission) the user payoffs are increasing since user 1 intends transmit longer, and so user 2 can longer jam. It is interesting that user 1's equilibrium strategy has a threshold structure between jamming and transmission mode and it is the same as if the malicious user is a constant jammer. The values of user 1's strategy does not depend explicitly on the detection probability in silent mode, and only on the domains of applying these values depends explicitly). The payoff to user 1 depends on this probability continuously. For user 2 this phenomena can be observed in reverse order. The payoff to user 2 has threshold structure on the probability and its value does not depend on the probability explicitly, while the equilibrium strategy for user 2 depends on it continuously. Also, Fig. 1 illustrates the domain, where user 1 gains from employing silent mode, incorporating in the transmission protocol some form of ambush mode to help the IDS to detect the jamming source. Of course, user 2 loses in this domain, and this domain essentially depends on the relation between urgency in transmission and detection probability.

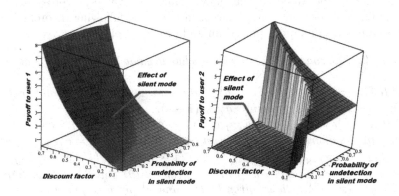

Fig. 1. Payoffs to user 1 and to user 2.

2.2   Random Jammer: Zero-Sum Game

To derive the maxmin anti-jamming transmission strategy we reformulate the game from previous section as a zero-sum game. In the zero-sum game, the cost function for user 2 is the payoff function for user 1. Thus, user 1 wants to minimize the payoff to user 2, and vice-versa. This situation can be described by the following zero-sum stochastic games Γ:

$$\Gamma = \begin{array}{c} \\ T_J \\ S \end{array} \begin{array}{c} S \qquad\qquad J \\ \begin{pmatrix} a_{T_J S}^1 + \delta\Gamma & a_{T_J J}^1 + \delta\gamma\Gamma \\ \delta\Gamma & a_{SJ}^1 + \delta\gamma_S\Gamma \end{pmatrix} \end{array}, \tag{11}$$

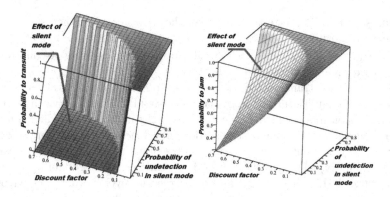

Fig. 2. Equilibrium probabilities to transmit for user 1 and to jam for user 2.

and a solution of the game is given as a solution to the Shapley (-Bellmann) equation [9]:

$$u = \text{val}(A^1(u)) = \max_{x^1} \min_{x^2} (x^1)^T A^1(u) x^2, \tag{12}$$

where $\text{val}(\Gamma)$ is the value of the game. Since the game is zero-sum, then $\max_{x^1} \min_{x^2}$ coincides with $\min_{x^2} \max_{x^1}$ in (12). The following theorem claims that the game has a unique equilibrium and gives it explicitly.

Theorem 2. *The considered zero-sum stochastic game has an unique stationary equilibrium.*

(a) If $(1 - \gamma\delta)a^1_{T_J S}/(1 - \delta) < a^1_{T_J J}$ then the unique (pure) equilibrium is (T_J, S) with value of the game $u = a^1_{T_J S}/(1 - \delta)$.

(b) If $(1 - \gamma\delta)a^1_{T_J S}/(1 - \delta) > a^1_{T_J J}$ and $(1 - \gamma_S\delta)a^1_{T_J J}/(1 - \delta\gamma) > a^1_{S J}$ then the unique (pure) equilibrium is (T_J, J) with value of the game $u = a^1_{T_J J}/(1 - \delta\gamma)$.

(c) If $(1 - \gamma\delta)a^1_{T_J S}/(1 - \delta) > a^1_{T_J J}$ and $(1 - \gamma_S\delta)a^1_{T_J J}/(1 - \delta\gamma) < a^1_{S J}$ then the value of the game is $u = u^1$ with u^1 given by (9) and the unique (mixed) equilibrium is (x^1, x^2) with x^2 given by (8), and x^1 given as follows:

$$x^1_{T_J} = \frac{a^1_{S J} - \delta(1 - \gamma_S)u}{a^1_{S J} + a^1_{T_J S} - a^1_{T_J J} - \delta(\gamma - \gamma_S)u}, x^1_S = \frac{a^1_{T_J S} - a^1_{T_J J} + \delta(1 - \gamma)u}{a^1_{S J} + a^1_{T_J S} - a^1_{T_J J} - \delta(\gamma - \gamma_S)u}.$$

Figure 3 illustrates what has changed in the user 1 transmission strategy for the zero-sum scenario when compared with the non-zero sum scenario. In Fig. 3(a), we denote by indices *ZS* and *NZS* the corresponding strategies for zero-sum and non-zero sum games. In the zero-sum game, user 1 applies more cautious strategy than in the non-zero some. Intuitively it is clear that a sleep mode cannot be an equilibrium strategy in the non-zero sum game since it contributes zero as a payoff. So, user 2 either uses jamming mode, or randomly sleep and jamming modes. In the zero-sum game, the silent mode can be an equilibrium strategy for user 2, if $u = a^1_{T_J} + \delta u \le a^1_{T_J J} + \delta\gamma u$, which takes place in the case (a) of Theorem 2.

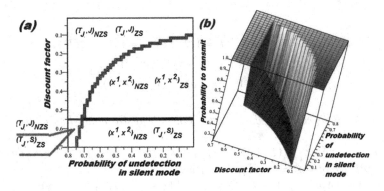

Fig. 3. (a) The domains where users apply different equilibrium strategies, and (b) probability to transmit by user 1.

3   Sophisticated SU Combines Malicious and Law Obedient Actions

In this section we assume that user 2 has a more sophisticated behaviour, where he might be a secondary user (SU) in a network and intends to use the network for two purposes: (i) to communicate as a law-obedient user, and (ii) to jam as a malicious user. Thus, he can choose between two modes: (a) transmission mode T, and (b) a jamming mode J. User 1 can choose between two modes: (a) transmission mode (T_T), where he transmits by applying the optimal power under assumption that user 2 is law obedient and uses the network the optimal way for transmission; and (b) a silent mode (S) to increase the probability of detection of the jamming event. The probability of detecting the jamming source is $1 - \gamma$, when user 1 is in transmission mode, and it is $1 - \gamma_S$, when user 1 is in silent mode. So, $\gamma_S < \gamma$. As a basic example of the payoff to user 2 in transmission mode we consider throughput, i.e. $v_T^2(\boldsymbol{P}^1, \boldsymbol{P}^2) = \sum_{i=1}^n \ln\left(1 + h_i^2 P_i^2/(\sigma^2 + h_i^1 P_i^1)\right)$. In transmission mode the users apply strategies composing Nash equilibrium for such a mode [9], i.e. a pair of strategies $(\boldsymbol{P}_{T_T*}^1, \boldsymbol{P}_{T*}^2)$ that for any $(\boldsymbol{P}^1, \boldsymbol{P}^2)$ the following inequalities hold: $v_T^1(\boldsymbol{P}^1, \boldsymbol{P}_{T*}^2) \leq v_T^1(\boldsymbol{P}_{T_T*}^1, \boldsymbol{P}_{T*}^2)$ and $v_T^2(\boldsymbol{P}^1, \boldsymbol{P}_{T*}^2) \leq v_T^2(\boldsymbol{P}_{T_T*}^1, \boldsymbol{P}_{T*}^2)$.

For example, the equilibrium strategies in transmission mode $(\boldsymbol{P}_{T*}^1, \boldsymbol{P}_{T*}^2)$ can be calculated by the results for general models using the Iterative Water Filling Algorithm (IWFA) [34,35]. For symmetric models the solution can be obtained explicitly [36,37]. Since user 2 knows that user 1 combines two modes (silent mode to detect the source of possible malicious activity and the transmission mode with the optimal power allocation versus law obedient action of the user 2), to gain greater jamming impact, in jamming mode user 2 applies the best response strategy to $\boldsymbol{P}_{T_T*}^1$, i.e. $\boldsymbol{P}_{J*}^2 = \arg_{\boldsymbol{P}^2} \max v_T^2(\boldsymbol{P}_{T_T*}^1, \boldsymbol{P}^2)$. This scenario can be described by the following non-zero sum stochastic game:

$$
(\Gamma^1, \Gamma^2) = \begin{array}{c} \\ T_T \\ S \end{array} \begin{array}{cc} T & J \\ \left(\begin{array}{cc} (a_{T_T T}^1 + \delta\Gamma^1, a_{T_T T}^2 + \delta\Gamma^2) & (a_{T_T J}^1 + \delta_\gamma \Gamma^1, a_{T_T J}^2 + \delta\gamma\Gamma^2) \\ (\delta\Gamma^1, a_{ST}^2 + \delta\Gamma^2) & (a_{SJ}^1 + \delta\gamma_S\Gamma^1, \delta\gamma_S\Gamma^2) \end{array} \right) \end{array}, (13)
$$

where

$$a_{T_T T}^k = v_T^k(\boldsymbol{P}_{T_T*}^1, \boldsymbol{P}_{T*}^2), k = 1, 2, \quad a_{T_T J}^2 = v_J^2(\boldsymbol{P}_{T_T*}^1, \boldsymbol{P}_{J*}^2),$$
$$a_{T_T J}^1 = v_T^1(\boldsymbol{P}_{T_T*}^1, \boldsymbol{P}_{J*}^2) + \delta(1-\gamma)\bar{v}^1/(1-\delta),$$
$$a_{SJ}^1 = \delta(1-\gamma)\bar{v}^1/(1-\delta), \quad a_{ST}^2 = v_T^2(\boldsymbol{0}, \boldsymbol{P}_{T*}^2).$$

Theorem 3. *The considered non-zero sum stochastic game has a unique stationary equilibrium.*

(a) *If* $(1-\gamma\delta)a_{T_T T}^2/(1-\delta) > a_{T_T J}^2$ *then the unique (pure) equilibrium is* (T_T, T) *with payoffs* $u^k = a_{T_T T}^k/(1-\delta)$ *with* $k = 1, 2$.

(b) *If* $(1-\gamma\delta)a_{T_T T}^2/(1-\delta) < a_{T_T J}^2$ *and* $(1-\gamma_S\delta)a_{T_T J}^1/(1-\delta\gamma) > a_{SJ}^1$ *then the unique (pure) equilibrium is* (T_T, J) *with payoffs* $u^k = a_{T_T J}^k/(1-\delta\gamma)$ *with* $k = 1, 2$.

(c) *If* $(1-\gamma\delta)a_{T_T T}^2/(1-\delta) < a_{T_T J}^2$ *and* $(1-\gamma_S\delta)a_{T_T J}^1/(1-\delta\gamma) < a_{SJ}^1$ *then the unique (mixed) equilibrium* $(\boldsymbol{x}^1, \boldsymbol{x}^2) = ((x_{T_T}^1, x_S^1), (x_T^2, x_J^2))$ *with payoffs* (u^1, u^2) *are given as follows:*

$$x_{T_T}^1 = \frac{a_{ST}^2 + \delta(1-\gamma_S)u^2}{a_{ST}^2 + a_{T_T J}^2 - a_{T_T T}^2 + \delta(\gamma - \gamma_S)u^2}, x_S^1 = \frac{a_{T_T J}^2 - a_{T_T T}^2 - \delta(1-\gamma)u^2}{a_{ST}^2 + a_{T_T J}^2 - a_{T_T T}^2 + \delta(\gamma - \gamma_S)u^2},$$

$$x_T^2 = \frac{a_{T_T J}^1 - a_{SJ}^1 + \delta(\gamma - \gamma_S)u^1}{a_{T_T J}^1 - a_{SJ}^1 - a_{T_T T}^1 + \delta(\gamma - \gamma_S)u^1}, x_J^2 = \frac{a_{T_T T}^1}{a_{T_T J}^1 - a_{SJ}^1 - a_{T_T T}^1 + \delta(\gamma - \gamma_S)u^1},$$

$$u^1 = \left(-c_1^1 - \sqrt{(c_1^1)^2 - 4c_2^1 c_0^1}\right)/(2c_2^1), \quad u^2 = \left(-c_1^2 + \sqrt{(c_1^2)^2 - 4c_2^2 c_0^2}\right)/(2c_2^2),$$

where

$$c_2^1 = c_2^2 = (1-\delta)\delta(\gamma - \gamma_S),$$
$$c_1^1 = a_{T_T J}^1(1-\delta) - a_{SJ}^1(1-\delta) - a_{T_T T}^1(1-\delta\gamma_S), \quad c_0^1 = a_{SJ}^1 a_{T_T T}^1,$$
$$c_1^2 = a_{T_T J}^2(1-\delta) + a_{ST}^2(1-\delta\gamma_S) - a_{T_T T}^2(1-\delta\gamma_S), \quad c_0^2 = -a_{ST}^2 a_{T_T J}^2.$$

Figures 4 and 5 illustrate the impact of the silent mode on user payoffs and their equilibrium strategies for $v_T^1(P_{T_T*}^1, P_{T*}^2) = 1.1$, $v_T^2(P_{T_T*}^1, P_{T*}^2) = 1.1$, $v_T^1(P_{T_T*}^1, P_{J*}^2) = 0.1$, $v_T^2(P_{T_T*}^1, P_{J*}^2) = 1.6$, $v_T^2(\boldsymbol{0}, P_{T*}^2) = 3$, $\bar{v}^1 = 4$ and $\gamma = 0.8$ as functions on discount factor δ and probability of non-detection in silent mode γ_S. It is interesting that user 1 never employs silent mode with certainty, he uses either just the transmission mode or chooses randomly between transmission and jamming modes. Thus, user 1 employs the silent mode versus a sophisticated adversary less often then versus a random jammer. Employing such a mode allows user 1 to increase his payoff and to reduce the payoff to user 2. There is one more interesting difference between the random and sophisticated jammer: payoff to user 1 versus sophisticated jammer is piece-wise continuous in terms of the discount factor δ and probability of non-detection in silent mode, while versus the random jammer it is continuous. Finally, note that the zero-sum version of the game (13) has the same structure as (11) with adaptation of matrix A^1 coefficients. Hence, Theorem 2 also can be applied for the zero-sum version of the game (13).

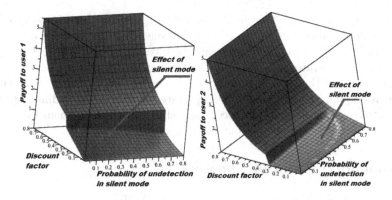

Fig. 4. Payoffs to user 1 and to user 2.

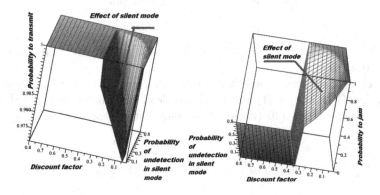

Fig. 5. Equilibrium probability to transmit for user 1 and to jam for user 2.

4   Conclusions

In this paper, using stochastic game modeling, we have studied anti-jamming strategies that may be employed against two types of jamming attacks: (i) a random jammer, where the malicious user combines a jamming mode with a sleep mode, and (ii) a sophisticated jammer, where the malicious user uses the network for two purposes: law-obedient communication with other users and to perform jamming attacks on the primary user. We have shown that incorporating silent modes in an anti-jamming transmission protocol, where the primary user does not transmit signals so as to help an IDS identify the source of jamming attack, can improve communication reliability. We have shown that in the maxmin anti-jamming transmission protocol, the primary user has to face more threats compared to the situation where the malicious user is a selfish one trying to gain by jamming the primary user. We have found that the payoff to the primary user or its equilibrium strategy can be discontinuous in the network parameters, such as in the detection probability of the IDS. This discontinuity means that the primary user has to take into account the technical characteristics of the network since some threshold values could increase the sensitivity of the transmissions protocol, while in other situations it produces only a minimal impact. In our future work, we are going to investigate how different discount factors, which illustrates differences in the urgency for the users to perform their action, can impact the optimal strategies. Also, we are going to investigate more sophisticated jamming and anti-jamming strategies that describe different types of malicious activity as well as the corresponding responses to them by the primary user, and to incorporate some learning algorithm in the users behaviour.

5   Appendix: Proof of Theorem 1

First note that (T_J, J) is an equilibrium if and only if

$$u^1 = a^1_{T_J J} + \delta \gamma u^1 \geq a^1_{S J} + \delta \gamma_S u^1, \tag{14}$$

$$u^2 = a^2_{T_J J} + \delta \gamma u^2 \geq \delta u^2. \tag{15}$$

Thus, u^1 and u^2 have to be given by (6). (15) always hold, and (14) holds if and only if (5) holds.

It is clear that there is no other pure equilibrium. Now look for mixed equilibrium. Let (7) hold. By (1) and (2), a couple of probability vectors $(\boldsymbol{x}^1, \boldsymbol{x}^2)$ is an equilibrium with payoffs (u^1, u^2) if and only if it is a solution of the equations

$$u^1 = U^1(u^1) \text{ and } u^2 = U^2(u^2), \tag{16}$$

where $(U^1(u^1), \boldsymbol{x}^2)$ and $(U^2(u^2), \boldsymbol{x}^1)$ are solution of the following LP problems:

$$\begin{aligned}
&\min U^1(u^1)\\
&L^1_{T_J}(u^1, x^2_S) := (a^1_{T_J S} + \delta u^1) x^2_S + (a^1_{T_J J} + \delta \gamma u^1)(1 - x^2_S) \leq U^1(u^1), \quad (17)\\
&L^1_S(u^1, x^2_S) := \delta u^1 x^2_S \qquad\qquad + (a^1_{S J} + \delta \gamma_S u^1)(1 - x^2_S) \leq U^1(u^1),
\end{aligned}$$

$$\begin{aligned}
&\qquad\min U^2(u^2)\\
&L^2_S(u^2, x^1_{T_J}) := \delta u^2 x^1_{T_J} \qquad\qquad + \delta u^2 (1 - x^1_{T_J}) \quad\ \leq U^2(u^2), \quad (18)\\
&L^2_J(u^2, x^1_{T_J}) := (a^2_{T_J J} + \delta \gamma u^2) x^1_{T_J} + \delta \gamma_S u^2 (1 - x^1_{T_J}) \leq U^2(u^2)
\end{aligned}$$

with the complementary slackness conditions (3) and (4).
First, consider LP problem (17). By (7), we have that

$$a^1_{S J} \geq a^1_{T_J J}. \tag{19}$$

Then, by (19), (see, Fig. 6) for any $u^1 \in [0, \bar{u}^1]$, where $\bar{u}^1 = (a^1_{S J} - a^1_{T_J J})/(\delta(\gamma - \gamma_S))$, $U^1(u^1)$ is a solution of the equations

$$L^1_{T_J}(u^1, x^2_S) = U^1(u^1) \text{ and } L^1_S(u^1, x^2_S) = U^1(u^1).$$

Thus,

$$U^1(u^1) = \frac{\delta^2(\gamma - \gamma_S)(u^1)^2 + \delta(a^1_{T_J J} - a^1_{S J} - \gamma_S a^1_{T_J S})u^1 - a^1_{S J} a^1_{T_J S}}{\delta(\gamma - \gamma_S)u^1 + a^1_{T_J J} - a^1_{S J} - a^1_{T_J S}}. \tag{20}$$

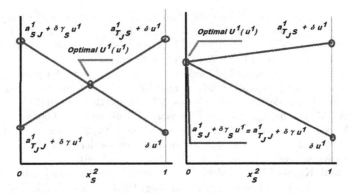

Fig. 6. LP problem (17) for $u^1 < \bar{u}^1$ (left) and LP problem (17) for $u^1 = \bar{u}^1$ (right).

It is clear that

$$U^1(0) > 0. \tag{21}$$

By Fig. 6(b),

$$U^1(\bar{u}^1) = a^1_{T_J J} + \delta\gamma\frac{a^1_{SJ} - a^1_{T_J J}}{\delta(\gamma - \gamma_S)} < (\text{by}(7)) < \frac{a^1_{SJ} - a^1_{T_J J}}{\delta(\gamma - \gamma_S)} = \bar{u}^1. \tag{22}$$

Thus, by (21) and (22), since U^1 is continuous, the Eq. (16) has at least one root in $[0, \bar{u}^1]$. By (20), this equation is equivalent to the following quadratic equation

$$c^1_2(u^1)^2 + c^1_1 u^1 + c^1_0 = 0 \tag{23}$$

with c^1_i, $i = 0, 1, 2$ given by (10). Since $c^1_0 > 0$ and $c^1_2 > 0$, by (21) and (22), the equation has the unique root in $[0, \bar{u}^1]$, while the second root of this quadratic equation is greater than $\bar{u}^1$. Thus, (8) and (9) is solution of the LP problem (17). It is clear that (8) and (9) gives solution of the LP problem (17). Since the complementary slackness conditions (3) and (4) obviously hold, and the result follows. ∎

References

1. Vadlamani, S., Medal, H., Eksioglu, B.: Security in wireless networks: a tutorial. In: Butenko, S., Pasiliao, E.L., Shylo, V. (eds.) Examining Robustness and Vulnerability of Networked Systems, pp. 272–289. IOS Press, Boston (2014)
2. Sharma, A., Ahuja, S., Uddin, M.: A survey on data fusion and security threats in CR networks. Int. J. Curr. Eng. Technol. **4**, 1770–1778 (2014)
3. Poisel, R.A.: Modern Communications Jamming Principles and Techniques. Artech House Publishers, London (2006)
4. Xu, W., Trappe, W., Zhang, Y., Wood, T.: The feasibility of launching and detecting jamming attacks in wireless networks. MobiHoc **2005**, 46–57 (2005)
5. Negi, R., Goel, S.: Secret communication using artificial noise. In: IEEE VTC 2005, pp. 1906–1910 (2005)

6. Xu, W.: Jamming attack defense. In: Tilborg, H., Jajodia, S. (eds.) Encyclopedia of Cryptography and Security, pp. 655–661. Springer, New York (2011)
7. Wu, Y., Wang, B., Liu, K.J.R., Clancy, T.C.: Anti-jamming games in multi-channel cognitive radio networks. IEEE JSAC **30**, 4–15 (2012)
8. Sagduyu, Y.E., Berry, R.A., Ephremides, A.: Jamming games for power controlled medium access with dynamic trafficc. In: IEEE ISIT 2010, pp. 1818–1822 (2010)
9. Fudenberg, D., Tirole, J.: Game Theory. MIT Press, Boston (1991)
10. Manshaei, M.H., Zhu, Q., Alpcan, T., Basar, T., Hubaux, J.P.: Game theory meets network security and privacy. ACM Comput. Surv. **45**, 25:1–25:39 (2013)
11. Theodorakopoulos, G., Baras, J.S.: Game theoretic modeling of malicious users in collaborative networks. IEEE JSAC **26**, 1317–1327 (2008)
12. Firouzbakht, K., Noubir, G., Salehi, M.: On the performance of adaptive packetized wireless communication links under jamming. IEEE Trans. Wirel. Commun. **13**, 3481–3495 (2014)
13. Garnaev, A., Baykal-Gursoy, M., Poor, H.V.: Incorporating attack-type uncertainty into network protection. IEEE Trans. Inf. Forensics Secur. **9**, 1278–1287 (2014)
14. Garnaev, Andrey, Hayel, Yezekael, Altman, Eitan, Avrachenkov, Konstantin: Jamming game in a dynamic slotted ALOHA network. In: Jain, Rahul, Kannan, Rajgopal (eds.) Gamenets 2011. LNICST, vol. 75, pp. 429–443. Springer, Heidelberg (2012)
15. Chen, L., Leneutreb, J.: Fight jamming with jamming - a game theoretic analysis of jamming attack in wireless networks and defense strategy. Comput. Netw. **55**, 2259–2270 (2011)
16. Liao, X., Hao, D., Sakurai, K.: Classification on attacks in wireless ad hoc networks: a game theoretic view. In: 2011 7th International Conference on Networked Computing and Advanced Information Management (NCM), pp. 144–149 (2011)
17. Altman, E., Avrachenkov, K., Garnaev, A.: Fair resource allocation in wireless networks in the presence of a jammer. Perform. Eval. **67**, 338–349 (2010)
18. Amariucai, G.T., Wei, S.: Jamming games in fast-fading wireless channels. IJAACS **1**, 411–424 (2008)
19. Nguyen, K.C., Alpcan, T., Basar, T.: Stochastic games for security in networks with interdependent nodes. In: GameNets 2009, pp. 697–703 (2009)
20. Wang, B., Wu, Y., Liu, K.J.R., Clancy, T.C.: An anti-jamming stochastic game for cognitive radio networks. IEEE JSAC **29**, 877–889 (2011)
21. DeBruhl, B., Kroer, C., Datta, A., Sandholm, T., Tague, P.: Power napping with loud neighbors: optimal energy-constrained jamming and anti-jamming. In: 2014 ACM Conference on Security and Privacy in Wireless and Mobile Networks (WiSec 2014), pp. 117–128 (2014)
22. Calinescu, G., Kapoor, S., Qiao, K., Shin, J.: Stochastic strategic routing reduces attack effects. In: GLOBECOM 2011, pp. 1–5 (2011)
23. Garnaev, A., Baykal-Gursoy, M., Poor, H.V.: A game theoretic analysis of secret and reliable communication with active and passive adversarial modes. IEEE Trans. Wirel. Commun. (2014, submitted)
24. Comaniciu, C., Mandayam, N.B., Poor, H.V.: Wireless Networks Multiuser Detection in Cross-Layer Design. Springer, New York (2005)
25. Verdu, S.: Multiuser Detection. Cambridge University Press, Cambridge (1998)
26. Trees, H.L.V.: Detection, Estimation, and Modulation Theory. Wiley, New York (2001)
27. Urkowitz, H.: Energy detection of unknown deterministic signals. Proc. IEEE **55**, 523–531 (1967)

28. Digham, F.F., Alouini, M.S., Simon, M.K.: On the energy detection of unknown signals over fading channels. In: IEEE ICC 2003, pp. 3575–3579 (2003)
29. Garnaev, Andrey, Trappe, Wade: Stationary equilibrium strategies for bandwidth scanning. In: Jonsson, Magnus, Vinel, Alexey, Bellalta, Boris, Marina, Ninoslav, Dimitrova, Desislava, Fiems, Dieter (eds.) MACOM 2013. LNCS, vol. 8310, pp. 168–183. Springer, Heidelberg (2013)
30. Garnaev, A., Trappe, W., Kung, C.-T.: Dependence of optimal monitoring strategy on the application to be protected. In: 2012 IEEE Global Communications Conference (GLOBECOM), pp. 1054–1059 (2012)
31. Altman, Eitan, Avrachenkov, Konstantin, Garnaev, Andrey: A jamming game in wireless networks with transmission cost. In: Chahed, Tijani, Tuffin, Bruno (eds.) NET-COOP 2007. LNCS, vol. 4465, pp. 1–12. Springer, Heidelberg (2007)
32. Garnaev, A., Hayel, Y., Altman, E.: A Bayesian jamming game in an OFDM wireless network. In: 2012 10th International Symposium on Modeling and Optimization in Mobile, Ad Hoc and Wireless Networks (WIOPT), pp. 41–48 (2012)
33. Altman, E., Avrachenkov, K., Garnaev, A.: Jamming in wireless networks: the case of several jammers. In: International Conference on Game Theory for Networks (GameNets 2009), pp. 585–592 (2009)
34. Luo, Z.-Q., Pang, J.-S.: Analysis of iterative waterfilling algorithm for multiuser power control in digital subscriber lines. EURASIP J. Adv. Sign. Process. **2006**, 10 (2006)
35. Yu, W., Ginis, G., Cioffi, J.M.: Distributed multiuser power control for digital subscriber lines. IEEE JSAC **20**(5), 1105–1115 (2002)
36. Altman, E., Avrachenkov, K., Garnaev, A.: Closed form solutions for symmetric water filling games. In: 27th IEEE Communications Society Conference on Computer Communications (INFOCOM 2008), pp. 673–681 (2008)
37. Altman, E., Avrachenkov, K., Garnaev, A.: Closed form solutions for water-filling problem in optimization and game frameworks. Telecommun. Syst. **47**, 153–164 (2011)

OpenMobs: Mobile Broadband Internet Connection Sharing

Nicolae-Valentin Ciobanu[1]([⊠]), Dragos-George Comaneci[1], Ciprian Dobre[1], Constandinos X. Mavromoustakis[2], and George Mastorakis[3]

[1] Faculty of Automatic Control and Computers, University Politehnica of Bucharest, 313, Splaiul Independentei, 060042 Bucharest, Romania
{nicolae.ciobanu1411,dragos.comaneci}@cti.pub.ro,
ciprian.dobre@cs.pub.ro
[2] Department of Computer Science, University of Nicosia,
46 Makedonitissas Avenue, 1700 Nicosia, Cyprus
mavromoustakis.c@unic.ac.cy
[3] Technological Educational Institute of Crete,
Estavromenos, 71500 Heraklion, Crete, Greece
gmastorakis@staff.teicrete.gr

Abstract. We witness an explosion in the number of applications being developed for mobile devices. Many such applications are in need or generate a lot of Internet traffic, and as such mobile devices are today equipped with more networking capabilities, from mobile broadband (3G/4G) to WiFi, Bluetooth, and others. However, when it comes to mobile broadband Internet access, for economic reasons, today mobile providers tend to switch from unlimited mobile data plans to tiered data pricing models, putting pressure on mobile data subscribers to be more careful how they consume their subscribed traffic. In this paper, we propose OpenMobs, a mean to reduce the costs associated with mobile broadband access to Internet, by sharing under-utilized networking resources among co-located users through free wireless connections. When two or more handsets are in the vicinity of each other, Open-Mobs forms an ad hoc mesh network to redirect traffic between mobile data plan subscribers, in the most economic and viable way. We present studies on the feasibility of such a system to minimize the costs users pay monthly to their mobile providers, and even financially compensates users' willingness to participate in the collaboration.

Keywords: Internet · Mobile broadband · Sharing · Traffic allocation

1 Introduction

Today mobile handsets and devices have come to outnumber traditional PCs several times, and applications for mobile devices exploded in number. But many such applications are in need or generate a lot of Internet traffic. For example, to address problems associated with the limited amount of resources (computation,

© Institute for Computer Sciences, Social Informatics and Telecommunications Engineering 2015
R. Agüero et al. (Eds.): MONAMI 2014, LNICST 141, pp. 244–258, 2015.
DOI: 10.1007/978-3-319-16292-8_18

storage, power) available within the mobile device, or to provide richer experience to their clients, many application developers appeal to resource providers (the 'Cloud') other than the mobile device. This is why today we do have various mobile applications connected to either Apple iCloud, Google's Gmail for Mobile, or Google Goggles. Of course, for this to happen, application developers rely on good networking connections with the Cloud.

The networking capabilities offered by mobile devices have become very diverse lately. Internet access options range from using free Wi-Fi at a hotspot, to having a mobile broadband (e.g., 3G) or a mobile hotspot access (the "any-where, anytime" Internet access offered over cellular networks). Among these, mobile broadband access is still widely used, since it allows the user to go online anywhere there is a cellular signal.

For mobile broadband access, a mobile data plan from a cell phone provider allows a client to access the 3G or 4G data network, to send and receive emails, surf the Internet, use IM, and so on from his mobile device. Mobile broadband devices such as mobile hotspots and USB mobile broadband modems also require a data plan from a wireless provider.

Unlimited data plans for cell phones (including smartphones) have been the norm most recently (sometimes folded in with other wireless services in a one-price subscription plan for voice, data, and texting). Still, today most providers, following the example set by AT&T in 2010 [11], use tiered data pricing, thus eliminating unlimited data access on cell phones. Tiered data plans charge different rates based on how much data the client uses each month. The benefit is that such metered plans discourage heavy data usage that could slow down a cellular network. Thus, it is no wonder today that most mobile broadband plans for data access on laptops and tablets or via mobile hotspots are typically tiered [10]. The downside is that users have to be more vigilant about how much data they are using, and for heavy users, tiered data plans are more expensive.

When it comes to choosing a suitable tiered mobile data plan [4], clients generally tend to go for oversized mobile data plans. For choosing, clients estimate their peak monthly traffic needs, which is natural considering that mobile operators charge the extra traffic above the data plan limits. In our work, we started by analysing this fact, through interviews and questionnaires, and found out that *today most clients do tend to pay for a lot of mobile broadband traffic, but most of the time they never use their entire payed data plan traffic.*

On the other hand, when users (accidentally) exceed their mobile plan rates, they are generally charged extra by the mobile provider. Also, in roaming, the extra costs for connectivity can be occasionally quite prohibitive. So, the research question we are addressing in this article is: *Can we come up with a solution that mediates opportunistic sharing of networking resources, when needed, between users?.* For the sharing of WiFi Access Point traffic, opportunistic networking today provides an answer [2]. For mobile broadband access, we want to let users share parts of their unused mobile broadband traffic with others. But users pay a monthly fee to their mobile providers, so they might be reluctant in 'giving away' traffic to others, for free. Thus, we propose letting the user become a *re-seller of broadband traffic that he gets from his mobile provider.* This means that a user can sell part of his under-used traffic, and sell it to clients in need, making a small profit in doing this (such that, at the end of the month, some of his monthly mobile data plan fee gets payed by others). For a buyer, it is attractive to have other users let him use their mobile data broadband access, if he ends up paying less compared to the fees charged by the mobile provider.

In the present work we present OpenMobs, a system designed to support the sharing of under-utilized resources available on mobile handsets in a distributed and opportunistic way. When two or more handsets are in wireless proximity, OpenMobs tries to forward part of one user's traffic through the mobile data plan of the other. To incentivize the payments between users, and motive them share resources in an accountable manner, a digital currency such as BitCoin [9] can be used as the form of payment for used resources. Here, we present extensive studies on the feasibility of such a system to minimize the costs users pay to their mobile providers at the end of the month.

Internet connection sharing has existed as an idea for many years, and every modern operating system has implemented its fair share of services in order to address it [12]. For smartphones, the latest venture that comes close to what the current work is trying to solve is Open Garden [6]. Open Garden leverages crowdsourcing to create seamless connectivity across 3G, 4G, Wi-Fi and Bluetooth. It enables users to create their own ad-hoc mesh networks with other Open Garden enabled devices (i.e., smartphones, tablets and PCs). Unlike the centralized idea proposed by Open Garden, OpenMobs allows users to share networking resources with minimal interaction with a centralized entity. OpenMobs tackles the problem of automatic sharing based on context, where the user node automatically chooses to use the opportunistic shared connection.

Our work can also be compared with the idea of offloading cellular networks through ad hoc vehicular wireless networks [8]. However, we do not rely only on the existence of wireless routers (it is even better when such devices exist), and optimize traffic consumption particularly considering the wireless mobile broadband charging fees. To the best of our knowledge, this is the first work to propose such a decentralized traffic sharing approach.

The rest of the paper is structured as follows. In Sect. 2 we first introduce the theoretical optimization problem linked to the allocation of networking resources, and propose a heuristic allocation approach for the maximization of compensation costs. Our approach is further evaluated in extensive simulation experiments in Sect. 3. Finally, in Sect. 4 we present the conclusions.

2   Traffic Allocation Model

2.1   Research Problem

The problem of sharing traffic can be modelled as follows: Given a set of users, each having a mobile data plan (defined by a data amount for which the user pays a monthly fee, and a cost model for computing an extra fee associated with the traffic consumption exceeding the data plan threshold set by the cell phone operator), and each consuming a certain amount of traffic each month, we want to find an equilibrium price auction model for bidding traffic between users, such that by re-routing traffic through other mobile phones and paying a fee for the temporary use of their data plans, users gain profits and/or pay less, compared to the case when each user acts selfish sticking to only the local data plan costs negotiated by each with their cell phone operators.

In this problem, any user can become a traffic provider for other users (*seller*). The traffic is auctioned, and any user is interested to buy traffic from other users (*buyer*) directly located in his wireless communication range (WiFi, Bluetooth or ZigBee could be employed at no extra costs), if the price is lower than the cost associated with sending the traffic over the 3G or 4G data network. As mentioned, such a situation appears, for example, when a buyer already consumed its entire monthly data plan traffic, and any extra traffic might be charged by the mobile operator at considerable higher fees. Or, when a buyer is in roaming, and the cost of transferring data over the mobile operator can be considerable higher compared to the costs negotiated with the mobile operator by another user (i.e., local to the mobile network).

This situation is illustrated in Fig. 1. In the example, $user_B$ needs to transfer some data (send and receive emails, surf the Internet, use IM, and so on) from its mobile device. For this, he can send data over 3G, using the cost associated with the data plan negotiated with the mobile provider ($cost_B$). Luckly, in his wireless communication range, $user_A$ is offering to transfer this data, over a WiFi connection existing between these two users, at a cost (bid_{AB}) lower than $cost_B$ (so $user_B$ actually pays less, the difference being his 'gain'). For $user_A$, this situation also brings a small profit ($gain_A$), since the offered cost bid_{AB} is higher than the actual cost ($cost_A$) negotiated by $user_A$ with her mobile provider for transferring this data.

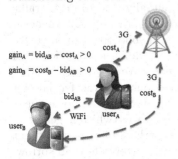

Fig. 1. Example scenario.

When applying equilibrium price auctions for the allocation of traffic, the two roles, buyer and seller, face distinct yet linked challenges. The buyer is interested to transfer traffic at the minimum cost possible, while the seller wants to maximize his profit (he will commonly pursue the objective of maximizing profit). Thus, we need to come up with specific equilibrium prices each time a user is interested to transfer some data, such that to avoid situations where a seller loses money at the end of the month, by selling traffic too cheap, compared to the cost he has to pay for his own traffic transfer needs. In this case, the profit is given by the difference between the revenue from the served bids, and the costs associated with all transfers over the mobile data network.

For the rest of this article, we assume that each user has a mobile data plan, negotiated with a local mobile provider/operator. Also, each user consumes a certain amount of traffic, each month, for his own personal needs (transfers generated from the local mobile phone, for emails, web, and others). We further assume that each user can participate in any auction, with any other users having different data plans and traffic needs.

2.2   Formal Notations

As a basis for the optimization approach presented in the following, we introduce a formal notation. First, we define the basic entities:

- $U \subset \mathbb{N}$ Set of participating users.
- $B \subset \mathbb{N}$ Set of buyers (willing to buy traffic from other users, where $B \subseteq U$).
- $S \subset \mathbb{N}$ Set of sellers (wanting to sell traffic to other users, where $S \subseteq U$).

According to the mobile data plan of user $u \in U$, he can monthly transfer traffic up to a specific amount (DP_u), at a constant fee $(CF_u$ - generally negotiated with the mobile provider). If the user exceeds the DP_u limit, the extra traffic is charged separately by the mobile operator, according to a cost algorithm $CO_u(T)$, that depends on the actual amount of traffic T being transferred.

Generally, the data plans differ between users. Thus, for any 2 users u_1 and u_2, it can happen that $DP_{u_1} \neq DP_{u_2}$, $CF_{u_1} \neq CF_{u_2}$ and so on (but, it can also happen that two users can get similar data plans, especially when they are subscribed to the same mobile operator).

Also, we assume that each user transfers a certain amount of traffic, T_u each month. Naturally, there is no problem when all users manage to stay within their mobile data plans $(T_u \leq DP_u)$ - but this is not always the case because of at least two reasons: (1) even if the user manages to provision a data plan satisfactory to his need, unscheduled events might actually lead to more traffic being generated than usual (*unforeseen networking needs*), and (2) whenever in roaming, or for different services provided by the mobile operator at 'extra costs', there are supplementary fees for the generated traffic, independently of the traffic included within the data plan (*extra costs*). We assume that other users are willing to sell traffic (actually, accept connections and transfer data for other users, through their local mobile data plan), because they do not manage each month to consume all the traffic they generate anyway (which is generally the case, as users tend to negotiate mobile data plans with mobile operators that are above their average traffic needs - the old saying 'better safe than sorrow' generally applies when we think what kind of mobile data plan is suitable to our monthly traffic needs).

Whenever two users, a buyer $(b \in B)$ and a seller $(s \in S)$ are in contact (they can exchange traffic at no costs over short- or medium- range wireless protocols, such as WiFi, Bluetooth or ZigBee), they can negotiate a price (CS_{bs}) for transferring data generated by b, over the wireless link to s, and from there over the mobile data network, using the seller's data plan. This price also depends on the amount of traffic T_{bs} that is transferred between these two users (otherwise, the buyers might transfer well above the data plan limits of the seller, which might reduce the seller's profit).

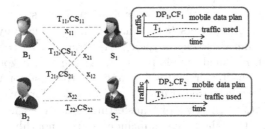

Fig. 2. Schematic overview of the optimization model, depicting the decision variables, and most relevant entities.

Finally, we assume users are mobile, such that with a high probability, over a longer period of time, any two users can meet at least once (such that $\forall b \in B$, $s \in S$ $T_{bs} \geq 0$ stands).

2.3   Optimal Allocation Approach

To compute an optimal solution to the indicated problem, we transfer the problem definition into a mathematical optimization model. The result is given in Model 1, and will be explained in detail in the following.

In Eq. 6, x is defined as a binary decision variable. Specifically, x_{bs} indicates whether the user b is willing to buy traffic from another user s. More specifically, when two users meet, each one presents his offer (the price he is willing to accept for the other to transfer traffic through his mobile data plan). Of course, this auction can be accepted or not by each user (which is interpreted by this binary decision variable). An overview of the optimization model, which highlights the relations between the decision variables and the most important entities, is depicted in Fig. 2.

Equation 1 specifies the objective of the optimization model, namely the minimization of the costs implied for transferring cell phone generated data over the mobile networks operated by different mobile providers (but doing it such that in the end no user loses money). This is similar to the concept of profit, as the difference between the fees paid to the mobile operator without using any optimization, versus the smaller fees paid to the mobile operator when users collaborate and re-sell traffic in their data plan, is a cost which is shown in their own pockets. Thus, the two components shown in Eq. 1.

Equation 2 specifies the cost for transferring data for all users, as a sum between the data plan costs (CF, fix costs paid by all user at the end of the month; this generally includes the traffic D, corresponding to the data plan negotiated with the mobile operator), and costs associated with extra traffic (CO is a cost model specified by the mobile operator; according to this, generally the user pays proportionally with the amount of traffic transferred over the data plan limits T'). The cost CO can be quite large, and in this case, the T' traffic could be redirected through the unused data plan offered by another user.

Equation 3 specified exactly this optimization. In this case, some traffic is transferred through other users (so we have sellers S, and buyers B). In this case, the cost is a sum between (1) the cost for transferring the local traffic by the buyer, through his local mobile provider, (2) the cost negotiated for traffic auctioned between the buyer and seller, and (3) the cost for transferring the local traffic plus the negotiated traffic, through the local mobile provider of the seller. In this equation, the cost of transferring data over the mobile operator depends, again, whether the traffic is included in the monthly data plan traffic, or exceeds the data plan traffic (which is presented in Eq. 4).

Finally, Eq. 5 links everything together, and presents the conditions needing to happen in order for a user to maximize his profit by selling data plan traffic (respectively, optimize the cost by buying traffic from a seller, at a cost lower than the one offered by the mobile operator). For users to gain from this collaboration (see Fig. 1), two conditions must simultaneous stand: (1) the buyer must buy at a cost smaller than the cost of transferring the same amount of data through the mobile operator (right inequality), and (2) the seller must sell at a cost that covers at least the cost necessary for him to transfer the sold data over the local mobile operator (left inequality).

For the seller, the cost could be 0 if he manages to sell traffic included in his mobile data plan, negotiated with the mobile operator. This condition is also captured in Eq. 5; in this case, his operating/transferring cost C_s is kept to 0 if the traffic generated by the seller and transferred over the mobile operator (T_s), plus all traffic that he manages to sell, is still less than the data plan traffic negotiated with the operator (DP_s). Actually, the seller still has to pay at the end of the month the fee associated with his data plan, but this is independent of the amount of traffic sold (and is included in $Cost_{initial}$). In other words, C_s establishes a hint over the *profit* the seller manages to accomplish.

In Eq. 5, the selling price needs a predictor on the amount of traffic the seller expects to deliver through his mobile network for the current month. A fog-of-war probabilistic model, similar to the one proposed in [8], can be used to deal with this uncertainty, considering the history of traffic associated with the user monthly, on a historical base. With this construction, Model 1 still constitutes a Linear Program (LP), or more specifically, Binary Integer Program (BIP). This class of optimization problems can be solved using well-known methods from the field of Operations Research, most notably, the Branch and Bound (B&B) algorithm [7]. While the B&B algorithm can be very efficient in some cases, it is still based on the principle of enumeration, i.e., in the worst case, all potential solutions have to be examined [5]. Specifically, for a BIP, the solution space grows exponentially with the number of decision variables. As can be observed from Model 1, the number of decision variables increases quadratically with the number of traffic auctions (Eq. 6), and linearly with the number of mobile data plan types. Accordingly, the computational complexity of the optimal allocation approach is exponential and corresponds to $O(2^{\|U\|^2 * \|DP\|})$, where $\|DP\|$ is the number of different tiered mobile data plans in use.1

Model 1 Optimal Allocation Model

$$\text{Maximize} \quad Profit_x = \{Cost_{initial} - Cost_{optim}(x)\} \geq 0 \qquad (1)$$

$$Cost_{initial} = \sum_{u \in U} CF_u + \sum_{u \in U} CO_u \left(T_u' \right) \qquad (2)$$

$$Cost_{optim}(x) = \sum_{b \in B} C_b \left(T_b - \sum_{s \in S} x_{bs} * T_{bs} \right)$$

$$+ \sum_{b \in B, s \in S} x_{bs} * CS_{bs} \left(T_{bs} \right) + \sum_{s \in S} C_s \left(T_s + \sum_{b \in B} x_{bs} * T_{bs} \right) \qquad (3)$$

where,

$$C_u(T) = \begin{cases} CF_u & \text{if } T < DP_u. \\ CF_u + CO_u \left(T - DP \right), & \text{otherwise.} \end{cases} \qquad (4)$$

$$\forall b \in B, s \in S, \quad x_{bs} = 1 \iff C_s(T) < CS_{bs}(T) < CO_b(T)$$

with,

$$C_s(T) = \begin{cases} 0, & \text{if } T_s + \sum_{\forall u, u \neq s} x_{us} * T_{us} + T < DP_s. \\ CO_s(T), & \text{otherwise.} \end{cases} \qquad (5)$$

$$x_{bs} \in \{0, 1\} \quad \forall b \in B, S \in S \qquad (6)$$

2.4   An Heuristic Allocation Approach

For real-life application scenarios involving thousands of users, the optimal allocation approach may be problematic due to its exponential growth in computational complexity. Thus, we have developed a heuristic approach that trades reductions in computation time against potentially sub-optimal solutions. The idea is to determine an equilibrium price auctioned between any two users.

In our approach, whenever two users, A and B, meet, each presents to the other a price he is willing to accept for traffic forwarding. This means that A computes a price, CS_{AB}, he is willing to accept from B (per data unit). If user B needs to transfer data (for email, or others), he decides whether is cheaper to transfer it through the mobile network (3G), or send it through A (over WiFi or other 'cost-free' wireless communication protocol). In this case, A gains a small fee, which is still larger than what it costs him to actually send the data coming from B, over A's mobile network. If this is true, than user A becomes the 'seller', and user B the 'buyer'.

The CS_{bs} price depends on several parameters (as described in Model 1): the mobile data plan of the seller (DP_s), the traffic already used from this data plan by the seller from the beginning of the current month[1] (P_s), and the amount of traffic the buyer is interested to transfer (XP_b). The idea is to sell cheap when the user has plenty of traffic left from the mobile data plan (such that to guarantee that at least someone buys - the seller wants to maximize his profit, and use the traffic remaining in the data plan that otherwise would be waste), and sell at a high rate if the seller does not have much traffic left in the mobile data plan (such that, in the unfortunate event that in the future he will also want to use his data plan for own traffic needs, the higher fees operated by the mobile provider for any extra traffic are still covered by the fees he gains from his traffic buyers - the seller wants to stay 'in profit', and not lose money at the end of the month).

Thus, the heuristic formula we propose for computing the cost is:

$$CS_{bs} = e^{\min\{th, \frac{P_s + XP_b - DP_s}{coef}\}} \tag{7}$$

where th is a high upper-limit threshold (that ensures the negotiated fee does not grow indefinitely), and $coef$ is a coefficient that reflects the mobility environment. This means that for $coef$, we start with a predefined traffic value (the predefined preference of the user to sell traffic). If, at the end of the month, the user losses money (because his preference in selling made him sell cheaper that the is charged by the mobile operator), the value of this coefficient doubles. After several iterations, as the experiments presented next show, the system actually reaches a state of eccuilibrium, and all $coef$ are stable and individually defined such that we have a positive profit.

3   Evaluation

3.1   Approach and Methodology

For testing the proposed heuristic allocation approach, we used three publicly-available mobility traces. UPB [2] is a trace taken in an academic environment at the University Politehnica of Bucharest, where the participants were students and teachers at the faculty. It includes Bluetooth and WiFi data collected for a period of 64 days, by 66 participants. St. Andrew [1] is a real-world mobility trace taken on the premises of the University of St. Andrews and around the surrounding town. It lasted for 79 days and involved 27 participants that used T-mote Invent devices with Bluetooth capabilities. Finally, MIT Reality [3] contains tracing data from 100 users from the University of Helsinki. The collected information includes call logs and Bluetooth devices in proximity, collected over the course of an academic year. Thus, each scenario emulates different running conditions: users meet scarcely, regularly, or frequently.

---

[1] Through the paper, a month is the time period usually charged by the mobile operator. As such, a month can actually begin with any day of the montly calendar.

On top of these traces, we simulated the behavior of users wanting to transfer data, with and without a system serving the proposed optimized heuristics. This system detects opportunistic wireless connections and tries to optimize the cost when possible, by transferring some of the traffic exceeding the mobile data plan, through other proximity-located users.

The main benefit of such a system is that it creates a virtual market of Internet traffic. Basically, it addresses the problem of rigid mobile subscription plans by providing opportunistic ad hoc sharing of traffic, below the normal rates. Those with excess traffic included in their mobile subscription plan can offer it to others for a much lower price than they would pay the network provider.

There is also a hidden benefit for the mobile network provider: the network usage can be more predictable since users will tend to use up their mobile subscription plan completely; at lower costs, users will be stimulated to use broadband communication more, which will result in profit for the provider.

Another benefit is present when travelling abroad since the rates offered by the local peers will be much less than the roaming rates offered by the mobile network provider.

Table 1. Data Service Plan parameters used in simulations.

Price/MB (EUR) for traffic included in plan	Price/MB (EUR) for for extra traffic outside the data plan	Amount of traffic included in data plan	Assignment probability
0.02	0.01	90 MB	0.05
0.012	0.01	200 MB	0.05
0.008	0.01	350 MB	0.10
0.007	0.01	450 MB	0.15
0.006	0.01	500 MB	0.30
0.004	0.01	1 GB	0.25
0.0037	0.01	1.5 GB	0.05
0.0032	0.01	2.0 GB	0.05

In these experiments, we were particularly interested whether there are benefits (profit) for the users, and whether users interact frequently enough in real-world so that the system is useful. We want to measure the benefits previously mentioned, and see if the degree of interaction that occurs between peers increases the benefits provided by the system.

Each of the cases was run several times on each trace, with varying random seed values, for a confidence level of 95 %.

In order for the simulations to resemble real usage as close as possible, we have chosen to allocate each mobile device from the trace a specific service subscription data plan, which has three associated parameters: price/MB when the user still has traffic in his normal data plan, price/MB when the user has exhausted the traffic in his data plan and the amount of included data traffic. Each data service plan also has an associated probability that is taken into account when generating the data plan associations for the mobile devices.

After associating a data subscription plan, the next step was to designate a level of data usage and traffic pattern per device. A traffic pattern has two associated parameters: the average amount of traffic used per month and a propensity to use that traffic when in a social context (when the device is in contact with other devices). The propensity parameter is represented as the probability that a device will consume traffic when in the presence of another device.

Table 2. Traffic usage pattern parameters used in the simulation.

Average Data Traffic per Month (MB)	Propensity to use traffic while in the presence of other mobile devices	Traffic Pattern Distribution Probability
200	0.5	0.25
400	0.5	0.25
600	0.5	0.25
800	0.5	0.25

The data service plans parameters used in our simulation are presented in Table 1. These plans and their distribution have been empirically determined based on the real data plan offered in Romania, by the Orange mobile operator. The Price/MB for traffic included in the data plan has been determined by factoring out the included data traffic as representing one fifth of the value of the mobile subscription plan. The 1/5 factor has been selected such that the price for traffic included in the plan will be less that the price for extra traffic for most of the service plans. Also, for each service plan there tends to be up to 5 components included in the offer (data traffic, internal voice traffic, external voice traffic, SMS, MMS).

The traffic usage pattern parameters used for the simulations are presented in Table 2. These parameters have been selected based on usual data traffic consumption patterns.

3.2   Results and Discussion

We used four metrics to evaluate OpenMobs's ability to support traffic sharing (all results below are averaged over all simulated months). The first one is *greediness*, which is the percent of monthly traffic a user uses, versus the traffic offered implicitly by his mobile data plan. In simulations, we have (a) users consuming less traffic than they are offered by the mobile provider, and (b) others consuming up to 10x times the traffic they could otherwise use (which happens because now users are motivated to use more, at lower offered prices). For the users in the first category, the gain is triggered by the traffic they sell. For the others, the gain is computed as the difference between what they would have paid without

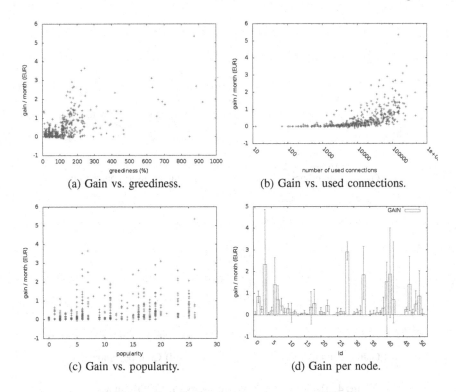

(a) Gain vs. greediness.

(b) Gain vs. used connections.

(c) Gain vs. popularity.

(d) Gain per node.

Fig. 3. Results for the experiments on UPB.

OpenMobs, and what they actually paid when using OpenMobs. As results in Figs. 3a, 4a, and 5a show, because costs in OpenMobs are optimized, users selling traffic gain a profit maintained within such limits that users buying would not lose money at the end of the month, compared to what they would pay if buying traffic directly from the mobile operator.

Another metric is the *usedConections*, which shows the link between the number of times a user buys or sells traffic, versus the gain OpenMobs brings at the end of the month. As seen in Figs. 3b, 4b, and 5b, users manage to gain at the end of the month proportionally to the number of times they are able to sell or buy traffic - thus, OpenMobs can actually incentivitize users to participate in the traffic sharing collaboration, just by the fact that the more clients use the system, the more profit they manage to gain.

The *popularity* shows the relation between the homophily of an user, and his monthly gain when using OpenMobs. Two users are considered to have a connection if they spend enough time in contact and share a number of friends in common [2]. The results in Figs. 3c and 4c show that a more popular user has a higher probability of making a certain profit from using OpenMobs – in the left part, the users with relatively few friends are clustered near the bottom, while in the right part of the plots, clients with more friends are scattered and tend to gain more from using OpenMobs.

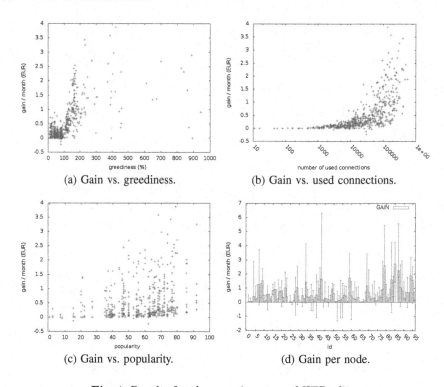

(a) Gain vs. greediness.   (b) Gain vs. used connections.

(c) Gain vs. popularity.   (d) Gain per node.

Fig. 4. Results for the experiments on MITReality.

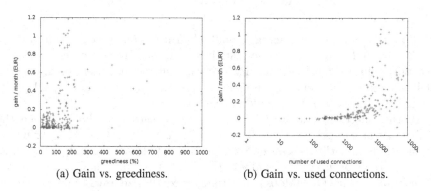

(a) Gain vs. greediness.   (b) Gain vs. used connections.

Fig. 5. Results for the experiments on StAndrews.

Finally, Figs. 3d and 4d show the relation between the average gain for each node (user), and the actual variance of the gain during the experiments. We recall that each experiment lasts for several month, and in the beginning users can actually lose (the lower values for gain). But, because OpenMobs adapts the strategy and corrects the coefficient used in the auctioned prices for selling traffic, in the end all users start gaining. This means that, in real life, when OpenMobs is used for even more consecutive months, it can actually start bringing more profit to each user – which we believe can act as another incentive for users to use and participate in the collaboration.

4 Conclusions

OpenMobs is a system designed to optimize the economical costs in accessing mobile broadband Internet through mobile handset devices. In this paper, we presented our approach to share under-utilized networking resources among co-located users through free wireless access. Whenever two or more users are in the vicinity of each other, OpenMobs forms an ad hoc mesh network and redirects traffic in the most economic and viable way. We presented extensive studies on the feasibility of such a system to minimize the costs users pay to their mobile providers at the end of the month, and even financially compensates users willingness to participate in the collaboration. We are currently well-underway with a real-world implementation of OpenMobs, on Android-operated devices. Also, ink the future, we aim to address also energy consumption as another parameter for our cost model.

Acknowledgment. The research is partially supported by COST Action IC1303 AAPELE, and by the national project MobiWay, Project PN-II-PT-PCCA-2013-4-0321.

References

1. Bigwood, G., Rehunathan, D., et al.: Exploiting self-reported social networks for routing in ubiquitous computing environments. In: IEEE International Conference on Wireless and Mobile Computing Networking and Communications, WIMOB 2008, pp. 484–489. IEEE (2008)
2. Ciobanu, R.I., Dobre, C., Cristea, V.: Sprint: social prediction-based opportunistic routing. In: IEEE 14th International Symposium and Works on a World of Wireless, Mobile and Multimedia Networks (WoWMoM), pp. 1–7 (2013)
3. Eagle, N., Pentland, A.: Reality mining: sensing complex social systems. Pers. Ubiquit. Comput. **10**(4), 255–268 (2006)
4. Hanlon, J.: Choosing the best broadband plan, August 2013. http://www.whistleout.com.au/Broadband/Guides/choosing-the-best-bradband-plan. Accessed 10 April 2014
5. Hillier, F.S., Lieberman, G.J.: Introduction to Operations Research. Tata McGraw-Hill Education, New Delhi (2001)
6. Laridinios, F.: Open Garden 2.0 makes sharing your WiFi and mobile connections easier and faster. http://techcrunch.com/
7. Lawler, E.L., Wood, D.E.: Branch-and-bound methods: a survey. Oper. Res. **14**(4), 699–719 (1966)
8. Malandrino, F., Casetti, C.: C Chiasserini, and Marco Fiore. Content download in vehicular networks in presence of noisy mobility prediction. IEEE Trans. Mob. Comput. **13**(5), 1007–1021 (2014)

9. Nakamoto, S.: Bitcoin: a peer-to-peer electronic cash system. Consulted 1, 2012 (2008)
10. Pinola, M.: Overview of Wi-Fi, 3G and 4G Data Plans. http://mobileoffice.about. com/. Accessed 10 April 2014
11. Pinola, M.: AT&T's new data tiers: cost less, less value? June 2010. http:// mobileoffice.about.com/. Accessed 10 April 2014
12. Tsiaras, C., Liniger, S., Stiller, B.: An automatic and on-demand MNO selection mechanism. In: IEEE/IFIP Network Operations and Management Symposium (NOMS 2014), Management in a Software Defined World. Krakow, Polland (2014)

On the Feasibility of Inter-flow Network Coding Over Random Wireless Mesh Networks

Pablo Garrido[✉], David Gómez, Francisco Santos, and Ramón Agüero

Universidad de Cantabria, Santander, Spain
{pgarrido,dgomez,ramon}@tlmat.unican.es,
francisco.santos@unican.es

Abstract. The attention that the scientific community has paid to the use of *Network Coding* techniques over Wireless Mesh Networks has remarkably increased in the last years. A large group of the existing proposals are based on the combination of packets belonging to different flows, so as to reduce the number of *real* transmissions over the wireless channels. This would eventually lead to better performances, together with an energy-aware operation. However, there are certain aspects that might prevent their use. In this paper we empirically study one of these deterrents; we propose an algorithm to establish the feasibility of applying *Network Coding* over random topologies, by identifying a set of nodes that might be able to act as coding entities. Besides, we discuss the appropriateness of such selection, by comparing the lengths of the corresponding paths. The results show that the probability of promoting these techniques is rather low.

Keywords: Inter-flow Network Coding · Wireless Mesh Networks · Random multi-hop topologies · TCP

1 Introduction

Network Coding was originally proposed by Ahlswede *et al.* in their seminal paper [2] more than a decade ago. Since then, the scientific community has made outstanding efforts in order to apply such techniques over different types of networks. It is worth highlighting the tremendous research effort that is being made towards the applicability of *Network Coding* over wireless networks, in general, and over mesh topologies, in particular.

Although there might be other sensible classifications, we can roughly separate the various proposals that have been made between those that code packets belonging to different flows (these are in fact those which were first proposed) from others that combine different packets (fragments) belonging to the same data flow (in this case, these solutions show some commonalities with fountain codes, such as *LT* or *Raptor*).

If we focus on the first of the aforementioned groups, there are some aspects that might deter the applicability of such solutions over real networks. The first

© Institute for Computer Sciences, Social Informatics and Telecommunications Engineering 2015
R. Agüero et al. (Eds.): MONAMI 2014, LNICST 141, pp. 259–274, 2015.
DOI: 10.1007/978-3-319-16292-8_19

one is the impact of random errors, which we already studied in our previous research [5,6], where we assessed the impact of packet erasure channels over canonical mesh topologies (i.e. the so-called X and *Butterfly* ones). In this paper we pay attention to another aspect that could limit the potential gains of these solutions. In particular, we look at *random network topologies* and we empirically evaluate the *real possibilities of using Network Coding* techniques over them. Namely, our analysis focus on the optimal choice of a coding element along the route, seeking the best intermediate node which is crossed by the various data streams, thus it (or they) could be able to merge the previously received packets into a single unit of information. We propose an algorithm to establish whether a particular random topology over might be considered as appropriate to use such technique. For the sake of simplicity, in this very first approach we only consider the presence of *two* data flows within the network; limiting as well the number of coding entities to *one* single node. The results show that, in spite of using flows that are chosen so as to favor the *merging* process, the probability of finding a suitable *coding node* is rather low and, in some cases, it would require using rather awkward routes, leading to performances that might be even lower than those seen by the legacy approach (i.e. traditional *store-and-forward* routing). Besides, we have included an additional testbed based on the `ns-3` simulation platform [1], quantifying the potential benefit brought about by combining the information of different flows along the network, thus reducing the number of transmissions required by legacy *store-and-forward* schemes. In this case, we have observed a performance increment of about 1.5 % when the length of the different routes is not altered by the usage of *Network Coding (NC)* techniques.

The rest of the document has been structured as follows: Sect. 2 outlines the main contributions found in the literature that address the same topics covered in this work. Section 3 presents and describes the solution that we have carried out to discover the potential coding opportunities within a random wireless topology. After that, Sect. 4 describes the empirical assessment used to evaluate the capability of the use of *Inter-flow NC* techniques over *Wireless Mesh Networks (WMNs)* to improve the performance exhibited by a traditional routing scheme. Finally, Sect. 5 properly concludes the documents and hints those issues that shall be tackled in the future.

2 Related Work

Although the research on routing protocols for multi-hop networks started already almost twenty years ago, we have seen that the relevance of such topologies has recently increased. They were originally conceived as communication alternatives for rather particular scenarios (for instance, natural disasters), thus limiting their actual potential and applicability. However, during the latest years, the use of mesh networks is proposed as a means to extend the coverage of more traditional topologies. Some key examples are the *IEEE 802.11s* standard or the *device-to-device* communication, that is currently under consideration by the 3GPP in the latest *LTE* specifications. In addition, we should also reflect the relevance of *machine-to-machine* communications and the key role that multi-hop topologies have in the corresponding wireless sensor networks. As a consequence, we have seen a reactivation of the technical activities in the *MANET* working group of the *IETF*, which has recently (as of June 2014) submitted various *Request For Comments*.

Regarding Network Coding, we have already mentioned that Ahwslede et al. introduced in [2] this promising technique, whose main principle questions the traditional *store-and-forward* paradigm, which has been dominating the packet switching-oriented networking realm during decades. This *legacy* concept was tailored at the initial steps of the Internet, when the routers suffered from an extremely limited capacity and their unique task was to redirect the packets to their next hop along the path, without carrying out any further processing. However, at the time of writing, these intermediate nodes have remarkably evolved, and they currently incorporate enough resources to perform more complex operations. The authors in [2] fostered the integration of a certain level of additional intelligence within the networking elements, allowing them to combine the information belonging to different flows, with the main goal of enhancing the network performance (i.e. improve throughput, mask losses, save energy, enhance the security, etc.).

Looming from such initial contribution, another branch, focused on the interplay between such techniques with wireless networks has also has also taken roots [3,9,15]; in this particular case, the inherent broadcast nature of the wireless channel is exploited. For instance, Katti et al. introduced *COPE* [9], a complete *NC* architecture, being one of the first works in putting into practice the theoretical concepts previously discussed in [2,10,12,17]. In a nutshell, they simplified all the coding/decoding tasks, proposing the use of simple bitwise *XOR* operations, exploiting the information that intermediate nodes had previously stored. Besides, they tailored their solution to take advantage from the spatial diversity of this type of communications, since the nodes were able to overhear the packets transmitted within their coverage area, even though not being the intended destinations; these packets might be useful to recover the original information that travels coded along the network. Another interesting work is the one carried out by Hunderbøll et al. [8]. They presented the so-called *Coding Applied To Wireless On Mobile Ad-hoc Networks (CATWOMAN)* framework, which was conceived to operate over *Better Approach To Mobile Adhoc Networking (BATMAN)* [13], integrating a fully-fledged *NC* solution within this routing protocol, using its control and management messages to identify coding opportunities by means of estimating the overhearing capability of the neighboring nodes. However, the authors did not consider the use of complex topologies, assessing the performance of their solution over rather simple scenarios, in which the role of the coding element could be straightforwardly selected.

In our previous works [5,6], we assessed the performance of an *Inter-flow* Network Coding implementation over canonical and simple wireless multi-hop topologies (i.e. *X*, *Butterfly*). We focused on the impact that some operational parameters (i.e. the configuration of the buffer that will temporary store the packets at the coding routers waiting for coding opportunities, the synchronization between the flows within the scenario, etc.) might have over the low performance exhibited by TCP over *WMNs*, mainly due to the way TCP reacts upon random losses. Although the results showed a relevant performance enhancement over ideal channels, when the wireless channels started to cause random errors, the interplay between TCP and *NC* was not as good as could have been expected, showing a remarkably lower performance than the one observed by the legacy TCP.

One of the most important characteristics of a generic *WMN* lies on its randomness, since the position and mobility of the nodes might be unpredictable. In such cases, the identification of a suitable node to carry out the coding functionality is far from being obvious (as it was, for instance, with the aforementioned canonical scenarios). In this sense, it is deemed necessary to provide a number of mechanisms to appropriately identify the most appropriate location of the coding entity (or entities) in real time, yet minimizing the required overhead that needs to be transmitted, as routing/coding signaling messages. Some works, such as [14,16] have already tackled this, posing an optimization problem to carry out the corresponding analysis. The first paper introduces two suboptimal code generation techniques: one uses linear programming, offering certain flexibility to select the objective functions; while the other use an optimization problem that establishes greater restrictions, posing an integer problem. The authors of the second paper proposes a distributed optimization problem, exploiting the information that is provided by neighboring nodes.

This work starts from the basis established by the contributions that are described hereinafter. On the first hand, Le et al. introduced *Distributed Coding-Aware Routing (DCAR)* [11] to overcome the main limitations of COPE [9], questioning its feasibility over dynamic topologies. Two main conclusions were derived: first, the choice of coding elements is tightly related to the pre-established routes (i.e. static conditions); second, the code structure in COPE is limited within a *two-hop region*. In order to sort these limitations out, they presented an *on-demand* and *link-state* routing protocol bringing about the discovery of high throughput paths by means of a novel routing metric (*Coding-Aware Routing Metric - CRM*). The protocol detects the potential network coding opportunities (i.e. the coding nodes along the network), being able to distinguish between "coding-feasible" and "coding impossible" paths. Additionally, they proposed a set of conditions that must be fulfilled by a node to become a coding element. Afterwards, Guo et al. [7] questioned whether these requirements are enough when there are various intersecting nodes along a path, and they proposed a new coding-aware routing metric, *Free-Ride-Oriented Routing Metric (FORM)*, able to exploit a larger number of coding opportunities, regardless of the number of flows and intersecting nodes. It is worth mentioning that, contrary to these two works, we do not focus on the protocol itself (i.e. we do not study its overhead, discovery messages, etc.), but our main objective is to carry out a thorough analysis of the corresponding coding conditions. To our best knowledge there are no other works that have carried out such a study. In order to do so, we propose an algorithm and we use it through an extensive simulation analysis in which we characterize the probability of finding coding opportunities over a number of different *randomly-generated WMN*.

3   Implementation

Before describing the algorithm that we have designed to identify the node(s) acting as coding element(s), we recall again that we have based this proposal on the conditions identified in [7,11]. We have broadened them and, exploiting graph theory, we have developed an algorithm that provides with the list of potential coding nodes (if any) in any wireless random topology.

We list below a set of assumptions that might help the reader to follow the analysis depicted afterwards.

- For the sake of simplicity, we consider the coding of two different flows.
- By exploiting the broadcast nature of the wireless channel, any node within the coverage area of a transmitter is able to overhear the packets it sends, even though they are not the real destination.
- As was already mentioned, we assume that there are always two active flows between two pairs of endpoints (i.e. $s_1 \to d_1$ and $s_2 \to d_2$); besides, if the algorithm found any coding opportunity, it would return a list of the potential coding nodes c_j, where $j = [0...N]$, being N the total number of them.
- We define $\mathcal{N}(u)$ as the set of one-hop neighboring nodes to node u.
- f_i denotes the ith flow within the scenario.
- Finally, the notations $\mathcal{U}(c_j, f_i)$ and $\mathcal{D}(c_j, f_i)$ are used to identify the upstream and downstream nodes, respectively. The former are defined as the nodes between the two sources (s_i) and a coding element (c_j), while the latter ones are those between c_j and the corresponding destinations (d_i).

When two flows converge at an articulation vertex, a "raw" coding opportunity is detected and a new *coded* packet is built using those that had been previously stored[1]. The coding and decoding calculations are based on simple *XOR* ($\oplus$) operations. Hence, from a *native* packet a belonging to an arbitrary flow f_m and another one, b, received from a different stream f_n, the coding node c_j will create a new *coded* packet, whose upper layer information[2] is built by means of combination of both native segment a and b, i.e. $a \oplus b$. At the receiving entity, this coded packet could be decoded *if and only if* the corresponding receiver had previously stored one of the constituent *native* packets[3]

---

[1] Recall that the *Inter-flow* coding scheme we are studying encodes packets belonging to different *data* streams.

[2] Since we will use our previously [5,6] implemented *NC* framework in a further simulation assessment (belonging to the future work), where we introduced a new layer between IP and TCP levels, a coding operation would involve both application-layer payload and TCP header.

[3] Typically, these are propagated within the topology, reaching the destination node thanks to the physical broadcast nature of wireless links.

(either a or b). In such case, the remaining packet could be straightforwardly obtained by means of the inverse operation: i.e. $a = (a \oplus b) \oplus b$ or $b = (a \oplus b) \oplus a$. However, when the receiver had not stored any of the *native* packets when it gets the *coded* one, it leads to a decoding failure event and the corresponding *coded* packet would be dropped.

As was hinted earlier, *an appropriate selection of the coding node is deemed essential; it needs to ensure that the final destinations are able to receive both the coded and native pieces of information*; otherwise, the consequences of decoding failures would have a dramatic impact over the overall system performance (i.e. the loss of a *coded* implies a twofold effect, since it holds information belonging the two different flows). Furthermore, those worthless transmissions might also cause more contention to access the shared channel, which would eventually bring about even worse performances.

With these assumptions, we broaden the conditions proposed in [11], leading to the requirements that need to be fulfilled by the two flows f_1 and f_2 to find a potential coding node c_j in an articulation point within their corresponding paths.

Definition 1. *Let f_1 and f_2 be two flows with an articulation point at node c. The conditions that leverage a coding opportunity are depicted below.*

- *There exists $u_1 \in \mathcal{D}(C, f_1)$ such that $u_1 \in N(v_2)$, $v_2 \in \mathcal{U}(C, f_2)$, or $u_1 \in \mathcal{U}(c, f_2)$.*
- *There exists $u_2 \in \mathcal{D}(C, f_2)$ such that $u_2 \in N(v_1)$, $v_1 \in \mathcal{U}(C, f_1)$, or $u_2 \in \mathcal{U}(c, f_1)$.*

In other words, *we have to ensure that the destination nodes are able to directly overhear the native packets belonging to the other flow*. It is worth highlighting that there exists a different approach to address the coding/decoding operation, based on the exchange of periodic reports which contain the essential information of each node (i.e. current neighbors, stored packets, etc.), as described in [9]. Nonetheless, this alternative would require an additional channel overhead and contention, thus clashing with the foundations of our *NC* approach [5,6].

Assuming ideal channel conditions (i.e. no packet losses due to propagation impairments, hidden terminals, etc.) as well as a perfect *MAC* scheduling (i.e. no collisions), the above constraints are *necessary and sufficient*. However, the authors in [7] questioned that these statements might not be appropriate if there exist various articulation points between the endpoints, proposing a number of modifications to discover the best set of nodes within a generic mesh topology.

In order to align the aforementioned requirements with the *NC* protocol operation we presented in [5,6], we have imposed the following constraints to deploy the corresponding scenarios: (1) we will only consider two data flows: $s_1 \rightarrow d_1$ and $s_2 \rightarrow d_2$; (2) we will limit the number of coding nodes c_j to 1; (3) only destination nodes can take care of the decoding process. Considering these limitations, the conditions described in Definition 1 need to be slightly updated, as can be seen below.

Definition 2. *Let f_1 and f_2 be two flows with an articulation point at node c. The simplified conditions that leverage a coding opportunity are enumerated below.*

- *There exists $u_1 \in \mathcal{U}(c, f_1)$ such that $u_1 \in N(d_2)$ and d_2 is the destination node of f_2, or $u_1 = d_2$.*
- *There exists $u_2 \in \mathcal{U}(c, f_2)$ such that $u_2 \in N(d_1)$ and d_1 is the destination node of f_1, or $u_2 = d_1$.*

To better illustrate this, Fig. 1 shows a generic multi-hop topology in which our proposed algorithm is able to find a coding node. We can differentiate the paths followed by the two flows f_1 and f_2, following the routes $s_1 \to 1 \to c_1 \to d_1$ and $s_2 \to c_1 \to 2 \to d_2$, respectively. Besides, it can easily be inferred that the particular locations of the nodes fulfill the conditions depicted in Definition 2, since both destinations d_i are able to overhear the packets sent from the sources of the other flows s_j, with $i, j \in [1, 2]$ and $i \neq j$. Hence, this particular scenario shows the conditions that would leverage the use of *NC*.

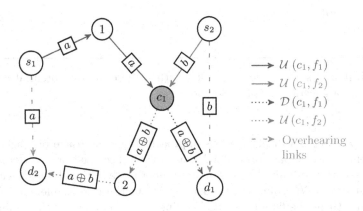

Fig. 1. Generic multi-hop topology

Once we have established all the necessary conditions (as well as the constraints imposed by our *Inter-flow NC* protocol) that any scenario must fulfill to leverage a coding scheme within the network, Algorithm 1 shows the procedure that we have implemented to identify the potential coding nodes within the corresponding graph. Essentially, the algorithm receives the following input arguments: the underlying graph $G(V, E)$ of the particular network topology/scenario, where V is the set of nodes of the network and E the edges/links that are established between them. In addition, it also needs the two pairs of endpoints $s_1/d_1, s_2/d_2$ that establish the corresponding flows. Finally, we introduce a last parameter, Δ, which limits the maximum number of additional hops that a route might take in order to find a coding router (compared to a traditional store-and-forward routing scheme). It is worth highlighting the key role

---

Data: $G(V, E), s_1, s_2, d_1, d_2, \Delta$
Result: List of possible coding nodes
Calculate f_1 and f_2 with Dijkstra;
for *each node i in $G \neq s_1$, s_2, d_1 and d_2* **do**
    Calculate $\mathcal{U}_K(i, f_1)$, $\mathcal{D}_K(i, f_1)$, $\mathcal{U}_K(i, f_2)$, $\mathcal{D}_K(i, f_2)$ with Yen's algorithm;
    for $j = 1 : K$ **do**
        $LU1 = [\ ]$;
        for *each node, n, in $\mathcal{U}_j(i, f_1)$* **do**
          | $LU1 = [LU1 \ n \ N(n)]$;
        end
        $LU2 = [\ ]$;
        for *each node, n, in $\mathcal{U}_j(i, f_2)$* **do**
          | $LU2 = [LU2 \ n \ N(n)]$;
        end
        if $(d_1 \in LU2)$ *and* $(d_2 \in LU1)$ **then**
            if $(Length(f_1) + \Delta \leq Length(\mathcal{U}(i, f_1) + \mathcal{D}(i, f_1)))$ *and*
            $(Length(f_2) + \Delta \leq Length(\mathcal{U}(i, f_2) + \mathcal{D}(i, f_2)))$ **then**
              | $CodingNodes = [CodingNodes \ i]$;
            end
        end
    end
end

Algorithm 1. Pseudo-code to check whether there is any potential coding node within a generic multi-hop topology

that this parameter will play in this approach, since the usage of longer paths has a tremendous impact over *WMNs*, as will be discussed below. Hence, it is deemed essential to limit the maximum number of "additional hops" generated by the use of our *NC* solution in order to prevent from insensible outputs. The algorithm returns the list of potential coding nodes that satisfy the coding conditions gathered in Definition 2, as well as the j routes between s_i and d_i (one route per flow and coding router c_j).

In order to find the corresponding paths between the endpoints, we use two different routing alternatives: *Dijkstra's* [4] and *Yen's* [18] algorithms. The second one, which provides a set of the K shortest paths, is used so as to be able to identify additional routes that might lead to better performances, since the former just returns a single path.

The main quality of this type of *NC* schemes is to combine packets belonging to different flows, thus saving a number of transmissions (up to 25 % in canonical topologies). However, due to the contention-based nature of the IEEE 802.11 medium access control, if these techniques led to longer routes, the corresponding performance enhancement would be mitigated, even leading to worse behaviors. For that purpose, the last part of our proposed algorithm introduces a novel constraint that establishes a sensible bound on the number of hops that has to be used in order to find a suitable coding router, mapped as Δ. As we will see later, all the routes provided by the *NC* approach will be, at least, equal in length to those ones corresponding to the legacy scheme; for that purpose, when the Δ constraint is enabled, all those paths which exceed the length of the legacy *Dijkstra's* path plus the aforementioned threshold will be automatically discarded, hence its resulting coding node c_j will not be part of the list of potential coding elements. In other words, even though in these cases the coding conditions introduced in Definition 2 are accomplished, the resulting routes might be considered as *false positives*.

4   Results

In this section we outline the process that we have followed to evaluate the behavior of our solution (based on Algorithm 1). In a nutshell, we have carried out an empirical assessment that can be structured according to the following stages: *(1)* randomly deploy the nodes within the scenario; *(2)* execute the routing algorithms whose operation was described in Sect. 3; *(3)* discuss the results provided by the proposed procedure, comparing them to those that would have been obtained by a traditional routing scheme.

After this step, the resulting output (i.e. the scenarios which have, at least, a potential coding node) will cater a second stage, where the routes generated by the algorithm will be used as the input of a simulation-driven assessment (through the ns-3 platform, using the *Inter-flow NC* implemented that we presented in [5,6]), where we will evaluate the potential benefit of combining the use of *NC* techniques with TCP over random wireless networks.

Before starting with the description of the algorithm assessment, we enumerate the characteristics of the scenarios that have been used for the analysis.

– A total number of 32 nodes is randomly deployed within a 100×100 meters squared area, following a *Poisson Point Process*.
– We discard any network whose corresponding graph is not connected; that is to say, we only analyze networks in which there is, at least, one path between any pair of nodes.
– We do not consider node mobility, and thus all nodes is stay *static* throughout the simulation.
– The coverage area of the nodes is modeled by a 20 m disk radius.
– Two pairs of endpoints define the two long-lived flows considered in the scenario (i.e. $s_1 \rightarrow d_1$ and $s_2 \rightarrow d_2$). All these nodes are selected so as to increase the likelihood of finding a coding entity at any of the articulation nodes between the two streams. Namely, we take the coordinates $(20, 80)$, $(80, 80)$, $(20, 20)$ and $(80, 20)$ as reference points, choosing the closest nodes to these positions as s_1, s_2, d_1 and d_2, respectively.
– For the sake of simplicity, we will assume that the flows f_1 and f_2 will be active throughout the process.

We have generated a total of 1000 scenarios complying with the above characteristics, using them as the input of the routing solutions. The algorithm proposed in this work returns the list of potential coding nodes (if any) as well as

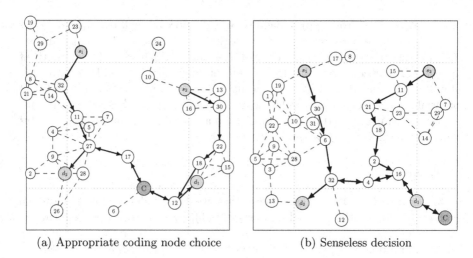

(a) Appropriate coding node choice   (b) Senseless decision

Fig. 2. Illustrative example of two random topologies

the length of the K paths for each of the two flows. For comparison purposes,
a traditional routing scheme establishes the shortest paths between the endpoints
by means of *Dijkstra's* algorithm.

As an illustrative example, Fig. 2 shows two of the random scenarios that were
studied. The topology on the left (Fig. 2a), corresponds to a situation in which
the coding router identified by the algorithm seems to be an appropriate one,
since node C is placed at an articulation point between the two paths, without
increasing their overall number of hops. Besides, the broadcast nature of the
wireless medium would allow the destination nodes d_1 and d_2 to directly overhear
the transmissions from nodes 27 and 18, respectively. This information will be
later used to decode the coded packets and retrieve the information originally
addressed to them. On the other hand, the topology on the right (Fig. 2b) leads
to a rather worse behavior, since the position of the coding node is far from being
adequate; we can see that the routes that connect C to the flow endpoints require
many unnecessary hops (i.e. 2 for the path $s_1 \rightarrow d_1$ and 5 for the other one), thus
significantly increasing the overall path lengths and likely jeopardizing the global
performance. On the basis of this first analysis, we can conclude that, although
the proposed algorithm is able to find the most appropriate coding router within
a random scenario, the results might require a second analysis, since the resulting
performance would be much lower than the one achieved using more traditional
routing mechanisms. In addition, this second scenario poses two main issues:
on the first hand, it reinforces the usage of a kind of limiter to avoid awkward
routes that would not provide any kind of benefit (tuning the aforementioned
Δ parameter, which will prevent the inclusion on insensible routes); besides, it
would be interesting to enhance the algorithm so that it could be able to detect
these undesired and illogical results, such as detecting i.e. the presence of cycles
along the routes.

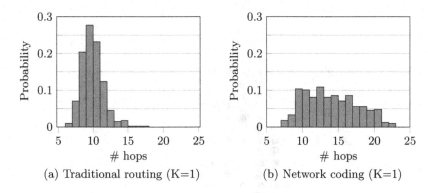

Fig. 3. *pdf* of the number of hops (Traditional routing *vs* Network coding)

The first aspect to be studied is the *probability density function (pdf)* of the number of hops required by the source nodes (s_i) to reach their corresponding destinations (d_i), as shown in Fig. 3. We can see that the traditional routing scheme (*Dijkstra*) is always able to find paths with ≤18 hops, with the presence of a peak centered at 9–11 hops; on the other hand, the *NC* scheme yields a more uniform set of probabilities, yet it is not a good performance at all, since the use of these techniques leads to longer routes (i.e. we can find cases in which a packet has to use up to 23 different hops before reaching its destination). This means that, in some specific scenarios, the coding scheme proposed by our algorithm would impose the use of a much larger number of hops, bringing about a performance degradation, rather than increasing it.

Figure 4 compares the number of hops that were obtained by the two approaches for every scenario. As can be seen, the *NC* scheme route lengths are bounded by the ones provided by the traditional approach. Although in many cases the increase of the route lengths might be acceptable, there are cases in which the paths that are required to foster the coding scheme are not sensible at all, hence such scheme should be discarded for those particular scenarios.

It is worth highlighting that, for the analysis carried out so far, the results obtained by the use of *Yen's* algorithm were similar, for different K values ($K = 1, 2, 3$). Hence, we only represent the results obtained for $K = 1$, which is equivalent to the ones achieved by *Dijkstra's*.

Figure 5 shows the probability of finding at least one coding router (in this case we do not consider the appropriateness of the resulting configuration). In the x axis we represent the difference between the number of hops of the routes provided by the two proposed routing algorithms. We can see that the use of *Yen's* algorithm with a higher K value could lead to some benefits, since the probability of finding a coding node increases as long as K gets higher. Anyway, although Algorithm 1 is able to establish a coding node in ≈47 % of the scenarios (without limiting the difference between the two path lengths), the corresponding topologies might deter the use of this technique, since the number of hops that are required for the *NC* scheme is much larger than the one established by the

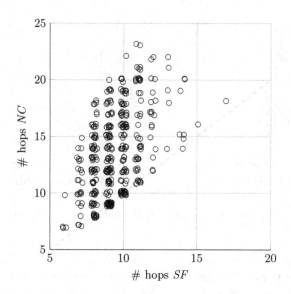

Fig. 4. Graphical representation of the difference between the path lengths (Traditional routing *vs* Network coding)

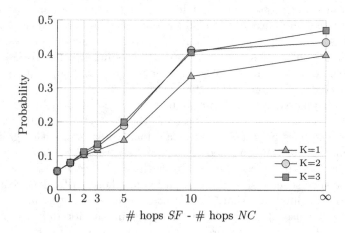

Fig. 5. Probability of finding at least a coding node.

traditional routing approach. Assuming that a difference of up to 2 hops between both solution could lead to a performance enhancement, since the number of saved transmissions compensates the use of longer paths to reach the destinations than the legacy *store-and-forward* scheme, the ratio of *NC* "feasible" scenarios would fall down until a rather poor percentage ($\approx$10 %).

In order to quantify the performance achieved by each solution, we have extended the analysis to a new scenario, based on the simulation of two long-lived TCP connections over random topologies (through the ns-3 platform), where we will empirically obtain a maximum value of Δ that might lead to a performance enhancement. It is worth recalling again that this stage only validates those scenarios where the algorithm has found at least a potential coding entity. Regarding the parameters that set up the scenario, the following issues have to be taken into account: first, from the output produced by the random scenario generator, we take the position of the whole set of nodes and the index of the endpoints (i.e. s_1, s_2, d_1 and d_2). Second, from the results offered by the algorithm, we need the *ID* of the coding node, c_1 (i.e. in this work we only consider the presence of a single coding node), as well as the routes between the pairs. Since we aim at comparing the performance achieved by our *Inter-flow* scheme with that of a traditional combination of TCP and a legacy *store-and-forward* scheme, we generate the following traffic: both sources s_1 and s_2 will send a total of 5000 packets to their respective destinations (d_1 and d_2, respectively). The length of these ones will be 1500 bytes at the network layer (i.e. including both TCP and *NC* headers), assuring a maximum utilization without leading to a lower layer fragmentation. With this setup, we repeat the analysis over 1000 different scenarios.

Figure 6 represents the *cumulative distribution function (cdf)* of the throughput for the different solutions. On the first hand, we appreciate in Fig. 6a the results of the first set of scenarios in which we have restricted our algorithm to discard all the potential coding nodes which would lead to longer paths to perform the *NC* operation. With these conditions, we observe as the *NC* solution offers a slight throughput enhancement throughout the curve ($\approx 1.5\%$). On the other hand, when we relax the Δ constraint (i.e. $\Delta = 1$), the behavior is rather different, as shown in Fig. 6b. In this case, we observe a first zone in which the throughput achieved by *NC* is significantly lower than that of TCP. This performance degradation could be assigned to the additional contention brought

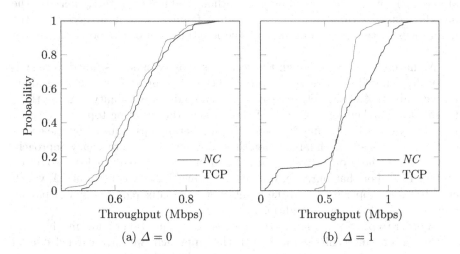

(a) $\Delta = 0$ (b) $\Delta = 1$

Fig. 6. Cumulative distribution function of the throughput

about by the extra hop that the two flows have to carry out in order to reach c_1, whose downstream coded flows, $\mathcal{D}(c_1, f_i)$, with $i \in [1, 2]$, are not able to compensate. Besides, it is also true that there is a second zone (right side of the figure) where the *NC* scheme performs better than TCP, showing a throughput enhancement of $\approx 2\%$.

Last, but not least, a higher value of Δ would lead to even worse behaviors, leading to situations in which the throughput of the *Inter-flow NC* scheme is remarkably lower than TCP's.

5   Conclusions

The use of *NC* techniques to enhance the performance over *WMNs* has drawn the attention of the scientific community during the last years. The corresponding research has covered various aspects, ranging from coding/decoding issues to the proposal of novel protocols able to promote these solutions. Some of the existing works can be grouped as *Inter-Flow* techniques, since they are based on the combination of packets belonging to different data streams. In this sense, we have used an algorithm to study the feasibility of *NC* over random wireless topologies.

In this work, we have started from the set of statements proposed in [7,11] to detect the potential network coding opportunities over generic scenarios, by exploiting the broadcast nature of the wireless medium (which allows the nodes to directly overhear transmissions within their coverage area). With the intention of combining these conditions with a holistic *NC* framework we have previously introduced in [5,6], we have tailored a new algorithm, which has to be adapted to its particular requirements. For instance, decoding tasks could only be tackled by destination nodes, hence they should be able to overhear the information of, at least, one of the "native" flows (i.e. without coding) to correctly perform the decoding tasks without leading to decoding failures. Like it predecessors, the main focus of this algorithm aims at the identification of the potential coding nodes.

We have seen that, although the scenarios that have been studied were synthetically tailored to increase the probability of finding at least a coding alternative, only 47% of the network topologies showed the possibility of using these techniques. Furthermore, in most of those cases, the resulting topologies would most likely deter from using *NC*, since the number of hops required by the corresponding routes are much larger than those obtained by a more legacy approach. In this sense, the probability of using *NC* over a reasonable topology would be around 10%. For that purpose, we have introduced a new constraint, Δ, which establishes an upper bound to the number of extra hops required by our particular coding and decoding conditions.

In order to provide a quantitative answer to the question of how much would be the performance enhancement with this approach, we have carried out an extensive simulation campaign (through the ns-3 platform), assessing the potential throughput benefit of combining the packets along the network. From the results generated by the aforementioned algorithm, we have recreated two different experiments (i.e. $\Delta = 0$ and $\Delta = 1$), studying the impact that longer paths bring about over our coding mechanisms. As hinted before, the use of alike routes (in terms of path length) leads to a (slight) throughput enhancement of $\approx 2\%$; however, in those topologies in which the introduction of a coding node implies the apparition of *extra* hops, the results are not so optimistic. This comes to demonstrate that there is to be a *trade-off* between the length of the downstream flows (which transport coded packets) and the number of additional hops, hence the *contention reduction* performed by the *NC* scheme could be able to compensate the *contention* increase produced by their underlying longer routes.

With respect to the remaining open issues arisen from this work, we have identified some action lines that shall be addressed in the future. The first and most straightforward step to be done is, as mentioned before, to enhance our proposed algorithm in such a way it could prevent yielding awkward routes (i.e.with the presence of cycles). Another interesting feature to be added consists in adapting our solution to be applied upon more general networks, where either the number of flows or coding nodes is not bounded, or the traffic present dynamic conditions. For instance, the use of COPE [9] shows a higher gain when the nodes code more than two packets together (belonging to different flows).

Acknowledgements. This work has been supported by the Spanish Government by its funding through the **COSAIF** project, *"Connectivity as a Service: Access for the Internet of the Future"* (TEC2012-38754-C02-02).

References

1. The ns-3 network simulator. http://www.nsnam.org/
2. Ahlswede, R., Cai, N., Li, S.Y., Yeung, R.: Network information flow. IEEE Trans. Inf. Theory **46**(4), 1204–1216 (2000)
3. Chachulski, S., Jennings, M., Katti, S., Katabi, D.: Trading structure for randomness in wireless opportunistic routing. In: Proceedings of the 2007 Conference on Applications, Technologies, Architectures, and Protocols for Computer Communications, SIGCOMM 2007, ACM, New York, NY, USA, pp. 169–180 (2007). http://doi.acm.org/10.1145/1282380.1282400
4. Dijkstra, E.W.: A note on two problems in connexion with graphs. Numer. Math. **1**, 269–271 (1959)
5. Gómez, D., Hassayoun, S., Herrero, A., Agüero, R., Ros, D.: Impact of network coding on TCP performance in wireless mesh networks. In: 2012 IEEE Proceedings of 23th International Symposium on Personal, Indoor and Mobile Radio Communications (PIMRC), September 2012
6. Gómez, D., Hassayoun, S., Herrero, A., Agüero, R., Ros, D., García-Arranz, M.: On the addition of a network coding layer within an open connectivity services framework. In: Timm-Giel, A., Strassner, J., Agüero, R., Sargento, S., Pentikousis, K. (eds.) MONAMI 2012. LNICST, vol. 58, pp. 298–312. Springer, Heidelberg (2013)
7. Guo, B., Li, H., Zhou, C., Cheng, Y.: Analysis of general network coding conditions and design of a free-ride-oriented routing metric. IEEE Trans. Veh. Technol. **60**(4), 1714–1727 (2011)

8. Hunderbøll, M., Ledet-Pedersen, J., Heide, J., Pedersen, M., Rein, S., Fitzek, F.: CATWOMAN: Implementation and Performance Evaluation of IEEE 802.11 Based Multi-Hop Networks Using Network Coding

9. Katti, S., Rahul, H., Hu, W., Katabi, D., Médard, M., Crowcroft, J.: XORs in the air: practical wireless network coding. IEEE/ACM Trans. Netw. **16**(3), 497–510 (2008)

10. Koetter, R., Médard, M.: An algebraic approach to network coding. In: Proceedings of 2001 IEEE International Symposium on Information Theory, p. 104 (2001)

11. Le, J., Lui, J.S., Chiu, D.M.: DCAR: distributed coding-aware routing in wireless networks. IEEE Trans. Mob. Comput. **9**(4), 596–608 (2010)

12. Li, S.Y., Yeung, R., Cai, N.: Linear network coding. IEEE Trans. Inf. Theory **49**(2), 371–381 (2003)

13. Neumann, A., Aichele, C., Lindner, M., Wunderlich, S.: ABetter Approach To Mobile Ad-hoc Networking (B.A.T.M.A.N.). IETF Internet Draft - work in progress 07, individual, April 2008. http://tools.ietf.org/html/draft-wunderlich-openmesh-manet-routing-00

14. ParandehGheibi, A., Ozdaglar, A., Effros, M., Médard, M.: Optimal reverse carpooling over wireless networks - a distributed optimization approach. In: 2010 44th Annual Conference on Information Sciences and Systems (CISS), pp. 1–6, March 2010

15. Sengupta, S., Rayanchu, S., Banerjee, S.: An analysis of wireless network coding for unicast sessions: the case for coding-aware routing. In: 26th IEEE International Conference on Computer Communications, INFOCOM 2007, pp. 1028–1036. IEEE, May 2007

16. Traskov, D., Ratnakar, N., Lun, D.S., Koetter, R., Médard, M.: Network coding for multiple unicasts: an approach based on linear optimization. IEEE Int. Symp. Inf. Theory **52**, 6 (2006)

17. Wu, Y.: Information exchange in wireless networks with network coding and physical-layer broadcast (2004)

18. Yen, J.Y.: Finding the lengths of all shortest paths in n-node nonnegative-distance complete networks using 12n3 additions and n3 comparisons. J. ACM **19**(3), 423–424 (1972). http://doi.acm.org/10.1145/321707.321712

Applications and Context-awareness

A Relational Context Proximity Query Language

Jamie Walters[✉], Theo Kanter, and Rahim Rahmani

Department of Computer and System Sciences, Stockholm University,
Forum 100, Kista, Sweden
{jamie,kanter,rahim}@dsv.su.se

Abstract. The creation of applications and services realising massive
immersive participation require the provisioning of current, relevant and
accurate context information. These applications benefit from access to
this highly dynamic information in real time. Existing approaches to
provisioning context information are limited by their interpretation of
context relationships as address book solutions thus limiting the discovering of related entities. We introduce the context proximity query
language (CPQL) for querying context related entities on distributed
across collections of remote endpoints. As a declarative query language
(CPQL) is similar in structure to SQL and describes the relationships
between entities as distance functions between their associated context
information. We simulate CPQL and show that it offers improvements
over existing approaches while scaling well.

Keywords: Context-Awareness · Immersive participation · Context ·
Context models · Internet of Things · Context proximity · Sensor
information · P2P context · Query language

1 Introduction

The increase in massive immersive participation scenarios drives our move towards a society of virtual and augmented reality supported by the massive
deployment of global sensor infrastructures enabled by open solutions such as [1]
and [2]. Such realities include immersive games such as Google Ingress [3]. These
immersed realities serve to fuse a dynamic and multifaceted experience of people, places and things. Solutions such as SenseWeb [4], IP MultiMedia Subsystem (IMS) [5] and SCOPE [6] were developed in response to this need to
provision information supporting such immersive realities. This context information enables the creation of interactive experiences that reflect the dynamic
relationships that exist among a users, environments and services.

They are however limited with respect to expressiveness and thus are not
capable of sufficiently answering the question of *Who you are, who you are
with and what resources are nearby* as required by Schilit and Adams [7]. While
semantic approaches such that described by Liu et al. in [8] offer some support
towards this problem, Adomavicius et al. in [9] suggested that these types of
approaches are limited and should be complemented by metric type approaches

© Institute for Computer Sciences, Social Informatics and Telecommunications Engineering 2015
R. Agüero et al. (Eds.): MONAMI 2014, LNICST 141, pp. 277–289, 2015.
DOI: 10.1007/978-3-319-16292-8_20

thus realizing the ability to answer the question of *nearness* as posited by both Schilit et al. in [7]. This would permit us to sufficiently offer support for the complementing metric-type similarity models which, according to Hong et al. in [10], is critical in realizing applications and services that can discover nearby sensors or points of information.

In achieving this we are firstly required to identify and select candidate entities and manage the subsequent volume of required context information. Petras et al. in [5] used centralized presence systems where an entity watches a list of other entities in its address book. While this reduces the volume of context information required to maintain relationships, the resulting relationships are not context centric and limits the ability to discover entities of interest with which to establish common context relationships. With the average address book estimated to be limited in size to $0.005 * population$ [5], this solution limits the number of entities that can be discovered. Subscribing to all users would not be a feasible solution as the volume of messages per status change would be approximated as $population x population$. This solution would not scale well and simply pruning the message queue as suggested by Petras et al. in [5] would offer little guarantee with regards to the quality of the context information.

Zimmermann et al. in [11] posits the notion of proximity as the overarching factor in establishing context relationships. This subsumes address book approaches, realizing truly context-centric networks where interactions, discovery and relationships are realised over the degrees of relationships between entities and their associated context information. In [12] we defined an approach to establishing context centric relationships between entities on an Internet of Things. This extended the approach of Zimmermann et. al in [11] to relational proximity thus subsuming spatial distance as the overarching indicator of context. However Zimmermann et al. in [11] provided no solution for discovering the candidate entities and establishing relationships in light of the highly dynamic nature of context information. Schmohl partially addressed this in [13], proposing a multi-dimensional hypersphere of interest in which entities entering are deemed to be candidates related and are evaluated and selected according to a proposed proximity measure. Here entities are discovered through the use of multi-dimensional indexing structures such as R-trees, kd-trees and space partitioning grids. These solutions are less optimal for multi-dimensional dynamic context environments as the cost of indexing increases exponentially with a linear increase in the number of dimensions. Queries therefore risk being executed against outdated indexes with no guarantees of information freshness. As a solution to this problem, Schmohl suggested in [13] that dimensions could be selectively. However applications depending on less popular dimensions would not stand to realize any benefit from this optimization.

Yoo et. al in [14] and Santa et. al in [15] proposed the use of publish-subscribe approaches as suitable alternatives with Kanter et. al in [16] showing that such approaches are scalable and can realize dissemination times on par with UDP signally used in SIP implementations. Frey and Roman in [17] extended this approach however this is based on events rather than the raw underpinning context information. Supporting the establishing of context-centric relationships over heterogeneous context information therefore requires new approaches to maximizing the identification of candidate entities while minimizing the overall resource costs.

In this paper we introduce an approach to discovering related context entities through the use of a context proximity query language and an approach for adaptively provisioning context information in order to minimize the communication overheads associated with provisioning context information to remote user endpoints. In Sect. 2 we summarize our approach to multi-criteria relational context proximity. In Sect. 3 we describe our existing approach to distributed context awareness. Section 4 describes our approach while in Sect. 6 we present our evaluation and some early results and Sect. 7 looks at our conclusions and discussions.

2   Relational Proximity

Relational proximity elevates the problem of entity organization to a multi-dimensional problem space. Deriving such an affinity or proximity value could, as suggested [18], be realized as an extension of existing two-dimensional approaches by using an $n - dimensional$ distance metric permitting us to derive a representation of proximity as a metric over multiple dimensions of context satisfying the requirements of Schmidt et. al in [19]. Such a proximity function f would consider a subset of available context information over a group of presentities in order to derive a proximity value P such that: $f[(a1, a2, a3)(b1, b2, b3)] \rightarrow P$.

The area of general proximity includes two significant approaches: *The Theory of Context Spaces* and *The Contextual Map*. The Theory of Context Spaces [20] involves identifying and grouping related entities according to their general context information. A proximity function is then subsequently applied to derive a metric, representative of the entities' degrees of affinity. This is given as the *scalar difference*: $\delta_{|P-Q|} = \sqrt{\sum_{k=1}^{N}(a_p^k - a_q^k)^2}$ and is used to determine the proximity between entities, P and Q over their attributes a_i and a_j within some context space. This is a variation of the Euclidean distance function over the current state with the dimension values normalized to between 0 and 1.

The Contextual Map approach as proposed by Schmohl in [13] is a means of modelling context spaces occupied by presentities and reasoning about the affinities between presentities. It considers the approach taken with geographical maps and applies to it to the dimensions of context, mapping all values and deriving a separation metric. Proximity is derived over areas of interest, n-dimensional hyperspaces with the entity at the centre. A threshold on each range is used to monitor entities that have a similar context on a specific range which can be grouped together.

Further, the notion of context proximity or affinity is derived using the Euclidean distance or separation between entities. Considering two entities, A and B, their proximity, P is calculated as: $\delta = \sqrt{\sum_{i=1}^{n}(A_i - B_i)^2}$. This cements the $n-dimensional$ hypershere around the entity with respect to the range and identifies those entities that closer or further away.

2.1   The MediaSense Approach to Relational Proximity

Relational proximity is derived between the states of entities as observed over a time window W. For solving this, the Earth Movers Distance as described by Rubner et al. in [21] is used; setting the distributions as the sets of observable context states for each window W, the weighted edges being the activity similarity between P and Q and the ground distance d_{ij} being the distance between pairs of states s_i, s_j derivable as:

$$d_{ij}(s_i, s_j) = \frac{\left(\sum_{k=1}^{n}\left[w_a * |F_a^D(a_i, a_j)|^r\right]_k\right)^{\frac{1}{r}}}{\left(\sum_{k=1}^{n}\left[w_a * |F_a^D(a_i, a_j)_{max}|^r\right]_k\right)^{\frac{1}{r}}}$$

where $a_i \in A_i^D, a_j \in A_j^D$

Here, w is the weighting for each attribute. The value of r can be adjusted to reflect the perceived distance between P and Q as shown by Shahid et al. in [22]. The distance is normalized with respects to the maximum distance between states in the encompassing application space. Our measure of proximity therefore logically subsumes existing $Lp-norm$ approaches.

The EMD algorithm is then applied to derive the largest possible transformation between P and Q that minimizes the overall context transformation cost, where:

$$WORK(P \rightarrow Q, F) = \sum_{i=1}^{m}\sum_{j=1}^{n}$$

subjected to the following constraints:

1. $f_{ij} \geq 0 \ 1 \leq i \leq m, 1 \leq j \leq n$
2. $\sum_{i=1}^{m} f_{ij} \leq P \ 1 \leq i \leq m$
3. $\sum_{i=1}^{n} f_{ij} \leq Q \ 1 \leq j \leq n$
4. $\sum_{i=1}^{m}\sum_{j=1}^{n} f_{ij} = min\left(\sum_{i=1}^{m} P \sum_{j=1}^{n} Q\right)$

The first constraint permits the transformation and hence the proximity from $P \rightarrow Q$ and not the opposite. The second and third constraints limit the transformation $P \rightarrow Q$ to the maximum number of context observations made for P or Q. The final constraint forces the maximum transformation possible between both entities. The context proximity, $\delta(P,Q)$, is the Earthmover's distance normalized by the total flow:

$$\delta(P,Q) = \left(\sum_{i=1}^{m}\sum_{j=1}^{n} f_{ij}d_{if}\right) * \left(\sum_{i=1}^{m}\sum_{j=1}^{n} f_{ij}\right)^{-1}$$

It is important to note, that $\delta(P, Q)$ is indifferent to the size of both sets of observations and permits partial similarity where the behaviour of P is subsumed by the behaviour of Q. This is a distinct advantage of this approach and excess observations are inherently discarded. However, where partial matching is desirable and the completeness of containment is important for relations such that $P \cap Q = P \cup Q$, we extend the proximity measure to be normalized relative to the maximum potential transformation of either P or Q, such that:

$$\delta(P, Q) = \left(\sum_{i=1}^{m} \sum_{j=1}^{n} f_{ij} d_{if} \right) * \left(\sum_{i=1}^{m} \sum_{j=1}^{n} f_{ij} \right)^{-1}$$

given that:

$$\sum_{i=1}^{m} \sum_{j=1}^{n} f_{ij} = max \left(\sum_{i=1}^{m} P, \sum_{j=1}^{n} Q \right)$$

3   Distributed Context Awareness

The MediaSense platform consists of a distributed overlay for provisioning context information to remote endpoints. Constructed over a distributed architecture, it permits the storage and retrieval of context information in response to the requirements of higher level applications and services. A fundamental point of departure from similar approaches is the use of a distribution approach and algorithms capable of responding to queries within a given range. This permits us to move depart from existing and previous DHT based approaches and provide answers to questions about degrees of magnitude of context information while continuing to exploit the benefits of distribution. The organizing and lookup algorithms have been shown to have complexity of $0.5 log N$.

The MediaSense architecture exposes an API supported by a SIP like protocol for persisting, locating and subscribing to entities of interest and defines a set of primitives as described in [23]. The underlying range look-up support allows for the discovery of entities based on ranges of raw context information by querying within the upper a lower limits of an interest area. This permits us to find entities based on an area of interest by defining range of context values encompassing this area of interest. However defining areas of interest meaningful to applications and services requires more expressive means of expressing context based queries than the primitive constructs of the associated protocol.

4   The Context Proximity Query Language

Given the approach to establishing context relationships as described in Sect. 2.1 and the distributed context provisioning platforms of the type described in Sect. 3, we are required to define methods for finding, establishing and maintaining the relationships between any group of entities which satisfy the requirements of application-defined proximity measures. Firstly, we create a query language for defining the proximity; the bounds of the hypercube of interest. The query is then executed across a distributed heterogeneous data store with the candidate entities selected for establishing a relationship. The resulting relationships are maintained by subscribing to the entities of interest and continually evaluating the relationships with each derived context state ranking each entity by its current proximity. New entities are continually added while non-relevant entities are consequently pruned.

4.1   Language Constructs

The context proximity language is designed as a declarative query language inspired by SQL and adopting a similar construct and syntax. Table 1 shows an overview of the language constructs as compared to SQL. The intuition being that users in remote endpoints should be able to declare what constitutes the definition of context proximity or degrees of nearness between any two given entities. The query language is therefore a multi-criteria extension of the interest based approach introduced by Forsstrom et. al in [24] with the interest area being defined as a multidimensional distance function over the a subset of the underlying context information.

Table 1. CPQL - SQL comparison

CPQL	SQL
get, sub	*select*
where	*where*
from	*from*
[table]	*[people], [place], [thing]*
order	*order by*

At the core of the query language are two main types of statements: a *get* statement or *sub* statement. Both a CPQL get and a *sub* are functionally similar to an *sql-select* and retrieves the current context entities that possess a state within the hypersphere of interest defined by the proximity algorithm. The fundamental difference however being that a CPQL *get* does a single retrieve on the current matching states and the query is then terminated. It's purpose is to locate only current entities matching query parameters. A *sub*, assumes the functionality of a continuous query continually retrieving all entities with a current state that currently satisfies the defined proximity function.

GET—SUB PRESENTITY
WHERE DISTANCE [DISTNAME] ¡ [VALUE]
[ORDER [ASC—DESC]]
DEFINING [DISTANCENAME]
$ASsqrt(pow(F_{lat}(P_{lat}, Q_{lat}), 2) + pow(F_{lon}(P_{lon}, Q_{lon}), 2));$

DEFINING [DISTANCENAME]
AS sqrt(pow($F_{lat}(P_{lat}, Q_{lat})$, 2) + pow($F_{lon}(P_{lon}, Q_{lon})$, 2));

GET—SUB PRESENTITY
WHERE DISTANCE [DISTNAME] < [VALUE]
[ORDER [ASC—DESC]]

Additional keywords such as *order* allows an ordered set of entities to be returned by the query interface.

Our approach is consisted of three main components as shown in Fig. 1; namely a query interface for defining or declaring a query, an engine to decompose the relational query into its the subsequent queries and a component for issuing the query to remote end points and retrieving the corresponding results to be collated and returned via the user interface.

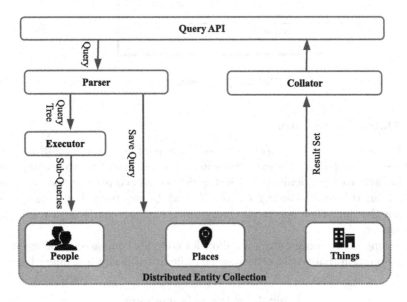

Fig. 1. CPQL architecture

5   The Architecture

5.1   Query API

The interactive API is at the top our solution and accepts user input definitions of complex multi-criteria proximity relationships. Implemented as a Java extension to the MediaSense platform, this component provides several key functionalities. Firstly, It allows us to define and introduce query comparators into the distributed architecture. Query comparators are further detailed in Sect. 5.2.

Each query comparator is assigned a unique id with which it is identifiable over the collection of comparators and persisted, through this API onto the MediaSense overlay. The user interface further permits the updating, and deletion of query comparators as well as the ability to determine if a current comparator exists with a known identifier. Secondly, it permits the declaration of queries for immediate execution which are forwarded to the query engine at each node. The user interface further permits us to create queries that can themselves be persisted locally or shared globally among remote end points. This allows us to create and share queries that define complex proximity relationships as well as the discovery and reuse of queries defined by other users. Finally, the user interface returns the subset of relevant context entities that satisfy the current query parameters which have been collated and filtered (Fig. 2).

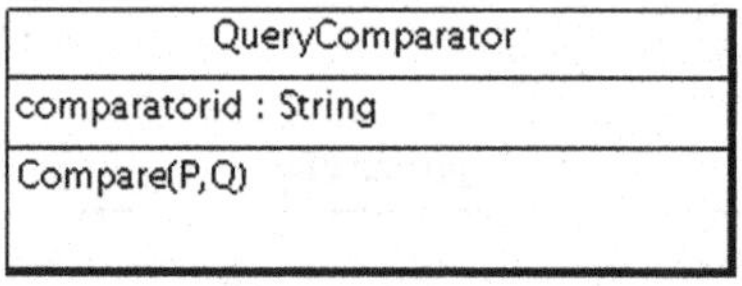

QueryComparator
comparatorid : String
Compare(P,Q)

Fig. 2. Query comparator

5.2   Query Comparators

Query comparators are encapsulated realizations of complex computing specifications for comparing context dimensions. Similar in nature to a comparator class in Java, each implemented object is defined as accepting a pair of context values from the corresponding entities P and Q and returning a comparison value for the dimension specified. Query objects return comparison results as a real number.

By using query comparators we allow for complex comparisons between context information that would otherwise be difficult to specify in a query language

Table 2. Overview of comparators

Comparator	Usage
Hamming Comparator	Compare string distances
Great Circle	Compare line of sight difference in distance
Urban Commuting	Compare the difference between distances in urban environments
Urban Public Commuting	Compare Distances in urban environments with public transportation
Simple Temperature	Compare temperature
Energy Temperature	Compare temperature as a function of the monetary cost of the energy to meet equilibrium

at runtime. Comparators can therefore be created, tested and verified independent of the query and added to the architecture for later usage. We can therefore implement comparators that range from simple subtraction for temperature comparisons to distance comparators that involve driving distances, fuel consumption and traffic times. This elevates the notion of distance between raw context information from simply arithmetic to more meaningful representations that reflect the perceived distances that could be observed at a higher more meaningful level. A list of comparators is shown in Table 2.

5.3   Parser

The parser resides locally on each node on the distributed platform. The parser is implemented as a Java Compiler parsing engine accepting queries as statements written in Java. Each query is parsed at the local parser for correctness and completeness and any subsequent errors returned via the user interface to the calling application. The resulting output of the parser is a Java based parse tree representation of the query which can be used for execution and comparing results sets. The resulting parse tree is routed to the executor.

5.4   Executor

The executor consists of two components, a global executor which resides local to the executing query and the query executor which is instantiated across all endpoints in response to a query being distributed on the platform.

Global Executor. The global executor for a given query R resides locally at the query's originating node. Each query received from the parser is sent to the global executor. The global executor decomposes the proximity function into its constituent dimensional queries. Each query finding a state possessing a context dimension that satisfies the parameters of the unified relational proximity function. Each dimension has an upper and lower limit, the range of the query. For simplicity, the upper and lower bounds of an application space is used, i.e., the bounds of each dimension that constitutes the n-dimensional hypersphere circumscribing the proximity function. The constituent queries are therefore range queries which are then executed on the platform. The queries are then routed using the platform's native lookup implementation. The query:

$getpresentity$

$where distance commutingdistance < 0.5$

$order by asc$

$defining distance commutingdistance$

$AS sqrt(pow(F_{lat}(P_{lat}, Q_{lat}), 2) + pow(F_{lon}(P_{lon}, Q_{lon}), 2));$

would produce the constituent sub-queries:

$$F_{lat}(P_{lat}, Q_{lat})$$
$$F_{lon}(P_{lon}, Q_{lon})$$

Query Executor. The sub-queries arrive at the query executor at each remote node that is capable of answering the query, i.e., nodes which are storing values within the range of the sub-query. Firstly, the sub-query executor fetches the comparator and compares the dimensions. If there are any matching states, the node routes a response to an intermediate collator. This is done by calling the *route(key)* function of the underlying distributed platform, where *key* is generated through a triple derived from the ID of the requesting entity, P, the matching entity Q and the executing query R such that $key = key(P_{id}, Q_{id}, Qry_{id})$. The function used to generate the key is specific to the implemented routing algorithm used by the distributed platform. All states responding to the query $(P_{id}, Q_{id}, Qry_{id})$ would arrive and be collated at the same node. This exploits the distribution platform for minimizing the volume of information sent to remote end points originating context proximity queries.

5.5   Collator

The collator consists of two parts: the intermediate collator and the global collator. The intermediate collator for each $(P_{id}, Q_{id}, Qry_{id})$ gets a collection of entity-dimensions matching the originating query. The intermediate node is responsible for filtering states that do not match the complete query. Each entity arriving at an intermediate node is compared and only returned to the global collator if all states satisfies the context query. This is then returned to the global collator at the query's originating node.

6   Evaluation

The CPQL query language provides for an approach to querying context information over a heterogeneous architectures. For evaluation we measured the number of entities returned to an endpoint with CPQL and the address book approach compared to the expected number of entities matching the context query provided. We simulated the query algorithm by creating a global population of context entities of size N where N is between 1000 and 10000 entities. Each entity is assigned a random number of context dimension constituting its profile. An application was created with three random dimensions (d_a, d_b, d_c) such that $d \in D$. Each simulation was run 20 times with a new configuration of dimensions and entities. The results are shown in Table 3.

The number of entities that satisfy the query requirements are shown. CPQL queries show a reduction in the number of entities located when compared to the total network size and are comparable to the number of expected entities

Table 3. Retrieving proximity entities

N	Expected	CPQL	Addressbook
1000	35	36	5
5000	177	168	25
10000	1485	1535	50
50000	2793	2700	250
1000000	7611	7691	500

to be returned. This is more than the address-book approach therefore adding an increased overhead, however returning a more comparable result set. This demonstrates that address book approaches are not sufficient in finding all related entities in a context network. Additionally, the relatively low numbers of entities returned compared to the total network size minimize the need to adopt pruning methods to reduce load in end points.

Figure 3 shows how the CPQL language scales with the number of applications. It shows that applications are in an environment with few commonly used dimensions of context information, CPQL does not scale well as the number of subscriptions increase to account for the diverse set of context information as the number of applications increase. However where, there few often used dimensions such as in platforms focused on specific problem domains, there is a high duplicate of dimensions. Here CPQL scales gracefully to account for the duplication in dimensions, i.e. end points are not required to subscribe to existing more than once to a source of context information. The CPQL is executed as a subscription on remote end points, the number of nodes having a subscription and therefore replying increases relative to the duplication in dimensions across the application domains. Even in low duplication, the number of nodes scales fairly well.

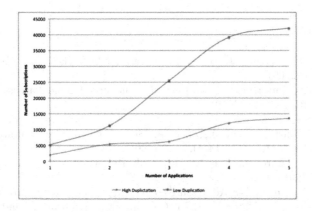

Fig. 3. Retrieving proximity entities

Additionally the number of queries needed to support each query is equal to the number of dimensions contained in the query. This can be compared to an address book approach where this is equal to the number of entities in each address book. The performance of CPQL however is related to the implementation of the language and the platform used. Overall communication costs required to execute queries and retrieve values are dependent on the implementation. However a reduction in the number of entities returned will result in an overall reduction in communication costs.

7 Conclusion

An Internet of Things supporting a fusion of users, applications and services demand access to context information that can provide support for realising immersive experiences with the same richness as the World Wide Web. This information resides in a distributed collection of endpoints including computers, sensor networks and mobile phones. The provisioning of this information must be relevant and liberated from the assumption network services enabling the brokering of information or presence models that do no scale well.

In response to this we presented the context proximity query language CPQL and describe its implementation on our distributed context provisioning platform. This allows for the ability to retrieve related entities occupying a state circumscribed by a context proximity function. Unlike previous address book approaches entities are discovered firstly as a function of their context relationships defined over their underlying context behaviours. Early results demonstrate that such approaches are superior to address book approaches being able to retrieve an entity set more closely matching the expected value. In low dimensionality spaces CPQL scales well with an increasing number of applications.

Future work could extend the language to add more complete subset of SQL for greater flexibility as well as adding map-reduce support for greater distributed aggregation of query results.

References

1. Strohbach, M., Vercher, J., Bauer, M.: A case for IMS. IEEE Veh. Technol. Mag. **4**(1), 57–64 (2009)
2. Kardeby, V., Forsström, S., Walters, J.: The updated mediasense framework. In: 2010 Fifth (ICDT) (2010)
3. Ingress
4. Kansal, A., Nath, S., Liu, J., Zhao, F.: Senseweb: an infrastructure for shared sensing. IEEE MultiMedia **14**(4), 8–13 (2007)
5. Petras, David, Baronak, Ivan, Chromy, Erik: Presence Service in IMS. Sci. World J. **2013**, 8 (2013) 606790
6. Baloch, R.A., Crespi, N.: Addressing context dependency using profile context in overlay networks. In: 2010 7th IEEE Consumer Communications and Networking Conference (CCNC), pp. 1–5. IEEE, January 2010

7. Schilit, B., Adams, N., Want, R.: Context-aware computing applications. In: First Workshop on Mobile Computing Systems and Applications, WMCSA 1994, pp. 85–90. IEEE, December 2008

8. Liu, L., Lecue, F., Mehandjiev, N., Xu, L.: Using context similarity for service recommendation. In: 2010 IEEE Fourth International Conference on Semantic Computing, pp. 277–284, September 2010

9. Adomavicius, G., Tuzhilin, A.: Context-aware recommender systems. RecSys 16(16), 335–336 (2010)

10. Hong, J.I., Landay, J.: An infrastructure approach to context-aware computing. Hum. Comput. Interact. 16(2), 287–303 (2001)

11. Zimmermann, A., Lorenz, A., Oppermann, R.: An operational definition of context. In: Kokinov, B., Richardson, D.C., Roth-Berghofer, T.R., Vieu, L. (eds.) CONTEXT 2007. LNCS (LNAI), vol. 4635, pp. 558–571. Springer, Heidelberg (2007)

12. Walters, J., Kanter, T., Rahmani, R.: Establishing multi-criteria context relations supporting ubiquitous immersive participation. Int. J. 4(2), 59–78 (2013)

13. Robert Schmohl. The Contextual Map. deposit.ddb.de (2010)

14. Yoo, S., Son, J.H., Kim, M.H.: A scalable publish/subscribe system for large mobile ad hoc networks. J. Syst. Softw. 82(7), 1152–1162 (2009)

15. Santa, J., Gomez-Skarmeta, A.F.: Sharing context-aware road and safety information. IEEE Pervasive Comput. 8(3), 58–65 (2009)

16. Kanter, T., Österberg, P., Walters, J., Kardeby, V., Forsström, S., Pettersson, S.: The mediasense framework. In: 2009 Fourth International Conference on Digital Telecommunications, pp. 144–147. IEEE, July 2009

17. Frey, D., Roman, G.-C.: Context-aware publish subscribe in mobile Ad Hoc networks. In: Murphy, A.L., Vitek, J. (eds.) COORDINATION 2007. LNCS, vol. 4467, pp. 37–55. Springer, Heidelberg (2007)

18. Adomavicius, G., Tuzhilin, A.: Context-aware recommender systems. In: Proceedings of the 2008 ACM conference on Recommender Systems - RecSys '08, p. 335 (2008)

19. Schmidt, A., Beigl, M., Gellersen, H.W.: There is more to context than location. Comput. Graph. 23(6), 893–901 (1999)

20. Padovitz, A., Loke, S.W., Zaslavsky, A.: Towards a theory of context spaces. In: Proceedings of the Second IEEE Annual Conference on Pervasive Computing and Communications Workshops, pp. 38–42. IEEE, March 2004

21. Rubner, Y., Tomasi, C., Guibas, L.J.: A Metric for Distributions with Applications to Image Databases, p. 59, January 1998

22. Shahid, R., Bertazzon, S., Knudtson, M.L., Ghali, W.A.: Comparison of distance measures in spatial analytical modeling for health service planning. BMC Health Serv. Res. 9, 200 (2009)

23. Walters, J., Kanter, T., Savioli, E.: A distributed framework for organizing an internet of things. In: Del Ser, J., Jorswieck, E.A., Miguez, J., Matinmikko, M., Palomar, D.P., Salcedo-Sanz, S., Gil-Lopez, S. (eds.) Mobilight 2011. LNICST, vol. 81, pp. 231–247. Springer, Heidelberg (2012)

24. Forsström, S., Kardeby, V., Walters, J., Kanter, T.: Location-based ubiquitous context exchange in mobile environments. In: Pentikousis, K., Agüero, R., García-Arranz, M., Papavassiliou, S. (eds.) MONAMI 2010. LNICST, vol. 68, pp. 177–187. Springer, Heidelberg (2011)

Socially-Aware Management of New Overlay Applications Traffic - The Optimization Potentials of the SmartenIT Approach

Krzysztof Wajda[1]([✉]), Rafał Stankiewicz[1], Zbigniew Duliński[1],
Tobias Hoßfeld[2], Michael Seufert[2], David Hausheer[3], Matthias Wichtlhuber[3],
Ioanna Papafili[4], Manos Dramitinos[4], Paolo Cruschelli[5], Sergios Soursos[6],
Roman Lapacz[7], and Burkhard Stiller[8]

[1] AGH University of Science and Technology,
al. Mickiewicza 30, 30-059 Kraków, Poland
wajda@kt.agh.edu.pl
http://www.smartenit.eu
[2] University of Würzburg, Würzburg, Germany
[3] TU Darmstadt, Darmstadt, Germany
[4] Athens University of Economics and Business, Athens, Greece
[5] Interoute, Pisa, Italy
[6] Intracom SA Telecom Solutions, Athens, Greece
[7] Poznan Supercomputing and Networking Center, Poznań, Poland
[8] University of Zürich, Zürich, Switzerland

Abstract. Today's overlay-based mobile cloud applications determine a challenge to operators and cloud providers in terms of increasing traffic demands and energy costs. The social-aware management of overlay traffic is a promising optimization approach, which shows potential for improvements by exploiting social information. This paper identifies key stakeholders and their roles in the service provisioning value chain and outlines major markets and optimization potentials. Accordingly, two scenarios are developed: the end user focused scenario aming at increased QoE for end users, and the operator focused scenario targeting at the highest operating efficiency in terms of low cost and high revenue for the operator. The energy efficiency plays a major role as a key performance metric in both scenarios. SmartenIT's socially-aware management approach is illustrated based on two example mechanisms for traffic optimization: the home router sharing mechanism (HORST) on the end user side, as well as the dynamic traffic management mechanism (DTM) on the operator side. The paper is concluded by a first sketch of SmartenIT's architecture and its mapping to the two scenarios.

Keywords: Application-layer traffic optimization · Economic traffic management · Social networks · QoE · Energy efficiency · Inter-cloud communications

© Institute for Computer Sciences, Social Informatics and Telecommunications Engineering 2015
R. Agüero et al. (Eds.): MONAMI 2014, LNICST 141, pp. 290–300, 2015.
DOI: 10.1007/978-3-319-16292-8_21

1   Introduction

In the current phase of Internet development we are observing significant coexistence and mutual stimulation of cloud computing and on-line networking. Fundamental solutions elaborated for traditional network management are probably not adequate for observed new situation. For evolving Future Internet concept and for contemporary overlay applications, we need novel characterization approaches, new business models, stakeholders characterization leading further to design of innovative network and traffic management mechanisms [12,13].

SmartenIT consortium has defined social awareness, QoE awareness and energy efficiency as the key targets for the design and optimization of traffic management mechanisms for overlay networks and cloud-based applications. Such three main targets, although defined in wide meaning, can be used as design goals for emerging proposals, e.g., to establish content distribution systems minimizing energy consumption by using energy awareness of its architecture elements and using social awareness translated into efficient structure of caches which minimizes volume of transferred data.

The remaining part of the paper is organized as follows. In Sect. 2, we introduce relevant definitions and terminology used to describe stakeholders in current service layer of networks. Section 3 provides descriptions of two different segments of the value chain of service provisioning, i.e., network-centric and user-centric cases. Section 4 aims at presenting the optimization potential for joint consideration of cloud and overlay, illustrated by description of HORST and DTM solutions. System architecture specified and being under practical development within SmartenIT consortium is presented in Sect. 5. Finally, Sect. 6 draws conclusions worked out after specification phase of SmartenIT project and briefly overviews next steps to come.

2   Definition and Terminology

In today's Internet marketplace, the Internet service layer stakeholders are those who buy and sell Internet services, namely Connectivity Providers, Data Centres Operators (DCO), Cloud Service Providers, Information Providers, and End-users. The Connectivity Providers operating at Layers 3 and below include: End-User Network Provider, Access, Transit, and Backbone Provider. The Information Providers are commonly referred to as Over-The-Top providers (OTTs). End-users may be classified as residential and business (small, medium, and large). A Connectivity Provider, commonly referred to as Network Service Provider (NSP), normally owns its network and is responsible for the provisioning of its functionalities. An Internet Service Provider (ISP) is an NSP also offering Internet services. DCOs own and manage a set of resources, including servers, storages, security devices, power management devices and the network infrastructure responsible for both, internal network traffic and external connectivity to other stakeholders.

The role of data centers (DC) is rapidly growing. Although the Internet is forecasted to reach the 'Zettabyte' era in 2016 [2], data centers have already entered it. While the amount of traffic crossing the Internet and IP WAN networks is projected to reach 1.3 ZBs (i.e., 10^9 TBs) per year in 2016, the amount of DC traffic is already 1.8 ZBs per year, and by 2016 will nearly quadruple to reach 6.6 ZBs per year. This represents a 31 % Compound Annual Growth Rate (CAGR). The higher volume of DC traffic is due to the inclusion of traffic inside DC (typically, definitions of Internet and WAN stop at the boundary of DC). Factors contributing to traffic remaining in DC include functional separation of application servers, storage, and databases, which generates replication, backup, and read/write traffic traversing DC. In the cloud systems era Cloud Service Providers are becoming the main direct customers of DCs. The resources provided on demand by DCs allow those providers to build new innovative services addressing requirements, like scalability, mobility, availability and reliability. Also, the flexibility of Cloud Service Providers may introduce new business models which result in cost reduction on the end-user's side. DCOs have been convinced that the use of cloud platforms to manage their resources is profitable for their business. Using systems like OpenStack they can apply the Infrastructure as a Service (IaaS) model to offer dynamically resources like CPU, memory and storage. According to the NIST definition [3], the consumer in this cloud model does not manage or control the underlying cloud infrastructure but has control over operating systems, storage, deployed applications, and possibly limited control of selected networking components which are in fact virtual items.

The SmartenIT approach provides consistent sequence of terms and concepts starting from most generally defined scenarios, providing more functionality-oriented use cases, up to detailed solutions [6]. We foresee an environment where both user-driven and operator-driven actions lead to a mutually accepted solution. Therefore a proper architecture is required for this. The Internet services provisioning is enabled by means of commercial business agreements among the Internet stakeholders, thus creating a multi-provider and user-centric environment, presented in the next section.

In the remainder of the paper we focus our analysis on the End User Focused Scenario (EFS), pertaining to the services and interactions visible to the end-users and the Operator Focused Scenario (OFS) reflecting the wholesale agreements among network and overlay service providers - that though not visible to the end users, greatly affect the Internet services. These two scenarios are also important from a technical point of view since they allow different potential for optimizations and respective traffic mechanisms that operate in different time scales and over different granularities of Internet traffic under a unified framework, the SmartenIT architecture.

3   The Multi-provider and User-Centric Environment

There exist two different segments of the value chain of service provisioning. On the one hand, there is the wholesale market with large time scale agreements regarding traffic aggregates of providers who interact in order to provision services to the users. On the other hand, users exhibit their demand in small time scales by means of flows. Consequently, two different scenarios are defined, one addressing the end-users' view of the system (EFS) and the other addressing the operators' view of the system (OFS).

The EFS is based on the involvement of the end-user and his devices as active instances in the system, e.g., for prefetching data to be consumed in the near future. As opposed to that, the OFS is focusing on the interactions among the different operators acting in SmartenIT framework, namely Cloud Providers, Service Providers, and Internet Service Providers. One key feature of Cloud Computing paradigm is the fact that cloud services are offered to the end-user in a transparent way, e.g. the user is not aware of physical location.

The SmartenIT scope clearly highlights the fact that multiple stakeholders are involved, each of them having its own interests, strategies and business goals. It must be noted that a SmartenIT solution would inevitably have to accommodate the possibly conflicting goals and needs of the stakeholders in an incentive-compatible way. Otherwise, the SmartenIT propositions would have limited or even no chance of being adopted in practice, resulting in limited or zero impact on the market.

3.1   End User Focused Scenario

The end user focused scenario has the goal of providing increased QoE and energy efficiency for end users by distributing and moving content and services in an energy and social aware way, while taking provider's interests into account. The scenario definition adds a number of innovative aspects to former definitions of service and content mobility, which are described in the following. First, besides mobility of services and content on the same level of aggregation (e.g., the migration of virtual machines between DCs or the caching of content in a CDN), to which we refer as horizontal mobility, we add an additional infrastructure layer to the existing solutions consisting of user-owned Nano Data Centers (uNaDas). uNaDas are WiFi routers, which provide extended functionality such as increased computation and storage capabilities. The devices are located at end-user's premises and enable vertical mobility, i.e., a movement of services and content into the user's home, thus making him part of the content and service delivery chain.

Consequently, optimizing placement means optimizing along the two dimensions of vertical and horizontal placement. Finding the right placement is an optimization problem to be solved in a socially aware and energy efficient manner. For this purpose, social data is either provided by the end user offering his local view on his social network account or from a direct cooperation with online social network providers given a suitable business model exists. The inclusion of social data allows predicting the necessity to move content, e.g., content consumed by friends can be prefetched to a user's uNaDa, in order to provide better QoE. Moreover, social data can be used to derive trust relations between users in a highly distributed and untrusted environment, which is the base for cooperation among users and their devices. In order to optimize the placement with respect to energy efficiency, information on energy consumption is needed.

This data can be derived from energy models providing an energy estimate of the placement. Energy models which estimate energy consumption from network measurements are existing in literature, e.g., [10]. Moreover, modelling the energy efficiency of placements allows also for the prediction of future energy consumptions.

Besides providing a platform for placing content and services, the uNaDa layer accounts for the increasing importance of mobile devices such as smart phones and tablets. Therefore, means for offloading from cellular technologies to the uNaDas, local WiFis are offered. The offloading capabilities are combined with possibilities to access the content stored on the uNaDa, thus the uNaDa may act as a wireless cache for relevant content.

The stakeholders in this scenario are Cloud Application Providers offering the content and services (e.g., YouTube, Vimeo or Amazon EC2), the Internet Service Provider, and the end user. Cloud Application Providers and end users have a clear incentive to collaborate in this scenario, as it will increase the QoE of the end user, which will in turn increase his willingness to pay for services and content [11]. Moreover, the cloud application can reduce the provisioning of own resources. On the contrary, the ISP can benefit from the solution, if it is implemented in an underlay aware way, which will reduce traffic over peered links and can relieve the cellular infrastructure.

3.2 Operator Focused Scenario

The Operator Focused Scenario (OFS) has the goal of achieving highest operating efficiency in terms of high Quality of Service, low energy consumption, low operating cost and highest revenues (where applicable). The scenario focuses on a certain number of well-known aspects that mixed together lay the foundation to drive potential SmartenIT innovation. First, the impact of inter-cloud communication on other involved stakeholders, i.e. the ISPs, and the reaction of those to the decisions of the DCOs which constitute the cloud layer are taken into account. Second, new coalition schemes between DCOs are considered, i.e. the so-called Cloud Federation, which enable collaboration so as to achieve both individual and overall improvement of cost and energy consumption, while simultaneously achieve footprint expansion by addressing a geographically larger set of users. Other key topics (to be intended as triggers of inter-cloud communication process among DCOs) of the selected scenario are content placement (to provide QoE enhancements), data replication (to achieve geographical fault-tolerance) and VM migration (to give support service mobility). Moreover some social awareness information (even if at a different aggregation level w.r.t EFS) can be seen as potentially impacting the actual scenario.

Whichever the trigger of inter-cloud communication process a trade-off rises due to the competing interests of the DCOs which constitute the source and destination end-points for each transmission flow, as well as the interests of the ISPs providing inter-connectivity to the DCOs. In particular, the DCO is interested in performing often data replication/migration in order to provide high QoS/QoE to its end-users [14], or the Cloud Service Providers that employ its (storage, computing) service to offer other services and applications to end-users. Moreover, data migration/re-location may often be imposed by the need to reduce overall energy consumption within the federation by consolidating processes and jobs to few DCs only.

On the other hand, the traffic generated by the data replication or migration performed by the DCOs significantly burdens the networks of the ISPs, which implies increase of operating cost for the ISP mainly in terms of transit inter-connection cost. Consequently, the ISPs would like to employ certain mechanisms and pricing models that will enable efficient traffic management, as well as sharing of revenues obtained by cloud services and applications.

Therefore, the OFS scenario defines a series of interesting problems to be addressed by SmartenIT, specifically:

- the interactions between the members of the Cloud Federation (from technical and business point of view)
- the interactions of DCOs and ISP in terms of traffic crossing ISP WAN links, fair optimization of resource allocation and sharing among the federated members, and
- energy efficiency for DCOs, either individually or overall for all member of the federation.

4   Cloud/Overlay Traffic Optimization

4.1   Home Router Sharing Based on Trust (HORST)

Home router sharing based on trust (HORST) [1] is a mechanism which addresses data offloading, content caching/prefetching, and content delivery. The HORST mechanism eases data offloading to WiFi by sharing WiFi networks among trusted friends. Moreover, it places the content near to the end-user such that users can access it with less delay and higher speed, which generally results in a higher QoE. The SmartenIT solution consists of a firmware for a home router and an OSN application. The HORST firmware establishes a private and a shared WiFi network (with different SSIDs) and manages the local storage of the home router as a cache.

To participate a user needs a flat rate Internet access at home where he has to install the HORST firmware to his home router. The owner of the home router uploads the WiFi access information of the shared WiFi to the OSN application. Each user can share his WiFi information to other trusted users via the app and request access to other shared WiFis.

HORST ensures resource contribution by incorporating an incentive mechanism coupling different resource contributions of end-users to the system, namely the provisioning of storage capacity and offloading capacity, to the receivable QoE, based on the vINCENT incentive mechanism presented in [4]. In order to enhance the overall system performance, the incentive includes social networking data as a base of trust, thus increasing market liquidity.

The HORST router has a social monitor component to collect social information from an OSN about the router's owner and his trusted friends. If a user approaches the home router of a trusted friend, he is provided with access data via the OSN app to connect to the shared WiFi. Every HORST system predicts the content consumption (i.e., when and where will which content be requested) of his owner based on history and information from the OSN, such as content popularity and spreading. If a predicted content, e.g., a video, is not yet available in the local cache, it will be prefetched (e.g., first chunks of a video as proposed by the Socially-aware Efficient Content Delivery (SECD) mechanism [7]). If the user is connected to a friend's home router, a prefetch command is sent to the HORST system on the friend's router. For prefetching as well as for actual requests which cannot be served locally, HORST chooses the best source (either another HORST home router or a cloud source) based on overlay information, and fetches the desired content. In regular intervals, HORST checks if the content in his own local cache is still relevant (either for local consumption or as a source for content delivery) and decides whether to keep or replace it.

Finally, HORST federates all home routers to form an overlay content delivery network (CDN), which allows for efficient content placement and traffic management. Thereby, ISP costs can be included in the local decisions at the home router, e.g., by taking into account the location of contents in terms of Autonomous Systems (AS). For the communication between the home routers and the distributed storage of meta-information, RB-Tracker [9] is used due to its efficiency. Thus, RB-Tracker builds the basis of HORST and hides the complexity of the overlay management.

4.2   Dynamic Traffic Management

The dynamic traffic management (DTM) mechanism [5,7] developed in SmartenIT is a solution for the OFS case. It aims at minimization of ISP's cost of inter-domain traffic by appropriate management of overlay traffic. The overlay traffic generated between DCs or between DCs and end-user devices often passes inter-domain links. DTM offers the ISP a capability to select the network path used for traffic transfer.

ISP aiming at inter-domain traffic cost reduction needs to answer two questions: when to transfer the traffic, and which inter-domain link to use for data transfer. If ISPs network is multihomed and the tariffs used on different inter-domain links differ, appropriate shifting of inter-domain traffic between them may result in lowering total costs [5]. Such traffic management is possible by creating tunnels between remote DCs (GRE or MPLS tunnels). Each tunnel should pass different inter-domain link. Appropriate selection of the tunnel results in transferring the traffic being sent between DCs via a given inter-domain link. The decision on link selection is taken by ISP dynamically according to the current situation and estimated cost of inter-domain traffic.

DTM consists of two main building blocks: (1) an algorithm to find the optimal solution to be achieved at the end of an accounting period. Using cost functions and information on the traffic distribution in the previous period, it makes a prediction for the next period and finds a better traffic distribution in which the ISP's cost is minimized; (2) the compensation procedure which determines how the traffic distribution should be influenced at a given moment to achieve the optimal solution at the end of the accounting period, i.e., decides on selection of inter-domain link. To make it possible to dynamically react to the situation in the network and predict costs periodical traffic measurements on links is needed. Finally, to make it possible to dispatch flows to appropriate tunnels SDN controller may be used.

5   System Architecture

Based on the description of scenarios, the identified properties of the SmartenIT approach and the high-level description of such solutions, this section provides an overview of the SmartenIT system architecture [8]. The component diagram in Fig. 1 shows all the core components of the architecture as well as the necessary interfaces. The color-coding of the components denotes whether a component already exists in external systems (white) or if it is SmartenIT-specific (blue). In the rest of this section, we highlight the most important components and provide a short overview of their functionality.

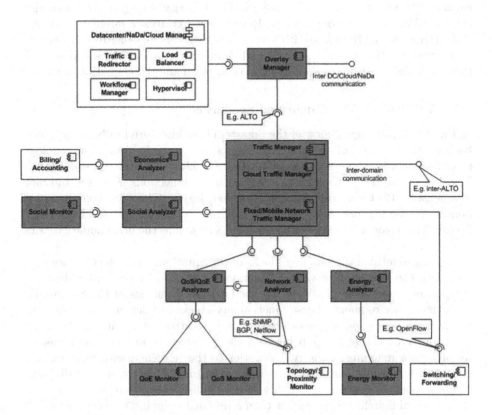

Fig. 1. The SmartenIT architecture - component diagram

The **Traffic Manager** is the central component of the architecture and includes all the decision-taking functionality. It encompasses the Cloud Traffic Manager and the Fixed/Mobile Network Traffic Manager components. The **Cloud Traffic Manager** makes high-level decisions, e.g., the caching of specific content to specific places, or the redirection of a user request to another (nano)data center. These decisions are communicated to the Overlay Manager which in turn informs the affected DCs. The **Fixed/Mobile Network Traffic Manager** takes low-level decisions, such as what QoS class should be assigned to a specific flow, which MPLS tags to be used, etc. These decisions are later materialized by the Switching/Forwarding component. The Traffic Manager provides a number of interfaces so as to interact with the rest of the system components and gather the required information or communicate the resulting decisions. The **Overlay Manager** allows the formation of overlays between remote (nano)data centers or even small Clouds, with DCs or uNaDas being the peers in these overlays. This component is responsible for the communication between peers so as to advertise offered resources, ask for resources, cache/move data, etc.

A number of Analyzers is included in the architecture, the purpose of which is to collect multi-dimensional metrics and process them so as to enrich the decision-taking functionality of the Traffic Manager. The **QoS/QoE Analyzer** addresses the QoS/QoE optimization aspects, while the **Network Analyzer** captures the network state and topology. The **Energy Analyzer** offers energy consumption considerations and the **Economics Analyzer** interacts with the Billing/Accounting Systems of ISPs or Cloud Operators, in order to address economic optimizations. Finally, the **Social Analyzer** consider the social aspects that can provide estimates for content consumption and dissemination patterns.

5.1   Adherence to the Identified Scenarios

In Fig. 2, the topological view of the SmartenIT architecture has been used as a basis for the mapping of scenarios and the respective mechanisms. The topological view includes three domains of entities: (1) **Data Center/Cloud Layer**: This layer comprises DCs and their virtual interconnections using the Internet as a network. (2) **Core and Access Network Layer**: This layer contains components in the ISP network and the private networks of DCOs. (3) **End User Layer**: This layer covers the end-users devices as well as the users home gateway (uNaDa).

Having identified the building blocks of the SmartenIT architecture, we proceed with the formation of various functionality stacks (by combining different components) and their placement on the envisioned entities of the SmartenIT deployment environment. These functionality stacks are depicted as a stack of blue/orange boxes and are associated to the respective entities in Fig. 2.

In order to bridge the gap between the architecture and the mechanisms, we provide a mapping of the two scenarios to the (enriched with functionality stacks) deployment environment, as depicted in Fig. 2. The topological diagram has been used to get a first overview of the traffic management solutions w.r.t the SmartenIT architecture, rather than a detailed mapping to components.

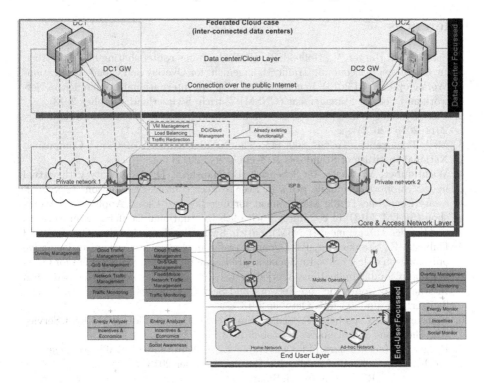

Fig. 2. Topological view of architecture with added scenario overlay [7]

With this in mind, scenarios and functionality can be aligned along a common axis. This further allows mapping each SmartenIT proposed mechanism to a set of envisioned functionalities, while at the same time showing the mainly addressed scenario. A detailed view of this mapping of all mechanisms to the respective scenarios/functionality is attached to the appendix of [7].

6   Conclusions and Outlook

In this paper, we briefly present the social-aware, QoE-aware and energy-efficient network management approach and system architecture worked out by EU SmartenIT project.

Specific solutions, defined by two main and complementary scenarios: ISP-oriented and end-user-oriented, are defined in details as, respectively, the DTM and HORST solutions. The relevant mapping of designed mechanism onto SmartenIT architecture modules is also provided. After succesfully achieving goals of specification phase, participants of the SmartenIT project are now implementing necessary modules in order to build fully operational system.

Acknowledgment. This work has been performed in the framework of the EU ICT STREP SmartenIT (FP7-ICT-2011-317846). The authors would like to thank the entire SmartenIT team for discussions and providing insights on major research problems.

References

1. Seufert, M., Burger, V., Hoßfeld, T.: HORST - home router sharing based on trust. In: Social-aware Economic Traffic Management for Overlay and Cloud Applications Workshop (SETM 2013), in conjunction with 9th International Conference on Network and Service Management (CNSM), Zurich, Switzerland, October 2013
2. Cisco Systems White Paper: Cisco Global Cloud Index: Forecast and Methodology 2011–2016 (2012)
3. Mell, P., Grance, T.: SP 800–145. The NIST Definition of Cloud Computing, National Institute of Standards & Technology (2011)
4. Wichtlhuber, M., Heise, P., Scheurich, B.: Hausheer, D: Reciprocity with virtual nodes: Supporting mobile peers in Peer-to-Peer content distribution. In: Social-aware Economic Traffic Management for Overlay and Cloud Applications Workshop (SETM 2013), in conjunction with 9th International Conference on Network and Service Management (CNSM), Zurich, Switzerland, pp. 406–409, October 2013
5. Duliński, Z., Stankiewicz, R.: Dynamic traffic management mechanism for active optimization of ISP costs. In: Social-aware Economic Traffic Management for Overlay and Cloud Applications Workshop (SETM 2013), in conjunction with 9th International Conference on Network and Service Management (CNSM), Zurich, Switzerland, pp. 398–401, October 2013
6. Biancani, M., Cruschelli, P., (eds.): SmartenIT Deliverable 1.2 – Cloud Service Classifications and Scenarios, October 2013
7. Burger, V. (ed.): SmartenIT Deliverable 2.2 – Definitions of Traffic Management Mechanisms and Initial Evaluation Results, October 2013
8. Hausheer, D., Rückert, J. (eds.): SmartenIT Deliverable 3.1 – Initial System Architecture, April 2013
9. Lareida, A., Bocek, T., Waldburger, M., Stiller, B.: RB-tracker: A fully distributed, replicating, network-, and topology-aware P2P CDN. In: IFIP/IEEE International Symposium on Integrated Network Management (IM 2013), Ghent, Belgium, pp. 1199–1202, May 2013
10. Schwartz, C., Hoßfeld, T., Lehrieder, F., Tran-Gia, P.: Angry apps: the impact of network timer selection on power consumption, signalling load, and web QoE. J. Comput. Netw. Commun. **2013**, Article ID. 176217, 13 pp. (2013). doi:10.1155/2013/176217
11. Reichl, P.: From charging for quality of service to charging for quality of experience. Ann. Telecommun. **65**(3–4), 189–199 (2010)
12. Stiller, B., Hausheer, D., Hoßfeld, T.: Towards a socially-aware management of new overlay application traffic combined with energy efficiency in the internet (SmartenIT). In: Galis, A., Gavras, A. (eds.) FIA 2013. LNCS, vol. 7858, pp. 3–15. Springer, Heidelberg (2013)
13. Hoßfeld, T., Hausheer, D., Hecht, F., Lehrieder, F., Oechsner, S., Papafili, I., Racz, P., Soursos, S., Staehle, D., Stamoulis, G.D., Tran-Gia, P. Stiller, B., Hausheer, D.: An economic traffic management approach to enable the TripleWin for users, ISPs, and overlay providers. In: Tselentis, G., et al. (eds.) FIA Prague Book – Towards the Future Internet - A European Research Perspective, pp. 24–34. IOS Press Books (2009)
14. Fiedler, M., Hossfeld, T., Tran-Gia, P.: A generic quantitative relationship between quality of experience and quality of service. IEEE Netw. Spec. Issue Improving QoE Netw. Serv. **24**(2), 36–41 (2010)

Implementing Application-Aware Resource Allocation on a Home Gateway for the Example of YouTube

Florian Wamser$^{(\boxtimes)}$, Lukas Iffländer, Thomas Zinner,
and Phuoc Tran-Gia

University of Würzburg, Am Hubland, Würzburg, Germany
{wamser,ifflaender,zinner,trangia}@informatik.uni-wuerzburg.de

Abstract. Today's Internet does not offer any quality level beyond best effort for the majority of applications used by private customers. If multiple customers with heterogeneous applications share a bottleneck link to the Internet, this often leads to quality deterioration for the customers. This particularly holds for home networks with small band Internet access and for home networks with resource limitation like a bad channel quality within a wireless network. For such cases, the best effort allocation of resources between heterogeneous applications leads to an unfair distribution of the application quality among the users. To provide a similar application quality for all users, we propose to implement an application-oriented resource management on a home gateway. Therefore, allocation mechanisms need to be implemented such as the prioritization of network flows. Furthermore, a component monitoring the application quality and dynamically triggering these mechanisms is required. We show the feasibility of this concept by the implementation of an application monitor for YouTube on a standard home gateway. The gateway estimates the YouTube video buffers and prioritizes the video clip before the playback buffer depletes.

1 Introduction

The success of tablet computers, game consoles, and Smart TVs reflects the increased user demand for Internet-based services at home. The users in the home network can access value-added services offered directly by the network provider, such as IPTV. Likewise, they also use Over-The-Top (OTT) services like YouTube, Netflix, or online gaming and browse the web or download files. All these services have specific requirements with respect to the network resources which have to be fulfilled to ensure a good Quality-of-Experience (QoE) for the users. Furthermore, multiple users may concurrently access different services via the central Internet access point in the home network, the home gateway.

As stated by the Home Gateway Initiative (HGI) [1], the network at home and the broadband Internet access link may constitute a bottleneck. This may be due to the insufficient availability of broadband access, i.e., the network provider

© Institute for Computer Sciences, Social Informatics and Telecommunications Engineering 2015
R. Agüero et al. (Eds.): MONAMI 2014, LNICST 141, pp. 301–312, 2015.
DOI: 10.1007/978-3-319-16292-8_22

offers only small band Internet access, or due to limitations within the home network, like the varying channel quality of the wireless networks.

Traffic in today's network structures is usually transmitted on a best effort basis. As a result, different services or applications with varying requirements and capabilities are treated equally on a per flow-basis, resulting in a unfairness in terms of QoE. Long lasting OS updates on a home computer may thus interfere with video streaming to a Smart TV which leads to video stallings and a degradation in the QoE of the user. In such a case, it is necessary to explicitly allocate the network resources unequally to the involved applications on network level to achieve a similar QoE across multiple applications, as introduced in [2].

This explicit network resource control is known as Application-Aware Networking. Scalability issues hinder the implementation of such mechanisms within aggregation and wide area networks, but the small size of the home network makes them a promising candidate. Most of the traffic is forwarded in home networks via the home gateway, making it possible to control the network resources, and therewith the application quality, at this entity. The applicability of this approach was shown in [3], however, performance studies on the potential of the approach on a home gateway are missing.

In this paper, we evaluate the potential of flexibly allocating network resources to different applications. We focus on a two-application scenario where YouTube flows and a file download compete for resources via a shared bottleneck link. YouTube maintains a playback buffer to overcome resource limitations on a short time scale. We take advantage of this in order to provide an accurate reaction against video stallings. We implemented a network-based buffer estimator for YouTube which allows the accurate monitoring of the application video pre-buffering state. If the local video buffer runs empty, the IP flow is prioritized, if the buffer is sufficiently filled, the prioritization is turned off, or other applications like browsing are prioritized.

The remainder of this paper is structured as follows. Section 2 summarizes the home gateway architecture and its components. In Sect. 3, the implementation details for the specific scenario are described. Section 4 highlights the evaluation setup, and Sect. 5 presents the results of our evaluation. The related work is summarized in Sect. 6, and the paper is concluded in Sect. 7.

2   Application-Aware Resource Control for a Home Gateway

In this section, we introduce the developed application-aware resource management framework running on the home gateway and its components.

The developed architecture consists of four components. These are a network monitoring, a network control component, an application monitor, and a decision component. The purpose of the architecture is a cross layer approach that manages the network resources in a more sophisticated way in order to increase the QoE of all network users. It manages the network resources based on the application information. Resource management actions are only triggered if they may improve the average application performance of all network users.

This means that they are triggered if an indication for, or the QoE degradation itself, has been detected and a resource management action may improve the QoE of one application while not degrading the quality of others. In the following, we describe the four components.

Network Monitoring. The network monitoring and control component firstly performs network monitoring of relevant QoS parameters and keeps track of the current network load. It provides a collection of relevant QoS parameters to the decision component. Thus, it supports the decision component by forcing appropriate resource management actions.

Network Control. This component implements possible resource control mechanisms for an explicit allocation of network resources to single flows or traffic classes. With respect to the capabilities of the home gateway, these mechanisms may range from additional entries in the routing table to the prioritization of application classes or flows, sophisticated resource allocation actions or even an active manipulation of the application layer content. The network control component implements the input from the decision component.

Application Monitor. The application monitor continuously estimates the current application quality based on the applications' network flows. The quality depends on the current application state which is a collection of application-specific quality indicators. These quality indicators describe whether the current resources offered by the network are sufficient for a good quality. The resulting application quality is forwarded to the decision component.

Decision Component. The decision component sequentially determines how the available resource control mechanisms shall be forced based on the current network and application monitoring data. It predicts how the resource control may change the application and network state. A resource control action is triggered if the confidence in the prediction is high, the degree of the QoE improvement is significant, and the effort performing the resource management action is acceptable.

3 Implementation Details and Application Design

This section highlights the implementation details of our approach.

3.1 Monitoring the YouTube Buffer State

Details of our approach to estimate the application quality of YouTube are discussed in this subsection.

To enable a smooth playback of YouTube videos for the customer with a fluctuating network bandwidth, the YouTube application buffers a certain amount of the video data. To further achieve an economically efficient service, the pre-buffered video data have to be kept as small as possible to minimize the waste of transport resources if the user aborts the video playback. This task is performed by different flow control algorithms. Thus far YouTube implements two different approaches on flow control: the "throttling approach" performed on the server side by controlling network bandwidth [4] and the "range request approach" performed by the client by requesting the required parts of the video similar to the MPEG-DASH approach [5].

YouTube supports multiple media container formats [6]. Each format encapsulates the content provided in a different way. The most common formats are Flash Video (FLV) [7], Third Generation Partnership Project (3GPP) [8] and MPEG 4 (MP4) [9] where MP4 can be implemented as a continuous or fragmented format, the last one currently being the default format for newly uploaded videos to the platform.

MP4 specifies that media and meta data can be separated and stored in one or several files, as long as the meta data is stored as a whole. The file is divided in so-called boxes. The standard files contain one "ftyp", "mdat" and "moov" box. Where "ftyp" specifies the file type, "mdat" contains the media data and "moov" the meta data. "moov" has several subboxes that contain the video header and timescale, information about substreams and the base media decode time.

Fragmented MP4 provides the ability to transfer the "mdat" box in multiple fragments instead of one big blop. As shown in Fig. 1 each fragment consists of a "moof" and a "mdat" box. The "moof" (movie fragment) box contains subboxes determining the default sample duration, the number of samples in the current track and a set of independent samples.

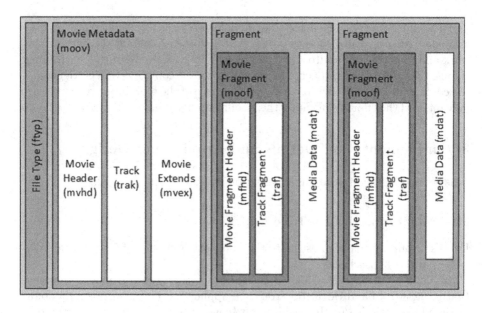

Fig. 1. MP4 fragment format

The fragmented MP4 is currently used for YouTube's range request algorithm and is currently the default format for newly uploaded videos. Therefore the application used for the YouTube buffer prediction focuses on this format.

To detect the requests to the server, the outgoing TCP traffic is monitored for HTTP GET requests. When a request is detected, video information like the video id, the format and the signature as well as streaming related information like the utilized flow control approach, are derived.

As for accumulating the currently downloaded amount of data for a certain video, the incoming traffic is monitored for the fragment boxes and incoming fragments are added to the estimation of the video's download process. The buffer estimation is then calculated as the difference between the available playback time of the already downloaded amount and the time passed since the begin of playback. We compute the application state for the video and the audio flow. User interaction like pausing, reverse jumping can not be taken into account. Forward jumping can be identified using the media data if the user jumps to a location which has not been downloaded yet.

3.2   Enforcing Resource Control

The most flexible way to control the network resources on a per-flow basis is the assignment of a dynamic rate limit to the individual flows. This enables a granular adjustment of each flow, but also results in a lot of state information required to maintain the single queues for each individual flow. A more simple approach is to define several priority queues and assign the flows to the different priorities with respect to the current application state, cf. Fig. 2. Since we evaluate a small home scenario, we implemented the priority approach by using five different queues with

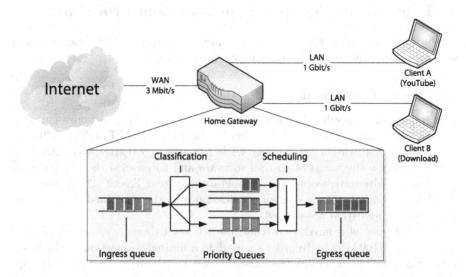

Fig. 2. Buffered playtime for audio and video

a queue size of 25 packets for each queue. To dynamically re-assign flows to different priorities, we use a Python wrapper script for the Linux Traffic Control [10] (TC) API via a simple TCP socket interface. With TC a stateful queuing is done that classifies the incoming packets and sorts them into the priority classes that are emptied by a scheduler according to the priorities.

3.3 Triggering Resource Control Actions

The network controller is implemented within the application monitor and executed periodically. If the YouTube video or audio playback buffer falls below 25 s, it is moved to a higher priority queue. If they overrun 40 s, the flow is moved to a lower priority. Thus, a reaction takes place if the application quality is endangered, i.e., the playback buffers threaten to run empty. Best-effort behavior is used, as long as the application quality for all applications is not endangered.

3.4 Application Design

The described components are implemented in two binaries. One is the resource enforcement application using priority queues. The other components are implemented as a C++ linux application. The multi-threaded design of the application together with the compiler optimizations provided by C++ allow low latencies and a high performance on the used end device. We use the local TCP/IP interface to perform the communication between the applications. The redirection of the YouTube flow through the user space, however, has a significant impact on the data plane performance, since the CPU of the home gateway becomes the bottleneck. This results in a CPU load of 40 % for a link capacity of 3 MBit.

4   Experimental Setup and Measurement Procedure

In the following subsection, the measurement scenario and the measurement sequence is described in order to evaluate the resource control.

4.1 Experimental Setup

The implemented application is designed to run on a typical home gateway. Among the available off-the-self gateway hardware, an AVM Fritz!Box 3390 has been chosen, featuring a MIPS 34Kc CPU running at 300 MHz with 22 MiB of RAM. To allow the usage of custom software and to provide the default linux libraries the alternative open source operating system Freetz [11] is used. On the Fritz!Box the resource control application and the combined decision and monitoring application are started.

The gateway is connected to the Internet via Ethernet with a theoretical bandwidth of 100 Mbit/s. In order to emulate a limited connection to the Internet, we restrict the downlink from the Internet to 3 Mbit/s. Two client laptops (Client A and Client B) are connected to the gateway via Ethernet with a link speed of 1 Gbit/s.

4.2 Measurement Procedure

For our investigations, we use the following procedure. The scenario begins with starting a YouTube video clip on Client A. After 15 s a download is started on Client B utilizing four parallel connections for the download. Hence, we can expect the download to get at least four times the bandwidth of the YouTube stream. As video clip, we always use the same video clip, "VAN CANTO - Badaboom (Official)"[1] in 720p. After 300 s we stop the measurement.

5 Evaluation Results

5.1 YouTube Buffer Level During Video Playback

At first, we have a look at the YouTube buffer level over time without any resource management. Using fragmented MP4, the audio and the video stream are transmitted separately resulting in different playback buffer states. If one of the playback buffers is empty, the video clip stalls until the stalling threshold of 5 s is reached.

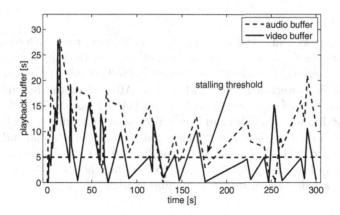

Fig. 3. Buffered playtime for audio and video without application monitoring and resource management

Figure 3 shows the playback buffer for the audio and video buffers. Both buffer levels increase until the parallel download is started. After that, the buffer level for both buffers decreases at about 20 s. In this example, the video buffer initially is empty at second 40, resulting in a short stalling period although the audio buffer stays at a sufficient buffer level. Since not enough network capacity is available to allow a smooth video playback in case of a concurrent file download, the video playback is interrupted several times. After 60 s, the audio buffer falls

---

[1] Video clip available at http://www.youtube.com/watch?v=Aeaz4s7q0Ag&wide=1&hd=1.

below the threshold of 5 s while the video buffer still maintains a higher buffer level. Consequently, the audio flow is also taken into account in the following.

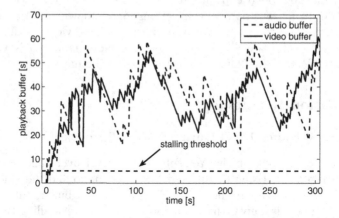

Fig. 4. Buffered playtime for audio and video with application monitoring and resource management

Figure 4 shows audio and video playback buffer over time with dynamic prioritization enabled. In contrast to the best-effort case, the buffer levels increase although the parallel download has started. Both flows are prioritized until the playback buffers overrun a threshold of 45 s. After that, the resource control mechanism is turned off, until the buffers fall below 25 s. The TCP flow control results in additional dynamics and it may take some time until a fair bandwidth share between the flows is reached. This is reflected by the minimal and maximal playback buffer levels at 15 s and 63 s. In addition, the re-assignment to different priorities may lead to packet reordering influencing the TCP control loop and resulting in a reduction of the TCP sending window, cf. [12].

5.2   Statistical Evaluation of the Investigated Scenario

After investigating the time series for the audio and video streams for the scenarios with and without prioritization, we focus on a statistical significant comparison between both approaches. For that, we conduct 10 runs and compare the CDFs for the buffer fillings. The results of this investigation is illustrated in Fig. 5 with a confidence level of 95 %. It can be seen that the application-aware approach using dynamic prioritization with respect to the application state clearly outperforms the approach without prioritization, i.e., the best effort case. This holds for both flows, the audio and the video flow. Stalling is minimized allowing a better user-perceived quality for the video streaming user. Further, it can be seen, that the buffer level for the audio buffer is typically higher as for the video buffer. Hence, we can conclude that a video stalling is more likely due to a video

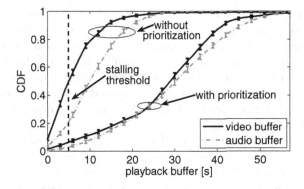

Fig. 5. Buffered playtime for audio and video

buffer under run. Figure 5 also shows that the majority of values are located between 20 and 50 s, closely related to the values of the control hysteresis.

6   Related Work

In the following, papers on different resource management approaches are summarized. We specifically address QoE cross-layer resource management and application-aware resource management.

Different common techniques for resource management are used in networking devices and current communication protocols [13–15]. They all make use of protocol-specific conditions to favor packets or IP flows, or to influence the data transmission. To identify relevant packets or streams other techniques are necessary. Approaches like deep packet inspection (DPI) or explicit signaling of the application [16] are used to identify different applications and to map them to QoS classes. Approaches like [17,18] tag the ToS (type of service), the diffserv (differentiated services) field in the IP packet or use a shim header [16] to prioritize the corresponding network traffic.

QoE Cross-Layer Resource Management. The goal of QoE resource management approaches is a resource allocation according to the QoE of the users. QoE models [19,20] for different applications form the basis as proposed in [21–25]. In order to incorporate QoE, a cross-layer optimization is typically used [21,22,25]. For example, in case of overload on the network layer, [21,22] prioritize important packets of MPEG videos, mainly I-frames, in order to still guarantee a high quality. In [26], a multi-layer video encoding with scalable video codec is used. The goal is to prioritize the different layers in different QoS classes to specifically drop video layers with less importance if the network is congested. In [23], QoE-based scheduling for wireless mesh networks is proposed. According to a MOS metric that maps QoE to QoS parameters, the video, data, and audio traffic is forwarded.

Application-aware resource management. In addition to the work mentioned above, application-aware resource management is seen as a step towards QoE-oriented or QoE-aware resource management. It allocates resources based on dynamic cross-layer information from the application, e.g., the buffered play-time in case of videos in order to increase QoE [27–29]. This approach can be seen as a continuation of former work which used a so-called utility function for network resource management to define a scheduling order with respect to different application cases [30–34].

In [35], a QoS manager is proposed which centrally passes the requirements for the whole network to a switch. The problem is addressed how various networking entities can work together to prioritize traffic flows in order to allow a prioritization for the entire network. For residential networks, [36] proposes to setup a QoS system that uses hints from individual hosts to make decisions about traffic prioritization. In [37], the concept for traffic prioritization is presented for small networks. The authors specify a prioritization of applications for active users and a de-prioritization for applications in the background.

7   Conclusion

Traffic in today's network structures is typically transmitted on a best effort basis. As a result, different services or applications with varying requirements and capabilities are treated equally on a per flow-basis. This may result in unfairness in terms of the user-perceived quality, in particular if the overall resources are limited. This holds especially for home networks where different users may compete for limited network resources.

In this paper, we presented an application-aware networking approach to overcome this problem. We investigated the feasibility of the approach for a scenario consisting of two users, a download user and a user watching a YouTube video clip. We implemented an application monitoring component for YouTube, a prioritization mechanism to control the resources, and a simple decision logic. The monitoring component is able to estimate the video and audio playback buffer. The resulting information are used to trigger a prioritization of the video streaming if the buffer runs empty. Hence, a good QoE for the video streaming user can be guaranteed. The components were implemented on a typical home gateway. The evaluation of the scenario indicates the potential of the mechanism to manage the application quality and therewith the QoE for multiple users in a multi-application scenario.

References

1. Home Gateway Initiative: Home Gateway QoS module requirements. whitepaper, Dec 2012
2. Eckert, M., Knoll, T.M.: ISAAR (Internet Service Quality Assessment and Automatic Reaction) a QoE monitoring and enforcement framework for internet services in mobile networks. In: Timm-Giel, A., Strassner, J., Agüero, R., Sargento, S., Pentikousis, K. (eds.) MONAMI 2012. LNICST, vol. 58, pp. 57–70. Springer, Heidelberg (2013)

3. Wamser, F., Zinner, T., Iffländer, L., Tran-Gia, P.: Demonstrating the prospects of dynamic application-aware networking in a home environment. In: Proceedings of the 2014 ACM Conference on SIGCOMM, pp. 149–150. ACM (2014)
4. Alcock, S., Nelson, R.: Application flow control in youtube video streams. ACM SIGCOMM Comput. Commun. Rev. **41**(2), 24–30 (2011)
5. Sieber, C., Hoßfeld, T., Zinner, T., Tran-Gia, P., Timmerer, C.: Implementation and user-centric comparison of a novel adaptation logic for DASH with SVC. In: IFIP/IEEE International Workshop on Quality of Experience Centric Management (QCMan), Ghent, Belgium (2013)
6. Wikipedia: Youtube – Wikipedia, the free encyclopedia (2014). https://en.wikipedia.org/wiki/Youtube. Accessed 20 May 2014
7. A.S. Incorporated: Video File Format Specification, Adobe Systems Incorporated Std., Rev. 10, November 2008. http://download.macromedia.com/f4v/video_file_format_spec_v10_1.pdf. Accessed 26 May 2014
8. Singer, D.: 3GPP TS 26.244; Transparent end-to-end packet switched streaming service (PSS); 3GPP file format (3GP), ETSI 3GPP Std., Rev. 12.3.0, March 2014. http://www.3gpp.org/DynaReport/26244.htm. Accessed 26 May 2014
9. MPEG 4 standards ISO/IEC 14496–1 ff, International Organization for Standardization Std., Rev. 2010 (1999). http://www.iso.org/iso/iso_catalogue/catalogue_ics/catalogue_detail_ics.htm?csnumber=24462
10. Hubert, B.: Linux Advanced Routing & Traffic Control, Linux Foundation. Accessed 26 May 2014
11. Freetz project: Freetz. http://freetz.org/
12. Zinner, T., Jarschel, M., Blenk, A., Wamser, F., Kellerer, W.: Dynamic application-aware resource management using software-defined networking: implementation prospects and challenges. In: IFIP/IEEE International Workshop on Quality of Experience Centric Management (QCMan), Krakow, Poland (2014)
13. IEEE 802.1Q 2011: Standard for Local and Metropolitan Area Networks - Media Access Control (MAC) Bridges and Virtual Bridge Local Area Networks, August 2011
14. IEEE 802.11e-2005: Standard for Information technology - Part 11: Wireless LAN Medium Access Control (MAC) and Physical Layer (PHY) specifications, November 2005
15. IEEE 802.16m-2011: Standard for Local and metropolitan area networks - Part 16: Air Interface for Broadband Wireless Access Systems, Amendment 3: Advanced Air Interface (802.16m-2011), May 2011
16. Paul, S., Jain, R., Pan, J., Iyer, J., Oran, D.: Openadn: A case for open application delivery networking. In: 2013 22nd International Conference on Computer Communications and Networks (ICCCN), pp. 1–7. IEEE (2013)
17. RFC 791: DARPA Internet program protocol specification (1981)
18. Nichols, K., Blake, S., Baker, F., Black, D.: RFC 2474: Definition of the differentiated services field (DS field) in the IPv4 and IPv6 headers (1998)
19. Agboma, F., Liotta, A.: QoE-aware QoS management. In: 6th International Conference on Advances in Mobile Computing and Multimedia, pp. 111–116. ACM (2008)
20. Fiedler, M., Hoßfeld, T., Tran-Gia, P.: A generic quantitative relationship between quality of experience and quality of service. IEEE Network **24**(2), 36–41 (2010). Special Issue on Improving QoE for Network Services
21. Gross, J., Klaue, J., Karl, H., Wolisz, A.: Cross-layer optimization of OFDM transmission systems for MPEG-4 video streaming. Comput. Commun. **27**(11), 1044–1055 (2004)

22. Khan, S., Peng, Y., Steinbach, E., Sgroi, M., Kellerer, W.: Application-driven cross-layer optimization for video streaming over wireless networks. IEEE Commun. Mag. **44**(1), 122–130 (2006)
23. Reis, A., Chakareski, J., Kassler, A., Sargento, S.: Quality of experience optimized scheduling in multi-service wireless mesh networks. In: IEEE Conference on Image Processing (ICIP), pp. 3233–3236. IEEE (2010)
24. Pries, R., Hock, D., Staehle, D.: QoE based bandwidth management supporting real time flows in IEEE 802.11 mesh networks. Praxis der Informationsverarbeitung und Kommunikation **32**(4), 235–241 (2010)
25. Ameigeiras, P., Ramos-Munoz, J.J., Navarro-Ortiz, J., Mogensen, P., Lopez-Soler, J.M.: QoE oriented cross-layer design of a resource allocation algorithm in beyond 3G systems. Comput. Commun. 339(5), 571–582 (2010)
26. Huang, C., Juan, H., Lin, M., Chang, C.: Radio resource management of heterogeneous services in mobile WiMAX systems [Radio Resource Management and Protocol Engineering for IEEE 802.16]. IEEE Wireless Commun. **14**(1), 20–26 (2007)
27. Thakolsri, S., Khan, S., Steinbach, E., Kellerer, W.: QoE-driven cross-layer optimization for high speed downlink packet access. J. Commun. **4**(9), 669–680 (2009)
28. Superiori, L., Wrulich, M., Svoboda, P., Rupp, M., Fabini, J., Karner, W., Steinbauer, M.: Content-aware scheduling for video streaming over HSDPA networks. In: Second International Workshop on Cross Layer Design, IWCLD 2009, pp. 1–5. IEEE (2009)
29. Staehle, B., Wamser, F., Hirth, M., Stezenbach, D., Staehle, D.: AquareYoum: Application and quality of experience-aware resource management for YouTube in wireless mesh networks. PIK - Praxis der Informationsverarbeitung und Kommunikation (2011)
30. Xiao, M., Shroff, N., Chong, E.: A utility-based power-control scheme in wireless cellular systems. IEEE/ACM Trans. Netw. **11**(2), 210–221 (2003)
31. Andrews, M., Qian, L., Stolyar, A.: Optimal utility based multi-user throughput allocation subject to throughput constraints. In: IEEE INFOCOM, vol. 4, pp. 2415–2424. IEEE (2005)
32. Song, G., Li, Y.: Utility-based resource allocation and scheduling in ofdm-based wireless broadband networks. IEEE Commun. Mag. **43**(12), 127–134 (2005)
33. Saul, A.: Simple optimization algorithm for mos-based resource assignment. In: VTC Spring 2008, pp. 1766–1770. IEEE (2008)
34. Pei, X., Zhu, G., Wang, Q., Qu, D., Liu, J.: Economic model-based radio resource management with qos guarantees in the cdma uplink. Eur. Trans. Telecommun. **21**(2), 178–186 (2010)
35. Zinca, D., Dobrota, V., Vancea, C., Lazar, G.: Protocols for communication between qos agents: Cops and sdp. In: COST
36. Katchabaw, M., Lutfiyya, H., Bauer, M.: Usage based service differentiation for end-to-end quality of service management. Comput. Commun. **28**(18), 2146–2159 (2005)
37. Martin, J., Feamster, N.: User-driven dynamic traffic prioritization for home networks. In: Proceedings of the 2012 ACM SIGCOMM Workshop on Measurements Up the Stack, pp. 19–24. ACM (2012)

Ambient Assisted Living (AAL) Architectures

Reliable Platform for Enhanced Living Environment

Rossitza Goleva[1(✉)], Rumen Stainov[2], Alexander Savov[3], and Plamen Draganov[3]

[1] Department of Communication Networks, Technical University of Sofia,
Kl. Ohridski blvd. 8, 1756 Sofia, Bulgaria
rig@tu-sofia.bg
[2] Applied Computer Science Department, University of Applied Science,
Marquardstrasse 35, 36039 Fulda, Germany
rumen.stainov@informatik.hs-fulda.de
[3] Comicon Ltd., Mladost 4, bul. Roman Avramov, Bitov kombinat, et.2,
1715 Sofia, Bulgaria
{comicon,plamen}@comicon.bg

Abstract. The aim of this paper is to present an idea of the platform for enhanced living environment that will allow flexible and reliable use of cloud computing and sensor networks for highly customized services and applications. The architecture is based on sensors using IEEE 802.15.4 and zigbee protocols. Furthermore, the access to the cloud could be done by any available wired or wireless technology. We propose an application layer service using peer port for reliable and scalable data transmission. The presented solution is dynamic, flexible and conforms to the health and home automation standards.

Keywords: Sensor-to-cloud · Zigbee · IEEE 802.15.4 · Peer port · Cloud computing · Internet of things · Opportunistic environments · Quality of service

1 Introduction

The aim of this work is to investigate the Quality of Service (QoS) and performance parameters of the sensor-to-cloud communication. We highlight the QoS parameters between the Modbus TCP programmable logic controllers (PLC) and the wireless sensor mesh network of zigbee 802.15.4 devices working at 868.3 MHz and at 2.4 GHz. The traffic parameters considered are throughput, delay, loss, topology discovery, and topology configuration time. The applicability of the solution is proven by a set of experiments in the lab with up to 20 sensors, few repeaters and one PLC. The solution could be applied for personal area network (PAN) setup and combined well with body area network (BAN), home/business automation network, health care network from one side and wide range of cloud applications for data storing and statistical analyses [1] from the other side. Due to the vitality of the information, the connection to the cloud is considered to be peer-to-peer (P2P) using a special type of reservation channel at the application layer called peer port (PP). The peer port application is simulated and experimented in the lab LAN as well.

© Institute for Computer Sciences, Social Informatics and Telecommunications Engineering 2015
R. Agüero et al. (Eds.): MONAMI 2014, LNICST 141, pp. 315–328, 2015.
DOI: 10.1007/978-3-319-16292-8_23

During our experiments, we check the network performance in the case of radio interference at the same radio frequency, with additional radio frequency noise, different number of devices and Modbus channels, in the sleeping/waking up modes, and different zigbee profiles.

The paper is organized in two main sections. The first one explains the details of the experiments in sensor network. The second part concerns trials in the lab of the application layer protocol and peer port implementation. The tests performed show the vitality of the solution and its further perspectives. Future research and implementation plans are discussed at the end of the paper.

2 State of the Art

Zigbee is a wireless technology for sensor networks based on IEEE 802.15.4 at physical and medium access control (MAC) layers of Open System Interconnection Reference Model (OSI RM) [2–3]. The technology has been created to work in the environment with high interference and with rather small capacity. Nevertheless, recently there are many zigbee applications with real-time video and voice transmission. The communication channel between zigbee devices and the PLCs is low capacity and the protocols are usually based on telegrams (questions and answers). Most of the applications are non-real-time [4]. The same is valid for P2P communication and especially for the peer port applications where the data and devices are mobile and the demand for reliability is high.

Zigbee is ideal for connections when there is a high interference and low signal-to-noise ratio. The range between 10 and 40 m is proper for BAN and PAN [5]. Transmission range of up to 300 m is also appropriate for sensor-to-cloud communications. One of the main sources of interference is the wireless LAN. When the power of the signal is high and the signal-to-noise ratio is good the transmission rate could be significant [6]. Signal modulation is changed at different frequencies and influences the transmission rate [7].

End-to-end delay is calculated as a difference between time stamp when the data is sent and time stamp upon data reception. The queuing delay could not be distinguished from the transmission delay. Furthermore, the time for data processing at both ends is usually bigger than the transfer delay. In this paper, we aim to estimate this time in two parts: sensor-PLC and PLC-cloud. When the number of sending sensors is small, QoS parameters are conformed. This is the reason to simulate very often the network in extreme environment [8–10].

Modbus is considered as an industrial standard for automation. It is used in the cases when transmission of real-time or near-real-time communication is necessary via serial connection. Combination with zigbee technology allows mesh and semi-mesh ad hoc network implementations. Modbus TCP is a standard for gateway between zigbee sensors and PLCs in other networks [9].

Physical layer QoS parameters could be directly measured [11]. They show the connection between power of the signal and signal/noise ratio from one side and the network performance from other side. The protocol influence on the network is not visible at this layer [9]. Most of the QoS parameters estimated in this work are at network layer. Some of the Quality of Experience (QoE) parameters [5] could be also calculated [12, 13].

Losses are calculated as a part of the totally sent data. It is not always possible to distinguish between the data sent successfully during first trial, during the second trial etc. For example, the enocean sensors repeat the same message three times in case of lack of acknowledgement (ack). The ratio between numbers of retransmissions over the total transmissions is calculated according to [14]. The availability of the service in zigbee and enocean technology is up to 99,99 %. This means only 52 min without service annually [15]. This reliable solution is thanks to the vitality of the sensors and their capability to structure and restructure clusters using flexible ad hoc On-Demand Distance Vector (AODV) routing.

Sensors work in a sleeping/waking up mode in a ratio 1:100. They are grouped in ad hoc clusters, form clusters, reshape clusters dynamically. The transmission is per hop or end-to-end [7, 16, 17]. This feature makes the technology very appropriate for PAN and BAN. During the experiments series zigbee, input/output zigbee (i/o zigbee), i/o zigbee controllers are used for home automation [18, 19]. Trials with enocean sensors are planned for further analyses and comparison. The experiments in the lab are setup with up to 20 sensors on 20 sq. m with a possibility for radio interference. The transmission interval is expected to increase exponentially with the amount of information to be sent and the sensor density.

The trials also include measurements when there is a direct transmission line between sensors in a mesh topology and when there is a lack of direct channel and sensors have to retransmit, i.e. having a semi-mesh topology [9]. Thanks to the reconfiguration by the ad hoc routing protocol, the clusters usually form mesh topology [20]. When mesh configuration is not possible, the sensors establish a communication channel using dynamic relays. This feature allows transmission in real-time or near-real-time because the time for reconfiguration is less than 30 ms. Additional 15 ms are necessary for the sensor to wake up and another 15 ms for the channel access. Practical applications show that these time intervals are up to 10 times bigger [9, 21, 22]. The channel capacity is usually up to 100 kbps. The protocol could tolerate up to 30 % losses. That is why the zigbee standards are applicable in Internet of Things (IoT) and Delay (Disruption) Tolerant Networks (DTN).

Zigbee works at about 1.10^{-5} Bit Error Rate (BER) and about 0 signal/noise ratio. Other technologies like WiFi and Bluetooth can reach up to 1.10^{-1} BER [23]. The communication channel is point-to-point at 868 MHz with up to 20 kbps rate. The rate at 2.4 GHz could be up to 250 kbps and there might be up to 26 communication channels accessed by Carrier Sense Multiple Access with Collision Avoidance (CSMA-CA) protocol. A beacon frame is used for waking up the sensors. Waking intervals race significantly without the use of a beacon [24–26]. Theoretically, the topology with clusters could be scalable and very big. Up to 255 clusters with up to 254 nodes could be connected. This allows the technology to be used in applications in business, hospital/hotel environments in a scalable manner [27–30].

3 Zigbee Experiment Setup

The protocol Modbus was created for PLC and remote terminals communication using the master/slave protocol. It is asynchronous and supports point-to-point and point-to-multipoint connections via RS232, RS485, RS422 interfaces of wired and wireless modems. In our experiments, we use Modbus RTU (Remote Terminal Unit) and Modbus TCP. The payload of the data unit is up to 252 bytes. Data units are encapsulated into TCP segments.

In addition to IEEE 802.15.4 physical and MAC layers, the zigbee protocol stack supports network layer routing and packet forwarding using peer-to-peer communication. Star topology is also supported. The zigbee protocol has an application sublayer (APS) for cluster, profile, and end-points addressing. At application layer there is a Zigbee Device Object (ZDO) for device, services, and network management. IEEE 802.15.4 defines Full Function Devices (FFD) and Reduced Function Devices (RFD). The zigbee router, the part of the end-devices and the coordinator are FFDs. Some of the end-devices are RFDs. The zigbee coordinator and routers are always awaken. FFD end-devices could sleep (Fig. 1).

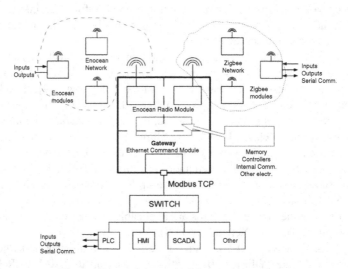

Fig. 1. The experimental zigbee setup topology.

IEEE 802.15.4 PHY supports up to 16 communication channels. The coordinator chooses a working channel upon network configuration. Both Modbus RTU and Modbus TCP are analysed.

The application profiles are private and public. For the Enhanced Living Environment (ELE) we choose a combination between the zigbee home automation and the zigbee health networking enriched by peer port support in a cloud.

EnOcean technology supports special type of sensors that obtain power supply from the alternative (e.g. solar) sources. It could reach a rate of up to 125 kbps.

The protocol repeats the same frames three times using the uniformly distributed intervals to avoid collisions.

The protocol is optimized for energy consumption. Transmission is limited in time. Rx and maximal Tx maturity times are accordingly 100 ms and 40 ms. The communication is near-real-time. The network could also have repeaters that have different time-slot organization. Repeaters also count how many times the message is repeated. The difference between repeater of type A and repeater of type B is the retransmission procedure. Type A repeater retransmits only the messages from the original devices whereas type B repeaters retransmit only the messages that are already retransmitted ones or are coming from the original device.

The QoS tests organized in the network are summarized on Table 1. The parameters estimated during the experiments are throughput, losses, and delay. All analyses of the topology lead to the wake up and sleep time estimation as well as time for network reconfiguration, network access, network routing. The detailed tests are made in normal and extreme working environment.

Table 1. List of measurements in zigbee network.

No	Description
1.	Duplex channel analyses via serial zigbee sensors without radio interference. Up to 3 radio channels for data to Modbus RTU. Different number of sensors per radio channel
2.	Measurements of full mesh topology with interference
3.	Analyses of the connection between zigbee i/o and zigbee i/o controllers in mesh and semi-mesh topologies
4.	Analyses of the two parallel channels to Modbus RTU
5.	Analyses of the throughput to Modbus RTU with different number of sensors and sensor density
6.	Zigbee-Home Automation QoS analyses
7.	Enocean QoS analyses with different sensor density at 868.3 MHz
8.	End-to-end QoS parameters' estimation
9.	Analyses of the topology reconfiguration by changing: the size of the cluster; the sensor density; the cluster division; the cluster unification; the route changing; the routing via different number of hops
10.	Topology reconfiguration analyses with radio interference
11.	Zigbee- Home Automation QoS analyses in full mesh and semi full mesh topologies
12.	Analyses of the enocean sensors to repeaters connection with and without clusters at 868.3 MHz

The data exchanged in the sensor network is discrete or analogue and uses serial communication for reliability. In the Fig. 1 the PLC can act as a client and a server at the same time. HMI (Human Machine Interface) and SCADA (Supervisory Control and Data Acquisition) are usually Modbus TCP clients. The data from sensors requires Modbus TCP client/server mode. In this case, it is possible to transmit critical sensor information to PLC immediately. Data from sensors can be sent periodically in sleep or waking up modes. Sensors can transmit only changes in data values for energy safe. It could be applied in sleep/waking up mode or in only wake up mode with delay critical data, i.e. alarms. The data could be requested by the gateway. It is useful for traffic management but needs additional functionality in the gateway. The functionality is useful when the end-user likes to send a command to the end-device, i.e. switching on or off. All types of data transfers could be combined depending on the customer request of specific scenario application. Data could be fragmented. Sleep mode is not useful in serial data transmission due to the additional delay. EnOcean sensors are STM310 and STM300 types and work at 868.3 MHz. Radio module has 3 analogue and 4 digital inputs, software and hardware control on waking up. The power supply could be conventional or alternative. Repeaters have a port for serial communication using RS-232 interface (Fig. 2). Retransmissions are limited to two. Transmission mode is pure broadcasting because the messages are not addressed. This allows formation of a typical mesh topology for PAN.

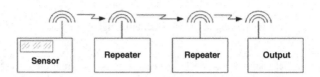

Fig. 2. Enocean sensors and repeaters configuration.

Topological schemas like tree or star are not considered in this paper. The MAC layer also can be adapted to support guaranteed and contention-based time slots, beacon or non-beacon-enabled networks. The binding table also allows service composition and decomposition. The connection to the cloud is done via zigbee gateway. Regardless of its possible interference to IEEE 802.11b/g, the WLANs and the zigbee networks can work together. This is feasible because 802.11 can change the frequencies from one side and zigbee can transmit in guard bands from other side. If necessary zigbee and IEEE 802.11 can use time division multiple access (TDMA) for interoperability. The compatibility with Bluetooth is supported by adaptive frequency hopping (AFH). Due to the retransmission capabilities zigbee technology could coexists with wireless phones and micro ovens (Fig. 3).

SynthNV and MixNV devices (produced by WindFreak Technologies) are used for radio interference together with "Dolphin Sniffer". The module is connected to the PC and managed by DolphinView software. A Faraday cage is applied for interference management. Test equipment also includes PLC M340 (Schneider Electric), operational panel HMI STU 855 (Schneider Electric), wireless switch WRT54G (Linksys, Cisco Systems), and SCADA IGSS software for test configuration (Fig. 3).

Part of the measurements in zigbee sensor network is shown in Table 2. Only two types of the experiments are presented in full mesh and semi mesh topologies with up to 4 sensor-to-sensor retransmissions and additional radio noise at the transmission channel. The transmission in 5 s corresponds to the case when the channel is one and there is more than one sensor to transmit or there is a noise at transmission frequency.

Fig. 3. Test setup.

Loss occurs also in the situation of contention or noise. In all other cases the transmission delays of up to 600 ms are acceptable for sensor data. In all cases the losses are acceptable because sensors retransmit the data in case of error.

Table 2. List of measurements in zigbee network.

No	Description	Bytes to transmit	Radio noise	Other sensors in the same channel	Transmission time, ms	Losses, bytes
1.	Duplex channel analyses via serial zigbee. Transmitted telegrams in 1 bytes.	1	0	0	182	0
		1	0	1	5400	1
		1	Yes	1	5700	2
		1	Yes	0	180	1
2.	Duplex channel analyses via serial zigbee with reduced radio coverage and retransmissions	1	0	0	402	0
		60	0	7	400	1
		120	0	0	550	0
		120	0	7	570	1

4   Peer Port Application

Mobile cloud computing and Internet of Things environments are interesting area for QoS and QoE because of its lack of guarantees. End users expect to have the necessary information and available communication line continuously. The difference between physical and logical platforms is invisible from user perspective. The traffic is often unpredictable because of network overlays, peer-to-peer communication, multicasting, multihoming and real-time video services. Overlay networks could be created depending on people, devices, places and peers as well as at different scale. Application layer technologies for distributed overlay may be heterogeneous, i.e. peer-to-peer (P2P) or client/server [31]. The sockets are often instable because of the user transparency in space and time. There are many authors that address traffic congestion mostly in client/ server applications [32, 33]. The self-similar, long-range dependant symmetric or near symmetric peer-to-peer traffic transmitted in real-time or in near real-time is still not well predicable [34]. Here we try to highlight an investigation of peer traffic at the application and the transport layers where the health and enhanced living environment services in the cloud are fed by the PAN sensor networks. Based on the existing information availability, proper connectivity and after active and passive information processing we propose a solution for cloud service development and implementation [35].

Peer-to-peer overlays allow reliable small-scale and large-scale data sharing, content distribution, and application-level multicast applications. They have specific features as selection of nearby peers, redundant storage, efficient search, location of data items, data permanence or guarantees, hierarchical naming, trust and authentication, anonymity, and redundancy. P2P networks routing is dynamic, efficient, self-organizing, and massively scalable in cluster organization. It is also robust in the wide-area, combining fault tolerance, load balancing and explicit notion of locality [36, 37].

Peers exchange messages of different length and using different protocol [38]. There are specific features of P2P traffic and applications like node naming and addressing, address resolution, packet sequencing, protocols for guaranteed delivery, timers and counters. Peers are self-organized and can generate, transmit, store, retransmit and receive packets at the same time. Routing in the overlay is adaptive in comparison to the packet layer. A message intended for one peer can be transmitted via intermediate peers to reach the destination peer. This relay or ad hoc functionality is combined with temporary replicas for information redundancy and service reliability. Multicast routing enables a message sent to a single multicast address to be routed to all members of the multicast group. It reduces network traffic from one-to-many applications such as video broadcasting or video conferencing. Since multicast routing at IP layer is not always supported by the Internet routers, application layer multicasting (ALM) or overlay multicast (OM) was invented [38].

In this paper, we propose a solution of data redundancy using peer port. The role of the peer port is to keep temporary a replica of the information for redundancy during the transmission [34, 39]. It works as a mirror port between controllers in Storage Area Networks (SAN) or like a relay point in LTE, ad hoc or in zigbee communication channels. Each node in the overlay network may become a peer port of many other peers and vice versa. Furthermore, there are no limitations how many replicas to store in the peer port and for how long [40]. The procedure is supported at application layer and is transparent to the protocol layers below the application layer. In Fig. 4 we present sending peers, receiving peers and peer ports [39, 41].

The need for peer port application is motivated by large variations in delay and loss due different platforms and network traffic. Available end-to-end bandwidth fluctuates during connection [42, 43]. When the socket is released or freezes, the lost packets are

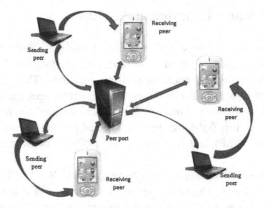

Fig. 4. Peer port is processing more than one request.

recovered from the replica in one of the peer ports. Usually, the replica occupies the resource at peer port until data acknowledgment.

The protocols applied in all peers in the overlay is sliding window [39, 41]. The go back N and selected repeat sliding window protocols are developed for point-to-point connections (referred further as standard protocol). Here, we propose a combination between point-to-point protocols and point-to-multipoint communication [40] at application layer. The data from sending peer is sent simultaneously to the receiving peer and to the peer port. The receiving peer sends acknowledgment (acks) or not acknowledgment (nacks) for a specified packet to the peer port. In case of confirmation, the peer port removes this packet, thus releases resources, and increases capacity to store information (Fig. 5). In an active network operation, P2P clients are many, i.e. there are many receiving peers and peer port must be flexible. In another case, upon reception of nack from the receiving peer, the peer port prepares the relevant packet to be sent, and sends it on communication channel.

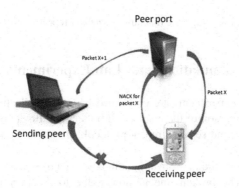

Fig. 5. Alternative communication, permanent data transmission.

5   P2P Scenario and Experimental Setup

The experiments in the lab are setup for behavior analyses of the peer port. A Java application and a ns-2 model are used for performance verification. The model contains one sending, one receiving and one peer port for simplicity. The services used during the trials are books, video, audio, archives, and text messages transfer. The protocol implemented is the well-known three-way handshake modified for the peer port (PP) by added multicasting. In Fig. 6 the scenario for selected repeat is presented. The standard link between sending (SP) and receiving peers (RP) is interrupted in both models randomly.

At transport protocol, there are also options to use UDP or TCP over the different point-to-point connections. The main experiment supposes TCP connections between the sending peer from one side and receiving peer and peer port from the other side. In addition, the connection between the peer port and the receiving peer is UDP. Other combinations of TCP/UDP were also explored. The buffer length is set to 1 MB and a 2 ms delay limit standard transmission between sending and receiving peers is considered. The packet payload is 60 and 500 bytes and reflects the behavior of the queues.

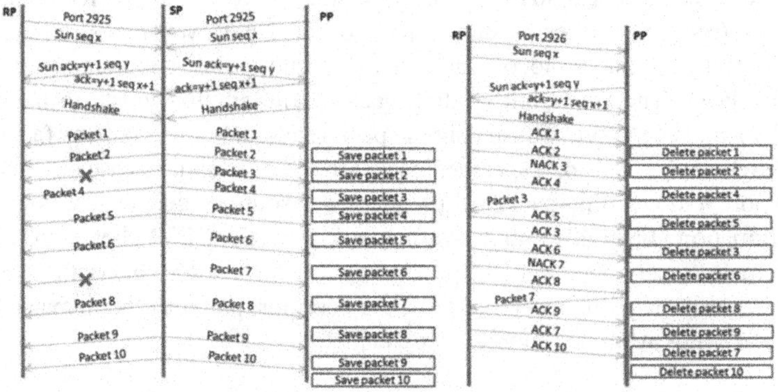

Fig. 6. Sequence diagram of selected repeat protocol.

6   Results from Simulations and Lab Experiments

Simulations and life experiments are performed by Java application in similar conditions for further comparison of the results. All buffers and timers of the three peers are equal. The go back N and selected repeat protocols are applied on a standard line and on peer port links.

On Table 3 we present data from simulations when a message is transferred directly and via peer port. The broken line is slower due to the peer port retransmission. Standard link is the fastest way to transmit. The time to do the replica at peer port is almost the same as the transmission time over standard line. The difference between standard line and replication to peer port is comparable to the additional delay over the broken link. Additional delay added due to the broken link and peer port might be significant in cases when the transmission is in real-time and the nodes are overloaded. On Table 4, we present the same results for myfile.wav transfer. Single packet transmission takes about 20–100 ms. The delay when using big file replica is much higher and not acceptable in real-time communication.

The difference in time for transmission over peer port and direct line of myfile.wav file is plotted on Fig. 7. The blue line on the figure represents standard line and the red line shows the transmission over the peer port. The grids on the graph represents the fluctuations of the length of the sending and receiving buffers due to the go back N protocol or selective repeat protocols. The plots are cumulative for simplicity. After the line was broken it was not recovered until the end of file transfer. Additional delay due to retransmission is far from the acceptable delay bound in real-time applications. Nevertheless, the technology is fully acceptable in continuous data replication between storage networks and sensor networks with non time-critical data. All multihoming solutions also could benefit from the solution.

Table 3. Simulated results for sending/receiving message with and without broken link.

Information	Bytes	Standard line time, s	Broken line time, s	Peer port time, s	Peer port vs. standard line deviation, s	Additional delay, s
Message 'Hello world'	40	0,105	0,13	0,10232	0,00268	0,025
	80	0,1142	0,1414	0,10264	0,01156	0,02722
	120			0,107	−0,107	
	134	0,11478	0,1524		0,114784	0,037594
	174			0,1074	−0,1074	0
	214			0,112	−0,112	0
	268			0,112	−0,112	0

Table 4. Simulated results for sending/receiving myfile.wav with and without broken link.

Information	Bytes	Standard line time, s	Broken line time, s	Additional delay, s
Myfile.wav	40	1,2023	1,3589	0,1566
	80	1,207	1,4586	0,2516
	656	1,2116	1,5953	0,3837
	1232	1,2162	1,5999	0,3837
	1808	1,2208	1,6007	0,3799
	2384	1,2254	1,6501	0,4247
	2960	1,23	1,7105	0,4805
	1063952	9,718	18,373	8,655
	1068560	9,7548	18,41	8,6551

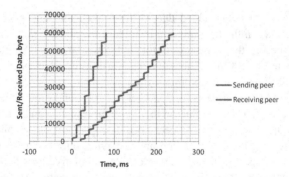

Fig. 7. The first 60000 sent/received packets from file archive over standard line and via peer port.

7 Conclusion

This paper presents an idea for combined sensor-to-cloud platform that is reliable enough to send PAN information. We set experiments in the lab dividing sensor and peer port QoS parameters. All experimental results demonstrate the feasibility of the proposed solution and its reliability. Sensor networks and peer port behavior could influence significantly the near-real-time and non-real-time services in the distributed overlays. We implement zigbee sensors in real trail as well as sliding window protocols in ns2 model and in a real-time Java application. We show the additional delay for telegrams and file transfers over the network. In non-prioritized environments, the additional delay could be significant. Only messages and continuous packet streams can conform to the QoS requirements. The future work aims to map the Quality of Service and the Quality of Experience parameters over cross-layer approach for distributed quality management [42, 43].

Acknowledgments. Our thanks to ICT COST Action IC1303: Algorithms, Architectures and Platforms for Enhanced Living Environments (AAPELE); Project No ИФ-02-9/15.12.2012, Gateway Prototype Modeling and Development for Wired and Wireless Communication Networks for Industrial and Building Automation; Comicon Ltd., Bulgaria.

References

1. ZigBee Document 075360r15. ZigBee Health CareTM, Profile Specification, ZigBee Profile: 0x0108. Revision 15, Version 1.0, March, Sponsored by: ZigBee Alliance (2010)
2. BlackBox ZigBee™ Test Client (ZTC), Reference Manual. Freescale Semiconductor Literature Distribution Center, Document Number: BSBBZTCRM, Rev. 1.2 (2011)
3. Severino, R., Koubâa, A.: On the Performance Evaluation of the IEEE 802.15.4 Slotted CSMA/CA Mechanism. IPP-HURRAY Technical Report, HURRAY-TR-080930, September 2008
4. Agarwal, A., Agarwal, M., Vyas, M., Sharma, R.: A study of Zigbee technology. Int. J. Recent Innov. Trends Comput. Commun. **1**(4), 287–292 (2013). ISSN: 2321–8169

5. Kaur, G., et al.: QoS measurement of Zigbee home automation network using various modulation schemes. Int. J. Eng. Sci. Technol. (IJEST) **3**(2), 1589–1597 (2011). ISSN: 0975-5462
6. Chen, F., Wang, N., German, R., Dressler, F.: Simulation study of IEEE 802.15.4 LR-WPAN for industrial applications. Wirel. Commun. Mob. Comput. **10**, 609–621 (2010). doi:10.1002/wcm.736
7. Zigbee Specification, Document 053474r17 (2008)
8. ZigBee RF4CE Specification, version 1.01, ZigBee Document 094945r00ZB (2010)
9. Rawat, P., Singh, K.D., Chaouchi, H., Bonnin, J.M.: Wireless sensor networks: a survey on recent developments and potential synergies. J. Supercomput. **68**, 1–48 (2013). doi:10.1007/s11227-013-1021-9. Springer Science + Business Media New York
10. Ciobanu, R.-I., Marin, R.-C., Dobre, C., Cristea, V., Mavromoustakis, C.X.: ONSIDE: Socially-aware and interest-based dissemination in opportunistic networks. NOMS **2014**, 1–6 (2014)
11. IEEE 802.15.4/ZigBee Measurements Made Easy Using the N4010A Wireless Connectivity Test Set. Agilent Technologies, Inc. (2009)
12. Tsitsipis, D.; Dima, S.M., Kritikakou, A., Panagiotou, C., Gialelis, J., Michail, H., Koubias, S.: Priority Handling Aggregation Technique (PHAT) for wireless sensor networks. In: 2012 IEEE 17th Conference on Emerging Technologies & Factory Automation (ETFA), pp. 1, 8, 17–21 Sept 2012. doi:10.1109/ETFA.2012.6489574
13. Tung, H.Y., Tsang, K.F., Tung, H.C., Rakocevic, V., Chui, K.T., Leung, Y.W.: A WiFi-ZigBee building area network design of high traffics AMI for smart grid. Smart Grid Renew. Energy **3**, 324–333 (2012) http://dx.doi.org/10.4236/sgre.2012.34043
14. 315 MHz Radio Communications in Buildings, EnOcean white paper
15. EnOcean Technology – Energy Harvesting Wireless, EnOcean white paper (2011)
16. EnOcean Wireless Systems – Range Planning Guide, EnOcean white paper (2008)
17. ZigBee-2007 Layer PICS and Stack Profiles, ZigBee Document 08006r03, Revision 03 (2008)
18. Alves, M., Koubaa, A., Cunha, A., Severino, R., Lomba, E.: On the development of a test-bed application for the ART-WiSe architecture. In: Euromicro Conference on Real-Time Systems (ECRTS 2006), (WiP Session) July 2006
19. EnOcean_Equipment_Profiles_EEP_V2.5, EnOcean Serial Protocol, March 4 (2013)
20. Woo, S.-J., Shin, B.-D.: Efficient cluster organization method of Zigbee nodes. Int. J. Smart Home **7**(3), 45–55 (2013)
21. ZigBee PRO Stack, User Guide, JN-UG-3048, Revision 2.4, NXP Laboratories UK (2012)
22. Krogmann, M., Heidrich, M., Bichler, D., Barisic, D., Stromberg, G.: Reliable, real-time routing in wireless sensor and actuator networks. International Scholarly Research Network ISRN Communications and Networking, vol. 2011, Article ID 943504, 8 p., (2011). doi:10.5402/2011/943504
23. Zigbee Home Automation Public Application Profile, ZigBee Profile: 0x0104, Revision 26, Version 1.1 (2010)
24. Singhal, S., Gankotiya, A.K., Agarwal, S., Verma, T.: An investigation of wireless sensor network: a distributed approach in smart environment. In: Second International Conference on Advanced Computing & Communication Technologies (2012)
25. Koubaa, A., Severino, R., Alves, M., Tovar, E.: H-NAMe: Specifying, Implementing and Testing a Hidden-Node Avoidance Mechanism for Wireless Sensor Networks. IPP-HURRAY Technical Report, HURRAYTR-071113, April 2008
26. Boonma, P., Suzuki, J.: Self-Configurable Publish/Subscribe Middleware for Wireless Sensor Networks. 978-1-4244-2309-5/09. IEEE (2009)

27. Jurčík, P., Severino, R., Koubâa, A., Alves, M., Tovar, E.: Real-time communications over cluster-tree sensor networks with mobile sink behaviour. In: the 14th IEEE International Conference on Embedded and Real-Time Computing Systems and Applications (RTCSA 2008), Kaohsiung, Taiwan (2008)
28. FP7-ICT-STREP Contract No. 258280, TWISNet, Trustworthy Wireless Industrial Sensor Networks. Deliverable D4.1.2, Hardware platform characterization/description (2012)
29. Cuomo, F., Luna, S.D., Monaco, U., Melodia, T.: Routing in ZigBee: benefits from exploiting the IEEE 802.15.4 association tree. ICC 2007 Proceedings (2007)
30. Terry, J.D., Jensen, C., Thai, S.: The Evolution of Spectrum Management: A Technical Framework for DSA Management. 978-1-4244-2017-9/08. IEEE (2008)
31. Coulouris, G., Dollimore, J., Kindberg, T.: Distributed Systems Concepts and Design. Adison Wesley, USA (2005)
32. El-Ansary, S., Haridi, S.: An overview of structured P2P overlay network. Swedish Institute of Computer Science (SICS), Sweden. Royal Institute of Technology – IMIT/KHT, Sweden (2004)
33. Lua, E.K., Crowcroft, J., Pias, M., Sharma, R., Lim, S.: A survey and comparison of peer-to-peer overlay network schemes. IEEE communication survey and tutorial, March (2004)
34. Mahlmann, P., Schindelhaue, C.: Peer-to-peer netzwerke: algorithmen und methoden. Springer, Berlin/Heidelberg, Germany (2007)
35. Huang, M.L., Lee, S., Park, S.-C.: A WLAN and bluetooth coexistence mechanism for health monitoring system. 978-1-4244-2309-5/09/$25.00 ©2009. IEEE (2009)
36. Stoica, I., Morris, R., Karger, D., Kaashoek, F., Balakrishnan, H.: Chord: A scalable peer-to-peer lookup service for Internet applications. In: Proceedings of ACM SIGCOMM 2001, August (2001)
37. Zhao, B., Kubiatowicz, J., Joseph, A.: Tapestry: An infrastructure for fault-tolerant wide-area location and routing. Technical Report UCB/CSD-01-1141, University of California at Berkeley, Computer Science Department (2001)
38. Buford, J.F., Yu, H., Lua, E.K.: P2P Networking and Applications. Morgan Kaufmann, USA (2009)
39. Stainov, R.: Peer ports for layered P2P streaming. In: Proceedings of the 6th International Conference in Computer Science and Education in Computer Science, CSECS 2010, 26–29 June, Fulda/Munich, Germany, ISBN: 978-954-535-573-8 (2010)
40. Stainov, R., Goleva, R., Genova, V., Lazarov, S.: Peer port implementation for real-time and near real-time applications in distributed overlay networks. In: 9th Annual International Conference on Computer Science and Education in Computer Science 2013 (CSECS 2013), 29 June, 2 July, Fulda-Wuertzburg, Germany, pp. 87–92 (2013)
41. Stainov, R.: Peer ports: mobility support in peer-to-peer systems. In: Proceedings of the 5th International Conference in Computer Science and Education in Computer Science, CSECS 2009, May 2009, Boston, USA (2009). ISBN 978-954-535-573-8
42. Sieber, C., Hossfeld, T., Zinner, T., Tran-Gia, P., Timmerer, C.: Implementation and user-centric comparison of a novel adaptation logic for DASH with SVC. In: 2013 IFIP/IEEE International Symposium on Integrated Network Management (IM 2013), pp. 1318, 1323, 27–31 May 2013
43. Tyson, G., Mauthe, A., Kaune, S., Grace, P., Taweel, A., Plagemann, T.: A middleware platform for supporting delivery-centric applications. ACM Trans. Internet Technol. 12(2) Article 4, 28 (2012). doi:10.1145/2390209.2390210. http://doi.acm.org/10.1145/2390209.2390210

General Assisted Living System Architecture Model

Vladimir Trajkovik[1]([⊠]), Elena Vlahu-Gjorgievska[2],
Saso Koceski[3], and Igor Kulev[1]

[1] Faculty of Computer Science and Engineering, University "Ss Cyril
and Methodious", "Rugjer Boshkovikj" 16, P.O. Box 393,
1000 Skopje, Republic of Macedonia
{trvlado,igor.kulev}@finki.ukim.mk
[2] Faculty of Information and Communication Technology,
University "St. Kliment Ohridski", Partizanska bb,
7000 Bitola, Republic of Macedonia
elena.vlahu@uklo.edu.mk
[3] Faculty of Computer Science, University "Goce Delcev",
ul. Krste Misirkov n.10-A, P.O. Box 201, 2000 Stip, Republic of Macedonia
saso.koceski@ugd.edu.mk

Abstract. Novel information and communication technologies create possibilities to change the future of health care and support. Ambient Assisted Living (AAL) is seen as a promising alternative to the current care models so a number of researchers have developed AAL systems with promising results. The main goal of AAL solutions is to apply ambient intelligence technologies to enable people with specific needs to continue to live in their preferred environments. In this paper, we are presenting a general architecture of system for assisted living that supports most of the use cases for such system.

Keywords: Assisted living · Wearable sensors · Environmental sensors · Social networks

1 Introduction

Advances in communication and computer technologies have revolutionized the way health information is gathered, disseminated, and used by healthcare providers, patients, citizens, and mass media. This led to the emergence of a new field and new language captured in the term "e-health".

The importance of healthcare to individuals and governments and its growing economy costs have contributed its emergence as an important area of research for scholars in business and other disciplines. The recent trend in healthcare support systems is the development of patient-centric pervasive environments in addition to the hospital-centric ones. Such systems enable healthcare personnel to be able to timely access, review, and update and send patient information from wherever they are, whenever they want. In that way, pervasive health care takes steps to design, develop, and evaluate computer technologies that help citizens participate more closely in their

© Institute for Computer Sciences, Social Informatics and Telecommunications Engineering 2015
R. Agüero et al. (Eds.): MONAMI 2014, LNICST 141, pp. 329–343, 2015.
DOI: 10.1007/978-3-319-16292-8_24

own healthcare, on one hand, and on the other to provide flexibility in the life of patient who lead an active everyday life with work, family and friends.

There are technical requirements (instrument usability, power supply, reliable wireless communications and secure transfer of information) for the healthcare systems based on wearable and ambient sensors [1]. However, there are also concerns about the technology acceptance in the healthcare. Many authors have considered this issue. For example, Cocosila and Archer [2] are investigating the factors favoring or disfavoring the adoption of mobile ICT for health promotion interventions.

Ambient Assisted Living (AAL) has the ambitious goal of improving the quality of life and maintaining independence especially of elderly and people with disabilities using technology [3]. AAL can improve the quality of life by reducing the need of caretakers, personal nursing services or the transfer to nursing homes. In this context, there are two goals: a social advantage (a better quality of life) and an economic advantage (a cost reduction for society and public health systems) [4, 5].

Most efforts towards building Ambient Assisted Living Systems are based on developing pervasive devices and use Ambient Intelligence to integrate these devices together to construct a safety environment [6]. But, technology limitation is that it cannot fully express the power of human being and the importance of social connections. In this concept, the usage of advanced information and communication technology (social networks) could be helpful in connecting people together and organizing community activities.

It is important for AAL systems to ensure high-quality-of-service. Essential requirements of AAL systems are usability, reliability, data accuracy, cost, security, and privacy. According to [7] to achieve this requirements it is important to involve citizens, caregivers, healthcare IT industry, researchers, and governmental organizations in the development cycle of AAL systems, so that end-users can benefit more from the collaborative efforts.

The electronic health record (EHR) is a collection of electronic health information about individual patients and population, operated by institutions (medical centers) [8]. It is a mechanism for integrating health care information currently collected in both paper and electronic medical records (EMR) for improving quality of care. A personal health record (PHR) is a record where health data and information related to the care of a patient is maintained by the patient [9]. PHR provides a complete and accurate summary of an individual's medical history that is accessible online. One of the advantages of AAL systems is integrating data from AAL systems and smart homes with data from electronic health or patient records. Although it is still in an early stage, aggregating data from different medical devices and integrating them with data in health records enable a comprehensive view on health data [10]. Presenting these health data can lead to more efficient and competent decisions of physicians, nurses, patients, and informal caregivers.

AAL systems are based on interoperability and integration of various medical devices. Nevertheless, the lack of standards and specification is one of the biggest obstacles for their commercial penetration on the market. In this context, AAL systems and platforms rely on different standards and specifications by various initiatives and groups, such as: Health Level 7 (HL7) [11] - supporting clinical practice and the management, delivery, and evaluation of health services; Continua Health Alliance

[12] which produces industry standards and security for connected health technologies such as smart phones, gateways and remote monitoring devices; ETSI [13] which provides harmonized standards for radio & telecommunications terminal equipment; AAL Europe [14] which is funding projects that involves small and medium enterprises (SME), research bodies and user's organizations (representing the older adults).

One major issue concerning AAL systems is the ethical problem due to the multitude and heterogeneous personal information continuously collected by AAL systems [15]. There is concern about possible negative consequences [16] such as:

- loneliness or isolation, resulting from the use of certain devices that replace human caretakers, which may be the user's only regular social contact;
- privacy issues - surrounding biometrics and "smart home" systems collect personal information;
- discrimination - wearable biometric monitors or mobility devices are highly visible and can make a person's disability very obvious.

These are the reasons why AAL systems need to be seen as tool for help and assistance rather than controlling device for what are people doing.

AAL is seen as a promising alternative to the current care models and consequently has attracted lots of attention. Although according to [17] there are three categories of Ambient Assisted Living interoperability services: (1) notification and alarming services, (2) health services, and (3) voice and video communication services, we found that systems for assisted living need to be more general and to support more services in order to be helpful not only for elderly and people with disabilities, but for all people who want to live healthy life in accordance with their everyday obligations.

The System for Assisted Living we present in this paper uses mobile, web and broadband technologies. Broadband mobile technology provides movements of electronic care environment easily between locations and internet-based storage of data allowing moving location of support. The most important benefits of our proposed system model are increased medical prevention, more immediate time response at emergency calls for doctors, 24 h monitoring of the patients' condition, possibility for patient notification in different scenarios, transmissions of the collected biosignals (blood pressure, heart rate) automatically to medical personnel, increased flexibility in collecting medical data. The proposed system model creates an opportunity for increasing patient health care within their homes by 24 h monitoring on the one hand, and increasing medical capacity of health care institutions on the other hand. This results in reducing the overall costs for patients and hospitals and improves the patient's quality of life.

2 Related Work

In the last several years Ambient Assisted Living is one of the most popular research areas among scientists. Thus, many sensors, technologies and systems are developed.

Ruiz-Zafra et al. [18] are presenting the m-health cloud-transparent platform called Zappa. Zappa is extensible, scalable and customizable cloud platform for the development of eHealth/mHealth systems. Its main advantage is the ability to operate in the cloud.

By using cloud computing, open technologies (open-source software, open hardware, etc.) and additional techniques the platform provides uninterrupted monitoring with the goal of obtaining some information that can be subsequently analyzed by physicians for diagnosing. In order to show the applicability of the platform the authors are introducing two m-health systems, Zappa App and Cloud Rehab, based on the Zappa platform.

In [4], Takacs et al. present a complex wireless and personalized AAL solution that includes telemonitoring, health management, mental monitoring, mood assessment as well as physical and relaxation exercises. Their approach is based on a novel computational and communication platform called Virtual Human Interface (VHI), specifically designed to bridge the gap between people and computers by using virtual reality and animation technologies. The main goal of the research is to create an open-architecture and reconfigurable system which is as independent as possible from individual manufacturers and wireless standards.

AlarmNet [19] is an assisted living and residential monitoring network for pervasive adaptive healthcare in assisted living communities with residents or patients with diverse needs. According to the authors (Wood et al.) the primary reason for developing AlarmNet was to use environmental, physiological and activity data of assisted living residents in order to improve their health outcomes. AlarmNet unifies and accommodates heterogeneous devices in a common architecture that spans wearable body networks, emplaced wireless sensors, user interfaces and back-end processing elements. Contributions and novelties of this work include extensible heterogeneous network, novel context-aware protocols and a query protocol for online streaming-SenQ.

Kleinberger et al. [5] are presenting an approach and several evaluations for emergency monitoring applications (research projects: EMERGE and BelAmI). The main goal of EMERGE is to support elderly people with emergency monitoring and prevention by using ambient, unobtrusive sensors and reasoning about arising emergency situations. Experiments were performed in laboratory settings in order to evaluate the accuracy of recognizing Activities of Daily Living (ADL). The interpretation of the evaluation results have proved that it is possible to measure ADLs accurately enough for detecting behavior deviations. But, according to the Kleinberger et al., to reach this objective it is very useful to include all stakeholders very early in the requirements analysis and development process for the prototypes and especially in the setup of the experiments.

Lopez de Ipina et al. in [20] present the CareTwitter AAL platform. They propose the adoption of passive RFID tags as tiny databases where a log of a person can be stored, so that other users with their NFC devices can access and manipulate the data in them. The data is encoded in the resident's RFID tags, and such care logs are then transferred into a public micro-blogging service Twitter. The CareTwitter platform stores a log for every new care procedure applied on a resident's RFID wristband, following a data-on-tag approach. CareTwitter makes data stay at any time with the resident and be available in real-time and without relying on wireless links. The experiments provided in the paper [20] have proven that the storage capacity of either a 1 K (wristband) or a 4 K (watch) Mifare RFID tag is sufficient for storing the care logs of a whole day. The integration of CareTwitter with Twitter proves the high potential of using interactions with everyday objects or people to automatically publish data into Internet, in this case, the log of residents in a care center, so that their relatives and friends can be kept up-to-date about them. The tweets published by CareTwitter are never made publicly available. Only users authorized by the residents or their family can follow them.

In [21] an Internet of things-based AAL architecture to support blood glucose management and insulin therapy is presented. This architecture offers a set of services for monitoring, interconnecting with the Diabetes Information System (glycemic index database), and ubiquitous access to the information based on the developed personal device (Movital), AAL environment gateway (Monere), web portal, and the management desktop application. The important aspect of presented solution is that most of the measurements and interactions with the patient are done at home. This enhances the self-monitoring blood glucose solutions and allows the interaction with the nurses and physicians through new technologies such as personal health card based on RFID and the Web diabetes management portal. According to the authors (Jara et al.), Internet of things allows the defining of solutions closer to the patient, physician and nurses, which allows an easier integration and acceptance of them. The evaluation of the proposed architecture has presented that nurses and physicians are very interested and open to these kinds of solutions, considering it very useful and suitable to be included in hospitals.

Mileo et al. [22] present a monitoring system, called SINDI, equipped with a pervasive sensor network and a non-monotonic reasoning engine. Proposed system, gathers data about the user and his/her environment, through a wireless sensor network. Combining different data sources, the system interprets the evolution of the patient's health state and predicts changes into risky states according to a graph-based computational model of medical knowledge and the clinical profile of the monitored patient. In this system, the results of context-aware interpretation of gathered data are used to predict and explain possible evolutions of the patient's health state in terms of functional disabilities, dependency in performing daily activities and risk assessment, as well as to identify correct interaction patterns. The advantage of the system is in providing various: suggestions (according to the medical practice and the results of the prediction reasoning task), alerts (when the system identifies behaviors or situations that are potentially dangerous for patient), alarms (when specific environmental or clinical conditions are detected), notifications (when the system receives new input or terminates the inference process) and reminders (according to an agenda).

We should also mention some of the recent developed assisted living technologies for commercial use.

BeClose [23] is an affordable, easy-to-use home monitoring and care giving technology for the elderly. This system indicates that everything is okay and provides independence and peace of mind for the user. The BeClose system consists of a base station and a variety of small sensors throughout users home. These electronic devices are designed to work together to make sure the user is up and about each day. If something is out of the ordinary, the system will alert users' family members and caregivers.

Basis has introduced Body IQ [24] in fall 2013. It is a proprietary technology that recognizes and displays users' activities automatically, like walking, running and biking, as well as sleeping. Body IQ ensures users to get credits for their efforts in real-time, including caloric burn, with no need to push buttons, switch modes or tag activities. It also automatically determines when users fall asleep and when they wake up.

Apple is said to be working on a wrist-worn device that would go far beyond telling time, allowing users to measure and track health and fitness data with a new wearable device – "iWatch". Apple's iWatch [25] is expected be able to operate independently of an iPhone or iPad. Reports have suggested that iWatch should debut in fall 2014.

According to previous brief review of literature and other works, not mentioned in this paper, there is need for general architecture of the system for assisted living to be proposed. The system for assisted living should be of help not only for elderly and people with disabilities, but for all people who want to lead healthy life.

3   General Architecture of the System for Assisted Living

The body sensor networks (BSN) are type of a wireless sensor networks (WSN) composed of sensors usually attached on human body or in some cases implanted inside the human body. The main purpose of BSN is to measure the physiological signals and to provide information about human behavior. Therefore, the number, the type and the characteristics of the sensors may vary and they mainly depend on the application and system infrastructure [26]. Two types of sensors could be applied: one capable to collect continuous time-varying signals such as accelerometers, pedometers, gyroscopes, electro-encephalograph (EEG) sensors, electromyography (EMG) sensors, visual sensors, and auditory sensors and the other to collect discrete time-varying signals such as glucose sensors, temperature sensors, humidity sensors, blood pressure sensors. State-of-the art sensors nowadays have high compact factor and thus high wearability and high biocompatibility. Wireless communication technologies such as Bluetooth or Zigbee, radio frequency identification devices (RFID), and Ultra Wide-band (UWB) could be employed to transmit the collected data.

The environmental sensors are reading the value of users' environmental parameters. Moreover, the sensor technology can be applied to collect environmental information regarding the location of people and objects, information about their interaction, etc. Additionally, by applying data fusion techniques on the data gathered both from BSN and environment sensors, reliable assessments of persons' behavior and the activities performed could be conducted. From sensor technologies perspectives, AAL applications are facing various challenges, among which, one of the most important ones is regarding the quality of collected data, which is the basis for further behavioral analysis [27].

3.1   Logical Architecture of the System for Assisted Living

In the System for Assisted Living that we are proposing in this paper, the body sensor networks are reading the value of users' health parameters. The environmental sensors are reading the value of users' environmental parameters. Additionally user can use applications that can measure (follow) users' physical activities. All the data is gathered by users' personal or mobile device, like a PC, laptop, tablet, smartphone or smart TV, and along with data from clinical centers, medical databases and social networks are sent for further processing by assisted healthcare algorithms. The processed data (by assisted healthcare algorithms) are sent back to the end users in order to allow wanted services. The logical architecture of System for Assisted Living is shown on Fig. 1.

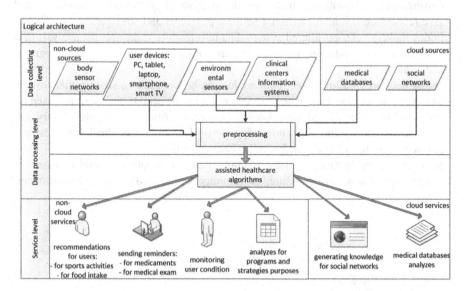

Fig. 1. Logical architecture of the System for Assisted Living

In the service layer different processes of different users can be integrated. This allows non-medical processes, medical processes, care processes and communications within social networks to be incorporated in the architecture of System for Assisted Living.

The whole interaction in the proposed system is request/reply based. If there is need for additional information then new request is raised. We should emphasize that the information generated from the social networks are reliable information and the information from personal profiles (age, weight, height, diagnose entered by end user) are unreliable information. This information should be confirmed by the medical records from clinical centers and then deployed on data generated by corresponding algorithms implemented in the social networks. In this way the tips (recommendations) generated from social networks are reliable or valid.

3.2 Physical Architecture of the System for Assisted Living

On Fig. 2 the physical architecture of System for Assisted Living is shown.

The System for Assisted Living deals with data relevant to following institutions:

– Clinical centers - monitor the health status and physical condition of users and provide recommendations and suggestions about the therapies and medicaments that users should take in order to improve their health.

- Medical databases - collect data from clinical centers and different databases, perform tests and experiments. They process and analyze collected data and based on their research draw conclusions, recommendations and suggestions for diagnosis, therapy and activities.
- Government organizations - make specific analysis of system data information and give recommendations for national actions, programs and strategies.
- Policy makers - can get filtered system data information, make specific analysis of it and give recommendations for non-government organizations, including programs and strategies.
- Social networks - allow direct communication between users, sharing their results and exchange of their experience. Social networks can send to the user tips based on the users' health condition, prior knowledge derived from users' health history and physical activities, and the knowledge derived from the medical histories and physical activities of users with similar characteristics.
- Services for environmental data - supply data for weather condition (weather temperature, atmospheric pressure, air humidity, wind speed) in users' environment.

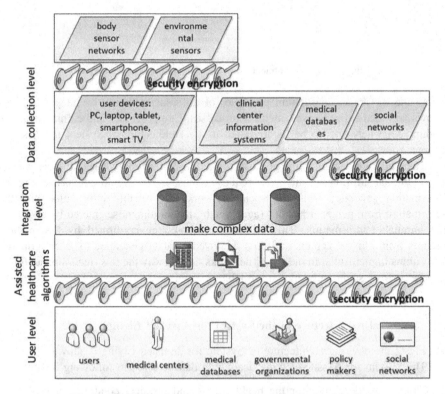

Fig. 2. Physical architecture of the System for Assisted Living

Data is collected from body sensor networks; users' PC, laptop, tablet, smartphone or smart TV; environmental sensors; clinical centers; medical databases; social networks.

In the integration level, collected data from different sources is being adjusted according to the standards and formats of the inputs of the assisted healthcare algorithms.

Collected data is processed according to the need or demand:

– for generating recommendation for users;
– for clinical centers - for monitoring the user condition or clinical purposes;
– for medical databases analyzes;
– for purposes of governmental organizations and policy makers;
– for generating knowledge for social networks.

Processed information is sent to: users (on their PC, laptop, tablet, smartphone or smart TV), clinical centers, medical databases, governmental organizations, policy makers or social networks.

The medical personnel can remotely monitor the users' medical condition, reviewing the data arriving from the users' personal or mobile device. In this way, medical personnel can quickly respond to the user by suggesting most suitable therapy as well as when to receive it, focusing on activities that are necessary for his rehabilitation and maintenance of his health, sending him/her (on his/her personal or mobile device) various tips and suggestions for improving his/her health.

The conclusions drawn from research data, while exploring medical databases, can be routed back to the clinical centers. These data can be used as additional knowledge for the individual analyzes of the users' condition. Clinical centers can exchange data and information with the social networks and thus have access to a larger group of users that can share research, recommendation and suggestion of the medical personnel.

Social networks allow direct communication between users and sharing their data. At the same time, the users' individual data can be compared with average data obtained using different collaborative filtering techniques. The social networks can learn from recommendation made by medical personnel and generate notifications and recommendation based on the most successful scenarios. These portals also can provide an interface and use data from a variety of medical databases and environmental databases (temperature, wind speed, humidity).

The complex structure of data from the social networks along with the data arriving from different clinical centers can be used by different medical databases for further analysis and research.

Governmental organizations and policy makers can get the data from social networks, clinical centers and medical databases, make specific analysis on it and give recommendations for national action by governments and non-government organizations, including programs and strategies.

The key stakeholders of the proposed System for Assisted Living are elderly and people with disabilities who needs monitoring of health condition, reminders for everyday obligations, and assistance in everyday routine and social inclusion. Family of the elderly and people with disabilities who need professionals to take care of their family members and want to remotely monitor health status can also use the system. People who want to lead healthy life can use system. By using the system they can monitor their own health condition and physical activities. In addition, Clinical centers can remotely monitor their patients and gather all kind of health data from different patients for further analyzes. Governmental, non-governmental organizations and Policy makers can get summarized health information from the proposed system that can help in generating health programs, strategies and policies. Industry, especially medical and pharmaceutical industries, can benefit from the proposed system by getting the health information that can help them in developing new devices, applications and therapies that are needed.

3.3   Security Issues

The fundamental goals of secure healthcare systems are safely exchanging the users' information and preventing improper use of illegal devices, such as intercepting transferred data, eavesdropping communicating data, replaying out-of-date information, or revealing the users' medical conditions. Specific security requirements will have a significant influence on the performance of the system:

- Data Storage and transmission: Local database (in users' devices) stores data received by sensors, in case there is always back up of data (they will be saved only some period). When there are problems in sending data to clinical center or social network some of data is not going to be send, so all transaction will be rolled back. When service is available the data will be sent. By this, the quality of service (QoS) facilities (demand for high reliability, guaranteed bandwidth and short delays) are provided [28].
- Data Confidentiality: Most patients do not want anyone to know their medical information, except their family doctor or medical specialist. The solutions are to use a cryptographic algorithm to encrypt medical information and protect the necessary data.
- Authentication: Only an authenticated entity can access the corresponding data that are available for that entity; unauthenticated entities are denied when they try to visit data information that they do not have the rights to obtain. For example, asymmetric cryptography (i.e. PKI) is often used, because these private keys are credentials shared only by the communicating parties.
- Access Control: In traditional network security models, access control determines whether a subject can access an object based on an access control list (ACL).
- Privacy Concerns: Every user can choose what information can be private or public. User can choose his records to be public: (a) for medical purposes, (b) to all visitors of the social network, (c) to users in his category, (d) to none. In order to have medical support the user has to agree to share personal information with clinical centers and medical databases, whose data are also protected.

System for Assisted Living has own security and privacy statements that explains how system protects users privacy and confidentiality and how will be treated users personal information.

3.4   Validity of Information

One of the most important issues in the system is information validity and confirmation. We divide system information validity in three categories.

Most reliable information (valid information) is information in the first category. This information originates from the clinical centers, medical databases, and sensors.

The second category (reliable information) is information generated from the social networks. This information can be confirmed (transferred in the first category) if confirmed by the medical records from clinical centers. This confirmation is then deployed on data generated by corresponding algorithms implemented in the social networks.

Information from personal profiles (age, weight, height, diagnose entered by end user) are third category information (unreliable information). Increase of validation of this information can be done by comparing them with average results using social network or by confirming them with the medical records coming from healthcare institutions.

4   Use Case Scenarios

The general use case scenarios for System for Assisted Living are shown in Fig. 3.

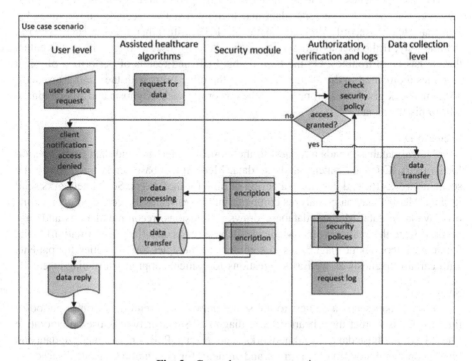

Fig. 3. General use case scenario

Scenario A:

The user switches on the application on his phone and starts his physical activities. Application reads the data (blood pressure, pulse, sugar level and type of activity, length of path, time interval). If irregularity occurs while reading the data, such as patient's blood pressure is quite higher than normal to perform the operation, the application sends signal and message with those data to the medical center. The application signals to user that there is some irregularity. Medical personnel review the submitted data and previous medical records of the patient. Based on the patient's diagnosis, treatment received and his activity currently carried out, along with the medical data received from the application, a recommendation is issued back to the application of the patient, to temporarily stop his activities and receive appropriate medicine (if by that moment it's not already received) or to reduce the pace of the activity itself. The application signals to the user that a message from the medical center has arrived. The user applies the recommendation from the medical center.

Scenario B:

Medical personnel review the patient's data (diagnosis, therapy received, activities done) and conclude that the patient did not receive his regular therapy and does not perform the recommended actions or has excessive over-activity. The medical center sends an urgent message to the patient to do an emergency medical examination.

Scenario C:

The user switches on the application on his phone and connects to the social network. He enters his personal data and therapy that has received and updates his Personal Health Record. User can share his PHR with other users of the network. Additionally, if the user assumes to have certain heart disease diagnosis he can enters that he has heart troubles. On the base on his PHR and results of performed physical activities (compared to the average results of the other users with the similar problem) social network give him a proposition if he has or not such diagnosis and advice him to talk to his physician.

Scenario D:

Medical database sends a request to the clinical centers to send data from a period for its users. Clinical Centers sends its data. Medical database sends a request to the social networks to send data from a period of time for their users. Social networks send its data. Medical database analyzes compares and investigates the collected data and its own available data. Medical database draws conclusions, recommendations and suggestions from the analyzed data. Medical database sends data (latest information) to the Clinical centers, about diagnostics, recommended therapies and activities for patients with certain diagnosis as well as suggestions for patients appropriately diagnosed.

Scenario E:

Policy maker sends a request to the social networks to send data from a period of time for its users that have heart disease diagnose. Social networks use collaborative filter to extract those data. Social networks send its data. Policy maker analyze data and give recommendation, make program and strategy for prevention of heart disease.

5 Conclusions

This paper presents a general model of assisted living system architecture. Generally, the main objectives of the proposed System for Assisted Living are:

(1) Help its users to actively participate in their health care and prevention, thereby providing: monitoring of users' health parameters and their physical activities (condition); 24-h medical monitoring; recommendation with tips on how to improve their health; opportunity for health care within users' homes; increased capacity of health institutions, resulting with reduction of overall costs for consumers and healthcare institutions.
(2) Alignment of the solution to the current state of technology.
(3) Collecting different types of data and combining them into complex structures of health data. The survey, analysis and research of such structures allows to understand the impact and the influence of applied therapy, physical activity, time parameters and other factors on the development of the health condition of the user. Such analysis can be further used by all stakeholders for diagnosis, treatment, therapy and prevention.

The presented architecture gathers all common features of assisted living system features and determines possibilities for various assisted living system deployments by presenting use cases scenarios derived from proposed architecture.

Acknowledgement. The authors would also like to acknowledge the contribution of the COST Action IC1303 - AAPELE, Architectures, Algorithms and Platforms for Enhanced Living Environments.

References

1. Korhonen, I., Parkka, J., Van Gils, M.: Health monitoring in the home of the future. IEEE Eng. Med. Biol. **22**(3), 66–73 (2003)
2. Cocosila, M., Archer, N.: Adoption of mobile ict for health promotion: an empirical investigation. Electron. Markets **20**(3–4), 241–250 (2010)
3. Cardinaux, F., Bhowmik, D., Abhayaratne, C., Hawley, M.S.: Video based technology for ambient assisted living: A review of the literature. J. Ambient Intell. Smart Environ. **3**(3), 253–269 (2011)
4. Takács, B., Hanák, D.: A mobile system for assisted living with ambient facial interfaces. Int. J. Comput. Sci. Inf. Syst. **2**(2), 33–50 (2007)
5. Kleinberger, T., Jedlitschka, A., Storf, H., Steinbach-Nordmann, S., Prueckner, S.: An approach to and evaluations of assisted living systems using ambient intelligence for emergency monitoring and prevention. In: Stephanidis, C. (ed.) UAHCI 2009, Part II. LNCS, vol. 5615, pp. 199–208. Springer, Heidelberg (2009)
6. Sun, H., De Florio, V., Gui, N., Blondia, C.: Promises and challenges of ambient assisted living Systems. In: Proceedings of the 6th International Conference on Information Technology: New Generations, Las Vegas NV, 27–29 April 2009, pp. 1201–1207 (2009)

7. Memon, M., Wagner, S.R., Pedersen, C.F., Beevi, F.H.A., Hansen, F.O.: Ambient assisted living healthcare frameworks, platforms, standards, and quality attributes. Sensors **14**, 4312–4341 (2014)
8. Gunter, T.D., Terry, N.P.: The emergence of national electronic health record architectures in the United States and Australia: Models, costs, and questions. J. Med. Internet Res. **7**(1), e3 (2005)
9. Tang, P., Ash, J., Bates, D., Overhage, J., Sands, D.: Personal health records: definitions, benefits, and strategies for overcoming barriers to adoption. JAMIA **13**(2), 121–126 (2006)
10. Knaup, P., Schöpe, L.: Using data from ambient assisted living and smart homes in electronic health records. Methods Inf. Med. **53**, 149–151 (2004)
11. http://www.hl7.org. Accessed 06 August 2014
12. http://www.continuaalliance.org. Accessed 06 August 2014
13. http://www.etsi.org/standards. Accessed 06 August 2014
14. http://www.aal-europe.eu. Accessed 06 August 2014
15. Viron, G, Sixsmith A (2008) Toward Information Systems for Ambient Assisted Living. In: Proceedings of the 6th International Conference of the International Society for Gerontechnology, Pisa, Tuscany, Italy, 4–7 June 2008
16. Hill C, Grant R, Yeung I (2013) Ambient Assisted Living Technology. An interactive qualifying project report submitted to the Faculty of Worcester Polytechnic Institute
17. Mikalsen M, Hanke S, Fuxreiter T, Walderhaug S, Wienhofen L (2009) Interoperability Services in the MPOWER Ambient Assisted Living Platform. In: Medical Informatics Europe (MIE) Conference, Sarajevo, 30 August–2 September 2009
18. Ruiz-Zafra, Á., Benghazi, K., Noguera, M., Garrido, J.L.: Zappa: An open mobile platform to build cloud-based m-health systems. In: van Berlo, A., Hallenborg, K., Rodríguez, J.M. C., Tapia, D.I., Novais, P. (eds.) Ambient Intelligence - Software and Applications. AISC, vol. 219, pp. 87–94. Springer, Heidelberg (2013)
19. Wood, A., Stankovic, J., Virone, G., Selavo, L., He, Z., Cao, Q., Doan, T., Wu, Y., Fang, L., Stoleru, R.: Context-aware wireless sensor networks for assisted living and residential monitoring. IEEE Netw. **22**(4), 26–33 (2008)
20. López-de-Ipiña, D., Díaz-de-Sarralde, I., García-Zubia, J.: An ambient assisted living platform integrating RFID data-on-tag care annotations and twitter. J. Univers. Comput. Sci. **16**(12), 1521–1538 (2010)
21. Jara, A.J., Zamora, M.A., Skarmeta, A.F.G.: An internet of things–based personal device for diabetes therapy management in ambient assisted living (AAL). Pers. Ubiquit. Comput. **15**, 431–440 (2011)
22. Mileo, A., Merico, D., Bisiani, R.: Support for context-aware monitoring in home healthcare. J. Ambient Intell. Smart Environ. **2**(1), 49–66 (2010)
23. http://www.assistedlivingtechnologies.com/remote-monitoring-elderly/11-beclose.html. Accessed 28 June 2014
24. http://www.mybasis.com/blog/2013/11/body-iq-intelligence-the-most-advanced-way-to-recognize-activity-sleep-and-caloric-burn/. Accessed 28 June 2014
25. http://appleinsider.com/futures/iwatch. Accessed 28 June 2014
26. Liolios, C., Doukas, C., Fourlas, G., Maglogiannis, I.: An overview of body sensor networks in enabling pervasive healthcare and assistive environments. In: Proceedings of the 3rd International Conference on PErvasive Technologies Related to Assistive Environments, Samos, Greece, 23–25 June 2010
27. Nugent, C.D., Galway, L., Chen, L., Donnelly, M.P., McClean, S.I., Zhang, S., Scotney, B. W., Parr, G.: Managing sensor data in ambient assisted living. J. Comput. Sci. Eng. **5**(3), 237–245 (2011)

28. Gama, O., Carvalho, P., Alfonso, J.A., Mendes, P.M.: Quality of service support in wireless sensor networks for emergency healthcare services. In: Proceedings of the 30th Annual International Conference of the IEEE Engineering in Medicine and Biology Society, pp. 1296–1299. IEEE Computer Society (2008)

Continuous Human Action Recognition in Ambient Assisted Living Scenarios

Alexandros Andre Chaaraoui[1]([✉]) and Francisco Flórez-Revuelta[2]

[1] Department of Computer Technology, University of Alicante,
P.O. Box 99, 03080 Alicante, Spain
alexandros@dtic.ua.es

[2] Faculty of Science, Engineering and Computing, Kingston University,
Penrhyn Road, Kingston upon Thames KT1 2EE, UK
F.Florez@kingston.ac.uk

Abstract. Ambient assisted living technologies and services make it possible to help elderly and impaired people and increase their personal autonomy. Specifically, vision-based approaches enable the recognition of human behaviour, which in turn allows to build valuable services upon. However, a main constraint is that these have to be able to work online and in real time. In this work, a human action recognition method based on a bag-of-key-poses model and sequence alignment is extended to support continuous human action recognition. The detection of action zones is proposed to locate the most discriminative segments of an action. For the recognition, a method based on a sliding and growing window approach is presented. Furthermore, an evaluation scheme particularly designed for ambient assisted living scenarios is introduced. Experimental results on two publicly available datasets are provided. These show that the proposed action zones lead to a significant improvement and allow real-time processing.

Keywords: Ambient assisted living · Human action recognition · Continuous recognition · Action zones · Real time

1 Introduction

Currently, ambient assisted living (AAL) is attracting great interest in public and administration. This is due to the dual challenge our society is facing with an increasing need of assistance for elderly and impaired people and the simultaneous difficulties in containing the budget deficit. AAL can play a key role in this matter, since it enables diverse care and safety services and can extend the independent living at home of the people. Specifically, vision-based technology is of special interest because it allows to provide valuable services from the detection of home accidents to telecare services [1]. To this extent, vision-based human behaviour analysis can be extremely useful in order to detect actions and activities of daily living which are valuable for health-status monitoring.

© Institute for Computer Sciences, Social Informatics and Telecommunications Engineering 2015
R. Agüero et al. (Eds.): MONAMI 2014, LNICST 141, pp. 344–357, 2015.
DOI: 10.1007/978-3-319-16292-8_25

In human action recognition (HAR), actions like *falling, walking, sitting* and *bending* are recognised. Great advances have been made in order to improve the recognition rate, support multiple views and view-invariant recognition [2,3] as well as real-time performance [4,5]. However, it can be observed that HAR has been addressed by classifying short video sequences that contain single actions. Therefore, two strong assumptions have been made: (1) segmented video sequences which only contain a single action each are provided, and (2) all the video sequences necessarily match with one of the learnt action classes. Whereas these assumptions are commonly made in the state of the art and most of the datasets provide such data, these do not hold true in practical situations as in AAL scenarios, but also regarding human-computer interaction, gaming or video surveillance. In people's homes, cameras will provide a continuous video stream which can contain actions at any moment. This leads to continuous human action recognition (CHAR). In other words, an unsegmented video stream has to be analysed in order to detect actions at any point. Another restriction, which comes along with dealing with the raw video stream of the cameras, is that actually these may not record the expected actions. The person could be performing an unknown action, or nothing at all. Therefore, the proposed system needs to be robust enough in order to discard unknown actions that otherwise would result in misclassifications.

In this paper, continuous human action recognition (CHAR) is addressed in order to overcome the aforementioned assumptions. The concept of *action zones* is introduced and a novel method is proposed to detect the most discriminative segments of action sequences. For continuous recognition, a method based on a sliding and growing window technique is presented. Finally, to perform continuous evaluation considering specific constraints of AAL scenarios, a suitable evaluation scheme based on segment analysis and F1 score is proposed. Experimental results on two publicly available datasets are provided.

2   Related Work

Determining the relevant segments of a continuous video stream may be trivial for a human, but it certainly involves a great difficulty for an automated computer vision system. This explains why few works deal with the related additional constraints. Some works try to find the boundaries of the actions in order to apply temporal segmentation. These boundaries can be detected based on discontinuities or extremes in acceleration, velocity or curvature [6]. Once the resulting video segments are obtained, sequence-based action recognition can be applied. Such a temporal segmentation is performed in [7], where atomic movements are localised in the video stream based on so-called 'ballistic movements'. These are defined as impulsive movements, which involve a sudden propulsion of the limbs, and rely on the acceleration and deceleration of start and end of the ballistic segments. A trajectory-based motion feature (*i.e.* the popular motion-history images from [8]) is employed along velocity magnitude features based on silhouette transformation, frame differences and optical flow. Two approaches are tested for the temporal segmentation. The first proposal handles alignment of the optical flow direction by means of dynamic programming. Whereas in the second, assuming that boundaries are characterised by zero velocity, movement begin-end detection is performed with a boosting based classifier. The first option performed better, since it does not classify specific temporal moments, but aligns a globally optimal segmentation taking into account movement direction. In [9], start and end key frames of actions are identified. Segmentation is performed based on the posterior probability of model matching considering recognition rounds. Depending on the accumulated probability, rounds are ended if a threshold is reached. Adjacent rounds classified as the same action classes are connected into a single segment. Lu *et al.* deal with temporal segmentation of successive actions in [10]. During the learning, only a few characteristic frames are selected based on change, which leads to an outstanding temporal performance of the recognition. Likelihood of action segments is computed considering pair-wise representations of characteristic frames. Although good results are obtained, no further instructions are provided on how an actual continuous video stream would be handled.

A very popular technique in video and audio processing is the sliding window approach. Sliding windows allow to analyse different overlapping segments of the stream in order to isolate a region of interest and then perform classification comparing the window to a set of training templates. If a variable size is also considered, both window position and size dynamically change so that all necessary locations and scales are taken into account. Some works have applied the sliding window technique to CHAR [8,11,12]. In [13], a sliding window is employed to accumulate and smooth the frame-wise predictions of a frame-based low-latency recognition. Low-latency CHAR is also considered in [14], where so-called *action points* are proposed as natural temporal anchors. These are especially useful for gaming. Two approaches are proposed. The first relies on a continuous observation hidden Markov model (HMM) with firing states that detect action points. And the second employs a direct classification based on random forests classifiers and sliding window. In conclusion, by means of sliding window techniques, the temporal segmentation is simplified, since no specific boundaries have to be detected. However, due to its computational cost it may only be used if the applied segment analysis can be performed very efficiently.

3   Human Action Recognition Method

As it has been previously mentioned, this work builds upon prior contributions in which HAR has been successfully performed for action sequences that have been segmented beforehand. Since in this work these contributions are extended to support continuous recognition, this section provides a brief summary of the related previous publications.

For pose representation a silhouette-based approach has been chosen due to its rich spatial information and low computational requirements. More specifically, a feature representation based on the distance between the contour points and the centroid of the human silhouette is employed. Furthermore, spatial alignment and a significant dimensionality reduction are performed to obtain a low-dimensional and noise-reduced feature (see [15] for greater detail).

Based on the method published in [16], the most representative feature representations involved in each action class (the so-called key poses) are obtained based on a clustering algorithm, and a bag-of-key-poses model is generated. In order to complement this spatial information related to the human posture, temporal cues are considered by means of modelling the evolution of the human silhouettes along the action sequences. To extract this kind of information, sequences of key poses are learned. These, in turn, are employed for action recognition, where temporal alignment of sequences is performed for matching using dynamic time warping (DTW). Also multi-view recognition is taken into account [5]. Concretely, intelligent feature fusion of single-view feature representations is performed with a feature concatenation operator in addition to a weighted feature fusion scheme that is based on *a priori* knowledge about the usefulness of each camera.

4 Learning of Action Zones

It can be observed that the method presented in Sect. 3 is clearly based on segmented recognition since it performs spatio-temporal matching of action sequences. Nevertheless, its accurate recognition and outstanding temporal performance led us to extend it for continuous scenarios. The first issue that has to be addressed is the existence of misclassifications. Action sequences may contain irrelevant segments which are common among actions and therefore ambiguous for classification. For this reason, we propose to extract *action zones*.

Definition 4.1. *Action zones correspond to the most discriminative segments with respect to the other action classes in the course of an action.*

Based on Definition 4.1, for instance, the *fall* action contains an action zone corresponding to the segment from where the body is partially bent, until it is completely collapsed. In other words, the part where the person is standing still is ignored as well as the part where the person is lying on the floor, since these are not discriminative with respect to other actions. In this way, the most relevant segments can be identified in order to ease the differentiation between actions. Furthermore, action zones are shorter than the original sequences. For this reason, the matching time will be significantly reduced. Since the underlying HAR method also presents a very low computational cost, a sliding window approach may be employed without prohibitively reducing the temporal performance.

Initially, the same learning is performed as detailed in Sect. 3. Since segmented sequences are still needed for the learning process, these can easily be obtained relying on the frame-wise ground truth and discarding the segments where no action is performed. Action zones may be located at different parts of the actions depending on the type of action and how the action ground truth has been labelled. However, based on the provided definition, action zones can be detected automatically by analysing the transition of key poses. For this purpose, we first compute the discrimination value of each key pose w_{kp}. All available pose representations are matched with their nearest neighbour among the bag of key poses and the ratio of within-class matches is obtained ($w_{kp} = \frac{matches_{kp}}{assignments_{kp}}$). Therefore, this value indicates how valuable a key pose is for distinguishing action classes. In this way, based on the transition of key poses and their discriminative value, our action zones, *i.e.* the most discriminative segments, can be detected.

Specifically, for each training sequence of action class a and a specific temporal instant t, the following steps are taken for the corresponding frame:

1. The feature representation $\bar{V}(t)$ of the current frame is matched with the key poses of the bag-of-key-poses model. For each action class a, the nearest neighbour key pose $kp_a(t)$ is obtained.
2. For the A action classes, the raw class evidence values $H_{raw_1}(t), H_{raw_2}(t), ...,$ $H_{raw_A}(t)$ are computed based on the ratio between the discrimination value $w_{kp_a(t)}$ and the distance $dist_{kp_a(t)}$, where $dist_{kp_a(t)}$ denotes the Euclidean distance between the pose representation and the matched key pose $kp_a(t)$. Hence, the discrimination value will be taken into account depending on how well the key pose defines the current pose.

$$H_{raw_a}(t) = \frac{w_{kp_a(t)}}{dist_{kp_a(t)}}, \quad \forall a \in [1...A]. \tag{1}$$

3. Normalisation is applied with respect to he highest value observed:

$$H_{norm_a}(t) = \frac{H_{raw_a}(t)}{H_{raw_{max}}(t)}, \quad \forall a \in [1...A]. \tag{2}$$

4. Gaussian smoothing is performed centred in the current frame, considering only the frames from a temporal instant $u \leq t$. In this way, we do not take into account future frames, as this would require to delay the recognition for a constant time interval. Convolution is applied to the history $H_{norm}(u)$ values with a Gaussian filter kernel in order to generate $H_{smooth}(t)$. Discrete kernel values are processed based on approximating the continuous values (see [17]):

$$G(u) = \frac{1}{\sigma\sqrt{2\pi}} e^{\frac{-(u-\mu)^2}{2\sigma^2}}, \quad / \quad u \leq t. \tag{3}$$

5. Attenuating the resulting value, the final class evidence $H(t)$ is obtained:

$$H_a(t) = e^{10H_{smooth_a}(t)}, \quad \forall a \in [1...A]. \tag{4}$$

Figure 1 shows the $H(t)$ evidence values that have been obtained over the course of a *bend* action. In comparison to the raw values, here outliers have been filtered and the differences between classes have become more pronounced. As it can be seen, the evidence of the *bend* class is significantly higher than the others in the central part of the sequence. This is due to the fact that the person is initially standing still. He or she then bends down and, finally, returns to the initial position. The segment that corresponds to the poses in

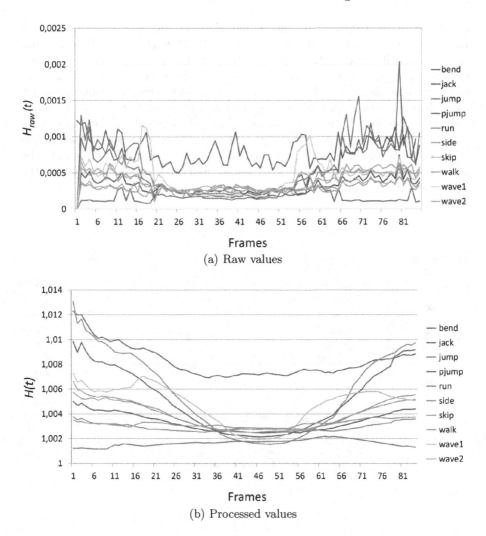

(a) Raw values

(b) Processed values

Fig. 1. Evidence values of each action class before and after processing are shown for a *bend* sequence of the Weizmann dataset.

which the person is bent down is the most discriminative one. The poses of this segment match with the most discriminative key poses of the *bend* action class, whereas the ratio between discrimination value and distance is lower for the other classes. For this reason, action zones can be detected by defining the thresholds $HT_1(t), HT_2(t), ..., HT_A(t)$ that have to be reached by the class evidence values of these segments. Specifically, an action zone will be collected from the frame on where:

$$H_{action}(t) > H_{median}(t) + HT_{action} , \tag{5}$$

where *action* corresponds to the action class of the current sequence and $H_{median}(t)$ indicates the median value out of $H_1(t), H_2(t), ..., H_A(t)$. An action zone will end if this condition ceases to be met. The median value is employed because the expected peak of $H_{action}(t)$ would influence the average. Moreover, this approach also works if action segments present a high evidence value for more than one action class, which may happen for very similar actions. A second example is shown in Fig. 2, where the class evidence values that have been obtained for the cyclic *jumping jack* action are detailed. Several short action zones could be found choosing the appropriate threshold HT_a. It can also be seen that the peaks correspond to the discriminative segments in which the limbs are outstretched.

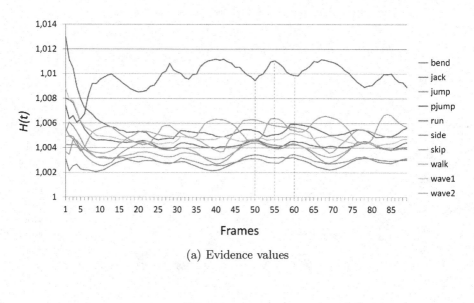

(a) Evidence values

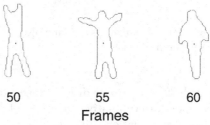

(b) Corresponding silhouettes

Fig. 2. Evidence values $H(t)$ of each action class and the corresponding silhouettes of one of the peaks of evidence are shown for a *jumping jack* sequence of the Weizmann dataset.

5 Continuous Recognition

In this proposal, continuous human action recognition is performed by detecting and classifying action zones. For the continuous recognition of the incoming multi-view data, a sliding window technique is employed. More specifically, a sliding and growing window is used to process the continuous stream at different overlapping locations and scales. At this point, a *null class* has to be considered in order to discard unknown actions and avoid false positives. This class corresponds to all the behaviours that may be observed and have not been modelled during the learning.

Algorithm 1 details the process: The sliding and growing window grows δ frames in each iteration and slides γ frames if the window has reached its maximal length $length_{max}$. If at least $length_{min}$ frames have been collected, the segment of the video stream (or video streams if available) S that corresponds to the window is compared to the known action zones. The best match is obtained by matching the segments of key poses using DTW. Then, a threshold value DT_a is taken into account in order to trigger the recognition. This value DT_a indicates the highest allowed distance in a per-frame basis. In this way, only segments which match well enough with an action zone are classified. Eventually, the unrecognised frames will be discarded and considered to belong to the *null class*.

6 Experimentation

6.1 Parametrisation

Special consideration has been given to the parameters $HT_1, HT_2, ..., HT_A$ and $DT_1, DT_2, ..., DT_A$. The first ones define the threshold that has to be surpassed by the class evidence $H_{action}(t)$ in comparison to the $H_{median}(t)$ value. Different values are admitted for each action class, since the class evidence behaves differently for each type of action. In the case of the second set of parameters, each action class is considered to require a specific similarity between sequence segments and action zones in order to confirm the match as a recognition and avoid false positives for 'poor matches'. This leads us to two sets of A parameters that are difficult to establish empirically, as exhausting tests are unaffordable.

Among the possible search heuristics, evolutionary algorithms stand out since they are proficient for scenarios where the shape of the solution space is unknown and this hinders the election of optimal algorithms. They can also deal with a large number of parameters in a moderate run time. Moreover, relying on a coevolutionary-based approach the intrinsic relationship between our two parameter sets can be considered. For this reason, a technique based on the cooperative coevolutionary algorithm from [18] has been employed for parameter selection. By means of this method, the best performing combination of HT and DT values can be found.

Algorithm 1. Continuous recognition: sliding and growing window

---

Let δ denote the number of frames the window grows in each step.
Let γ denote the number of frames the windows moves when slid.
Let S denote the video stream.

$start = 0$
$length = 0$

repeat
⎯⎯⎯⎯⎯⎯⎯⎯⎯ Sliding and growing window ⎯⎯⎯⎯⎯⎯⎯
    $length = length + \delta$

    if $length > length_{max}$ **then**
        Discard γ frames considered to belong to the *null class*
        $start = start + \gamma$
        $length = length - \gamma$
    end if
⎯⎯⎯⎯⎯⎯⎯⎯ Compare to action zones ⎯⎯⎯⎯⎯⎯⎯
    if $length \geq length_{min}$ **then**
        $dist_{min} = max\_value$
        for all $action\_class \in training\_set$ **do**
            for all $action\_zone \in action\_class$ **do**
                $dist = d_{DTW}(action\_zone, S[start : start$
                $+length])$
                if $dist < dist_{min}$ **then**
                    $dist_{min} = dist$
                    $a = action\_class$
                end if
            end for
        end for
⎯⎯⎯⎯⎯⎯⎯⎯ Recognise or continue ⎯⎯⎯⎯⎯⎯⎯
        if $dist_{min} \leq length \times DT_a$ **then**
            Recognise segment $S[start : start + length]$
            as action class a
            $start = start + length$
            $length = 0$
        end if
    end if
until end of stream or forever

6.2   Continuous Evaluation

For action recognition based on segmented sequences, the evaluation scheme is straightforward. Since the ground truth label of each sequence is known, the ratio of correctly classified sequences in the test is commonly used as accuracy score. Nevertheless, for continuous evaluation, several new constraints appear. Depending on the application scenario, one might be interested in the number of repetitions of each action. This happens in gaming (*e.g.* three *punches*), whereas in video surveillance the fact that the action happened is more relevant (*e.g.* *punching*). In AAL, it is especially important not to miss any actions, because this could result in safety issues (*e.g. falling down*). A delay of a few seconds may be acceptable if this improves the recognition avoiding false negatives. As a result, the applied evaluation scheme varies between authors.

A common option is to apply frame-by-frame evaluation as in [10], but the reliability of this approach is arguable. This is due to the lack of correlation between frames and actions. It could happen that only a few last frames of an action are not recognised correctly. This would result in a high frame-by-frame recognition rate (*e.g.* 90 %), although only one correct class label and one or more incorrect predictions have been returned by the system. This means that 50 % or more of the returned labels were erroneous. For this reason, other levels of evaluation have been proposed, such as event analysis, where only the activity occurrence and order is considered, or the hybrid segment analysis [19]. In this last approach, a segment is defined as "an interval of maximal duration in which both the ground truth and the predicted activities are constant". In this way, despite the fact that segments may have different durations, alignment is given since each ground truth or prediction change leads to a new unit of evaluation.

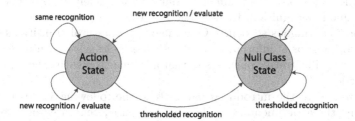

Fig. 3. This finite-state machine details the logic behaviour of the applied segment analysis.

This last level of analysis has been employed in this work, as it provides a clear way to align the recognitions with the ground truth and avoids the disadvantages of the frame-based analysis. Figure 3 shows how the *null class* has been considered in the segment analysis. As it can be seen, only new recognitions (*i.e.* different from the last predicted action class) are taken into account for evaluation. The thresholded recognitions are retained and their segments are considered to belong to the *null class*. In addition, recognitions are accepted for a delay of τ frames after the ground truth indicated the end of the action. Note that this is only allowed if no prediction was given until that moment, *i.e.* the *null class* state was active since the action started and until the delayed recognition has occurred. Otherwise, the action would have already been classified (correctly or wrongly).

In view of the multi-class classification that is performed and that now a *null class* has to be contemplated, results are measured in terms of true positives

354   A.A. Chaaraoui and F. Flórez-Revuelta

(TP), false positives (FP), true negatives (TN) and false negatives (FN). These values are accumulated along a cross validation test. A leave-one-actor-out cross validation (LOAO) is proposed in which each sequence includes several continuously performed actions of an actor. In order to consider both precision and recall rates, the F_1-measure is used as follows:

$$F_1 = 2 \times \frac{precision \times recall}{precision + recall} \tag{6}$$

$$precision = \frac{TP}{TP + FP} \tag{7}$$

$$recall = \frac{TP}{TP + FN} \tag{8}$$

6.3 Results

Our approach has been validated on the multi-view INRIA XMAS (IXMAS) [20] dataset and the single-view Weizmann [21] dataset. The former provides continuous multi-view sequences of different actions performed by the same actor, whereas the latter provides segmented single-view sequences. In order to support continuous recognition, the sequences of the same actor are concatenated into a single continuous sequence. Consequently, unnatural transitions are created due to the gaps of information. Nevertheless, tests have been performed on this dataset for illustrative purposes so that a comparison with other approaches can be made.

With regard to the introduced parameters, the following values have been used during the experimentation (these have been chosen based on experimentation):

1. The threshold parameters have been established by the coevolutionary parameter selection algorithm as follows: $HT \in [0.05, 1.5]$ and $DT \in [0.002, 0.02]$. In Fig. 4, the class evidence values of a sample sequence can be seen, where the action zone that has been obtained using these HT class evidence thresholds is highlighted.
2. The Gaussian smoothing applied to the $H(t)$ class evidence considers $\sigma = 10.486$ frames. Since approximate discrete values are applied for the convolution, a total of 22 history frames are taken into account and the rest is considered zero.
3. Regarding the sliding and growing window, in each iteration the window grows 5 frames ($\delta = 5$), and when the maximal length $length_{max}$ is reached, the window slides 10 frames ($\gamma = 10$).
4. A delayed recognition is accepted within a period of 60 frames, corresponding to approximately 2 s ($\tau = 60$). This time interval has been considered acceptable for this AAL application.

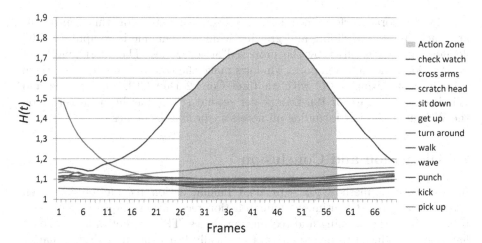

Fig. 4. Evidence values $H(t)$ of each action class and the detected action zone are shown for a *scratch head* sequence of the IXMAS dataset.

Table 1. Obtained results applying CHAR and segment analysis evaluation over a LOAO cross validation test. Results are detailed using the proposed approaches based on action zones (1) or segmented sequences (2).

Dataset	Approach	$length_{min}$	$length_{max}$	F_1
IXMAS	1	3	30	0.705
IXMAS	2	10	120	0.504
Weizmann	1	3	20	0.928
Weizmann	2	10	120	0.693

Table 1 shows the scores that have been achieved by our approach over the ideal value F_1-measure of 1.0. The IXMAS dataset presents several known difficulties as view invariance and noise which explain the score difference. Furthermore, the segments labelled as *null class* in which 'other actions' are performed can easily lead to an increase of false positives. In order to show the benefit gained from the action zones approach (approach 1), tests have also been performed using the entire segmented sequences instead (approach 2). In this way, larger segments are considered by the sliding and growing window and these are compared to the original action sequences provided by the ground truth. It can be seen that the proposed continuous recognition based on action zones provides a substantial performance increase and leads to higher scores in general.

Comparison with other state-of-the-art works is difficult in CHAR, due to different evaluation schemes. In [10], frame analysis is employed and 81.0 % accuracy is reported on the IXMAS dataset. In the case of the Weizmann dataset, for example in [9], CHAR is performed and a score of 97.8 % is reached. Segment analysis is employed in this case, although the rate of correctly classified segments is computed based on a 60 % overlap with the ground truth.

The temporal performance has also been evaluated for this continuous approach. While the sliding and growing window technique is computationally demanding, this is offset by the proposed action zones. The short lengths of both action zones and temporal windows make the comparisons between them very efficient. Using a PC with an Intel Core 2 Duo CPU at 3.0 GHz and Windows x64, a rate of 196 frames per second (FPS) has been measured on the Weizmann dataset including all necessary processing stages.

7   Discussion and Conclusion

In this work, a method for segmented human action recognition has been extended to support continuous human action recognition. Improvements have been made at the learning and recognition stages. The concept of action zones has been introduced to define and automatically learn the most discriminative segments of action performances. Relying on these action zones, recognition can be carried out by finding the equivalent segments that clearly define the action that is being performed. For this purpose, a sliding and growing window approach has been employed. Finally, segment analysis is used introducing special considerations for the specific AAL application of our work. Tests have been performed relying on the whole segmented sequences or only on the action zones, and significant differences can be seen. By means of action zones, higher accuracy scores are obtained. Real-time suitability of this continuous approach has also been verified. This is indispensable for most of the possible applications, and a necessary premise for online recognition.

In future works, further evaluation should be applied to ease the comparison to other approaches. It could be useful to implement other state-of-the-art techniques and test them in the same conditions as our proposal. Furthermore, a consensus should be reached about the appropriate evaluation schemes. It has also been observed that regarding CHAR, there is a lack of suitable benchmarks including foreground segmentations or depth data. Therefore, new datasets should be created along the corresponding evaluation schemes.

References

1. Cardinaux, F., Bhowmik, D., Abhayaratne, C., Hawley, M.S.: Video based technology for ambient assisted living: a review of the literature. J. Ambient Intell. Smart Environ. **3**(3), 253–269 (2011)
2. Poppe, R.: A survey on vision-based human action recognition. Image Vis. Comput. **28**(6), 976–990 (2010)
3. Aggarwal, J., Ryoo, M.: Human activity analysis: a review. ACM Comput. Surv. **43**(3), 16:1–16:43 (2011)
4. Shotton, J., Fitzgibbon, A.W., Cook, M., Sharp, T., Finocchio, M., Moore, R., Kipman, A., Blake, A.: Real-time human pose recognition in parts from single depth images. In: IEEE Conference on Computer Vision and Pattern Recognition, CVPR 2011, pp. 1297–1304 (2011)

5. Chaaraoui, A.A., Padilla-López, J.R., Ferrández-Pastor, F.J., Nieto-Hidalgo, M., Flórez-Revuelta, F.: A vision-based system for intelligent monitoring: human behaviour analysis and privacy by context. Sensors **14**(5), 8895–8925 (2014)
6. Kellokumpu, V.P.: Vision-based human motion description and recognition. Ph.D. thesis, University of Oulu, Faculty of Technology, Department of Computer Science and Engineering (2011)
7. Vitaladevuni, S., Kellokumpu, V., Davis, L.: Action recognition using ballistic dynamics. In: IEEE Conference on Computer Vision and Pattern Recognition, CVPR 2008, pp. 1–8 (2008)
8. Bobick, A., Davis, J.: The recognition of human movement using temporal templates. IEEE Trans. Pattern Anal. Mach. Intell. **23**(3), 257–267 (2001)
9. Guo, P., Miao, Z., Shen, Y., Xu, W., Zhang, D.: Continuous human action recognition in real time. Multimed. Tools Appl. **68**(3), 827–844 (2014)
10. Lu, G., Kudo, M., Toyama, J.: Temporal segmentation and assignment of successive actions in a long-term video. Pattern Recogn. Lett. **34**(15), 1936–1944 (2013). Smart Approaches for Human Action Recognition
11. Hu, Y., Cao, L., Lv, F., Yan, S., Gong, Y., Huang, T.: Action detection in complex scenes with spatial and temporal ambiguities. In: IEEE 12th International Conference on Computer Vision, ICCV 2009, pp. 128–135 (2009)
12. Kavi, R., Kulathumani, V.: Real-time recognition of action sequences using a distributed video sensor network. J. Sens. Actuator Netw. **2**(3), 486–508 (2013)
13. Bloom, V., Argyriou, V., Makris, D.: Dynamic feature selection for online action recognition. In: Salah, A.A., Hung, H., Aran, O., Gunes, H. (eds.) HBU 2013. LNCS, vol. 8212, pp. 64–76. Springer, Heidelberg (2013)
14. Nowozin, S., Shotton, J.: Action points: a representation for low-latency online human action recognition. Technical report, Microsoft Research Cambridge (2012). Technical Report MSR- TR-2012-68
15. Chaaraoui, A.A., Flórez-Revuelta, F.: Human action recognition optimization based on evolutionary feature subset selection. In: Proceeding of the Fifteenth Annual Conference on Genetic and Evolutionary Computation Conference, GECCO 2013, pp. 1229–1236. ACM, New York (2013)
16. Chaaraoui, A.A., Climent-Pérez, P., Flórez-Revuelta, F.: Silhouette-based human action recognition using sequences of keyposes. Pattern Recogn. Lett. **34**(15), 1799–1807 (2013). Smart Approaches for Human Action Recognition
17. Russ, J.C.: The Image Processing Handbook. CRC Press, Boca Raton (2006)
18. Chaaraoui, A.A., Flórez-Revuelta, F.: Optimizing human action recognition based on a cooperative coevolutionary algorithm. Engineering Applications of Artificial Intelligence: Advances in Evolutionary Optimization Based. Image Processing (2013). doi:10.1016/j.engappai.2013.10.003
19. Ward, J.A., Lukowicz, P., Gellersen, H.W.: Performance metrics for activity recognition. ACM Trans. Intell. Syst. Technol. **2**(1) 6:1–6:23 (2011)
20. Weinland, D., Ronfard, R., Boyer, E.: Free viewpoint action recognition using motion history volumes. Comput. Vis. Image Underst. **104**(2–3), 249–257 (2006)
21. Gorelick, L., Blank, M., Shechtman, E., Irani, M., Basri, R.: Actions as space-time shapes. IEEE Trans. Pattern Anal. Mach. Intell. **29**(12), 2247–2253 (2007)

Cloud Based Assistive Technologies and Smart Living Environment System

Vlatko Nikolovski[✉], Petre Lameski,
Boban Joksimoski, and Ivan Chorbev

Faculty of Computer Science and Engineering,
University of Ss. Cyril and Methodius, str. "Rugjer Boshkovikj" 16,
P.O. Box 393, 1000 Skopje, Republic of Macedonia
{vlatko.nikolovski,petre.lameski,boban.joksimoski,
ivan.chorbev}@finki.ukim.mk

Abstract. This paper describes a cloud based architecture for processing data and providing services for smart living environments and support for assistive technologies. Based on scalable cloud technologies and optimized software architectures, it provides infrastructure for an extendible set of various functionalities. The paper describes the core processing module along with several related proof-of-concept services. Several use case scenarios are presented including a mobile app voice navigation tool for the blind, text to hand sign speech video sequencing tool for the deaf, image processing tool for a smart home, etc. Details are presented about the software development tools used and their integration in a functional multiplatform application. Guides for future works and extension of the system are discussed.

Keywords: Assistive technologies · Smart living environments · Cloud processing · Voice navigation · Text to sign language speech

1 Introduction

The advantages of the cloud based architectures delivering high computing yet scalable environment and resource sharing, provides a powerful resource for expansion of services and platforms for smart living environments and assistive technologies. Systems using the main principles of cloud computing, provide infrastructure for an extendible set of various functionalities and services. This paper describes a cloud based system for assistive technologies and smart living services. Descriptions are given of the core processing module along with several related proof-of-concept assisted living services, concerning security in the cloud, interoperability and interconnectivity between various devices and their interaction with the end-users. The presented core module relies on the principles and standards of cloud computing delivering better characteristics and platforms compared to similar solutions based on traditional principles. Several use case scenarios are presented in details regarding the software development tools used and their integration in a functional multiplatform application. The described architecture is not limited to the concept subsystems described. Various smart living room functionalities are planned and can be developed

R. Agüero et al. (Eds.): MONAMI 2014, LNICST 141, pp. 358–369, 2015.
DOI: 10.1007/978-3-319-16292-8_26

on top of the backbone core module described. Broadening assistive living systems to encompass smart living-room features increases their viability and sustainability. The border between such systems is thin and a universal approach brings efficiency and quality. Guidelines for future work and extensions are discussed.

This article is structured as follows: Sect. 2 presents related work. Section 3 describes the architecture of the Core Cloud based system and interaction between components. Also security issues are discussed. In Sect. 4 several composite modules are presented and their interaction with the Core system. Section 5 concludes the paper.

2 Related Work

The digital revolution has dramatically increased the usage and function of consumer smart devices, simultaneously reducing their cost. The interoperability among IT-based services as well as wireless smart devices are an indispensable tool for assisted living as well. Numerous IT companies contributed in support and deployment of new smart environments, smart cloud-based services and wireless devices, improving user convenience and better living.

2.1 Assistive Technology Frameworks

Assistive technology systems have often been developed strictly targeting a specific domain and set of functions. It is only recently that generic frameworks capable of providing a variety of assistive services are emerging. The Assistive Technology Rapid Integration and Construction Set system, also known as AsTeRICS [1] is an Open Source platform which provides creation of flexible solutions for people with disabilities. The AsTeRICS platform implements interfaces and protocols for connectivity and interaction between various input and output components.

One aspect of assistive systems - telehealth is on the forefronts of development, due to economic reasons. The term telehealth describes Integrated Information Systems built for delivery of health care services at a distance, using ICT technologies. Telehealth combines variety of distance health care services and applications for home care, long-term care, health promotion, prevention, self-care and integration of social and health care services [2, 3]. Notable examples of such Telehealth systems include the EIP-AHA, initiative of the European Union in at least 30 European regions [4], and the 3 Million Lives project in the UK [5].

The NavChair Assistive Wheelchair Navigation System presented in [6], provides assisted mobility to the wheelchair operator regarding door passage, obstacle avoidance and maintenance of a straight path. Another similar assistive system for people with motor disabilities is proposed in [7], based on the VHAM prototype for mobile robots in healthcare, to provide "smart" wheelchair.

Various assistive technologies and systems are developed for navigation of visually impaired people. The interaction between multiple input sensors (accelerometers, gyroscopes, proximity) and ICT technologies (GPS, "Voice search") provides possibilities for implementations of systems for indoor and outdoor navigation [8].

Notable examples include the Electronic Cane [9] and the Navigation Tool for Blind People based on a microcontroller with two vibrators and two ultrasonic sensors [10].

2.2 Cloud Platforms

Cloud computing is a concept of sharing computing resources, providing high processing power and scalability [11]. The Cloud computing model delivers applications or infrastructures as network services, making them accessible from everywhere on the network, anytime of the day. The resources required by the deployed services, such as CPU power, internal memory and network load are allocated dynamically on demand, providing autonomous and highly dynamic scalable environment [12, 13]. Many companies are launching different platforms diverse in features and pricing, fighting to attract users. Amongst others, Amazon was one of the first and so far one of the biggest providers of Cloud computing services [14].

Windows Azure Cloud Service [15] is an internet-scale computing and services platform managed by Microsoft. It includes many separate features, such as: Web hosting services; Mobile hosting services; Media files hosting; Development environment with advanced testability; Big data hosting; Extensive computing power;

Google Cloud Platform [16] is another powerful cloud computing platform, build on the same infrastructure as the Google Search Engine and the Youtube streaming services. The platform provides easy integration with familiar development tools, managed scalability, computing, storage allocation and management.

3 System Architecture

The proposed cloud based system provides an integrated environment for development of composite, user-driven Assistive and Home Enhancement Technology services. The system defines a protocol for interaction and communication between interconnected components, provides enhanced security, authentication and accounting protocols, allowing managed Plug&Play functionality of various components and services.

The Core module shown on Fig. 1 is fully developed on top of the Windows Azure platform [15]. The interconnectivity is based on the Pure HTTP protocol [17], providing two way communication. In addition, the system defines REST-full HTTP endpoints independent of consumer platforms, due to the simple nature of the HTTP protocol and JSON data format [18]. The components supported by the system are divided in three main categories, based on their functionality: sensors, processors and triggers. Due to the cloud oriented architecture of the system, the client platforms pose no limitation in interconnectivity and interoperability. Therefore, we have so far developed components/clients based on Android, Windows and Linux operating systems that interact with the cloud system correctly.

The system provides a Graphical Design Tool (GDT), implemented as a Web Application, for design and modeling Assistive and Home Enhancement services and workflows. The GDT tool is a simple, yet functional user interface, where the user can develop a model using drag&drop techniques, intuitively describing the rules (wires) for interaction between the components. In addition, multiple components are

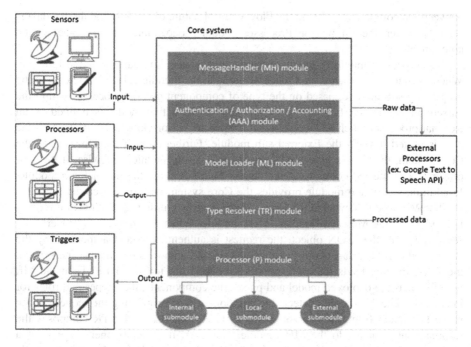

Fig. 1. Core system architecture.

supported for integration in terms of sensors, processors and triggers including smart phones, tablets, personal computers, laptops, game consoles. Each component used in a model has a unique identifier (UID) and must be defined as one of the three possible types: sensor, processor or trigger.

3.1   Core Cloud Modules

The core system is composed of five modules, each with different functionalities. The Message Handler module processes HTTP request messages on their way in (DE serializing JSON data), and HTTP response messages on their way out (serializing data into JSON objects). In addition, the Message Handler module synchronizes the communication between the Core and components.

The AAA module provides security protocols. The authentication is based on OAuth 2.0 protocol with Bearer tokens [19]. After the data flow is authenticated and authorized, the AAA module loads the authorized account profile from the database.

The Model Loader module activates the model created with the GDT tool. In addition, the ML module processes defined components (sensors, processors and triggers) and rules for interaction between them, from the model. Furthermore, the ML registers the components and rules into the TR module.

The TR module resolves the type of each registered component, and deploys a protocol for interaction between the components, based on the data provided by the ML module. Furthermore, the TR module controls the data flow rules for communication between the components. Due to the Flow Control nature of the TR module, the data is send to either the Output or Processor module, depending on the type of the component.

The Processor module consists of three sub modules: Internal, Local and External. When the data flow reaches the Processor module, the module delegates the data to the proprietary sub module, based on the type of component used as processor within the parsed model. In addition, if the component in the active model is defined as an external processor, such as Google Text to Speech API or Google Translate API, the data is routed through the External sub module. Furthermore, if the processor is the Core system, the data is processed from the Local sub module. Likewise, if the processor is a connected component, the data is routed through the Internal sub module. In addition, every sub module provides the Core system with processed data.

The Message Lifecycle in the Core system is shown on Fig. 2. Each HTTP request is handled by the Message Handler (MH) module. When the message is properly deserialized from the JSON object, the request is authenticated and authorized by the AAA module. After successfully authentication and authorization against the system, the AAA module loads the corresponding profile from the Database. Then the ML module loads the deployed model and parses the components, their types and rules for interaction. The TR module detects the component type originating the request. If the request is made from a sensor or a trigger type component, the TR composes the response and sends it to the MH module. However, if the component type is of a processor type, the request is processed to the Processor module. The Processor module resolves the type of the processor component and routes the request to the appropriate sub module. When the corresponding module finishes processing, it sends a response to the MH module. The MH module then sends back the response to the component.

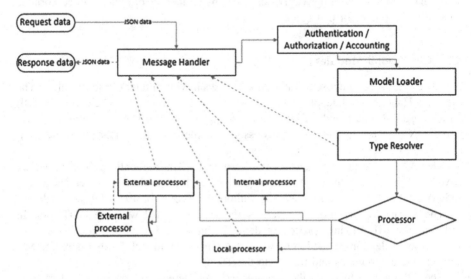

Fig. 2. Core system architecture.

3.2 Core Cloud Module Security Considerations

Cloud Computing might suffer from a number of security issues and concerns mainly divided in two broad categories: security issues by providers and security issues by customers. A risk management protocol must be defined to balance the issues and security risks between these two categories and the benefits of cloud computing services. Based on the Windows Azure Security policy, the vendor provides its own strategies and solutions for securing the services which are provided to the end users. Microsoft Azure delivers a secure environment and managed cloud infrastructure through implementation of different security policies: live monitoring and logging of services, patching deployment environments, built-in antivirus/antimalware protection and intrusion detection and DDoS prevention.

Aside of the security from the provider, the core system implements its own standards and protocols for Cloud-based security for the services that the core system provides. The security is managed through three different layers, securing the client, the server applications and communication channels (Fig. 3).

The authentication and authorization is based on OAuth protocol, with implementation of an OAuth Authentication Server in the Cloud. Every client application must obtain a Bearer token from the authentication server to be authorized to use the core services. The Core server checks the client token on every request, consolidating the Authentication server for the validity of the token. This way, every request must be authenticated.

The communication channel provides data encryption trough the HTTPS protocol. In addition, the Core service and client applications have their own implementation for encryption of the communication between them.

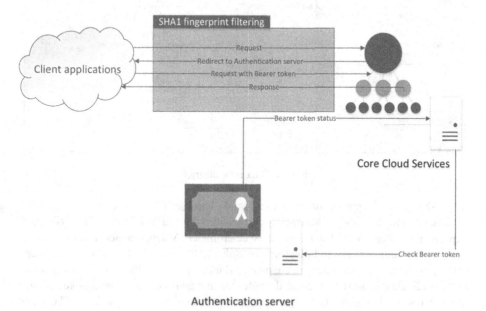

Fig. 3. Authentication and authorization

Every client application deploys SHA1 certificates which are obtained from the Core service. The Core service verifies that each request originates from a client application that matches one of the certificate fingerprints, to ensure integrity of clients and to prevent code injection.

4   Services Related to the Cloud Module

4.1   Voice Navigation Tool

The system is used for building a tool for navigation of visually impaired persons (VNT). The VNT tool is an android application, using data inputs from the GPS and other sensors [20] usually implemented in android devices, such as: gyroscope, accelerometers, magnetometer and a gravity sensor. The Core Cloud Module processes the data inputs from the VNT and forwards voice message to the VNT tool.

The route definition function which is part of the VNT tool, (from A to B), is based on a Google Maps plugin. Based on the techniques proposed in [5] for filtering signals and data acquisition from sensors, the Core Cloud Module provides a sensor fusion environment, where each movement is calculated and mapped within the route coordinates, as in the Google Maps plugin.

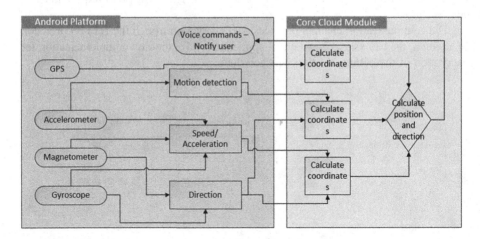

Fig. 4. Data flow diagram

A Data flow diagram is described in Fig. 4. The user defines the desired route for navigation into the Google Maps plugin, provided by the VNT tool. The VNT then exposes the values provided from the Accelerometer, Magnetometer and Gyroscope sensors, also and wireless and bluetooth modules to the Core system. The Core system calculates the movement based on the provided input data from the VNT tool and maps the coordinates against the defined route for navigation. The calculations of the movements are based on techniques for sensor fusion presented in [21]. The Core system then transforms the calculated direction into voice with the Google Text to

Speech API. In addition, the end-user is provided with voice direction messages for navigation through a defined route.

4.2   Video Processing Home Behavior Detection

Image and video processing is becoming an increasing part of many intelligent systems. The increasing age of the human population increases the burden on healthcare funds everywhere in the world. The limited movement ability with the increased risk of falling and the increased cost of rehabilitation of elderly people demands a way to optimize and improve the care for this growing portion of the population.

With the introduction of surveillance behavior understanding [22], the costs for observation of elderly hospitalized and home cared patients could potentially be reduced. It would reduce the staff expenses needed for patient observation and would give patients an improved health-care quality. There are already some approaches available in the literature that detect sudden falling of patients [23]. The introduction of the cheap and readily available 3D sensors like Kinect [24] could further improve the use of such systems by providing the hardware needed to get better scene observation and detect the human behavior through video surveillance even better.

The processing of the increased data available through the camera and 3D sensors, on the other hand, demands increased processing power. Moving the profiling and processing of the sensor data to the cloud would yield the needed increased processing power. There are already available commercial cloud solutions for Video surveillance like the one presented in [25] and many others. However, these solutions are mostly concerned with the security aspects of video surveillance and the ability of the user to monitor their own premises at any time. The lack of video surveillance solutions that allow some sort of automation in the anomaly detection is present and needs to be addressed by the community.

An example module in our system introduces a cloud based approach to behavior anomaly detection in patients. The Kinect sensor gathers data from the patient behavior throughout the day. This data is uploaded to the cloud module where a profile for each patient is created and updated in real time.

The system runs in two modes: Profiling and Detecting. During the Profiling the system generates the behavior model of the users. The behavior consists of time labeled frame sequences. These frame sequences are the relative joint coordinates obtained by the Kinect sensor. Each sample contains a time window of T seconds obtaining N frames per second. Each frame contains the tracked position of each joint of the human body. A clustering is performed on the data during the Profiling period for 4 h segments of the day: morning, noon, afternoon, evening, early night and late night. Each period of the day is given K clusters with centroids and based on the profiling data a threshold for normal behavior is given to each centroid.

After the profiling period, the system is switched to the Detecting mode. The execution subsystem compares the input to the generated clusters of the user and labels the behavior as either anomaly or normal based on the distance to the centroids of the nearest cluster. If the behavior is labeled as anomaly, the system notifies the responsible nurse or doctor by sounding the alarm. The nurse and the doctor receive the video feed and choose to react if the alarm is valid and the patient is in danger, or label the feed as false alarm. If the signal is labeled as a false alarm, the system gathers the behavior data for the patient of the period of day when the alarm was sounded and adds the data to the model, thus updating the behavior model. The system gathers all the behavior data online and updates the model for each 24-h period. If a period had a real alarm, then the data of that period is ignored.

This subsystem is intended to assist both patients and doctors. The patients receive a better health service and assistance, while medical personnel get help in the observation of patients and can care for more patients in the same time. The subsystem is still in the prototyping phase of development and is being tested on non-patient behavior.

4.3   Text to Sign Language and Voice to Text

As part of improving the home automation specifically created for deaf and hard of hearing, several modules are introduced that ease the communication and narrow the language barrier for people.

The voice-to-text subsystem enables parsing of an input sound file and is responsible for conversion of the sound patterns into textual data. The subsystem expects an input sound file and accompanying metadata in a compressed file format. The voice data is uncompressed and sent for further processing. Currently the system utilizes public voice-to-text converters like the Web Speech API from Google, but local modules can also be developed. The recognized text can then be utilized for different purposes.

We are using small inexpensive computers like RaspberryPI and accompanying microphones, recording speech samples that occur in the homes and sending them to the cloud for processing. There is a node.js application based add-on for the Kodi Entertainment System (formerly XBMC), that listens for prolonged sound sequences, records, compresses and send the data to our cloud service.

The text-to-sign language module is closely correlated to the voice to text module. The text-to-sign module is able to convert textual data to transformation parameters in a given sign language.

There are also WebGL and OpenGL ES client environments that renders predefined 3D virtual male, female and child avatar, capable of excessive range of motion and facial gestures. For controlling the avatar, the application utilizes the support of skeletal animation that is widespread in the CGI industry. A bone system is created for every avatar and is connected to the mesh using the smooth skin weights method (Fig. 5). Facial expression is important and there is a complex system of morph targets and bones for mimicking expressions of the human face. Each sign gesture for a particular language is encoded as a set of transformations that are applied to specific joints or vertices, using rotation parameters and morph-target key frames. The input text is processed for the terms and rules. The module is creating a sequence of animation data parameters in a JSON file format that is sent to the client.

Similar project have been developed in the past, implementing similar articulate gesturing approaches [26].

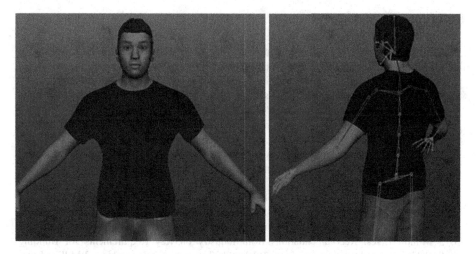

Fig. 5. The model and skeletal system of the male avatar

5   Conclusion

This paper describes a work in progress system platform and architecture with several proof-of-concept modules that offer a glimpse of what modern mobile devices utilizing the scalable and omnipresent cloud systems can offer. The core processing system along with several satellite modules are described. Text to sign language animated avatar is available for the hard of hearing people as a lightweight browser web application. Anomaly behavior of stay-at-home elderly or patients is developed using readily available MS Kinect. Voice navigation tool for the blind, not limited to GPS signals is also presented.

The initial results obtained from the modules in their early stages show promise. Combining the processing power, low price, scalability and reliability of the cloud platforms along with the evermore capable sensor available in smartphones and home environments is a combination we expect to bring forward assisted and enhanced living. The cloud environment enables easy upgrade of versions and algorithms that become instantly available to the user of the system. Transferring the burdening processing of raw sensor data to the cloud enables advanced algorithms to be used while saving battery power in the sensors and demanding insignificant processing capabilities in smartphones and other client devices. All these advantages are expected to promote this architecture and similar ones into the forefront of ambient assisted living systems.

Acknowledgment. The research is partially supported by COST Action IC1303 Algorithms, Architectures and Platforms for Enhanced Living Environments (AAPELE) and the work was partially financed by the ATCSN-15 project (Assistive Technologies for Children with Special Needs for 2014/2015) at the Faculty of Computer Science and Engineering at the Ss. Cyril and Methodius University, Skopje, R. of Macedonia.

References

1. Nussbaum, G., Veigl, C., Acedo, J., Barton, Z., Diaz, U., Drajsajtl, T., Garcia, A., Kakousis, K., Miesenberger, K., Papadopoulos, G.A., Paspallis, N., Pecyna, K., Soria-Frisch, A., Weiss, C.: AsTeRICS - toward a rapid integration construction set for assistive technologies. In: Gelderblom, S., Miesenberger, A. (eds.) Everyday Technology for Independence and Care, pp. 766–773. IOS Press, Amsterdam (2011)
2. Bashshur, R.L., Reardon, T.G., Shannon, G.W.: Telemedicine: a new health care delivery system. Annu. Rev. Public Health 21, 613–637 (2000)
3. Wade, V.A., Karnon, J., Elshaug, A.G., Hiller, J.E.: A systematic review of economic analyses of telehealth services using real time video communication. BMC Health Serv. Res. 10, 233 (2010)
4. Strategic Implementation Plan of the Pilot European Innovation Partnership on Active and Healthy Ageing - Innovation Union - European Commission. http://ec.europa.eu/research/innovation-union/index_en.cfm?section=active-healthy-ageing&pg=implementation-plan
5. 3 Million Lives: Recommendations from Industry on Key Requirements for Building Scalable Managed Services involving Telehealth, Telecare, & Telecoaching. 3 Million Lives (2012)
6. Levine, S.P., Bell, D.A., Jaros, L.A., Simpson, R.C., Koren, Y., Borenstein, J.: The NavChair assistive wheelchair navigation system. IEEE Trans. Rehabil. Eng. 7, 443–451 (1999)
7. Pires, G., Honorio, N., Lopes, C., Nunes, U., Almeida, A.T.: Autonomous wheelchair for disabled people. In: Proceedings of the IEEE International Symposium on Industrial Electronics, pp. 797–801. IEEE, Guimaraes (1997)
8. Yelamarthi, K., Haas, D., Nielsen, D., Mothersell, S.: RFID and GPS integrated navigation system for the visually impaired. In: 53rd IEEE International Midwest Symposium on Circuits and Systems (MWSCAS), pp. 1149–1152. IEEE, Seattle (2010)
9. Kim, S.Y., Cho, K.: Electronic cane usability for visually impaired people. In: Park, J.H., Kim, J., Zou, D., Lee, Y.S. (eds.) ITCS & STA 2012. LNEE, vol. 180, pp. 71–78. Springer, Heidelberg (2012)
10. Bousbia-Salah, M., Fezari, M.: A navigation tool for blind people. In: Sobh, T. (ed.) Innovations and Advanced Techniques in Computer and Information Sciences and Engineering, pp. 333–337. Springer, Netherlands, Dordrecht (2007)
11. Höfer, C.N., Karagiannis, G.: Cloud computing services: taxonomy and comparison. J. Internet Serv. Appl. 2, 81–94 (2011)
12. Grossman, R.L.: The case for cloud computing. IT Prof. 11, 23–27 (2009)
13. Calheiros, R.N., Ranjan, R., Buyya, R.: Virtual Machine Provisioning Based on Analytical Performance and QoS in Cloud Computing Environments. Presented at the September (2011)
14. Amazon Web Services (AWS) - Cloud Computing Services, http://aws.amazon.com/
15. Azure: Microsoft's Cloud Platform, http://azure.microsoft.com/en-us/
16. Google Cloud Computing, Hosting Services & Cloud Support — Google Cloud Platform, https://cloud.google.com/
17. RFC 2616 - Hypertext Transfer Protocol – HTTP/1.1, http://tools.ietf.org/html/rfc2616
18. RFC 7159 - The JavaScript Object Notation (JSON) Data Interchange Format, http://tools.ietf.org/html/rfc7159
19. RFC 6750 - The OAuth 2.0 Authorization Framework: Bearer Token Usage, http://tools.ietf.org/html/rfc6750

20. Sensors Overview | Android Developers, http://developer.android.com/guide/topics/sensors/sensors_overview.html
21. Ruotsalainen, L., Kuusniemi, H., Chen, R.: Visual-aided two-dimensional pedestrian indoor navigation with a smartphone. J. Glob. Position. Syst. **10**, 11–18 (2011)
22. Borges, P.V.K., Conci, N., Cavallaro, A.: Video-based human behavior understanding: a survey. IEEE Trans. Circuits Syst. Video Technol. **23**, 1993–2008 (2013)
23. Rougier, C., Meunier, J., St-Arnaud, A., Rousseau, J.: Fall detection from human shape and motion history using video surveillance. Presented at the 2007
24. Kinect for Xbox One, http://www.xbox.com/en-US/xbox-one/accessories/kinect-for-xbox-one
25. Cloud Video Surveillance, http://www.ivideon.com/
26. Elliott, R., Glauert, J.R.W., Kennaway, J.R., Marshall, I.: The development of language processing support for the ViSiCAST project. In: Proceedings of the Fourth International ACM Conference on Assistive Technologies, pp. 101–108. ACM Press, Arlington (2000)

AAL: Human Interaction Technologies

Phylogenetic Introduction to Phraseology

Multimodal Interaction in a Elderly-Friendly Smart Home: A Case Study

Susanna Spinsante[(✉)], Enea Cippitelli, Adelmo De Santis, Ennio Gambi,
Samuele Gasparrini, Laura Montanini, and Laura Raffaeli

Department of Information Engineering, Marche Polytechnic University,
Ancona, Italy
s.spinsante@univpm.it,
http://www.tlc.dii.univpm.it

Abstract. This paper discusses different and multimodal user-system interfaces proposed in the framework of a smart home designed to support the independent living of elderly and frail users. It is shown how different technologies and solutions may be complemented and integrated to provide effective interaction both for routine activities of daily living and anomalous situations.

Keywords: Multimodal interaction · Smart TV · Near Field Communication · Touchscreen · Depth sensor

1 Introduction

Population aging is more and more a global fact, that results from public health and medical progresses against diseases and injures, but also represents one of the most challenging phenomena that families, states and communities have to face. The need of sustaining the relevant part of population represented by older adults, from a social and an economical point of view, asks for new approaches: a market segment including people aged 50 and older emerges, the so-called "gray market" or "silver market", challenging companies and societies [1] with new requests and needs. Within this market, an important role is expected to be played by assistive technologies to help older people to maintain their ability in performing the activities of daily living (ADLs) and, therefore, their independence. Ambient Assisted Living (AAL) and Ambient Intelligence (AI) will support new generations of older adults, for longer and improved quality living. Several public institutions, at a national and wider level, are carrying on specific initiatives to promote the flourishing of new actors in the silver market, to create sustainable economic systems able to offer products, services and solutions to face the emerging needs.

In this scenario, this paper presents the approach to multimodal user-system interaction adopted in the framework of an AAL architecture designed for a elderly-friendly smart home. Such an architecture, named TRASPARENTE[1]

---

[1] The acronym TRASPARENTE means *transparent* and stands for "assistive network technologies for residential autonomy in the silver age".

© Institute for Computer Sciences, Social Informatics and Telecommunications Engineering 2015
R. Agüero et al. (Eds.): MONAMI 2014, LNICST 141, pp. 373–386, 2015.
DOI: 10.1007/978-3-319-16292-8_27

covers several aspects of the home living, such as independent living, home security, health monitoring and environmental control. It is one of the ongoing projects supported through an action co-funded by the Italian Marche Region administration, for the development and implementation of AAL integrated platforms, to monitor ADLs and detect any abnormal behavior that may represent a danger, or some kind of symptoms of an incipient disease.

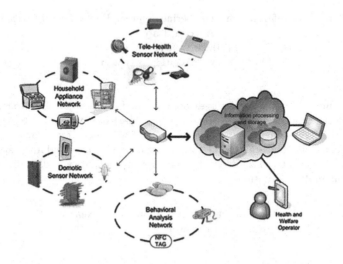

Fig. 1. Domains in the TRASPARENTE architecture.

The TRASPARENTE architecture is composed by several sub-systems related to different domains, as shown in Fig. 1: home automation, behavior detection, telemedicine, human-system interfaces. Each subsystem has its own devices generating specific data, all managed by centralized server applications that provide a unique integrated platform for data processing. Each element needs to collect proper data from a wide range of heterogeneous sensors, differing for type, transmission and network technologies (Controller Area Network - CAN - bus, Ethernet, Wi-Fi, Wireless SubGHz), processing capabilities, and storage. The processing operations are performed by the local server, according to the functionalities implemented. This approach builds upon previous research experiences [2], and is shared by the industrial partners involved within the project. In the TRASPARENTE architecture, several interfaces are provided to support both user driven and event driven interaction, and to meet the needs of different users and conditions. Smart TVs, portable touchscreen devices, Near Field Communication (NFC) devices, and depth sensors are used to enable user interaction with the system, to send commands, to acquire data, to request information. The data flow is bidirectional and involves mostly the local Wi-Fi and Ethernet networks. Data are formatted as JavaScript Object Notation (JSON) elements by higher-level applications; the local server replies with JSON objects to any client application request, regardless of the original data format.

The paper is organized as follows: Sect. 2 presents the technological solutions adopted for supporting user-driven interaction within the reference architecture, whereas Sect. 3 discusses how event-based interaction is managed within the system. Preliminary evaluations of the selected solutions are provided in Sect. 4; finally, Sect. 5 draws the main conclusion of the paper.

2   User Driven Interaction

This section presents the technological solutions designed and implemented to support user driven interaction, i.e. all those actions explicitly requested and performed by the user, towards any of the architecture domains and sub-systems.

2.1   Smart TV Interface

Among the several devices supporting user driven interaction, the choice of the smart TV is motivated by the usually limited familiarity of elderly with personal computers or portable devices, the need for simplified and intuitive controllers, and for technology that overcomes visual and hearing impairments. The TV is one of the most common and familiar home appliances, so it is expected that the learning process can be taken up positively. The commercial spreading of smart TV is increasing, and other projects may be found that employ this platform to design applications for elderly, such as social TV applications [3,4].

In TRASPARENTE, the smart TV application enables functions for control and monitoring, and for issuing requests for information, by addressing a specific service exposed by the local server. The smart TV and the local server are connected to the same home network, via Ethernet or Wi-Fi, and communication is performed according to the HyperText Transfer Protocol (HTTP). When launched for the first time, the application needs to download the system configuration file from the server, which is saved in a common memory area of the smart TV, to be used later for all the functionalities. Once the system configuration is available, the application may issue proper command instructions to the server, that processes the request and forwards it to the correct device (via CAN bus or any other technology), to execute the corresponding action.

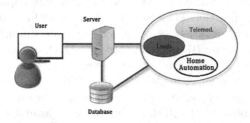

Fig. 2. Server-centric communication model in the proposed architecture.

The smart TV application can be also used to show information about the power consumption of the appliances, being these data acquired periodically by meter nodes, and stored in specific databases. Any request towards databases is not issued directly, but through the server application, as shown in Fig. 2. The same procedure applies to telemedicine-related services, such as consultation of the values collected by some electro-medical devices. A further functionality provides the visualization of automatic reminders for drugs assumption on the TV screen. It is activated when the application is launched, so while the user is watching TV, a pop-up window appears in a corner of the screen at the time of drug intake, indicating name, and quantity of the assumption. The reminders list is stored in a database and can be managed through the application itself.

To ensure the user's satisfaction and willingness of using the application provided, some basic rules [5] have been considered in the design of the smart TV application, dealing with graphic appearance and feedback on user's actions: contents have been organized for an efficient utilization of the available screen area; text size, background, and icons have been properly selected to better identify the available functionalities. Other aspects of basic importance are the insertion of short clear instructions to guide the user, and a robust design with respect to possible input errors and exceptions. Pop-up messages are shown to notify the user about the outcomes of the different operations, to identify possible problems and suggest a solution. Finally, for smart TV equipments supporting voice recognition, it is possible to define a set of custom commands and associate them to the corresponding browsing or control functions.

2.2 Portable Interfaces

The touchscreen-based interaction is very simple, as it does not require an advanced mental model and features a direct approach: the input device is also the output device. Typically, touchscreen interfaces do not require special motor skills [6], but a careful and accurate design. The touchscreen interface designed for TRASPARENTE runs both on tablets and smartphones: smartphones feature great portability, but, due to the small size of the screen, do not fit with subjects affected by visual impairments or poor motor skills. Tablets represent a good compromise between mobility and acceptable screen size.

The application runs on Android O.S. versions later than 3.0 (Honeycomb), released in 2011 and optimized for tablets. The interface supports all the control and monitoring functionalities for the smart home in a single application, providing the user with a variety of services designed to simplify his life. Specifically, it allows the user to: (i) send commands to the home automation system; (ii) display the status of specific subsystems (e.g. lights, sensors, etc.); (iii) monitor the energy consumption of loads (appliances); (iv) display reminders for the subject's drug therapy; (v) start audio/video communication sessions via Session Initiation Protocol (SIP). All these functions are available through a single menu. As for the smart TV interface, control and monitoring rely on a central processing server, accessed on a Wi-Fi link, once the system configuration is downloaded from the server; through HTTP messages, on/off light switching, opening/closing of blinds and windows, and specific scenarios can be controlled. An initial check on the network connection is executed, and dialog boxes for notifications are provided at the application start. A service running in background is responsible for periodically interrogating the central database, using the Wi-Fi connection, to monitor the patient's drug therapy and send reminders to the user when it is time to take medications. The service uses pop-ups, rather than notifications, to alert the user, in order to maintain a graphical uniformity with the Smart TV application presented above.

Finally, the portable device application supports audio/video communication sessions via SIP. This functionality is proposed as a solution for people with mobility problems, to perform routine tasks such as answering the entry-phone or opening the door. It is based on an existing open-source application (in its beta phase), called *csipsimple* [7], selected for the stability of its SIP stack [8]. The original application has been modified to integrate the video player and the Open Graphics Library (OpenGL) [9] library, to support video connection with the video entry-phone, not originally provided. The entry-phone call is delivered to all the portable devices on the Wireless Local Area Network (WLAN), so the user can see who is calling anywhere he is, and decide to answer, refuse or open the door. The video-calling system architecture is shown in Fig. 3.

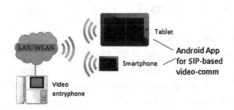

Fig. 3. Video-calling system architecture.

The peculiarity of portable touchscreen devices requires an adequate design of the graphical user interface, trying, however, to maintain consistency with the style adopted for the smart TV application. Some specific guidelines for the interaction have been elaborated, that cover four main aspects:

- Target elements design: the size of buttons, graphics and target elements has a great influence on the interaction accuracy [10]. It is expected, therefore, to use buttons of at least 9.2 mm size for smartphones, and even larger for tablets. Once the target has been captured, a visual or acoustic feedback to the user is generated.
- Graphic elements design: to facilitate the understanding of contents, each button has an icon and a text label that specifies its meaning. The graphics is simple and intuitive, there are no animations.
- Navigation: during navigation it is important to keep the user always able to know "where he is"; for this reason, each page features a title and an additional help button to provide navigation aid.

– Layout design: due limited screen size, the use of text is minimal, preferring key words to long sentences.

2.3 NFC Interface

The use of NFC to simplify user interaction and management of more complex procedures has been already addressed in the literature [11–13]. NFC is not designed to transfer large amounts of data, but rather to provide a quick and easy-to-implement wireless communication, which can serve as a bridge between already existing services, or may allow the creation of new specific types of services. In TRASPARENTE, the use of NFC technology is twofold. The former is a service to display on the TV screen the nutritional values of food, or the indications about drugs. An NFC reader detects passive tags placed in foods and drugs boxes, and sends a message to the smart TV application. The message contains a two-digit code to distinguish food from drug, and a code to identify the specific product and search for the corresponding information in the proper database. In case of a drug, the expiry date is also included. The resulting message structure is:

CODE - ID, for food;

CODE - EXPIRYDATE - ID, for drugs.

The centralized server hosts a local database management system to store data from the different subsystems. For the nutrition-related service, a table contains the amounts of carbohydrate, protein, salt, vitamins, etc. for hundreds of foods. For each drug, 4 fields are extracted: name, instructions, contraindications, and dosage. Data saved in the NFC tag follow the NFC Data Exchange Format (NDEF) protocol, so the board has to read the tag, convert the values to a string, and forward it to the smart TV application through a HTTP POST request. Once received the message, the TV application queries the local database and displays the results. This procedure is represented in Fig. 4.

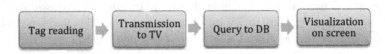

Fig. 4. Flow of operations to show product (food or drug) information from the NFC-based interaction.

The latter service controls the home automation system by means of a so-called Smart Panel, designed to provide a pictorial and instantaneous representation of the commands, that may be issued by simply tapping the NFC reader close to the panel itself. Each graphic element in the panel is coupled to a tag. Irrespective of the specific format chosen for the panel, it supports both single and multiple commands: a single command (single control) causes a state change in a single device of the home automation system, and may be composed either through single and multiple tag readings. A multiple command (scenery control) implements a so-called *scenario*, i.e. it causes a state change in several devices and equipments managed by the home automation system, up to a whole room or the whole building. The Smart Panel has been designed in different versions, as shown in Figs. 5 (a) and (b), providing the same set of multiple commands for scenery control, but differing in the section related to single commands. They also provide an info tag, describing how to use the home automation system. The supported multiple commands are: (i) *Goodbye Home*: turns off all the lights, closes all the shutters and windows. It pilots habitual actions performed when a user leaves the home; (ii) *Welcome Home - Night*: turns on the lights of the hall, the living room, and the kitchen. It pilots habitual actions carried out when a user come back home during the night; (iii) *Welcome Home - Day*: raises all dampers. It pilots habitual actions carried out when a user enters the home during the day; (iv) *Good Morning*: turns up the shutters in the kitchen, the bathroom, and the dining room. It pilots habitual actions performed when a user wakes up in the morning.

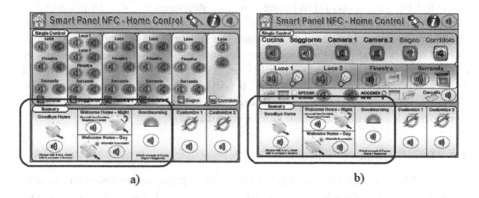

Fig. 5. Different versions of the Smart Panel.

3 Event Based Interaction

In the TRASPARENTE architecture, proper solutions are used to handle event based interaction, i.e. those situations in which the system has to react to some conditions that are not explicitly determined by the user, but result from anomalous or unexpected events. The most innovative contribution relies in the adoption of a consumer device, the Kinect by Microsoft, to implement both an automatic fall detection system, and a drink intake monitoring application.

3.1 Automatic Fall Detection

The fall event is one of the leading cause of injury for older adults: studies have shown that 33 % of people over 65 years experience a fall each year [14]. A fall detection solution could limit the amount of time that the person remains on the floor and reduce the onset of complications. Fall detection methods may resort to three approaches [15]: wearable device based, ambience sensor based, and vision based. The last one included Red Green Blue (RGB) cameras only until a few years ago, but nowadays new low-cost devices have enabled different opportunities, such as the Microsoft Kinect depth-based sensor. Moreover, depth cameras increase the acceptability of AAL solutions, because people are not immediately recognisable from the depth maps [16].

The solution proposed exploits raw depth information from a Kinect device positioned on the room ceiling, to identify people and detect if a fall occurs. Although some native skeleton models are available for Kinect, they are inoperable when the sensor is in top location. A new approach is proposed, based on the following processing steps: (i) preprocessing and segmentation; (ii) distinguish object phase; (iii) identification and tracking of people. First, the raw depth frame is processed to prepare data for subsequent steps. A reference frame, created when the system is switched on, is exploited to extract the foreground scene. The distinguish objects phase classifies different groups of pixels, performing object identification and indexing. The last step analyses objects features and recognizes if people are present. It mainly evaluates three features, starting from the point at the minimum distance from the sensor, for each object: (i) head-ground distance gap; (ii) head-shoulder distance gap; (iii) head size. If a cluster of pixels verifies all the previous conditions, it is labeled as a person and tracked in the subsequent frames. The fall event is notified when the distance value of the central point associated to the person exceeds an adaptive threshold. A detailed description of the entire solution can be found in [17].

3.2   Drink Intake Monitoring

In the AAL scenario, dietary habits monitoring is an active research branch. Thanks to the advances in image sensors and computer vision, today it is possible to design sophisticated algorithms to automatically recognize the patient behaviors. In [18], the consequences of a not sufficient assimilation of water are discussed. An automatic solution may overcome the problem. In the proposed application, Kinect is placed on the room ceiling, at a distance of 3 m from the floor. A model, characterized by 17 joints, is automatically fitted to the person shape. At each frame, the system monitors the distances between head and hands, to identify a *drink intake* action. Related works, such as [19,20], follow the same idea but with a camera placed in front of the patient.

The algorithm includes an initial phase of preprocessing operations applied to the raw depth frame, to allow an efficient extraction of the blob associated to the person. Then, using the depth sensor intrinsic parameters, the depth region of interest is transformed in a Point Cloud (PC), from the 2D frame domain ($[row$ $column$ $distance]$) to a 3D representation ($[x$ y $z]$). An unsupervised machine learning algorithm, named Self Organizing Map (SOM) [21], takes as input the PC, to provide the coordinates of 17 joints associated to the person. The SOM fits the predefined model, visible in Fig. 6, with the specific PC distribution.

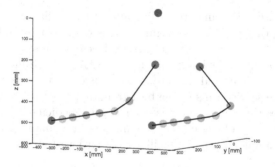

Fig. 6. Model of the person for the drink intake monitoring application.

This process is iterated for each frame, to manage the different aspect ratio of different human bodies.

Differently from supervised neural network solution, this method does not require any learning phase and it is a relevant advantage in AAL solutions. Before the first use of the SOM, it is necessary to superimpose the initial model to the PC, according to the orientation of the person into the scene. The subject to monitor, indeed, is free to sit at any side of the table, so the orientation issue must be taken into account by the system. Starting from the recognition of the table in the depth frame, and using the line version of Hough transform [22], the algorithm is able to rotate the model in the appropriate direction. Dishes and glasses are too much tiny or small to be identifiable in the depth frame, so the RGB stream is used to overcome this limitation. Taking into account that these objects have usually a specific shape, the circular version of the Hough transform [23] is exploited. Finally, to allow data fusion of depth and RGB streams, a mapping algorithm that compensates the different camera's point of views is applied. This operation ends with the association of an RGB pixel to the corresponding one in the depth frame [24].

4   Preliminary Evaluations

Applications for smart TV and portable devices have essentially the same structure and enable access to the same services, however the interaction to the system using each tool is different. Referring to the smart TV interface, interaction is mainly supported by the use of the TV remote controller. On one hand, this brings a number of advantages, related to the familiarity for all categories of users. On the other hand, it is not a practical device to use, when dealing with operations that require many steps, such as text input, or browsing the available contents. These limitations have been considered during the design stage, to make the interaction as simple as possible.

The touch-based interaction takes into account the specific needs of an elderly user. A study by Apted *et al.* [25] examined how older people interact through single and multi touch gestures. The results show that older users need a time of learning and interaction understanding almost twice than younger users, then recovered during the use of the system. For this reason the usability criteria set out in Sect. 2.2 have been met. At the current development stage, the application for touchscreen portable devices is partially available. The functionality related to drug therapy is ready and numerous tests have been performed to evaluate its reliability. The service runs in the background at the start of the device, and effectively notifies the user when it is time to take medicines, while an Android *activity* allows him to add/edit/delete reminders in a simple and intuitive way (as shown, for example, in Fig. 7), facilitating text insertion by auto-completion.

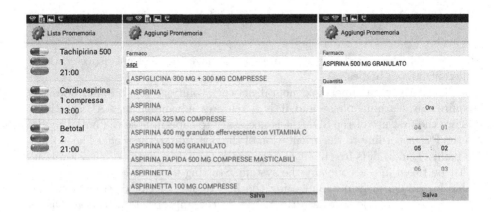

Fig. 7. Drugs management application on Android device

Part of the application that enables video calls between different SIP clients is also available and functioning (see Fig. 8). Currently, video entry-phone/tablet, and tablet/tablet calls are enabled. The system works properly, allows to start/ close communication, sending the audio and video stream, and to open the entrance door through a relay. The development of the remaining functions, and their integration in a single application, are ongoing.

The complete architecture is at a developing stage, so not all the functions designed have been implemented yet. A test environment has been set up in the laboratory, where the single parts of the architecture are going to be gradually integrated. As for the smart TV interface, some of the single functionalities have been tested individually: (i) request and storage of the system configuration; (ii) home automation system control; (iii) reminders visualization and management; (iv) request and visualization of medical parameters. In the future, all the functions will be implemented and merged in a single application for the overall validation.

The adoption of NFC both to request information on food and drugs, and to control the home automation system, simplifies the user interaction, since it just requires to tap the reader near to the NFC tag area. The communication among NFC devices, local server, and the involved subsystems, has been

Fig. 8. Video-calling application on Android tablet: the video entry-phone is calling.

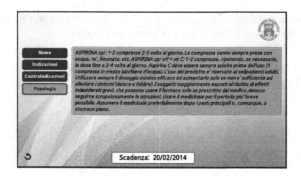

Fig. 9. A page of the smart TV application showing medicine dosage.

successfully tested. Figure 9 shows information about drug dosage obtained from the database, corresponding to a sample medicine.

The fall detection solution provides the distance between the point associated to the person and the sensor, positioned on the ceiling. Low depth values represent a standing person while high distances denote a fall. Figure 10(a) shows the values of this distance, for each frame where a person is identified. When the evaluated depth overcomes the threshold of 2600 mm, which is automatically tuned considering the distance between the sensor and the floor, the system detects a fall. Looking at Fig. 10(a) a person who enters the scene, simulates a fall, and raises again before exiting can be noticed. Figure 10(b) shows the depth map for one of the frames where a fall occurred (red spot in Fig. 10(a)), where the point associated to the person is the magenta spot.

For the food intake monitoring, the algorithm has been tested on a database of 17 different situations, for a total of 4800 depth frames. The test users, in good health, are between 21 and 38 years old. In all the realizations the drink intake action is always recognized (31 out of 31) with a simple threshold of 250 mm applied to the distance between head and hands. Figure 11(a) shows the PC, for the 300-th frame, of a person drinking, and the corresponding model calculated by the algorithm described above. Figure 11(b) depicts the distance between head and left hand for each frame. As visible in the graph, in the frame

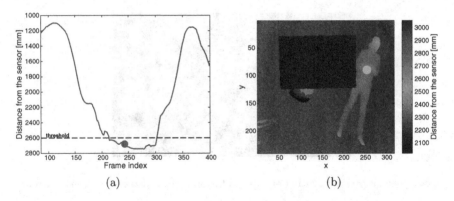

Fig. 10. (a) Distance values of the point associated to the person during a simulated fall, (b) depth map with a fallen person (Color figure online).

interval 260:330 this distance reaches a minimum, in particular it equals 169 mm at the 300-*th* frame. Ongoing improvements of the algorithm are finalized to:

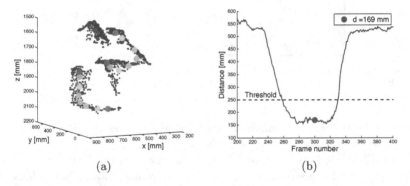

Fig. 11. (a) PC with superimposed the skeleton model for the 300-*th* frame, and (b) distance between head and left hand for all frames.

- improve the recognition of specific objects such as glasses and dishes;
- adopt more robust techniques to recognize the drink intake action, than the simple threshold-based solution described above;
- populate the current database of test users to confirm the promising results described above.

5 Conclusion

The paper presented the ongoing activities of an experimental research project aimed at designing and prototyping an assistive architecture for elderly-friendly smart homes. Focus has been put on the different interfaces the architecture will include, to handle both user driven and event driven interaction. They are based on different technologies but, when possible, implement a common design (as for the smart TV and portable devices), or exploit consumer devices (such as Kinect or NFC tags and readers) in innovative applications. Preliminary tests and evaluations on the selected interfaces provided promising results, upon which further developments are being carried out.

Acknowledgment. This work was partially supported by the Regione Marche - INRCA project "Casa intelligente per una longevita' attiva ed indipendente dell'anziano" (DGR 1464, 7/11/2011). The authors would also like to acknowledge the contribution of the COST Action IC1303 - AAPELE, Architectures, Algorithms and Platforms for Enhanced Living Environments. The authors alone are responsible for the content.

References

1. Kohlbacher, F., Herstatt, C. (eds.): The Silver Market Phenomenon - Marketing and Innovation in the Aging Society. Springer, New York (2011)
2. Spinsante, S., Gambi, E.: Remote health monitoring by OSGi technology and digital TV integration. IEEE Trans. Cons. Elect. **58**(4), 1434–1441 (2012)
3. de Abreu, J.F., Almeida, P., Afonso, J., Silva, T., Dias, R.: Participatory design of a social TV application for senior citizens – the iNeighbour TV project. In: Cruz-Cunha, M.M., Varajão, J., Powell, P., Martinho, R. (eds.) CENTERIS 2011, Part III. CCIS, vol. 221, pp. 49–58. Springer, Heidelberg (2011)
4. Alaoui, M., Lewkowicz, M.: A LivingLab approach to involve elderly in the design of smart TV applications offering communication services. In: 5th International Conference, OCSC 2013, Held as Part of HCI International 2013, Las Vegas, NV, USA (2013)
5. Nielsen, J.: Traditional dialog design applied to modern user interfaces. Commun. ACM **33**(10), 109–118 (1990)
6. Wood, E., Willoughby, T., Rushing, A., Bechtel, L., Gilbert, J.: Use of computer input devices by older adults. J. Appl. Gerontol. **24**(5), 419–438 (2005)
7. csipsimple - SIP application for android devices - google project hosting. http://code.google.com/p/csipsimple
8. PJSIP - open source SIP, media, and NAT traversal library. http://www.pjsip.org
9. OpenGL - the industry standard for high performance graphics. http://www.opengl.org
10. Parhi, P., Karlson, A.K., Bederson, B.B.: Target size study for one-handed thumb use on small touchscreen devices. In: Proceedings of 8th Conference on Human-computer Interaction with Mobile Devices and Services (2006)
11. Vergara, M., Daz-Helln, P., Fontecha, J., Hervas, R., Sanchez-Barba, C., Fuentes, C., Bravo, J.: Mobile prescription: an NFC-based proposal for AAL. In: Proceedings of 2nd International Workshop on NFC (2010)
12. Isomursu, M., Ervasti, M., Tormanen, V.: Medication management support for vision impaired elderly: scenarios and technological possibilities. In: Proceedings of 2nd International Symposium on Applied Sciences in Biomedical and Communication Technologies, pp. 1–6 (2009)
13. Rashid, O., Coulton, P., Bird, W.: Using NFC to support and encourage green exercise. In: Proceedings of 2nd International Conference on Pervasive Computing Technologies for Healthcare, Tampere, Finland (2008)

14. Centers for Disease Control and Prevention: Falls Among Older Adults: An Overview (2013)
15. Mubashir, M., Shao, L., Seed, L.: A survey on fall detection: principles and approaches. Neurocomputing **100**, 144–152 (2013). Special issue: Behaviours in video
16. Demiris, G., Parker Oliver, D., Giger, J., Skubic, M., Rantz, M.: Older adults' privacy considerations for vision based recognition methods of eldercare applications. Technol. Health Care **17**(1), 41–48 (2009)
17. Gasparrini, S., Cippitelli, E., Spinsante, S., Gambi, E.: A depth-based fall detection system using a kinect® sensor. Sensors **14**(2), 2756–2775 (2014). doi:10.3390/s140202756. http://www.mdpi.com/1424-8220/14/2/2756
18. Scales, K., Pilsworth, J.: The importance of fluid balance in clinical practice. Nurs. Stand. **22**, 50–57 (2008)
19. Haker, M., Böhme, M., Martinetz, T., Barth, E.: Self-organizing maps for pose estimation with a time-of-flight camera. In: Kolb, A., Koch, R. (eds.) Dyn3D 2009. LNCS, vol. 5742, pp. 142–153. Springer, Heidelberg (2009)
20. Klingner, M., Hellbach S., Kstner M., Villmann T., Bhme H.J.: Modeling human movements with self organizing maps using adaptive metrics. In: Proceedings of Workshop New Challenges in Neural Computation 2012 (2012)
21. Kohonen, T.: The self-organizing map. Proc. IEEE **78**, 1464–1480 (1990)
22. Duda, R.O., Hart, P.E.: Use of the hough transformation to detect lines and curves in pictures. Commun. ACM. **15**, 11–15 (1972)
23. Hough circle transform, OpenCV. http://docs.opencv.org/doc/tutorials/imgproc/imgtrans/hough_circle/hough_circle.html
24. Herrera, C.D., Kannala, J., Heikkilä, J.: Joint depth and color camera calibration with distortion correction. IEEE Trans. Pattern Anal. Mach. Intell. **34**, 2058–2064 (2012)
25. Apted, T., Kay, J., Quigley, A.: Tabletop sharing of digital photographs for the elderly. In: Proceedings of the SIGCHI Conference on Human Factors in Computing Systems, New York (2006)

Analysis of Vehicular Storage and Dissemination Services Based on Floating Content

Mihai Ciocan[1], Ciprian Dobre[1]([⊠]), Valentin Cristea[1],
Constandinos X. Mavromoustakis[2], and George Mastorakis[3]

[1] Faculty of Automatic Control and Computers, University Politehnica of Bucharest,
313, Splaiul Independentei, 060042 Bucharest, Romania
mihai.ciocan@cti.pub.ro
{ciprian.dobre,valentin.cristea}@cs.pub.ro
[2] Department of Computer Science, University of Nicosia,
46 Makedonitissas Avenue, 1700 Nicosia, Cyprus
mavromoustakis.c@unic.ac.cy
[3] Technological Educational Institute of Crete, Estavromenos,
71500, Heraklion, Crete, Greece
gmastorakis@staff.teicrete.gr

Abstract. Floating Content is an attractive model for deploying and sharing information between mobile devices in a completely decentralized manner. For vehicular city-scale applications, the model has many applications. In this paper we conduct an analysis of the feasibility of such a model to support the sharing and dissemination of localized information, using realistic mobility traces in two different cities. As our experimental results reveal, the feasibility in urban environments is influenced by several factors. A high density inside the anchor location sustain the life of the information regardless the radius size. Having a big radius may cluster more vehicles and thus, increases the probability of floating. The radio range can also affect information sharing. A small radio range compared to the information availability range may prevent the application to spread content in the entire zone and rely on vehicle density. For all these, we provide experimental evidence.

Keywords: Floating content · Collaborative sharing · Vehicular networks · Mobile data dissemination

1 Introduction

Mobile devices (i.e., smartphones, smart tablets, etc.) have become a staple of our society. Today, thanks to smartphone sensors and the possibility to combine their capabilities over advanced wireless technologies, information in the form of context becomes common input for applications running in our hand. Mobile applications can offer navigation in unfamilar places (e.g., Google Maps, Waze), or can socially connect people (i.e., Facebook, Twitter).

© Institute for Computer Sciences, Social Informatics and Telecommunications Engineering 2015
R. Agüero et al. (Eds.): MONAMI 2014, LNICST 141, pp. 387–400, 2015.
DOI: 10.1007/978-3-319-16292-8_28

The evolution of location-aware mobile technology, in particular, has greatly influenced the mobile application industry. Facebook Messenger provides the users with the location of their communication partners. Its latest feature, Nearby Friends, sends notifications when the user comes within a short distance of a friend (if he chooses to share his location). Other location-aware applications tackle the increasing curiosity people have on others' activities (e.g., Tiner or Skout facilitate an interaction with nearby strangers).

Prior to the worldwide spread of smartphones, location was mainly used for space orientation. Applications such as Google Maps, Google Earth or Waze, can display information around the current position of the user. But, although mobiles devices have bigger storage sizes today, they are still limited when storing big amount of map data. Thus, navigators generally have to rely on the data network services to provide the user with detailed geographical views. However, recently navigation services have become social, and act as real communities where people share information with certain location importance. Maps support point-of-interest tagging, photo and text description, and even online street navigation. They are able to share information in real time.

Traditional social network applications (i.e., Facebook, LinkedIn) dependent on a centralized infrastructure to overcome distances and connect people located around the world. But a centralized infrastructure can introduce issues regarding content and location relevance and security [1]: (i) *location privacy* concerns (an application may need to provide the user with the exact location); (ii) *content privacy* issues (shared information can be stored by a private company, and be subject to censorship); (iii) *connectivity* to the infrastructure (can be a problem for traveling users who may have to deal with high roaming charges and unavailability of data services); (iv) *geographic validity* (locally relevant shared content may be of little interest to the rest of the world); (v) *temporal validity* concerns (shared content might be only valid for a limited amount of time); (vi) *user identification* (used to create some sense of responsibility towards the service provider, it can also raise a privacy issue since the shared information is associated with the owner, and companies can futher give access to their records to security agencies).

To respond to such problems, smart cities of tomorrow will probably rely on the use of a *content sharing service*, entirely dependent on mobile devices in the vicinity, and that will probabyl use principles of opportunistic networking [9]. Bringing social media and content sharing into ad-hoc networks seems the natural choice towards the next frontier in mobile industry [10].

The second context for the work being presented in this paper relates to *vehicle-to-vehicle wireless communication*. Research in advanced communication infrastructures at city-level has advanced today towards new applications for providing advanced levels of safety, entertainment and comfortable driving to a huge number of individuals that use vehicles on the roads every day [1]. Today car manufacturers introduce wireless communication equipment in their cars, and provide services designed to help drivers in case of accidents or collisions (e.g., Volvo introduced "Volvo on Call", and BMW their "BMW Assist" services).

However, most implementations of such services rely on a centralized infrastructure. Naturally, the next step would be to modify the equipment in order to make use of inter-vehicle communication, a type of ad-hoc network which mainly uses broadcast as a method of information distribution [10]. The only limitations vehicles may have are the available transmission capacity which depends on the rate and the size of the information broadcasted.

The biggest challenge, still, with such solutions, is how to *make the information stay alive and "float"*, to achieve the main purpose of the sharing process which is to reach a high number of vehicles. In this paper we study the feasibility of having such a distributed storage and dissemination service, addressed to overcome all the mentioned before problems.

We present an analysis of the floating content model to provide the innovative means to socially connect together participants within the city of tomorrow, and where storage and dissemination services on top of vehicular ad hoc networks will provide the means for AAL/ELE applications to connect together people and allow them to interact towards a common goal, such as for example monitor their well-beings, or discover in real-time vital location-based information such as accident in front, or the location of the nearby hospital.

The rest of the paper is organized as follows. First, we present the adaptation of a Floating Content model, towards a realistic vehicular mobility scenario. In Sect. 3 we present implementation details for this model, followed in Sect. 4 by experimental results. Finally, Sect. 5 presents conclusions and future work.

2 Floating Content

Our experiments are based on a model of sharing information originally proposed in [7]. Here, we extend this model with an analytical construct designed to describe the evolution of information over time, and add criticality conditions, adapted for the case of a vehicular ad hoc network. We consider a network that uses intermittent connectivity (a complete path cannot be established apriori to transmission from source to destination; vehicles can forward messages when they meet, one hop at a time, until the data eventually reach the destination) and forwarding mechanisms (to select the appropriate next hop, and avoid epidemic solutions because of possible congestion over the network) to facilitate communication.

2.1 Service Model

We assume users to be mobile nodes who are interested in the content generated by other nodes. They use mobile devices able to handle the amount of data being exchanged during their participation in the ad-hoc network. Also, we assume a completely decentralized storage/dissemination infrastructure.

We assume nodes are uniformly distributed and travel independently, with a constant speed. We also assume mobile devices are equipped with wireless interfaces (Bluetooth or WLAN) to enable network communication. Analysis of performance for 802.11p standard displayed in [3] have shown that using a bitrate of 6 Mbps and a payload of 500 bytes yields a delivery rate of up to 80 %. This indicates the acceptable reliability and performance of IEEE 802.11p, and confirms the viability of floating up to several megabytes of data (from 10 KB for text messages to 10 MB for photos). This standard is used also in our simulations, discussed further on. Making intuitive judgements, we can determine that contacts cannot last more than several tens of seconds, in vehicle case even less due to their high speeds.

The devices also need to be equipped with accurate systems to determine their position (e.g. using GPS tracking, cellular base stations, cell tower triangulations using WLAN access points or Wi-fi tracking). Many factors need to be considered, like accuracy needed, battery consumption etc. In order to provide the best location based service, the equipment must acquire the most accurate location coordinates. Finally, nodes need to synchronize their clock time so that users can process exchanged information (this can be done with the help of GPS or cellular networks).

2.2   System Operation

As [7] presents, a node generates the information I, which has a size of $s(I)$ and a defined lifetime (Time to Live, or TTL, determining a validity period for the information, before it becomes obsolete). The information is tagged with the anchor zone, defined by its geo-located center P and two radii (see Fig. 1): r identifies the *replication range*, inside which nodes replicate the information to other nodes they meet on their way, and a defines the *availability range* inside which the information is still stored with limited probability. These parameters are specific for each unit of information, and are defined by the creator of each

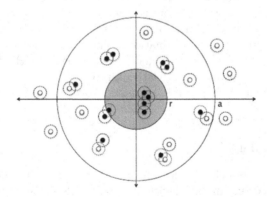

Fig. 1. Moving nodes inside an anchor zone. Black nodes are information-carrying nodes, white nodes will eventually get the information from the black ones. The probability of a node carrying an item tends to 1 inside the replication zone, and decreases until reaching an availability distance a after which no more copies are found (after [7]).

particular message. Outside the availability zone there exist no copy of the item in the node data storage.

When two nodes meet in the anchor zone defined for a particular data, they share it. As such, all nodes inside the anchor zone should have a copy of the item (obtained while meeting other nodes already in the anchor zone), while nodes which are leaving the anchor can remove it at their own discretion. Let us consider two nodes A and B that meet. Node A does have an item I tagged with an anchor zone centered in point P and radii a and r. Let h be the distance of node A from the center P. When node A meets node B, item I gets replicated to B with the probability $p_r(h)$:

$$p_r(h) = \begin{cases} 1 & \text{if } h \leq r \\ R(h) & \text{if } r < h \leq a \\ 0 & \text{otherwise} \end{cases}$$

$R(h)$ is a decreasing function which determines the probability of replication between the outer replication border and the availability border of the anchor zone. The area between *replication range* and *availability range* acts as a buffer zone, that prevents immediate deletion of items. As shown in [7] and because of simplicity and more traceability, in our evaluation we assume no buffer zone.

2.3 Analysis of the Floating Content Model

The features of floating content offer exciting opportunities, but also introduces problems. The major challenge is that the communications service makes no guarantees that data will stay around until its lifetime expires. For example, during the night the content is expected to disappear. People's daily activities cause density fluctuations over the day, which may be a problem for the residing information in certain places. Thus, the information is expected to remain available for no more than a few hours.

Multiple use cases can emerge from the floating content concept. One of them can use infrastructure-less local data availability for advertising or selling goods. This type of market could have a dynamic catalog of available merchandise, being able to operate updates on the fly. Another one is information sharing between tourists and visitors about local attractions, or notifications about services a hotel is offering. Spreading news and keeping it localized, time-bounded and most important anonymous, can be another use case of floating content for which best-effort operation perfectly suits the needs.

Overall, floating content can be used in many ways, considering two important aspects of it. First, floating information is location-aware, so developers should consider multiple data-oriented architectures. The second aspect is that spreading the information while containing it to an anchor zone relies on a best effort approach, a problem which the Internet infrastructure solves with repair mechanisms that can recover lost packets. In Floating Content, data that expires becomes pretty much unrecoverable.

392   M. Ciocan et al.

2.4   Analytical Model

Similar to our paper, the Floating Content model has been a subject of analysis in [5]. The most important objective of this work has been finding a pattern to guarantee that a specific information remains in its anchor zone until the expiry of its lifetime with a high probability. It is called the *criticality condition*, and it depends on aspects such as mobility patterns and replication policies of the nodes inside the anchor zone.

While moving inside the anchor zone, a node may come in contact randomly with other nodes. We can assume there are two nodes moving permanently inside the zone. Let v be the frequency at which they come in contact with each other. Assuming the population of nodes in anchor is N, the total number of pairs is $\frac{1}{2}N(N-1) \approx \frac{1}{2}N^2$ and the total rate of encounters is $\frac{1}{2}N^2v$. A part of these encounters, more exactly $2p(1-p)$, replicate an item to nodes that does not have it yet, thus the total rate of such events is $p(1-p)N^2v$. This rate shows the type of monotonicity of the size of the population which have the item I. Let $\frac{1}{\mu}$ be the time spent by a node in the anchor zone. It results that the total exit rate of nodes is $N\mu$, and the exit rate of tagged nodes is $Np\mu$. The growth rate is determined by the formula:

$$N\frac{d}{dt}p = N^2p(1-p)v - Np\mu \tag{1}$$

The two terms on the right are equal when in equilibrium, leading to the stationary value $p^* = 1 - \mu/(vN)$. In order to have a positive solution, $p^* > 0$, it requires that,

$$N\frac{v}{\mu} > 1. \tag{2}$$

Equation (2) is called *criticality condition*. The left side value represents the average number of collisions a randomly chosen node has during its sojourn time. Considering the sign of the Eq. (1), it can be seen that the solution is stable. When $p > 1 - \mu/(vN)$, it tends to increase, and when $p < 1 - \mu/(vN)$, it tends to decrease. The information disappears (even in the fluid model) when the derivative is negative, leading to the solution $p = 0$. Moreover, since we need to prevent accidental disappearance of the information carrying population by stochastic fluctuations, $Np = N - \mu/v$ must be large.

2.5   Information Evolution During its Lifetime

Inspired by the mathematical modeling of the spread of infection diseases [4], we decided next to extend further the analyze, by looking into the evolution of information spreading as if it was a virus. The reason we decided to perform analysis using this model is because the protocol proposed uses broadcasting as a way of transmission, known as epidemic routing.

Our approach is very similar with the SIR model [6]: S stands for susceptibles (nodes interested in information, which do not have a copy yet); I stands for the infected ones (nodes who have a copy, and can send it further to neighbours); R stand for the removed (nodes which deleted their copy of the message, either because their availability time expired, or they are out of the anchor range).

As shown in [4], we define r as the infection rate. The number of the infected is proportional with the current number of susceptibles and infected, or rSI. We define a as the removal rate. The number of removed is proportional to the infected nodes only, or aI. The number of each class can be, now, computed using the following conditions: $\frac{dS}{dt} = -rSI$, and $\frac{dI}{dt} = rSI - aI$, and $\frac{dR}{dt} = aI$.

These equations ensure that the total population $N = S + I + R$ and $S_0 > 0$, $I_0 > 0$ and $R_0 > 0$. Also, when a susceptible gets infected i.e. receives the message, it becomes immediately infectious.

From these equations, at the beginning of information exchanging, when $t = 0$ the following equation results:

$$\frac{dI}{dt}\bigg|_{t=0} = I_0(rS_0 - a) \gtreqqless 0 \; if \; S_0 \gtreqqless \frac{a}{r} = \mu \tag{3}$$

There are two cases which emerge from (3): $S_0 < \mu$ implies that the number of infectives drop from I_0 to 0 and no epidemic can occur, $S_0 > \mu$ the number of infectives increases and the information spreads. μ can be considered as a threshold which determines whether the information will live or not. The presented model helps us to understand how the information develops in time, how the number of neighbours and the radius size influence its spread.

3   Floating Content Implementation

We decided to evaluate the conditions to use a Floating Content storage service within a city, by considering realistic vehicular mobility trace data. We used the Omnet++ network simulator, due to its extensibility and modularity. Also, we used the open-source framework for running vehicular network simulations called Veins, and Simulation of Urban Mobility (SUMO), a microscopic road traffic simulation package designed to handle large road network. Thus, we were able to perform bidirectionally-coupled simulation of road traffic and network traffic. Movement of nodes in Omnet++ simulation is determined by movement of vehicles in road traffic simulator SUMO. Nodes can then interact with the running road traffic simulation.

We assumed the use of the IEEE 802.11p standard for vehicular communication. Also, to estimate the feasibility of floating content, we positioned anchor zones every 200 m in a grid across the simulation area (which corresponds to a somewhat dense scenario for these zones). Every anchor zone had its own independent module to record multiple statistics during the simulation: the total number of vehicles crossing the anchor, the average sojourn time of a vehicle, the number of contacts of a vehicle during its sojourn time.

We simulated different scenarios using mobility datasets collected in San Francisco [8] and Beijing [11]. The territory of San Francisco, California covers an area of about 121 km^2, whilst Beijing encompasses an area of about 16.807, 8 km^2. In case of Beijing, we slightly over 1000 cabs (corresponding to cars crossing our selected area), during one week (from 2nd February 2008, to 10th February 2008). For San Francisco, we simulated the movement of all 500 cabs in the datasets, over the period of 12 days (from 17th May 2008 to 29th May 2008).

In the end, we are interested in *criticality*, defined as the product between (i) the maximum number of nodes that exists at a given time in an anchor zone, (ii) the average number of contacts in during the sojourn time, and (iii) the average sojourn time of vehicles in an anchor zone.

The environment for our simulation required by Omnet++ was generated using OpenStreetMap [2]. We decided to use two different city scenarios (SanFrancisco and Beijing) to show that floating content in urban environments is feasible regardless of particularity of road architecture (we have other results for different cities, such as Erlangen, but here we present only these 2 cities due to page limits). To analyse the model, we first vary the anchor zone radii, between [200 m, 500 m]. Although in theory IEEE 802.11p aims to provide both V2V and V2I communications in ranges up to 1000 m, due to obstacles and inferences we consider ranges between [200 m, 500 m] to reflect more realistic somewhat-dense urban traffic conditions [3]. Figure 2 shows how anchor zones are distributed.

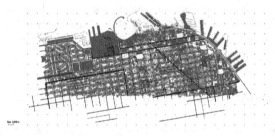

Fig. 2. Anchor zones every 200 m over the simulation area.

4   Experimental Results

We analyzed the feasibility of information sharing using the floating content model, considering the particularity of the road network as well as the spatial distribution of vehicles, and also the evolution during the simulation, following the SIR model.

4.1   Beijing

Figure 3a displays an area within the Beijing city, where we conducted our simulations. The figure is a snapshot that displays the road network from an area of $6.7 \times 5.2 \,\mathrm{km}^2$. The map is coloured with respect to the amount of time a car has to wait due to the traffic lights placed in intersections. Road segments coloured in red have a waiting time of about 40 s, more than the ones coloured in black, where there is a continuous flow of vehicles (corresponding to a waiting time close to 0s).

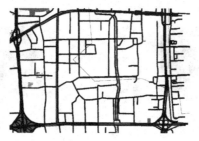

(a) Beijing traffic waiting time heatmap.

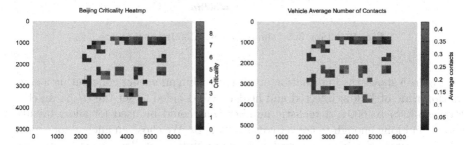

(b) Beijing Criticality Map $r = 200m$. (c) Average Number of Contacts Map $r = 200m$.

Fig. 3. Beijing 300 s simulation with 200 m anchor size.

Figure 3b shows the *criticality* heatmap, and Fig. 3c presents the average number of contacts a vehicle encounters during its sojourn time. The similarity between them is visible. The black (and gray, corresponding to value 0) areas state that the *criticality* factor is nearly 0, thus the probability of information floating is very low. Such areas occur in places between streets or outside the traffic road network, where neither vehicles, nor their radio range can reach them. In the 200 m scenario, the anchor zones with a higher probability of floating scatter the map. In the blue coloured areas, results show an average *criticality condition*, slightly above 1, which corresponds to the criticality threshold. According to Fig. 3c, 9 out of 10 vehicles do not have any interaction with other vehicles, during their sojourn time. The reason is the small amount of time spent in that location, and lack of neighbours at the time a beacon is sent out.

The bright yellow area, occurs naturally in the road intersection. The expectations for an information to live rise with respect to the average waiting time on a road segment. The *criticality factor* rise well over 8 as well as the average number of contacts a vehicles has during its sojourn time.

Increasing the anchor range yields better floating results. Figure 4 shows that information has a high probability of living along the road network. Also, the small light yellow areas in Fig. 4b reflect that every node has at least one contact during its sojourn time. The *criticality condition* increases 4 times than the one computed for a range of 200 m.

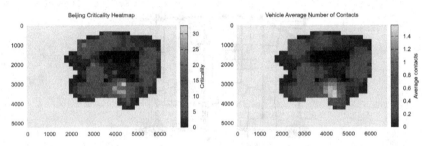

(a) Beijing Criticality Map $r = 500m$.   (b) Average Number of Contacts Map $r = 500m$.

Fig. 4. Beijing 300 s simulation with 500 m anchor size.

Figure 5 shows the information evolution within an anchor zone during a simulation time of 1000 s: infected and healed. We decided to set the *ttl* parameter (time-to-live) to 600 s, a realistic number that could be used for short lasting events and long enough to collect consistent data. We chose an anchor zone with a high number of information exchanges to provide a detailed picture of its evolution and avoided the ones which disappeared before the expiry time because of stochastic fluctuations.

We recorded the number of replicas an information has during the simulation denoted by *Replicas* label. The other two labels are 2 classes which belong to the epidemic SIR model: *infected* denote the information carrying nodes, and *healed* the ones which previously had a copy of the information and deleted it. The deletion could occur if the distance between the vehicle and the geo-location origin was bigger than the anchor radius or the information availability expired.

It is important to determine whether the information will spread or not. And if it does, for how long, and how it will develop in time. As we mentioned before, if $S_0 > S_c = a/r$ the content will spread. The plot in Fig. 6 confirms the condition for a 500 m anchor radius: the threshold μ is around 0 during most of the information lifetime, and the amount of susceptibles is greater than the

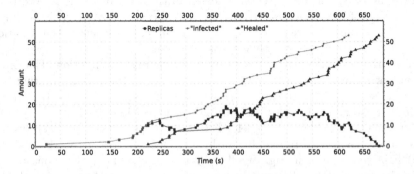

Fig. 5. Information life evolution with 500 m range. The number of copies is equal with the total number of "infections" minus the total number of "healings".

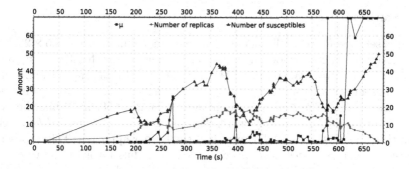

Fig. 6. When $S > \mu$ the number of replicas the number of replicas can increase, on the other hand, when $S < \mu$, the number of replicas decrease towards 0; μ represents the epidemy threshold; the anchor zone radius is 500 m.

threshold. This means that they could possibly receive a copy in the near future and become "infected". The end time period states that the number of susceptibles become less than μ, and thus the replication process reaches the end. The reason the threshold suddenly becomes larger is due to the application deleting the item once the lifetime expires. The "infected" will become susceptible again, fact confirmed by the figure (see the slight increase).

Figure 7 depicts how the information develops with respect to radius size. Establishing the optimum range enables the equipment and application to save battery energy and have a better resources management.

Anchor zones with $r \in [100\,\text{m}, 200\,\text{m}]$ yield a short life expectancy. In our scenario the content lasts for about 100s, just 1/6 of the due time. Such distances are probably more suitable if used indoor public places like shopping malls, metro stations, usually overcrowded places were the message exchanging is possible.

Ranges within $[300\,\text{m}, 400\,\text{m}]$ increase the life time up to 500 s, but the information disappears ahead of time. The range of 500 m keeps the item alive until its termination time. As long as the range is big enough to hold a considerable amount of vehicles inside, the information will last.

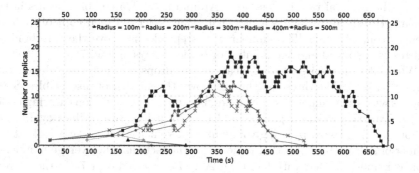

Fig. 7. Information life evolution with respect to radius size.

4.2   San Francisco

The area selected from San Francisco to be used in simulations has $4.5 \times 2.5 \, \text{km}^2$, and contains a road network made up from road streets with different numbers of lanes on each way. We removed the bicycle, pedestrian, cityrail and public transport segment roads, and left only the segments for regular road vehicles.

Figure 8 depicts the results using an anchor range of 500 m. While the average number of contacts slightly increases from 2 to 2.5 the *criticality* reaches 120 in the top spots, nearly 2.5 times than the former approach. This is possible because the anchor zones now cover larger areas, thus involving more cars in the exchanging process. The bigger radius make the anchor zones more diffusive inside the heatmap confirming that a user may receive much more items spread on a larger area. In the 200 m scenario, the areas are more concentrated, with the need of being close to the high traffic zones in order for the replication to be possible. The big values that appear over a big portion of the map are an indicator that even in the probabilistic system used the information will float.

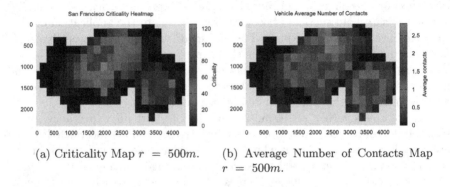

(a) Criticality Map $r = 500m$.   (b) Average Number of Contacts Map $r = 500m$.

Fig. 8. San Francisco 300 s simulation with 500 m anchor size.

Again the epidemic model SIR is confirmed, as shown in Fig. 9. During its lifetime the removal rate is close to 0. Around $t = 475$ s a spike occurs in the epidemic threshold μ which is a sign that vehicles deleted their copy of the item when got out of range. The number of susceptibles is above the threshold, so epidemy is sustained and the number of replicas stays around 70.

When lifetime expires, the replication rate drops to 0 and the deletion rate starts increasing. The threshold thus gets over the number of susceptibles. Same happens with the number of susceptibles, because the information carrying nodes start information deletion process and transform into susceptibles again. The anchor zone is crossed by a higher number of vehicles if we take a look at the number of susceptibles. Another indicator is the fact that the average number of replicas is much higher, with less than 20 in Beijing and over 70 in the current scenario.

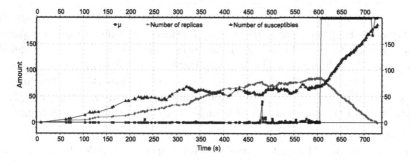

Fig. 9. When $S > \mu$ the number of replicas the number of replicas can increase, on the other hand, when $S < \mu$, the number of replicas decrease towards 0; μ represents the epidemy threshold; the anchor zone radius is 500 m.

Figure 10 describes how the spread develops in time with respect to anchor radius size. It indicates that when $r \in [300\,\text{m},\ 500\,\text{m}]$, the information floats the entire due time. Intuitively, the distinctive aspect is the average number of replicas proportionally with the range size. A lower radius kills the item prematurely, existing no peer to exchange messages with.

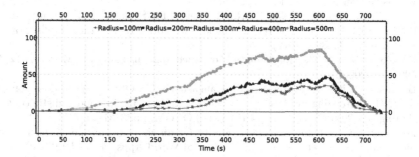

Fig. 10. Information life evolution with respect to radius size.

5   Conclusion

We have presented an analysis of distributed storage and dissemination services based on floating content design, that works exclusively on mobile devices without relying on a central infrastructure network. We performed our evaluations using realistic scenarios and the results revealed that floating content could be feasible in urban environments.

There are several important factors that influence information floatability. A high density inside the anchor location sustain the life of the information regardless the radius size (but the number of copies would be small for small radii). Having a big radius may cluster more vehicles and thus, increase the probability of floating. The radio range could also affect information sharing. A small radio range compared to the information availability range may prevent the application to spread content in the entire zone and rely on vehicle density. We believe information sharing applications between mobile entities will experience a growth in the near future, a prediction supported by the improvements made in wireless communication, the increase spread of mobile phones worldwide, and the construction of vehicles with communication equipment.

Acknowledgment. The work presented in this paper is co-funded by the European Union, Eurostars Programme, under the project 8111, DELTA "Network-Aware Delivery Clouds for User Centric Media Events".

The research is partially supported by COST Action IC1303 AAPELE, and by project MobiWay, PN-II-PT-PCCA-2013-4-0321.

References

1. Bojic, I., Podobnik, V., Kusek, M., Jezic, G.: Collaborative urban computing: serendipitous cooperation between users in an urban environment. Cybern. Syst. **42**(5), 287–307 (2011)
2. (Muki) Haklay, M., Weber, P.: Openstreetmap: user-generated street maps. IEEE Pervasive Comput. **7**(4), 12–18 (2008)
3. Han, C., Dianati, M., Tafazolli, R., Kernchen, R., Shen, X.: Analytical study of the ieee 802.11 p mac sublayer in vehicular networks. IEEE Trans. Intell. Transp. Syst. **13**(2), 873–886 (2012)
4. Hethcote, H.W.: The mathematics of infectious diseases. SIAM Rev. **42**(4), 599–653 (2000)
5. Hyytia, E., Virtamo, J., Lassila, P., Kangasharju, J., Ott, J.: When does content float? characterizing availability of anchored information in opportunistic content sharing. In: 2011 Proceedings of IEEE INFOCOM, pp. 3137–3145 (2011)
6. McCluskey, C.: Complete global stability for an sir epidemic model with delay-distributed or discrete. Nonlinear Anal. Real World Apps **11**, 55–59 (2010)
7. Ott, J., Hyytia, E., Lassila, P., Vaegs, T., Kangasharju, J.: Floating content: information sharing in urban areas. In: 2011 IEEE International Conference on Pervasive Computing and Communications (PerCom), pp. 136–146. IEEE (2011)
8. Piorkowski, M., Sarafijanovic-Djukic, N., Grossglauser, M.: CRAWDAD data set epfl/mobility (v. 2009-02-24), February 2009. Downloaded from http://crawdad.org/epfl/mobility/
9. Podobnik, V., Lovrek, I.: Transforming social networking from a service to a platform: a case study of ad-hoc social networking. In: Proceedings of the 13th International Conference on Electronic Commerce, p. 8. ACM (2011)
10. Smailovic, V., Podobnik, V.: Bfriend: context-aware ad-hoc social networking for mobile users. In: 2012 Proceedings of the 35th International Convention MIPRO, pp. 612–617. IEEE (2012)
11. Yuan, J., Zheng, Y., Zhang, C., Xie, W., Xie, X., Sun, G., Huang, Y.: T-drive: driving directions based on taxi trajectories. In: Proceedings of the 18th SIGSPATIAL International Conference on Advances in Geographic Information Systems, pp. 99–108. ACM 2010)

An Approach for the Evaluation of Human Activities in Physical Therapy Scenarios

Manuel P. Cuellar[1], Maria Ros[1(✉)], Maria J. Martin-Bautista[1], Y. Le Borgne[2], and Gianluca Bontempi[2]

[1] Department of Computer Science, University of Granada, Granada, Spain
{manupc,marosiz,mbautis}@decsai.ugr.es
[2] Département d'Informatique, Université Libre de Bruxelles, Machine Learning Group, Brussel, Belgium
{yleborgn,gbonte}@ulb.ac.be

Abstract. Human activity recognition has been widely studied since the last decade in ambient intelligence scenarios. Remarkable progresses have been made in this domain, especially in research lines such as ambient assisted living, gesture recognition, behaviour detection and classification, etc. Most of the works in the literature focus on activity classification or recognition, prediction of future events, or anomaly detection and prevention. However, it is hard to find approaches that do not only recognize an activity, but also provide an evaluation of its performance according to an optimality criterion. This problem is of special interest in applications such as sports performance evaluation, physical therapy, etc. In this work, we address the problem of the evaluation of such human activities in monitored environments using depth sensors. In particular, we propose a system able to provide an automatic evaluation of the correctness in the performance of activities involving motion, and more specifically, diagnosis exercises in physical therapy.

Keywords: Human activity recognition · Depth sensors · Time series matching

1 Introduction

Human activity recognition is one of the most complex tasks within Ambient Intelligence [1]. However, in the last few years there have been approaches that provide a successful gesture and activity recognition in different domains. The most successful techniques that have provided the best results in this field are data-driven approaches, and more specifically those based in Hidden Markov Models [16] or time series matching methods [15,17], among others. The integration of unobtrusive sensors in our daily life allows smart spaces to detect users and their activities, with the aim of providing assistance to people, as for instance in the projects [13,14]. The technologies used to acquire the information of the human activity are wide: smartphone accelerometer data, passive/active sensors located in the environment, cameras, and depth sensors. Despite these advances,

© Institute for Computer Sciences, Social Informatics and Telecommunications Engineering 2015
R. Agüero et al. (Eds.): MONAMI 2014, LNICST 141, pp. 401–414, 2015.
DOI: 10.1007/978-3-319-16292-8_29

few approaches aimed at the simultaneous detection and evaluation of the user activity, nevertheless, this application is of big interest to fields such as sports or physical therapy. Recent works have shown that the activity acquired with depth sensors is not as accurate as other physical activity monitoring technologies such as Vicon systems [3,4], but they provide enough accuracy for motion monitorization systems at home [2].

This work focuses in this research line, and describes a system that uses a depth sensor to acquire information about a performer of diagnosis exercises in physical therapy, detects the exercise being executed, and provides an evaluation of its performance. Traditionally, recovery from injuries has been carried out following a sequence of steps starting with initial medical intervention, a period of rest, and finally a rehabilitation program monitored by experts [5]. However, due to staff shortages, economic resources and space limitations, the latter is usually limited to scheduled sessions, daily or weekly, in physiotherapy centres.

During the last decade, the advances in computer and sensor technologies have enabled the development of telerehabilitation systems to improve the patient recovery [6–8]. Projects such as Stroke Recovery with Kinect project [20], is an example of the interest of this new research field from not only the academia, but also from the research industry. We can find two types of approaches: Those focused on technology exploitation either to improve the performance rehabilitation exercise, either to obtain a better monitorization of the movement to provide the therapist with accurate data for the latter analysis and diagnosis, and those that are designed to automatically assist the user to perform the exercises correctly.

For the first type, we cite example projects such as Rehabilitation Gaming system (RGS) [9,10] and ICT4Rehab [11], between others. In RGS, it is proposed a complete methodology to use videogames for stroke rehabilitation. The game is designed to automatically adapt the difficulty to each patient, in order to allow an unsupervised and personalized rehabilitation. The main conclusion of this work is that they proved the correlation between virtual and real kinematic movements, therefore enabling games as a powerful tool in rehabilitation. On the other hand, the project ICT4Rehab uses videogames for muscle spasticity rehabilitation in children. They develop a set of serious games to exercise rehabilitation movements suggested by therapists, which evaluate automatically the performance of each patient after playing a game. Considering the increasing number of approaches and articles, we may conclude that serious games have arisen as a promising tool in rehabilitation research [12]. However, despite the motivation factor for the patient and the accuracy of movements that sensors may measure and provide to a computer-aided therapist, these approaches do not usually provide personalized support to the patient, and the medical expert is still required during the execution of exercises and the later diagnosis.

In our approach, we attempt to solve this limitation including an evaluation method for diagnosis exercises performed by patients and monitorized using a depth sensor camera. Our final goal is to build a decision support system able to assess the patient semantically and to automatically evaluate his/her performance. However, as a first step, we need to establish a suitable measure to evaluate exercises and to distinguish between correct and incorrect performances. The remaining of the manuscript is focused in this idea: First, Sect. 2 provides an overview of the prototype application developed to fulfil the data acquisition requisites. After that, Sect. 3 shows the technical details for exercise representation, detection and our approach for performance evaluation. Section 4 shows the experimental results of our proposal over a real dataset with participants, and finally Sect. 5 concludes.

2   System Overview

Our main objective is to develop a system able to acquire and automatically evaluate diagnosis exercise performances in physical therapy. To that end, we have built a prototype application called *PReSenS* (Proactive Rehabilitation Sensing System) [19], able to acquire and save template exercises involving motion or posture holding, to create exercise plans for patients, and acquire and save their exercise performances. We use a depth sensor to fetch the skeleton joint 3D rotation data from the human body from both physical therapists and patients in real-time. The typical system operation comprises 3 stages: First, the physiotherapist saves exercise templates using the recording editor (1 template for each exercise). These are stored into a remote database containing the information about exercises, patient plans and patient performances. In a second stage, the physical therapist proposes an exercise plan to the patient, who performs the exercises. In this stage, the system is able to provide the patient with a preliminary automatic evaluation of the plan execution, and stores this information into the remote database. Finally, in a last stage, both patients and physiotherapists can access the system remotely using a web front-end, to make an in-depth motion signal analysis and/or to obtain suggestions and professional evaluations to help performers to improve. Figure 1 summarizes these stages and describes the general architecture of the system.

In this paper, we focus on the problem of automatic performance evaluation of diagnosis exercises in physical therapy, highlighted in stage 2. According to interviewed experts in the field, most of these exercises can be classified in two main categories: motion exercises and posture holding. A physical therapist use to evaluate the performance of these types of exercises according to different absolute measures such as the angle between joints, amplitude of moves, etc., and asks their patients to perform an exercise either for a number of repetitions or for a limited period of time before its evaluation. We included these features in *PReSenS* so that the system fits the requirements of professionals in the field as accurately as possible.

3   Exercise Representation and Evaluation

Before providing an evaluation of a motion or posture holding performance, a previous and necessary step is to know which features must be evaluated and how

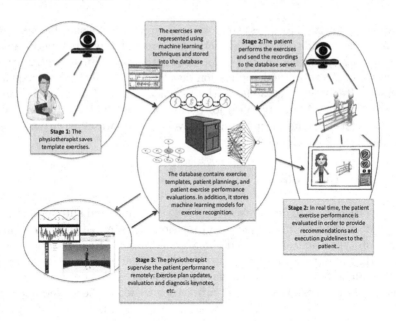

Fig. 1. Scheme of *PReSenS* use

to aggregate them to calculate the final evaluation report. We need to evaluate a sequence of postures of the human body, and its representation is key to success and to accurately fit a physical therapist methodology. In this work, we consider 2 types of data capable of being considered for evaluation: absolute and relative. Absolute features encompass absolute angles of joints/bones with regard to the underlying 3D base coordinate system. Assuming this base to be the vectors $(1, 0, 0), (0, 1, 0), (0, 0, 1)$, in *(X, Y, Z)* coordinates, for each joint we can obtain the features of the angles between coordinates XY, YZ, XZ. On the other hand, relative features are the angles between bones that share a joint, considering the 2D plane defined by the two vectors that represent each bone. Absolute features help to detect the position of a bone/joint in respect to the absolute coordinate systems (for instance, to know tilts), while the relative ones help to know relation between joints when the absolute coordinates are not relevant (for example, an angle of 90 degrees between the arm and the forearm). The use of angles to represent postures is not only close to the therapist methodology, but it also has some desirable advantages since the angles between joints are not influenced by external characteristics such as patient height, width, or constitution.

We are able to obtain 3-D rotation data from 20 joints of the human body directly from the depth sensor used in *PReSenS*: center/left/right hip, spine, center/left/right shoulder, head, right/left elbow, wrist, hand, knee, ankle and foot), so our possible feature set include 79 basic variables, considering only the bones involved in a joint and assuming the hip as the starting joint. We store each posture data using a compressed format containing joint quaternion rotations in the *PReSenS* database, that can be processed to acquire these features. In particular, Eq. 1 shows how to transform a quaternion rotation $q = (q_X, q_Y, q_Z, q_W)$ to a 3D vector $V = (V_X, V_Y, V_Z)$, which can be easily used to compute absolute and relative angles.

$$V = F(q) = (1 - 2q_Y^2 - 2q_Z^2, 2q_X q_Y + 2q_Z q_W, 2q_X q_Z - 2q_Y q_W) \tag{1}$$

Once we have a suitable representation for an activity as a sequence of angles of the joints of interest, indexed in time, we need to perform 2 tasks to evaluate the exercise: First, to detect the activity and to bound the signal acquired from the sensor to a specific time range of interest. Second, to evaluate the exercise performed in the range detected, to obtain a performance score. These two steps are explained in the next Subsects. 3.1 and 3.2, respectively.

3.1 Exercise Performance Detection

As the first step to detect the activity being performed by an user, we selected time series matching methods to solve the problem of exercise detection because they provide a set of advantages in the scope of our work: (1) they allow to select and change the dimensionality of a template/performance exercise without re-training, (2) they ease the management of specific dimensions (features of interest being monitorized) for kinematic analysis, (3) they require a single template to be saved by the therapist before its use, etc. Moreover, their accuracy in fields, such as gesture recognition and activity detection in previous works, has provided promising results that make them suitable to be used in the problem addressed.

To achieve a fast and effective activity detection, the system *PReSenS* uses a single template for each exercise, acquired from the monitorization of the physical therapist using the depth sensor. This template is a recording of a suitable exercise performance carried out by the therapist, and will be used to match and find similar activities during the patient performance. It is composed by a multidimensional signal of features of interest to evaluate the exercise, which must be previously selected by the therapist. For instance, if an exercise is *Left leg up*, only the joints involving the move should be selected to avoid monitorization of irrelevant body parts, as for example, the head.

After the template is recorded into the system, a performer can execute an exercise plan including such activity. We detect the associated exercise using time series matching algorithms. In particular, we have implemented a modified variant of the subsequence matching Dynamic Time Warping algorithm (DTW) [18] in *PReSenS*, with a ground truth segmentation method able to detect the beginning and the end of the exercise. However, due to space limitations, we are not able to describe in depth this method in this paper. For this reason, for the remaining of the manuscript we will assume that we have an algorithm that provides a matching between the therapist template and the patient's performance and it returns the matching between these two multidimensional signals.

3.2 Performance Evaluation

We believe that the simplest way that a system may provide an automatic evaluation of an exercise performance is using a score value; for instance, between 0 and 100. The evaluation process will consist of scoring the correctness of a specific exercise performance, obtaining a degree of similarity after comparing the performance with the therapist's template. We are able to carry out this comparison since in the previous subsection we found a matching between an exercise performance and its corresponding therapist's template. Thus, next we describe how to compare these two signals to compute a final single score value.

We need to evaluate 2 types of exercises: Posture holding and motion. A posture holding exercise template is represented as a single posture, while a motion template is an ordered sequence of postures in time. Finally, a patient's performance is always an ordered sequence of postures in time. For posture holding comparison, each posture in the patient's performance is compared with the single template posture, while motion exercises are compared using the matching between data series provided by the method described in the previous section using DTW. In order to obtain a single evaluation score, we have to evaluate each posture in a move separately, and then to aggregate all these evaluations in the move into the final score value.

We use the basis of membership functions and aggregation coming from Fuzzy Sets theory to compute the evaluation of a posture. More specifically, we use the Gaussian-shape function (GF) and the Generalized Bell function (GBF) (Eq. 2). Each function returns a membership value $\mu \in [0, 1]$ of a number X being approximately A (Gaussian function), or being between approximately $C - A$ and $C + A$ (generalized bell function). The σ values help to define each fuzzy membership function depending on the context and application. Figure 2 shows examples of both functions with different parameters for a better description. The paradigm of fuzzy theory helps us here to represent the inherent uncertainty nature of the addressed application.

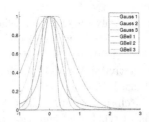

Fig. 2. Example of Gaussian-shape membership function with values $\sigma = \pi/12$ (Gauss 1), $\sigma = \pi/6$ (Gauss 2) and $\sigma = \pi/3$ (Gauss 3), with mean $\mu = 0$; and Generalized Bell membership function with values $A = \pi/12, \sigma = 5$ (GBell 1), $A = \pi/12, \sigma = 1$ (GBell 2), $A = \pi/6, \sigma = 5$ (GBell 3)

$$f_{GF}(X) = e^{\frac{(X-A)^2}{\sigma}}$$

$$f_{GBF}(X) = \frac{1}{1 + |\frac{X-C}{A}|^{2\sigma}} \tag{2}$$

For the posture of the exercise performance at time t, each joint feature i, $J_i(t)$ (angle/s of interest described in the previous section) in a patient's posture is compared and evaluated in respect to its corresponding matching posture in the template $J_i'(t)$. We remark that this value is independent to signal shifting, since both patient and template signals have been aligned using DTW. The difference between these features $J_i(t) - J_i'(t)$ is input to either a GF or GBF membership function, selected previously by the therapist during the exercise template creation, and it returns the degree of similarity of the feature in the range $[0, 1]$. The therapist would select the GF function if a single feature value must be used to match the posture joint, or GBF if a range of values (angles) is accepted as valid for the maximum evaluation value. After that, the score of the posture at time t, $P_{score}(t)$, is obtained as the aggregation of these values considering a relevance value of each feature joint to perform the exercise, r_i, according to Eq. 3, where N is the number of features considered in the problem. The final score of the exercise is then calculated as the average score of all postures in the patient performance, and its range is the interval $[0, 1]$, where 1 means a perfect match between the patient motion and the template.

$$P_{score}(t) = \sum_{i=1}^{N} r_i f_i(J_i(t) - J_i'(t))$$

$$subject\ to: \sum_{i=1}^{N} r_i = 1 \tag{3}$$

$$Score = \frac{1}{T} \sum_{t=1}^{T} P_{score}(t)$$

This method to calculate a score/evaluation of an exercise performance is simple enough to allow near real-time processing of the exercise performance, and accurate enough to provide robust evaluations. In the next section, we show the effects of using the GF or the GBF to obtain the evaluation of an exercise performed by a set of participants.

4   Experiments

4.1   Data Acquisition and Experimental Design

In this experimentation, we aim to evaluate the accuracy and quantity of information that the proposed scoring functions may provide. To achieve this objective, we required patients with complete mobility degrees capable of performing correctly every exercise. The data for the experimentation were obtained from a sample of 10 healthy participants (5 men and 5 women) covering an age range from 21 to 40 years old.

Participants were asked to perform correctly a set of repetitions of diagnosis exercises widely used in physical therapy, covering 3 motion and 2 posture holding exercises:

- **Arms up,** 10 repetitions (motion). The participants must perform a 180 degrees move of both arms simultaneously, from the bottom to the top. The relevant features for this exercise are: left/right hip, shoulder, and elbow relative angles in respect to their parent bones (6 features).
- **Left arm extension and flexion,** 10 repetitions (motion). The participants must perform a complete extension and flexion of their left arm, being perpendicular to the torso. The features being monitorized here are: shoulder center, left shoulder and elbow relative angles in respect to their parent bones (3 features).
- **Left leg up,** 10 repetitions (motion). The participants must up and down their left leg up to 60 degrees in respect to the body vertical line without moving the torso. Here, we selected the following relevant features: Spine, left/right hip, knee and ankle relative angles in respect to their parent bone (7 features).
- **Flamenco,** 10 s (posture holding). The participants must hold the balance over the right leg, while maintaining the left one up with an angle of 90 degrees in respect to the torso. All body bone relative angles in respect to their parent joint are monitorized features in this exercise.
- **Cross arms,** 10 s (posture holding). The participants must hold a cross-like posture, their arms completely extended with an angle of 90 degrees in respect to the torso. We monitorize the following relevant features: spine, shoulder center, left/right shoulder, elbow and wrist (6 features).

Fig. 3. Snapshot of the exercise performance *PReSenS* view: A template move is shown in the upper right corner (Flamenco exercise in the image), together with the current participant performance evaluation (center right) and the remaining time for the exercise. On the left, it is shown the current posture of the patient with an avatar, and a countdown to start the exercise execution.

Before recording each participant performance, we thought them about the right way to perform the exercises, and performed some preliminary tests so they got used to the prototype application and success during the exercise execution. After that, we asked them to perform the required exercises following a template known move shown in the prototype application (Fig. 3). After all participants finished, we migrated the data from a MySQL database to plain text for the experimental analysis using Matlab R2011a. The experimental data and Matlab scripts to perform all the next experiments can be downloaded for free from http://decsai.ugr.es/~manupc/presens.

We used a Toshiba laptop Core i7, 2 MB cache L1, Windows 7, 8 GB RAM, and a Kinect for Windows depth sensor for the experiments. Our prototype application was implemented in C# using the Kinect SDK API provided by Microsoft to access the sensor data. The sensor signals were acquired at 30fps with a resolution of 640×480 pixels (RGB camera) and 80×60 (depth camera), using average smooth filtering to remove signal noise with value 0.5. The skeleton data for each exercise performance were stored into a MySQL database for their later processing.

In our experiments, all motion signals acquired from the participants were summarized using Piece-Wise Aggregation Approximation (PAA) with a rate of 1 (no summarization), 2 (half reduction) and 3 (a third) of the original signal length, to study the effect of summarization over the scoring of an exercise in the experiments. The standard deviation for the Gaussian membership function was set to a constant value of $\pi/12$ radians, and the amplitude and slope for the Generalized Bell functions were set to $\pi/12$ radians and 5, respectively. We chose these values for all joints for reading clarity of this experimentation, since they represent normal and assumable differences between correct performances for the exercises proposed. These membership functions are shown in Fig. 2 for clarity. In addition, all joints were assigned the same relevance r_i to simplify the experimentation, without loss of generality.

4.2 Results

In this section we are looking for answers to the following questions: (1) How does data series summarization influence in the evaluation of motion exercises in physical therapy?, and (2) How different is the selection of one membership function or another to evaluate an exercise performance, in terms of final results and scoring?. The first question is key to achieve a near real-time human activity detection and evaluation, since summarization techniques help to reduce the complexity and computational time of the operations involved in such tasks. On the other hand, the second question aims at finding a suitable model to evaluate a posture in a motion performance.

Our first interest focuses in knowing if data signal summarization influences in the score of an exercise performance. To know that, we applied PAA with rates 1, 2 and 3 over the signals before the calculation of the score, and performed a paired t-test with 95 % of confidence level for each activity using the Gauss scoring function, to know if the data distributions differ significantly.

We obtained 10 probability values (coming from the comparison of each activity with PAA values = 1–2 and PAA values = 1–3). All data distributions passed the test except the activity *Left leg up*, where we obtained a p-value <0.05 and then we conclude that summarization affects this activity. To check it, we plotted the boxplots in Fig. 4, showing the data distributions coming from the difference between the scores using a PAA value = 1 and a PAA value = 2 (left), and a PAA value = 1 and PAA value = 3 (right). Accordingly to the results of the test, we verify that there are significant differences in both distributions; however, they are in the order of 10^{-4}, which means that, if we provide the score using a range between 0.00 and 100.00, the second decimal unit will be affected if we use summarization. The same results were obtained using the Generalized bell function as scoring criterion.

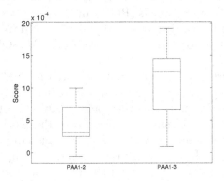

Fig. 4. Score calculation differences between the application of PAA with values 1 and 2 (left), and PAA with values 1 and 3 (right)

On the other hand, we checked the benefits in computational cost provided by PAA. We measured the time (in ms) required to perform PAA, template and patient performance matching, and scoring, for each activity. Table 1 summarizes the average computational time spent for each PAA value and activity, to process one second of performer activity. We notice different influences of PAA regarding motion and posture holding exercises: While in the first group we achieve a significant speed improvement, the second group increases the computational time required. This means that applying PAA to posture holding exercises is more expensive than the direct comparison with the template. However, for motion exercises, the computational cost is decreased by an average rate of 8.12 when a PAA value = 3 is used. In summary, benefits of PAA to improve the computational cost when calculating the score of an exercise are high, especially if we want to achieve a near real-time system behaviour. However, its use may decrease the accuracy of the evaluation score. This is a design decision that every system developed, based on this approach, should consider before its implementation. In our case, *PReSenS* was implemented with a PAA value = 3 since we agree to loose one centesimal unit of precision calculating the score for the good of near real-time behaviour.

Table 1. Time (in secs.) required to obtain a score of an activity performance for each second, depending of the summarization rate PAA

PAA	Arms up	Left arm ext.	Left leg up	Flamenco	Cross arms
1	0.1348	0.0813	0.0754	0.0004	0.0004
2	0.0353	0.0218	0.0236	0.0007	0.0007
3	0.0161	0.0099	0.0098	0.0005	0.0005

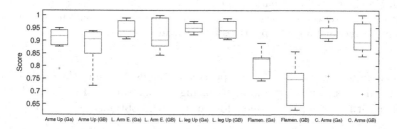

Fig. 5. Final score distribution for all diagnosis exercises and membership functions (Ga = Gauss function; GB = Generalized Bell function)

Our second interest is to know the effect of selecting a Gauss or a Generalized Bell membership function to evaluate an exercise, from a practical point of view. To do this, we calculated the score for every user performance in each activity, using either a Gauss or a Generalized Bell membership function for every feature of interest in the exercises. Figure 5 shows the boxplots of the scores obtained using both methods for each activity. As we may observe, GBF provide a wider range of scores than GF. This is a desirable effect for a scoring function, since it allows to better distinguish between good and not-so-good performances. Since the variance is higher in the GBF scores, also it is the information provided by the scoring method. As result, the average score obtained with the GBF is always lower than the score calculated with the GF. This is explained by the inherent shape of both functions: While the slope of the GF is softer from the maximum membership 1 to 0, we are able to adapt this slope for the GBF and, in our experiments, was set to a maximum value. Thus, we evaluate with high membership the postures whose angles are in the specified range, and low membership when a posture overcomes the limits allowed. As a result, GBF seems to have some desirable properties that make more suitable than GF to evaluate the exercises proposed in this experimentation.

Regarding the score values, we may see that they range from a very good scores (exercises *Arms up, Left arm extension and flexion, Left leg up,* and *Cross arms*), to lower ones in *Flamenco*. This is due to the difficulty of holding the balance in the last one, and also that all joints were monitorized in this experiment with the same relevance. The scores obtained have values accordingly to a human expert evaluation of the participants during the exercise performance, and may be justified directly by the kinematic analysis of the signals acquired.

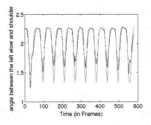

Fig. 6. Matching between a participant performance (blue) and the template (red) for the *Arms up* exercise. The picture shows the angle between the left elbow and the left shoulder (in radians) for 10 repetitions (Color figure online).

As an example, we show in Fig. 6 a portion of the evolution of the angle between the left elbow and the left shoulder during the execution of activity *Arms up*, together with its template values, for an user who obtained a score of 94.05.

4.3   Final Remarks

In this work, we have proposed a method to evaluate diagnosis exercise performances in physical therapy. The previous section has shown that using techniques for data summarization may help to achieve a near real-time evaluation of a patient performance, and also has put in manifest some desirable features of Generalized Bell functions as membership evaluation methods to score a posture feature. We have performed the experiments with the underlying assumption of time series matching between the user performance sensor signal and a template exercise; however, further questions remains: How different is to use a time series matching algorithm in respect to plain and simpler methods like Euclidean distance to compare signals? How different is the score value if we consider a wider or narrower set of features to be monitorized? Additionally, if the timing coordination between the user performance and the template exercise provided by the therapist is an aspect to be evaluated, how to adapt the techniques proposed in this work to solve this problem? How to use the scoring information to semantically assess a patient about how to improve his/her performances? In addition, some patients have certain diseases that do not allow them to perform all exercises correctly (for instance, the arm cannot be completely extended). How to adapt a previous template for each user without the need to save a particular template for these patients? These answers will be provided in a future work that extends our research.

5   Conclusions

In this work we have described *PReSenS*, a system able to acquire motion data of an user performing diagnosis exercises in physical therapy, using a depth sensor camera. We have proposed a method for automatic evaluation of exercise performance, providing a simple evaluation value as a score. We have discussed how to evaluate each feature of interest to be monitorized for an exercise, and how to aggregate these features to obtain the final evaluation score. In addition, we have proposed two evaluation functions based on fuzzy sets theory, to model the inherent uncertainty of the problem addressed. As a result, we have shown that Generalized Bell evaluation function may provide more information than the Gauss evaluation function, due to its capabilities to delimitate the correct range of a joint move. In addition, the use of time series matching algorithms in combination with data summarization techniques may help to achieve an accurate and fast evaluation methodology that can be used in near real-time applications. Summarization techniques allow to reduce the computational cost of evaluation, although their use may provide loss in accuracy in centesimal units.

Acknowledgements. We thank the administrative staff, students and teachers from the Faculty of Education, Economy and Technology of Ceuta for their patience and help as volunteers for our experimentation. This work was mainly supported by the Contrato-Programa of the Faculty of Education, Economy and Technology of Ceuta, the project TIN2012-30939 and the IC1303 AAPELE action.

References

1. Hein, A., Kirste, T.: Activity recognition for ambient assisted living: potential and challenges. In: Proceedings of 1st German Ambient Assisted Living - AAL-Congress (2008)
2. Fernandez-Baena, A., Susin, A., Lligadas, X.: Biomechanical validation of upper-body and lower-body joint movements of kinect motion capture data for rehabilitation treatments. In: Proceedings of Fourth International Conference on Intelligent Networking and Collaborative Systems, pp. 656–661. IEEE Press, New York (2012)
3. Bonnechere, B., Jansen, B., Salvia, P., Bouzahouene, H., Omelina, L., Cornelis, J., Rooze, M., Van Sint Jan, S.: What are the current limits of the Kinect sensor? In: Proceedings of 9th International Conference on Disability, Virtual Reality & Associated Technologies, pp. 287–294 (2012)
4. Bonnechere, B., Sholukha, V., Moiseev, F., Rooze, M., Van Sint Jan, S.: From Kinect to anatomically-correct motion modelling: preliminary results for human application. In: Proceedings of the 3rd European Conference on Gaming and Playful Interaction in Health Care, pp. 15–26. Springer Fachmedien Wiesbaden (2013)
5. Beam, J.W.: Rehabilitation including sportspecific functional progression for the competitive athlete. J. Bodywork 6(4), 205–219 (2002)
6. Zheng, H., et al.: SMART rehabilitation: implementation of ICT platform to support home-based stroke rehabilitation. In: Stephanidis, C. (ed.) HCI 2007. LNCS, vol. 4554, pp. 831–840. Springer, Heidelberg (2007)
7. Zheng, H., Davies, R., Hammerton, J., Mawson, S.J., Ware, P.M., Black, N.D., Eccleston, C., Hu, H., Stone, T., Mountain, G.A., Harris, N.: SMART project: application of emerging information and communication technology to home-based rehabilitation for stroke patients. Int. J. Disabil. Hum. Dev. 5, 271–276 (2006)
8. Zhou, H., Hu, H.: A survey - human movement tracking and stroke rehabilitation. Technical report, University of Essex (2004)

9. Cameirao, M.S., Badia, S.B., Oller, E.D., Verschure, P.F.: Neurorehabilitation using the virtual reality based Rehabilitation Gaming System: methodology, design, psychometrics, usability and validation. J. Neuroeng. Rehabil. **7**, 48 (2010)

10. Cameirao, M.S., Badia, S.B., Duarte, E., Verschure, P.F.: Virtual reality based rehabilitation speeds up functional recovery of the upper extremities after stroke: a randomized controlled pilot study in the acute phase of stroke using the Rehabilitation Gaming System. Restor. Neurol. Neurosci. **29**, 287–298 (2011)

11. Omelina, L., Jansen B., Bonnechere, B., Jan, S., Cornelis, J.: Serious games for physical rehabilitation: designing highly configurable and adaptable games. In: 9th International Conference on Disability, Virtual Reality and Associated Technologies, pp. 195–201 (2012)

12. Graaf, A., Anderson, F., Annett, M., Bischof, W.: Gaming motion tracking technologies for rehabilitation. In: Gaming Motion Tracking Technologies for Gaming, pp. 60–73 (2010)

13. Boger, J., Hoey, J., Poupart, P., Boutilier, C., Fernie, G., Mihailidis, A.: A planning system based on markov decision processes to guide people with dementia through activities of daily living. IEEE Trans. Inf. Technol. Biomed. **10**(2), 323–333 (2006)

14. Jasiewicz, J., Kearns, W., Craighead, J., Fozard, J.L., Scott, S., McCarthy, J.: Smart rehabilitation for the 21st century: the Tampa Smart Home for veterans with traumatic brain injury. J. Rehabil. Res. Dev. **48**(8), 7–28 (2011)

15. Corradini, A.: Dynamic time warping for off-line recognition of a small gesture vocabulary. In: Proceedings of IEEE ICCV Workshop on Recognition, Analysis, and Tracking of Faces and Gestures in Real-Time Systems, pp. 82–89. IEEE Press, New York (2001)

16. Crandall, A.S., Cook, D.J.: Using a hidden markov model for resident identification. In Proceedings of the 6th International Conference on Intelligent Environments, pp. 74–79. IEEE Press, New York (2010)

17. Leon, O., Cuellar, M.P., Delgado, M., Le Borgne, Y., Bontempi, G.: Human activity recognition framework in monitored environments. In: Proceedings of 3rd International Conference on Pattern Recognition Applications and Methods, pp. 487–494 (2014)

18. Muller, M.: Information Retrieval for Music and Motion. Springer, Heidelberg (2007)

19. Cuéllar, M.P., Le Borgne, Y., Galiano-Castillo, N., Arroyo, M., Pegalajar, M.C., Martin-Bautista, M.J., Bontempi, G.: PReSenS: towards smart rehabilitation with proactive sensing for remote and automatic medical evaluation. In: 7th IADIS International Conference on Information Systems, pp. 314–318 (2014)

20. http://research.microsoft.com/en-us/projects/stroke-recovery-with-kinect/

AAL: Devices and Mobile Cloud

Towards Cross Language Morphologic Negation Identification in Electronic Health Records

Ioana Barbantan$^{(\boxtimes)}$ and Rodica Potolea

Computer Science Departament, Technical University of Cluj-Napoca,
Gh. Baritiu St 28, Cluj-Napoca, Romania
{ioana.barbantan,rodica.potolea}@cs.utcluj.ro

Abstract. The current paper presents an approach for analyzing the Electronic Health Records (EHRs) with the goal of automatically identifying morphologic negation such that swapping the truth values of concepts introduced by negation does not interfere with understanding the medical discourse. To identify morphologic negation we propose the RoPreNex strategy that represents the adaptation of our PreNex approach to the Romanian language [1]. We evaluate our proposed solution on the MTsamples [2] dataset. The results we obtained are promising and ensure a reliable negation identification approach in medical documents. We report precision of 92.62 % and recall of 93.60 % in case of the morphologic negation identification for the source language and an overall performance in the morphologic negation identification of 77.78 % precision and 80.77 % recall in case of the target language.

Keywords: Cross language · Morphologic negation · Electronic health records · Dictionary

1 Introduction

The evolution of technology acquaints us frequently with specialized gadgets that can influence our everyday life. We gain access to devices that manage our eating and exercise habits, monitor our heart rate and inform us of the calories we burn and consume or translate our activity to statistical dimensions. The English language became ubiquitous; we use English terms when referring to our computer components and the actions we can carry out using them or when sharing our thoughts and feelings on the social media. The devices nowadays have English imprints on them; when entering a store we usually find the Open/Closed sign more often than the corresponding information for the native language in each country. For the young generation these aspects do not represent issues as a large percentage of the young population in every country is familiar with the English language. Issues arise when these devices are used by elderly people whose existence was not overwhelmed by the adoption of the English language and the rapid evolution of technology. Usually, the main topic of interest for this category of population is represented by the development of their health.

As technology evolves, the number of medical devices that we gain access to grows as well; nowadays, we can easily send our health status by means of these devices to

© Institute for Computer Sciences, Social Informatics and Telecommunications Engineering 2015
R. Agüero et al. (Eds.): MONAMI 2014, LNICST 141, pp. 417–430, 2015.
DOI: 10.1007/978-3-319-16292-8_30

our medical doctors that automatically fill up our electronic health records with this new information. The problem is what to do when the persons that need to use the devices are not familiar with the language in which the instructions are presented or the information displayed on them.

The EHRs capture the medical history and current condition with detailed information about symptoms, surgeries, medications, illnesses or allergies. They are an important source of new information and knowledge if exploited correctly. From these documents we can retrieve new ways of how diseases interact with each other, the influence of demographics on the patients' conditions and many more. But in order to do this, the documents need to be clear, carry trustworthy information and should be unambiguous. In most cases the EHRs are unstructured documents and may contain recurrent information. The problem we address in this paper is defining a strategy for identifying negation in EHRs, towards retrieving relations among medical concepts. We propose an approach for adapting for the Romanian language to our already established methodology for English [1]. In both languages negation is of syntactic and morphologic types and a correspondence between the negation concepts is easily noticeable.

The main contribution of the paper addresses the existing drawback of several negation identification approaches that do not consider negation represented using negation prefixes in both languages. We propose a strategy that includes negation prefixes in identifying and dealing with the negative concepts in the EHRs. In order to tackle morphologic negation, our strategy is based on interpreting the structure of the words and evaluating the existence of the words with and without prefix in the language by taking into account the definitions provided in a dictionary specific to the source respectively the target languages.

The rest of the paper is organized as follows. In chapter II we present similar systems dealing with EHRs and negation. In chapter III the EHRs are briefly introduced along with the two most common negation types. Our solution is detailed in chapter IV where we describe the RoPreNex strategy and present the experiments we performed in chapter V. The last two chapters include the conclusion of our work and future enhancements for the approach we propose.

2   Related Work

Both in Romanian and English languages the task of identifying negation is mostly focused on negation expressed with specific words like *nu, fara, nici* in Romanian or *not, without, nor,* the English corresponding words. Morphologic negation is disregarded and there are even cases when it is otherwise inferred. For example, the authors in [3] talk about negation prefix when dealing with the word *not* and refer to it as negation prefix, whereas they are dealing with syntactic negation based on Givon's negation classification [4]. They present a system that identifies the n-words that represent negative quantifiers in order to determine the negative concord for the Romanian language.

A cross-lingual approach for document summarization is proposed in [5]. The authors evaluate how a cross language approach could help in spreading the news around the world when dealing with ordinary but not breaking news that are easily propagated among websites. The authors use as source language Romanian and translate the summarized information into English. The translation is performed using a bidirectional English-Romanian translation tool. The authors evaluate the performance of their approach by asking a set of questions to judges. The questions are regarding the Romanian summarizations and then the same set of the questions were asked for the translated summaries. An accuracy of 43 % is reported in the case of giving correct answers for the summarized documents. Most of the questions that could not have been answered are due to the fact that the translated summaries were not clearly understood.

Negation in medical documents is subject of interest in the medical domain as the diagnosis process the stated and missing or denied symptoms are weighted differently. There are several approaches dealing with identifying and labeling negation, like NegEx [6], Negfinder [7], or the tool presented in [8] developed for the BioScope negation annotated corpus. The main drawback of these tools is the absence of treating morphologic negation, hence leaving out several negated terms, especially when dealing with medical documents.

One reason for not considering morphologic negation is motivated by the authors in [9] by the few occurrences of these terms or by considering the prefixes as not determining negations [10]. In [7] negation is defined only when the negation terms negate subjects or object concepts (no, without, negative) and specify that even though there are concepts that have negative connotations (like akinesia) they are disregarded and report these cases as miscellaneous errors. These approaches are valid when dealing with data that is not domain dependent or in cases when the negation algorithm is meant to find all concepts that can be determined by a single negative identifier. In the case of medical records, (domain dependent documents) the negations are prevalent as in the medical language negation prefixes are broadly used. In medical documents is it expected that negation is clearly formulated as these documents should be clear and carry as few ambiguous terms as possible.

The analysis of morphologic negation is presented as a future enhancement for the work of the authors in [9], where they predict a growth in the performance of identifying the scope and focus of negation by removing the prefix and determining the validity of the obtained word. They introduce how negation in Natural Language is characterized and present an approach of automatically determining the scope and focus of negation. The frequency of the negation-bearing words in the corpus they use leads to considering negation only the determiners not and n't. The scope of negation was identified with 66 % accuracy.

Negation in medical documents is approached by Averbuch et al. in [11] that report that including negation in information retrieval improves precision from 60 % to 100 % with no significant changes in recall. They also state that the presence of a medical concept in the record, like a symptom, does not always imply that the patient actually suffers from that condition as the symptom can be negated.

Capturing word's semantics and relationships with the help of a dictionary in order to categorize a text is presented in [12]. The text is disambiguated and represented as features using the concepts and hypernymy relations in WordNet. The authors compare the results of text categorization when using a bag of words approach for document representation and when using the WordNet information for selecting the features.

They evaluate the methods on two datasets and notice that the WordNet approach exceeds in all test conditions the bag of words approach.

Negation has application in sentiment analysis when the opinion (positive, negative or neutral) is in question. In sentiment analysis the goal is to identify the polarity of assertions that can be positive or negative [13]. Usually this is done using specific words for the polarity categories [14]. The BioScope negation annotated corpus is used for evaluation in order to extract the polarity of the sentences using a Conditional Radom Field approach and a dependency parser [9]. The authors report achieving a 75.5 % F1 score on the BioScope corpus, a medical corpus and 80 % F1 score when using a product reviews corpus.

3   Theoretical Background

This section attempts to set the background of the work presented in this paper by introducing the main concepts we operate with: EHRs and the need to structure them, the role of handling negation in EHR concept extraction and structuring and the cross language strategies.

3.1   Electronic Health Records

The EHRs are unstructured or semi-structured text documents carrying medical information about patients. The HL7 standard announces as their main purpose being to provide the medical history and current condition [15]. The access to these medical documents is restricted to the medical personnel and the sharing of the information from these documents needs authorization.

The content of the EHRs can be organized into categories like symptoms, procedures, surgeries, medications, illnesses or allergies. If exploited correctly, the EHRs can offer information about future epidemics, or can be used to predict the status of patients having similar conditions.

The standard indicates that the EHR information should be captured using standardized code sets or nomenclature or even unstructured data. When the raw data is unstructured there are no straightforward mechanisms to infer knowledge out of data. When the presence of a symptom is noticed in an EHR, a semantic analysis is required to determine whether the occurrence is an affirmative or a negated one.

3.2   Negation

When performing the anamnesis for a patient the medical doctors are interested whether the patient suffers or not from different symptoms, and based on the responses from the patient, a diagnosis is established. When querying a data source for patients with similar conditions, it is important for the machine to distinguish between the negated and affirmed symptoms. Negation can be expressed in different ways as the patient can state he has fever or he is afebrile. In this case it is important to treat all types of negations that occur in documents.

Givon classifies negation as syntactic negation in the case of explicit negation and morphologic negation when using prefixes [4]. Expressing the symptomatology of a patient the following three sentences can be used.

- *The patient has no symptoms.*
- *The patient is asymptomatic.*
- *The patient doesn't have symptoms.*

As underlined in the three examples, negation can be expressed using explicit terms like no and n't but can also be expressed with a prefix a (*aymptomatic*).

Syntactic Negation is introduced by specific negation terms like *no, without, deny, not, rule out* in case of the English language or *fara, neaga, eliminia* in case of Romanian are commonly found in natural language (the two lists of terms are not correspondent). Unlike morphologic negation that is associated with a single word, syntactic negation can determine several words like in the case of an enumeration of symptoms: *The patient presented without fever, neck pain or tiredness.*

Morphologic Negation is expressed with specific negation prefixes placed in front of the words to alter their meaning by swapping their truth value. They support enhancement of the vocabulary by increasing the number of words. The prefixes can also be used in learning new terms as presented in the study in [16]. The separation of a word into prefix and root form helps in understanding the meaning of the words. Table 1 captures the negation prefixes in the English and Romanian languages and their correspondence.

Table 1. Correspondence of English and Romanian negation prefixes.

English negation prefix	Romanian negation prefix	Meaning	English example	Romanian example
In, il, im, ir	In, i	Negative prefixes	Insufficiency	Insuficient
A, an	A	Not, without, lacking	Afebrile	Afebril
Non		Absence, negation	Nonsurgical	Nechirurgical
Dis	Des, dez, de, ne	Negation, removal, expulsion	Discontinue	Discontinuu
Anti	Anti, Contra	Opposing, against	Anti-inflammatory	Antiinflamator
Un	Ne	Not, reversal, cancellation, deprived of	Uncomplicated	Necomplicat

3.3 Cross Language Approach

We define our approach for solving specific Natural Language Processing (NLP) tasks in a new language (we will call it target language) once a solution is set up in some other language (we will call it source language). In our case the source language is English, the target language is Romanian, and the task is negation identification in

EHRs. However, the approach is not limited to specific languages and/or tasks. Once in a source language an efficient solution for text processing has been identified, the approach defines a way of adapting it to the target language.

A cross language strategy to perform sentiment analysis for identifying subjective sentences is proposed in [17]. While translating queries from English to Indonesian the authors in [18] show that using a collection of dictionaries rather than a single dictionary significantly improves the results.

The English language covers a large amount of everyday life subjects, so, we should try to benefit in any possible way from this. The concepts used in Computer Science especially but also in other scientific and professional fields tend to be English. The medical domain makes no exception. Terms like *bypass* or *follow-up* became familiar to every single one of us [19].

4 Methodology for Morphologic Negation Identification in EHRs

In our work so far, we have implemented several strategies for identifying negation in medical documents (needed to further structure the EHRs). In [20], we employed a vocabulary of terms and a binary bag of words feature vector, while in [1] we replaced the vocabulary obtained with a dictionary of the English language. Our current work proposes cross-language strategy that deals with identifying morphologic negation in a target language based on an already established strategy for a source language.

4.1 Cross Language Strategy for Morphologic Negation Identification

Given the source language solution for negation identification, we define a methodology for adapting the solution for a target language. However, the methodology makes no restriction to the choice of languages. Provided the linguistic resources for other languages are available, the same strategy may be applied. Our specific goal is to instantiate the cross language methodology that identifies morphologic negation in both the source and target languages using the linguistic resources in the corresponding language. The source language is English, for which we have proposed and evaluated the PreNex strategy [1] and the target language is Romanian, which represents the subject of our current approach.

The resources we employ in our analysis consist in a dataset of EHRs available in English. The strategy starts by translating them into Romanian using an online translation service in order to obtain standardized documents and a reliable comparison. We propose a dictionary based approach where we identify morphologic negation. The dictionaries we use are WordNet[1] for English and DexOnline[2] for Romanian.

---

[1] http://wordnet.princeton.edu/.

[2] http://dexonline.ro/.

4.2   Dictionary Based Negation Extraction

In our previous approach, we proposed identifying morphologic negation from English medical documents, namely from the MTsamples [2]. We proposed a dictionary based approach [1] that exploits the meaning of the words by using an English language dictionary, namely WordNet and proposed several rules that semantically exploit the meaning of the words.

The rules for negation identification used in the PreNex approach are:

Definition recurrence rule: the root of a prefixed word is contained in the prefixed word's definition.

Definition content rule: both the root of the prefixed word and the prefix word are defined in WordNet and the definition of the prefixed word contains a negation identifier.

Hyphen rule: the prefix is followed by hyphen or space – the case is handled by removing the special character and sending the entity to be analyzed with the previous rules.

Compound words: progressively build a word from consecutive letters on an n-gram basis; remove the prefix and perform an analysis of the root. If the word can be split into two words with definitions in WordNet, we consider the word negated with negation prefix.

The rules were added progressively and as it can be noticed in Table 2, at each step improvements in the precision and recall were obtained. The first rule identifies negation prefixes with a precision of 95.07 % and a small recall of 29.09 %. The following rules added introduce degradation in precision, but the decrement of 2.45 % becomes irrelevant in relation to the increase of 64.51 % achieved for recall. We report as final results in the case of the PreNex strategy, precision of 92.62 % and recall of 93.60 %.

Table 2. PreNex performance.

PreNex rules	Precision (%)		Recall (%)		F-measure (%)	
(1): R1	95.07		29.09		44.55	
(2):(1)+R2	91.56	-3.55	74.78	45.69	82.35	37.77
(3):(2)+R3	92.81	1.25	89.01	14.22	90.87	8.54
(4):(3)+R4	92.62	-0.19	93.60	4.59	93.11	2.23
Overall improvement	-2.45		64.51		48.55	

The false positives introduced by the proposed solution are "infusion", "absolute", "intensity" or "another".

4.3   Dataset

In order to evaluate our approach we used a dataset of English EHRs provided by [2]. These are semi-structured documents that contain medical information about hospitalized patients. They present the evolution of the patient from the point they were admitted in the hospital to the point of discharge. The documents capture the symptoms, medical history, the procedures performed and the administered medication. There are cases when the patient is required to return to the hospital for a follow-up examination, in which case the conditions and details about the appointment are also established in the document.

As our current goal is to analyze medical documents for the Romanian language, we propose an adaptation of the morphologic negation identification proposed for English. As we want to make sure that the documents we send for analysis are compliant with the medical standards, we translated the documents to Romanian. Also, the amount of available annotated EHRs for Romanian is not satisfactory for a reliable analysis. In order to obtain the Romanian version of the EHRs, we used an online translation tool to obtain the correspondence of the medical documents between the two languages. There were cases where the translation tool employed could not translate all terms due to the fact that the words were not found in the English dictionary or in the English-Romanian dictionary. This issue was encountered in the case of the word *nontender or nonfasting* which are domain specific terms, in our case, the medical one.

The proposed methodology of evaluating the negation identification for the Romanian language follows the steps in Fig. 1. First, the corpus of documents used in the English language is translated for a reliable comparison. Then we preprocess the documents and apply the proposed negation identification rules. The last step employed is the proposed adapted strategy for identifying negated concepts.

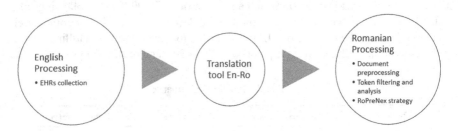

Fig. 1. Input data preparation.

4.4   RoPreNex Algorithm

In the current approach we propose identifying morphologic negation in medical documents written in Romanian, by adapting the strategy proposed for the English language. As presented in Table 1, a correspondence between the English and Romanian negation prefixes is noticeable.

We propose the RoPreNex algorithm to identify morphologic negation in Romanian medical documents, presented in Fig. 2. The rules consider the existence of the words and their root form in the DexOnline dictionary and also the content of their definition. DexOnline represents the Romanian language dictionary and consists of a collection of Romanian dictionaries. The dictionary interlinks the words with their definitions and has also integrated synonyms and the newest words that appeared in the language after 2004, when the integration of the dictionary on paper completed.

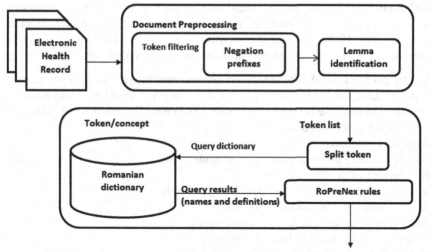

Fig. 2. RoPreNex flow.

There are several changes that had to be applied to our PreNex algorithm. As the DexOnline dictionary also contains definitions for the words that are not frequently used in the language (like regionalism or rural expressions) we must include an additional verification step such that these words do not interfere with our search. In case of the rural expressions, the words are truncated or the first letters may be removed in which case we might deal with a false case of root word.

The Romanian lemmatization tools are less efficient than the ones existing for English. Moreover, they should be accessed via a web service, which induces time overhead (also a less reliable solution), so we propose a lemmatization process that is able to bring the words in the documents to their dictionary form. The approach works as follows. For each word in the documents that was selected as possible negated concept, we remove its prefix and before determining its truth value, we preprocess it. The approach we propose considers the termination of the words. Usually the difference between the words in the document and their dictionary form appears in the added termination that announces the inflections (e.g. *e* is added for the plural of nouns or *em* in the case of verb tenses). When a match between the preprocessed word from the document and the words in the dictionary, we send to the negation identification rules the currently preprocessed word.

The RoPreNex strategy is presented in the algorithm below. For the morphologic negation identification task we proposed the following rules *Literal words, Definition content, Undefined prefixed word*.

Literal words. The DexOnline dictionary also contains definitions for the words that are not used in common language like regionalism or rural expressions. In this case the words are shortened and the first letters are removed when expressing the words, case in which they could falsely represent prefixes. This rule is a preprocessing step applied for the words in the dictionary. The following rules are the actual negation identification rules.

Definition content. The definition content rule identifies negation based on the definition of the word. First, we identify the prefix, remove it from the word, and obtain the root of the word. If the root and the prefixed word exist in DexOnline, we check whether the word's definition contains at least one negation identifier.

Undefined prefixed word. The undefined prefixed word rule is applied in the cases when the prefixed word is not defined in the dictionary as it could represent a domain specific term. In this case we remove the prefix and determine whether the root of the word is defined in the dictionary.

Algorithm notations:

ω – the possible prefixed word with negation prefix

$\tilde{\omega}$ – the root of ω

ρ – the prefix of ω { anti, dez, des, de, ne, in, a, im, contra }

definition(ω) – the definition of a word

defined(ω) – the word is defined in dictionary

literal(ω) – the word is in its literal form

The algorithm of determining whether ω is prefixed with a negation prefix works as follows:

```
Input = ω -possible prefixed word with negation prefix

ρ = prefix of ω

ω̃ = Remove ρ from ω

//Literal words

If (literal(ω)) (literal(ω̃))

    ω <- lemma(ω)

    ω̃ <- lemma(ω̃)

    //R1. Definition content

    If (definition(ω) && definition(ω̃))

    If (definition(ω) contains one negation identifier)

        Then ω is negated with prefix

    Endif

    Endif

    Else //R2. Undefined prefixed word

    If (!defined(ω) and defined(ω̃))

        Then ω is negated with prefix

    Endif

Endif

END
```

5 Morphologic Negation Evaluation RoPreNex

This section presents the experiments performed with the proposed morphologic negation identification strategy for Romanian medical documents, and a comparison with PreNex, our original solution for English [1]. We evaluate our approach on the translated MTsamples dataset, presented in more detail in Sect. 4.3.

Table 3. RoPreNex algorithm rules coverage.

Rule	% of covered cases
Definition content	78.57
Undefined prefixed word	21.43

In our proposed strategy, most of the prefix negated concepts are identified by the *Definition content* rule, as most of them are defined in both representations: as prefixed word and root form, Table 3, line 2. A smaller percentage of the prefixed concepts are not defined in the dictionary, and for this case we had to introduce the second rule *Undefined prefixed word*, Table 3, line 3 which covers 21.43 % of the correctly identified concepts.

5.1 RoPreNex Performance

The rules we propose for identifying morphologic negation in Romanian medical documents are promising as can be seen in Table 4, last line. The performance of each rule is presented also in Table 4. Even though the *Undefined prefix word* rule has a small value for recall, as it misses some of the words it was supposed to identify, the great value for precision makes it an important rule for our approach. Making a tradeoff between the quality and number of correctly identified negated concepts, we report an overall performance of precision of 77.78 % and recall of 80.77 %. The PreNex strategy outperforms the current RoPreNex strategy with only 14.85 % in case of precision and 12.83 % in case of recall, as presented in Table 5. To the best of our knowledge a tool for dealing with morphologic negation has not been developed for the Romanian language, that is why we report our results to our English version of the algorithm.

The performance of our proposed strategy is satisfactory taking into account the fact that the documents we evaluated were translated and not original and the fact that we did not include any language specific methodologies for text analysis.

Table 4. RoPreNex performance.

Rule	Precision (%)	Recall (%)
Definition content	76.74	84.62
Undefined prefixed word	81.82	69.23
Overall performance	77.78	80.77

Table 5. Performance of negation identification strategy for Romanian and English strategies.

Approach	Precision (%)	Recall (%)
Romanian approach (RoPreNex)	77.78	80.77
English approach (PreNex)	92.62	93.60

5.2   Discussion

The reported performance of our proposed approach is promising, and we encountered the following problems addressed at the level of translation tool employed, at the word level, and at dictionary level.

Translation level issues. The translation tool we employed in our approach did not manage to perform a one-on-one translation. There were cases when in the translated document we encountered English words like *nontender* or *nonfasting*.

Word level issues. Other issues we came across were related to the fact that for the Romanian language we could not employ a lemmatizer that could help in normalizing the words such that we could obtain their dictionary format. Using our lemma implemented approach we managed to increase the recognition rate, but when the inflectional form of the word changes the root's structure it still remains an issue that has to be addressed. We also found cases when the words are shortened in the source language and the translation tool could not translate the word in the target language, like in the case of the word *noncontrib*.

Dictionary level issues. The DexOnline dictionary we used in our approach is populated with most of the words that exist in the Romanian language and also with the newest terms entered in the language. But, there still are cases when the dictionary fails to capture information about specialized terms like *atraumatic*.

The false positives introduced by our algorithm are usually represented by words that have a negation specific prefix but are not actually negated words. Like in the case of the word *informat* whose English correspondent is *informed*. In this case the word matches all rules we defined as the word and its root are both defined in the dictionary, but do not represent a negated entity.

6   Conclusions and Further Work

In this paper we propose a methodology for identifying morphologic negation in Romanian medical documents. It is the adaptation of our proposed solution on English documents, towards a cross-language NLP strategy for medical documents mining. The results we report for identification are promising as to our best knowledge there are no similar approaches for identifying morphologic negation for the Romanian language. The results obtained by our proposed methodology are precision of 77.78 % and recall of 80.77 % %, which are only 14.85 % in case of precision and 12.83 % in case of recall below the corresponding English results. We consider our methodology reliable when applied on medical documents as the false positives that are introduced are not medical related concepts. Our current work consists in enhancing the identification performance of morphologic negation for the Romanian language.

We consider improving the performance of this strategy by first preprocessing the documents by employing a spell checker for each language or a distance measure algorithm that could correct the form of the misspelled words. Another task that we consider is represented by treating the abbreviations and word shortenings as the medical terms can appear with a code mostly in the case of the diseases.

Acknowledgments. The authors would like to acknowledge the contribution of the COST Action IC1303 - AAPELE.

References

1. Barbantan, I., Potolea, R.: Exploiting Word Meaning for Negation Identification in Electronic Health Records, IEEE AQTR (2014)
2. MTsamples: Transcribed Medical Transcription Sample Reports and Examples. Last accessed on 23.10, 2012
3. Iordachioaia, G., Richter, F.: Negative concord in Romanian as polyadic quantification. In: Muller, S. (ed.) Proceedings of the 16th International Conference on Head-Driven Phrase Structure Grammar Georg-August-Universitat Gottingen, pp. 150–170. CSLI Publications, Germany (2009)
4. Givon, T.: English Grammar: A Function-Based Introduction. Benjamins, Amsterdam, NL (1993)
5. Orasan, C., Chiorean, O.A.: Evaluation of a cross–lingual romanian–english multi–document summariser. In: Proceedings of LREC 2008 Conference, Marrakech, Morocco (2008)
6. Chapman, W., Bridewell, W., Hanbury, P., Cooper, G.F., Buchanan, B.G.: A simple algorithm for identifying negated findings and diseases in discharge summaries. J. Biomed. Inform. **34**(5), 301–310 (2001)
7. Mutalik, P.G., Deshpande, A., Nadkarni, P.M.: Use of general-purpose negation detection to augment concept indexing of medical documents: a quantitative study using the UMLS. J. Am. Med. Inform. Assoc. **8**(6), 80–91 (2001)
8. Vincze, V., Szarvas, G., Farkas, R., Móra, R., Csirik, J.: The BioScope corpus: biomedical texts annotated for uncertainty, negation and their scopes. In: Natural Language Processing in Biomedicine (BioNLP) ACL Workshop Columbus, OH, USA (2008)
9. Blanco, E., Moldovan, D.: Some issues on detecting negation from text. In: Proceedings of the Twenty-Fourth International Florida Artificial Intelligence Research Society Conference (2011)
10. Councill, I.G., McDonald, R., Velikovich, L.: What's great and what's not: learning to classify the scope of negation for improved sentiment analysis. In: Proceedings of the Workshop on Negation and Speculation in Natural Language Processing, Uppsala, pp. 51–59 (2010)
11. Averbuch, M., Karson, T.H., Ben-Ami, B., Maimond, O., Rokachd, L.: Context-sensitive medical information retrieval, In: Proceedings of AMACL, pp. 282–286 (2003)
12. Elberrichi, Z., Rahmoun, A., Bentaalah, M.A.: Using WordNet for text categorization. Int. Arab. J. Inf. Technol. **5**(1), 16–24 (2008)

13. Turney, P.D.: Thumbs up or thumbs down? Semantic orientation applied to unsupervised classification of reviews. In: Proceedings of the 40th Annual Meeting of the 14. Association for Computational Linguistics (ACL), Philadelphia, pp. 417–424 (2002)

14. Rokach, L., Romano, R., Maimon, O.: Negation recognition in medical narrative reports. Inf. Retrieval **11**(6), 499–538 (2008)

15. Fischetti, L., Mon, D., Ritter, J., Rowlands, D.: Electronic Health Record – system functional model, Chapter Three: direct care functions (2007)

16. Stahl, S.A., Shiel, T.G.: Teaching meaning vocabulary: productive approaches for poor readers. Read. Writ. Q. Overcoming Learn. Difficulties **8**(2), 223–241 (1992)

17. Riloff, E., Wiebe, J.: Learning extraction patterns for subjective expressions. In: Proceedings of the Conference on Empirical Methods in Natural Language Processing (EMNLP-03) (2003)

18. Hayuran, H., Sari, S., Adriani, M.: Query and document translation for english-Indonesian cross language IR. In: Peters, C., et al. (eds.) Evaluation of Multilingual and Multi-modal Information Retrieval. Lecture Notes in Computer Science, vol. 4730, pp. 57–61. Springer-Verlag, Heidelberg (2007)

19. Frinculescu, I.C.: An overview of the english influence on the Romanian medical language. Sci. Bull. Politehnica Univ. Timişoara Trans. Mod. Lang. **8**, 1–2 (2009)

20. Barbantan, I., Potolea, R.: Towards knowledge extraction from electronic health records - automatic negation identification. In: International Conference on Advancements of Medicine and Health Care through Techonology. Cluj-Napoca, Romania (2014)

Energy Consumption Optimization Using Social Interaction in the Mobile Cloud

Katerina Papanikolaou[1]([⊠]), Constandinos X. Mavromoustakis[2],
George Mastorakis[3], Athina Bourdena[3], and Ciprian Dobre[4]

[1] Department of Computer Science and Engineering, European University
Cyprus, 6 Diogenis Str. Engomi, P.O. Box: 22006, 1516 Nicosia, Cyprus
k.papanikolaou@euc.ac.cy
[2] Department of Computer Science, University of Nicosia,
46 Makedonitissas Avenue, P.O. Box: 24005,
1700 Nicosia, Cyprus
mavromoustakis.c@unic.ac.cy
[3] Department of Informatics Engineering, Technological Educational Institute
of Crete, Estavromenos, 71500 Heraklion, Crete, Greece
gmastorakis@staff.teicrete.gr, bourdena@pasiphae.eu
[4] Faculty of Automatic Control and Computers, University Politehnica
of Bucharest, 313 Splaiul Independentei, 060042 Bucharest, Romania
ciprian.dobre@cs.pub.ro

Abstract. This paper addresses the issue of resource offloading for energy usage optimization in the cloud, using the centrality principle of social networks. Mobile users take advantage of the mobile opportunistic cloud, in order to increase their reliability in service provision by guaranteeing sufficient resources for the execution of mobile applications. This work elaborates on the improvement of the energy consumption for each mobile device, by using a social collaboration model that allows for a cooperative partial process offloading scheme. The proposed scheme uses social centrality as the underlying mobility and connectivity model for process offloading within the connected devices to maximize the energy usage efficiency, node availability and process execution reliability. Furthermore, this work considers the impact of mobility on the social-oriented offloading, by allowing partitionable resources to be executed according to the social interactions and the associated mobility of each user during the offloading process. The proposed framework is thoroughly evaluated through event driven simulations, towards defining the validity and offered efficiency of the proposed offloading policy in conjunction to the energy consumption of the wireless devices.

Keywords: Resource sharing · Centrality · Social collaboration · Energy conservation · Dynamic resource migration · Dependable mobile computing · Temporal execution-oriented metrics

1 Introduction

As social networking is experiencing an exponential growth and is becoming part of our daily routines, the communications overlay it creates can be exploited, by a number

© Institute for Computer Sciences, Social Informatics and Telecommunications Engineering 2015
R. Agüero et al. (Eds.): MONAMI 2014, LNICST 141, pp. 431–445, 2015.
DOI: 10.1007/978-3-319-16292-8_31

of applications and services [1]. Users are connecting to social networks by using small mobile devices, such as smart phones and tablets that are able to form opportunistic networks. Such networks form a potential infrastructure for increased resource availability to all users in the network, especially to those that face reduced resource availability (e.g. energy, memory, processing resources etc.). Opportunistic wireless networks exhibit unique properties, as they depend on users' behavior and movement, as well as on users' local concentration. Predicting and modeling their behavior is a difficult task but the association of the social interconnectivity factor may prove part of the solution, by successfully tapping into the resources they are offering. Resource sharing in the wireless and mobile environment is even more demanding as applications require the resource sharing to happen in a seamless and unobtrusive to the user manner, with minimal delays in an unstructured and ad hoc changing system without affecting the user's Quality of Experience (QoE) [2]. This forms a highly ambitious objective as on one hand wireless environments cannot reliably commit to sharing resources for establishing reliable communication among users since there is no way of guaranteeing resource allocation and on the other hand, if that was to be overcome their limited capabilities exacerbate further the problem. The mobility factor imposes additional constraints as network topology is constantly producing fluctuation in bandwidth usage and resource availability. The dependency on device capabilities restricts solutions to particular devices, lacking generality in its applicability. In this context and by considering all the above-mentioned issues, this work uses social interactivity as a method for modeling and achieving resource sharing in the wireless mobile environment.

As social platforms are used by a staggering majority of 87 % of mobile users for communication and message exchange, they form an underlying web interconnecting mobile users and possibly enabling reliable resource sharing [3]. Using social connectivity and interactivity patterns, we should be able to provide adaptability to device capabilities and operating environment, enabling devices to adapt to frequent changes in location and context. One of the ever lacking resources in the wireless mobile environment is that of energy. As energy is stored in batteries, it forms the only source for mobile device operation and as new and more power demanding applications are created every day, energy usage optimization forms a challenging field, approached by both hardware and software solutions.

This work proposes a model of energy usage optimization for mobile devices in an opportunistic wireless environment, using the social interaction model. The social interaction model is based on the social centrality principle. With the social centrality principle users are able to share resources when a shared contact threshold is satisfied. Energy intense processing and other actions are disseminated using the proposed model enabling nodes running low on energy resources to extend or alleviate their energy demands and thus extend their life and availability. In the proposed model, the centrality principle and the "ageing" timing rule are applied, in order produce a more efficient use of the available energy. Thus, opportunistic energy conservation takes place enabling efficient management of the energy available to other wireless peer users, and guaranteeing end-to-end availability for the longest time possible, in a wireless mobile environment.

This introduction of the social interaction model for achieving optimum resource usage forms the key innovation of the proposed framework. The framework evaluates the energy state of each node, according to its type, energy demands and usage combines this with its social centrality, determining if the node is to receive or provide energy to the network. Through the proposed framework, the ability to adaptively perform tasks for another node increases and depends on the node's current energy state, as well as on its "friendship" degree. Furthermore, the proposed framework strengthens or relaxes the energy usage and the task allocation scheme, according to the social contacts and the user's interaction parameters. In Sect. 2, we describe the related work, while Sect. 3 elaborates on presenting the proposed social-enabled mechanism for opportunistic and socially oriented energy sharing and process off-loading. Section 4 presents the performance evaluation of the proposed scheme through the experimental evaluation and Sect. 5 concludes this paper, by proposing future potential directions for further research.

2 Related Work

Social networking started as an online tool for forming connections and information sharing. Its appeal and huge popularity primarily came from the fact that the social activity was enhanced in the online line environment with the use of multimedia, giving users instant access to information. Another aspect of the online environment was the ability of the social network users to share their location with others, instantly advertising their present coordinates either using programs such as FourSquare or having automatic tracking, by exploiting the mobile devices GPS capabilities. The use of user mobility in opportunistic networks will help to realize the next generation of applications based on the adaptive behavior of the devices for resource exchange. The problem of energy usage optimization that considers energy as a finite resource that needs to be shared among users, providing most processing power whilst maintaining group connectivity, will greatly benefit by using the social centrality model. Opportunistic networks will greatly benefit from the capability of the mobile devices to gather information from any hosted application, in order to better utilize network resources. The task allocation and load balancing can be strictly or voluntarily associated with the social communication. Works such as [4] propose architectures, which rely on the local information derived by the devices and their local views, in optimizing load balancing and energy management, as well as even some self-behaving properties, like self-organization. In [4] resource manipulation optimization is offered. However, this occurs without considering social parameters, such as friendship, contact rate or the temporal parameters (i.e. users' location).

The contribution of this work is to combine the energy management scheme with the proposed social parameters and model for each node, in order to optimize the energy management and load sharing process. In the game theoretic approach [5], the energy usage optimization problem is translated to a contention game, where the nodes compete to access the energy resources, reaching to the Nash equilibrium; an approach that improves on the random and individualized approach. In [5] the proposed system supports fine grained offload to minimize energy savings with minimal burden on the programmer. The model decides at runtime which methods should be remotely executed driven by an optimization engine that achieves the best energy savings possible under the mobile devices current connectivity constraints. In [6] energy offloading is viewed as potentially energy saving but the overheads of privacy, security and reliability need to be added as well. The integration of social connectivity into the process is an unexplored area. Social connectivity takes into consideration users associations, location profiles and social interactions as a basis for creating an index for users' resources over time for subsequent resource offloading.

In this work, a social-oriented methodology is used for minimizing energy consumption for highly demanding applications with high memory/processing requirements. The social-oriented model with the associated friendships as the basis for social mobility, utilizes the introduced social-centrality, for selecting and offloading energy hungry partitionable tasks (parts of executable applications and processes) under the availability optimization objective. In addition, this work considers the motion coefficients for each user (using normalized [0..1] parameter) and encompasses these characteristics into the proposed energy utilization scheme for enabling maximum temporal node availability without reducing the processing capabilities of the system as a whole. The proposed scheme uses both the pre-scheduled opportunistic offloading [7] and the social interactions that take place among the collaborative users and their associated strength of friendship. The scheme improves on predicting user mobility under the end-to-end availability. In order to assess the effectiveness of the proposed scheme, exhaustive simulations take place considering the offered energy by the social-collaborative network within the mobility context. The results of these lead to thorough measurements of the energy consumption optimization for mobile nodes/users.

3   Probabilistic Motion and Social Oriented Methodology for Efficient Energy Consumption

Wireless mobile networks allow unrestricted access to mobile users under a changing topology. The implications of mobility cannot be determined over time as the network topology is dynamically changing. In our work, the mobility model used is based on the probabilistic Fraction Brownian Motion (FBM) where nodal motion is done according to certain probabilities in accordance with location and time. Assume that we need to support a mobile node that is low on energy reserves and requires an energy heavy application to run. This implies that in a non-static, multi-hop environment, there is a need to model the motion of the participating nodes in the end-to-end path such that the requesting nodes can move through the network and conserve its resources. We also assume a clustered-mobility configuration scenario presented in [2], where each node has its own likelihood for the motion it follows. To predict whether a node will remain within the cluster, we aggregate these probabilities. This also shows the probabilities for the other nodes remaining in the cluster. The mobility scenario used in this work is modelled and hosted in a scheme that enables the utilization of social feedback into the model. Unlike the predetermined relay path in [7] and the known location/region, the mobility scenario used in this work is a memoryless FBM [8], with no stationary correlation among users' movements. FBM can be derived probabilistically from the random walk mobility model and can be expressed as a stochastic process that models the random continuous motion. The mobile node moves from its current location with a randomly selected speed, in a randomly selected direction in real time as users interact. However, in real life the real time mobility that the users exhibit, can be expressed as an ordinary walk, where the users spot-out some environmental stimuli and are attracted to them. Their decisions may be relayed to their respective social communication. In the proposed scenario, the walking speed and direction are set for the mobile users and are both chosen from predefined ranges, $[v_{min}, v_{max}]$ and $[0, 2\pi)$, respectively [9]. The new speed and directions are maintained for an arbitrary length of time randomly chosen from $(0, t_{max}]$. The node makes a memoryless decision for new speed and direction when the chosen time period elapses. The movements can be described as a Fractional Random Walk on a weighted graph [1], with the total likelihood $P_{i,j}^L$ in L^n.

We model the movement of each device using a graph theoretical model, in which a device can move randomly according to a topological graph $G = (V,E)$, that comprises of pair of sets $V(or\ V(G))$ and $E\ (or\ E(G))$ called edges. The edges join different pairs of vertices. This walk considers a connected graph with n nodes labeled $\{1, 2, 3, ...,n\}$ in a cluster L^n with weight $w_{ij} \geq 0$ on the edge (i,j). If edge (i,j) does not exist, we set $w_{ij} = 0$. We assume that the graph is undirected so that $w_{ij} = w_{ji}$. A node walks from a location to another location in the graph in the following random walk manner. Given that node i is *in reference*, the next location j is chosen from among the neighbors of i with probability:

$$p_{ij}^L = \frac{w_{ij}}{\sum_k w_{ik}} \tag{1}$$

where in (1) above the p_{ij} is proportional to the weight of the edge (i, j), then the sum of the weights of all edges in the cluster L is:

$$w_{ij}^L = \sum_{i,j:j > 1} w_{ij} \tag{2}$$

Then the stationary distribution according to [1] is given by

$$\pi_i^L = \frac{w_i^L}{2w} \tag{3}$$

where, it can be seen that the preceding distribution satisfies the relationship $\pi P = \pi$, when the movement is performed for a node/device i to location j (stationary distribution of the Markov chain as each movement of the users usually has a selected predetermined path (i e. corridor etc.)) associated as follows:

$$\sum_i \pi_i P_{ij} = \sum_i \left\{ \frac{w_i}{2w} \times \frac{w_{ij}}{w_i} \right\} = \sum_i \left\{ \frac{1}{2w} w_{ij} \right\} = \frac{1}{2w} \sum_i \{w_{ij}\} = \frac{w_j}{2w} = \pi_j \tag{4}$$

Equation 4 above denotes that the stationary probability of state of i is proportional to the weight of the edges emanating from node i. By using the motion notation we can express the track of requests as a function of the location (i.e. movements and updates p_{ij}^L) as: $R_i(I_{ij}, p_{ij}^L)$ *where* R_i is the request from node i, I_{ij} is the interaction coefficient measured in Eq. 2. We use the representation of the interactions by utilizing notations of weighted graphs (Eq. 1).

Different types of links or involvements are expressed in different ways in social connectivity modeling. Consequently, several types of centralities are defined in the directed or undirected graphs [1]. Users may have or not a certain type of association with any other user in the global network and this is modelled with the concept of the social network. Nodes carry weights that represent the degree of associativity with other nodes. These weights are associated with each edge linking two nodes and are used to model the interaction strength between nodes [10]. This models the degree of friendship that each node has with the other nodes in the network. The weights are assigned and used to measure the degree of the strength of the association of the connecting parts. Consequently the degree of social interaction between two devices can be expressed as a value in the range of [0, 1]. A degree of 0 signifies that the two nodes/devices are not socially connected and therefore no social interaction exists between them. As social interaction increases so does the weight reaching 1 indicating very strong social interaction. The strength of the social interaction and the energy state of each node will form the basis for offloading processes to other nodes in the network. In this work, we propose such a model for efficient energy management prolonging node lifetime based on the social association scheme.

We propose that the strength of social interaction will also affect the offloading process, which as the next sections show will affect the energy conservation mechanism. The social interaction can be represented by the 5×5 symmetric matrix (Eq. 2 matrix is based on the social population in the network), the names of nodes correspond to both rows and columns and are based on the interaction and connectivity. The latter matrix, forms the Interaction Matrix which represents the social relationships between nodes. The generic element i,j represents the interaction between two individual elements i and j, the diagonal elements represent the relationship an individual has with itself and are set to 1. In (5), the I_{ij} represents all the links associated to a weight before applying the threshold values which will indicate the stronger association between two nodes.

$$I_{ij} = \begin{bmatrix} 1 & 0.766 & 0.113 & 0.827 & 0 \\ 0.132 & 1 & 0.199 & 1 & 0.321 \\ 0 & 0.231 & 1 & 0.542 & 0.635 \\ 0.213 & 0 & 0 & 1 & 0.854 \\ 0 & 0 & 0.925 & 0.092 & 1 \end{bmatrix} \tag{5}$$

3.1   The Use of the "Friendship" for Process Execution Memory-Oriented Offloading

The elements of the Matrix I_{ij} (5) represent the measure of the social relationship "friendship" between the users. This is determined by the amount of direct or indirect social interaction among the different users belonging to the network as follows:

$$f^d_{i \to j} = norm[c(t) \cdot P(t)]^{0..1} \forall i, j \tag{6}$$

Where $f^d_{i \to j}$ is defined as the direct friendship evaluation from node i to node j, $P(k_t)$ is the probability $P(k)$ of a node being connected to k other nodes at time t in the network decays as a power law, given by: $P(k) = k^{-\gamma}$ where for the value of the power γ is estimated as follows $2 < \gamma < 3$ as explored in various real networks [11]. This results in a large number of nodes having a small node degree and therefore very few neighbors, but a very small number of nodes having a large node degree and therefore becoming hubs in the system. $c(t)$ consists of the duration of the communication among "friends", and is determined as a function of the communication frequency and the number of roundtrip "friendships". The roundtrip "friendships" are determined by the "hop-friendships" of the node i to a node k, as Fig. 1 presents. These are the "friends-of-friends" where according to the node i any "friend-of-friend" can reach–on a roundtrip basis- the node i again.

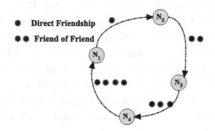

Fig. 1. Roundtrip "friendship" of a node i via other peers, and the "reach-back" notation to the node via the intermediate peers.

Then, the $c(t)$ of any of the "friendship" peers can be evaluated as the: $c(t) = \frac{1}{N} f^d_{i \to j}$, where N is the number of peers away from i, for reaching a friendship within $f^d_{i \to k}$ for a specified time slot t. Each element in the I_{ij} is re-estimated and varies through time according to the enhancement of the relation of the individuals as follows:

$$I_{ij} = \frac{I_{ij} + \Delta I_{ij}}{1 + \Delta I_{ij}} \tag{7}$$

Where I_{ij} is the association between two individuals that is strengthened or weakened (if less than $\nabla I_{ij} = I_{ij_{(\tau)}} - I_{ij_{(\tau-1)}}$) and ∇I represents the difference from the previous I_{ij} association between i, j. As associations and friendships vary over-time resulting in the strengthening or weakening of different links we incorporate this element by adding a time-varying parameter enabling an association to fade if two individuals are not in contact for a prolonged time period. This is expressed using the flowing equation:

$$\Delta I_{ij} = \frac{a}{t_{age}} + b, \forall t_{age} < T_{RL} \tag{8}$$

where t_{age} is the time that has passed since last contact and is measured until the individuals abandon the clustered plane L. The empirical constants a and b are chosen be the network designer [12] with typical values of 0.08 and 0.005 respectively. The proposed model encompasses the impact of the mobility on the interaction elements I_{ij} as the derived matrix consisting of the elements of w_{ij}^L and I_{ij} as follows:

$$M_{ij} = I_{ij} \cdot p_{ij}^L \tag{9}$$

where the element w_{ij} derived from the p_{ij}^L matrix of the plane area L, is the likelihood of an individual to move from i to a certain direction to j, as Fig. 1 shows.

3.2   Cloud Offloading Model Using Social Centrality

The determination of the importance of each node in a wireless mobile network is a very important task. This importance is based on the node's position, connectivity and interactivity patterns, as well as on motion thought time. A large number of connections and interactions signify an important and social central node. The term of centrality that has been introduced in [1] combines user behavior of each individual device with respect to its placement and behavior with the other devices within the cluster [2]. From a group of nodes a subset of the individuals is sampled and used to produce a subgraph, consisting only of those individuals and the links among them. The subgraph produced is used for performing the centrality approximation with the centrality scores of the sample being used as approximations. In social networks the high connectivity degree nodes serve as bridges in order to provide connectivity to lower degree nodes. A node's degree can be measured by $D_c(aj) = \sum_{i=1}^{n} d(ai, aj)$, where $d(ai, aj) = \begin{cases} 1 \forall ai, aj \in D \\ 0 \forall ai, aj \notin D \end{cases}$, D denotes the direct connectivity. As the maximum number of connected nodes for any graph is $n-1$, the formula to calculate the centrality of the node by using the proportion of the number of adjacent nodes to the maximum number $(n-1)$ is as follows:

$$D_c'(aj) = \frac{\sum_{i=1}^{n} d(ai, aj)}{n - 1} \tag{10}$$

Centrality is used to indicate the relative importance of a node in a network of nodes [13] and its relative contribution to the communication process as derived by the duration and distance covered with the frequency and parameterized in the context of avoiding network communication partitioning. Adding to this, social centrality measures the social closeness of two or more nodes. With social centrality we measure the number of times a node is chosen to host the "best-effort" parameters, process offloading in our case, for time t in L. A node with high social betweenness centrality β_{ai} will have to strongly interact with the other nodes belonging to social cluster L, measured as:

$$\beta_{ai} = \frac{\sum_{1}^{j} P_{aj \to ak}}{\sum_{1}^{k} P_{ij} \forall P \in ai} \tag{11}$$

with $P_{aj \to ak}$ representing the number of paths in the cluster via which the requested memory/capacity resources can be served between nodes aj and ak and P_{ij} represents the number of paths in the social cluster that include ai, $\forall P \in ai$. Based on the latter, we introduce the social-oriented stability parameter $\sigma_{c(t)}$ for a specified time t, as:

$$\sigma_C(t) = \left[\frac{R_{ij|t} \cdot (1 - norm(\beta_{ai})) \cdot N_{C(i \to j|t)}}{\inf(C_r) \cdot R_{C(t)}} \right] m_{ij}(t) \qquad (12)$$

where R_{ij} is the normalized communication ping delays between i and j nodes at time t, β_{ai} is the normalized [0..1] social betweenness centrality showing the strong ability to interact with other nodes in the cluster L, $N_{C(i \to j|t)}$ is the successfully offloaded capacity/memory units over the total allowed capacity, C_r is the multi-hop channel's available capacity, $m_{ij}(t)$ is the interaction measures derived from Eq. 8 at the time interval t, and $R_{C(t)}$ is the end-to-end delay in the cluster's pathway. The social-oriented stability parameter $\sigma_c(t)$ indicates the capability and transmitability of the node i to offload a certain process according to the ranked criteria of each process in L for time t.

3.3 Energy-Consumption Model Using Social-Oriented Capacity Measurement

Energy consumption is important for wireless nodes as non-optimized energy usage can lead to uncertainty in availability and reliability for each node and consequently the whole of the network. In this work, we use the social centrality aspect of the network as the substrate for efficient energy conservation. As the social centrality degree differs per node, processes are offloaded so as to minimize the total energy consumption and provide a total higher node availability for the most popular nodes, thus maintaining network connectivity. The system will decide when and where to offload processes, according the current energy state of each device. The degree of social centrality allows the node to offload resources according to the social model and the estimation of the each node's energy consumption as in Eq. 14. So ultimately, in order to achieve energy conservation, resources may be offloaded to the cloud or any other peer-neighboring device (so that the device that needs to run the executable resource will potentially conserve energy). Thus, the measurable energy consumption can be evaluated according to the:

$$E_{r(a_j)} = E_C(a_j) \cdot \frac{C}{S_{a_j}} \qquad (13)$$

where C is the parameter indicating the number of instructions that can be processed within T_t, S_{a_j} represents the processing time at the server-device and $E_C(a_j)$ represents the relative energy consumption which is expressed as:

$$E_C(r_i) = \frac{Cost_{C(r_i)}}{S_C(r_i)} W_C \qquad (14)$$

where S_C is the server instruction processing speed for the computation resources, $Cost_C$ the resources instruction processing cost for the computation resources and W_c signifies the energy consumption of the device in mW.

Each mobile device should satisfy an energy threshold level and a specified centrality degree in the system in order to proceed with process execution offloading. By using N devices within *2-hops vicinity coverage* which is evaluated based on the measurements regarding the maximum signal strength and data rate model [14]) the following should be satisfied:

$$\frac{Cost_{c(r_i)}}{S_{c(r_i)}} \cdot W_c \Big|^{r_i} > \frac{Cost_{c(r_i)}}{S_{c(r_i)}} \cdot W_c \Big|^{1,2..N} \tag{15}$$

$$W_{r_i} > W_c \forall f_{i \to j}^d \text{ devices} \tag{16}$$

The energy consumption of each device should satisfy the (15)–(16) for each of the resources (executable processes) running onto the device MN_{m-1} hosting the r_i resource. The $r_1, r_2, r_3, .. r_i$ parameters represent the resources that can be offloaded to run onto another device based on the resources' availability as in [15]. In this respect, the r_i with the maximum energy consumption is running in a partitionable manner to minimize the energy consumed by other peer-devices. These actions are shown in the steps of the proposed algorithm in Table 1.

Table 1. Centrality-based offloading scheme

1: **Inputs:** MN_m, Location, resources $r_1, r_2, r_3, .. r_i \forall MN_m$ with certain mobility direction w_{ij}^L

2: for all Cloud devices that have association of $f_{i \to j}^d$ and satisfy $c(t) = \dfrac{1}{N} f_{i \to j}^d$

3: find from $r_1, r_2, r_3, .. r_i$ the r_i that can be offloaded to run onto another device

4: for all MN_{m-1} do{

5: Estimate $\sigma_C(t) = \left[\dfrac{R_{ij|t} \cdot (1 - norm(\beta_{ai})) \cdot N_{C(i \to j|t)}}{\inf(C_r) \cdot R_{C(t)}} \right] m_{ij}(t)$

6:   if ($\sigma_C(t)$ is valid and above a threshold){

7:     search for MN_{m-1} device that satisfies

$$\frac{Cost_{c(r_i)}}{S_{c(r_i)}} \cdot W_c \Big|^{r_i} > \frac{Cost_{c(r_i)}}{S_{c(r_i)}} \cdot W_c \Big|^{1,2..N}, \ W_{r_i} > W_c \forall 1,2,3,...N$$

8:     offload ($r_i, MN_{k(i)}$) //to $MN_{k(i)}$ to execute resource *(i)* onto k node

9:   end **if**

10:   end **for**

11: end **for**

The resource allocation will take place, towards responding to the performance requirements as in [2] and [15]. A significant measure in the system is the availability of memory and the processing power of the mobile cloud devices, as well as the server-based terminals. The processing power metric is designed and used to measure the processing losses for the terminals that the r_i will be offloaded, as in (17), where a_j is an application and T_k^j is the number of terminals in forming the cloud (mobile and static) rack that are hosting application a_j and $T_{a_j}(r)$ is the number of mobile terminals hosting process of the application across all different cloud-terminals (racks).

$$C_{a_j} = \frac{T_k^j}{\sum_k T_{a_j}(r)} \forall \min(E_c(r_i)) \in f_{i \to j}^d \tag{17}$$

Equation 17 shows that if there is minimal loss in the capacity utilization i.e. $C_{a_j} \cong 1$ then the sequence of racks $T_{a_j}(r)$ are optimally utilized. The latter is shown through the conducted simulation experiments in the next section. The dynamic resource migration algorithm is shown in Table 1 with the basic steps for obtaining an efficient execution for a partitionable resource that cannot be handled by the mobile device in reference and therefore the offloading policy is used to ensure execution continuation. The entire scheme is shown in Table 1, with all the primary steps for offloading the resources onto either MN_{m-1} neighbouring nodes (or–as called- server nodes (as in [15])) based on the delay and temporal criteria of the collaborating nodes.

4   Performance Evaluation Analysis, Experimental Results and Discussion

Performance evaluation results encompass comparisons with other existing schemes for offered reliability degree, in contrast to the energy conservation efficiency. The mobility model used in this work is based on the probabilistic Fraction Brownian Motion (FBM) adopted in [15], where nodes are moving, according to certain probabilities, location and time. The simulated scenario uses 80 nodes that are randomly

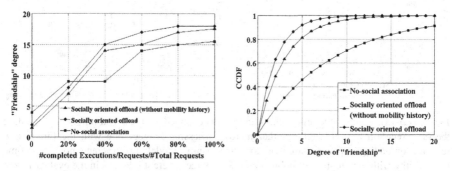

Fig. 2. (a) and (b). Friendship degree with the completed requested offloads and the CCDF with the degree of friendship.

initialized with social parameter and through the transient state during simulation the system estimates the social betweenness centrality in regards to the ability to interact with other nodes in *L,* and successfully offload memory or processing intense processes to be partially executed onto socially-collaborating peers based on the criteria depicted in Table 1 pseudocode.

"Friendship" degree with the completed requested offloads is shown in Fig. 2 (a) for three different schemes. It is important to mark out that by using the social interactions the number of completed offloading processes are greater and outperforms the applied scheme with no social interactions at all. In Fig. 2(b) the Complementary Cumulative Distribution Function (CCDF or tail distribution) with the degree of "friendship" is shown within the respective values of ageing factor (Eq. 8).

The proposed social-enabled scheme allows the distribution of partitionable resources to be offloaded to "friendship" peers, whereas the degree of the "friendship" among peers plays a catalytic role for offloading executable resources in respect to the location of each user. These measures were extracted for social centrality parameter >0.6. In addition, when resources are offloaded, a critical parameter is the execution

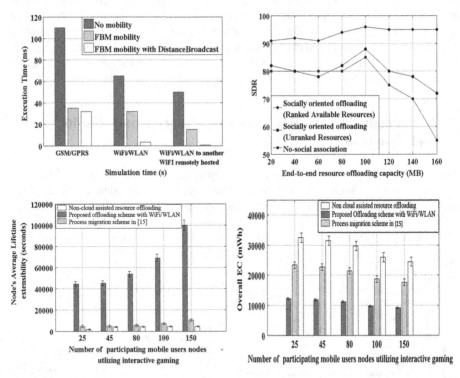

Fig. 3. (a)–(d). Comparative evaluations and results obtained for the social offloading regarding the (a) Execution time through simulation; (b) Successful delivery rate with the End-to-End resource offloading capacity based on the "friendship" model; (c) Average node's lifetime extensibility with the number of mobile devices for three different schemes in the evaluated area (evaluated for the most energy draining resources); and (d) Energy Consumption (EC) with the number of mobile users participating during an interactive game.

time, while nodes are moving from one location to another. Figure 3(a) shows the execution time during simulation for mobile nodes with different mobility patterns and it is evaluated for GSM/GPRS, Wi-Fi/WLAN and for communication within a certain Wi-Fi/WLAN to another Wi-Fi/WLAN remotely hosted. The latter scenario -from a Wi-Fi/WLAN to another Wi-Fi/WLAN- shows to exhibit significant reduction, in terms of the execution time duration, whereas it hosts the minimum execution time through the FBM with distance broadcast mobility pattern. Figure 3(b) shows the Successful Delivery Rate (SDR) with the End-to-End resource offloading capacity based on the "friendship" model whereas in Fig. 3(c) shows that the proposed scheme extends the average node's lifetime significantly when the number of mobile devices increases.

As interactive game playing requires resources in GPU/CPU-level, the lifetime is an important metric for the evaluation of the overall performance of the scheme and the impact on nodes lifetime. Measurements in Fig. 3(c) were extracted for the total number of 150 mobile terminals that are configured to host interactive gaming applications, using Wi-Fi/WLAN access technology. The proposed scheme outperforms the other compared schemes, by significantly extending the lifetime of each node. This is as a result of the offloading procedure incorporated into a social centrality framework that takes place on each node, which evaluates the energy consumption of each device according to the Eqs. 15–17 for the associated cost for each one of the executable processes. It is also worthy to mention that the proposed scheme outperforms the scheme in [15] by 11–48 %, extending the lifetime of the mobile devices, when devices reach 150 by a maximum of 48 %. The Energy Consumption (EC) with the number of mobile users participating during an interactive game (demanding in GPU/CPU processing) is shown in Fig. 3(d). During the interactive game-playing process, the processing requirements of each device dramatically increase. Figure 3 presents the evaluation for the energy consumed (EC) for three schemes, including a non-Cloud oriented method for 150 mobile terminals. The proposed scheme outperforms the other compared schemes, with the associated EC to be kept in relatively low levels.

5 Conclusions

This paper proposes a resource manipulation method comprising of an executable resource offloading scheme, incorporated into a social-aware mechanism. The proposed scheme allows partitionable resources to be offloaded, in order to be executed according to the social centrality of the node ("friendship" list). According to the model, which targets the minimization of the energy consumption and the maximization of the lifetime, each mobile device can offload resources in order to conserve energy. The scheme is thoroughly evaluated through simulation, in order to validate the efficiency of the offloading policy, in contrast to the energy conservation of the mobile devices. Future directions in our on-going research encompass the improvement of an opportunistically formed mobile cloud, which will allow delay-sensitive resources to be offloaded, using the mobile peer-to-peer (MP2P) technology.

Acknowledgment. The work presented in this paper is co-funded by the European Union, Eurostars Programme, under the project 8111, DELTA "Network-Aware Delivery Clouds for User Centric Media Events".

The research is partially supported by COST Action IC1303 Algorithms, Architectures and Platforms for Enhanced Living Environments (AAPELE).

References

1. Hu, F., Mostashari, A., Xie, J.: Socio-Technical Networks: Science and Engineering Design, 1st edn. CRC Press, 17 November 2010. ISBN-10: 1439809801
2. Mavromoustakis, C.X.: Collaborative optimistic replication for efficient delay-sensitive MP2P streaming using community oriented neighboring feedback. In: 8th Annual IEEE International Conference on Pervasive Computing and Communications (PerCom 2010), Mannheim, Germany March 29–April 2 (2010)
3. Tang, J., Musolesi, M., Mascolo, C.C., Latora, C., Nicosia, V.: Analysing information flows and key mediators through temporal centrality metrics. In: 3rd Workshop on Social Network Systems (SNS 2010), Paris, France, April (2010)
4. Sachs, D. et al.: GRACE: A Hierarchical Adaptation Framework for Saving Energy. Computer Science, University of Illinois Technical Report UIUCDCS-R-2004-2409, February 2004
5. Cuervo, E. et al.: MAUI: Making smartphones last longer with code offload. In: 8th International Conference on Mobile Systems, Applications, and Services MobiSys 2010, pp. 49–62. ACM, New York (2010)
6. Shaolei, R., van der Schaar, M.: Efficient resource provisioning and rate selection for stream mining in a community cloud. IEEE Trans. Multimedia 15(4), 723–734 (2013)
7. Khamayseh, Y.M., BaniYassein, M., AbdAlghani, M., Mavromoustakis, C.X.: Network size estimation in VANETs. J. Netw. Protoc. Algorithms 5, 136–152 (2013)
8. Camp, T., Boleng, J., Davies, V.: A survey of mobility models for Ad Hoc network research. Wireless Commun. Mobile Comput. (WCMC) 2(5), 483–502 (2002). Special Issue on Mobile Ad Hoc Networking: Research Trends and Applications
9. Lawler, G.F.: Introduction to Stochastic Processes. Chapman & Hall, London (1995)
10. Scott, J.: Social Networks Analysis: A Handbook, 2nd edn. Sage Publications, London (2000)
11. Mavromoustakis, C.X., Dimitriou, C.D., Mastorakis, G.: On the real-time evaluation of two-level BTD scheme for energy conservation the presence of delay sensitive transmissions and intermittent connectivity in wireless devices. J. Adv. Netw. Serv. 6(3 & 4), 148–161 (2013)
12. Mastorakis, G. et al.: Maximizing energy conservation in a centralized cognitive radio network architecture. In: Proceedings of the 18th IEEE International Workshop on Computer Aided Modeling Analysis and Design of Communication Links and Networks (CAMAD), Berlin, Germany, 25–27 September 2013, pp. 190–194 (2013)
13. Mavromoustakis, C.X., Dimitriou, C.D.: Using Social Interactions for Opportunistic Resource Sharing using Mobility-enabled contact-oriented Replication. In: The Proceedings of the 2012 International Conference on Collaboration Technologies and Systems (CTS 2012), in Cooperation with ACM, IEEE, Internet of Things, Machine to Machine and Smart Services Applications (IoT 2012), Denver, Colorado, USA, pp. 195–202 (2012)

14. Ciobanu, R-I. et al.: ONSIDE: Socially-aware and interest-based dissemination in opportunistic networks. In: Sixth IEEE/IFIP International Conference on Management of the Future Internet (ManFI 2014) in conjunction with the IEEE/IFIP Network Operations and Management Symposium (NOMS 2014) in Krakow, Poland, 5–9 May 2014
15. Mousicou, P., Mavromoustakis, C.X., Bourdena, A., Mastorakis, G., Pallis, E.: Performance evaluation of Dynamic Cloud Resource Migration based on Temporal and Capacity-aware policy for Efficient Resource sharing, accepted to MSWiM. In: The 16th ACM International Conference on Modeling, Analysis and Simulation of Wireless and Mobile Systems, Barcelona, Spain, 3–8 November 2013, pp. 59–66 (2013)

3D Printing Assistive Devices

Aleksandar Stojmenski[1(✉)], Ivan Chorbev[1], Boban Joksimoski[1],
and Slavco Stojmenski[2]

[1] Faculty of Computer Science and Engineering,
University of Ss. Cyril and Methodius, "Rugjer Boshkovikj" 16,
P.O. Box 393, 1000 Skopje, Republic of Macedonia
aleksandar.stojmenski@gmail.com, {ivan.chorbev,boban.
joksimoski,}@finki.ukim.mk
[2] Medical Faculty, University of Ss. Cyril and Methodius, "50 Divizija",
1000 Skopje, Republic of Macedonia
stojmenski@on.net.mk

Abstract. A revolution brought about by invention of 3D printing technology is emerging on the horizon. The 3D printer has potential to become a primary tool for building almost everything we need in the future. This paper presents the creating of custom made medical accessories and assistive devices that can help people that have a certain types of traumatic physical injury, fine motoric or hearing disabilities. Having in mind that fractures and other physical or motoric injuries are likely to occur in 2 % of the population every year, our efforts are in creating 3D printed immobilizers and assistive devices. These are more comfortable than standard casts and devices, far more accessible and affordable than off the shelf products. With the use of 3D scanners, accurate and detailed virtual model of both the traumatized or disabled region is easily created. Henceforth, the accompanying 3D model is custom-fit and can be easily printed. The 3D printed devices are often custom printed in structure that ensures easy appliance and removal, multiple use and skin respiration. Other benefits include a robust material that is water resistant and lighter, thinner and better looking than standard devices. The immobilizers and devices that were made in cooperation with the Traumatology clinic, Non-profit organizations focused on working with handicapped are presented in detail. Other types of medical accessories including hearing aid and printing assistive devices are covered in this paper.

Keywords: Assistive devices · Additive manufacturing · Immobilizers · Hearing aid · 3D printing · 3D scanning · Rapid prototyping · Medicine · Hand disabilities · Hearing disabilities

1 Introduction

While 3D printers have been present since the 1980s, mass usage and production started around 2010 and their popularity has increased rapidly since. The first 3D printer was made in 1983 by Chuck Hull who patented it using the word stereolithography [1]. In those days, 3D printers used to be large, expensive and highly limited in their performance in contrast to today's 3D printers that are easily affordable, not of such a massive physical scale and have satisfactory performance.

© Institute for Computer Sciences, Social Informatics and Telecommunications Engineering 2015
R. Agüero et al. (Eds.): MONAMI 2014, LNICST 141, pp. 446–456, 2015.
DOI: 10.1007/978-3-319-16292-8_32

In general, the printing is done in three phases. The first phase is modelling and results in creation of 3 dimensional model that the printer is going to "print" or additively manufacture. This model can be generated in almost all of the 3D modelling software's available (such as Maya, Blender, 3D Studio max...). We have utilized Autodesk Maya and we are recommending it for usage, although every modelling software can be used for creating the meshes used.

The second phase is printing. In this phase the printer reads the design from the computer model, usually as an .STL file and creates the final shape. Most commercial 3D printers use plastics as a material to build the final shape in this phase. There are three types of plastics: PLA (Polylactic Acid) is a biodegradable thermoplastic that has been derived from renewable resources such as corn starch and sugar canes and is the easiest material to use, ABS (Acrylonitrile butadiene styrene) is the second easiest material and is robust and solid, PVA (Polyvinyl Alcohol Plastic) is the hardest type of plastic and is the kind of plastic that we are using in the process of printing the hand immobilizer and assistive devices. Also, there are various types of materials that different printers can use. Those include powders, resins, titanium, stainless steel, silver, gold etc. [2, 3].

The third phase is the completion, when all the supports for building the object are removed and assembling the model is made in case it is made out of more than one part.

The design of forearm and thumb orthoses (immobilizers) is currently limited by the methods used to fabricate the devices, particularly in terms of geometric freedom and potential to include innovative new features. 3D printing technologies, where objects are constructed via a series of sub-millimeter layers of a substrate material, may present an opportunity to overcome these limitations and allow novel devices to be produced that are highly personalized for the individual, both in terms of fit and functionality. The immobilizer's that we present are showing an easier way to handle temporal disability of the hand.

Digital technology has made a large impact on hearing instrument processing and fitting, and it is now making a large impact on hearing aid shell manufacturing. Current manufacturing processes of custom-fit shells of hearing aids may be highly intensive and manual process, and quality control of the fitting of hearing aids may be tough. Using additive manufacturing technologies the process of creating hearing aid shells for people with hearing disabilities can be facilitated. The measures could be taken from modern ear 3d scanners such as OTOSCAN [4].

The third sort of accessories that are covered in this paper are assistive devices for people with temporal or permanent fine motoric handicap. We manufactured various types of customized assistive devices that facilitate the process of eating, washing, hair brushing, writing and other everyday activities to people with disabled hands. Also, we manufactured assistive technology gadgets that would help people that are having complete arm disability to use modern communication devices such as tablets and computers. The main contributions of this paper are related to the modeling process and developing 3D printed devices that are customized to fit every person's hand.

2 Background Work

Although 3D printers were not commercialized, scientists have been working on many issues that can be solved using 3D printing, including aiding medicine. Back in 2003, a team of scientists started researching artificial bone replacement using inkjet 3D technologies. They printed the bones layer by layer with bio printing using regenerative medicine [5]. When the first 3D printers that can print metal appeared, their method was implemented for a jaw later implanted on an 83-year-old woman [6]. As technology improved, a general improvement in the field of medicine and 3D printing has appeared, printing human tissue that can lead to printing and replacement of human organs [7]. Recently, a number of papers have been published presenting foot orthoses (FOs) and ankle foot orthoses (AFOs) fabricated using AM techniques, successfully demonstrating the feasibility of this approach [8, 9].

Another useful application domain is generation of graspable three-dimensional objects applied for surgical planning, prosthetics and related applications using 3D printing or rapid prototyping [10]. Graspable 3D objects overcome the limitations of 3D visualizations which can only be displayed on flat screens. 3D objects can be produced based on CT or MRI volumetric medical images. Using dedicated post-processing algorithms, a spatial model can be extracted from image data sets and exported to machine-readable data. That spatial model data is utilized by special printers for generating the final rapid prototype model.

There are several examples of the use of 3D printing in biomedicine in the recent past. Titanium printed pelvic was implanted into a British patient [11]. In order to create the 3D printed pelvis, the surgeons took scans of the man's pelvis to take exact measurements of how much 3D printed bone needed to be produced and passed it along to a 3D printing company. The company used the scans to create a titanium 3D replacement, by fusing layers of titanium together and then coating it with a mineral that would allow the remaining bone cells to attach.

Besides titanium, plastic printing is also used. A plastic tracheal splint has been printed for an American infant [12]. In an infant with tracheobronchomalacia, they implanted a customized, bio-resorbable tracheal splint, created with a computer-aided design based on a computed tomographic image of the patient's airway and fabricated with the use of laser-based three-dimensional printing. Also, 3D printed skull replacement has been used on a woman in the Netherlands. The patient has fully regained her vision, she has no more complaints, she's gone back to work and there are almost no traces that she had any surgery at all.

The hearing aid and dental industries are expected to be the biggest area of future development using the custom 3D printing technology.

3 Immobilization

Getting the anatomically accurate measures is crucial for creating good immobilization. The data required for this step can be acquired using different methods:

- **Computer Tomography:** the best method for acquiring measures is by using pictures from computer tomography (CT images in DICOM format). Depending on the slices and the quality of the images, using programs like 3D doctor [13] and voxelization techniques, it is possible to recreate the 3d model of the injury. The obtained model usually has a high level of detail and gives a very good overview of the bone itself and the place of the injury. The shortcomings of this method are that it is difficult to remesh the model for creating a lower point count, needed for better performance.
- **3D scanner:** The second method we tried is using a 3D scanner. Using this method a real life object can be scanned and digitalized into a 3D model. There are two types of 3D scanners, ones that rotate the object around them and others that rotate themselves around the object. This method is probably most efficient, but we currently have access to a scanner that rotates the object around itself and it has limited use for scanning parts of the human body. The scanner that we used is MakerBot Digitilizer. Another alternative for this method is to scan the object using an application from AutoDesk called 123D Catch. This application creates a 3D model from variety of images and provides satisfying results.
- **Manually:** The third and definitely most accurate method is manually taking measures from the key parts of the injured part (wrist girth, elbow length, etc.) and using a script to regenerate our model according to the given parameters. This method uses a previously modelled and parameterized body part (e.g. arm, finger, toe, etc.). Using the input measures, we are able to recreate the injured part (arm in our example) using combination of morph targets and other mesh deformators present in our preferred modeling toolkit (sculpt, wrap, etc.).

After obtaining the 3d model that represents the injured body part, we are able to create the specific immobilizer using 3d modeling techniques and deformers. The steps in creating the immobilizer are described as follows:

1. **Creating generic immobilizer for a body part:** This step is done once, and the model obtained is later specialized for each patient. The first step is algorithmically creating pentagonal and hexagonal polygonal plane grids in 3D modeling software. The grid is projected on a body part of a generic 3d human model. In accordance with an orthopedist, we are adjusting the number of divisions and density of the cellular structure. Minor modeling is used to correct the projection errors and fine tuning the mesh. Usually it takes 2–3 days to get a correct model that can be used.
2. **Specializing the immobilizer:** After obtaining the model of the injury, we are adjusting the pre-generated generic model using technique called shrinkwrap [14]. This aligns the model in accordance to the model of the specific injury. The length of the process depends on the complexity of the model and usually takes couple of minutes. After creating the immobilizer model, it is checked for mistakes in the shrikwrap process. If the model passes the inspection, it is further solidified (strengthened) on the pressure points, and it is ready for pre-printing process.

The patients with broken or cracked bones face difficulties while having a shower, getting dressed, lifting their broken part of the body that is covered with tough and bulky materials. Even some of them are having problems with the adjustment of the immobilizer that doesn't always fit their arms (or any other body part that is being prototyped). Having those in mind and the fact that a fracture occurs every 3 s and that 2 people out of 100 are likely to have a fracture per year [15], we made an effort to facilitate those 4 weeks to the people that experience an undislocated fracture on the distal part of the typical place of radius. There are fractures, which don't need reposition of the fracture fragment, but only immobilization during 4 weeks in the correct position causing temporal disability and need of assistive devices. Because we think that there is chance for additional compression on the soft tissues of the distal part of forearm, we performed 2 mm bigger anatomical model to prevent compression.

Also, on the end parts of the model we used a soft material, which cannot make stasis in the forearm. We first made a 3D scan of the hand so that we are sure that the immobilizer will fit perfectly in the patient's hand. Afterwards, we adjusted our model to the dimensions we received by the 3D scanner as shown on Fig. 1 and we flushed it to printing.

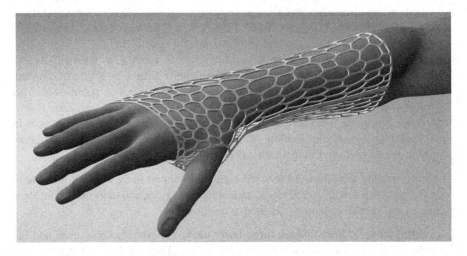

Fig. 1. 3D hand immobilizer.

The model is printed with lightweight, but solid plastic that is hypoallergenic and not itchy. The lightweight plastic is thin enough to fit every piece of clothing that fits the regular hand. Our model has gaps so that the skin is able to breathe and in order to control the degree of swelling of the arm and the soft tissue damage or wounds of the skin. Also, those gaps make the washing of the hand easier. The model is easily applicative and can be removed just as easy because it is divided in two parts (upper and lower) with supports on both of the sides as shown on Fig. 2. Also, it is fully recyclable so there is no medical waste.

4   3D Printing Assistive Devices

In cooperation with a non-profit organization, "Open the Windows" we made few devices that can ease the everyday functioning of people with disabilities. Initially we

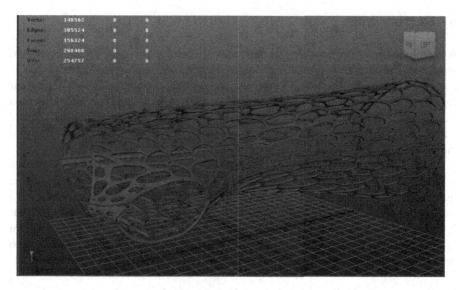

Fig. 2. 3D immobilizer in Maya.

created a cuff that would stick to a palm with partial hand disability. Then we started attaching different parts of helping devices for everyday usage. We created a spoon for eating as shown in Fig. 3A.

Fig. 3. (A) 3D spoon model attached to a cuff in Maya; (B) Penholder 3D model in Maya

We made a toothbrush that could not be used as 3D printed because of the firmness of the material. Instead, a regular toothbrush can be used and attached to the holder with a screw. Almost every regular toothbrush can be attached to the model. The holder itself is ergonomic and custom designed to a specific persons palm or hand. The toothbrush is based on the same holder as the spoon. It can be made generic to be able to hold any tools similar to a toothbrush including hair brush, shoe brush and other devices for eating such as fork, knife.

We manufactured a holder that would facilitate writing with pen or pencil to the same group of people with partial hand disabilities. We could not use the model of the holder that we described because we needed different positioning of the hand and the thumb. The model that we made enables easy writing with the holder while feeling no discomfort on the hand. The model of the holder can be seen on Fig. 3B.

5 Hearing Aids

A hearing aid is an electronic device that picks up sound waves with a microphone and sends them to the ear through a tiny speaker. Hearing aids are frequently formed in an attempt to fit a given situation. A typical custom-fitting process starts with taking ear canal measures of a patient at the office of an Otolaryngologist. The sample is then shipped to a manufacturer's laboratory. At the manufacturer's laboratory, skilled technicians using manual operations make each shell. The quality and consistency of the fit of each shell vary significantly with the technician's skill level.

A 3D scanner scans the ear impression using a laser light source that has precision in microns. Because a laser loses its effectiveness in marking the contour of the impression if it is transparent, powder and liquid materials should not be used to take an ear impression. Rather, an opaque substance, like silicon, should be used to take ear impressions. The material is presented in Fig. 4 and the color of the silicon is light green so it could be easily scanned because the darker is the object the harder it is to scan using our 3D scanner.

Fig. 4. Ear canal impression

After the model is obtained using 3d scanning technologies, the same could be printed using additive manufacturing technologies, facilitating the waiting time for the patient and the developing time for the manufacturer.

6 Evaluation

In order to evaluate the efficiency of our immobilisation model, we sent an application to the Ethical committee of Macedonian association of orthopaedics and traumatology asking if we could apply the immobilizer with accordance to people having a broken hand condition. The status of the application is pending. Aside from the ethical committee, few doctors already evaluated our model and assessed that the model is fully anatomically correct, fits very good on the arm and may be widely applicable in their everyday work. This can be concluded from the survey that we've made about the experience that the doctor's had with the immobiliser. The results that are shown on Fig. 5 are from a questionnaire in which we gathered information from a test group consisted of five doctors. Each question was in a form of statement graded by the users with one of the grades: Strongly Disagree, Disagree, Undecided, Agree, Strongly Agree. The questions that we used could be seen in the Appendix.

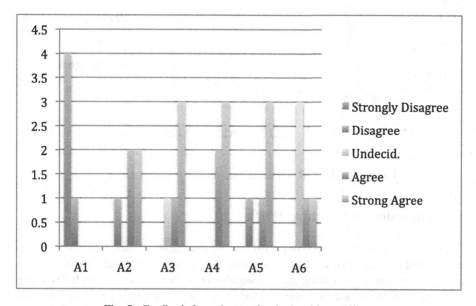

Fig. 5. Feedback from doctors for the hand immobilizer

It is very important that the place where the bone fracture took part is more densely covered with smaller polygonal objects so it can be more firm in contrast to the other part of the model where we want elasticity to relax the hand and also handle big tissue swelling. Using the model, the doctors confirmed that there are no signs of any local irritation or allergic reactions.

The assistive devices covered in this paper were given for usage in the Macedonian non-profit organisation from where we got the descriptions of general needs for the disabled people. We made a questionnaire and the devices that we manufactured were evaluated positively since the visitors there already used similar, but not customized devices. The overall test group that responded to the questionnaire contained 10 people that had hand disabilities. The results of the questionnaire are shown in the following figure (Fig. 6).

The ear impression presented in this paper eases the traditional work of the manufacturer in terms that he could easily specify the thickness of the wall of the hearing aid device and also specify different areas with different thickness using computer aided design.

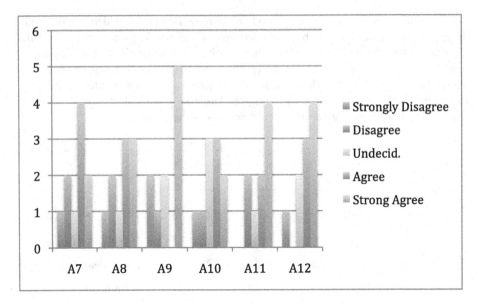

Fig. 6. Feedback of user experience for the assistive hand holder

7 Conclusion and Future Work

Orthotics continues to be recommended for the treatment of various medical conditions. Traditionally, many different manual techniques were used to manufacture orthotics and shells for hearing aid hardware's. Those techniques are gradually being replaced by modern additive manufacturing techniques. This paper provided a concise description of the techniques required to design and manufacture a hand immobilizer, a hearing aid shell and different types of bones for learning purposes.

Doctors completed tests for the immobilization model and it was concluded that this model is more comfortable for the patient than splint immobilization. It is lightweight, but it also enables good immobilization of the fracture and doesn't cause any allergic reactions or irritation to the skin. Among other benefits, the doctors can have good control over the degree of swelling and the wounds of the skin. We plan to obtain a better 3D scanner so that we could fill the gap of getting good measures for the model and develop a routine use of these techniques, facilitating the work to the doctors and helping the patients in recovering their bone fracture.

Most assistive devices for the hand-disabled people employ holders and similar griping structures. This paper covers the manufacturing process of assistive devices for eating, writing, tooth brushing and computer or tablet usage. In the future we will develop other devices and also examine their usability.

Looking into the future, the technology for custom hearing aid manufacturing is expected to continue to refine itself in the complexity of the software manipulation, as well as the ease and accuracy in which the scanning is done. No matter what method is used for manufacturing the hearing aid shell, one must always remember that with the development of the micron precision 3D ear scanners, the human factor or modeler can be even avoided when taking an ear impression. Therefore, an accurate ear impression is the first crucial step in ensuring an accurately fit hearing aid shell.

Acknowledgment. The research is partially supported by COST Action IC1303 Algorithms, Architectures and Platforms for Enhanced Living Environments (AAPELE).

Appendix: Questionnaire

The questions in the questionnaire for the hand immobilizer were as follows:

A1. There are signs of any local irritation or allergic reaction.
A2. Those immobilizers may replace the traditional ones.
A3. There is no itchiness while wearing the immobilizer.
A4. The immobilizer provides good skin respiration, washing and tissue control.
A5. The immobilizer is fully anatomically correct.
A6. 3D printed immobilizers may be widely applicable in my everyday work.

The questions in the questionnaire for the assistive holder were as follows:

A7. The holder is comfortable and is applied with ease.
A8. The holder may facilitate the way you do daily actions.
A9. I have used similar devices but they weren't custom fit for my arm.
A10. The holder could be easy changed and adjusted to any every day usage purpose.
A11. I would like other types of 3D printed hand holders.
A12. The holder is tightly tied to the hand and is not loose while using it.

References

1. 30 Years of Innovation. www.3dsystems.com, http://www.3dsystems.com/30-years-innovation
2. What materials do 3D Printers use? Find out now at 3D Printer Help. http://www.3dprinterhelp.co.uk/what-materials-do-3d-printers-use/
3. pramoddige: 3D Printing Materials 2015–2025: Status, Opportunities, Market Forecasts. http://3dbusinesses.com/listings/3d-printing-materials-2015-2025-status-opportunities-market-forecasts/
4. OTOSCAN® 3D. http://earscanning.com/
5. Saijo, H., Igawa, K., Kanno, Y., Mori, Y., Kondo, K., Shimizu, K., Suzuki, S., Chikazu, D., Iino, M., Anzai, M., Sasaki, N., Chung, U., Takato, T.: Maxillofacial reconstruction using custom-made artificial bones fabricated by inkjet printing technology. J. Artif. Organs Off. J. Jpn. Soc. Artif. Organs. **12**, 200–205 (2009)
6. 83-Year-Old Woman Gets the World's First 3-D Printed Jaw Transplant. http://www.popsci.com/technology/article/2012-02/83-year-old-woman-gets-worlds-first-3-d-printed-jaw-transplant
7. Mironov, V., Boland, T., Trusk, T., Forgacs, G., Markwald, R.R.: Organ printing: computer-aided jet-based 3D tissue engineering. Trends Biotechnol. **21**, 157–161 (2003)

8. Faustini, M.C., Neptune, R.R., Crawford, R.H., Stanhope, S.J.: Manufacture of Passive Dynamic ankle-foot orthoses using selective laser sintering. IEEE Trans. Biomed. Eng. **55**, 784–790 (2008)
9. Mavroidis, C., Ranky, R.G., Sivak, M.L., Patritti, B.L., DiPisa, J., Caddle, A., Gilhooly, K., Govoni, L., Sivak, S., Lancia, M., Drillio, R., Bonato, P.: Patient specific ankle-foot orthoses using rapid prototyping. J. Neuroeng. Rehabil. **8**, 1 (2011)
10. Rengier, F., Mehndiratta, A., von Tengg-Kobligk, H., Zechmann, C.M., Unterhinninghofen, R., Kauczor, H.-U., Giesel, F.L.: 3D printing based on imaging data: review of medical applications. Int. J. Comput. Assist. Radiol. Surg. **5**, 335–341 (2010)
11. UK Surgeon Implanted A 3D-Printed Pelvis - Business Insider. http://www.businessinsider.com/uk-surgeon-implanted-a-3d-printed-pelvis-2014-2
12. Zopf, D.A., Hollister, S.J., Nelson, M.E., Ohye, R.G., Green, G.E.: Bioresorbable airway splint created with a three-dimensional printer. N. Engl. J. Med. **368**, 2043–2045 (2013)
13. 3D-DOCTOR, medical modeling, 3D medical imaging. http://www.ablesw.com/3d-doctor/surgmod.html
14. van Overveld, K., Wyvill, B.: Shrinkwrap: an efficient adaptive algorithm for triangulating an iso-surface. Vis. Comput. **20**, 362–379 (2004)
15. Facts and Statistics. International Osteoporosis Foundation. http://www.iofbonehealth.org/facts-statistics

Author Index